The Magic of Houdini®

Will Cunningham

*with contributions by Peter Bowmar,
Jason Iversen, and Dave Johnson*

THOMSON
™
COURSE TECHNOLOGY

Professional ■ Technical ■ Reference

Important: Thomson Course Technology PTR cannot provide software support. Please contact the appropriate software manufacturer's technical support line or Web site for assistance.

Thomson Course Technology PTR and the author have attempted throughout this book to distinguish proprietary trademarks from descriptive terms by following the capitalization style used by the manufacturer.

Information contained in this book has been obtained by Thomson Course Technology PTR from sources believed to be reliable. However, because of the possibility of human or mechanical error by our sources, Thomson Course Technology PTR, or others, the Publisher does not guarantee the accuracy, adequacy, or completeness of any information and is not responsible for any errors or omissions or the results obtained from use of such information. Readers should be particularly aware of the fact that the Internet is an ever-changing entity. Some facts may have changed since this book went to press.

Educational facilities, companies, and organizations interested in multiple copies or licensing of this book should contact the publisher for quantity discount information. Training manuals, CD-ROMs, and portions of this book are also available individually or can be tailored for specific needs.

ISBN: 1-59863-082-2

Library of Congress Catalog Card Number: 2005929819

Printed in the United States of America

06 07 08 09 10 BU 10 9 8 7 6 5 4 3 2 1

Publisher and General Manager, Thomson Course Technology PTR:
Stacy L. Hiquet

Associate Director of Marketing:
Sarah O'Donnell

Manager of Editorial Services:
Heather Talbot

Marketing Manager:
Heather Hurley

Acquisitions Editor:
Megan Belanger

Marketing Coordinator:
Jordan Casey

Project Editor:
Kezia Endsley

Technical Editor:
Jeff Wagner, Side Effects Software

Editorial Services Coordinator:
Elizabeth Furbish

Interior Layout Tech:
William Hartman

Cover Designer:
Mike Tanamachi

Front Cover Image:
Jon Campbell, Josh Burton, Scott Englert, William Atkin, Scott Spencer, Matthew Parrot, Benjamin Willis, and David Bokser

Back Cover Image:
Steven Ong

Indexer:
Larry Sweazy

Proofreader:
Carla Spoon

THOMSON
COURSE TECHNOLOGY
Professional ■ Technical ■ Reference

Thomson Course Technology PTR, a division of Thomson Course Technology
25 Thomson Place ■ Boston, MA 02210 ■ http://www.courseptr.com

This book is dedicated to all you folks who can put it to use. Learning is living, baby!

Acknowledgments

First and foremost, I want to thank Genevieve, my loving partner in life and crime (all alleged!), for supporting this enormous effort. A less compassionate soul would have rebelled against my long hours at work followed by long hours on this book. You are a keeper! I want to also thank Danielle, my mammy, for always believing in me, even during those times when she must have wondered if all my neurons were correctly connected. Thank you to my sister Stacie for her valuable legal advice.

In addition, I would like to thank Megan Belanger, the acquisitions editor, for convincing me completely that choosing Thomson was the right choice. It has been an absolute pleasure working with you, even during those hectic last months. Thank you to Kezia Endsley, the production editor, for abiding by my sometimes warped sense of expression and only offering correction where needed. Thank you to all the good folk at Side Effects for creating this amazing software and supporting the creation of this book so thoroughly. In particular, appreciation must be extended to Jeff Wagner, as the technical editor, for applying his wealth of knowledge and expertise in correcting mistakes and offering abundant suggestions for how to relate the material more effectively.

And finally, I would like to thank the contributing authors Peter Bowmar, Jason Iversen, and Dave Johnson. Their vast knowledge and production experience has added immensely to the quality of the project. Thank you also to Doug Bloom for first showing me this wonderful software package and being a great mentor ever since. In fact, at numerous points during its development, I almost felt like the book was really just an excuse for me to be able to constantly ask questions of some of the best Houdini users in the land. In particular, Peter helped bring this book to fruition by answering literally hundreds of questions over the course of the effort, contributing amazing material, and by always offering a nudge in the right direction when I came upon a challenging fork in the path. In light of his crucial contribution, it is fitting for him to have a space here to speak his feelings on the matter.

"Peter grovels in apology to his lovely wife Elva and wonderful daughter Sufiah for the time this book has taken from his family. Hopefully becoming a millionaire after the huge sales of this book will help to ease their suffering. For Elva and Sufiah, Peter."

I am afraid he may have to find another way to make the necessary remunerations as his expectations of the windfall from sales is just a touch heady! It has been a challenging escapade and I have learned much in the process. Hopefully, you too will find the book to be a worthwhile adventure!

Will

About the Author

Will Cunningham was born a seeker of knowledge and experience. As the years stroll by, he continues to believe that it is vitally important to never lose a sense of wonder and curiosity about the world in which you live. From the dusty desert floor to high Andean passes, he has discovered that life is a ripe peach for the eating, as long as you remember your napkin.

Professionally, Will studied at the Academy of Entertainment and Technology and later served as a Houdini Technical Intern at Side Effects Software. Eager to create effects for the big screen, he jumped into production with BlackBox Digital on the feature film *The Prince and Me*. Since then, he has worked for a number of production houses on a variety of projects including *Bee Season* and *The Lion, the Witch, and the Wardrobe*. He is currently with Sony Pictures Imageworks doing effects work for the fully CG feature Open Season. He is also an instructor at the Academy and has been instrumental in helping to build its effects curriculum over the last several years. He is currently working on creating material for an intermediate Houdini class that will be offered in the Spring semester of 2006.

About the Contributors

Peter Bowmar started blowing things up as an excuse to make movies (or making movies as an excuse to blow things up) very soon after seeing *Star Wars* in 1977. He hoodwinked Ryerson Polytechnic (now Ryerson University) in Toronto, Canada, into giving him a B.A.A. in Film in 1991. Soon after, he moved to Singapore, helping to start up the new Film Sound and Video department at Ngee Ann Polytechnic. It was here he was first exposed to Houdini. Leaving Singapore, he moved to Los Angeles and started working for Side Effects Software doing mostly support, demos, and training. After over five years at SESI, he moved on to Rhythm and Hues, joining as an FX Technical Director and leaving as a Senior Technical Director. Peter is currently working toward his master's degree in Animation (using Houdini, of course) at Bournemouth University, in the United Kingdom. He is married to the wonderfully patient and supportive Elva, and they have an extra special daughter named Sufiah.

Jason Iversen, born in Zimbabwe in 1972, started out on his windy career path as a database programmer at a life insurance company and wandered through game programming, virtual reality applications, and architectural visualization to end up firmly committed to CGI by working at a commercials Post Production facility in South Africa as an animator. It was here he was introduced to PRISMS, the predecessor of Houdini. He grew up with Houdini since the moment he received a CD-ROM one day with "Houdini 0.9alpha" hand-written on the label. He now works on feature film projects as a CG Supervisor at Digital Domain in Venice, California, and is still a practicing devotee to Houdini in all its abstract goodness. He blames Tron for where he ended up...personally, not the movie.

Dave Johnson's animation career spans 15 years and he is currently the Senior Technical Director and Lead Animator producing industrial films in support of marketing and engineering for Northrop Grumman Corp. An avid Houdini evangelist, he is a certified Houdini instructor, has taught Houdini for over five years, and is an expert in production pipeline development. He has a B.A. in Music Education and Composition from Azusa Pacific University. He lives in Southern California with his lovely wife and four children.

Contents

Introduction xix

chapter 1
Introduction and Welcome 1
Why This Book Was Written 2
History of Computer Animation at a Blink 2
History of Houdini at a Glance 2
Houdini's Procedural Paradigm 4
Houdini's Family of Products 5
My Perspective 6
Summary 6

chapter 2
3D Concepts Reviewed 7
Where Is 3D? 7
The Building Blocks of 3D Space 8
    Points and Vertices 9
    Primitives 9
    Planar and Non-Planar Geometric Forms 10
    Convex and Concave Polygons 10
Through the Looking Glass 11
    Perspective Projection and Orthographic Projection ...11

Coordinate Spaces in Houdini 12
Transformations and Order 13
Transformation and Deformation 13
Summary 14

chapter 3
The Houdini Interface 15
The Introductory Method 15
Four Basic Interface Zones 15
Help Pane 16
The Three Most Common Panes 18
    The Viewer Pane 19
        Stowbars *19*
        State Indicator *19*
        View Indicator *19*
        Selection Options *19*
        Display Options *20*
        Viewing Options *20*
        Moving the View Around *20*
        The View State and Operational States *21*
        Transform Handles *21*
        Moving Between Viewpoints *24*

The Network Editor Pane 24

Object Node Functionality *25*

Performing an Operation in the View Pane *25*

Performing an Operation in the Network Editor Pane *26*

Networks *26*

The Parameters Pane 27

The Number Ladder *28*

The Various Contexts 28

OBJs (Objects Operators) 29

SOPs (Geometry Surface Operators) 29

DOPs (Dynamic Operators) 30

POPs (Particle Operators) 30

SHOPs (Shader Operators) 30

VOPs (VEX Builder) Are VEX Operators 30

CHOPs (Motion and Audio Channel Operators) 31

COPs (Compositing Operators) 31

ROPs (Outputs Rendering Operators) 31

Summary 32

chapter 4
Object Operators (OBJs) 33

Objects as Containers 33

Object States 33

Just a Box o' Running 34

Creating the Track (the Path State) *34*

Getting the Box on the Track (the Follow Path State) *35*

Creating a HUD Slider *35*

Persistent Handles *36*

Creating and Configuring box2 (the Copy State) *36*

How a Sphere Becomes a Baton (the Parent and Blend States) *37*

The Shading Selector *38*

The Primitive Olympics *38*

Eyes on the World 39

Conjure the World and Gravity *39*

Speed the World Through Space (the Sticky State) *39*

Witnessing Your Creation (the Look At State) *40*

Improving Your World (the Morph State) *41*

Higher on the Mountain (an Interface Medley) 42

Viewport Layouts and Adjusting the Construction Plane Grid 42

Snapping 42

The Pose State 44

Auto-Numbering Nodes 45

Homing the View 45

Locating Objects 45

The Update Button 46

Summary 47

chapter 5
Surface Operators (SOPs) 49
Salutations to the SOP Node 49
Polygonal Modeling 50
  Making a Totem Pole 50
    The Basic Head 50
    The Bird 52
    The Boy 55
    The Bull 58
    Assemble the Totem 58
    Further Play in the Network Editor 59
Procedural Modeling 61
  Duplicating DNA 61
    Channel Referencing 65
  Soccer Is for Kicks 68
    Panes Ease the Pain 69
    The Details View and Attributes 70
    Grouping Is the Goal 71
    Presets 73
Learning the Brush Operations 74
  Sculpt It! Comb It! Paint It! 74
    Ye Ole Copy SOP 77

NURBs Modeling 80
  The Wisdom of Worms 80
    Create the Apple 81
    Create the Worm 84
    Squirm the Worm 84
    Create the Sign 85
Summary 87

chapter 6
Additional SOPs Practice 89
Attack of the Be-Tentacled Sphere 89
  Create the Mothersphere 89
  Create the Tentacle 90
  Create the Aperture 91
  Ewwww! It Moves! 93
Creating Stonehenge 95
  Create the Arch 95
  Create the Circle of Arches 96
  Create the Moon 97
  The Message Is Friendship 99
  It Lives! 100
SOPs That Confound the Melon 102
  Object Merge SOP 102
  Blast SOP, Delete SOP, and Dissolve SOP ...103

Copy SOP, Primitive SOP, Duplicate SOP, and
   Copy/Paste 104
Understanding Point and Primitive SOPs 105
Using the Edit and Transform SOPs 106
Summary 107

chapter 7
Animation..109
Manually Set Keyframes 109
Autokey Your Way to Freedom 111
Discovering the Channel Editor 112
The Zones of Utility 113
   The View Area 113
   Channel List 115
   Channel Groups 116
Houdini Takes Me Away 117
   Creating Desks 118
Flipbook to Preview Animation 120
Simple Rigging 120
Create Zee Skeleton 120
   Gimbal Lock 122
   Editing Bones 123
      Changing a Bone's Position 123
      Splitting Bones 123
      Parenting Bones 124

Rigging the Hand 125
   Create Zee Skeleton 125
   Capture Geometry 127
   Add a Little Automation 129
Rigging the Dragonfly 130
   Create Zee Skeleton 130
"Capture" Geometry 132
   Isolate the Pieces 133
   Parent the Pieces 134
Chops-ify the Dragonfly 135
Summary 137

chapter 8
Particle Operators (POPs)..139
Salutations to the POP Node 142
Particle Operations Are Cooked in a
   Simulation 142
Simulations Are the Result of Interconnected
   Forces 142
Particle Simulations Are Interactive 143
The Real Time Toggle 143
Particle SOP or Pop Merge SOP or Popnet SOP ..144
   Particle SOP 144
   Pop Merge SOP 145
   Popnet SOP (Called POP Network in the Tab Menu)...146

Impulse or Constant Birthing 146

Select a Source or Set a Context Source 148

    Select a Source 148

    Set a Context Source 148

Each Particle Has Its Own Space 148

Z Axis Aligned to Velocity 149

$F and $FF 151

POP Activation Field 151

Popnet Oversampling 151

Initial Velocity, Force POP, Wind POP, and
    Fan POP 152

    Initial Velocity 152

        Explicitly Set Initial Velocity *152*

        Inherit Initial Velocity *153*

    Ye Old Force POP 155

    The Wind POP 156

    The Fan POP 157

Particle Charge 157

Collision Detection 159

The Particle Primitive 162

POP Events and the Popevent() Expression 164

    POP Event Generated with a Collision POP 165

    POP Event Generated with an Event POP 167

The Dotted Line Connection 168

Poppoint() Expression 169

Getting Colors and Alpha from POPs to
    Render 172

Exercise: Flying Arrows 175

    Overview 175

        Create the Ground Geometry *176*

        Create the Arrow Geometry *176*

        Create the Birth Geometry *178*

        Create the Particle Simulation *178*

        Attach the Arrow Geometry to the Particles *180*

        Add Variation Using the Copy Stamp
        Technique *181*

Summary 183

chapter 9
Shader Operators (SHOPs) **185**

Shader Contexts 186

Adding Instances of Default Surface and
    Displacement Shaders 186

The Shader Viewer 187

    The Top Stowbar 187

    The Left Stowbar 187

    The Bottom Stowbar 187

Contents

Applying Shaders 188
  Apply Shaders at the Object Level 188
  Apply Shaders Using the Shader SOP 189
  Apply Shaders to Groups Using the Shader SOP 190
   Create the Groups 190
   Create the Shaders 191
   Apply the Shaders 192
UV Coordinates 193
  A Simple UV Study 193
   UV Texture SOP 194
   UV Project SOP 195
  How to Layer Textures 196
   How It Works 197
   The Layered Surface SHOP 197
Texturing the Dragonfly 199
  Apply UV Coordinates 199
   Apply UV Coordinates to the Legs 199
   Transfer UV Coordinates 200
   Apply UV Coordinates to the Wings 202
   UV Coordinates for the Wing Hinges, Eyes,
    and Antennae 203
   Apply UV Coordinates to the Body 204

Apply Shaders and Textures 204
  Create the Groups 205
  How to Save UV Images 206
  Quick Reloading of Textures 207
  Rest Position 208
  Assign the Shaders 208
Summary 214

chapter 10
VEX Operators (VOPs)...........................215
What Are VEX Operators? 215
VEX, Expressions, and Hscript 215
Salutations to the VOP Node 216
Creating a Soccer Ball Surface Shader 216
  Analyze the Look 216
  Consider Approaches for Achieving the Look 216
  Visualize Groups on Existing Geometry 217
  Apply UV Coordinates 217
  Add a Custom Attribute 218
  Add the VOP Network 219
  Add a New Material 220
  Apply the New Shader and Render 221
  Use IPR to View Changes 221
  Access a Custom Attribute 222

Use a Custom Attribute 222
Work with Different Data Types in VOPs 224
Add a Texture Map 224
Get and Use the UV Coordinates 225
Apply Lighting to the Texture Map 225
Composite the Label Over the Base Materials 226
Add User Parameters to the SHOP 227
Organizing the User Interface 229

Saving the VOPnet to Disk as a New SHOP Type ..229
VOPnet Management 231
Summary 232

chapter 11
Digital Assets..............................233
Kick the Tires! 233
Preparing for Assetization 235
Collapsing Into a Subnet 236
Creating the Asset 236
Building the Asset's User Interface 238
Expose the Desired Parameters 238
Verify External References 241
Expose the Remaining Parameters 241
Organize the User Interface 242

Refine the User Interface 244
Create a Menu 245
Understanding the Channel References 246
Modify a Channel Reference 247
Special Controls 248
Disabling Parameters 251
Expose Handles 251
Create Help 253
Operator Comments 253
Tooltip Help 253
HTML Help 254
Conjure an Icon 255
Behind the Curtain 256
New Operator Type 256
Design Philosophy 258
OTL Files 258
Versioning Assets for Safety 258
The Operator Type Manager 260
OTL Installation 260
Locked/Unlocked Status of an Asset 261
Takes and HDAs 262
Multiple Definitions Using the Search Path 262
Embed an OTL 263
Summary 264

chapter 12
Dynamic Operators (DOPs) 265

Total Perspective Vortex 265

    Ye Grand List 266

    Divide and Conquer 266

    Salutations to the DOP Node 266

    Objects Level Objects and DOPs Objects 267

In the Beginning, There Was the Void (and RBDs) 267

Objects versus Data versus Subdata 269

Volume Representation 271

Taking Control 272

    Constraints 272

    Multiple Constraints 274

    Limiting Your Constraints 275

Affectors and Active and Passive States 276

    Affector Matrix 276

Crowd Psychology 278

    All for One and One for All! 278

    Pulling in Point Instances 279

Fractured Objects 280

    Create Primitive Groups Based on Connectivity 281

Keep It Together! Use Some Sticky Stuff! 281

Animating Values in DOPs 283

Cloth 284

    Getting Started with Cloth 284

    Two-State Constraints 285

    Cloth and Collisions 286

    Cloth in a Vacuum = Yawn 287

    Per-Point Attributes and the Cloth Solver 288

    Gleaning Some Meaning 290

Getting Wired 290

    Springs and Damping 291

    Pin the Tail on the Ferengi: Wire Constraints 292

    A Hairy Solution 293

    Feel the Power... Lines 294

Reuse and Recycle—Use the POP Solver 296

The Power of Feedback—The SOP Solver 297

The Script Solver 299

Static Solver and the Copy Data Solver 300

Only One Solver? 300

Now What? 303

    The Three Rs: Readin', Ritin', and Renderin' 303

    The Freedom of Data Act 304

    Controlling Visibility with the Rendering Parameters DOP 304

    Object Merge SOP Skullduggery 305

    Extracting and Processing Simulation Information 306

    Enough Impact? 308

Summary 310

chapter 13
Render Outputs (ROPs).....................**311**
File Structure 311
    The Hip-Centric Approach 311
    The Job-Centric Approach 312
Render Dependencies 314
Common ROP Options 314
    Valid Frame Range 315
    Render Control 315
    Start/End/Inc 315
    Render with Take 315
    Initialize Simulation OPs 315
    Pre-Render, Pre-Frame, Post-Frame, Post-Render
        Scripts 316
Using Local and Global Variables 317
Common ROPs 317
    Mantra ROP 318
    Render Command Options *319*
    Geometry ROP 321
    Channel ROP 321
    Object Scene and OpenGL ROPs 321
    Wren ROP 322

Motion Blur 322
    Transformation Blur 323
Deformation Blur 324
    Velocity Blur 325
    Velocity Motion Blur—The Remix 326
How Rendering in Mantra Worketh 327
Mantra Rendering Is All About the
    Micro-Polygons 329
Rendering from a File 331
Summary 334

chapter 14
And So It Ends?..............................**335**
Occupations in the Computer Graphics
    Industry 335
Houdini in Production 337
A Parting Word 338

Index..**339**

Contents

Introduction

Houdini has long been a dominant tool used in the creation of some of the most awe-inspiring animation and cinematic effects ever made. It is preferred by numerous studios for their most demanding challenges. If you go to the theatre and see something that blows your mind, it is a good bet that Houdini had a hand in it. Now you can conquer the amazing technology of Houdini with confidence. With this book, you will learn how to apply each of Houdini's breath-taking features to your projects as you take on modeling, character animation, particle effects animation, dynamic simulation animation, shading, digital asset creation, and rendering. *The Magic of Houdini* is full of exercises, tips, and illustrations to help you tackle each new skill. Get ready to experience the mystery, the majesty, the magic of Houdini!

What You'll Find in This Book

For many years now, aspiring Houdini artists have had to struggle through a dearth of documentation and resources to learn the software. This book aims to provide the first thorough introduction to vast 3D package. We all know how dry reading a technical book can be. So, I have endeavored to be humorous and informal while, at the same time, providing accurate and pertinent information for the task at hand. The material covered includes:

◆ A brief review of 3D concepts

◆ Interface work

◆ The objects context

◆ The surface operators context

◆ Simple rigging

◆ Animation techniques

◆ The particle operators context

◆ Expression language usage

◆ The shader operators context

◆ The VEX operators context

◆ Creation and management of digital assets

◆ The dynamic operators context

◆ The render outputs context

◆ Descriptions of industry job positions

Introduction

Who This Book Is For

This book is intended for people new to the world of 3D, people coming from other 3D packages, and also people who are knowledgeable in some parts of the program and want to explore new areas. The level of difficulty will progress from beginner to intermediate and touches on several advanced topics in the later chapters of the book.

Why This Book Was Written

Because it was sorely needed! This project swirled and coalesced from the origins of several years spent teaching and never having exactly the material I wanted to use for instruction. It grew from meager, isolated exercises into a cohesive, comprehensive whole that should serve well in getting essential information to a beginner and also giving more knowledgeable users a resource for studying areas new to them. Houdini is a vast package of immense capabilities. Hopefully, this book will help you through some areas you have yet to explore and give additional insight in areas you are already familiar with.

Basically, this book is the compilation of almost everything I wish I had when I was trying to scale the peaks of a package with a steep learning curve and few resources to get you going. In addition, it takes a few steps beyond that and introduces topics like VOPs and DOPs, which are areas in which even the most seasoned professionals can often use more practice. They might sound strange, but VOPs and DOPs are acronyms for various contexts within Houdini. VOPs means VEX Operators and DOPs means Dynamics Operators. As you progress through the book, you will become familiar with these and a number of other contexts.

You are about to embark upon a voyage of great discovery and adventure. As on any worthwhile adventure, there will be some moments of giddy exhilaration and some moments of dejected frustration. This book endeavors to make those peaks more frequent and those valleys easier to stride through. Let's get started!

chapter 1
Introduction and Welcome

You are about to embark upon a voyage of great discovery and adventure. As on any worthwhile adventure, there will be some moments of giddy exhilaration and some moments of dejected frustration. This book endeavors to make those peaks more frequent and those valleys easier to stride through. Figure 1.1 shows a Japanese torii gate at dusk with gears originating in the distance and making their way to and through the gate. I have had the distinct pleasure of helping to build a number of torii gates in the physical world and have always had an affinity for the clean geometry and the meaning they embody.

Simply put, a torii is a visual indication, a marker in the path, that you are leaving one world and entering another. There are times, perhaps when wandering about in the dusky, dark unknown, when a marker of this kind is a much-appreciated guide. This book is similar in that it too serves as a vehicle for exploring new vistas. The gears are the building blocks of knowledge that's covered as you progress

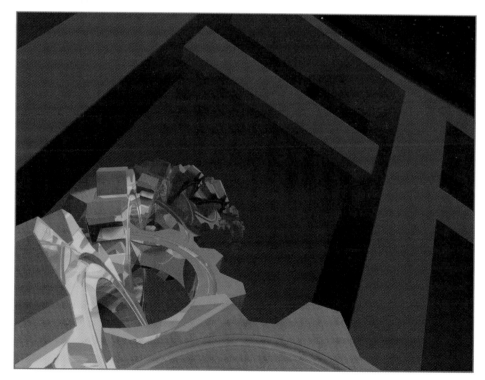

Figure 1.1
Welcome to the adventure!

through the book, all the while moving toward a more clear and certain understanding of the tools at your disposal. Saddle up! The sunlight is burning low and there is much to explore!

Why This Book Was Written

Because it was sorely needed! This project swirled and coalesced from the origins of several years spent teaching and never having exactly the material I wanted to use for instruction. It grew from meager, isolated exercises into a cohesive, comprehensive whole that should serve well in getting essential information to a beginner and also giving more knowledgeable users a resource for studying areas new to them. Houdini is a vast package of immense capabilities. Hopefully, this book will help you through some areas you have yet to explore and give additional insight in areas with which you are already familiar.

Basically, this book is the compilation of almost everything I wish I had when I was trying to scale the peaks of a package with a steep learning curve and few resources to get you going. In addition, it takes a few steps beyond that and introduces topics like VOPs and DOPs, which are areas where even the most seasoned professionals can often use more practice. They may sound strange, but VOPs and DOPs are just acronyms for various contexts within Houdini. VOPs mean VEX Operators and DOPs mean Dynamics Operators. As you progress through the book, you will get familiar with these and a number of other contexts.

History of Computer Animation at a Blink

Somewhere and some time in the volumetrically foggy past, you must have been dazzled by the artistry of this medium. Most everyone in this industry can trace his or her enthusiasm back to some seminal moment in days gone by where the magic of the movie moment was enthralling and lasting. The past few decades have introduced and cemented the use of computer graphics across the visual medium. What was once limited to research and graduate projects has spread to become fully integrated in the fields of television, research visualization, art, print media, video games, the Internet and, of course, feature films. Movies like *Tron* (1982) and *The Last Starfighter (1984)* were among the first to beautifully integrate computer animation with live-action on the big screen.

As the technology progressed, more and more films began to incorporate the new medium in order to enrich an environment, create an entirely imaginary one, add effects that were too costly, dangerous, or impractical to perform in real life, and more. Then *The Abyss (1989)* entered the stage and indelibly made 3D animation a part of the production process. The stunning effects achieved by Industrial Light Magic in this film brought those beautiful pseudopods and for the first time showed that a totally fabricated 3D character could evoke and embody emotion. Since that time, we have been the fortunate viewers to a maturing process that continues to hold me in thrall.

History of Houdini at a Glance

Having been a Houdini Intern in days gone by for Side Effects, I've met most of the folks who work there and they are all very cordial and civilized. I nevertheless continue to believe that all the programmers, at least, live in a dark cave somewhere outside of Toronto and do nothing but work to improve the software. During the various company gatherings and my chances to meet the Canadian contingent of employees, I was continually impressed that the long years of isolated living in near lightless conditions hadn't made any of them socially inept or unduly increased the size of their eyes and pupils.

Speaking of one such employee, I asked Kim Davidson, one of the founders and shakers at Side Effects, to put together a brief bit on this topic and he was gracious enough to oblige. The following sidebar is the result of that effort, in Kim Davidson's own words.

A WORD FROM KIM DAVIDSON

"Houdini's history starts in the early days of computer animation when there was no commercial software and no real-time graphics hardware. In 1987, Greg Hermanovic and I worked at Omnibus Computer Graphics, which was then the largest computer animation producer in the world. All of the animation at Omnibus was done on large mainframe computers with software that we had written ourselves and which Omnibus' President John Pennie named *PRISMS*. In addition to producing hundreds of commercials, Omnibus was an early contributor to film, creating the reflective and morphing spaceship for the Disney feature, *Flight of the Navigator* (1986).

Side Effects Software was cofounded by Greg and me with the goal of developing PRISMS as a commercial package. From our Omnibus experience, the spirit of Side Effects Software and the philosophy behind Houdini was born. Since we started by writing our own software and using it in production, we were in the customer's shoes right from the beginning. In fact, Houdini's procedural animation approach was created as a result of our production experiences where it was, and will always be, crucial to meet the changing needs of the creative director.

One could say that procedural animation was born out of laziness as much as necessity. We would record our production steps, so that when the creative director made changes, we could go back and make fast edits. We then created many standard steps that could be connected in any order to provide maximum flexibility. We also made sure we could animate anything and everything. These steps with the accompanying animatable controls evolved to become Houdini's operators, and this is the essence of procedural animation.

After cofounding Side Effects Software, Greg and I continued to develop software and produce animation, first with PRISMS and then with Houdini. Greg's particular interest was in real-time animation and he influenced CHOPs, a motion editing component of Houdini. My own interest was in advancing the character animation components. Our diverse user base helped to ensure that Houdini evolved as a complete and integrated animation solution. What our users create with Houdini inspires us to innovate each and every day.

I was asked to write a brief history and to recall some important events. There are so many and I've only just begun. However, this, the first ever book, marks an important milestone. Currently, most artists have learned Houdini in production under the tutelage of other Houdini users. This book, along with the Houdini Apprentice edition, will provide a way for you to develop Houdini skills on your own. Since we've spent the last few years making Houdini easier to use than ever, this seems the perfect time for such a book. It will allow more artists to understand and experience the creative freedom provided by Houdini's unique procedural approach to animation.

I hope you enjoy learning and using Houdini as much as we enjoy developing it."

Kim Davidson
President, CEO, and Cofounder, Side Effects

1. Introduction and Welcome

It is rare to encounter a company that is among the top competitors in its field and yet also maintains a very friendly and informal air. This attitude prevails throughout the Houdini community as well and is part of what makes it such a great package to use.

As Kim just touched on, PRISMS and then Houdini have been used in some of the most innovative films ever created, including *What Dreams May Come, The Matrix, Titanic, The Lion, the Witch, and the Wardrobe,* and more. It is a good bet that if you go to the theatre and see something that blows your mind, Houdini had a hand in it. In 1998, Side Effects received a Technical Achievement award from The Academy of Motion Pictures, Arts, and Sciences for the procedural modeling and animation components of PRISMS, (which were passed along and continue to be refined in Houdini). In 2002, the Apprentice edition was released and so finally the masses had legal access to the software for learning and tinkering. This free learning version has almost all the functionality of the complete Master version and so is a great way to learn the package—and you don't have to worry about the FBI coming to your house inquiring about what you've downloaded recently! In 2003, The Academy of Motion Pictures, Arts, and Sciences awarded numerous folk at Side Effects the Academy Plaque in honor of their contributions to the movie-making process. In 2005, Side Effects finally incorporated an integrated Rigid Body Dynamics and Soft Body Dynamics context in the package, much to the profound happiness of its users!

> Check out `http://www.sidefx.com/company/history/index.html` for more information about Houdini's history and its innovations in the industry. As they say, it's always good to know your roots.

Houdini's Procedural Paradigm

As I have now mentioned proceduralism several times, it's a good time to explain it in detail. It's one of the fundamental features and advantages of the Houdini package.

One of the defining aspects of the Houdini workflow centers on its *procedural paradigm.* Well, that certainly sounds impressive; but, what does it actually mean and why is it beneficial? Simply put, Houdini is designed so that every operation is a self-contained black box (or node) of utility. The term black box is used to describe a situation in which you don't necessarily need to know exactly how something is happening inside the box so long as you understand what is happening to its inputs and outputs. For example, I might not really know how a Copy `PolyBevel` operation does what it does, but I do know that if I feed star geometry into one input and sphere geometry into the other input, it ends up doing something very useful. Figure 1.2 shows the result of this simple network. Figure 1.3 shows the network of nodes used to create the field of stars. In the example, the flow of information is from top to bottom and the lines between the nodes indicate the connection between nodes, and so how the data is flowing. So, data from the circle node flows to the `group_points_to_pull` node to the `xform_make_star` node and finally into the left input of the `copy_data_to_sphere` node. The `sphere_template` node feeds data into

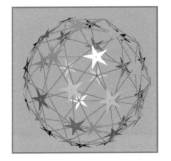

Figure 1.2
A spherical field of stars.

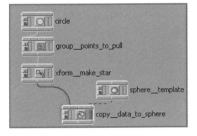

Figure 1.3
The network of nodes used to create the field of stars.

the right input of the `copy_data_to_sphere` node. Basically, the star geometry feeds into the left input of the final node, and the sphere geometry feeds into the right input of the final node.

Each of these nodes takes one or more inputs, acts upon them in some way, and then passes the result as the final output or to the next node in the line. Inherently, this approach lends itself to the creative approach of problem-solving because the user has the freedom to add, delete, or modify an operation at any stage in the process in order to see how it affects the end result. Replacing the star geometry with a teapot, the network automatically updates itself and you get the image in Figure 1.4. Figure 1.5 shows the modified network of nodes used to create the new image.

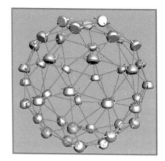

Figure 1.4
A spherical field of teapots.

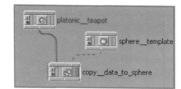

Figure 1.5
The network of nodes used to create the field of teapots.

Webster defines procedure as "a series of steps followed in a regular definite order." This is partly reflective of Houdini's usage of procedural in that all projects, grand and small, are built upon a series of steps as described. However, the Webster lexicon is partly not reflective of the Houdini usage in that the user is not restricted to a regular definite order. One of the great liberties of this package is that there are many paths available to reach a single objective. It is simply up to the experience, ability, and artistry of the user to determine which path is the most efficient, extensible, and aesthetically pleasing for the project at hand.

Houdini's Family of Products

Side Effects offers five flavors of Houdini, each with different capabilities and prices attached. Basically, they break down as follows. For more specific information, visit the Website at `http://www.sidefx.com`.

◆ Houdini Master is the total package. It contains modeling, animation, character, advanced effects, dynamic simulations, compositing, texturing, shading and materials, VEX building, and rendering tools.

◆ Houdini Select has a subsection of those capabilities. It comprises modeling, animation, basic effects, texturing, shading and materials, VEX building, and rendering.

◆ Houdini Escape is the same as Select, but with the addition of the character tools.

◆ Houdini Halo contains the compositing tools only.

◆ Houdini Apprentice is the free learning edition of the software. It is a very capable version with only a few limitations. A couple of the more noticeable ones are listed here:

    It places a watermark in the lower-right corner of all renders.
    Renders are restricted to a maximum resolution of 640×480.
    It doesn't allow writing out of geometry sequences.
    No Renderman or Mental Ray support is included.

In addition to those flavors, it is also possible to purchase in a a nongraphical version of Master. It is typically used to run simulations or renders on a render farm.

My Perspective

Alas, you encounter the unabashed opinions of the author! Over the past several years, I have studied a number of 3D packages and found them all to be reasonably capable; however, in Houdini, I found creative freedom. Strap on your tissue holsters, I am talking feelings here. From the beginning and continuing to this day, I have always felt that Houdini offers the tools to fit my mindset and creative approach instead of forcing my approach into the confines of the tools.

I am also fascinated with the way in which Houdini seems to stimulate both the creative and analytical aspects of my mind. The art at the beginning of this chapter juxtaposes these two approaches, with the torii gate being a stylized and creative symbol interacting with the mechanical and interlocking gears. When in harmony, these two aspects of the mind and approaches can produce powerful and pleasing results. You can easily see an example of this in the interface when comparing the Viewer pane (as shown in Figures 1.2 and 1.4) and the Network Editor pane (as shown in Figures 1.3 and 1.5). Each pane essentially represents the same information. However, the Viewer expresses this in a way that appeals to the visual, spacial, creative right brain, whereas the Network Editor shows causal relationships, orders of flow, and details that appeal to the analytical left brain.

This sort of symbiotic relationship pervades the program and provides continuous opportunities to focus the whole of the brain on the task at hand.

Initially, I looked upon the vast and darkened landscape of this package's methodology with excitement and more than a little trepidation. As we all know, out under the moon surrounded by dimmed sky, the strangest things can and likely will happen. Today, I can still see quite a number of unexplored peaks in the distance. And I happily look forward to encountering each of them, knowing that a solid grasp on the basics will capably take me into whatever adventures lay ahead. I hope you can find the same enjoyment on your own quest in this ever-expanding electronic multiverse.

So, please proceed with eager intention and bold demeanor! Yeehaa! <Cue the clarions.>

Summary

Houdini is a software package with roots in the birth of the CG industry. Although it has evolved over time, the basic feature of its procedural workflow has stayed the same. This paradigm of connecting nodes together to form more complex networks offers great flexibility and creative control in the production process and is used to create many of the stunning images you see in your favorite films.

chapter 2
3D Concepts Reviewed

Where Is 3D?

So you are determined and excited now, right? That is good, because before you can jump into the glory of creating an alien world or a terrestrial apocalypse, you must first ensure that you have a solid understanding of the 3D concepts that comprise your new environment. Most of you have, at one time or another, had the experience of measuring a mattress. After all, how else can you ensure that every square foot of your room is covered in springy good times? After taking these measurements, you usually describe them in terms of a width, height, and depth. Now imagine you are floating above and looking down on one mattress. From this perspective, the left to right measurement indicates width, the top to bottom measurement indicates height, and the measurement from the top side to the back side of the mattress indicates depth.

This sort of visualization is easily understood in terms of 3D coordinate systems as well. Houdini uses a rectangular coordinate system that is basically the same as the one Rene Descartes created way back in the 1600s. In fact, the story goes that Rene was lying in bed while watching a fly. At some pivotal moment, he realized that he could exactly describe the fly's position by using just three numbers. He devised a system wherein each of the axes described above was designated with a letter: x for width, y for height, and z for depth. The point at which each of these axes intersects is called the *world origin*. This point divides each axis into a positive and a negative side. Houdini uses a right-hand coordinate system, which means that x values become larger to the right of the origin and smaller to the left, y values become larger above the origin and smaller below it, and z values become larger the nearer the viewer and smaller as they are farther away from the viewer. Figure 2.1 shows this type of system.

Using this system, you can give any point (or fly) a position in 3D space using the world coordinates x, y, and z (x,y,z). For example, (0,1,0) indicates a point one unit above the origin. (-4, 3, -2) indicates a point that is four units to the left of the origin, three above it, and two units forward, or "into" the monitor.

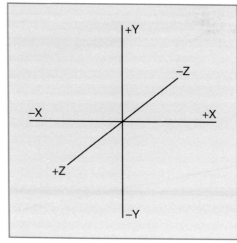

Figure 2.1
Slightly above and to the right of the default view in a right-hand coordinate system.

When using the terms left, above, and into, it is important to remember that these are somewhat loose terms. They describe the default state of the coordinate system in relation to the viewer. However, if the view is changed in some way, those terms might no longer be accurate. The new view might be showing positive Y going down, to the left, or some other direction. So, it is important to remember that the generic terms only apply when the axes are being viewed in the default, home position.

Another important point to consider is that the units in Houdini are arbitrary real-world distances. One unit to the right doesn't necessarily mean 1 meter, 12 inches, or 1 mile to the right. The units are adjusted to whatever seems most useful for the particular project at hand.

The Building Blocks of 3D Space

Now that you have an expansive playground before you, how do you begin to create sandboxes and swings to populate it? Every complex 3D model is comprised of smaller and smaller building blocks, just as we humans have bodies comprised of organs, which are comprised of cells, which are in turn comprised of atoms, which are then comprised of quarks, which are likely comprised of ever smaller phenomenon we have yet to discover. Fortunately, the aspiring 3D artist can treat the *point* as the smallest measurable unit.

So, place a single point out there in the void and suddenly your universe is populated! Place another point out there in a different location and you begin to play. Connect these two points and you have now created what Houdini calls an *edge*, which is a polygon face or curve. Experience the grandeur of evolution! Place yet another point off to the side somewhere and connect it to one of the points. Check out Figure 2.2 to see where this is going. Houdini calls this an *open polygon*.

Polygons are created from one or more connected straight edges. These edges are defined by the vertices that comprise them. Now, make the final evolutionary leap and connect the unfinished side, thereby creating a triangle composed of three edges and three vertices. You now have a *closed polygon*, because you can define the shape's inside and outside.

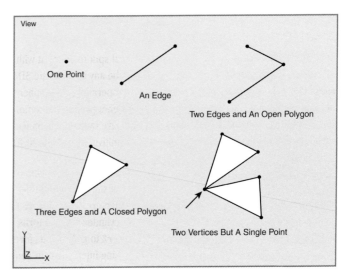

Figure 2.2
The building blocks of 3D space.

Points and Vertices

It is important to note that vertices and points aren't exactly the same things. As stated before, a *point* is a position in space defined by coordinates. *Polygons* (or other primitive types) are built on top of these points using vertices. A point can exist all by itself and be happy. In order to have a vertex (happy or otherwise), you need to have a primitive that it is a part of; in this case, a polygon. Vertices cannot live by themselves as points can. So, a vertex must reference a point, or a position in space, in order to build a polygon primitive.

Several primitives can have unique vertices that each reference the same point. In Figure 2.2, two triangular polygons share a point, or position in space. Each of them has their own unique vertex at that position in space and that position information is contained in the point. In other words, a point is considered the generic holder of a position in space, whereas several vertices can occupy that position and be unique to its accompanying polygon.

Primitives

As the term primitive was just used, this is a great spot to define it with relation to Houdini. In the 3D universe, a *primitive* is often considered to be any of the basic 3D geometric forms that packages offer as building blocks for more complex operations. The sphere, box (cube), tube (cylinder), and cone are examples. In Houdini however, a primitive is a more inclusive term. On the one hand, it is a type of geometry. Anytime you have two points connected by an edge, you have created a primitive. So, a single polygon is a primitive, or a single NURBs patch is a primitive.

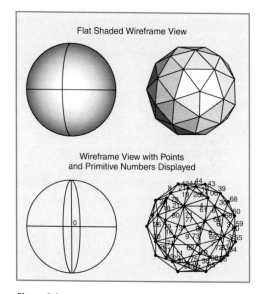

Figure 2.3
Left sphere of primitive type primitive and right sphere composed of many primitives.

However, just to make things nice and confusing, there is also a type of geometry called primitive. When geometry is of type primitive, it is actually a single point that defines a shape. This single point is used in a relatively simple equation to then create the shape. There are only a few shapes that are of type primitive, including the sphere, cylinder, and the torus. For example, a sphere of type primitive uses the equation $x2 + y2 + z2 = r2$ to generate its form. Using geometry of this type can be useful in saving memory and increasing interactivity in complex networks because their forms are represented by relatively simple equations. These types of primitives can be transformed in different ways Because they are defined by a single point, they cannot be subsequently deformed and so are of limited usefulness. To understand the difference between transformations and deformations, check out that section later in this chapter.

See Figure 2.3 to view spheres using the two distinct definitions of the word primitive. The sphere on the left is of type `primitive`. The sphere on the right is composed of many polygonal primitives.

2. 3D Concepts Reviewed

Planar and Non-Planar Geometric Forms

Two of the basic forms for geometric creation are the triangle and the quad. A *triangle* is comprised of three connected edges and three vertices. A *quad* is created when you add one more point off to the side and connect it. A quad is comprised of four connected edges and four vertices. An important point to consider when modeling with complex polygons (quads or greater) is that it is possible to make them non-planar.

A polygon is either planar or non-planar. A polygon is *planar* when all of its vertices lie on the same plane in 3D space. A polygon is *non-planar* when one or more of its vertices do not lie in the same plane in 3D space. Consider the triangle you just created. Assume two of the vertices are stationary. Now, you take the third vertex and move it up and down. Anywhere you move it, all three vertices will always lie along the same plane or be "flat" when viewed edge on. A triangle polygon is always planar because of this. Imagine taking a notebook sheet of paper and folding it diagonally into a triangle. Lay it flat on a table and the three corners lie within the same plane and so are planar. Now pick up one corner (pretend the paper is very stiff); you can see that all three corners still lie within a single plane when viewed edge on, and so the polygon is still planar.

Take a quad, on the other hand, and assume three of the four vertices are stationary. Now take the remaining vertex and move it perpendicular to the plane that the quad lies on. When viewed edge-on, you can see that this polygon is now non-planar. In other words, unfold that sheet of paper so you again have a four-sided page lying flat on a desk. All four of its corners lie within the same plane and so it is planar. Take one corner of the paper and lift it up. Now you have one point that no longer lies within the same plane as the other three. The paper is now non-planar. Figure 2.4 shows the triangle from above and from the side, and also the quad from above and from the side. The quad has its upper-left point pulled up and so had made it non-planar.

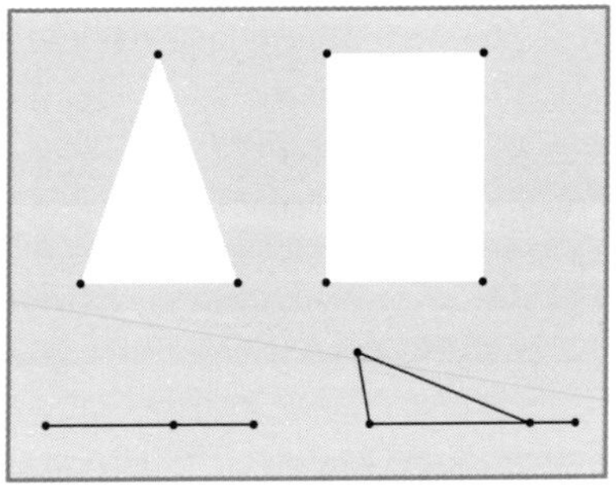

It is important to keep this difference in mind, because some modeling, rendering, and dynamics operations don't function correctly when applied to non-planar surfaces. To fix the quad (or notebook paper), you can either move the single point back in line with the other three points or split it diagonally with an edge and create two connected triangles, which, as I said before, are always planar.

Figure 2.4
The triangle is planar and the quad is non-planar.

Convex and Concave Polygons

Another important characteristic of polygons is whether they are convex or concave. A *convex polygon* is one in which any horizontal or vertical axis intersects it no more than twice. A circle, box, and triangle are examples. A *concave polygon* is one in which any horizontal or vertical axis intersects it more than twice. A star and crescent moon are examples of concave polygons. Some modeling and rendering operations don't function correctly when applied to concave polygons. So, it is important to know the difference when working with geometry. See Figure 2.5 to get a look at this.

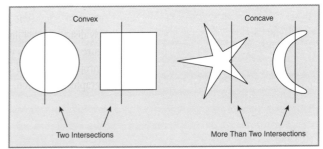

Convex   Concave

Two Intersections   More Than Two Intersections

Figure 2.5
Convex and concave polygons.

Through the Looking Glass

So, now that you grok the underlying principles of the space you are about to inhabit, how do you go about getting a peek at it? The large backlit screen you use is the door, but where is the key to that door? You view every 3D scene from a particular viewpoint, whether it is from the camera or some other arbitrary view. This viewpoint is limited by the extents of the viewport. By default, the viewport sees the x axis as running horizontally with larger values to the right, the y axis running vertically with larger values above, and the z axis running "out" and "into" the plane with larger values out towards the viewer and beyond. The *clipping plane* surrounds the viewpoint and is perpendicular to it. Normally, the clipping plane is the same as the viewport window with which you are viewing the 3D environment. It is called a clipping plane because you can't see farther to the right, left, above, or below than its borders allow and you also can't see behind it.

Even if you change the default homed, your viewpoint is always in the center and is always bounded by the limits of the clipping plane. This is exactly the same way you experience vision. You can move around and up or down and your viewpoint is always "centered" and your field of view is bounded by the capabilities of your eyes. You can't see something behind you. You can't see anything behind your clipping plane without rotating your viewpoint or moving back far enough so that the object comes into view.

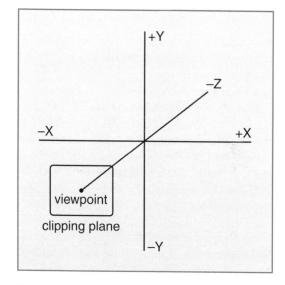

Figure 2.6
The viewpoint and the clipping plane (or viewport).

Perspective Projection and Orthographic Projection

Houdini has a number of preset viewpoints, including front/back, top/bottom, right/left, and perspective. An important difference between them is that the *perspective viewpoint* is a perspective projection, as its name implies. This means that if you project lines along the same axis off into the distance, they converge at a distant vanishing point. The other viewpoints use an *orthographic projection*, which simulates the vanishing point being infinitely distant so that lines on the same axis are parallel and so never converge. Figure 2.7 illustrates the difference in how a cube looks viewed through each of the projection methods. You can see that depth is not clearly represented in the orthographic projection.

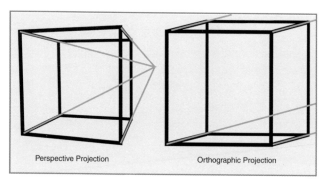

Figure 2.7
Perspective and orthographic projections.

Coordinate Spaces in Houdini

When manipulating objects in the 3D world, you always do so within the context of a particular space. The space that encompasses the 3D environment is called the *world* or *global space*. The point at which the three axes intersect is called the *world origin* and is identified as (0,0,0) or 0 in x, 0 in y, 0 in z. Another common coordinate space is called *object* or *local space*. Object space is the coordinate system that is attached to a particular entity or object and moves with it as it moves around world space. The object space origin is generally in the center of the object to which the space is referring but can be repositioned if needed. All the work you do inside an object is being done in a space "local" to the container object.

For example, suppose you are creating that playground of memories, when the days were long and carefree. It might make the most sense to position the various playground essentials in world space, because they are stationary in relation to the world origin. Then, object space can be used to animate each implement of youthful enjoyment. Each swing on the swing set would have its origin repositioned to the top of its geometry. Then the swing and chains would be rotated back and forth. The tetherball could have an object rotation that would make the ball and string swing about the central pole. The seesaw would have an object rotation taking its participants from butt-bumping depths to sky-walking heights. In these cases, it wouldn't make much sense to try to animate these motions in world space, because their offset from the world origin could result in nonsensical and unexpected movement.

Consider the seesaw, for example, as shown in Figure 2.8. You could build the seesaw and then place it wherever you wanted on the playground in world space. You could then animate how the seats go up and down by placing the pivot correctly in object space.

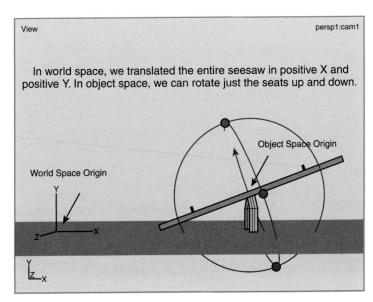

View   persp1:cam1

In world space, we translated the entire seesaw in positive X and positive Y. In object space, we can rotate just the seats up and down.

Object Space Origin

World Space Origin

Figure 2.8
World space and object space.

Transformations and Order

A *transform* is an umbrella term that includes making a change to geometry with a translation, rotation, and/or scale. So, if you have made a change in any one or more of these three areas, you have made a transformation. When you are first getting used to these terms, it is easy to confuse a translate and a transform. Keep in mind, though, that a transform doesn't necessarily involve moving an object, whereas a translate means just that.

> *Translate*: Move something in one or more of the x, y, and z axes.
>
> *Rotate*: Turn something around a central point in one or more of the x, y, and z axes.
>
> *Scale*: Make something bigger or smaller in one or more of the x, y, and z axes.

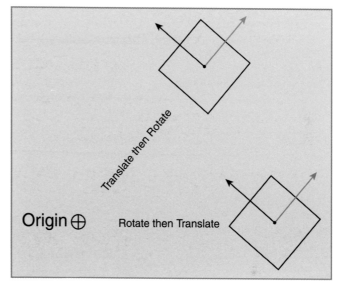

Figure 2.9
The order of transforms is important.

The order of how transformations are applied is important. Figure 2.9 illustrates this concept. Notice that the box ends up in a different spot depending upon the order of how the transforms are applied.

Transformation and Deformation

As you have already learned, a transformation is a translate, rotate, and/or scale (t, r, and/or s) change. A *deformation* is similar in that you are moving parts of geometry around using t, r, and/or s. However, it is different in that you are affecting the geometry in a non-uniform way. Transformations are applied to an object's origin, a single point. Deformations are many individual transformations applied to the actual geometric points used to define the geometry. Each point comprising the geometry can be transformed in a unique way, depending on the operation. This means that not all parts of the geometry are being affected in the same way. The upper half might be scaled larger, whereas the lower half is rotated and translated forward a bit. It is clear then that deformations are much more expensive to compute the transformations. In addition, knowing the difference between these two ideas is useful when working with velocities and motion blur, which are covered in Chapter 13, "Render Outputs."

2. 3D Concepts Reviewed

Summary

It is very helpful to have an understanding of the basic principles underlying the world of 3D before attempting your first cannonball into its warm waters. Don't worry if any of the concepts just discussed seem a little vague. As you progress through the book, you will find concrete instances in which to apply them.

chapter 3
The Houdini Interface

The Introductory Method

So many parts of the interface are interrelated and all of them have yet to be discussed, so breaking them into distinct categories of explanation is a difficult proposition. Throughout this book, I've made much effort to present each section in a manner that requires as little intermingling with yet-to-be-covered topics as possible. Although this is the goal, it's not an easy one and there are times where converging topics require a more relaxed approach. In addition, occasionally it's just more interesting to throw in a little bit of spice! The spice of life, oui? This chapter is about the interface and every subsequent chapter depends on it, so it's a little looser than usual and uses examples and explanations that are covered in more detail in later chapters.

Now that you have the basic concepts of a 3D environment in place, you can proceed to the point of this whole exercise—further playing in the land of Houdini! If you haven't already, you need to install the Apprentice version, which can be downloaded from the Side Effects Website at www.sidefx.com. Look in the Learning menu and choose the Apprentice option.

Four Basic Interface Zones

Go ahead and start Houdini and witness the wonder unfolding. The Houdini interface consists of four basic zones—the main menu bar at the top, one or more pane windows in the middle area, the playbar at the bottom, and the message bar just below that. Refer to Figure 3.1 to see the default setup of Houdini; it shows each of these zones, colored for clarification. The main menu bar is composed of drop-down menus that give you access to a large array of options. The pane windows are where the work of Houdini goes on. A pane is a generic window that can be configured in a number of ways to show the desired information.

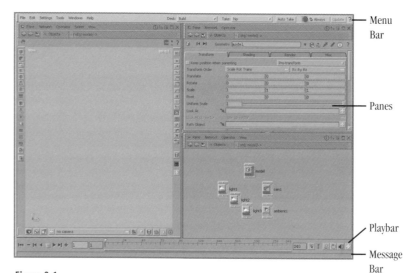

Menu
Bar

Panes

Playbar

Message
Bar

Figure 3.1
The four basic interface zones, colored for clarity.

15

The playbar allows you to control the timeline and make adjustments to it such as setting the frame range and frame rate. The message bar shows brief tips on how to use the currently selected operation.

The main menu bar is in blue at the top. The panes are in red in the middle of the screen. The playbar is the long strip in green just below the panes, and the message bar is in gray at the very bottom.

Help Pane

As on any playground or swimming pool, you sometimes have to refer to the manual to learn or refresh your memory as to how a tire swing, diving board, or Isosurface SOP works. Houdini has long been perceived as having a dearth of supporting documents. Often, the documentation that you could find required previous understanding (in which case, you wouldn't need the help) or a degree in technospeak to translate. Fortunately, Side Effects has been making great strides in the last few releases to fully and clearly document the various functions and features. Houdini comes with an integrated browser that has hyperlinked help topics that often contain example files that can be loaded directly from the browser.

To access the Help browser, click on the question mark in the upper-right corner of the Houdini window. The question mark is just to the right of the Always and Update buttons, as shown in Figure 3.2.

By default, the Help pane pops up alongside the Network Editor and Parameter panes. When you're jumping back and forth to the Help browser, it is often much easier to tear off the Help pane and have it accessible as a stand-alone window. To do this, simply click on the Tear Pane button. It is located in the upper-right area of any pane. The Tear Pane button is enclosed in a blue box in Figure 3.3.

Now you have the Help pane in a separate window that can be minimized or maximized as needed without affecting the size of any other panes you might be using. Figure 3.4 displays the Help pane in all her useful majesty. Now that you know the slightly more tedious way of getting to the Help browser, it is time to learn the simpler way. Close the current window and then click on the Help menu in the main menubar and choose Help Contents. This pops up a separate pane window automatically.

Figure 3.2
Access to the Help browser is in the upper-right corner of the Houdini window.

Figure 3.3
Tear the pane using the Tear Pane button.

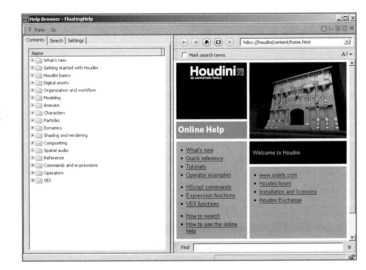

Figure 3.4
The Help pane.

The Help pane is divided into the listing of Contents and the display area (or browser). Depending on the size of the pane, the format may place the Contents on the left with the browser on the right or it may place the browser above and the Contents below. If you find yours is displaying the latter, widen the pane window until the Contents pop over to the left side. So now, anything you choose on the left is displayed on the right. The display area is a fully functioning Web browser that you can use to access outside Internet content. As with any pane, you can change the Help pane into any one of the other available pane types. To change the pane type, LMB on the word Pane in the upper-left corner of a pane window and choose a different option.

The Go menu contains shortcuts for jumping to the software change log, information about licensing and installation, the Houdini community, and the Houdini forum. The software change log is a great spot to read about bug fixes, find small changes to operators, and learn about new feature additions. The information includes any changes and lists in which build the change has been instituted. The licensing and installation page contains a quick review of licensing processes and a rudimentary troubleshooting procedure.

The Houdini community page is a great resource for both aspiring and experienced users. It lists Houdini's latest news and includes links of third-party resources found on the Web. If you're a new user, visit these sites to see what each has to offer. Two that I visit regularly are www.odforce.net and www.3dbuzz.com. Both have good forums with a wealth of information. The odforce forum tends to be frequented by professionals and newbies alike and contains some great discussions, example files, and effects challenges. The 3dbuzz forum is geared more towards beginner issues. The Side Effects forum is another required stop for the interested Houdnik.

> In this book,
>
> LMB = Left mouse button
> MMB = Middle mouse button
> RMB = Right mouse button
>
> In cases where the text says just to click or select, it is assumed to be referring to a LMB action. Also, the method of clicking is very important. A click of any of the buttons should be a quick tap. In some cases, if you perform a rather slow click, things won't work the way they should. So, anytime you should do a click (and not a click and hold), click the button with a fast tap.

> *Houdnik* is a Houdini beatnik; that is, a Houdini user who lovingly embraces the unconventional and creative methodologies employed by the software and enjoys waxing poetically on those same attributes. Thanks to Valerie Berney for that moniker.

Side Effects is an amazing resource and often contains the advice and responses of those kind folk who, as mentioned, live in a cave up near Toronto and create this software. Another of the buttons takes you to the Houdini mail list archive. This is an invaluable list where real production issues are often bandied back and forth between some of the most knowledgeable Houdini folk in the land. Many of its posters are professionals in the industry and use Houdini on a daily basis. For the beginner, this is an often overlooked resource because of the complexity of the issues being discussed. If the topics don't readily make too much sense, check back now and again as you continue the learning process. Over time, you will understand more and more and likely come to prize the camaraderie and openness that characterizes this discussion list as well as most any Houdini forum.

The Go menu also has a Houdini forum option that takes you to the same place as that great big button does on the Houdini community page.

3. The Houdini Interface

At the bottom of the browser is a Find feature. You can use it to search the help documentation for topics of interest. For example, if you want to know more about how the various brush operations work, type **brush** and your search is filtered as you spell out the word. Topics of interest are listed in the left window under the Search tab. Click the topics to see their associated content in the display area on the right. The Settings tab contains options for setting a home page for the display area, setting font type and sizes, and a few Help browser interface options.

The display area on the right has many of the same interface options as a normal Web browser, with buttons to jump backward and forward, go to the home page, refresh the current page, stop loading the current page, search for content within a page, and a URL bar where you can manually type in a particular Web address. In addition, there are helpful links to What's New, Tutorials, Expression Functions, and more.

Now that you have an inkling of where to go when you need help, you're ready to strut. Webster defines strut as "to walk with a pompous and affected air." What I mean is to move forward with that kind of style and flair, but without the bombastic attitude. Can you dig it?

The Three Most Common Panes

By default, Houdini is arranged in three panes—the Viewer pane, the Network Editor pane, and the Parameters pane. Figure 3.5 shows each of these areas. The Viewer pane is where you control the viewport and can change how things are displayed. The Network Editor pane shows you a node-based view of what your networks look like. Each of the boxes in this pane is considered a node (or tile). The Parameters pane shows you the specific information about a particular node.

A pane is a generic window that you can configure to display a number of different types of information. The Network Editor pane could just as easily be set to show parameters (in which case, it becomes the Parameters pane) or the view into 3D space (in which case, it becomes the Viewer pane).

To change the pane type, just click the Pane menu in the upper-left corner of any pane and choose a different type. LMB on the Pane menu in the Viewer pane and choose Network Editor. You now see the same information as in the other Network Editor pane that was already displayed. Now change it to a Channel Editor pane. This pane is used for manipulating animation channels. As you can see, you can configure a pane to display whatever type of information you want. Change it back to a Viewer pane to continue this chapter.

Viewer Pane

Parameters Pane

Network Editor Pane

Figure 3.5
The three most common panes.

The Viewer Pane

The Viewer pane is where you control the viewport and can change how things are displayed using projection methods with different shading modes, as well as determine what kind of geometric information to display, such as point numbers and normals, and much more.

Stowbars

Stowbars are common to all panes and allow you to hide or display the associated contents. If you don't see all the options, as shown in Figure 3.6, you might need to LMB on a stowbar to unstow the information. Stowbars provide a quick way to maximize screen space by collapsing options you don't need to see.

State Indicator

The state indicator tells you what type of state you are in. No, it isn't a palm reader or a clinical behaviorist, so it won't have much luck in diagnosing your personal state, but it is highly accurate in describing what state you are in within Houdini. Some actions can only be performed in particular states. The two basic categories are View state or an operational state. Adjustments to the viewpoint are made while in the View state, whereas adjustments to a particular operation are performed while in the chosen operational state.

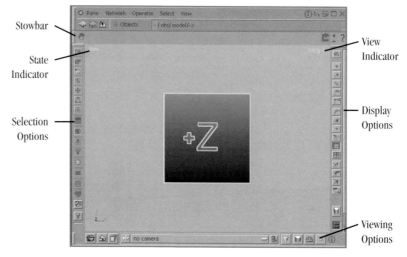

Figure 3.6
The Viewer pane.

View Indicator

The view indicator tells you which view you are currently using to peer into the scene. You can choose to view the scene through a number of views, including perspective, top, left, back, and so on.

Selection Options

This is where you set selection options such as using a mask, choosing secure selection, redoing a selection, and more. For example, you can turn on a point selection mask so that your selection is limited only to the points of a piece of geometry as opposed to its edges, faces, and so on.

Display Options

This is where you set the display options like the visibility of points, hulls, primitive numbers, and more. For example, you can turn on the display of primitive normals to see whether they are facing in the expected direction.

Viewing Options

This is where you set the viewing options like camera view, shading mode, quick rendering, and more. For example, you can turn on the view of a construction grid if it helped out in lining up geometry to a common ground plane.

Moving the View Around

To have any degree of creative fun and success in your new world, you must first be able to see it and move around in it.

1. Start a new session of Houdini and you should see the default box in the Viewer pane. Verify that you are in the View state by looking in the upper-left corner of the viewport (as shown in Figure 3.6).

3. Now that you see something in the viewport, you can practice seeing different sides of it. After all, it is always a good mental exercise to consider the different sides of a situation.

Use the following mouse buttons to adjust the viewpoint as stated. Experiment with each of these methods to gain an intuitive understanding of what each does. If you happen to lose sight of the geometry, home the view with the h key.

LMB = Tumble (rotate around)

MMB = Dolly (move in or out)

RMB = Track (move up, down, left, or right)

Notice that as you move the viewpoint around, the floating origin in the lower-left corner of the viewport moves as well. This keeps you informed as to how the global axes are oriented, as shown in Figure 3.7.

X axis = red

Y axis = green

Z axis = blue

> Most of the hotkeys discussed in this section depend on where the pointer is when they are used. So in the current section, you need to make sure the pointer is over the Viewer pane when using the hotkeys. As a general rule, the same hotkey can have different functions depending on where the pointer is.

> Use the h key to home your view in either the viewport or the Network Editor pane. The position of your pointer determines which pane is homed. When homing in the viewport, you must be in View state.

Figure 3.7
The floating axis indicator shows you how the global axes are oriented.

The View State and Operational States

As stated previously, you must first be in the View state in order to change the viewpoint. You can verify the current state with the status indicator in yellow as shown in Figure 3.8. This will either say View, if you are in the View state, or *Operation*, whereby *Operation* is the name of the operation you are currently in. For example, it can say Transform or Polyextrude. So, the *very* important lesson to remember is that if you are in an operational state (also called a working state because it is doing some kind of work), you can't make adjustments to your viewpoint. Likewise, if you are in the View state, you can't access the operation-specific GUI handles.

If you are in an operational state, you can temporarily go into the View state by pressing the spacebar. While the spacebar is pressed, you will see that the status indicator has changed from a working state to the View state. To go from an operational state to the View state, ensure your pointer is over the viewport and press the Esc key. To go from the View state to an operational state, again ensure your pointer is over the viewport and press the Enter key. Being in an operational state gives you access to the GUI handles.

Figure 3.8
The status indicator showing the View state.

> Press and hold the spacebar to temporarily enter the View state. Press the Esc key to exit from an operational state to the View state. Press the Enter key to go from the View state to an operational state.

> It is very important to always be aware of what state you are in within Houdini. You must be in the View state to move the viewpoint around. You must be in an operational state to have access to the GUI handles in the viewport.

Transform Handles

Transform handles give you access in the GUI to moving geometry around using translates, rotates, and scales.

1. In the Network Editor pane, select the node called *box* by LMB on the icon area of the node or box-selecting the entire node. You know the node is selected when it is highlighted in yellow. Go into an operational state by pressing Enter. You should see the manipulator handle for the box, as shown in Figure 3.9. You can also see that you are in an operational state called Geometry.

2. Try to move the viewpoint just using the mouse buttons and you will find that you cannot. As stated earlier, that's because you are in a working state. Hold down the spacebar and try again. This temporarily puts you in View state and so allows you to move the viewpoint around.

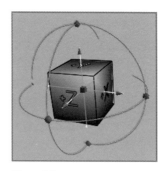

Figure 3.9
One of the transform handles.

3. The Houdini Interface

3. Home the view again. Depending on the particular operation, the GUI handle might appear different. In the Geometry working state, you have access to a translate/scale handle, a translate/rotate handle, and a translate only handle. The hotkeys are e, r, and t, respectively.

4. Toggle on the translate/scale handle and examine the different parts of the handle, as shown in Figure 3.10.

   LMB and drag on one of the interior white lines to translate the box in a particular axis. LMB and drag on the purple box in the center to have the freedom to translate in all three axes at once. You can use Ctrl+Z to undo any changes. By default, Houdini has a very large number of undos.

> With your pointer over the viewport, press the e key to toggle to the translate/scale handle. Press the r key to toggle to the translate/rotate handle. Press the t key to toggle to the translate only handle.

> In your initial forays into the land of Houdini, it is sometimes pretty easy to accidentally press a key and do something unintended. You can always use Ctrl+Z to sequentially undo changes. You can also access a list of possible undos. Go to the main menu by selecting Edit>Undo History. There, you can specifically select a particular spot in the history to undo (or redo) to.

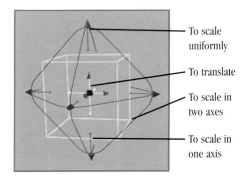

To scale uniformly

To translate

To scale in two axes

To scale in one axis

Figure 3.10
The translate/scale handle.

5. LMB and drag on one of the red cones (or arrows) on the outside edges of the handle to uniformly scale the box in all axes. Now LMB and drag on one of the red interior lines just inside these arrows to scale in a particular axis. Now LMB and drag one of the outside red edges of the handle to scale uniformly in two axes. For example, grab the red edge pointed to in Figure 3.10 and you can scale the box in X and Y simultaneously.

6. Press the r key and you still have access to translation, but now you have access to rotation, too. LMB and drag on one of the red curves to rotate in a particular axis or LMB and drag on the red intersections of the curves to rotate freely in all axes.

7. Press the spacebar to move the viewpoint around a bit.

8. Press the t key and you will only have access to translation handles. This handle operates the same in that you can constrain movement to a particular axis or move freely in all three axes at once.

9. Finally, press Esc to exit the working state and then home the view.

10. The h hotkey homes the view on all visible geometry. In this case, the view is homed on the box. If you have multiple pieces of visible geometry widely spaced, h pushes the viewpoint back as far as needed to encompass them all. This is just like trying to fit everyone in the frame when taking a group photo. The photographer must keep backing up until everyone is in frame.

The g key homes the view on selected geometry only. Homing on selected geometry is especially helpful when you want to get up close to a particular area of the geometry for a closer look. Homing the view on the selection sets the viewport's pivot around that selection and so makes it much easier to maneuver around it to get a better view.

11. Ensure that the box node is selected and press enter to jump "into" the Object. With your pointer over the viewport, press s to go into the Select state. Press the 1 hotkey to use the point selection mask. Now choose one of the corner of the default box, as shown in Figure 3.11. Press g to home the viewport on the selected point. Tumble the view around to see that the pivot is now centered on this selection. This makes it easier to examine particular areas in detail.

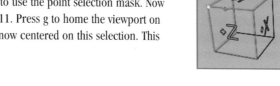

Figure 3.11
A point is selected on the default box.

12. It is also possible to frame the view, which achieves a slightly different goal than homing it. Press u to jump back "up" to the Object level. Dolly out a bit and tumble the view. Make sure you are in the View state and press f to frame the viewport. Notice the difference between framing and homing the view. Figure 3.12 shows the difference between the two methods. You can use Shift+F to frame the current selection, just as you can use g to home the current selection.

> Over the viewport and in the View state, press h to home the view, press g to home the selection, press f to frame the view, or press Shift+F to frame the selection.

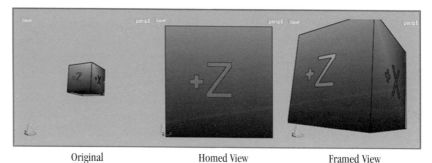

Original   Homed View   Framed View

Figure 3.12
The difference between framing and homing the viewport.

Moving Between Viewpoints

Houdini offers a number of defaults viewpoints that help to get desired angle on the 3D world.

1. Looking in the upper-right corner of the viewport, you can see the word *persp1* in yellow, which tells you that you are using the perspective viewpoint. You can view the 3D world from a number of default views, including top, front, right, UV view, and so on. Use the hotkey spacebar+*number,* whereby *number* is 1 through 5, to quickly jump to a particular view. Cycle through these and come back to space+1, which is the hotkey for the perspective view. As its name states, the perspective view is a perspective projection and shows geometry as you see the world. The top, right, back, and other, views show the geometry in an orthographic projection.

> Press spacebar+*number* (whereby *number* is 1 through 5) to quickly select which view is shown in the viewport: 1 is the perspective view, 2 is the top view, 3 is the front view, 4 is the right view, and 5 is the UV view.

2. You can also have several views up at once, which is often helpful in modeling. To go to quad view, use the spacebar+T hotkey. Quad view shows you four views at one time. By default, these are perspective, right, front, and top when looked at in a clockwise fashion. In the front viewport, drag the box around. The changes in position are reflected in the other viewports as well. It is easier to get very precise placement using multiple views in this way.

> Press spacebar+T to jump into quad view. Press spacebar+T again with your pointer over a particular view to expand that view.

3. You can expand a particular view by pressing spacebar+T again while the pointer is over the desired view. With your pointer over the front view, press spacebar+T to expand it. Go back to quad view and then jump back into perspective view.

The Network Editor Pane

The Network Editor pane shows you a node-based view of your networks and, when organized well, is a good visual indication of the flow of information.

1. Open a new session of Houdini, or if you are continuing from the previous exercise, just continue.

2. In the viewport, you should see the default box. You can also see that there are tiles in the Network Editor that represent the lights, camera, and geometry in the scene. These are just different methods for viewing the same information.

Object Node Functionality

You are currently in the Objects context and so each node is a particular Object type. To verify this, ensure that the context menu says Objects, as shown back in Figure 3.8. There are numerous Object types available and you can see that several Objects exist in the file, including light, geometry, and camera objects. Although nodes have slightly different functions in different contexts, they are very similar. Select the model (containing the box geometry) node and examine it, as shown in Figure 3.13.

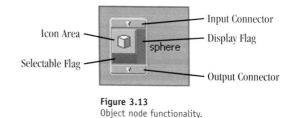

Figure 3.13
Object node functionality.

◆ Every node has an input and output connector. These are used to connect nodes to form networks of nodes. LMB the icon area of a node to select it. You can also click outside the box and drag a selection box around it in order to select it. The blue flag is called the Display flag and controls whether the geometry contained in the object is displayed in the viewport. LMB on the Display flag and observe that the box disappears in the viewport, and then toggle it back on. The brown flag is the Selectable flag and controls whether the object can be selected in the viewport.

◆ Select the model Object and press Enter to jump into it and thus enter the SOPs (Surface Operations) context. You can tell that you are in a different context because the menus are a different color and the context menu says SOPs instead of Objects. A *geometry object* is basically like a container for holding geometry. You create the object, jump inside, and then, in the SOPs context, create all the interesting geometry that makes minds melt and hearts palpitate. There is already a file SOP, which is why you see a box in the viewport.

Performing an Operation in the View Pane

One node does not provide a very interesting network. With your pointer over the viewport, press the Tab key and type the first three letters of the Transform SOP (t, r, and a). This is a sweet little shortcut for getting to exactly the SOP you want if you already know the name of it. Each letter you enter further narrows the field of possible choices. Usually, just typing the first few letters of the operation is sufficient to find what you want. Select the Transform operation. Read the blue Help bar at the bottom, which says "Select the geometry to transform and right-click to complete." Select the

> To choose an operation in Houdini, press the Tab key to bring up the Tab menu. Conventionally, it's called the Tab menu because of how you access it. Practically, this is the Operators menu and is where you choose from a plethora of operators to use.

box in the viewport and RMB to complete the operation. Remember that clicking in Houdini can be somewhat finicky. You want to make sure to quickly tap the mouse button to click it and not do it in a slow, moving-in-molasses kind of way. Notice you are now in a Transform working state and have access to the manipulator handle. Using the handle, uniformly make the sphere noticeably larger and move it over in positive X. Press the Esc key to exit to the View state.

The basic paradigm of performing an operation in Houdini is to:

1. Bring up the Tab menu (by pressing Tab) and select the desired operator.

2. Select the geometry to apply it to.

3. RMB to complete the selection. Remember that it needs to be a quick tap!

4. While you're in the operational state, make the desired changes.

Performing an Operation in the Network Editor Pane

You can also perform an operation in the Network Editor. There are times when using one of the methods is preferable to the other. For example, let's add another transform and see how the two methods differ.

1. With your pointer over the Network Editor pane, choose a Transform operation. Houdini shows you an outlined node and is waiting for you to LMB to drop it. Put it beneath the xform1 node. A couple of things become immediately apparent. You don't see the handle in the viewport, because you are still in the View state. The newly created node is not connected to the previous nodes and the Display flag (the blue flag) is still on the previous node. Connect the xform2 node to the network by LMB on the output of xform1 and then LMB again on the input of xform2. Turn on the Display flag for xform2. The new transform operation is now a part of the network and you can see its effect in the viewport.

2. You don't yet see the handle because you are still in the View state. With your pointer over the viewport, press Enter to go into the operational state. Notice that the pivot for the handle is not in the center of the sphere. When you add a node in the Network Editor, the pivot is placed at the Object's origin. When you add a node via the Viewer pane, the pivot is placed at the center of the selected geometry. That's fine for now. Move the box to some other location and rotate it a bit for good measure.

As you can see, performing a transform is certainly faster and easier when you do it in the Viewer pane; doing it in the Network Editor pane adds several extra steps. Generally speaking, you will want to work in the Viewer when you want interactive control of selected regions of the scene data. You will want to work in the Network Editor when building procedural networks where rules and procedures dictate geometry selections and modifications.

Networks

Networks are one of the core features and amazing aspects of the Houdini workflow. Because you build up a network with a series of distinct operations, you will always have a history of your work. You are not locked into a decision that might have seemed right earlier in the process, but turned out to be incorrect later. You can always go back up the chain, make changes, and then see how those changes propagate down the chain. This means you have a great deal of freedom to experiment and you never have to worry about permanently breaking something.

Let's look at some basic techniques for navigating and taking advantage of networks.

1. With your pointer over the viewport, press the Page Up key. You now see the scale and translate change you made in xform1, but not the translate or rotate added in xform2. This is because the Display flag has jumped up one node. Press Page Up again and the box is back in its original state because the Display flag has jumped up again. The network should now look like Figure 3.14.

Figure 3.14
The network at this point.

   You will see a grey wireframe view of the sphere as it is in xform2. That is because when you press Page Up, it also turned on the pink Template flag for that node. The Template flag views the state of the network at a particular node, but you cannot affect it in the viewport.

> With your pointer over the viewport, Page Up and Page Down quickly move the Display and Render flags up and down the network and turn on the Template flag for the first node they jumped from. With your pointer over the Network Editor, Page Up and Page Down jump the selected node up and down the network, but leave the Display and Render flags where there are. Changing which node is selected changes what is shown in the Parameters pane.

2. Press Page Down over the viewport to move the Display flag back down to the xform1 node. Using the handle, scale and translate the original sphere. You can see that the templated box inherits the changes made farther up the chain. Use Page Down to bring the Display flag back down to xform2 and turn off the Template flag. You will learn all about the SOP node's functionality in Chapter 5.

The Parameters Pane

The Parameters pane shows you the specific information about a particular node. Let's use the three-node network created in the previous section to check it out.

1. The xform2 node is highlighted in yellow. This tells you that it is the currently selected node and so its parameters are displayed in the Parameters pane. With your pointer over this pane, press the Page Up key and you can see that it has different functionality in this pane. The Display flag stays in the same spot. Now, just the selected node changes and so the parameters shown change. This is a quick way to jump up and down the chain to access the parameters associated with a particular node. You can, of course, just LMB on the node's icon to select it as well.

2. In the parameters for xform2, hold your pointer over the Shear label. A popup window tells you the name of each channel. In this case, you have shear1, shear2, and shear3 from left to right. In the shear1 field, type **2**. You can immediately see its effect in the viewport. RMB on the same field to undo the change. RMB on a field gives one level of undo.

> Use RMB to have quick access to one level of undo in a field. This undo feature is field-independent, so let's say you make a change to the sx field (which is scale in X) and then make other changes. You can later come back to the sx field and RMB to undo back to its previous value.

The Number Ladder

The number ladder is a great way to quickly make value changes to a field or group of fields. Technically, it is called the XCF ladder. X stands for extra, C for coarse, and F for fine. So, if you happen to see that term anywhere in the documentation, you can know that I call it the number ladder.

1. If you don't know exactly what the number is you are looking for, you can use the number ladder to interactively adjust the value. MMB and hold down on the shear1 field and drag the mouse left and right. You can interactively see the changes in the viewport. The increment of the change is based on where your pointer is before you drag left and right. So, for large changes, you might want to move the pointer up to 100 units and then drag left or right. The number ladder is shown in Figure 3.15.

2. Making changes in the viewport or in the Parameters pane are just two ways of accessing the same information. Drag the sphere around the viewport and the parameters will update. Likewise, adjust the parameter values and the viewport reflects those changes. You can also access the number ladder in the viewport. MMB on the part of the handle which corresponds to the axis you want to affect. The number ladder pops up and you can make changes.

Figure 3.15
The number ladder.

> Notice that every time you change a value from its default, it appears in bold. This works on most every interface feature including toggles, radio buttons, sliders, and so on. On the xform2 node, toggle off Recompute Point Normals and you'll see a dot next to it indicating it is no longer at its default value or state. This is a very useful forensic tool, because it allows you to more easily see what has changed about an operation. Basically, it makes understanding and troubleshooting files easier because you can see exactly what changes were made to them.

The Various Contexts

You have already read in a number of spots weird words like SOPs and POPs. But, what exactly are these silly-sounding names? These strange utterances are short names for the contexts available. Houdini is comprised of a number of contexts. Each of the different contexts has different capabilities and you move back and forth between them to achieve different objectives. Each context has a unique color associated with its menus. This section briefly describes what each of the contexts do so that when you hear them elsewhere in the book, you will have a general understanding of what you can do with each of them. For example, if you see the word POPs, you will know that particles are involved.

OBJs (Objects Operators)

The Objects context, shown in Figure 3.16, is considered the top level of your Houdini file. Some Object types are like containers that hold geometry operations and other things inside them. For example, you can lay down a geometry object and name it **apple**. Inside the apple object, you can put all the geometry and shaders you used to create it. This can help keep your files organized and can also enable you to create a digital asset out of the object. For more information on digital assets, refer to Chapter 11, "Digital Assets."

Figure 3.16
The context menu showing the Objects context.

There are numerous Object types each with different capabilities. You create the camera and lights for your scene at this level, create bones for rigging a character, and more. Generally though, the Objects context (also sometimes called level or editor) is where high-level operations and organization occur. You might say this is where you set the table with plates, napkins, utensils, and condiments.

In this context, networks don't function the same as in many other contexts. In this context, connecting a node to another node is creating a hierarchical chain of parent and child. In this relationship, the child inherits all of its parents and its predecessors transforms (translates, rotates, and scales). So, you can easily see how bone objects are used to create skeletal rigs with a foot being parented to an ankle, and an ankle parented to a leg, and so on. In most other contexts, connecting nodes forms a network for passing and computing the aggregate of the operations. This is an important difference to remember.

There are also what I call *Object states*. These are a bit confusing as they are operations that you can access in the Tab menu over the viewport, but not in the Tab menu over the Network Editor. These states often don't create accompanying nodes at the Object level and sometimes don't create nodes at all. I discuss this in more detail in Chapter 4, "Object Operators."

SOPs (Geometry Surface Operators)

The Geometry context, shown in Figure 3.17, is always tied to an Object level node and is contained within it. This is where all the operations occur that actually create and manipulate the geometry that you unwaveringly weave—perhaps it's a Christmas sweater. This context is often considered the meat and potatoes for beginners and experienced users alike, because they spend much time here whiling away the hours in wonderment. For the vegetarians amongst you, it can just as easily and credibly be considered the tofurkey and potatoes context. Hey, I've had tofurkey on a number of occasions and it is certainly an adventure!

Figure 3.17
The context menu showing the Geometry context.

3. The Houdini Interface

DOPs (Dynamic Operators)

In this context, you can create dynamic simulations using solvers that simulate rigid body dynamics, soft body dynamics, and so on. This is where you define the objects being used, the forces at play, and the type of dynamics solution you want to utilize. Just like SOPs, DOP networks can only exist within containers like objects. The DOPs context menu is shown in Figure 3.18.

Figure 3.18
The context menu showing the Dynamics context.

POPs (Particle Operators)

As you progress a little further in your knowledge of the package, the POPs context will likely gain in importance and usage and will become considered the salad and gravy context. The gravy is for the potatoes, not the salad. I say the gravy is for the potatoes because POPs are often intimately connected with SOPs and use them as birthing sources, affecting forces, destinations for passing attributes, and more. Ahh, the life of a particle is such a thing to behold. The POPs context menu is shown in Figure 3.19.

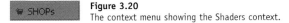

Figure 3.19
The context menu showing the Particles context.

Houdini's particle operators are undoubtedly the strongest and most open set of tools available for creating a wide array of original and challenging effects. Particle simulations are quite adroit in mimicking natural phenomenon and imagined phenomenon, and can be used for all sorts of trickery where it seems no other solution will do.

SHOPs (Shader Operators)

The Shaders context, whose menu is shown in Figure 3.20, is where you will define the nodes that control the surface appearance of your geometry objects, the characteristics of how lights produce shadow, how atmospheres fill a scene, how photons behave, and more. SHOPs is another context where nodes aren't connected into networks that pass along information from one to the next. Generally, each node is separate from the others and referenced in other networks for usage.

Figure 3.20
The context menu showing the Shaders context.

VOPs (VEX Builder) Are VEX Operators

VEX stands for Vector Expression language and is an expression language used widely throughout Houdini. To understand the differences between VEX and the expression language and Hscript, check out the section called "VEX and Expressions and Hscript" in Chapter 10. VOPs is a graphical way of accessing and utilizing the VEX language. VOP nodes basically contain little segments of VEX code that you can connect into networks to perform the same functions as hand-writing the code in a text editor. For many tasks, it is often much faster and simpler to get rolling with an idea in VOPs using the graphical method. The context menu is shown in Figure 3.21.

Figure 3.21
The context menu showing the VEX Builder context.

You'll use VOPs most often to create your own surface and displacement shaders. However, you can also use them to create customized particle operators, geometry operators, and more. Once you get comfortable in Houdini, VOPs are likely to become the green beans and cornbread of your contextual smorgasbord.

CHOPs (Motion and Audio Channel Operators)

The CHOPs context, whose menu is shown in Figure 3.22, is a very interesting and often overlooked aspect of the package, perhaps because it is so unique. CHOPs allows you to create, import, modify, and export analog waveform data. This context is fantastic for automagically creating the secondary motion of a tail whipping or creating the natural randomness found in the flapping of a butterfly's wings.

Figure 3.22
The context menu showing the Motion and Audio context.

You will notice that quite a number of channel operators have names traditionally associated with editing sound like delay, pitch, and resample. In fact, CHOPs can also be used to import, edit, and export audio in the .wav format. One seriously sweet result of this confluence of utilities is that you can use CHOPs to drive animation based on music. Now, you just need Side Effects to also support the import of the .mp3 format and you will be in for some eye-popping, zombie-staring, up-into-the-early-morning enjoyable effort. In their defense, I don't believe that a single one of their current clients is screaming for this capability, and likely not even murmuring for it.

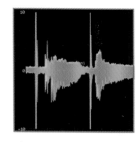

Figure 3.23
Waveform of me saying, "Pecan Pie!"

Figure 3.23 contains a recorded waveform as displayed in CHOPs which is me zestily saying "Pecan Pie!". Hey, that's better than a friend of mine who once taught a class on CHOPs by having his students manipulate a recorded waveform of him belching. You know who you are, Papa C! Ahh, welcome to the intriguing and often disturbing world of Houdini artists!

COPs (Compositing Operators)

In the COPs context, you can manipulate 2D images. Most often, this means compositing render passes but you can also generate texture maps and even manipulate attribute data baked into the image. For example, you can render

Figure 3.24
The context menu showing the Compositing context.

an image with the normal attribute data baked in and then change the lighting of the scene in 2D. Even more interestingly, you can pass data back and forth into COPs and back out in order to achieve some truly original and powerful functionality. For example, you can pass in the rendered view of a camera, analyze it in COPs, and then send out information to other parts of the package, which can then react based on that analysis. In this way, it is possible to model a human and have him or her interact with the environment using a reasonable approximation of actual vision. Figure 3.24 shows the COPs context menu.

ROPs (Outputs Rendering Operators)

The Outputs context, whose menu is shown in Figure 3.25, is where you create and configure drivers to control how images are rendered, how geometry is written out, and more. Houdini comes with a free, production quality renderer

Figure 3.25
The context menu showing the Outputs context.

called Mantra. It is here in ROPs that you can specify how a frame is to be sent to Mantra. For example, for test renders, you can specify a lower super sampling so that the quality is lower and the speed is faster. You can also choose to write out RIB for renderman-compliant renderers.

3. The Houdini Interface

Summary

Houdini's approach to the interface is both a unique and powerfully flexible one. Being able to totally customize your screen real estate using panes is especially helpful. Although it might seem like this chapter gruelingly rambled through one interface gizmo after another, in truth I have just touched the surface of the subject. However, in the interests of preserving both your attention and your neural connectivity, I'll move on to discuss the first context and sprinkle in further interface explanations along the way as you progress through the book.

chapter 4
Object Operators (OBJs)

Here you are in your first official context. It just feels special, doesn't it? As described in the summary of the various contexts in Chapter 3, the important thing to remember about the Objects context is that it is generally considered the place where high-level organization occurs. For example, say your were recreating the solar system within the confines of the 3D space Houdini conjures. Each planet is its own object with the sun relatively at the middle of the scene. Yes, yes. I am saying I agree with the heliocentric view of our immediate celestial environs. All the geometry and shaders for each planet are contained within its Geometry object and that object is named appropriately.

This chapter jumps into SOPs and dabbles in it every so lightly. It's difficult to do much anything of interest solely in the Objects context without jumping into some other context and so you will get some preview practice with SOPs.

Objects as Containers

Objects can act as containers for other networks. A few examples of objects used in this way are the Geometry object, the Light object, and the Camera object. One interesting way to use objects this way is when you're changing the visual display of a light. Let's say you want to change or add some custom functionality to a particular light. You can simply jump inside the Light object and change the geometry located within it. Going further, you can add geometry that had channel references back up to the parameters at the object level. In this way, you can easily create custom parameters at the top level and then have them control the geometry inside the object. For example, let's say you set up a custom attenuation of the light's intensity over distance. You can tie that parameter to geometry inside the object which then allows you to easily visualize in the viewport where the attenuation began, how strong the falloff was, and where it ended (meaning where the light intensity reached 0). Doing this is much faster than repeating the tweak and render cycle to achieve the desired result.

Object States

With your pointer over the viewport, you can perform a number of operations that, in a desire for differentiation, I call *Object states*. These operations differ from the container objects in that they do something more than just create an object to be used as a container. Some link objects and create no additional nodes. Some modify parameters of existing objects only. Some create numerous objects in one fell swoop. Some affect access to various GUI handles only. You look at a few of the more common object states over the next few pages.

Just a Box o' Running

And we both know who will put it there—you will, right now. In this exercise, you create a little track for two boxes to run around. Once you get that going, you'll give them a little sphere to pass off from one to the other, just as a baton is passed from one runner to another. During the course of the exercise, you are introduced to the following Objects context topics: the Path state, the Follow Path state, the Copy state, the Parent state, and the Blend state.

Creating the Track (the Path State)

Before a box can run, it needs a track upon which to waddle. You will create that now. Open a new session of Houdini to proceed. Delete the default model node and lay down a Geometry object.

1. Rename the new Geometry object box1. You can rename a node in a number of different ways. In the Network Editor, click the word *model* next to the geometry object and type the new name. You can also rename the node in the Parameters pane. At the top of that pane, you will see the object type (Geometry in this case) with the name field just to the right.

2. Scale the object down to 0.5 in all axes. Instead of typing in 0.5 in each of the fields in turn, use the number ladder to adjust all the fields at once. MMB on the Scale label and drag to the left until all three scale fields are at 0.5.

3. With your pointer over the viewport, press spacebar+2 to change the perspective view to a top view and dolly out a bit to get a wider view. Still with your pointer over the viewport, bring up the Tab menu and choose Path. The Path tool allows you to easily create a path by connecting vertices using Bezier curves. LMB to drop a control vertex and continue to drop vertices to create an oval track for the boxes to run around. Make sure to drop the last point next to the first point so that the transition is smooth. Finally, as per the instructions in the message bar, RMB to complete the operation.

4. In the Network Editor, you will see that the Path state has created a path object and several pathcv objects. The path object contains the path geometry and references to the pathcv objects that control the shape of the line geometry. Let's adjust the individual vertices to gain finer control of the shape of the path. In the Network Editor, select one of the pathcv objects. You should see the transform handle for that object in the viewport now. If not, check to see if you are in the View state. Recall that you can only adjust the viewpoint when you are in the View state. You need to be in the Operational state in order to have access to the transform handles. If necessary, press Enter to go into the PathCV working state. Now you can use the hotkeys e, r, and t to access the various transform handles to adjust the path. Your oval racetrack should look something Figure 4.1.

> You must know by now, but, in the interests of frustration-free learning and spreading the good mojo both near and far, it must be said one last time. Remember to quickly tap the mouse button or you might get unexpected behavior.

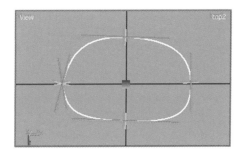

Figure 4.1
The oval track.

Getting the Box on the Track (the Follow Path State)

With your pointer over the viewport, choose a Follow Path operation. Remember that you can type the first few letters of the operation you desire to narrow the menu to those options. The message bar is recommending that you select one or more objects to change their "path" object… and what the message bar wants, it gets!

1. Select the box object. You are going to assign it a path to follow. Note, do not RMB after you select the box, as that will finish the operation. It seems the message bar doesn't always ask for exactly the right thing… so what the message bar wants, it gets so long as that will actually work! Now, it asks you to select a path object. Select the path (not the `pathcv`) to assign the box to follow the track. Notice how it jumped to the beginning of the track, as defined by the order in which you laid down `pathcvs`.

2. Look in the parameters for the `box1` object on the Transform tab. You see a path object parameter with `obj/path1` in its field. The Follow Path object state doesn't create any new nodes. It just plugs a channel reference into the Path Object field on a particular object. We can just as easily (or maybe more easily) click the + sign at the far right of the field and use the Tree view to select the path object.

Creating a HUD Slider

In the Position field, move the slider back and forth and you can see that `box1` goes back and forth around the track. So that you can easily have access to this parameter, you'll create a HUD (heads-up display) slider for it. In the value field, double-click the 0 so that it is enclosed in a box. LMB and hold on that box and drag the pointer over to the viewport and release the LMB. As soon as your pointer leaves the value field, you should see an arrow with a + next to it. This is telling you that you are using the drag-and-drop technique and there is currently something to drop. It can sometimes be tricky to get it working. The key is to make sure that the 0 is enclosed in a box before dragging. Figure 4.2 shows the HUD handle you just created.

Figure 4.2
HUD handle for the position parameter.

The HUD slider offers the same control as the slider in the Parameters pane. The nice part is that it is a persistent handle and so won't go away when you choose another object. By default, you can drag to 0 to the left and as high as you want to the right. You only want `box1` to go halfway around the track, so change the handle parameters. RMB on the slider and choose Handle Parameters. Change the range to 0 to 0.5 and toggle on lock high. This will make it so that 0.5 is the highest it will go no matter if you continue to drag right in the viewport. Drag the slider back and forth; now `box1` stops halfway around the track. HUD sliders are handles, so you must therefore be in operational state to have access to them. Hold down the spacebar to temporarily enter a view state; you will see that the sliders go grey and are not accessible.

> There are several ways to create a HUD slider in the viewport. You can select the value and drag it into the viewport. You can also drag the label of the parameter into the viewport. If you get a menu, choose the HUD Slider option. Note that if you drag a label that has more than one associated channel (like Transform, for example), it will create a slider for each parameter.

Persistent Handles

Normally in Houdini, you have access to a particular operation's GUI handles only when that node is displayed. It is often useful to still have access to a handle even if you have a different node displayed. One way to achieve this is to use persistent handles, which are available no matter what operation (or node) is displayed. You still have to be in an operational state of some kind to be able to affect the persistent handle. If you press Esc and go to the View state, you will no longer have access to any GUI handles, persistent or otherwise. By default, a HUD slider is a persistent handle, but you can also promote other handles to become persistent by RMB on them and choosing Persistent from the popup window.

Look in left viewport stowbar at the bottom and you should see a blue handle icon. This is a convenient way of temporarily turning off the display of the handle or accessing options specific to the handle. LMB on the icon and the HUD slider will disappear in the viewport. LMB it again to bring it back. Note that this just affects the display in the viewport. The handle still exists. RMB on the icon and you will get a menu of handle options. If you were to uncheck the Persistent box, the handle would be discarded and you would have to recreate it. The icon for persistent handles are blue and outlined in red. The icon for regular handles are grey.

You can change the outline color for the persistent handle in the Handle List pane. Go to the main menu Windows>Floating Pane to pop up a window and change it to the Handle List pane. This is a great pane for managing situations with numerous handles. At the bottom, you will see the HUD slider you created. Hit the blue square below the E (for expose) and you can turn on and off its display in the viewport. Click on the red square and you can change the outline color for the icon. The other options are used when creating handles in various levels of a subnet or digital asset. Hover the pointer over the various letters and you can see what each of them do. Make sure the HUD slider is visible and close the floating pane. See Figure 4.3.

Figure 4.3
The handle icon in the left viewport stowbar.

Creating and Configuring box2 (the Copy State)

With your pointer over the viewport, choose the Copy operation. Select box1 and RMB to complete. In the Network Editor, you now have another geometry object named box2. The object level copy state is just like pressing Ctrl+C or Ctrl+V; it just copies and pastes whatever is selected. Select the box2 node and delete it. Now select the box1 object and copy and paste it. You get the same result either way.

The box2 object is already tied to the track and thus retains this information. Look at the Follow Path parameter to verify this. Just as you did before, drag over a HUD slider for box2's Position parameter and place it just under box1's HUD. When you place HUD slider close to each like this, they dock to each other. Try dragging around just one of the sliders and you can see that they are stuck to each other, or docked. If you don't want this behavior, RMB on either of them and toggle off Docked. To dock them again, just drag and drop one next to the other as you did before.

Change the range of box2's HUD to 0.5 to 1 and lock the high value. This becomes your second runner who will wait for the first to arrive, accept the baton, and then gloriously cross the finish line at the end. Of course, you will have to indulge your imagination a bit. To some, the muggles among us, it will just appear as an oval line, two boxes, and a small sphere. This is, after all, the Magic of Houdini and you are an active apprentice! Drag both sliders back and forth to verify that box1 can only go from the start to halfway around and that box2 can only go from the halfway point to the ticker tape. Your viewport should now resemble Figure 4.4.

How a Sphere Becomes a Baton (the Parent and Blend States)

In the Network Editor, create a Geometry object. Press Enter to jump inside it and delete the default file node if it exists. Bring up the Tab menu and choose a Sphere SOP. Press the u hotkey to jump back up to the Object level and rename the node baton. Dolly out in the viewport if needed so that you can see the entire scene.

Over the viewport, press Enter to access the transform handles. Uniformly scale the baton object down to around 0.3 in all axes. You can change all three axes to this value or you can change the Uniform Scale parameter to 0.3. They both will get the sphere to the desired size.

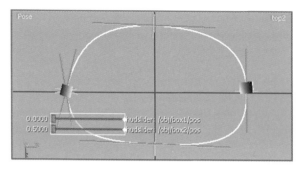

Figure 4.4
The current look of the viewport.

To quickly jump "into" a container type node, select it and press Enter. To quickly jump "up and out of" a container type node, press the u hotkey. Your pointer must be over the Network Editor pane for this to work as expected.

Over the viewport, choose the Parent state and follow the message bar instruction setting the baton as the child and box1 as the parent. In order to more easily see the sphere, change its translate X value to 0.7. The sphere jumped over to the same position as box1. Why did it do that? When you create a parent-child relationship, you create a situation where a child inherits the transforms of the parent. In the Network Editor, the baton node is now connected to the box1 node. All the Parent state did was connect one node to another. Drag the position of the box1 (using the HUD slider) back and forth and you'll see that the sphere goes with it. LMB on the input of the baton node and then click in a blank area anywhere in the Network Editor to disconnect the nodes. Notice that baton jumped back to its previous position , because it is no longer inheriting the transforms of the parent.

You can easily do the same thing as the Parent state using the nodes in the Network Editor. LMB on the input of the baton node and you again have the dotted line that follows your pointer. Houdini is waiting for you to connect this node to another node. LMB on the output of the box1 node and the baton is parented to it again. What if you wanted the baton to stay in its original position when parented? That is easily accomplished.

Unparent the baton node. On the Transform tab in the parameters for the baton, toggle on Keep Position When Parenting, and then re-parent the node. The baton stays in its position and yet is still parented to box1. The translate and rotate fields are now populated with values. What has happened is the baton was given a pre-transform (or initial offset) so that it initially stays in the same spot. Drag box1's position slider back and forth to see that the baton is still a child. But, how do you get the baton to be passed from box1 to box2? Press Ctrl+Z several times until the baton has no pre-transform and is no longer parented.

4. Object Operators (OBJs)

Over the viewport, choose a Blend state and follow the message bar's guidance. Select box1 and then hold down Shift. Then, select box2 and RMB to complete. The Blend state creates a blend object and parents it to whatever object(s) specified, which are box1 and box2 in this example. You can now blend between being parented to box1 or to box2.

Parent the baton to the blend node. The blend state is somewhat special in that it automatically creates HUD sliders for you. However, they aren't persistent. In the Network Editor, select the baton node and the blend sliders disappear. That's fine for now and you have to just remember to select the blend node in order to get access to the sliders. Select it again and drag the sliders back and forth and <drum roll> the baton is now blending between parents.

The Shading Selector

At times, it is easier to achieve a particular objective using a specific shading method. Use the shading selector to quickly select a shading mode. The Shading Selector button is located on the bottom stowbar in the Viewer pane and is the button shown in Figure 4.5. To choose different shading modes, just LMB and hold, and then select the desired option. Figure 4.6 shows a polygonal sphere using different shading modes.

Figure 4.5
The Shading Selector button.

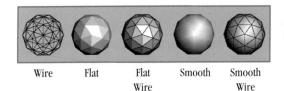

Wire Flat Flat Wire Smooth Smooth Wire

Figure 4.6
A polygonal sphere viewed in different shading modes.

To quickly jump into wireframe shading, press the hotkey w with the pointer over the viewport. Press it again to jump back to the currently selected shading mode. With your pointer over either the Network Editor or the Parameters pane, the w hotkey brings up the Tree view, which is just another view for navigating the Houdini file's structure.

The Primitive Olympics

Over the viewport, press w to go into wireframe shading mode. Your viewport should now resemble Figure 4.7.

And finally, let the runners run and the baton…ermmm, bat…which is to say, let the baton be passed. Using the HUD sliders, make box1 run from the beginning to half way around the track, then pass off the baton, and then make box2 finish the race in a glorious fashion. This might require you to jump up and down, whistling and chortling and thereby affording the box2 runner the adulation it so richly deserves. And besides, any excuse to chortle is a good one.

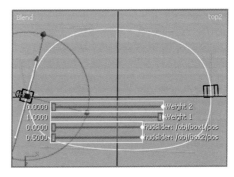

Figure 4.7
Baton blended fully to box1.

Eyes on the World

You are just beginning your adventure into the world of creation in Houdini. So, with a metaphorical abandon only known to the innocent, let's slosh around a ladle of galactic soup and see what cosmic wonders your protean efforts will provide. I think what I mean is that it's time to begin the exercise. The next sections cover the following Objects context topics: the Sticky state, the Look At state, and the Morph state.

Conjure the World and Gravity

You now need to create a world and some gravity so that your eyes have a place to behold.

1. Open a new session of Houdini using the default setup of lights and such. Rename the default "model" geometry object world and jump inside it.

2. Use the Tab menu to lay down a Sphere SOP. In the Parameters pane, change its Primitive Type to NURBS and its Rows and Columns to 20 each in order to give the geometry more detail.

3. Jump back up to Objects and drop another geometry object, naming it gravityGrid. Jump inside it and delete the default file node. Drop a Grid SOP. Change its Primitive Type to NURBS and its Size in X and Y to 20 each. You might not be able to see the grid in the viewport because it is edge on to the homed view. If needed, tumble the viewport a little and dolly out to get a proper perspective.

4. In this step, you apply UV coordinates to the grid because the Sticky state requires them in order to work correctly. Over the viewport, choose a UVProject SOP and select the grid and RMB to complete. In the Parameters pane, go to the Initialize tab and click the Initialize button. This allows Houdini to apply the UVs in whichever way is most appropriate for the geometry at hand. For more information about UVs and shading, refer to Chapter 9.

5. Over the Network Editor, choose a VEX Mountain SOP. Make sure that it is connected to the uvproject node and also that it has the Display flag (the blue one) on. Change the Height parameter to 20 to give the grid hills and valleys. Figure 4.8 shows what your SOP network should now look like.

Figure 4.8
The completed SOP network for the gravityGrid object.

Speed the World Through Space (the Sticky State)

It seems like I foggily remember from a long-ago physics class that mass moves through gravity much like an object moves along a blanket. Where the blanket is wrinkled or rippled, the object follows these deformations. You can now make your world object fly across the gravityGrid while it sticks to the hills and valleys.

1. Jump back up to Objects. Over the viewport, choose a Sticky operation. From the message bar, you can see that you need to select the gravityGrid and RMB to complete the operation. Go into wireframe viewing to more easily see what is happening.

2. Create a HUD slider for the stickyuv1 parameter. How do you know which parameter that is? In the Parameters pane for the sticky1 object, hold your pointer over the UV label for a second or two. The channel names of the associated parameter fields are shown in a popup window. So for the UV label, the channel names of the two fields to the right of it are stickyuv1 and stickyuv2. Hold your pointer over Rotation just below that and you can

see its channel name is stickyrot. In the next chapter, you learn why channel referencing is useful. So, now you know one way to find out the name of a particular channel. Before you continue, remember to create a HUD slider for the stickyuv1 channel. Bring up the HUD's handle parameters and lock the low and high values.

3. Drag the slider back and forth and you can see that there is a handle moving across the surface of the gravityGrid; however, the world is still just sitting there. Parent the world object to the sticky1 object so that world will inherit the sticky object's transformations. Play with the slider again and now the world is cruising along with the perturbations of gravity. You don't need to see the default handle associated with the Sticky state, so turn off its display. In the selection stowbar (the left stowbar in the Viewer pane), turn off the display of the handle using the handle icon button at the bottom.

Witnessing Your Creation (the Look At State)

But what is a world that none can see or experience? Some would argue that such a world really doesn't even exist because all of our worlds are merely projections from the inside going outward. Think about that for a bit and then continue.

1. Now, you can create a pair of eyes with which to watch your world speed by. Lay down a new Geometry object, jump inside it, and delete the default file node. Drop a Sphere SOP and jump back up to Objects. Rename it eyeball.

2. In the Network Editor, copy and paste the eyeball object and rename the new node pupil. Parent the pupil node to the eyeball node. Then scale the pupil down to 0.5 in all axes and change its translate in Z to −0.8. This will push it out of the eyeball a bit.

3. In the Network Editor, draw a selection box around both the eyeball and pupil, and then copy and paste them. Change tx (the channel name for translation in X)of the eyeball object to −1 and the tx of the eyeball1 object to 1. This pushes each off to the side so they are next to each other.

4. Drop a Null object and parent both eyeballs to it. Rename the Null object eyes. Change the eyes object's ty to 10 and tz to −10. Now the eyes have a better view of the action, or at least they could; however, they aren't currently looking in the right direction.

5. Over the viewport, select the Look At state and read the message bar. The eyes object is already selected, so just RMB to finish the selection. Read the message bar again and select the world object as the object to look at and RMB to complete.

6. Turn off the Display flag of the gravityGrid object (because gravity is invisible to our eyes, of course) and then drag the HUD slider back and forth. Go back to shaded view and check it out with lighting. The eyes now wake up and are watching the movement of the world. Your network should look like Figure 4.9.

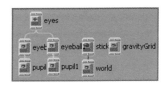

Figure 4.9
The final state of the Object network.

Improving Your World (the Morph State)

Currently, the world you created is a little too perfect. It is smooth as a metal marble and lacking in any surface detail. You can give it a few mountains for fun (and it's a good excuse to talk about the Morph state).

1. Over the viewport, select the Morph operation and then select the world object to edit. Watch the message bar at the bottom because sometimes it will automatically complete the object selection and move on to the next step and sometimes it won't. If it still says to select the object to edit, go ahead and RMB to complete. If it already says to select geometry to edit, you are ready to continue to the next step. Go back into wireframe and select the world. Notice that the entire object is selected, which isn't what you want. You just want to select individual points and then pull them out to create little mountains. Well, actually monstrously large space hugging mountains relative to the size of the world, but no matter.

2. In the Selection Options stowbar, notice that the selection mask is on Select Primitives, which is why it selects the entire object when you click it. Choose the first one, which is Select Points. You now want to see which points you can pick from. In the Display Options stowbar, turn on the display of points which is the first button. Dolly in on the world and select a single point and RMB to access the handle.

3. You need to pull the geometry directly out from the surface as if you were pulling directly out from the center of the sphere. Notice that the handle isn't aligned so that it would easy to do. You have to pull one way and then another to try and get it to come straight out. If that sounds too tedious, RMB on the handle and choose Toggle Peak Handle. This is the handle choice you want. The peak handle lets you pull along the axis created by a point directly in the center of the geometry running out to the point(s) selected. Pull it out to create a terrestrial mountain.

4. Create a few more mountains. A quick way to do this is to use the q hotkey to repeat the current operation. Press q and go through the Morph operation again to create a different mountain. Rinse and repeat until you think it looks just right. Figure 4.10 shows the eyes on the world.

> The y hotkey will toggle to the peak handle. The peak handle allows you to pull along the axis created by a point directly in the center of the geometry running out to the point(s) selected.

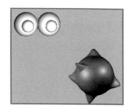

Figure 4.10
The eyes on the world.

> The q hotkey repeats the current operation. So, if you have an operation that you want to perform many times in a row, it's much faster to press q than to access the operation numerous times from the Tab menu. One point to realize is the q key doesn't work if you aren't in an operational state. This means that when you press q in the View state, nothing happens because there is no current operation.

Higher on the Mountain (an Interface Medley)

Have you ever had the opportunity to climb up the face of an ancient structure like a pyramid or a ziggurat? From Machu Picchu in the Andean mountains to Teotihuacan in the heart of Mexico, I've been fortunate enough to visit a few of these places and there is something truly mystical about the experience. Whether it's the exertion, the heights, or the imprints of memories gone by, the mind becomes quiet and feels the electricity, feels the magic of the place. In this exercise, you build your own ziggurat and place a few devotees on its levels. In the imaginary scene from the yesteryear of Latin America, the higher up the ziggurat they go, the higher up they are in the religious hierarchy until you have the head priest at the top crying out into the heavens. In this exercise, you'll learn about: viewport layouts and adjusting the construction plane grid, snapping, the Pose state, setting a favorite operation, auto-numbering nodes, homing the view, locating, and the Update button. Vamos a la cima!

Viewport Layouts and Adjusting the Construction Plane Grid

Depending on what you are doing, it can sometimes be useful to view a particular set of layouts together or to use a construction plane for alignment.

1. Open a new session of Houdini. Rename the default Geometry object `ziggurat` and jump inside it.

2. Over the viewport, press spacebar+t to go into quad view. Set up a viewport layout so that you are looking at a per-spective view and a right view. From looking at quad view, you can see that we want the two viewports on the right. So, click on the Viewport Layouts button and choose Right Pair Views. The Viewport Layouts button is in the stowbar at the bottom of the Viewer pane and is shown in Figure 4.11.

Figure 4.11
The Viewport
Layout button.

3. In the right viewport, adjust the grid spacing so that you can use it to calibrate the building of the ziggurat. Over the viewer, press d to bring up the Display Options window. Go to the Grid tab and change Grid Spacing to 10 and 10. You can MMB on the little bar between the fields to use the number ladder and interactively adjust if desired. Close the window. Dolly out a bit so you get a good view of the area.

Snapping

Snapping can help you accurately move things around.

1. Turn on snapping so that when you build the curve for the ziggurat, it will automatically snap to the grid and so make it simple to create a uniform structure. The Snapping button is in one of the stowbars at the top of the Viewer pane and is shown in Figure 4.12. Click on it and toggle the check mark on for snap. Notice that you can also use the hotkey Ctrl+J to do the same thing.

Figure 4.12
The Snapping
button.

2. Over the right viewport, choose a Curve operation. Use the LMB to lay down a point and use RMB when you are finished. Create a curve similar to that shown in Figure 4.13. Note that the curve is created on the negative side of the Z axis and the positive side of the Y axis. This will make it easy to revolve in the next operation. Even after pressing RMB after laying down the last point, you can go back and select a point to move it around or even add additional points if necessary. Check out the message bar to find out how.

Figure 4.15

The completed ziggurat in
wireframe shading mode.

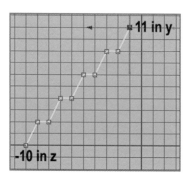

Figure 4.13
The ziggurat profile.

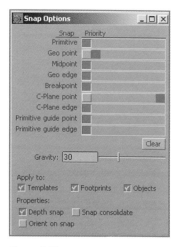

Figure 4.14
The Snap Options window with C-Plane
points having highest priority.

3. Note how the points in the picture are all aligned to the intersections of the grid. Even though you currently have snapping toggled on, yours aren't snapping to those spots. That is because you need to set up the correct snap priority. Click on the Snapping button and choose Snap Options. There are a number of different things you can snap to and each option can have a priority. This enables you to have snapping on for many things at once with some things being more "magnetic" than others. The background grid is called a construction plane and you want to snap to its points. So, drag the box to the right of C-Plane point to the far right. Gravity is the area of influence over which the snapping occurs. So, a higher gravity will reach out farther to grab your pointer. Leave it as is and your window should now look like Figure 4.14.

4. Close the window and now select one of the points and move it around. Your points snap to the construction plane points and so make it easier to build the profile shown in Figure 4.13. After you're finished, use the hotkey to turn snapping off. You no longer need to display the construction grid in the background. Over the viewport, press d. Go to the Grid tab and turn off Display Ortho Grid.

5. Over the Network Editor, append a revolve operation. Make sure the Display flag is on this node so that you can see its contribution to the network. In the Parameters pane, go to the Detail tab and change Divisions to 4 and toggle on End Caps. Look at that! You have created a ziggurat in just a few minutes. It needs a good deal more work, of course, before you could fittingly place it in a humid jungle or in the clouds of a mountain pass. Figure 4.15 shows your newly fashioned ziggurat in wireframe shading mode.

4. Object Operators (OBJs)

The Pose State

The Pose state is useful for gaining access to the handles associated with a particular object.

1. Jump back up to Objects and lay down another Geometry object. Rename it person1 and then jump inside and delete the file node.

2. Drop a Box operation and then change its size in Y to 5. That's your person. He won't think or move much, but he'll do for now.

3. Jump back up to the Object level change the Translate in Y on the light1 object to 200 to shed a little more light on the surroundings. Go to quad view and home all the views. Now, you want to place the person properly on the ziggurat. Anytime you need access to the handle associated with a particular object, use the Pose state. This is useful because different objects have different handles. For example, if you were to use the Transform state to select a cone light, you would get a transform handle. That would be fine if you wanted to move it. But, what if you wanted the cone handle to change the falloff or angle of the cone? In that case, use the Pose state because it brings up whatever handle is associated with the selected object. Over the perspective viewport, choose the Pose operation. Go to flat wire shaded mode and move person1 to be on the first ledge in the middle of the one of the sides. Ahh, this first person is just a youngling on the path to spiritual enlightenment. You might find it helpful to restrict the handle to only translations by pressing the t hotkey.

> The Pose state is a quick way to access the handles associated with a particular object. By default, this is set as the Favorite operation.

4. Let's get your person aligned properly with the ziggurat so that, when the times is right, he can walk forward up to a higher ledge and so progress on the path. RMB on the handle and choose Start Orientation Picking. In the top view, click the first corner and then click the second corner as shown in Figure 4.16. Then RMB to complete the process. The person1 object is now aligned with the orientation of the ziggurat, as shown in Figure 4.17. This person would have no chance of gaining the upper levels of sacred knowledge without first aligning himself to the possibilities before him. Check out the Rotate in Y for the person1 object and you can see that the value is no longer at the default of 0. Orientation picking is a quick way to align one entity to another.

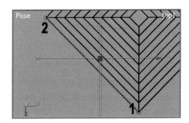

Figure 4.16
Orientation picking.

> The favorite operation is just a quick way to designate a particular operation as a favorite and then access it using the s key. Over one of the viewports, press Esc to exit to the View state. Now press s to choose the Pose state. Most often you will want to leave the Pose operation as the favorite operation, because it is a very handy way of selecting objects. In the Viewer pane, choose the Pane menu>Toolbars and Controls and toggle on the Operator Toolbar option. You now have an additional stowbar near the top of the Viewer pane. RMB and hold on the Pose icon at the far left and you can see that you can choose a different Objects level operation. For now, leave it as Pose. Before continuing, turn off the Operator Toolbar.

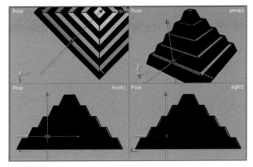

Figure 4.17
The person1 object on the first ledge and aligned to the structure.

Auto-Numbering Nodes

When you copy and paste nodes in Houdini, they will automatically be renamed with a number added to the original node's name. If a node of that number already exists, the number is incremented until an original combination is found.

1. Now, create a person at each ledge all the way up to the top. In the Network Editor, select the `person1` object and copy and paste it. The newly copied object is named `person2`. This is useful because you can use a wildcard like `person?` to refer to all of the person objects.

2. Press Ctrl+V a few more times to create persons 1 through 5. Use the favorite operation (the Pose state) to move each person to a higher ledge with `person5` being at the very top. One problem with this is that all of the boxes are on top of each other and so selecting a particular one in the viewport is difficult. Remember that Houdini has numerous ways of accessing the same information. Over a viewport, press s and then select the `person2` node in the Network Editor. Now you can move `person2` to the second ledge. Next, select the `person3` node and you can move it to the third ledge. Use the various viewports to get your placement correct. Rename `person5` (the one on the top) `highPriest`.

Homing the View

Over the perspective viewport, press spacebar+t to expand it. Recall that you can use the h key to home the view. Using the h key homes on all visible geometry. So, if you have two pieces of geometry that are far apart from each other, using h pushes the viewpoint back far enough to encompass both pieces. You will also remember that pressing the g key homes on the selection. Note that it homes on whatever the selection is, which means that you can choose a single point on the object and home the view on it. Remember that for either of these to work, you must first be in the View state. In fact, it is a very good idea to always press the spacebar first to ensure that you are in the correct state.

Let's say you wanted to move the `highPriest` object to an exact spot on the ziggurat top. Use h to home the viewport. At this distance, it isn't easy to get exacting placement of the `highPriest`. If it isn't already selected, use s to select the `highPriest` object and then press g to home the view on it. Now you can easily tumble, dolly, and/or track to get the object placed just right.

Locating Objects

Using locating makes it easy to see what objects are named in the viewport:

1. After you home on the `highPriest` object, you can see that it is outlined in yellow, as shown in Figure 4.18. This display option makes locating object selections in the viewport easier.

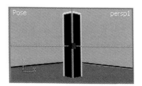

Figure 4.18
Selected object is highlighted in yellow.

2. This yellow highlight can be useful at times and not so much at other times. Let's turn it off for now. Go to the main menu and choose Settings>Main Preferences. Change the drop-down menu to Objects and Geometry. Toggle off Highlight Object Selections in Viewport and press Accept.

3. Press Esc to exit to the View state and then h to home the view on all visible geometry. Now, even though you have the `highPriest` node selected in the Network Editor, there is no indication about which one is in the viewport.

4. Object Operators (OBJs)

45

4. There is another way to see which objects are which: using the Locating button in the Viewer pane. Over the viewport, choose a Transform operation and toggle on the Enable Locating button in the left stowbar of the Viewer pane. This button is shown in Figure 4.19. Remember that you can determine what a button does just by leaving your pointer over it for a moment to activate the popup identification window.

Figure 4.19
The Enable Locating button.

5. Now, just move the pointer over an object in the viewport; it will be highlighted in white and its name will appear. Turn off the locating button and exit the View state before moving on.

The Update Button

Although it won't have any particular usefulness to you in this particular exercise, the Update button is still great to know about early on in the learning curve. I say that because every once in a while, you will open someone else's file and find that the Update behavior is set to Never. You then try to add objects or make adjustments. When you don't see anything happening, you wonder why your luck is so bad and why the gods hold you in disfavor. Well, they don't. It's just that you need to remember to check the Update button. (Later, when you get into more complex and heavy files, it is sometimes helpful to purposely set the Update behavior to Never so that you can make several changes and then have Houdini cook those changes. Otherwise, Houdini tries to cook those changes as soon as you make them, which can get very tedious.)

> The term *cook* in Houdini means to process the data in a network. It is sometimes beneficial to discretely control how Houdini chooses to cook networks.

1. Lay down a new geometry object and name it moon.

2. Jump inside it and delete the default node. Lay down a Circle operation and then jump back up to the Objects level.

3. Use the Pose state to access the transform handles and scale up the circle. Notice that as you drag on the scale handle, you interactively see the changes in the circle's scale.

4. On the far right of the main menu bar, change the Update button from Always to Never. Now, go back and scale the circle up and down. You don't see any changes. That is because you have explicitly told Houdini not to cook changes until you discretely tell it to by clicking the Update button or changing back to either Always or Changes. Click the Update button now and you will now see the changes you've made.

5. Click Never and it toggles to Changes. Now drag the scale up and down and you will see the modifications as soon as you let go of the LMB and thus finish the change. Unless you have specific reason for wanting it otherwise, it's generally a good idea to leave this option set to Always for maximum interactivity. So, click on Changes to toggle it back to Always. You now immediately see the modifications to the circle as you make them.

6. Scale the moon object up to 100 in all three axes. Pull it up to 60 in Y and push it back to –200 in Z. Practice using a combination of the e, r, and t hotkeys in the viewport and also the number ladder in the parameter's pane to make adjustments to the moon object. Your completed exercise should look similar to Figure 4.20. You have devotees ascending the ziggurat, ever closer to the celestial wonder of the moon above.

Figure 4.20
The completed scene.

Summary

In this chapter, you explored the Objects context and continued the introduction to various aspects of the interface. The Objects context is where high-level operations and organization occur. Generally speaking, Objects context operations are divided into containers and states, where containers are objects that hold other networks and states act upon nodes in some way other than just laying a single container node. Object states can create multiple containers, create SOPs inside those containers, or change parameters on existing objects. You dabbled a little in SOPs in order to spice up the journey. Now, that you have a good understanding of the Objects context, you're ready to move on to the next logical context: SOPs.

4. Object Operators (OBJs)

chapter 5
Surface Operators (SOPs)

Where the Object context is considered the high level organization of a file, the SOPs context is considered the guts of it. This is the context where you get down into the nitty-gritty details of making things happen. At the beginning of the book, you read about the procedural nature of Houdini and how networks are a series of connected operational nodes. You didn't really get to see this extensively in the Object context. Here in the SOPs context, you'll get a lot of practice with connecting nodes to form networks and seeing how information is cooked (or passed) through a network.

At its most basic, SOPs is where you can model a piece of geometry like turning a box into a bottle or a torus into a tofurkey, with a little more work of course! As you gain experience with these operations, you'll delve into a technique of modeling called *procedural modeling*. Basically, procedural modeling involves using SOP networks to build geometry in intelligent and reusable ways. You'll look at numerous examples of how to utilize this technique of modeling. As you continue your travels into this heady realm of ideas and intrigue, you'll start to use expressions and attributes to achieve truly amazing feats.

Salutations to the SOP Node

The SOP node is shown in Figure 5.1. This node has some of the same functionality as the Object node. You can see that there is a blue Display flag, input and output connectors, and a node icon showing what type of node it is. The SOP node introduces a few more features as well. The purple Render flag tells Houdini where in the network it should render. Usually, the Display and Render

A quick word is required here near the beginning of your adventure. Side Effects is very responsive to customer needs and releases new builds of the software at least weekly to accommodate customer requests. As such, the software is in a state of constant evolution. Because of this, you may find some things in this book or in the available files that produce errors or don't work in the manner described. Welcome to the world of 3D software! Usually, you can press on and everything will work out fine. If not, put your mind to work and try to identify what has changed. All of that said, I have made every effort to ensure that all of the material in the book and in the files is current for the production release build of Houdini 8, which is 8.0.313.

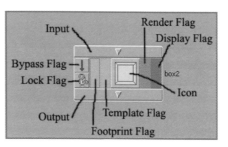

Figure 5.1
The SOP node.

flags are on the same node and so what you see in the viewport will also be what you render. However, by separating the two, it is possible to view one thing in the viewport and render something different. The footprint and template flags are alternate ways of showing different parts of a network in the viewport. The bypass flag allows you to essentially "turn off" a particular node. By turning it off, it is no longer computed as part of the network. The lock flag is a way of locking everything computed above a particular node to that node. So, if you lock a node somewhere in the middle of a network, any changes then made above the locked node are no longer cooked down, at least until the lock flag is toggled off. You'll go through using each of these new features later in this chapter.

Polygonal Modeling

There are several geometry types to choose from when modeling including polygons, NURBs, mesh, and so on. Each of them requires particular techniques and operators. The most common geometry type used for modeling in Houdini are polygons. They are great to use because they are easy to control, are supported with a wide variety of operators, and can come out just as smooth and curvaceous as you wish.

Making a Totem Pole

A totem pole is a physical object that graphically tells a story. It could be a history of a people, a history of a great leader, or an accounting of a magical event. Because you are right now creating a history with Houdini, you'll record the event by creating your own totem pole. And besides, a totem pole is very suited to polygonal modeling. You are going to create the totem tale by creating a basic head, which will then be tweaked into a bird at the top, a boy in the middle, and a bull at the bottom.

The Basic Head

First, you need to the build the basic head template.

1. Start a new session of Houdini and rename the default geometry Object `totem`.

2. Jump inside it and lay down a `Box` operation. Look in the parameters for the box and you'll see that it is of type Polygon by default, which is just what you want. Go into quad view by pressing spacebar+T over the viewport. You can see the box from multiple perspectives. Change the shading mode to flat wire shaded to get a clearer view of the various polygons.

3. Over the viewport, open the Tab menu and click on the Polygon menu. Inside it you will find operators that are generally associated with polygonal modeling. This doesn't mean that operators you find here won't work with other geometry types. It also doesn't mean that there are no other operators that will work for polygonal modeling. Basically, it's more of a suggestion saying, "Hey, you are using polygons. You might want to check out these operators." Choose a `PolyExtrude` operation. Go to the primitive selection mask by choosing it in the left stowbar or pressing the hotkey 4. Select the top face of the box and RMB to complete. Use the transform handle to extrude the face up in world Y and uniformly scale it down a little so that it looks something like Figure 5.2.

4. Turn on the display of points. Over the viewport, choose a `PolySplit`. The `PolySplit` operation basically cuts a polygon along the chosen line. Move your pointer over different areas of the box and you'll see that it turns into a small x when you are over an edge and into a small circle when you are over a point. Read the message bar and you can see that either

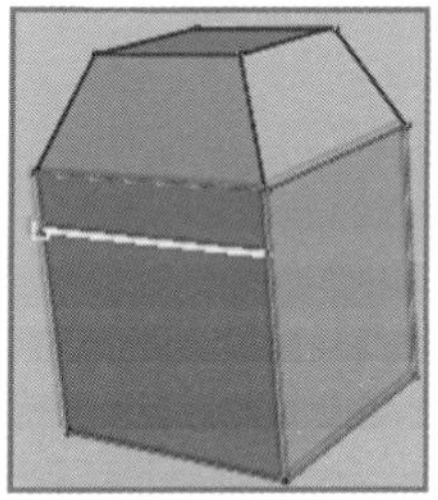

Figure 5.2
The box after a
`polyextrude` and a
`polysplit`.

of these is a valid starting point. Basically, you just LMB select one location after another until you have cut as many faces as you wish and then RMB to complete the split. You're just going to split the front face of the box as shown in Figure 5.2. LMB on the left edge of the front face. There is now a dotted line going to wherever you drag the pointer. Drag it up and down along the right edge of the front face and you'll see that you could LMB again and so make a split anywhere along the edge. You want the split to go perfectly across the front face, so Ctrl+RMB over the viewport and choose Snap to perpendicular. Now, the tool will snap to the location on the edge so that the split is perpendicular. Choose the edge and RMB to complete the operation.

5. Over the viewport, bring up the Tab menu again and look at the bottom of it. There is a short list of recently used operators. Choose the PolySplit and split the face about the same distance from the bottom as you just did from the top.

6. You are going to do a number of splits and there is a quicker way than pressing Tab and choosing PolySplit at the bottom of the menu. Over the viewport, press q to repeat the current operation, which is PolySplit right now. You want to split the middle and lower front faces exactly in two. Because they are connected faces, you can split both of them in one operation. Ctrl+RMB, toggle on Snap to edge midpoint, select the lower and upper edge, and split them so it looks like Figure 5.3. It doesn't matter if you start at the top or bottom edge. Notice that the middle edge is automatically cut for you.

> The q hotkey is used to quickly repeat the current operation. Look in the upper-left corner of the viewport to verify which operational state you are currently in. Note that if you are in the View state, pressing q will do nothing because you aren't in an operational state.

7. Press q again and create the splits shown in Figure 5.4.

8. You can polyextrude several faces at once. Select a PolyExtrude and choose the two eye socket shaped polygons on the front of the box. You will need to first change the selection option from edges to faces by pressing the hotkey 4 and then pull them out as shown in Figure 5.5.

9. Press q to apply another polyextrude. The two faces are already selected, so just RMB to finish the selection. Use the arrows on the handle to uniformly scale the faces "inward."

10. To finish the basic head, apply another polyextrude and push the faces back into the box. Doing so creates the eye sockets as shown in Figure 5.6. Your network should now look like Figure 5.7. The graphic shows what the nodes look like when you dolly out the view.

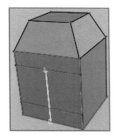

Figure 5.3
The box with a few more splits.

Figure 5.4
The box with a few more splits.

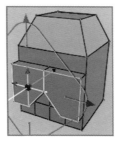

Figure 5.5
The extruded socket polygons.

Figure 5.6
The completed base head.

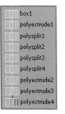

Figure 5.7
The current state of the network.

11. All of the nodes created thus far are related to the basic head. To clean up the workspace a little, you can collapse these into a subnetwork. Box-select all of the nodes, then Ctrl+RMB anywhere in the Network Editor, and then choose Collapse Selected Into Subnet. Whoa! It now looks like there is only one node. However, you still have all of the nodes. They are just hidden inside this node. Select the subnet node and press Enter to jump inside it. Whichever node has the Display and Render flag will pass information up to the subnetwork node. To see this, set those flags on the `box1` node and then press u to jump back up and out of the subnet. It looks like there is only a box SOP. Jump back in, set the flags on the last node in the chain, and jump back up. Rename this node `basicHead`. If you ever wanted to pull them back out of the subnet, just RMB on the subnet node and choose Extract Contents. For this exercise, let's leave it as is.

The Bird

And now you must tell the story of the flight of your people and so build the bird:

1. In the Network Editor, RMB on the output connector of the `basicHead` node and up pops the Tab menu. Choose a Null operation. This is a quicker way to choose an operation in the Network Editor because it will automatically wire in the new node. You still need to update the Display and Render flags to the new node. Rename this node `birdHead`. The Null operation doesn't add anything to the network. It is just used as a placeholder, usually for easy visual identification of a particular node.

2. Over the Network Editor, copy this node by pressing Ctrl+C and paste it twice by pressing Ctrl+V twice. Rename the second null `boyHead` and third null to `bullHead`. Put the Display and Render flags back on the `birdHead` node. Your network should now look like Figure 5.8.

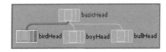

Figure 5.8
The current state of the network.

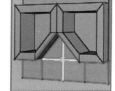

3. Over the viewport, choose a Dissolve and change the selection option to edges. Then select the four edges in the nose area of the bird head (the top one), as shown in Figure 5.9, and RMB to complete. You have just turned four polygons into a single one. Notice that there is a point in the bottom edge that you don't need. Toggle on Remove Inline Points and it is removed.

Figure 5.9
The four edges in the nose polygon.

4. Over the viewport, choose a `PolyExtrude` and select the nose polygon. You are going to polyextrude it a couple of times to create a beak. Pull out the face and uniformly scale it down a little.

5. Choose the face for another `PolyExtrude`. This time, you are first going to rotate the face down and then pull it out. Press r to use the rotate handle. If you tried rotating the face down right now, it would be difficult because the handle is at an angle. To fix this, RMB on the handle and toggle off Local. This changes the handle from Local to Global control. Rotate the face down some, pull it out, and then scale it down. Use the e and r hotkeys to switch between the translate/scale and translate/rotate handles. Repeat this again to create the tip of the beak. The bird's beak should look like Figure 5.10.

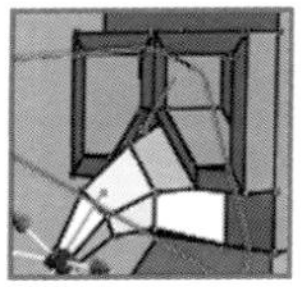

Figure 5.10
The bird's beak.

6. Now, you are going to create some wings for the bird. Over the viewport, choose a `PolyExtrude` and select the two polygons using the Shift key to add the second face. These will be the "sides" of the head. Scale down the faces in world Z.

7. You don't need the little edges that were created in the previous step, so choose a Dissolve and select all four (two on each side of the head) and remove them. Remember to turn on the edge selection mask in order to select edges. You can select multiple edges by holding Shift down and then selecting the desired edges. Toggle on Remove Inline Points to get rid of the stranded points. Your bird head should now look Figure 5.11.

8. Over the viewport, choose a Delete operation and select the middle polygon on each side. You want to keep these for making the wings and get rid of everything else. In the parameters, change the Operation to Delete Non-Selected and now you have just the two faces. Copy and paste this node and change this node's Operation back to Delete Selected. You will use this node later to merge back in the rest of the head. Put the Display flag back on the `delete1` node and continue.

9. Over the viewport, choose a `PolyExtrude` and select both faces. Remember to go back to a primitive selection mask to choose faces. Try to pull the handle out in world X to create the wings. When you pull one way, one wing is pulled out, but the other is pulled "into" the head. You want to be able to pull one way, but have each polygon extrude "out," away from the head. You need to switch the handle back to Local control so that changes are applied to each individual polygon. Undo the erroneous extrusion and then RMB on the handle. Toggle back to local control and pull the faces out. Pull out a few more `polyextrudes` until your wings look something like Figure 5.12.

10. In the Network Editor, append a subdivide to the last `polyextrude` and update the Display and Render flags. The wings are now rounded and smoother. Change the Depth to 2 to subdivide it further. This is a very common method of making polygonal geometry more organic and smooth. One useful way of modeling is to be able to continue making adjustments to the polygonal cage while at the same time seeing how those changes look after the subdivide is applied.

11. Over the viewport, press the PageUp key and go into wireframe shading mode. What are you now seeing? Look over in the Network Editor to find out. The Display flag is on the last `polyextrude` node and so you are seeing the polygonal cage in wireframe. The pink Template is now placed on the subdivide node

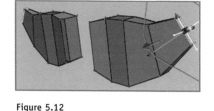

Figure 5.12
The polygonal wings.

Figure 5.11
The "side" polygons should look like this.

If your viewport is showing strange looking geometry like that shown in Figure 5.13, it might help to adjust your clipping distances. Usually pushing the Near Clipping Plane a little more forward will help. If you do see this, bring up the display options and go to the Optimization tabs. Turn off the Automatically Adjust toggle and change the Near value to something like 0.1. Sometimes, you may need to go as high as 1 to clear up the problem.

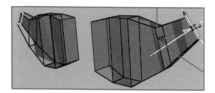

Figure 5.13
The wings displayed with strange artifacts.

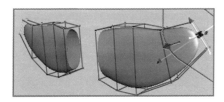

Figure 5.14
Wireframe polygonal cage with smooth shaded subdivision.

and you are seeing the smoothed cage in a grey wireframe. The Template flag allows you to see the state of a network at a node other than where the Display flag is. Let's change the Template shading mode to smooth shaded to make it easier to see. Over the viewport, press the Display Options button in the right stowbar (or just press d) to bring up the display options. On the first tab, Guides and Markers, go to the far right of the Templates line and change to Smooth Shaded. Close the window and your viewport should now look like Figure 5.14.

12. Over the viewport, use the PageUp and PageDown keys to move the Display flag up and down the network. You can easily adjust the handle for a particular `polyextrude` while seeing the effect on the final subdivision. This is a very easy and intuitive way of modeling because you have the simplicity and predictability of polygons while at the same time being able to see how the changes affect the final, smoothed form. Play with this technique for a few minutes to tweak the shape of your wings.

13. Over the Network Editor, use the PageUp and PageDown keys. Notice that the functionality is slightly different. The Display flag stays put, the selected node changes, and so what is displayed in the Parameters pane also changes. After you are finished tweaking, return the Display flag to the subdivision node and turn off the template flag.

14. You now need to combine the wings with the rest of the bird head. The Merge SOP is used to bring different network branches together. However, you want to merge the two geometry streams (the wings and the head) before the subdivide so that you can then subdivide them as a whole. This helps to avoid any potential topology problems that could arise. Drop an unconnected Merge SOP. Disconnect the subdivide node by clicking on its input connector and then in a blank spot in the pane. Reconnect it after the merge node by clicking on its input connector and then on the merge node's output connector. Wire the last `polyextrude` and also the `delete2` node (which contains the head geometry) into the merge. The merge node can take numerous inputs and brings them all together to be passed on down the chain.

15. Turn on the display of point numbers and look at the points where the wings attach to the head. Notice that there are overlapping numbers and so multiple points. This can sometimes cause problems with the subdivide and would definitely cause issues if you were to ever capture and then deform the geometry. Insert a Fuse SOP between the merge and the subdivide nodes by RMB on the merge node's output and choosing the operator. Put the Display flag on the fuse node and the point numbers show there is only one point at each of the attachment points.

16. Move the Display flag down to the subdivide node and change its Depth to 2. Your network should now look like Figure 5.15. Bird head, check!

Figure 5.15
The current state of the birdHead network.

5. Surface Operators (SOPs)

The Boy

The story of youth must be told so that the old remember their history. As such, you will build the boy's head.

1. On to the boy who would be a head. Move the Display flag over to the boyHead node. Why don't you give him a nose? Over the viewport, choose a Transform and select the four polygons that occupy the nose area. Pull them out to be even with the eyes, as shown in Figure 5.16.

2. Just as happened in with bird geometry, notice that there are multiple number at the intersection points of the eyes and the nose polygons. Append a Fuse SOP to join the points and fix it. Turn off the display of point numbers for now.

3. Over the viewport, select a PolySplit operator. Ctrl+RMB over the viewport and toggle on Snap to midpoint and Snap to perpendicular. This will help to accurately cut the polygons. The polysplit will show an x on any edge and a circle on any point that is a viable target. Split the lower nose polygons by clicking on the edge of one side and then the edge on the other side, RMB to complete. Note that you don't have to click the edge in the middle; it will automatically be split. You should end up with what is shown in Figure 5.17.

4. Use two more polysplits to split vertically so that you get what is shown in Figure 5.18.

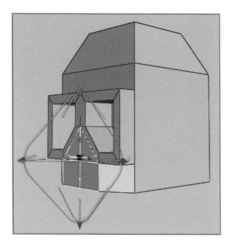

Figure 5.16
The nose area polygons are even with the eyes.

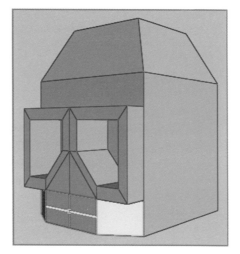

Figure 5.17
After polysplitting the lower nose polygons.

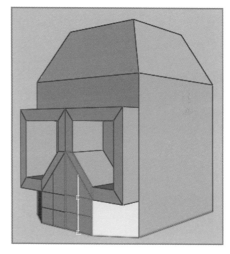

Figure 5.18
The nose area polygons after three polysplits.

5. Over the viewport, choose a SoftTransform and use a point selection to choose the three points shown in Figure 5.19. RMB to complete the selection. The geometry is now colored so you can better visualize the falloff of the SoftTransform operation, with hotter colors receiving more influence and cooler colors receiving less. In the Parameters pane, move Soft Radius to zero and you can see the whole head turns blue. Pull the edge out to create the nose. Currently, it's a little too harsh. Usher in the utility of the SoftTransform operation! Slowly, move the Soft Radius value back up until you have a good-looking snout. A value of 0.25 worked for me.

6. Look underneath the head; there are some problems with the polygons on the bottom. Basically, this single giant polygon needs to be split up a couple of times so that each individual one would follow the topology. But, let's try another way so you can see a new operator. Over the viewport, choose a Delete and, using a faces selection mask, delete the entire bottom polygon so that there is a big hole.

7. Turn on the display of points to better see where they are. Over the viewport, choose a PolyKnit operator. This is a sweet little operation that brings out the grandmother in all of us. You select the points of the polygons you want to knit in a particular order and then RMB to complete. Just like the with the PolySplit operation, when your pointer is over a point, a red circle displays to let you know it has found an appropriate location. Figure 5.20 shows the result of this work and also shows the order in which to select the points. You don't want to hold Shift down when selecting these points, because you are creating a selection order and not just adding more points to the selection. Note that you are skipping some of the points and they are automatically being correctly constructed.

8. Turn on the display of primitive normals, located in the right stowbar of the Viewer pane. This shows the normal of each face, or primitive. Of the four polygons just created, the largest one has its normal facing into the head. It is important for correct rendering to ensure that all normals are pointing in the direction they should be. Specifically, you need to make that one point outward like the rest of the model. Over the viewport, choose a Reverse and select the errant face and, you know by now, RMB to complete. The polygon now has its normal facing correctly.

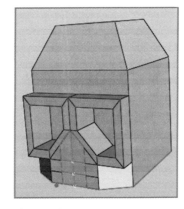

Figure 5.19
Select these three points.

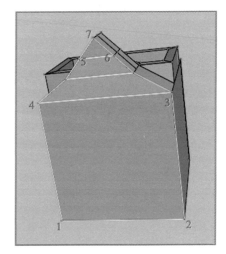

Figure 5.20
Selection order for the polyknit.

9. Turn off the display of primitive normals and points. Because this may very well be the boy who would be a head who would be a king, give him a crown to signify his station. Over the viewport, choose a PolySplit and select the just one of that slant in at the top of his head, RMB to complete. You only selected one edge and so nothing really happened. At the top of the viewport, change Path Type to Quad Strip and toggle on Close Path. Le Magic has le worked. Houdini jumped around each of the faces and split them until it returned to the original edge, as shown in Figure 5.21.

10. Over the viewport, choose a PolyExtrude and select the four faces shown and extruded in Figure 5.22. Before you pull them out, RMB on the handle and toggle off Local control. Then, use the handle edge shown in the figure to extrude the faces in the X and Z axes.

11. Append a Subdivide and set the Depth to 2. Such is the boy who would be a head—who would be a king! The boyHead network should look like Figure 5.23.

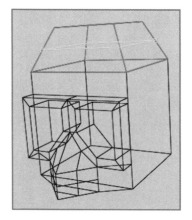

Figure 5.21
The powerful mojo of polysplit.

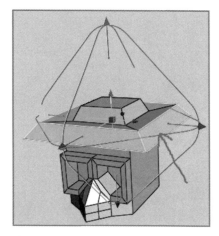

Figure 5.22
Polyextrude the four faces to create a crown.

Figure 5.23
The boyHead network.

The Bull

For every nation or people, there are times of strife and challenge. It is fierce determination and gumption that see them through to better days. Honoring this, you will build a bull head.

1. Move the Display flag to the `bullHead` node. `Polysplit` the forehead polygon down the middle, creating a left and right forehead primitive.

2. Use a Delete Operator to delete every primitive except for the character's left forehead primitive that you just created.

3. You are going to create a horn in much the same way as you did the wings earlier. This time, append a Subdivide first, change the Depth to two, and update the Display flag. Now, you'll see the smoothed result as you add `polyextrudes` to the polygonal cage. So, press PageUp over the viewport to turn on the template flag for the subdivide node and the Display flag for the delete node. You could do this manually as well.

4. Go into wireframe shading mode and, over the viewport, choose a `PolyExtrude`. As you pull and adjust the cage, the smoothed result is shown as well. Nice feedback, yes! Sometimes when modeling in this way, you may need to turn on the display of primitive normals because the faces are no longer visible. Selecting a primitive's normal will select the primitive.

5. Finish tweaking the horn and let's copy it over to the other side. In the Network Editor, insert a Mirror SOP after the last polyextrude node. By default, it should mirror across the X axis and so you now have two horns.

6. Turn off the display of primitive normals; you don't need them any longer. You need to bring together the horns and the head now. Copy and paste the delete node that isolated the forehead primitive (`delete4` for me). Change the Operation to Delete Selected to get everything but that primitive.

7. Make sure the Display flag is on the new delete node and select a Delete operator in the viewport. Use it to delete the other forehead polygon because you don't need it either.

8. Drop a Merge and pipe in the mirror node with the bull's head geometry just as you did with the bird.

9. Append a Fuse to join points that sit on top of each other.

10. Append a Subdivide and set the Depth to 2 to complete this part of the totem. Your network should look like Figure 5.24.

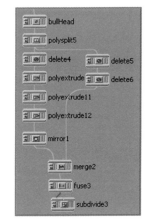

Figure 5.24
The completed bull head network.

Assemble the Totem

You have created the various pieces of the story and now they must be assembled into a cohesive history.

1. You have three network chains, each containing one of the totem heads. All that is left is to stack them up and merge them.

2. In the Network Editor, append a Transform SOP to each of the branches.

3. Then drop a Merge and feed all three branches into it. Put the footprint flag on this node.

4. Drop an unconnected Tube SOP and adjust it to become the central pillar of the totem pole. Then adjust each of the heads to get them where you want them. Wire the tube node into the merge. The network should now look like Figure 5.25. The completed totem should resemble Figure 5.26.

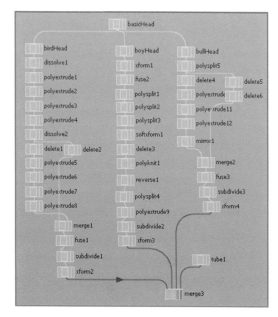

Figure 5.25
The state of the completed network.

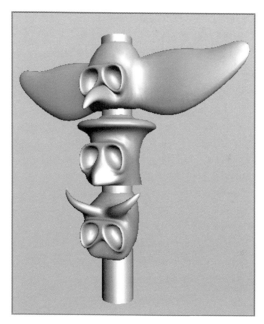

Figure 5.26
The completed totem.

Further Play in the Network Editor

In the interests of getting familiar with additional organizational tricks, let's take this exercise a little further. Let's pretend you look over at the network of nodes and say to yourself, "Egads man! The very sight of it is unsettling!" Fortunately, Houdini has numerous ways to wrangle and organize the appearance of nodes in the Network Editor. All of the following interface tricks will occur over the Network Editor, so you can assume all clicking to be done will need to be done in that pane.

1. There are two main ways to view nodes in the Network Editor. You are currently viewing them in Worksheet view. Press t to switch to List view. This is just a different way of looking at the same information. The columns represent a category of information about the node with the icon, and then name, the Display flag status, Render flag status, and so on. Reflecting just what you saw in the Worksheet view, here too you can see that the merge3 node has the display (blue) and render (purple) flags. All of the yellow blocks are on for hidden nodes, which are all the nodes inside the basicHead subnet.

2. Select the name of a node here and then go back to Worksheet view to verify that the node is selected. You can tell that a node is selected by the yellow box around it. Jump back to List view, Ctrl+RMB, and choose Alphabetical List Order. Now all of your operators are listed in alphabetical order. This makes it very simple to choose all the nodes that begin with a particular letter or set of letters. Jump back to Worksheet and notice that changing the ordering to alphabetical didn't affect how the nodes are laid out.

When using the Worksheet view, it is easy to see the connections between nodes and so understand the flow of data. Contexts that involve building networks default to this view because seeing the connections is important. Some contexts, like ROPs and SHOPs, are displayed in the List view by default. This is because they are generally comprised of individual, unconnected nodes and so using List view makes more sense.

3. Say you have a stupendously large network and navigating around it by panning in the Network Editor is frightfully tedious. There is a faster way! First, dolly in on your network so that it goes beyond the edges of the pane. Then, press o to bring up the overview window, which will pop up in the lower-left corner of the editor. Drag the box around inside it to quickly navigate to various parts of the network. Figure 5.27 shows this overview popup window.

> If you forget what any of the hotkeys are, pressing RMB over an icon or UI widget typically brings up a context menu for that item. You can also Ctrl+RMB anywhere in a main area, such as the Network Editor or the path browser, to bring up a general context menu. The general context menu is a subset of the pane's menus.

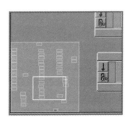

Figure 5.27
The Network Editor overview window.

4. You can color nodes to visually group them or signify other things. For example, you might find it useful to color the final merge node to green to signify that this is the node that should have the Display and Render flags on it. Nodes that are no longer in use could be colored red or black. To color a node, press c to bring up the color palette. It will pop up in the same spot as the overview window. Then select the desired node and choose a color for it. Press c again to close the color palette.

5. Another way to visually organize nodes is using network boxes. Select the entire birdHead chain of nodes (from the birdHead node to the xform1 node) by dragging a box around them. Then Ctrl+RMB and choose Create Network Box from Selected. Drag the box and all of its contents around by clicking and dragging on the bar at the top. It's easy to add or remove nodes to a box. Select the last node inside the box, the xform1 node, and drag it out of the box. Now dragging on the bar won't affect that node. Just drag it back in to make it a member of the network box.

6. In the upper-right corner of the box, there are minimize and close buttons. The close button will delete the network box and dump its contents back into the editor. So, closing it would put the network back to the way it was before you added the box. The minimize button will shrink the contents down to a box. It's a little bit like creating a subnet, but you'll see that there aren't any input or output connectors. Collapsing into a subnet is actually creating a new node that contains other nodes. A minimized network box is just visually collapsing the network contained within it. Name this box birdHeadBox.

7. You can color network boxes just as you can regular nodes. Bring up the color palette, select the box, and then choose a color for it.

8. Go ahead and put all the nodes in the boyHead network (from the boyHead node to the xform2 node), minimize it, and finally color it as well. Name it boyHeadBox.

9. There may be times when you are working on a network when you want to make some part of it invisible so you or others don't accidentally change settings. You can hide nodes in the Network Editor. Honestly, I think there are probably better ways to achieve that objective. But, let's say you receive a file that has hidden nodes. Now, you'll be able to recognize what is happening and expose them if you wish. Select the entire bullHead part of the network and Ctrl+RMB to choose Hide Selected. Presto, where is the rabbit-o? The nodes are still there because you still see the bull's head in the viewport. In the Network Editor, there are dotted lines that seem to go to nowhere. That is the visual clue that there are hidden nodes. The first time I saw that I thought the file was broken or the computer needed to be rebooted. Now, you won't have to experience that pain! Figure 5.28 shows the network after all of your tinkering.

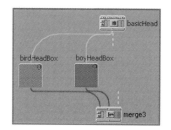

Figure 5.28
The network after a few UI tricks.

As you can see, it isn't always wise to use every trick in the book in organizing your networks. In this case, you've actually made it more difficult to understand! But, you now have some more tools in your arsenal when a need arises.

Procedural Modeling

Through tremendous effort of will and courage, you have made it through a good chunk of introductory explanation and even the first few exercises. Now, you say, can we make a person shoot fire out of his… fingertips already! Well, just as the miracle of the physical form starts small and builds to increasing degrees of complexity, so must you reign in your initial aspirations for grandiose effects making and get some practice with the basics. In fact, let's do exactly that by creating a strand of DNA. How was that for a contrived sequitir?

You will create the DNA using a technique called procedural modeling. Basically, this just means modeling the Houdini way. In other words, you will consciously take advantage of one of Houdini's core features: proceduralism. This aspect of Houdini was discussed in the Chapter 1. As it relates to modeling, you will create a network in which you can make changes at any time to any part of the network and see the effect of those changes cook all the way down to the last node in the network. Cook is just another way of saying process. The implication here is that you always have access to modifying your construction history, as it is contained within the aggregate effect of all the individual nodes. It sounds complicated. It ends up just being cool. Enough high-falutin' talk of pageantry. Let's do something!

Duplicating DNA

As have been previous exercises, this one too will be very explicit in stating and describing every step of the process. As you progress through exercises, the detailed step-by-step method will give way to a goal-oriented approach. Several chapters and exercises from now, you shouldn't need to be reminded how to rename a node, set a keyframe, or make a transformation. With some of the exercises in this book, you won't just walk through each of the nodes in their final order pretending that this is exactly how you went about creating them.

Also, while doing the exercises (in this book and from anywhere, really), always use common sense and keep an eye out for values that don't seem to work for your particular project. If you change values somewhere early in the exercise, values given later may not be meaningful. In addition, it's entirely possible that I have misstated a number here or there. Rest assured, I have painstakingly tried to make certain that all exercises work exactly as intended. That said, keep a logical and artistic eye out for what works in your particular situation.

1. Ensure that Houdini is up and you are starting with a blank slate by clicking the main menu File>New, if necessary.

2. If the model geometry exists, rename it DNA. If not, throw down a geometry object and do the same.

3. Jump into the `celluloidDNA` object to access SOPs. Two easy ways for doing this are to either RMB the object and choose Edit Network or, with the desired node selected, simply press the Enter key. With the pointer over the Network Editor pane, press the h key to home the view on all existing nodes. Sometimes Houdini will have a File node here by default. If so, delete it. Remember to select a node, LMB on the icon part of it or box-select the entire node. If you click on other areas of the node, you will be acting on the node in some way other than just selecting it.

4. Drop a Grid operation. The default Orientation of ZX orients the grid edge-on. Change the Orientation to XY for a better view. Sometimes when you do this, the grid may seem to have disappeared. What has happened is that the amount of light hitting the grid at this angle to the viewpoint just so happens to approximate the same color as the viewport background. Over the viewport, press the hotkey w to switch to wireframe shading mode. You can now see that the grid is still there and ready to do your bidding. Mush, grid! Mush!

The grid node will be used as the "backbone" for the DNA, meaning that you will determine its basic structure here. Enter the value shown in Figure 5.29. Remember to use Houdini's built-in forensic feature of setting non-default values in bold or putting a black dot by it (as in the case of a menu). This will help you to quickly identify which values need your attention.

It is best to never leave a blank space in filenames or paths when using Houdini. Although windows is designed to accommodate it, Houdini has grown up in a Unix environment and having spaces in the wrong spot can lead to broken and unexpected behavior. In most cases, if you try to name something using characters other than alphanumeric characters, the non-alphanumeric characters are automatically converted to underscores. However, just to be safe, it is best add an underscore or period for segmentation of a path or filename instead of a blank space. In some cases, you will consciously choose to use spaces as delimiters, which is a fancy way of saying separators. So, you can enter a number of commands delimited by spaces to inform Houdini that they are separate commands.

Figure 5.29
Values for the grid node.

5. Append a Polywire SOP. One way to do this is to RMB on the output of the grid node and then choose the desired operation. Note that when you do it this way, it will automatically connect the nodes, but you will still have to update the Display and Render flags to the current node. Change the Wire Radius to 0.05. Jump back and forth from smooth shaded mode to wireframe by pressing the w hotkey.

6. In the viewport, choose a Twist operation. Box-select the entire grid and RMB to complete the operation. Note that it automatically connects the nodes and places the Display and Render flag on the current operation. For simpler operations like this, it's a little faster to do in the viewport. When using a node that has multiple connections, it can sometimes be easier to drop it in the Network Editor. Set the Strength to 200. Set the Primary Axis to Y so that it twists around the correct axis. You now have the respectable beginnings of a DNA strand and with just three operations!

7. Currently, it looks very angular instead of having smooth curves. Drop a Subdivide SOP in between the `polywire` and `twist` nodes. There are a few different ways to do this. First, pull the twist node down a little to make room. One way is to RMB on the twist's input or the polywire's output and choose the desired operation. This will insert the subdivide into the network while keeping the Display and Render flags on the twist node. Delete the subdivide and let's insert it another way. Put the Display flag on the polywire node and then, in the viewport, add the Subdivide operation. Update the Display flag to the last node. This is a case where it is easier to add the operation in the Network Editor.

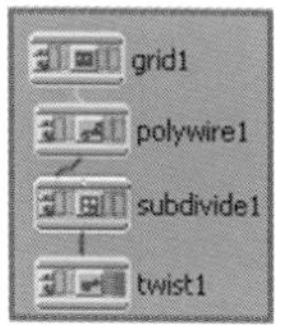

Figure 5.30
The current state of the network.

The DNA now, rounded curves, but the interior rungs are a little rounded. In the subdivide's parameters, toggle on OVERRIDE Crease Weight Attribute and drag the slider around to see what it does. Set it to a value of two. Figure 5.30 shows your network at this point.

8. Let's pretend that, at this point, you remember the Divide operator and are wondering if it might do a better job rounding the DNA than the subdivide did. With Houdini, you should always pursue these moments of introspection because it has a huge number of operators and you'll gain proficiency as you gain a better understanding of what particular operators are useful for.

You are going to add a Divide by branching (as opposed to inserting) it under the polywire node. MMB on the polywire output and choose Divide. Notice that the node is added as a branch off to the side and not inserted into the current network chain. Delete this node and let's add it again by branching in the viewport. Place the Display flag on the polywire node. In the viewport, bring up the Tab menu and press s to bring up the D operators. Hold the Shift key and select the Divide operator. Finish the operation as you normally do and you'll see that the node has been branched. Update the Display flag to it, toggle off Convex Polygons, and toggle on Smooth Polygons. Play with Weight and Divisions to see how they affect the geometry. It does a reasonably good job, but let's stick with the subdivide. So, delete it and return the Display flag to the twist node.

9. You now have a reasonably good-looking DNA strand that been created using procedural modeling. Go up to the grid's parameters and change the Size in X and Y. Change the number of Rows. On the polywire node, change the Wire Radius. On the subdivide node, change the Crease Weight or Depth. Although, don't go over three on Depth or your machine may start to chug. If it does, press Escape to kill the cooking. Adjust the Strength parameter on the twist node. You can see that every time you make a change, it is immediately being cooked down to wherever the Display flag is. In this case, the changes are cooking all the way down the network to the twist node. Make sure to change back all the values to those stated previously and then continue.

This is the simplest form of procedural modeling. You always have access to the history because it is contained within each of the nodes (or procedures). That is simply sweet. There is no other way to say it, really. Houdini does have some operators and ways of working that are not procedural and sometimes you can't avoid doing things that way. But, if you change your way of thinking to be procedural, your networks will be more open and modifiable and you'll be the happier for it.

10. For the sake of silly exploration, let's make the DNA bend back and forth and then settle to a stop, kind of like a spring does when you shake it around. Append another Twist operation to the network. If you do it in the Network Editor, always remember to update the Display flag. Rename this node `bend`. In the parameters, change Operation to Bend and adjust the Strength parameter back and forth. You'll see that it bends the DNA to the left and right. But, let's say you want the base of it to be pretty stable and have it wobble more towards the top.

5. Surface Operators (SOPs)

The bend is applied around the Pivot point, which is currently in the middle of the strand. So, it is bending the strand in half. The light blue geometry is called guide geometry and serves to give you a visual clue as to what the operator is doing. In this case, it tells you the primary and secondary bend axes and also where the pivot point is. Figure 5.31 shows this guide geometry. Change the pivot in Y to –2.5 and then play with the Strength. Now, the base stays put and it wobbles higher up on the strand.

11. On the grid node, change its height (Size in Y) to 10. Notice that the pivot is no longer situated at the base. Ideally, you want to figure out a way to have the pivot be at the bottom of whatever geometry is fed into the bend node. Fortunately, that is easy to do using a local variable. Change the pivot in Y field from –2.5 to `$YMIN` and check out the results. The pivot has jumped down to the bottom again. Change the height of the grid again and notice that no matter what you change it to, the pivot always stays at the bottom.

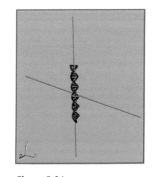

Figure 5.31
Helpful guide geometry is colored light blue.

Anything that has a $ sign preceding it is a variable. In this case, `YMIN` is a local variable, which means that it can only be used locally or within the context of the specified SOP. Check the help for any SOP to see what local variables it can use. Access operator help by clicking on the ? mark in the upper-right of the parameters for the node. `YMIN` gets the minimum extent of the bounding box in the Y axis. A bounding box is just an imaginary box that is extended in each of the axes so that it fully encloses the given geometry. So, the pivot will always stay at the minimum Y extent of the bounding box feeding into it. Using local variables in this way is just taking procedural modeling to the next level and allows adjustments to automatically accommodate changes further up the chain. Notice that the Pivot Y field has turned, which is Houdini's way saying the field now contains an active channel. Change the strand's height back to 5.

12. You still have to get the strand to wobble back and forth and settle to a stop. Before you do that, let's add one more node to the network. You no longer need to see the guide geometry and it can be a little distracting. Over the viewport, press d to bring up the Display Options. Turn off the display of the guide geometry button. This button is shown in Figure 5.32. Remember that you can leave your pointer over most anything in Houdini and get a tooltip popup with information. The blue guide geometry in the viewport disappears.

Figure 5.32
The first button controls the display of guide geometry.

13. Turn it back on and exit the window. You're going to do it another way. Append a Null SOP to the chain and rename it `displayRender`. Always remember to update the Display flag if necessary. A Null operation doesn't do anything and is just a placeholder for organizational purposes. In this case, it serves two purposes. It gets rid of the guide geometry and also tells anyone looking at the file that this node should have the Display and Render flags. In this simple network, there isn't much doubt as to where they should be. However, when you get into making insanely large networks later, having a node labeled as such can help to make things clearer. The network should now look like Figure 5.33. Notice that when you dolly out beyond a certain point, the nodes are displayed in low detail.

Figure 5.33
The final state of the network.

14. Now, on to the wobble! You aren't going to cover keyframe animation until Chapter 7, "Animation." But, you can also animate using expressions. In the Strength field of the bend node, enter `sin($F)` and click Play on the playbar to see what happens. The strand is wobbling back and forth ever so slightly. The sin expression is a periodic function that cycles from between –1 and 1 by default. Change the expression to `sin($F)*100` and play it. You have increased the amplitude of the sin wave. Now, change it to `sin($F*10)*100` and play it. Multiplying by 10 inside the parentheses increased the frequency. It's wobbling now, but it's not slowing down over time.

15. You can create an expression that will act as a multiplier to the `sin()` expression so that you have `sin()` times a multiplier equals something. At the beginning, the multiplier will be 1 and at the end of the frame range, it will be 0. Let's pretend the `sin()` expression equals 5 for a moment.

    At first, 5 x 1 = 5, and so full wobbling

    Halfway through the frame range 5 x 0.5 = 2.5, and so half-powered wobbling

    At the end, 5 x 0 = 0, and so the wobbling will stop

16. Rather than create one large expression in the Strength field, you can break out the two parts (the `sin()` expression and multiplier expression) and then read them in as channels. That sounds a little confusing, but you'll get it in a moment. In the parameters for the bend node, add a spare parameter by clicking on the button shown in Figure 5.34 and choose Float. This button is located in the upper-right of the Parameters pane. Name the channel `sinexp` and the Label Sin Expression. Then click Add. A Spare tab has been created that has the new parameter. Drag the slider back and forth. Nothing happens. Wahoo! To delete a spare parameter, click the X button and then click Yes. Leave this one though, because you do want it.

Figure 5.34
The Add Spare Parameter button (third button from the left).

17. Let's copy the `sin()` expression from the Strength field and paste it here. There are a few ways you can do that. One way is to double-click in the expression field to box select the entire function and then Ctrl+C. Then Ctrl+V in the Sin Expression field to paste it. Notice the field turns from grey to green to indicate a channel is now present.

18. The field is currently in expression view because you can see the expression. Click on the Sin Expression label (just click on the words) and the field will toggle to number view. This view shows you the value that the expression evaluates to. Figure 5.35 shows the expression view and what it evaluates to in the numbers view while on frame 50.

Figure 5.35
The expression and number view of the Sin Expression field.

Channel Referencing

Channel referencing is a core feature of Houdini and is used everywhere, all the time. Hence, it is a topic you need to grok early and fully.

1. In the interests of an ever-expanding Houdini skill set, let's try copying this expression over a few other ways. RMB on the Sin Expression and choose Delete Channels. The field goes back to grey, which means that no channel is present. Click on the label and you'll see that you can't go back to expression view because no expression is present. RMB on it again and choose Revert to Defaults to set the field back to 0.

2. RMB on the Strength parameter and choose Copy Parameter. Jump back to the Spare tab and RMB on the Sin Expression field. You have five different choices for pasting, each of which has unique functionality. Choose Paste Copied Values. This pastes whatever the current value of the copied field is. Notice the field is still grey and that it didn't paste the expression. RMB and choose Revert to Defaults. Now RMB again and choose Paste Copied Expressions. Now, it pasted the expression, which is what you want.

3. Now, you want the Strength field to channel reference the Sin Expression field. This just means that the Strength field will go look at the Sin Expression field and then use whatever value it has in it. RMB on the Sin Expression field and choose Copy Parameter. RMB on the Strength field and choose Paste Copied Reference. The `sin()` expression has been replaced with `ch("/obj/DNA/bend/sinexp")`, which is a channel reference. More specifically, it has created an absolute channel reference. You can see that because the path starts all the way up at the Object level (/obj), jumps into the DNA object (/DNA), then looks for the bend node (/bend), and finally, looks for the `sinexp` channel on that node (/sinexp).

Most often, you will not want to use absolute path references because they can easily be broken. For example, what if you decided to rename the DNA object to `DNAWobble`? This channel would no longer work because it would still be looking for the DNA object. In reality, Houdini tries to automatically update these references when you make changes that they depend on. But, it doesn't always work and it's best not to depend on it.

4. A much better method is to use relative path referencing. RMB on the Sin Expression field and choose Copy Parameter. Then RMB on the Strength field and choose Paste Copied Relative Refs. Notice that you can just paste over the current reference without having to delete the channel first. Now the channel reference is `ch("./sinexp")`, which is a relative path reference. This says to look for the `sinexp` channel (/sinexp) within the same node and put whatever it evaluates to here. The . before the slash is a path reference to the current node. Now, no matter what you changed the DNA object's name to, this path never looks that high and so doesn't care. Click on the Strength label to switch to number view and you can see what the channel reference evaluates to. Verify this by going to number view on the Sin Expression field. They should be the same value.

Channel referencing is an extremely powerful feature of Houdini and is used throughout the package on every project. It may seem a little daunting at first, but the quicker you get completely comfortable with it, the faster your skills will progress.

Houdini uses Unix-like paths that use some operators that you need to know. The dot (.) means here or this node. The double dot (..) means go up one directory or node. The slash (/) indicates a new directory below the path.

---

5. Add another spare parameter, which will contain the multiplier expression. Make sure it is a Float type and name the channel multiplier and the label Multiplier. As stated earlier, you want to create an expression that evaluates to 1 in the beginning and then goes down to 0 by the end of the frame range. It turns out that the `fit()` expression will do just the trick. Let's look at the help for the fit expression. One way is to bring up a Textport by going to Windows>Textport (hotkey Shift+Alt+T). Type **exhelp fit** and press Enter. The syntax is as follows:

```
float fit (float num, float oldmin, float oldmax, float newmin, float newmax)
```

This means that the fit expression will return a float (floating point number) when you enter a number, and then the old minimum, and then the old maximum, and then the new minimum, the new maximum. When you are trying to understand an expression, it's often easiest to just put in some simple numbers so it is easier to see what is happening. There is an example in the help that does it for you in this case.

```
fit(3,1,4,5,20)=15
```

Basically, the expression takes the relationship of the number between the old min and max and creates a new number that preserves the relationship using the new min and max. Keep this in mind and close the Textport window.

6. How do you get it to work for you? As this will be a longer expression, let's use the expression editor. Click in the Multiplier field and press Alt+E. The expression editor is a great tool for doing longer expressions because you have more space to work in, you can format the expression with returns and such, and it tries to help you avoid syntax mistakes by highlighting, for example, matching parentheses. Figure 5.36 shows the expression editor. Type the following expression.

```
fit($FEND - $F, $FSTART, $FEND, 0, 1)
```

and press Apply. This will save the changes to the field without closing the expression editor. Pressing Accept saves the changes to the field and also closes the editor.

That looks like a bunch o' gobbledegook! Immediately, you can see that there are four variables being used because of the preceding $ signs. Remember earlier when you used the YMIN local variable? Well, now you are using global variables. These are global variables, which means they are meaningful anywhere in the package. Open the Help browser in the main menu Help>Help Contents. In the find field, type **variables** and then choose the first topic in the list. Here you will find a list of variables and where they are meaningful. You will notice that these are listed as playbar variables and are not global variables. Most folks just lump these two together as global variables. Reading there, you can see that FEND is the end frame, F is the current frame, and FSTART is the start frame.

Figure 5.36
The expression editor.

7. Let's substitute in the numbers where possible to make it easier to understand.

```
fit(240 - $F, 1, 240, 0, 1)
```

So, at frame 1, 240 – 1 = 239. Then give you a new number in the range of 0–1 that has the same relationship as 239 does in the range of 1–240. The new number is .9958. Make sure you are on frame 1; you can see that by changing the Multiplier field to a number view. You can see that as the current frame number gets larger, the number being fitted to the new range gets smaller. Play through the frame range and you can see you have achieved your greatest desire. Or at least, you have created a multiplier that starts at 1 at the beginning and then goes to 0 by the end of the frame range. Close the expression editor.

8. Why then is the strand still swaying about like it's 1 a.m. at a New Year's Party? That is because the Strength field isn't yet using the multiplier. If you tried to use the RMB Copy Parameter and Paste Relative Refs technique, the existing channel reference would get overwritten. So, you have to manually enter the multiplier channel reference. You know that the channel name is multiplier because you named it earlier. But, say you didn't know or forgot. Hold the pointer over the a particular label and a tooltip popup window will tell you what the channel name is. Figure 5.37 shows the tooltip for the Multiplier parameter.

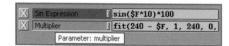

Figure 5.37
Tooltip window showing the name of the channel.

9. Jump over to the Strength field and let's finish the expression. Currently, it reads ch("./sinexp"), which is a channel reference to the sinexp channel of the current node. Click in the field and add a space and then a * at the end because you want to multiply the sin() expression function by the multiplier expression. Add another space and then enter ch.

Notice that a window pops up, offering you a number of different expressions that begin with ch. Quite a nice feature. But, it gets better. You want a channel expression, so go ahead and type in (". and another window pops up as shown in Figure 5.38. This window shows all of the possible channels that you could reference. Select the /multiplier at the bottom and it fills that in for you. Finish the expression with the closing " and) and you should have ch("./sinexp") * ch("./multiplier"). Notice also that it tries to help you get the syntax correct by highlighting matching quotations and parentheses. You can't beat that with a handy stick! , unless a stick is handy. Can I get a rim shot?! As a brief aside, I think it's scientifically proven somewhere that writing material for a book in long, uninterrupted stints leads to speaking in tongues or just speaking silly gibberish.

10. Click Play and witness the wonder as the DNA strand sways back and forth and slowly comes to a rest. Figure 5.39 shows this swaggering strand.

Soccer Is for Kicks

Let's continue the adventure in procedural modeling by creating a soccer ball that illustrates several new operators. In particular, this exercise will introduce you to the power of grouping. Figure 5.40 shows the result of this exercise.

1. Start a new session of Houdini and drop a Geometry object. Rename it soccerball and jump inside to the SOPs context.

2. Drop a Sphere SOP and change its Primitive Type to Polygon.

3. Append a Divide operation and toggle on Compute Dual. If you chose to create it in the Network Editor, remember now and forevermore to update your Display flag so that you can see its effect in the viewport! Already, you see the beginnings of what looks like a soccer ball. What exactly is Compute Dual doing? I have no idea. I know what the help says it is doing: "Convert the polyhedron into its point/face dual." What that actually means escapes me. This brings up an practical point about using Houdini operators. Just by playing around, you will discover what various operators and parameters do, and it's not always important to understand exactly what is happening beneath the hood. If you can make it do what you want, that is sometimes all you need.

Anytime you want to know what the channel name(s) is for a particular parameter, just hold your pointer over the parameter label and wait a second for the handy tooltip popup window.

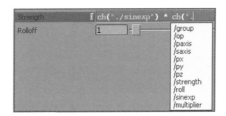

Figure 5.38
A handy window offering help in finishing the expression.

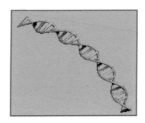

Figure 5.39
Ye swaggering strand of DNA.

Figure 5.40
Ye soccer ball.

4. Append a `PolyBevel` and drag the Relative Inset's slider back and forth to get an idea how it works. Leave the value at 0.6.

5. You now have the basic structure of the ball. It's time to think about how you are going to get some of the patches to be black and some of them to be white. The Measure SOP seems like a good choice. Append a measure operation and rename the node `measureArea`. Change the Type to Area. Though it doesn't look like much has happened, you now have created a Primitive Attribute called area and it is storing the area for every single primitive on the ball. An attribute is basically just a characteristic. I discuss them in more detail later in the chapter. MMB on the node icon to access the info window and you should see 1 Primitive Attributes: `area[1]`, among other things. MMB on the `polybevel` node and notice that the listing is not present. This verifies that the Measure operation has added the attribute.

Panes Ease the Pain

What if you wanted to find out what the actual value was for each primitive? You can view this information in the Details View pane. You want to be able to see the Details pane while still seeing the three panes you currently have displayed. Fortunately in Houdini, panes are just generic windows that can be configured however you like. A Viewer pane could just as easily become a Network Editor pane, a Parameters pane, or any other pane type.

1. In the Viewer pane, go the Pane menu and choose Network Editor. Press h to home the view and you'll see that this window is now displaying the same information as the other Network Editor pane. Look in the Pane menu and you can see that there are a number of different pane types available. Change back to a Viewer pane.

2. Still in this pane, choose Split Top/Bottom, which is also in the Pane menu. In the newly-created bottom Viewer pane, go in the Pane menu again and choose Split Left/Right.

3. Pane linking is another important tool in configuring panes. In the upper-right of every pane, you'll see a circle that usually has a number in it. Figure 5.41 shows the Pane Linking button. This sets panes to be linked together or otherwise. That means all panes configured to the same number will, for example, jump up to the Object level if you change one of them. In any one of the panes, click on the Context menu and change it to from SOPs to Objects. Notice that all five panes followed and changed to display the Objects context.

Figure 5.41
The Pane Linking button is the circle containing the number one.

4. For the two new Viewer panes, change each of their pane linking buttons to 2. In the Network Editor, press Enter to jump back down into SOPs for the `soccerball` object. Notice that the two Viewer panes didn't follow along because they are no longer linked with the other three panes. Close one of the panes that is using the 2, change the remaining to a Details View, and then set its pane linking button back to 1. You should now have four panes that are all linked together. This four-pane approach is a very common way of working with the fourth pane sometimes and sometimes not linked with the other three panes.

The Details View and Attributes

This pane is one in which you will spend more and more time as you traverse the peaks of this package. The reason is because it is incredibly useful, as it shows you the exact information stored for various attributes. This is where you go to get the gritty up-close look at what is happening in your network. Currently, you can see that there are five columns of information as shown in Figure 5.42.

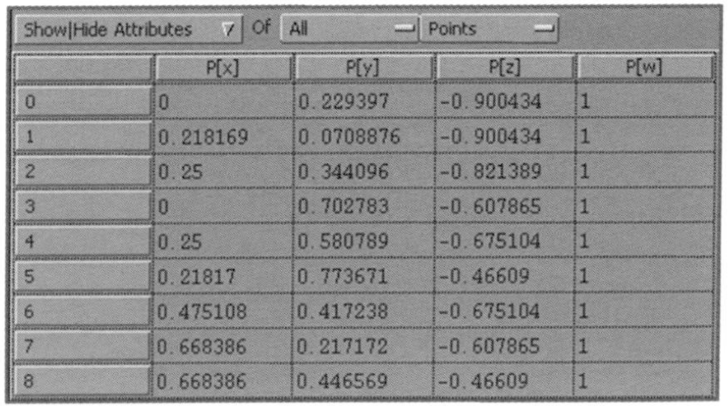

	P[x]	P[y]	P[z]	P[w]
0	0	0.229397	-0.900434	1
1	0.218169	0.0708876	-0.900434	1
2	0.25	0.344096	-0.821389	1
3	0	0.702783	-0.607865	1
4	0.25	0.580789	-0.675104	1
5	0.21817	0.773671	-0.46609	1
6	0.475108	0.417238	-0.675104	1
7	0.668386	0.217172	-0.607865	1
8	0.668386	0.446569	-0.46609	1

Figure 5.42
The Details View pane.

1. The details view is basically a spreadsheet in which you can cross-reference from geometry types on the left to their attribute information along the top. Because it is currently set to Points, point numbers are listed along the far left and point attributes are listed along the top.

2. Click on the Show/Hide Attributes button and you'll see that P is the only point attribute that exists and you are looking at it. Click on the P in that menu and it disappears from the spreadsheet. Go back and click it again to display the attribute. P is a point attribute, which stands for position. Remember that an attribute is basically just a characteristic. So, this is saying that each point has a characteristic that is its position in space. The first three attribute columns stand for position in X, Y, and Z. The last columns stands for weight, which isn't changed that often. So, point 4 is at 0.25 in X, 0.580 in Y, and −6.75 in Z.

3. In the Viewer pane, go into wireframe shading by pressing w and turn on the display of point numbers. Tumble around until you find point number 4. You know exactly where that point is in space by looking up its position information in the Details View.

4. MMB again on the measureArea node. You would think that it should list something like 1 Point Attributes: P[4] there, but it doesn't. That's fine because the position attribute is a default attribute given to geometry upon creation. All other attributes that are subsequently added will be listed in the info popup.

5. You know that the measureArea node added a Primitive attribute called area, but it isn't displayed in the Details View. That is because you are currently looking at point attributes. Change the button that reads Points to Primitives. It is now listing primitive numbers on the far left and primitive attributes along the top. Click on the Show/Hide menu and you can verify that there is only one primitive attribute, which is called area and it is displayed. Here you can see the exact value of the area of every primitive in the soccer ball.

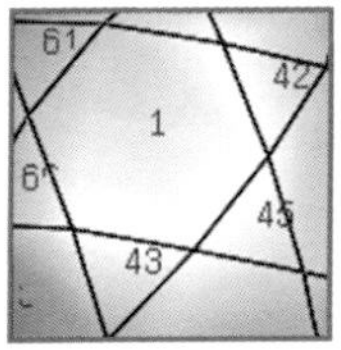

Figure 5.43
Looking at the size of primitives 1 and 43.

6. In the Viewer pane, turn off point numbers and turn on the display of primitive numbers. Jump out of wireframe shading to see the primitive number more easily. As shown in Figure 5.43, primitive 1 is one of the large patches and primitive 43 is one of the small patches. Looking up primitive 1 on the left, you find that its area is 0.208733 and primitive 43 has an area of 0.0340373.

Click on the polybevel node and you'll see that the area attributes disappear. That is because they do not exist at that node. You didn't add them until the measureArea node. Click back on it again and they are visible in the Details View again.

5. Surface Operators (SOPs)

Grouping Is the Goal

Now that you have an attribute that stores the area of every primitive on the soccer ball, it should be pretty easy to get all the larger ones to be white and all the smaller ones to be black. The Group SOP is the ticket. You first need to group the patches based on their area and you can then apply colors based on membership in the groups.

1. Append a Group operation and rename the node GRcolorBlack. In the parameters, the Group Name will default to group1, which is not very descriptive. Note that the Group Name and the name of the node are two different things. You could type in GRcolorBlack or something similar, but there is an easier way. There is a tricky local variable called OS, which is just a reference to the name of the node. Type $OS in the Group Name field. Remember that all variables are preceded by a $ sign. The Entity is already set to Primitives, which are what you want to group. Figure 5.44 shows the state of the network at this point.

2. MMB on the group node and the info popup tells you that there is now 1 Primitive Groups 122 in GRcolorBlack. Look a little higher up and you'll see that there are a total of 122 primitives in the soccer ball. So, currently every primitive is a member of the GRcolorBlack group, which isn't what you want. You want only the small patches to be members.

3. You'll use a really sweet expression to determine the criteria for grouping. Change the Operation parameter to Group by Expression. You need to find an expression that can read the area of each of the primitives in the soccer ball. The prim() expression can do exactly that! Whip up a Textport and look up the help on it by typing exhelp prim. Basically, you specify a path to the node you want to read from, then give a primitive number to look at, give the attribute a name, and then give the index number of the attribute to read. The index number is usually 0, 1, or 2. The index is easiest to understand in terms of the position point attribute, which is comprised of three components being X, Y, and Z. So the index number for X is 0, for Y is 1, and for Z is 2.

> Yes, it is a little confusing to say that the position attribute is comprised of three components, yet to access the third component, you enter an index of 2. You just have to remember that index numbers start counting from 0.

4. Let's give it a trial run to make sure it's working like you expect. You'll use the primitive expression to look up the area for primitive number 8. You can, of course, easily verify if it is working by looking up that value in the Details View pane. Your Textport prompt should read /obj/soccerball ->. This tells you that you are inside the soccerball object. If for some reason yours reads differently, just type cd /obj/soccerball and press Enter to get into the correct directory. Typing cd just means to change directories to, in this case, soccerBall.

5. Type ls and press Enter, which lists the contents of the current directory. You should see listed all the SOPs that you have previously created in this exercise. So, you want to use the primitive expression to read the area attribute from the measureArea node. Easy enough!

6. Well, there is one more trick to getting your test run to work and that is the necessity of using the echo command with the primitive expression enclosed in backticks ('). The problem is that you want to see what the prim() evaluates to and the Textport isn't going to do that without a little extra cajoling.

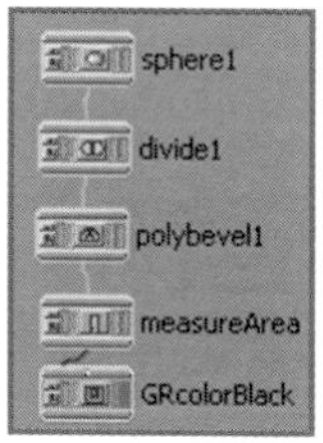

> Be careful to enter backticks (') and not apostrophes (') when you are telling Houdini to evaluate the interior contents.

Figure 5.44
The current state of the SOP network.

Putting an expression within backticks tells Houdini that you want to evaluate the expression and then return a value. You then tell Houdini to echo that value to the Textport window. Echoing to the viewport just means to display it.

7. Enter `echo 'prim("./` in the Textport and wait a smidge. The expression popup window shows you various options that can be entered next, as shown in Figure 5.45. Choose `measureArea` and then finish the expression so it reads

```
echo 'prim("./measureArea", 8, "area", 0)'
```

and press Enter. You should see a value that matches the value for Primitive 8 as shown in the Details View. For me, it is 0.125119. Hallelujah! You have just verified that you can get the primitive expression to read the area of a particular patch. Close the Textport window.

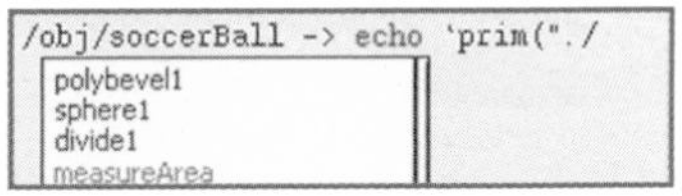

Figure 5.45
The ever-present and helpful expression popup window.

8. That has been an altogether excellent adventure but, now you need to get back to actually creating a group using the `prim()` expression. On the `GRcolorBlack` node, in the Filter Expression field, type `prim("../measureArea", "$PR", "area", 0)`. Notice that it is different from the way you entered it in the Textport in two ways. The path is `../` instead of `./` and you are telling it to look at `$PR` instead of primitive number 8.

Because the expression is in the `GRcolorBlack` node, it needs to first step out of the node using `../` and then look for the `measureArea` node. Earlier in the Textport, you were inside the `soccerball` object and just used `./`, which means look in the current directory. The quicker you get familiar with how Houdini (and Unix) uses directory navigation, the better off you'll be!

The second difference is that you are using the local variable `PR`, which stands for primitive number. Because you used a variable, you had to enclose it in parentheses and, as always, precede it with a `$` sign. It's about to get amazing so put on your rainbow-colored glasses. Using `PR` will make the primitive expression cycle through every primitive being fed in and evaluate the expression for each one individually. Earlier, it was only evaluating once for primitive 8. By using `PR`, it basically loops and evaluates the expression for every primitive. In this example, that would be 122 times. Holy dandelions! Switch to your puffy, white cloud-colored glasses if necessary!

9. MMB on the `GRcolorBlack` node to check the group status. It says there is 1 Primitive Group called `GRcolorBlack` which has 0 members. So, you aren't finished just yet. You're reading in the area of every primitive individually. You next need to set a criteria that will group out the smaller patches. You could say something like, "If the area of the primitive is less than x, make the primitive a member of this group." But, how do you determine what x should be? Back to the Details View!

You saw earlier that primitive 43 is one of the smaller patches. So go look up its area. It is 0.034. Next, scroll through the list to get an idea of what the area of the big patches are. It looks like the big patches have an area of either 0.125 or 0.21. So, you should be able to use 0.1 as a good value for grouping out the small patches. Your filter expression should now look Figure 5.46. MMB on the node and you'll see that the group now has 80 primitives in it, which are all the small patches.

```
prim("../measureArea", "$PR", "area", 0) < 0.1
```

Figure 5.46
The filter expression for the `GRcolorBlack` node.

Presets

Creating and saving presets is a handy way of speeding up your workflow.

1. Next, let's group the larger patches together. Append another Group operator and rename the node GRcolorWhite. In the Group Name, type $OS so that the field grabs the operator's name. You will likely find that you want your Group nodes to have $OS in the Group Name by default, instead of having to enter every time. You can do that! Go to the Presets button in the Parameters pane. It is located in the upper-right corner and is a little arrow that points down, as shown in Figure 5.47.

Figure 5.47
The presets menu button is the down arrow.

2. Click the Presets button and choose Save as Permanent Defaults. Now, every time you lay down a Group operator, the Group Name will automatically be $OS. Pretty sweet, huh? This will be the case even in future sessions of Houdini. Append another Group operator and you can see that the Group Name automatically has $OS in it. Go ahead and delete the node, as you don't need it.

   If you wanted to make a preset that lasted only for this session, you would choose Make current values temporary defaults. If you want to restore the factory defaults only to the current node, choose Revert to Defaults. If you want to restore the current node and make new nodes be created with factory defaults as well, choose Revert to and restore permanent defaults. Choosing this last option would make it so that dropping new nodes would no longer have the $OS in them.

3. You need the GRcolorWhite group to be the opposite of the GRcolorBlack group. You could easily just copy the prim() expression and switch the less than to a greater than sign. That would give you a group of all primitives whose areas are greater than 0.1. But, there is another way as well, which is a little trickier. Go to the Combine tab. On this tab, you can create logical complements of existing groups. So, you can tell it to create a group called GRcolorWhite that consists of all primitives that are not members of the GRcolorBlack group. It might be time to pop out one lens each from your rainbow-colored glasses and your white, puffy cloud-colored glasses and combine them too in the spirit of this new knowledge! Click on the arrow and choose $OS, then click on the button to display the exclamation point (which means *not*), and finally, click on the arrow to the right and choose GRcolorBlack. Yours should now look like Figure 5.48.

Figure 5.48
Using the combine tab on the group operator.

4. MMB on the node and the info popup will show that you have created a GRcolorWhite group that contains 42 primitives, which are all of the larger patches.

5. Finalmente! It's time to apply the colors based on the groups. Append a Primitive SOP and rename it applyBlack. For the Source Group at the top of the Parameters pane, click the arrow and choose the GRcolorBlack group. Go to the Attributes tab and change Color to Add Color. RMB on the Color label and choose Delete Channels. There are three components to color, which are red, green, and blue. Set all three channels to 0, which will create a black color. All of the little patches are now black.

6. Append another Primitive SOP and rename it applyWhite. It looks like the large patches are already white, but that is just their default viewport color. Set the Source Group to GRcolorWhite and change the Color field to 1, 1, 1, which will create a white color. It doesn't look much different in the viewport. To verify that it's working, change the middle field (green) to 0. All of the large patches turn purple. Return the value to 1.

7. The ball is a little too flat right now. In the Network Editor, append a PolyExtrude operation and rename polyexBlack. Set the Group to GRcolorBlack. Change the Translate in Z to 0.05 and the Inset to –0.02. The makes for some pretty nice patches. Press Enter in the viewport to access the handle if you want to make some adjustments that way.

8. Again in the Network Editor, append a PolyExtrude and rename it polyexWhite. Set the Group to GRcolorWhite. Change the two parameters as you just did for the black patches. Figure 5.49 shows the final state of the network. That is it! If your melon feels like the seeds are about to spurt out, you might want to go for a brisk walk. I find when you are in the zone of trying to grok something new and challenging, your brain seems to pool at least half the blood in your body. After a while, everything starts feeling a little other-worldly. A brief bit of physical activity helps to realign the meridians. And besides, you computer nerds can almost always use a little more time in the real world to help balance out all the time you spend in the 19" world. Which reminds me, I'd really like to upgrade to a 25" world!

Figure 5.49
The final state o' the network.

Learning the Brush Operations

Brush operations in Houdini are a great way to interactively affect geometry. You can sculpt as a sculptor does. You can paint as a painter does. You can comb as a hairstylist does. Welcome to marvelous country. You've come a long way, baby! You'll be using a mouse in the following exercise. But, if you have Wacom tablet, plug it in and take it for a spin. You can get a very fine degree of control with a tablet rig by modulating the application pressure.

Sculpt It! Comb It! Paint It!

Yes, work with me here, darling! You are going to work the magic, as they say. You are going to take a bland, boring, flat grid and through the miracle of cosmetic brush applications, turn it into a maaaaarvelous looking bit of scenery. Oh yes, darling. Do come along. You simply must see this! Figure 5.50 shows the end result of the "from flat to fabulous" miracle makeover.

1. Fire up a new Houdini session. Drop a Geometry and rename it terrain. Jump into it and delete the file node if it exists. Drop a grid operation. Change the Primitive Type to NURBs, the Rows to 30, and the Columns to 30.

2. Over the viewport, choose a Sculpt operation and choose the entire grid to apply it to. Move your pointer over the grid and you'll see the dotted outline of a circle. That is the size of your brush. Hold down the LMB and move around the grid. It looks kind of like in the cartoons when a certain rabbit is digging his way to the destination. Release the LMB. Hold it down again and continue sculpting. If you keep clicking in one spot, you can pull the geometry up to towering heights.

Figure 5.50
I just want to jump around with my shoes off and let it tickle my toes!

3. Now, hold down the MMB and do the same thing. The MMB will push geometry back down. You can change the amount of displacement per click by adjusting the FD value for the LMB and the BD value for the MMB. When you to start from a clean slate again, click the Reset All Changes button and you get to start from scratch.

4. Adjust the size of the Radius up and down to change the size of your brush. Go to the Brush tab and change Shape to Square. Reset the Changes and play around with that. The brush is now more angular. Even cooler, change the Shape to Bitmap and the Radius to 0.5. Reset the changes and just click once in the center of the grid. You're painting with a butterfly brush now! You can choose which channel of the bitmap you want to paint with. By default, it is set to Alpha. Feel free to take a few minutes to play with the various parameters to get a feel for what each does. When you are finished, change back to the Circle brush and change the Radius to 0.1. Reset the changes and sculpt something like what is shown in Figure 5.51. It by no means needs to be exacting. Basically, just sculpt some mountains and leave a flat valley area up front.

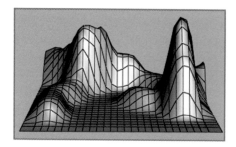

Figure 5.51
The result of the sculpt operation.

5. Append a Convert SOP change and change the Level of Detail in U and V to 1.4. This converts the NURBs grid to a polygonal grid and increases the smoothness a little.

6. Append a Point SOP. The Point SOP is one the most powerful SOPs available because it allows you to modify attributes on a per point basis. As you continue through the book, you'll often come back to this operation because it is so useful for a wide variety of things. For now, you are going to color every point on the grid black and give each point a Point Normal that points up in the Y axis. Change Keep Color to Add Color and delete the channels by RMB on the Color label and choosing Delete Channels. Change the triplet (r, g, b) to 0, 0, 0, which turns the grid to black. Go into wire-frame shading to make it easier to see. Change Keep Normal to Add Normal and delete the channels. Set this triplet to 0, 1, 0. This gives every point on the grid a point normal pointing up in the Y direction. To verify this, turn on the display of point normals in the right stowbar of the Viewer pane. They may turn out to not be large enough or entirely too large to be very helpful. Over the viewport, press d to bring up the Display Options and go to the Miscellaneous tab. Adjust the Scale Normals slider to around 0.15. MMB on the node to verify that you have added two point attributes, color (Cd) and normal (N), each of which are comprised of three components. Figure 5.52 shows the grid with point normals displayed and scaled down a bit.

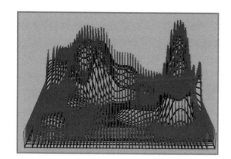

Figure 5.52
The grid with point normals displayed.

7. Append a Comb SOP to the network. In the viewport, make sure you are in an operational state and start combing around. All of the brush operations basically use the same interface and just affect different things. Press Reset All Changes to start over. Adjust Comb Lift to 1 and now combing will make the normals trend towards their face normal, which is perpendicular to the primitive surface from which they originate. Setting it to 0.5 combs them to halfway between their normal direction and laying flat on the grid. Setting the Opacity to around 0.3 can give you a more controllable brush stroke. Play around a bit and try to end up creating a swirl in the flat terrain up front and path of flattened normals going through the valley between the mountains. Yours should now look roughly like Figure 5.53. Later, you will copy little L-systems to each of the points and the direction of the point normal will determine how the L-system is oriented. So, the ones up front will kind of lay down and swirl around, a bit like a crop circle.

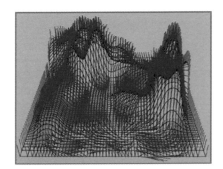

Figure 5.53
The combed point normals.

8. Append a Paint SOP to the network. Again, the interface is basically the same, only this time you are painting point colors. Change FG to 1, 0, 0, which means you will be painting pure red. By default, MMB will paint back to black. Turn off the point normals display and go back into shaded mode to more easily see what you are doing. Later, you will use the amount of red that an area contains to determine how many L-systems will be copied to that area. To mimic how it often works in nature with more vegetation growing in the valleys than the peaks, paint more red there and less in the heights. Switch to smooth wire shaded; yours should now look roughly like Figure 5.54.

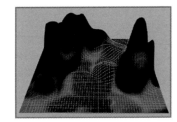

Figure 5.54
The painted population areas.

9. Now, let's create an attribute based on the amount of red you just painted. Remember that an attribute is just a characteristic. In this case, you will be creating a point attribute and so the attribute will describe how much each point in the grid contains, from 0 being black to 1 being full red. Append an AttribCreate SOP and rename it attribGrow. In the Name field, type in **grow** and leave the Class field to Point, as you want to create a point attribute. In the value1 field, type point("../paint1", $PT, "Cd", 0) and take a second to think about what you did. It likely rings a bell because you used a very similar expression, the prim() expression, in the soccerball exercise. The point() expression does that same exact thing as the prim() expression, only it references points instead of primitives. It is going to the paint1 node and looking at each point number, using $PT, and retrieving the first component, using 0, of the Cd attribute, which is the red component.

Both of these expressions are used all the time because they allow you to directly and easily access various characteristics of geometry. So, you are giving each point an attribute called grow and it will be equal to how much red is contained in that point.

10. Split the Viewer pane top and bottom and change the bottom pane to a Details View. Click Hide All Attributes and then choose grow and Cd. This makes it easier to compare the two attributes by not displaying attributes that you aren't interested in. Scroll down a little and you can see that all you are doing is stuffing Cd[0] into grow.

11. Append a Scatter SOP. The geometry vanished. What happened? Turn on the display of points and you can see something really sweet has happened. This operation has distributed points onto the grid based on the area of each primitive. Because all of the primitives have similar areas, the points are pretty uniformly distributed across the grid. Turn down the number of points to 2000 and toggle off Scatter Based on Primitive Area. In the Alternative Attribute field, type the attribute you just created, which is grow. Instantly, you'll see that the distribution of points no longer seems uniform. Slide Attribute Bias all the way over to 1 and now points are being distributed based solely on the amount of red contained in the surrounding points. Areas with more red, like in the valley, have far more points than areas that have less red, like higher up in the mountains. Each of these points will have an L-system copied to it. This is a great way to create an organically populated area of trees or grass. Your network should now look like Figure 5.55.

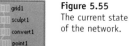

Figure 5.55
The current state of the network.

12. Off to the left side and unconnected, drop a Line SOP. It's fine at the defaults. This will be low-res geometry you use to visualize the look whilst working on it. Later in the exercise, you'll create a Switch SOP that will switch to a more complicated geometry only at render time. This keeps the computation load down and so makes working with it more interactive while still getting something more interesting going for the actual render.

13. Append a Switch SOP to the line node and leave it at the defaults.

Ye Ole Copy SOP

Welcome to the Copy SOP! It rocketh all planes of the multiverse and has at one point, early in its history, brought peace to the warring tribes of the Dantooine System. In fact, I feel it deserves a poem...

Oh Copy SOP

Oh beacon of hope to the seven cities

Please do continue the peace in the lands of Dantooine

Please do rocketh the multiverse, if you know what I mean

I feel better having said that and I hope you do too. If you haven't gathered already, the Copy SOP is an amazing piece of ingenuity. Let's see why. Append a Copy SOP to the switch node. Notice that this node has two inputs. MMB on the left input and it reads Primitives to Copy. Do the same on the right input and it reads Template to Copy To. Make sure the left input is connected to the stamp node and that the right input is connected to the scatter node. Your network should now look like Figure 5.56.

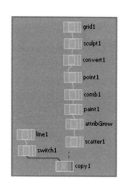

Figure 5.56
The state of the network.

So, what did it do? It copied what is coming into the left input to every point coming into the right input. So, one line is being copied to every point in the scatter node. Though, looking in the viewport, things look a little screwy. There are two problems: scale and orientation. The lines are way too big for the terrain and they aren't being copied with the correct orientation. They are inheriting the point normal information that you set earlier because the Rotate to Normal toggle is on, but you can easily see the ones in front are laying down flat in a swirl as you did to the point normals. You can fix the orientation of the line before it is fed into the copy node. Turn on the Footprint (the burgundy one) flag on the convert node so that you can see the terrain as you continue working.

1. RMB on the left input of the copy node and insert a Transform SOP. Leave the Display flag on the copy node and make sure the transform node is selected so you adjust its parameters. As always, you'll immediately see the changes you make cook down the chain. First, change the Uniform Scale to 0.1 to get the lines at a better scale. Now, change the Rotate in X to 90. You now have appropriately sized trees or grass or whatever and they are also correctly inheriting the point normal attribute. The problem was that the copy node expects the input to be facing down the positive Z axis when it copies using the Rotate to Normal option.

2. Notice that all the lines are exactly the same size. This doesn't make it look very natural, as it is unlikely you would find everything to be the same size in real life. You can use the Copy operation to randomly add variation to the copies, and this, as they say, eeeez zeeee spice of life! First, let's get the stamping working and then you'll determine a good range of scale for the copies. In the transform node (which is probably called xform1), enter `stamp("../copy1", "height", 0.1)` in the Uniform Scale field.

   Figure 5.57
   The Stamp tab of the copy node.

   Bring up a Textport and type `exhelp stamp` to get help on the `stamp()` expression. You reference which node is going to do the stamping, the name of the variable to be stamped, and a default value in case that variable isn't found.

3. In the copy node, go to the Stamp tab and type **height** in the first Variable field. Toggle on Stamp Inputs and see what happened in the viewport. All the lines disappeared because the value of height is currently zero. Move the slider back and forth, and you'll see that it sets the Uniform Scale of every copy to that value. Now, let's make it more interesting by using a simple expression instead of a constant value. Type `rand($PT) * 0.1` in the Value 1 field and check out what happens. Every point that comes in through the right input of the copy node has a unique point number, which can be accessed through the local variable PT. You can then use that point number as a seed for the `rand()` expression, which will return a random value between 0 and 1 based on the seed. So, every copy has randomly set Uniform Scale from 0 to 1. You then multiply that by 0.1 to get them all back down to a better range of scale. So the final range is from 0 to 0.1. Look around the geometry and you'll see that some lines are very small and some of the larger lines must have resolved to around 0.1. Figure 5.57 shows the Stamp tab and what you entered.

   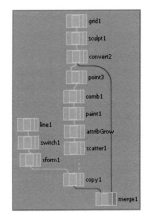

   Figure 5.58
   The current state of the network.

4. You want to see both the trees and the terrain underneath them. Append a Merge SOP to the end of the network chain. You use a merge to bring together various network branches into one branch. Even though a merge node has just one input, it can accept any number of inputs. LMB on its input and LMB on the output of the convert node. This will create a connection that passes down the geometry information from the convert node to the merge node. As always, make sure the Display flag is in the right place, and now you'll see the trees and the hilly terrain. Turn off the footprint flag on the convert node; the network should now look like Figure 5.58.

   Figure 5.59
   The Quick Render button (first on the left) has the blue icon.

5. Let's do a quick render to preview the work when rendered. RMB and hold on the quick render button, which is the blue icon in the lower-left of the Viewer pane (as shown in Figure 5.59) and choose View: Mantra. This is a simple way to get a low quality preview render of what is displayed in the viewport. You can see that the lines look a little strange.

The problem is that the Mantra renderer recognizes that you are trying to render a line primitive and so automatically attaches a width attribute (or characteristic) to them. By default, it chooses a value of 1, which is obviously too big for the scene.

6. Append an `AttribCreate` SOP below the merge node and rename it `attribWidth`. Type **width** in the Name field and enter **0.001** in the `value1` field. Remember that you just hold your pointer over the Value label to figure out what each of the channel names are. The `value1` channel is on the far left. Now, let's do another test render. Houdini will remember what the last chosen output driver was. Each of the choices you see when you RMB and hold is an output driver. Chapter 13, "Render Outputs," goes into more detail on them. Because you already chose the View: Mantra driver, you can just LMB click on it and Houdini will choose it again. This time, the lines look better.

7. Remember from earlier that you want to wire an L-system into the switch node so that you can preview a less dense geometry and then render a more dense one. Lay down an L-system SOP and wire it into the switch node. Set the Display flag to the L-system node and choose Bush in the Presets menu. There are quite a number of interesting presets for this operators. Most just change the rule set, which changes how the system is created. Some also animate various parameters like the crack and lighting presets. L-systems are great tools for mimicking the various kinds of branching behavior found in nature. I highly recommend reading the Houdini help on this node, as it is very informative and comes with a number of exercises to get you going. When you are done investigating, make sure to choose the Bush preset.

8. Set the Display flag on the switch node. Using the Select Input field, you can cycle through the connected inputs and decide which you want to pass down the chain. Note that the numbering starts with zero, so that choosing zero will pass through the first input. In this setup, zero will pass through the line geometry and one will pass through the bush. So, when you are working with the network, it will be set to 0. At render time, a simple pre-render script could change it to 1, and then a post-render script could change it back to 0. Set the input to 0 before you continue.

   You aren't going to mess with the render scripts themselves; that topic is covered in the Chapter 13. Let's do take a Textport moment though and check out the Hscript command that would be used.

9. Bring up a Textport window and go into the terrain Object. Remember that to navigate the directory structure is a simple thing. First, you have to figure out where you are. The prompt will tell you. It may currently read `/->`, which means you are at the root level. Type `ls` and you'll see all the root level directories, assuming of course that you are at the root level. Type `cd obj/terrain` to jump into the Object context and then into the terrain Object.

   To set a parameter on a node, you use the `opparm` command. Type `opparm switch1 input 1` in the Textport and press Enter. It's quite simple. Give the name of the node, the name of the parameter, and then the value you want to set. Look over at the switch node and you'll see you've just changed the input to 1. Press the Up arrow and change the command to `opparm switch1 input 0` and again check out the switch input. It has been set back to 0. It's that easy!

10. To end this exercise on a responsible note, append a Null SOP at the end and rename it `displayRender`. Figure 5.60 shows the final state of the network.

11. But wait! This is, after all, Houdini. Go back and change the switch to pass through the second input. Everything will automatically update using the trees instead of the lines. Oh, glory be!

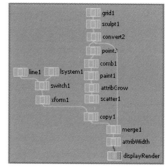

Figure 5.60
The final state of the network.

NURBs Modeling

I am so into the loving of curvaceous, bodacious lines. If the previous statement is something you find your-self saying from time to time, you will likely be a big fan of using Houdini's NURBs modeling operators. Generally speaking, NURBs are especially suited to creating smoothly deformed, organic-looking geometry. This is because you push around control vertices that then affect areas of the NURBs hull, rather than just the single point being manipulated, as happens with polygonal geometry. Figure 5.61 shows a point pulled upward in a polygonal curve and then shows the same thing with a NURBs curve (bottom). If you are inter-ested in a more technical explanation, the Houdini documentation has an excellent description of the nuts and bolts of this geometry type.

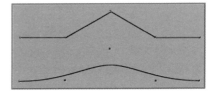

Figure 5.61
Comparing a polygonal curve (top) and a NURBs curve (bottom).

The Wisdom of Worms

Up to this point in the book, I have yet to really pay the proper respects to worms. Yes, it is surprising, I agree. Not a single word in praise of them to this point, and yet, worms so richly deserve it. Consider for a moment a few factors in support of this notion. Worms dig little tunnels that serve to aerate the soil. This improves the condition of the soil and so makes it easier for humans to grow food in the abundance needed in order to support an exploding global population. Thanks, worms! Consider also that worms eat, digest, and expel much of the trash that is plowed into the ground each year. The worm droppings enrich the soil and, again, make it easier to grow food in abundance. Thanks, worms! There is one more factor that is, perhaps, the biggest reason worms should be held in high regard and that is because worms are incredibly wise! Think about it this way. If Adam took one bite of the apple and so gained the knowledge of the ages, consider what worms must know. They love apples. Worms have been munching on apples ever since the two became acquainted. In honor of worms and their place in the grand scheme of life, let's model an apple with a worm crawling across it. Figure 5.62 shows the fruit of your imminent effort.

Figure 5.62
Worms = Wise?

Create the Apple

First, you create the apple for the worm to dine upon.

1. Open a new session of Houdini, drop a Geometry Object, and jump inside it.

2. Go to the right viewport. You can do that by first going to quad view with spacebar+T, and then spacebar+T again over the right viewport. A faster way is to use the hotkey spacebar+4. Note this will go to whatever viewport is in the lower-right of the quad view which, by default, is the right viewport. You should be seeing a construction grid in the background. Bring up the Display Options by pressing d over a viewport and go to the Grid tab. Change the Grid Spacing to 0.5 and 0.5. You can use the number ladder to adjust both values at once by MMB on the little bar in between the fields. Make sure Display Ortho Grid is toggled on and close the window.

3. Back in the right viewport, bring up the Tab menu, choose a Curve operation, and change the Primitive Type to NURBs at the top. Click on the Snap button in the upper-right and go to Snap Options. Drag the C-Plane point all the way to the right and drag the C-Plane edge about halfway over. This sets a snapping priority that is kind of like an order of magnetism. Construction plane points will be the most magnetic, construction plane edges will be slightly less magnetic, and geometry points will be the least magnetic. Close the window, leaving snapping off for now. Draw an outline for an apple core, which you will then revolve in the next step. Create something that is approximately the same shape and scale as that shown in Figure 5.63. After you RMB to complete the curve, you can go back and adjust any control vertex by clicking on its purple box. After you get the basic shape down, toggle snapping on and make sure the first and last points are snapped to the Y axis. This will ensure the revolved geometry doesn't contain holes at the top or bottom. Then, turn snapping back off.

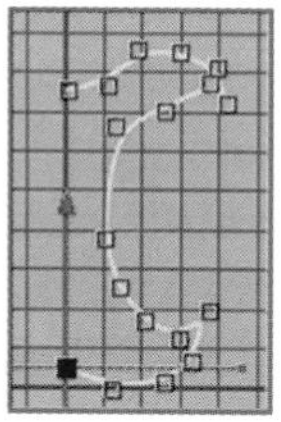

Figure 5.63
A NURBs curve creating an apple profile.

4. Append a Revolve operation and leave everything at the defaults. It revolved the profile around the Y axis and created a closed shape that looks much like an apple core.

5. It is a bit too perfect though. Switch back over to a perspective view by pressing spacebar+1. You can easily model in some irregularity using the Edit SOP. Turn on the display of points and choose an Edit operation in the viewport. This operation has a kind of somewhat non-procedural, special functionality. The goal is to push and pull points here and there to give the apple core a more irregular shape. You could use a Transform SOP for every one of these adjustments. In this case, every time you chose and adjusted a point or group of points, a transform node would be created recording this information. You could then jump up and down the network and have a perfectly procedural, historical record of every change that was made and you could go up and down the network making modifications to any of the individual transform nodes.

If you make numerous adjustments, your network can quickly grow cumbersome. Of course, you'll recall that there are many tools to organize your networks. However, sometimes you don't care to have a record of all the individual adjustments. This is where the Edit SOP announces its utility. You can make an unlimited number of transforms with one edit node. The Edit operation records the aggregate changes made and passes that information along down the network. So, if you make 10 changes, you only have a record of what the network looks like cooking all 10 changes and you can't step back through from step 10 to step 1. If you just made the changes, you can, of course, use undos to jump back to previously done work. But, you won't be able to later come back to this node and sort out individual transforms as you would had you used 10 separate Transform operations to get the same result.

Press the 1 hotkey to ensure you are using the point selection mask and choose a single point that you want to move. RMB to accept the selection and access the handle. Translate the point to give the apple a more organic shape. Just above the viewport, you'll see a Soft Radius parameter. Slide the value to 1 or more to see how translation made to the single point is inherited by surrounding points.

6. Now you want to make another transform to another point or points. Press the button in the Viewer pane's left stowbar that says Reselect Geometry for Current Operation, or the hotkey ` (called backtick). This leaves the change you just made and lets you choose new points to manipulate. Choose another area, RMB to accept the selection, and continue molding your masterpiece. The reason you have to press ` each time you want to make a new selection is because Secure Selection is toggled by default. It is also located in the left stowbar, just above the Reselect Geo button. Turn off Secure Selection and now you can skip pressing the `. When you are ready to move around different points on the apple, just select them, RMB to accept, and move them around. Select some new ones, RMB to accept, and move those around. Each selection you make can have its own unique Soft Radius setting. So, you can change it for a particular selection and it won't change the settings you had on previous transforms. It's easy to see why this operation isn't quite as procedural as using a long chain of Transforms. With the Edit operation, you only get the aggregate affect of all the changes.

> When you aren't concerned with having a perfectly procedural network and you want to make numerous transforms, the Edit SOP is the tool to use.

> I generally prefer to have Secure Selection toggled on so that I don't accidentally lose the current selection. However, when using the Edit SOP to make numerous transforms, it's quicker to temporarily turn Secure Selection off.

7. When you are selecting multiple points, using a box selection technique doesn't always work so well. In the left stowbar, you can toggle the picking technique between box, lasso, and brush picking. Try out lasso and brush picking to see how they work. Another selection interface tool that comes in handy is the Add, Toggle, Remove, Replace button. By default, it is on Replace. So, if you have one point selected and then select another, the original selection will no longer be selected. You can hold down Shift as you make selections to explicitly add them to the selection even while Replace is chosen. Hold down Ctrl to explicitly remove only a particular selection from the current selection. Change Replace to Add and you don't have to hold down Shift. Any selection you make will be added to the current selection. Change Add to Remove and now any point you select is removed from the selection. Change Remove to Toggle and now you click on points to first add them and then click again to remove them. If you ever find yourself in a situation where you can't choose or un-choose anything, it's worth a look over at this button to see what it is set to. Usually, Replace is a good method to use so set it back to that before continuing. Play around with the various tools just described until your apple core looks something like the one in Figure 5.64. Make sure to toggle back on Secure Selection after you finish using the Edit operation.

Figure 5.64
The apple core made a little more organic.

8. Next, you are going to create a bite mark in the apple. Go to the top viewport, go to wireframe shading, and choose another Curve operation. Change it to NURBs, create a curve similar in shape, and scale to the one shown in Figure 5.65. You'll see in the Network Editor that this has started a new network branch.

Figure 5.65
The first curve of the bite geometry.

9. Append a Duplicate SOP and change the Number of Copies to three. You now have four copies of the curve. You can't see them currently because they are on top of one another. Using the Parameters pane (because it seemed easier than doing it in the viewport), adjust the Rotate in Y and the Pivot in X and Z so that you end up getting something that looks like Figure 5.66. Values of ry –40, px 0.25 and pz 0.325 worked for me.

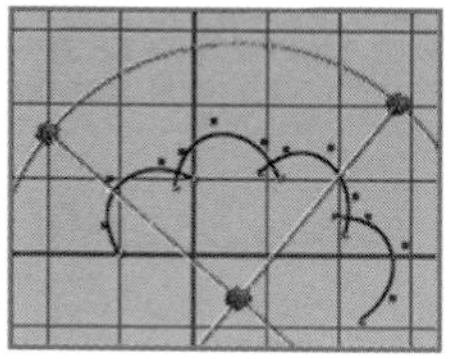

10. Turn on the display of point numbers. MMB on the duplicate node and it says you have four primitives. You need to turn these four primitives into one so that you can then skin them correctly. Append a Join SOP and toggle on Multiplicity. This handy operation joined all the primitives correctly and turning on Multiplicity made the connecting points sharper. You have a pretty good-looking bite mark curve now.

Figure 5.66
Create the bite curve.

11. Append a Transform and use it to line up the curve to along the X axis as shown in Figure 5.67.

12. In the Network Editor, append a Duplicate SOP and change the Number of Copies to five. Rotate it in X to around 35 degrees.

13. Append a Skin SOP and you have a primitive that should be able to take a good bite out of the apple. Go ahead and turn off the display of points and point numbers.

14. Go to the perspective viewport. Turn on the Template flag of the edit node so that you can see the apple core. Over the viewport, choose a Transform and choose the bite geometry. Position it so that it is penetrating the apple core on the upper lip off to the right a bit (as viewed from the homed view position). Basically, you want to get it into a similar position as shown in the render at the beginning of this exercise.

Figure 5.67
The curve transformed to line up with the X axis.

15. Append a Surfsect operation and wire in the bite geometry network into its left input and the apple geometry network into its right input. Your network should now look like Figure 5.68. Surfsect is the Boolean operation for NURBs and Beziers geometry. Its counterpart for polygons geometry is the Cookie SOP. By default, the Operation is set to Union, which should give something like Figure 5.69. Change the Operation to User Defined and toggle on Keep Inside A and Keep Outside B. So, you want to keep the outside of the apple core and the inside of the bite geometry.

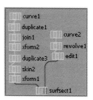

Figure 5.68
The current state of the network.

Figure 5.69
Surfsect using the union operation.

Ideally, you should now have an apple core that looks like a big bite has been taken out of it. However, sometimes the surfsect needs a little jostling to convince it to work. If necessary, adjust 2D Tolerance up a little bit and the Boolean should work. Be careful adjusting 3D Tolerance and Marching Steps, as they can quickly bring your machine to an ungraceful crash. Check out the Help to find out more about them. Displaying profiles generated by the surfsect can be very memory intensive if they are in large numbers. Turn off their display in the viewer's right stowbar, which is the display options.

Create the Worm

You don't want the apple to feel lonely, so you'll commence to creating a worm for company.

1. Drop an unconnected Tube SOP somewhere in the Network Editor. Change it to NURBs and the radii to 0.1 and 0.1. On the Details tab, change the Rows to 20.

2. Append a Cap operation and change First U Cap and Last U Cap to End cap rounded. This closes both sides of the tube and makes the ends slightly rounded to resemble a worm.

Squirm the Worm

The worm must do more than merely exist. It has dreams and ambitions. It must traverse the landscape of the eaten apple!

1. Next, let's get the worm to crawl on the apple core. Luckily, the Creep operation is perfect for getting one thing to crawl over the surface of another thing. Drop a Creep SOP and connect the cap node to its left input and the edit node to its right input. On the Initialize menu, choose Keep Proportions. As you can see, it tries but doesn't exactly succeed in keeping the worm roughly the same. You need to manually make some scale adjustments to get the worm back to a good size. Adjust the Scale in X, Y, and Z until your worm looks good again. The values I used were 0.3, 0.1, 1.3.

2. Using the number ladder to adjust the Translate in Y up and down and you'll see the worm crawls up and down the core. You'll probably also see that sometimes the scale of the worm gets a little screwy. Like he may get really short sometimes or really fat other times, depending on where he is on the apple. This is because the Creep operation is sliding projected geometry (the worm) over the UVs of the base geometry. Because the UVs are perfectly uniform across the apple, the worm is distorted as he is moves across them. To get the UVs to be perfectly uniform would be quite a feat; however, you can do a heck of a lot better than it is currently.

3. You can take a grid with uniform UVs and paste that on to the surface of the apple. Then have the worm creep across that grid. You'll still get a little stretching or squashing here and there, but it works out much better than before. Lay down an unconnected Grid SOP and change it to NURBs. Change the Size to 5, 5 and the Rows and Columns to 20 each.

4. Drop an unconnected Paste SOP and connect the grid node to its left input and the edit node from the apple to its right input. Change Along Vector to Parametrically. Next, set U Range to 0.2 and 0.4, and V Range to 0 and 1. Look in the viewport and you'll see that this determines the U and V range over which the grid will be pasted. You can also immediately see that the uniformity of the UVs of the grid is better than that of the apple. Look closely at the lips of the apple and you'll see that the pasted grid isn't following it with enough detail and so is cutting into the apple. Because the worm will now follow the grid, it would make it look like the worm was sinking into the apple. Change the Belt Width to 0.3 and the Belt Divisions to 6. Now, the grid correctly follows the crisp edge of the lip.

5. Append a Delete SOP to the paste and enter a 0 in the Group field. You don't have any groups. This is a quick way of specifying a primitive by its number. The apple should be primitive number 0 and so you are left with the pasted grid geometry. Connect this delete node into the right input of the creep node. Your network should now look like Figure 5.70.

6. Make a HUD slider for the Translate Y parameter on the creep node. Do you remember how? 'Tis easy as a summer day is lazy... ideally, I mean. Double-click in the parameter field to box select the value. Then, LMB and drag and drop in the viewport. Now, you can easily move the worm back and forth using the slider.

7. Append a Merge operation to the creep node and pipe in the surfsect node as well so that you can see both the worm and the apple. Slide the worm so that it is halfway over one of the lips of the core. Do a test render using the default mantra driver. RMB on the quick launch button and choose View: Mantra. As the worm goes over the lip, it can get sharp edges in its body as shown in Figure 5.71.

8. RMB on the creep node and insert a Smooth operation. Change the Iterations to 60 and do another test render. Ahh, much improved! Figure 5.72 shows the worm in its happier, smoother state.

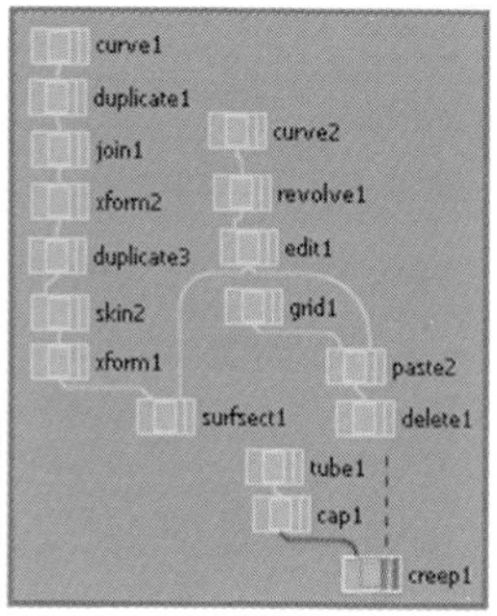

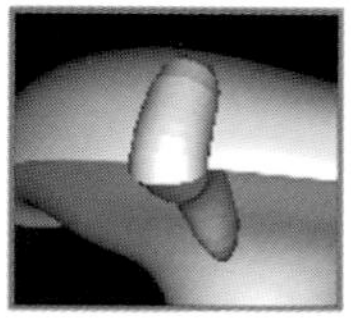

Figure 5.71
The worm's body has some unsightly sharp edges.

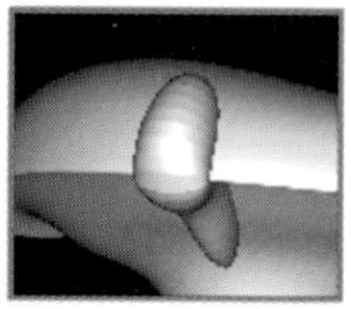

Figure 5.72
The worm's body after a comforting Smooth operation.

Figure 5.70
The current state of the network.

Create the Sign

Sure, you could easily end this discussion of NURBs right now and feel good that you covered a good deal of material. But, there are a few more NURBs related SOPs that I want to talk about and so I have contrived a way to do it. You'll create a sign that ponders the nature of worms.

1. Drop an unconnected grid somewhere off to the side. Change it to NURBs, its Orientation to XY, and its Size to 4.2 and 3.

2. Also unconnected, drop a Font Operation to the side. The field where you enter text is where it says Frame: $F. Delete that and enter WORMS\n=\nWISE? and check out the viewport. Home the view if necessary. The \n is how you specify an enter in single line fields. So, you should see

    WORMS
      =
    WISE?

    in the viewport. Toggle off Hole Faces. Later, this will help the sweep to create pleasing geometry. After you add the sweep, come back if you want and toggle it on and off to see the difference. Go ahead and delete the field, and let's do it an easier way. Press Alt+E on the field to bring up the expression editor. Type WORMS and then press Enter. Type = and then press Enter. Type WISE? and then press Enter. Press Accept and the editor will take care of the carriage returns for you!

3. Lay down an unconnected Project SOP and connect the font node into its left input and the grid into its right input. This operation lets you project one geometry onto a surface in order to create a profile on that surface. Change Axis to Minimum Distance. You now have the profiles of the words on the grid.

4. Append a Profile SOP and you have now extracted the profiles from the grid.

5. Lay down an unconnected Circle SOP and change it to NURBs Curve and the Radii to 0.05 and 0.05.

5. Append a Sweep operation, making sure the that the circle is connected to its left input and the profile node is connected to its middle input. Switch to the Output tab and change the Skin Output to Skin with Preserve Shape and Auto Closure. Wahoo! You have bubble letters! The sweep node is sweeping the circle along the backbone of the profile.

6. Let's make the letters a little smoother. Append a Refine SOP and toggle on First U and Second U. Change them to 0 and 1 respectively. Change U Divisions to 15. Toggle on First V and Second V and change them to 0 and 1, respectively. With the Refine operation, you add divisions (and so detail) over a specific UV range. In this case, you are adding detail over the entire range. Your network should now look like Figure 5.73.

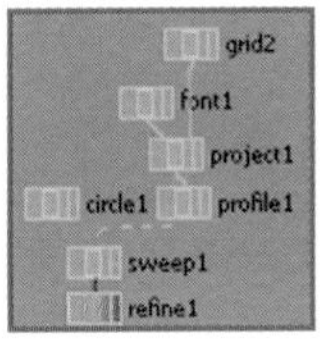

Figure 5.73
The state of the sign network.

7. You have the bubble letters. Now, you need the sign with the words cut out. RMB on the font node and choose Reference Copy. This creates a copy of the node that has all its parameters channel referenced back to the original node. So, any changes you make to the original node will automatically be passed over to the reference copy. RMB on the Hole Faces parameter and choose Delete Channels. Toggle it on. This is the only parameter you want to be different. Making a reference copy is better than copying and pasting the node because, if you later wanted to change the text, you only have to change it once.

> Make a reference copy when you want to create another node that inherits all the values of the current node. In addition, making a reference node can help you determine what a particular channel reference is if that is all you want.

8. Make a reference copy of the project node and wire the copied font node into its left input. Append a Trim operation to this branch; you now have the grid with the words cut out of it.

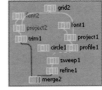

Figure 5.74
The current state of the sign network.

9. Append a Merge and make sure that both the trim node and the refine node are fed into it. You now have the cut-out sign with the bubble letters. Oh, when I said contrived, I meant nothing less! Your network should now look like Figure 5.74.

10. Over the viewport, add a Transform and select the sign. As discussed earlier in the book, doing this over the viewport automatically centers the pivot point and so makes the sign easier to position. Turn on the Footprint flag for the merge node containing the apple core and worm. Move the sign around so that you like its position and that be the end. To get the render at the beginning of this exercise, I adjusted the position of the camera and the lights, and changed the quality settings of the mantra output driver. This is discussed in more detail in Chapter 13.

11. Finally, connect the transform node to the merge at the bottom. Append a Null SOP and label it `displayRender`, and you have finished yet another tour of training. Figure 5.75 shows the final state of the entire network.

Summary

So you have had your first meal of faux meat and potatoes. The SOPs context is the main course in the Houdini meal. This chapter introduced many of the basic features and operators available and it's crucial for you to solidly understand and feel comfortable in the context. The next chapter continues upon this path and introduces you to ever more mind-boggling uses for the various tools at your disposal. Press on! There is a good deal more to be digested!

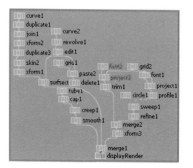

Figure 5.75
The final state of the entire SOP network.

5. Surface Operators (SOPs)

87

chapter 6
Additional SOPs Practice

L o and behold, there is more to be learned in the land of SOPs. Lest you get too comfortable in your confidence of surface creations, know that there is much yet to cover in this context. In this chapter, you take the basic principles learned in the previous chapter and weave them together with an artistry known only to spiders and writers.

Looking in the Tab menu, you can see there are a fantastic number of surface operations. The publisher politely suggested that I keep this book under 1,000 pages, so I won't be covering them all here. However, this chapter covers two more exercises that introduce you to new SOPs and new ways of using SOPs you are already familiar with. Call it an extended exploration!

Attack of the Be-Tentacled Sphere

Now it is time to create a model of a beast so fearsome, so loathed throughout the galaxy that most never even have the guts to call it by its rightful name. Instead, they quake in their starboots and can say nothing more than "The Be-Who-Must-Not-Be-Named." You must embrace this fear and so conquer it! At the very least, you must build a small model of the real thing and not fear the model, as shown in Figure 6.1!

Create the Mothersphere

This fierce beast must have a home for all its constituent horrors and it is up to you to create it.

1. Fire up a fresh session of Houdini. Throw down a geometry object, rename it `tentacles`, and jump inside.

2. Drop a Sphere SOP, change the Type to Polygon, and change the Frequency to 4.

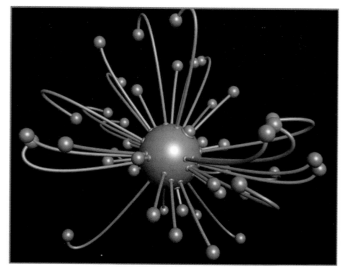

Figure 6.1
The fearsome be-tentacled sphere.

3. Append a Facet operation and toggle on Post-Compute Normals. Notice that this creates the Normal point attribute. Turn on the display of point normals to see them. You may have to scale up the normals' display size to see them clearly. Turn them off and continue. Adding the point normal attribute ensures that the copy operation will copy over the tentacles and point them all outward from the surface of the sphere.

4. Turn on the display of points so you can create the points to which you will later copy the tentacles. Append a Scatter and change the Number of Points to 5. Turn on the Template flag on the facet node and you can see that you've created five points on the surface of the sphere. Turn off the Template flag and move along.

Create the Tentacle

Now you will create the appendage with which it will strike fear into the hearts of even the most brave.

1. Go to the top viewport and, if necessary, turn on the grid display. Change the grid spacing to 0.5. Create a NURBs curve that looks something like that shown in Figure 6.2. Notice that you are creating it so it points down at the positive Z axis. You do this to ensure that the orientation is correct when it is copied later. Note also that the first point in the curve is at the top of the figure and the last point is the filled-in box at the other end.

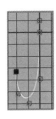

Figure 6.2
The backbone of the tentacle.

> It is almost always best to build geometry down the positive Z axis. That is because numerous operations, such as the Copy for example, expect incoming geometry to be situated in that manner.

2. Append a Resample SOP and leave it at the defaults. Notice that this operation converted the curve to a polygon and then evenly distributed the points along the length of the curve

3. Append a Carve SOP and toggle off First U. Toggle on Second U and slide the value back and forth. By animating this parameter later, you will get the tentacles to "grow" out of the mothersphere. Hence, this will be referred to as the grow slider from now on. You will be using this one a good deal throughout the exercise. So, turn it into a HUD slider for easy access.

4. Lay down an unconnected Circle SOP and rename it tentacleWidth. Change it to a NURBs Curve and the Radii to 0.05.

5. Append a Sweep SOP and make sure that the tentacleWidth is connected to its left input and that the carve is connected to its middle input. On the Output tab, change Skin Output to Skin with Auto Closure. Go back and change the grow slider: you now have a growing tentacle. The tentacle part of your network should look like Figure 6.3.

6. Drop an unconnected Align SOP and rename it alignCircleToCarve. Wire in the tentacleWidth node to its left input and the carve node to its right input. Change the Right UV to 1 and again play with grow slider. It really is all about playing. Well, that and doing good in the world, as my mother always reminds me. The circle primitive follows the leading edge of the tentacle.

7. Drop an unconnected Sphere SOP and rename it bulb. Change its Type to Polygon, its Radii to 0.2 each, and its Frequency to 4.

Figure 6.3
The current state of the tentacle network.

8. Drop an unconnected Align SOP and rename it `alignBulbToCircle`. Wire in the bulb node to its left input and the `alignCircleToCarve` to its right input. Immediately, you'll see something crazy happened. Toggle off Individual Alignment, as you want to align the entire sphere together and not each individual primitive face. The next thing you'll see is that you can't see. That is, the guide geometry is getting in the way. Bring up the display options and, on the Guides and Marker tab, toggle off their display for a moment. Turn on the Footprint flag for the `sweep` node so that you can see the tentacle as well as the bulb. Play with the grow slider and see what it looks like. The bulb doesn't exactly line up correctly with the tentacle.

9. In the parameters for the `alignCircleToCarve` node, go to the Transform tab and you can make manual adjustments to the alignment. Aligning the circle correctly will then pass down to and so correctly align the bulb as well. I changed mine to Translate in X to 0.1, Translate in Y to 0.2, and Rotate in Y to 90. Do whatever works for your situation.

10. Append a Group SOP to the `alignBulbToCircle` node and rename it `GRbulbs`. If necessary, change the Group Name to `$OS` so that it inherits the name of the node. Make sure Enable is toggled on under the Number option and MMB to verify that a primitive group has been created that contains the bulb primitives. You will use this group later to isolate the bulbs and the tentacles from each other.

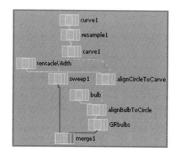

11. Append a Merge SOP and also wire in the `sweep` node. You now have the completed tentacle together. Turn off the Footprint flag on the `sweep` node. Your tentacle network should look like Figure 6.4.

12. Drop an unconnected Copy SOP and connect the scatter node to its right input and the merge to its left input. Turn on the Footprint for the `facet` node. Play with the grow slider and you should see five tentacles growing outward from inside the mothersphere. In the copy node, toggle off the Rotate to Normal parameter. The orientation of the tentacles gets screwed up. Toggle it back on.

Figure 6.4
The state of the tentacle network.

There are two main things that you set up to ensure that the tentacles were oriented correctly by the copy operation. The `facet` node initializes point normals that point outward from the mothersphere. Turn on the bypass flag for the `facet` node. Again, the tentacles are screwed up. Toggle it back off. The other thing was that you built the curve for the tentacle going in the positive Z axis. The copy operation requires this little bit of forethought to ensure that the copied geometry is correctly oriented.

Create the Aperture

You'll see in the rendered image at the beginning of this exercise that there is a little ring at the base of each of the tentacles. Just like a camera aperture opens and closes, you are going to create an effect where the tentacles push up through the mothersphere and create little apertures around the opening. If that wasn't described clearly enough, you will see it in a moment.

1. Append a Delete SOP to the copy node and rename it `deleteTubes`. For the Group at the top of the parameters, click the arrow at the far left and choose the `GRbulbs` group. Change the Operation to Delete Non-Selected. The bulbs are isolated and await your bidding.

2. Append a Cookie SOP and make sure that `deleteTubes` is connected to its left input and the `facet` node is connected to its right input. The Cookie operation is the polygonal version of the Boolean operation. Adjust the grow slider so that the bulbs are intersecting with the mothersphere. Turn off the Footprint flag on the `facet` node. Change the Operation to User Defined and toggle on and off the various options to see how a Boolean operation

works. You are actually going to use a different feature of the Cookie. So, place the checkmark on the Creases option. Move the grow slider around and you will see that the cookie is now creating curves out of the creases where the two inputs are intersecting.

3. Lay down an unconnected Circle SOP and rename it apertureWidth. Change it to a NURBs Curve and its Radii to 0.05 each.

4. Drop an unconnected Sweep operation and connect apertureWidth to the left input and the cookie node to its middle input. On the Output tab, change the Skin Output to Skin with Preserve Shape and Auto Closure. Play with the grow slider and you will see that the bulbs now create a pore-like, squishy thing as they push up through the mothersphere. Now, you are really getting somewhere. Fear not the pores of the Be-Who-Must-Not-Be-Named! The network now looks like Figure 6.5.

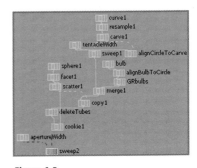

Figure 6.5
The current state of the network.

5. Copy and paste the deleteTubes node and rename it deleteBulbs. Change the Operation to Delete Selected, thereby isolating the tentacle tubes.

6. Copy and paste the cookie node and connect the deleteBulbs node into its left input. Alas, you aren't getting the curves like with the bulbs. The problem is that the Cookie operation is for doing Booleans on polygonal geometry. The tubes are still NURBs geometry. MMB on the deleteBulbs node and you can see that it lists five NURBS surfaces.

7. RMB on the input of the deleteBulbs node and insert a Convert SOP. Toggle to the Divisions Per Span option and set U and V to zero. Make sure the Display flag is on the appropriate cookie node (probably cookie2) and now play with the grow slider. You get the curves generated from the intersections of the tubes and the mothersphere.

8. You want to have both the curves from the bulb cookie and the tube cookie to go to the sweep node. What do you do? You throw down a Merge, pipe in both cookie nodes, and then connect the merge to the middle input of the sweep. Oh yes, the procedural workflow is the sweet nectar.

9. You'll notice that when you drag the grow slider to 0.02, the align operations break down and bulbs jump out to weird positions. The simple solution is just to never carve down that far. RMB on the HUD slider and choose Handle parameters. Change the Range to 0.03 to 1 and lock both the low and high values.

10. Another strange thing you may have noticed is that at particular values on the grow slider, the apertures disappear and the sweep shows an error. You can tell this because it turns the node icon red. MMB on the node to read the error message. The error says that the backbone doubles back on itself. The problem is that sometimes the cookie operation creates curves that aren't useful.

Even if you don't happen to see this error, be safe and insert a Facet SOP between the sweep and merge nodes. Toggle on Remove Degenerate. This will remove any bad primitives. Insert a Refine SOP between the facet and sweep nodes. Toggle on First and Second U and set them to 0 and 1, respectively. Change Tolerance U to 0.001 and you'll see that this simplifies the curves. That takes care of another potential problem, as sometimes the cookie passes through curves that have their points jumbled. Any bad results that the cookie may try to pass off will now be deleted or fixed before going into the sweep node.

11. Append a Merge to the sweep and get all the geometry wired in that you want to display. The three things that should be merged are the aperture, mothersphere, and tentacle geometries. So, pipe in the sweep2, the facet1 node, and the copy1 nodes. Make sure the Display flag is on this merge and you should see all of your geometry at once now. If you have any Template or Footprint flags on elsewhere in the network, turn them off.

Notice that a yellow flag on the merge node indicates a warning. MMB and it says that a mismatch of attributes on the inputs was detected and that some attribute values may not be initialized to expected values. Look in the viewport using a shaded mode and you will see that the tentacles and bulbs are black, whereas the rest of the geometry looks normal. Oh, my free spirit plays wiz zee words to foreshadow zee ahnsuur! The issue is with the point normal attribute. Figure 6.6 shows what the problem looks like.

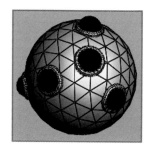

Figure 6.6
The spheres have normals that have been incorrectly initialized.

12. MMB on each of the nodes coming into the merge. The facet1 node is passing in a Normal point attribute. The sweep and the copy node do not have a Normal point attribute. The problem arises because the merge node sees that the facet has it and so initializes the other inputs to have it as well. However, it doesn't initialize the attribute correctly and so it basically screws up the normals for the other geometry. The answer is to put all the inputs on equal footing before going into the merge. Actually, it looks like the aperture geometry is fine. But, let's set it up as well just to be thorough.

RMB on the sweep2's output, insert a Facet SOP, and toggle on Post Compute Normals. It's a little trickier to get a Facet operation inserted before the copy1 node. Copy and paste the facet3 node. Connect it to the copy1 node's output and connect this new facet to the merge node. You'll notice that the merge now has four inputs and you just want three. In its parameters, click the X for the copy1 entry and that input will be disconnected. Wahoo! The geometry looks fine and the warning is gone.

> Another way you can rewire the merge node is using selectable links. This is set in the Settings>Main Preferences>Worksheet Tiles and Trees>Connect Tiles with Selectable Links toggle. With it on, you can click on the wires that connect nodes to rewire them. You can then click on the third wire going into the merge (the one that came from the copy1 node) and rewire it into the output of the new facet4 node directly. One danger to be aware of when using this option is that you can inadvertently unwire nodes when you mean to be tracking the Network Editor.

13. To honor the muses of organization, append a Null SOP and rename it displayRender. It might be a good time to verify the layout of your network. Jump over to Figure 6.7 to see the final state of the network.

Ewwww! It Moves!

Because the network is a fearsome spectacle even now, proceed another few steps and copy stamp in a little variation.

1. First, you will copy stamp the growth of each tentacle to get some variation in the lengths. In the carve node, enter stamp("../copy1", "growth", 0) in the Second U field.

6. Additional SOPs Practice

2. In the copy node, go to the Stamp tab and toggle on Stamp Inputs. Enter `growth` for the first variable and adjust the slider to verify that the stamp is working. There are a large number of ways you get variation by entering an expression in the Value field. Enter `rand($PT) * $FF/$NFRAMES` and play through the frame range. Let's break down the expression to make it easier to grok. The `rand($PT)` gives you a random number between 0 and 1 for each tentacle. This part of the expression will produce different growth lengths for each tentacle. The second part of the expression makes the tentacles grow over time. `$FF` is a global variable for the floating point frame number. `$NFRAMES` is a global variable for the total number of frames. Substitute some numbers in there for different times in the frame range and you will see that it will return larger values as you progress through the range, thereby making the tentacles grow.

3. The tentacles grow over time and to different lengths, but they are still all rotated the same way. Let's add some variation there also to finish the exercise. Insert a Transform SOP between the `merge1` node and the `copy1` node. Rename it `stampRotate`.

4. Because you created the tentacle pointing "up" in the positive Z direction, that is the axis you want to rotate around. Change the Rotate in the various axes to intuitively verify that this is the case. Enter `stamp("../copy1", "rotate", 0)` in the Rotate Z field.

5. In the Stamp tab of the copy node, enter `rotate` for the second variable and, as always, adjust the slider to see if the stamp is working. Use the number ladder to rotate in larger increments as the slider defaults to a range of 0 to 1 and you won't see much happening in that range. Enter `rand($PT) * 360` in the second value field. The first part returns a random value between 0 and 1. Multiplying that by 360 gives each tentacle a random amount of rotation between 0 and 360 degrees. And for the final step to illustrate to the good things that come from proceduralism, go back to the scatter and change the number of points to 20 or so. Everything automatically cooks and updates. Now, your sphere is all the more menacing. Do you feel like you've come to understand the Be-Tentacled Sphere? Perhaps maybe even come to appreciate how it sees the universe? Your network should now look like Figure 6.7.

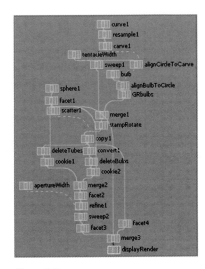

Figure 6.7
The final state of the network.

The `rand()` expression returns a pseudo-random number based on a given seed value. It isn't truly random because it will return the same value when given the same seed. If it were truly random, it would return a different value each time it was computed even when given the same seed value. In most cases with computer graphics, you wouldn't really want something that was truly random, as that would mean you couldn't predictably duplicate a particular result. Just think if you used the `rand()` expression somewhere in your network and the client approved the look. The next time you run it, the look changes because `rand` is returning a different value. Doh!

Creating Stonehenge

In this exercise, you will explore the mysteries of Stonehenge. There is a legend that if you can find the key, this archaeological wonder is the doorway to a greater intelligence. Lace up your boots and bring along your plumb bob and leaf trowel because you have some digging to do… digging into this mystery, that is! Figure 6.8 is a render of this adventure.

Create the Arch

First, you need to create the arch for the magical mound.

1. Get rolling in a spanky fresh new session of Houdini. Drop a Geometry object, rename it `stoneHenge`, and jump inside.

2. Drop a `box` object and leave it at the defaults.

3. Append a Transform SOP and rename it `archSize`. Go to a quad view to more easily see the next few steps. Change the parameters to match those in Figure 6.9. Notice that the Translate Y field contains an expression that keeps a little bit of the arch below the ground plane no matter how large you scale it vertically.

4. Append a Duplicate SOP and enter `-(ch("../archSize/tx")) * 2` in the Translate X field. Breaking down the expression, you see that it channel references the `tx` field of the `archSize` node. That value is then negated and then multiplied by two. What does that do? It automatically places the opposing pillar the same distance from the Y axis. Change the `tx` channel in the `archSize` node and you will see the opposing automatically update.

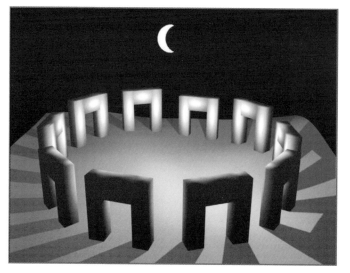

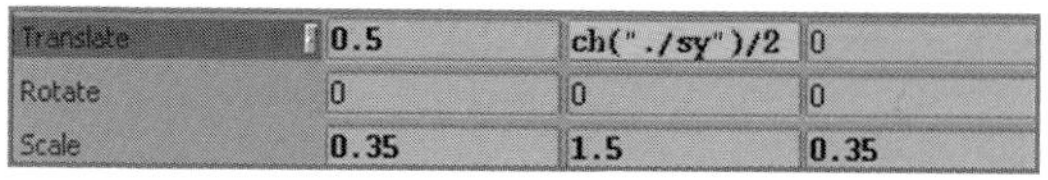

Figure 6.8
Stonehenge under a full moon.

Translate	0.5	ch("./sy")/2	0
Rotate	0	0	0
Scale	0.35	1.5	0.35

Figure 6.9
The parameters for the `archSize` node.

5. Turn on the display of points. Append a Facet SOP and toggle on Unique Points. This option "unshares" each point in the boxes. Now, each box has its own unique point at every corner.

6. Over the viewport, choose a Delete operation and select the two interior sides, the ones that face each other. In the parameters, change the Operation to Delete Non-Selected.

7. Append a Transform SOP and enter `$YMAX` in the Pivot Y field. This places the pivot at the maximum extents in Y of the bounding box feeding in to this node. Change the Scale in Y to 0.3.

8. Over the viewport, choose a `PolyKnit` SOP. You can sew together polygons with this operation. A little red circle appears when the pointer is over a valid sewing point. Click on the corners in the following order: 4, 1, 2, 5, 7, 3, 0, 6, 4, 1 and RMB to complete the selection. Figure 6.10 shows you what this looks like just before completing the selection. If your point numbers are in a different position than those shown in the illustration, change the numbering of your selection so that you still follow how it works in the example; that is, the front-right corner to front-left corner to back-left corner, and so on.

Jump out of wireframe and, oo laa laa, you have sewed together an arch between the two pillars!

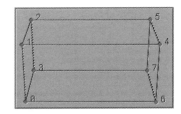

Figure 6.10
The `polyknit` operation.

9. Append a Merge and wire in the `polyknit` (should already be) and also the duplicate node. You now have one completed pillar. The interesting part about how you built it is that you have taken advantage of the procedural nature of Houdini. Leave the Display flag on the merge node and go up and change the `tx`, `sx`, `sy`, or `sz` of the `archSize` node and also the `sy` channel of the `xform1` node. As you tweak the arch's size, everything automatically updates so that the model doesn't break. Yes, you are truly beginning to understand the mind of Houdini! The network should look like Figure 6.11.

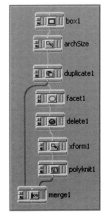

Figure 6.11
The arch network.

Create the Circle of Arches

Now, you arrange a number of arches in a ceremonial circle.

1. Ahhh, but one arch does not a Stonehenge make. No, that will never do! Drop an unconnected Grid SOP and change it to NURBS and its Size in X and Y to 10.

2. Append a VEX Mountain SOP and change the Frequency 1, 2, and 3 to 0.1. Remember to hold the pointer over a label to see what the channel names are. In this case, they are `freq1`, `freq2`, and `freq3`. Lots of freqs in dis house! Jesss dah way you like it! This operation just pushes points around using noise. That gives a gently rolling field in which to place your circle of arches.

3. Lay down an unconnected Circle SOP and rename it `circleSize`. This will determine the circumference of the circle and the number of arches. Change the Type to NURBS Curve and the Orientation to ZX. Change the Center in Y to 5 to push it up a goodly distance above the ground.

4. Drop an unconnected Ray SOP and wire `circleSize` into the left input and the `vex_mountain` node into the right input. This operation lets you project one piece of geometry onto another piece. So it has projected (or ray'd) the circle down onto the ground. Notice that the circle is no longer flat. It is conforming to the undulations in the ground geometry.

5. Branch a Transform from the `circleSize` node. Do you recall how? MMB on the node's output and choose the desired operation to branch instead of insert. Change the Scale in all axes to 0.9.

6. Drop another unconnected Ray SOP and wire it up so that this smaller circle also gets ray'd down to the ground. This inner circle will allow you to create point normals for the larger circle. The copy operation that comes later will then use these point normals to make sure that each arch is facing inward towards the center.

7. Drop an unconnected Point SOP and rename it setNormals. Wire ray1 into the left input and ray2 into the right input. Change Keep Normals to Add Normals and then delete the channels. Enter $TX2-$TX in the nx field and $TZ2-$TZ in the nz field. What did you do?... something super advanced, in a technologically disco kind of way. Turn on the display of point normals and scale them up in the display options, misc folder, if necessary. You have given point normals that point towards the center of the circle to the larger circle.

Leave the Display flag here and go up to xform2 and change the Scale from 0.9 to 1.1 in all axes. The point normals now point outward from the circle. Ohhhh, the Power! So, it takes the position in X of the inner circle and subtracts the position in X of the outer circle and then assigns that to the nx field. After doing the same to the nz field, you get some very useful point normals. If it hasn't happened already, let your path of adoration and admiration of the Point SOP begin here.

8. Drop a Copy SOP and wire the merge into its left input and the setNormals node into its right input. Simple as kidney pie with a second helping of fish and chips! Change the Radii and the Divisions on the circleSize node and watch in amazement as proceduralism cooks your changes down to the copy node. It really is finger-lickin' good. Chicken, on the other hand, I can do without. Your network should now look like Figure 6.12.

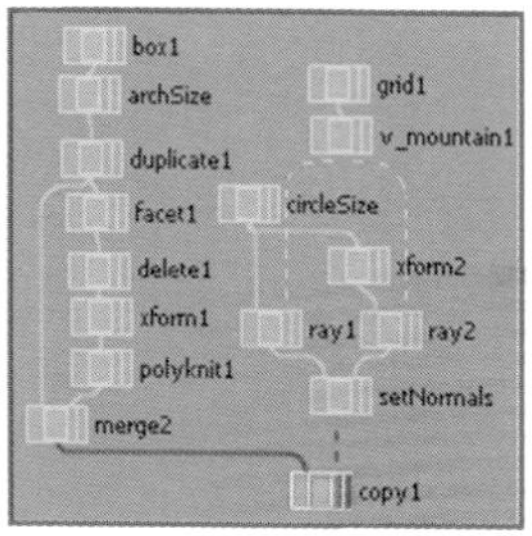

Figure 6.12
The network creating the circle of arches

Because you used the ray operation, you can also change the Height parameter on the vex_mountain node; the arches will stick to the ground as the elevation of solid earth is moved up and down like the surface of an ocean! Oh, the grandeur. I feel faint. And, I am recovered, but still impressed.

> When the burning ember of discovery,
> When the flame of your new fancy has ebbed,
> When you are ready,
> Please continue.

Create the Moon

No arcane magic was ever performed under a blistering hot sun. No feat of ancient wisdom and might would ever unfold under a cloudless blue sky. The night reserves those momentous moments. The veil of shadows must ever conceal its secrets. However, the moon, I think you would agree, has every right to be a spectator in your creation. So, you shall conjure one now.

1. Jump back up the object level. Drop another Geometry object and name it moon.

2. Jump inside and lay down a COP2 Network. In Houdini, you can pretty much lay down any kind of network inside of any other type of network. This paradigm is called *Networks in Networks* and was instituted to make packaging up digital assets a straightforward process. (You read more about it in Chapter 11, "Digital Assets.") For now, you should have created a COP network here inside the moon object. Rename the node createZeeMoon and jump inside it.

   You are going to create simple COP network that will have a black background with a white circle rising. Why, you ask? Well, I had to contrive a way for you to check out the Trace SOP and it will be fun to do a little mucking about in the compositing editor as well.

3. Drop a Shape COP and change its Type to Circle. On the Transform tab, scale it down to 0.1 and 0.1. On the Image tab, toggle on Override Size and change it to 500 and 500.

4. RMB on the shape node and choose Reference Copy. As you learned earlier, this creates a copy of the node with all the parameters channel referenced back to the first one. So, any future changes you make to the first shape node will automatically be referenced into the second one.

5. Append an Invert COP to the shape2 node. The layout of COPs differs from other contexts because it flows from left to right instead of from top to bottom. So, RMB on the output (the on the right side) of the shape2 node and choose an Invert operation. Just like in SOPs, always make sure to update the Display flag when appropriate. The white circle is now black and the surrounding area is now white.

6. Append a Transform COP to the invert and change Translate in X to 0.12 to push it over a little.

7. Append a Multiply COP and notice that it has two inputs, a top and a bottom. Connect the shape1 node into the bottom input. Keep the Display flag on the multiply node and go back and adjust the tx channel on the xform node. Make sure to do it in small increments like 0.01 so you can see the magic. The full moon is carved into a crescent moon.

8. Append another Transform SOP and change the ty channel to –0.45. That should put the moon at the bottom of the viewable area. Alas, you have taken a small deviation into COPs. Let's make another slight deviation into animation and call it a preview of the next chapter. Make sure you are on frame 1 and RMB on the ty field and choose Set Keyframe. The field should turn green to indicate the keyframe has been set.

9. Now go to frame 120 and again RMB on the ty channel field and choose Set Keyframe. Change the value to 0.3. Scrub through the frames and you will see the moon travel up over time until frame 120.

10. Append a Null COP and rename it moonOut. This last node will make it easy to know which node to pick in the Trace operation. Your COP network should look like Figure 6.13. Jump back up to the SOPs context.

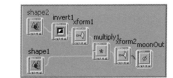

Figure 6.13
The COP network.

11. Drop a Trace SOP and toggle from File to COP. Click the + button at the far left and navigate to and choose the moonOut node. Zee image of zee moon has been imported, traced, and turned into geometry! Although it is a little small. Jump up to the object level and change the Scale in all axes of the moon object to 10. While you are here, push the moon back a little by changing Translate in Z to –5.

    Jump back in and go to the Filters tab on the trace node and toggle on Resample Shapes. Set the Step Size to 7. This cleans up the geometry by removing unnecessary complexity.

12. Scrub through the timeline and you can see that the trace is following the movement created in COPs. Tracing works best on an image that has good contrast. It has no problem with the black-and-white example. Jump back into the COP network so you can do one last little bit of twiddling.

13. Remember you adjusted the tx channel on the xform1 node to turn the full moon into a crescent moon. Go to frame 150, RMB on the tx field, and choose Set Keyframe. The value should be 0.12, which you set previously.

14. Go to frame 180, again RMB on the tx field, and choose Set Keyframe. Change the value to 0.03.

15. Jump back up to SOPs and scrub through the timeline. Isn't the Trace SOP almost illegally fun? Append a Null SOP and rename it moonOut. Always keep an eye towards good organization; it will save you and others who view your file much time and frustration.

The Message Is Friendship

What would intelligence be without the flame of friendship? Let's hope you never have to find out.

1. Once activated, what might this greater intelligence say? I can imagine at least three things, but you will go with the first. Jump into the stoneHenge object and lay down an unconnected Font SOP. Delete the default text and enter HELLO WORLD_.

2. Append a Transform SOP and change the rx channel to –90.

3. Append a Ray SOP and make sure the transform node is connected into the left input and the vex_mountain node is connected into the right input. The letter gets ray'd down onto the geometry; follow its curvature. I know you already did this earlier with the circle, but I have to say again that this operation spanks butt.

4. Append a PolyExtrude operation and change the Translate in Z to –0.3.

5. Over the viewport, choose a Group operation. Use the primitive selection mask (hotkey 4) and choose the entire underscore geometry. Rename the node GRunderscore. If it isn't already, change the Group Name to $OS.

6. Append a Delete SOP and choose the GRunderscore group. This should delete the underscore and leave the words. Rename the node del_.

7. Branch a Delete SOP from the GRunderscore node. Remember that to branch a node, you need to MMB on the output. In this one, also choose the GRunderscore group and then change the operation to Delete Non-Selected. So, this one should have deleted the words and left the underscore geometry. Rename the node delWords. The message part of your network should resemble Figure 6.14.

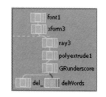

Figure 6.14
The message part of the SOP network thus far.

8. Append a Group SOP to the delWords node and rename it GRblink. Change the Group Name to $OS if necessary. If it was necessary, make this the default already using the Presets menu! Change the Operation to Group by Expression. Enter if($F%20 < 10, 1, 0) in the Filter Expression field. Scrub through the timeline and you will see the underscore blinking.

Breaking down the expression, if the current frame number mod (%) 20 is less than 10, return a value of 1. Otherwise, return a value of 0. When the expression returns 1, the geometry is part of the group. When it returns 0, the geometry is not a part of the group.

Delete the whole expression and enter $F%20. Toggle to number view and scrub through the frame range. The value returned counts up to 19 and then starts again at 0. Using the mod sign (%) is a quick and easy way to create a repeating cycle. Undo to go back to the full expression. The modulus operator is simply the remainder of the division of the value.

9. Append a Visibility SOP and set the Group to GRblink. Scrub the time-line and you will see the underscore blinks on and off, much like a cursor, you might say. The Visibility operation is a great way to visualize in the viewport what geometry is a part of a particular group and what is not. If you are looking at another person's file that contains a group, but you are having problems understanding what the group is doing, branch off a Visibility node and you will immediately be able to see what is in the group and what is not. Changing the Apply to parameter will quickly toggle the visibility between the two entities. Another good use for it is when you have a lot of geometry and you want to temporarily "get rid" of parts of it to clear up the area you are focusing on. For example, if you were modeling the neck of a character, it might make it easier to select all of the head and use a Visibility operation to temporarily get it out of the way. After finishing up on the neck area, you would just delete the visibility node in the network and all would be back to normal. In this case, you are just using it to pull off a gag in the viewport.

> When using the Visibility SOP, it is important to remember that visibility is affected only in the viewport. The geometry will still be visible in a render.

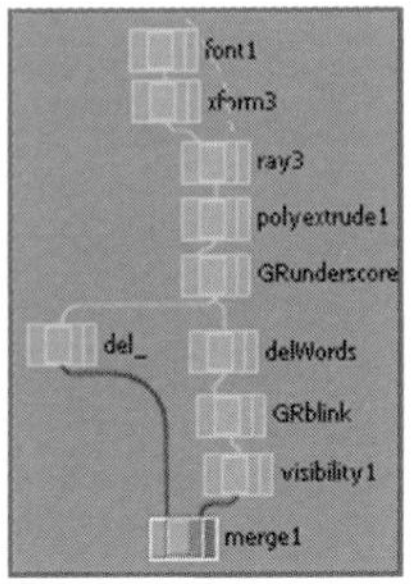

Figure 6.15
The current state of the message part of the network.

10. Append a Merge and make sure the visibility and del_ nodes are connected to it. Your network should now look like Figure 6.15.

It Lives!

As you read earlier (and will now forever testify to be true), magic happens at night. And no, I am not talking about in a Barry White kind of way.

> Earth magic, baby. Ahhh, yea.
> I can't never get enough. It's just not enough.
> *<insert Barry White riff>*

You will now make it so that Stonehenge stands by day and the Grand Poobaa of the Extra-Terrestrial Intelligentsia reveals itself to the world at night. Its friends just call it GP, or The Poob.

1. To summarize, you want the arches to disappear and the words to appear when the moon crests o'er yon grassy vale. First, you need to be able to reference where the moon is. You have such power within your mortal grasp! Off to the side, drop an unconnected Object Merge SOP and rename it getMoon. Enter a . (period) in the Transform Object field. In the Object 1 field, navigate to and choose the moonOut node inside the moon object. Scrub through the timeline and you can see that you have imported the moon geometry and its transformations. There is a little bit of tricky thinking that one must step through in order to understand what an Object Merge is doing. In the "SOPs That Confound the Melon" section that comes later in the chapter, you can read more about it. For now, you must gracefully accept its utility and move on.

2. Append a Primitive SOP and change the Scale in all axes to 0. Because there is but a single primitive with the Pivots set to be centered ($CEX, $CEY, $CEZ), all the points are shrunk down to the center point of the primitive. MMB on the node and it says you still have a good number of points, whereas you really just want a single one.

3. Append a Fuse SOP and toggle off Remove Degenerate. You now have just a single point that represents the position of the moon in the night sky.

4. Append a Null SOP and rename it `moonPosition`.

5. Find the `copy1` node, which should contain the circle of arches. Append to it a Transform SOP. Enter **$YMIN** in the Pivot Y field and set the Scale in Y to 0. This will be the ending state of the arches, when they are hidden in the ground.

6. Drop an unconnected `BlendShapes` SOP. Wire in the `copy1` node and then the transform node you just created. This is a sweet operation, in that Barry White kind of way! Git Sum! You can blend a number of different attributes between two or more inputs. Change the Blends parameter to 2 and drag the `blend1` slider back and forth. The arches shrink and grow because the blend is blending the point positions of the two inputs.

   Toggle on the See One/See All button in the lower-right area of the Viewer pane so that you can see the `moon` object. Figure 6.16 shows the icon. Also, turn on the Footprint flag for the `vex_mountain` node so that you can see the ground.

Figure 6.16
The See One/See All button.

7. Your task, should you choose to accept it, is to figure out when the arches should start shrinking into the ground. Then, you need to figure out how long they should take to sink into the ground. You are going to be reading the Y position of the single point in the `moonPosition` node to figure this out. RMB on that node and choose Spreadsheet. Watch the `P[y]` column as you scrub through the timeline. To me, it looks like the moon crests the ground at around 0, which looks like a good place to start the arches sinking. Scrubbing through the timeline a little more whilst watching the `P[y]` column, it looks like a good range for total shrinkage is 0 to 2.

8. Let's use a `point()` expression to retrieve the position (P) of the `moonPosition` point in Y and then wrap that in a `fit()` expression to force it to your bidding. Enter `fit(point("../moonPosition", 0, "P", 1), 0, 2, 0, 1)` in the `blend1` field and scrub the timeline. The arches start shrinking when the `moonPosition` point is at a `P[y]` of 0 and then finish shrinking when it reaches a `P[y]` of 2. Remember that the `point()` expression begins counting index (or component) numbers at 0. So Y, even though it is the second component of x, y, z, is referred to as 1 because the `point()` expression looks at x, y, z as 0, 1, and 2.

9. Now, The Poob must speak. You are going to do basically the same setup for the words. Append a Transform SOP to the merge node containing the words (and underscore). Enter **$YMIN** for its Pivot in Y field and set the Scale in Y to 0.

10. Drop a `BlendShapes` SOP and make sure that the merge node is connected first and the transform node is connected second. You can change the ordering of connections using the arrows in the node's parameters as shown in Figure 6.17. Set the Blends field to 2 and scrub the slider back and forth to verify the blend is working.

    Enter `fit(point("../moonPosition", 0, "P", 1), 2, 2.8, 1, 0)` in the `blend1` parameter field. This is doing the same kind of thing as the previous expression, only just the opposite. He he. When the moon is at a `P[y]` of 2, set the blend value to 1, which means the words are scaled to 0 in Y. When the moon is at a `P[y]` of 2.8, set the blend value to 0, which means the words are scaled to 1 in Y.

Figure 6.17
Use the indicated arrows to change the ordering of inputs.

11. In a final, spell-binding act of daring do, let's create an expression-driven Switch SOP. Drop an unconnected switch and wire in the blendshapes1 node first (the one with the arches) and then wire in the blendshapes2 node (the one with the words). Move the slider from 0 to 1 and back and you'll see that it switches the input that it passes down the network. Enter if(point("../moonPosition", 0, "P", 1) < 2, 0, 1) in the Select Input field and tell me what it is doing. I can't hear you. But, that does make sense because it is not likely that I am sitting next to you whilst you are doing the exercise. In any case, think through it and you will see that it is very similar to the previous expressions.

12. Append a Merge operation and ensure that the switch and the vex_mountain nodes are wired into it.

13. You are becoming a stickler for good network organization. I can feel it! And so, append a Null SOP and rename it displayRender. Play the timeline and witness the first *real* proof of an advanced interstellar civilization! Figure 6.18 shows the final state of the stoneHenge object's SOP network.

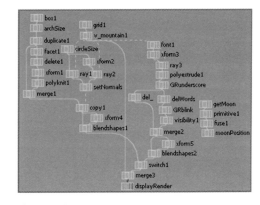

Figure 6.18
The final state of the network.

SOPs That Confound the Melon

In this section, I take a few minutes to go over a few SOPs in particular. These weren't covered earlier in detail because it would have taken you too far off the path of the exercise. Here, however, there is no path but detail! The following topics are covered because I recall them appearing murky at best when first learning about them. Hopefully, you can avoid some of that frustration by getting the answers right now at the outset.

Object Merge SOP

The Object Merge SOP is a useful tool for bringing the SOP contents of one object into another object. It all seems pretty simple until you really start to think about what the Transform object is doing. At least for me, that part gets a little murky. But, with a short exercise and some discussion, I'll wager you can regain a solid footing.

1. Open a new session of Houdini and lay down three Geometry objects. Name them sphere, box, and cone.

2. Jump into the sphere object and drop a Sphere SOP. Jump into the box object and drop a Box SOP. Jump into the cone object and drop a Tube SOP. Change the rad1 channel to 0 to change the tube into a cone. Delete the file nodes in each of the objects if they exist.

3. Jump back up to the objects' context. Leave the sphere at the world origin. Translate the box object in positive Y by five units. Translate the cone object in positive X by three units. Home the perspective view, dolly out a bit, and you should see what is shown in Figure 6.19.

4. Jump into the sphere object and lay down an unconnected object Merge SOP. Append a Merge SOP and wire the sphere node into it as well. As always, update the Display flag.

Figure 6.19
Zee perspective view.

6. Additional SOPs Practice

5. In the Object 1 parameter for the object merge node, navigate to and choose `tube1` node inside the `cone` object. Toggle the See One/See All button so you can see the other two objects. Currently, the merged cone is sitting on top of the sphere at the world origin. Why didn't it inherit the transform of the `cone` object and so be right on top of it? Because the Transform Object field is empty, only the SOP information is being imported. And so, the +3 units in X aren't being inherited.

6. Now, it starts to get a little murkier. In the Transform Object field, navigate to and choose the `sphere` object. The cone has moved over on top of the other cone. Go to wireframe shading and turn on the display of primitive numbers. The numbers verify that there are two cones occupying the space. Usually, this is what you want. Delete the `/obj/sphere` path and replace it with a . and you will get the same result. A period just means to inherit the current object's transforms.

   But, why if you set it to inherit the sphere's object transforms do you get the +3 units in X from the `cone`'s object transforms? Think of it this way. This specifies the object `merge`'s world origin to be the same as the `sphere` objects. Then, it evaluates the `cone`'s object transform relative to this new world origin. The `cone` object is 3 in positive X from the specified world origin and so the imported cone sits on top of the `cone` object.

7. Change the Transform Object field to `/obj/cone` and the cone jumps back to be on top of the sphere. The reason is different this time, though. Earlier, it was because no object transforms were being considered. This time, the object merge's origin is set to +3 in X. It then evaluates where the `cone` object is relative to that new world origin. It is right on top of it, and so no transforms are applied. The result is that the cone sits on top of the sphere.

Figure 6.20
The merged cone using the box's object transforms.

8. To get even loopier, change the Transform Object field to `/obj/box`. Whoa! Exploding brain mass engage! You are object merging a SOP from one object into another object using the object transforms from yet another object. Now, this is getting silly. Yet, you can make sense of it. First the object merge's world origin is set to +5 in Y. Then, the `cone` object is evaluated relative to that new world origin. The cone is five units down and three units to the right. So, the merged cone is now below the `cone` object as shown in Figure 6.20. Once you get into the details, it becomes readily understandable. And, if not, go through the exercise one more time as repetition does help comprehension!

Blast SOP, Delete SOP, and Dissolve SOP

I recall first being introduced to these three operations. I quickly came to the point of near total confusion and would always end trying them all when I wanted to do something that involved deleting things. Well, there is an easier way, and that is to understand how they are different.

1. Start a fresh batch of Houdini and jump into the default geometry object. Throw down three Sphere SOPs and change them all to a Polygon Primitive Type. Set the Frequency on each to 1.

2. Place the Display flag back on the first one. Make sure you are using a primitive selection mask (the hotkey is 5). Turn on the display of primitive numbers. Over the viewport, select a Blast operation, and select and blast primitive 15 and 16. It deleted the two primitives and left a hole.

3. Put the Display flag on the sphere2 node. Over the viewport, select a Delete operation, and select and delete primitives 15 and 16. Again, it deleted the two primitives and left a hole. So, they do the same thing? Well, yes. However, look at the parameters for each node. The delete node offers all kinds of options that the blast does not. Basically, you can forget about the Blast SOP and just use the Delete SOP. Sometimes you will use the extra functionality and sometimes not.

4. Put the Display flag on the sphere3 node. Over the viewport, select a Dissolve operation, and select and dissolve primitives 15 and 16. This time, all of the edges that comprised the two primitives were deleted, but the primitives adjusted in order to repair the hole. That is the main difference between this operation and the previous two. This is most often used to delete unnecessary edges. Notice it has a useful option to remove inline points. Let's use it in this manner to see how it works.

5. Drop an unconnected Grid SOP and change its Rows to 3 and its Columns to 7. Change the Orientation to XY so that it is facing you. Over the viewport, select a Dissolve and switch to the edges selection mask (the hotkey is 2). Choose the inner four edges, as shown in Figure 6.21.

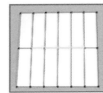

Figure 6.21
Choose these four edges and dissolve them.

6. Houdini dissolved the edges and left the primitives that the edges were a part of. Turn on the display of points if necessary and notice that Houdini stranded points in the vertical edges. Toggle on Remove Inline Points and Houdini will take care of them too.

Copy SOP, Primitive SOP, Duplicate SOP, and Copy/Paste

Here is another gaggle of SOPs that gave me some confusion initially. They can all kind of copy things. Let's look at each to see the differences.

1. Start a new session of Houdini and jump into the default geometry object. Drop a Sphere SOP and change the Type to Polygon. Change the Radius in all axes to 0.2.

2. Drop an unconnected Grid SOP and change the Size in X and Y to 5.

3. Drop an unconnected Copy SOP. Wire the sphere into its left input and the grid into its right input. This operation copies one full copy of the left input to every point in the right input.

4. Drop an unconnected Primitive SOP. Wire the sphere into the left input and the grid into the right input. Toggle on Do Transformation. You'll see a contorted piece of geometry.

5. Insert a Facet SOP between the left input and the sphere node. Toggle on Unique Points. Now, it is easier to see what it is doing. This operation copies one primitive in the left input to a point in the right input until all primitives in the left input are used. You can see this because all the points on the grid have a piece of the sphere copied to them except for the last two rows. There are 80 primitives in the sphere and 100 points in the grid.

6. Branch off a Duplicate SOP from the sphere node. Change the Number of Copies to 3 and change the Translate in X to 1. This operation merely makes multiple copies of the input.

7. And finally, select the sphere node, press Ctrl+C, and then press Ctrl+V. This just does a copy and paste job in the old-fashioned sense of the phrase. That's all there is to it. No need for any future confusion.

Understanding Point and Primitive SOPs

This section could probably occupy the contents of an entire book all on its own because these two SOPs have real, ultimate power. The big difference between the two is that, as the names imply, one lets you access point attributes, whereas the other lets you access primitive attributes. The amazing part about them is that they allow you to get down and dirty and apply and modify attributes on a per point (or per primitive) basis if desired. So, you could say, "Primitive number 5,573, I hereby decree that you will be purple." Or "Point number 102,972, I hereby decree that you will have a velocity in X of 110,199." In addition, you can utilize the power of various local variables to affect all points (or primitives) on an individualized basis. Let's check out a simple example of each.

1. Start up Houdini and jump into the default Geometry object.

2. Jump into it and drop a Grid SOP.

3. Append a Point SOP and add `+ rand($PT) * 0.4` to the `ty` channel so that it reads `$TY + rand($PT) * 0.2`. The local variable `TY` says to take the position in Y of each point individually in the grid. The `PT` variable is the point number for each point. So, each point will get a different, random amount of noise because it will feed the `rand()` expression its own point number. Then multiply that value by 0.4 to scale it down a little bit. Take that value and add it to the original position, which is stored in `$TY`. Your grid should look like the one shown in Figure 6.22.

Figure 6.22
The grid with some noise applied.

4. Branch a Facet SOP from the `grid` node. Toggle on the Unique Points parameters.

5. Append a Primitive SOP to the `facet` node. Toggle on Do Transformation. Enter `$BBX * 90` in the Rotate Z field. `BBX` is a local variable that sets a range from 0 to 1 using the X extents of the bounding box of the geometry. So, multiplying that by 90, you can see that the left edge of the grid is pretty flat (where `BBX` is 0) and the primitives are progressively more vertical as they get closer to the right edge (where `BBX` is 1.).

6. Go to the Attributes tab and change Keep Color to Add Color. RMB on the Color label and delete the channels. Set all three to 0 and then enter `$BBX` in the green field. Remember that the fields are red, green, and blue from left to right. The left side of the grid is black and gets progressively more green towards the right edge. Your grid should now look like Figure 6.23.

Figure 6.23
The grid after some adjustments with the primitive node.

In a similar fashion as these last few exercises, many operators have small examples of the particular operation in the context of a network and often with comments. If you are uncertain how a particular operator works, be sure to check out its help documentation and look for these examples.

Using the Edit and Transform SOPs

These operators aren't all that confusing but they do have some important points to take note of.

1. Open a new session of Houdini, drop a Geometry object, and jump into it.

2. Drop a Sphere SOP and change its Type to NURBS. Turn on the display of points.

3. Let's say you wanted to turn the sphere into a beautifully modeled head. That process is certainly going to require many adjustments to points here and there to get everything just right. Over the viewport, select a Transform operator, choose a few points, and drag them around. Still over the viewport, press q to repeat the transform and choose another set of points and move those around. Doh! Say you made a mistake with that last adjustment and want to grab a few more points to move. Press the Reselect Geometry for Current Operation button, which is the one with the red arrow on it in Figure 6.24. This is in the left stowbar of the Viewer pane. Now select all of the points you meant to the first time around and RMB to complete. The new selection gets the changes previously applied!

Figure 6.24
The reselect geometry for current operation and secure selection buttons.

> When you want to apply an operation that you have previously done to a new selection, press the Reselect Current Geometry for Current Operation and you can reselect what should be a part of the selection to affect. Note that you must be in the working state of the particular operation that you want to affect. This is helpful when you accidentally didn't select everything you wanted to, or selected more than you wanted to and already applied the operation.

4. Every time you want to move a different set of points, you will have to add a new Transform. This will create a very explicit history of nodes recording what was done in each step. It is easy to see how this can quickly lead to enormous and unwieldy network. In addition, it is painful having to add a new operator each time you want to choose some new points to move around. There is a simpler way!

5. The way is the Edit SOP. Over the viewport, choose an Edit SOP, grab a few points, and move them around. Press the Reselect Geo button to make a new selection. RMB and then transform that around. Note that the each transform is saved and not lost, while still only leaving one node in the network. Press Reselect Geo again and choose another set of points. RMB and move those around. So, the Edit operation allows you to make as many changes as you want within a single node and stores the aggregate effect of those changes. You won't be able to later come back and trace through each little adjustment as you would with a huge network of transform nodes.

6. Although this is somewhat easier, it could be even easier yet. You have to press that Reselect Geo button every time to make a new selection. Toggle off the Secure Selection button, which is the button just above the Reselect Geo button. Now, you can just grab some points, RMB, and move them around. Select some different points, RMB, and move those around. Alas, it is a relatively painless process!

> I usually work with Secure Selection enabled so that I don't accidentally deselect what I am working on or accidentally select something that I don't want to affect. However, there are times when turning it off helps to speed up the workflow. This is especially true when you are using an Edit operator to do lots of pushing and pulling work.

Summary

You made it! Surely you are bloated with knowledge by now! Trust me when I say that we both feel like the SOPs material started years ago. But, your long labors and diligent dallying will certainly be rewarded; all of the concepts you learned here readily transfer over to the other contexts covered later in the book. Hopefully, you have seen and explored enough to have confidence with the context and are ready to move on.

chapter 7
Animation

Way back in the days of yore, there were legions of people called *Animators*, *InBetweeners*, and *Inkers*. The Animators were the actors, the InBetweeners were the meticulous workhorses, and the Inkers were the ones who put the finishing touches and color on the work. They used lots of paper, pencils, erasers, ink, celluloid, and time. Computers have affected these keys players significantly and have, to a large degree, replaced the InBetweeners and the Inkers. But, the process they developed for creating this art form still flourishes in basically the same form. Animation using a computer begins with the Animator (you) setting the main poses, or keyframes, and the computer then automatically handles the in-betweens using interpolation based on some function. As you have seen in previous chapters, animation can also be created through the use of expressions. You will cover the more traditional path of animation in this chapter.

Manually Set Keyframes

Try this example:

1. Open a fresh Houdini session and rename the default Geometry object `sphere`.

2. Jump into it and drop a Sphere SOP.

3. Jump back up to the Object context and home the view. Dolly back a little so you get a little more virtual real estate to play in. Over the viewport, choose the Pose state in the Tab menu. Make sure the model object is selected and RMB to accept the selection.

4. Using the handle, move the sphere to the left edge of the viewport. Notice that the numbers in the parameters pane change as you drag it around. In this case, the Translate X parameter is updating to reflect the changes made in the viewport.

5. RMB in the Translate X field and choose Set Keyframe. The background of the parameter will change from grey to green as shown in Figure 7.1. This signifies that this field contains a channel and that you are on a keyframe in that channel.

Figure 7.1
An active channel on a keyframe is colored green.

6. Go to the next frame by pressing the right arrow key. The background will change to teal (that light blue-green color), which indicates there is a channel, but that you are not on a keyframe. Figure 7.2 has a picture of this scenario.

Figure 7.2
An active channel that's not on a keyframe is colored teal.

7. Go to the last frame in your range. Drag the sphere to the right edge of the viewport, which should be in the positive X direction. The color of the Translate X field changes to brown. This means that the value has changed, but the keyframe hasn't been committed (or saved) yet, as shown in Figure 7.3.

Figure 7.3
An active channel that shows a proposed change is colored brown.

8. RMB on the Translate X parameter and choose Commit Changes. The parameter turns green indicating that you are now on a keyframe. Isn't it a good feeling to know that you can see green for playing with a computer?

9. Now for the magic of computer interpolation. Go back to frame 1 and press Play. You will see your sphere move gently across the screen from where you set it on frame 1 to where you set it on the final frame. The computer completed the in-between frames automatically with a grace and aplomb known to but a few, like Twiki in the 25th century. The same thing would have taken a human InBetweener much, much longer. Beedie beedie beedie, indeed.

> One of the benefits of Houdini is that there is almost always more than one way to do something. Keyframing is no exception. There are hotkeys and mouse menus everywhere. When you are first learning Houdini, try a number of different approaches until you find the one that makes sense to you.

10. Go to the first frame and set a keyframe on the Translate Y channel. Alt+LMB click on the field. This is the hotkey for setting a keyframe. Go to the last frame and again set a keyframe in the Translate Y field.

11. Slide the frame indicator to around one-third of the way forward in the frame range. Move the sphere up to the top of the viewport. The Translate Y field turns brown, indicating that a change has been made but not yet committed. If you moved to a different frame before committing the change, you would lose the change. Alt+LMB on the field to save the keyframe.

12. Go two-thirds of the way through the frame range. Drag the sphere down to the bottom of the viewport and set a keyframe. Doh! Say you made a mistake and didn't actually want that keyframe. You can RMB on the field and choose Remove Keyframe or use the hotkey Ctrl+LMB. Okay. Okay. After deliberation, you realize that it is a good spot for a keyframe. So, go ahead and keyframe it again.

13. Drag back to the first frame and keyframe all of the Scale channels at once. Alt+LMB on the Scale label and all three fields will be keyframed at once.

14. Go to the next keyframe for the Translates, which is when the sphere is at the top, and change the scale of the sphere. A quick way to jump forward or backward through keyframes of a particular parameter is to LMB (to go backward) or RMB (to go forward) on the little box that sits between the parameter label and its fields. This box button is shown in Figure 7.4. Jump back and forth using this technique and stop on the keyframe with this sphere at its height.

Figure 7.4
Use this button to quickly jump forward or backward to keyframes.

15. RMB on the handle and choose Key Scales, which sets a keyframe in all of the Scale channels. Using the scale handle, scale it up to around two in all axes. Remember the hotkey for accessing the translate/scale handle is e.

16. Jump to the next Translate keyframe where the sphere is at the bottom of the viewport. Again, key all three Scale channels. Adjust them to around 0.5 using the number ladder this time. Remember to adjust all fields of a parameter at once, you need to MMB on the label and make the desired change.

17. Go to the final frame and again keyframe the Scale channels and set them all to 1. Play the animation and you'll see the sphere go from left to right, bobbing up and down, growing and shrinking, and finally returning to its original size.

18. Pretend you never wanted to change the Translate Z channel. You don't want it keyframed and you don't want the value to change either. RMB on the field and choose Lock Parameter. The field turns red, indicating that it is locked, as shown in Figure 7.5. In addition, the Z portion of the translate handle in the viewport disappears.

| Translate | 10.4326 | 0 | 0 |

Figure 7.5
The locked channel is colored red.

Autokey Your Way to Freedom

Using autokey can save quite a few clicks as you work. For example, when animating a rigged character, you just want to move the parts into position to block in the key poses. Having to constantly worry about RMB and LMB all the time to manage keyframing can get a little taxing. Autokey can help make this process much more smooth and fluid. With all great power comes great responsibility, as you have likely heard. You must be wary of the powerful mojo of this magic though. It is easy to forget it's on and so mistakenly set loads of keys that you don't desire. Generally, I would say it's best to use autokey for a session while you are focused on animating something and then turn it back off before finishing the session, going to lunch, or ending your day. In fact, as soon as you are finished with this exercise, make sure to go back and turn it off.

1. Go to the main menu Settings>Main Preferences and change the drop down to Animation. Toggle on Add Keyframes on Parameter Change. Also make sure the checkmark is on for Auto-commit Parameter Change at Keyframes. Press Accept to apply the changes and close the window.

   The first option sets it so that every time you change a parameter value, a keyframe will be set. The second option does the same thing for you when a channel already exists. It's the technical difference between setting a keyframe and committing a change.

2. Go to the first frame and delete all of the animation you have created thus far. This is more than just deleting the keyframes that exist on frame one. You will delete the all of the animation data in the channel. RMB on the Translate label and choose Delete Channels. Do the same for the Scale label. All the fields should be gray again, indicating that none of them contain active channels.

3. Now, move the sphere somewhere in space. Que pasa? It didn't set any keyframes. You first have to make the channel active by setting a keyframe. Then any future changes will automatically be recorded. Keyframe all Translates. Change the frame number and move the sphere. Whichever parameters were modified in the change are automatically keyed. Move forward in time again and move the sphere. Again, the changes are automatically keyframed.

4. Most importantly, go back to the Main Preferences, turn off Add Keyframes on Parameter Change, and accept the change before moving to the next topic.

Discovering the Channel Editor

You have set quite a few keyframes by now and you have seen how the computer automatically interpolates the in-betweens. What method is it using to do this interpolation? This information and a plethora of other details can be found in the Channel Editor. This editor is the main tool for visually setting and modifying animation channels. The Channel Editor features three methods for viewing data: Graph, Table, and Dopesheet. You examine the Graph view in the following exercise because it is by far the most commonly used of the trio. For information about the Table or Dopesheet views, check out the Help documents.

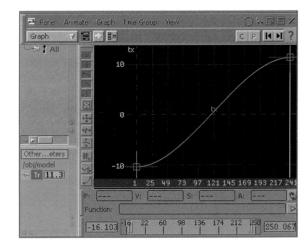

1. Delete any active channels you may have on the object containing the sphere. RMB on the `tz` field and choose Unlock Parameter, if necessary.

2. Go to frame 1 and set a keyframe in `tx`. Drag the sphere over to the left side of the viewport.

3. Go to the last frame and set another keyframe. Drag the sphere over to the right side of the viewport. Play the timeline and you again have a sphere that goes from left to right.

4. RMB on the `tx` field and choose Scope Channels. The Channel Editor pops up with the `tx` channel scoped, as shown in Figure 7.6. The term *scope* or *scoping channels* simply means that Houdini is placing the chosen channels in the channel editor and the channel list so that you can work on them. Note that the Channel Editor is just another pane type. It can be accessed in the Pane menu as well.

Figure 7.6
The various zones in the Channel Editor.

The Zones of Utility

There are a few different zones of utility in the Channel Editor. The menus are along the top. The view area (highlighted in red) shows the animation data as curves and keyframes. It contains information about these keyframes and curves at the bottom. In the stowbar to the left, you will find various toggle buttons to control what is displayed in the view area. The channel list area is highlighted in green. The channel group area is left at the default grey color.

The View Area

This area shows keyframes and the curves that connect them. Keyframes are represented as white boxes as shown in Figure 7.7. Values are displayed running vertically along the left edge of the view area. The timeline is displayed in the purple band running horizontally along the bottom edge of the view area. Display options are in the stowbar to the left of the view area.

Figure 7.7
A keyframe is indicated with a white box.

1. In the example, you can see that there is a keyframe at frame 1 with a value of around −10 and another keyframe at 240 with a value of around 11. It is very easy to adjust keyframes in the Channel Editor. The vertical line is the time handle. Slide this left and right to adjust when the keyframe will happen. The white box is the value handle. Slide this up and down to change the value at this keyframe. These two handles are exclusive of each other. So, you would not be able to adjust the keyframe in time by grabbing the white box or vice-versa. The white horizontal line is the slope handle. This affects how the curves come into and out of the keyframe. Go ahead and play with these handles to get a feel for how they work.

> If you demand to be able to move the keyframe in both time and value at once, you can do so. Hold down Ctrl and LMB the white box. You can now adjust both the time and value of the keyframe at the same time.

2. Navigation in the view area is very similar to other viewports in Houdini. RMB to pan and MMB to dolly. A really nifty feature of the MMB is that you can independently dolly in the vertical (value) axis or the horizontal (time) axis. Hold down the MMB and drag left and right; you will dolly in and out on the timeline while maintaining the visual scale of the values. Hold down MMD and drag up and down and you will dolly in and out on values while maintaining the visual scale of the timeline. And, of course, you can scale both of the axes at the same time, meaning you don't have to release the MMB and then depress it again to affect the other axis. Using MMB in this way is a very efficient way of getting the animation information into a format you can use. If you ever lose the channel offscreen or something similar, just press h to home the view on the selected curve or curves. LMB does not adjust the view because there is no tumble capability in a 2D view.

3. Notice that the fields below the view area are greyed out. Use the LMB to box select one of the keyframes. The fields are now populated with information about the keyframe and also about the curve that connects the two keyframes. F stands for the frame at which the keyframe sits. V stands for the value that the keyframe contains. S stands for the slope of the handles coming into and out of the keyframe. A stands for acceleration. The acceleration field is only valid for functions that use acceleration values, such as the bezier() function. Move the selected keyframe in time and value, and you will see those changes reflected in the appropriate fields. Move the slope handle up or down, and you will see that change reflected in the S field.

The Function field shows what kind of function the curve is using. The curve is actually called an interpolation segment because it tells the software how to interpolate between two keyframes. By default, a cubic function is used to define the interpolation segment.

4. Deselect the keyframe in the view area and select the interpolation segment. Only the Function field contains information. Click the arrow button to the left of the field and you can change what kind of function defines the segment. This menu contains a number of the most commonly used functions. Choose linear(). This is great for things that have a constant acceleration, such as the second hand on an old electric clock. It goes in a straight line from one keyframe to the next. Change the function to constant(). This maintains the keyframe value until the next keyframe. This can come in handy if you are controlling a switch, such as a camera switcher or a Switch SOP's input channel, which both use integers instead of floating point numbers. For motion that needs to smoothly start and end from a stationary position, the cubic() function works great, as long as you make sure the slope of each of the end keyframes is set to 0. Or you can use the ease() function, which always starts and ends smoothly.

> Many character animators use the constant() function to rough out the blocking of an animation. Using this method makes the posturing and timing of the sequence easier to see because the computer does not add any motion through interpolation. You can change the default segment function in the Settings>Main Preferences>Animation folder.

5. You are not just limited to the defined functions though. Oh no! You can also go in and create your own functions to define interpolation segments. Delete the constant() and enter sin($F*4)*4 and your view area should look something like Figure 7.8. Try changing the interior 4 to another number to affect the frequency of the sin wave and the exterior 4 to change the amplitude of the sin wave. Play the timeline and you'll see the ball go back and forth in the X axis. You can grab and scrub through the timeline using the time bar, which is the big vertical white line in the view area. As you drag it, the current frame number will temporarily pop up next to it. Take it one step further in hilarity and good times by multiplying this expression by the easeout() function so that you have easeout() * sin($F*4)*4. Now, the sin wave values are easing out of the first key frame. Good times. Good times.

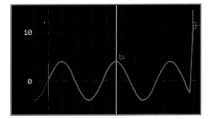

Figure 7.8
You can define your own function for an interpolation segment.

6. Change the segment's function back to linear(). Move your pointer over the segment around the middle and set a keyframe by using Alt+LMB. You now have three keyframes and two interpolation segments. Every segment can be defined by a unique function. Select the second segment and choose the cubic() function. Drag the slope handle leaving the middle keyframe down to affect the second segment. You can see that the first segment stays in a straight line.

7. Alt+LMB on the one of the segments and drag left and right while still holding the hotkey combo depressed. A keyframe box slides back and forth along the segments and becomes a keyframe when you release.

8. Select the keyframe and press the Delete key to remove it. Move the time bar in the channel editor to some random frame by simply selecting and dragging it. Press the C button that is located above the view area to copy the value of the curve at the frame. Move the time bar to some other location and press the P button. It will paste that value to this time and create a keyframe.

9. You can use the arrow buttons to the right of the C and P buttons to jump forward and backward through keyframes.

10. Look over in the stowbar to the left of the view area. It contains various buttons to control what information is displayed. Toggle on and off a few to see what they control. Make sure all the default ones are back on before you continue.

11. Finally, at the bottom is a display much like the playbar, as it shows the frame range. It too can be used to control the horizontal extents of the view area. You MMB and drag left and right just as you do in the view area. The range that is displayed in the graph is the same as the range that is shown here.

Channel List

The channel list is a handy way to access channels that you want to adjust in the channel editor.

1. The channel list is in the lower-left corner of the Channel Editor. It's just like having your parameters right there with you the whole time, like a good friend. Currently it contains only the tx channel. Back in the parameters for the sphere Object, set a keyframe at frame 1 and 240 (or whatever your last frame is) for the Translate Y and Z channels. RMB on the ty channel and choose Scope Append Channels. This will add your new ty channel to the Channel Editor and you can see both the tx and ty channels at the same time. Notice that the curve is flat because it is currently keyframed from 0 to 0. Do the same for the tz channel so that you can now see all three Translate curves in the Channel Editor.

2. In the Channel Editor, move the time bar to frame 150. In the channel list, click on the ty channel. The other two will be removed from the display; however, they are still scoped as you can see them in the channel list. Ctrl+RMB anywhere in the view area and choose Add keyframes at current time.

3. Select the new keyframe by drawing a marquee around the entire key. Then, Ctrl+RMB and choose Tie/Untie Selection. Deselect the key clicking anywhere in the black area. Now grab the slope handle on the left side of the keyframe and drag it up. Do the same to the one on the right. Play back your animation and you'll see your sphere move along as it did before, but with an unnatural bounce in the middle. If you don't see much of a bounce, check out the scale of the values on the vertical axis in the Channel Editor. If necessary, angle the slopes up more to get more extreme bumps in the path.

4. Select the tz channel in the channel list. Change the keyframed value at frame 1 to 5 and the keyframed value at frame 240 (or your last frame) to −10. Hold down Shift and select the tx and ty channels. Your Channel Editor should now look something like Figure 7.9.

5. Go to frame 1. Back in the Object parameters for the sphere, keyframe all three Scale channels. Go to frame 240 (or your last frame) and set a keyframe here for all three as well. RMB on the Scale label and choose Scope Channels to scope all three channels at once. The channel list now displays the three scale channels.

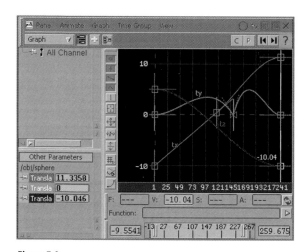

Figure 7.9
The current state of the Channel Editor.

6. But, what if you wanted to still have the ty channel scoped too? Scope the ty channel and it replaces the scale channels in the channel list. LMB the thumbtack to the left of the ty channel in the channel list. This pins the channel to be displayed at all times. Scope the scale channels again and you will see that the ty channel stays put. Toggle off the thumbtack.

7. Select the ty and sz channels in the channel list so that they are the only two displayed in the view area. Anywhere you feel the urge, set a keyframe on the curves. Notice that both curves get a keyframe. You may not want that. Hold down Shift+Alt and LMB on one or the other channel curves and the keyframe will be limited to the one chosen.

8. Another handy feature of the Channel Editor is its ability to template certain channels in the view area. Suppose that it would be useful to be able to see the ty channel while manipulating the sz channel. But, you don't want to accidentally change the ty channel in any way. Go to View menu and toggle on Show Template Field. A Template field appears up in the menu bar. Type ty in it and the ty curve becomes a dotted line in the view area, as shown in Figure 7.10. Now, nothing you do in the view area will affect the templated channel. It is just like turning on the Template flag for a node. Delete the ty from the Template field and you can manipulate it again.

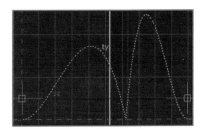

Figure 7.10
The ty channel is templated.

Channel Groups

The channel groups area is in the upper-left area of the Channel Editor, as shown back in Figure 7.6. You can group channels for easier access. You can group any channels together, even from unrelated nodes in different networks.

1. Continuing from the previous exercise, select the sz and ty channels in the channel list. Drag and drop them from the channel list into the channel groups area. You have just created a channel group. Another method is to Ctrl+RMB over the channel groups area and choose Create Group(s) from Displayed.

Figure 7.11
Proof that you made a new channel group.

2. Expand the All Channel Groups branch to see the new group. Click on the new group label and any channels contained within the group are scoped. Click again on the label and rename the group so_useful. Your channel groups should look like Figure 7.11.

3. The 2 in parentheses means that the group contains two channels. Like individual channels, groups can be tacked so that they are always scoped. Toggle the thumbtack for the so_useful group.

4. Back in the sphere's Object parameters, scope all the translate channels. The channels in the so_useful group stay scoped and now tx and tz are also scoped. Your channel list should look like Figure 7.12.

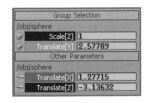

Figure 7.12
The channel list showing a tacked group.

5. Click the so_useful group. Note again that only the channels in the group are scoped. Toggle off the thumbtack. The little key icon will set a keyframe on all members of the group at the current frame. Click it and a keyframe will be placed on each curve at the time bar.

6. To remove a channel from a group, scope the group and then RMB on the channel in the channel list and choose Remove Channel(s) from Group(s). In the same way, you can add a channel to the scoped group.

Houdini Takes Me Away

Takes are an interesting method for layering parameter changes and creating animation. Basically, you have the root take, which is always named hip. You can then create additional takes, which are children of this root take. So, the children inherit all of the node and parameter information from the parent, root take. You can have multiple levels of parent-child takes in the hierarchy so that a child may also be the parent of a take as well. In a child take, you specify particular parameters that you want to include in the take and thereby change from the inherited information. Figure 7.13 shows the scene you will be experimenting with in this section.

The fundamentally important feature of using takes is that they offer an easy and non-destructive way of creating variations in a file. You can access a particular take in the Take menu at the right in the main menu bar as shown in the Figure 7.14. You can also access takes in the Take List pane. The advantage to using the pane is that it shows you the hierarchical relationship between multiple takes and also shows you the parameters that a particular take modifies. Figure 7.15 shows you an example of the Take List pane with multiple levels of parent-child takes and displays the included parameters of take1 on the right. Next, you stroll through a simple example so you can get a feel for what takes can do.

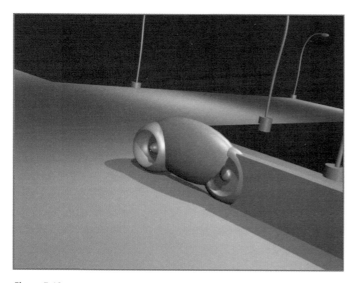

Figure 7.13
A wall-spewing electron bike.

Figure 7.14
The Take menu selector.

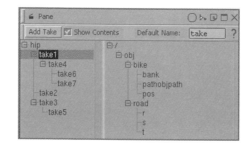

Figure 7.15
The Take List pane.

7. Animation

Creating Desks

You first need to create a desk that is suitable for playing with takes and then save out that desk so that you can easily come back to it in future sessions.

1. Open a new session of Houdini.

2. Go to the Desk menu selector on the right of the main menu bar. It is next to the Take menu. Change it from Build to CHOPs; notice that the layout of the panes changes. Go to Particles and again the layout changes. Depending on what you are doing in Houdini, there is usually a particular layout of panes that will be especially useful and it is much quicker to jump to a desk that is already configured rather than split them top and bottom and left and right, and then configure the linking, and then the pane information. All of the options you see in the menu are the default desks that come in the package. But, you are not limited to using just these. You can also save your own custom desks and jump to those as well.

3. Now, you'll create a simple four-pane setup that you'll use for exploring takes. Go to the Settings>Desktops menu. Click Add Desktop and you will see that a new desk called Desk1 is created. Click on the name field, call it Takes, and then choose Accept.

4. In the Desk menu, choose the new Takes desk. It jumps to a single Viewer pane. This is the default simple beginning. Split that pane left and right, and then split each of those panes top and bottom. So, you should end up with four panes total.

5. Set the pane type of the upper-right one to Network Editor, the lower-right one to Parameters, and the lower-left one to Take List. You can leave the upper-right one as a Viewer pane.

6. Use the link panes button (the little circle in which you choose a number) and set the Viewer, Network Editor, and Parameter panes to 1.

7. Open the Settings>Desktops menu again and click Apply Changes at the bottom. Now, in any future session, you can jump to the Takes desk and it will automagically configure your panes as they are now.

And now, you return to the previously scheduled programming, "Takes in the Wild."

1. Rather than do the usual pushing around of a box, you can use something a little more interesting. Open the takesStarter.hip file and re-select the Takes desk from the menu. You will see an electron bike sitting at a crossroads. Jump into the road Object and you will see that there are networks that strip out a path for going straight, turning left, and turning right. You are going to create a take for each of these options. Jump back up to the Object level.

2. In the Take List pane, make sure the root (hip) take is selected and then click the Add Take button. Click on the name and rename it goForward.

3. Ensure that take is selected in the list and check out the bike node and its parameters. The node's Display flag is dimpled and its parameters are greyed out. This is normal and tells you that you are in a take and that the greyed out parameters are being inherited from the parent take, which is the root hip take in this instance.

4. In the Transform tab of the bike Object's parameters, RMB on the Path Object parameter and choose Include in Take. You will see a couple of things happen. The parameter is no longer greyed out and so you can modify it. Also, that parameter has been added in the right window in the Take List pane as shown in Figure 7.16.

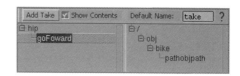

Figure 7.16
The goForward take with the pathobjpath parameter included.

5. RMB on the Position parameter and choose Include in Take. Do the same for the Auto-Bank factor parameter. Note that these two parameters still seems to be greyed out even though they are in the list for the goForward take. That is because they require a valid path object to be set first before they can be adjusted.

6. Click the + button in the Path Object field, navigate into the road Object, and choose the straightPath node. Now, the other two parameters are able to modified.

7. Go to frame 1 and set a keyframe in the Position field. Set the value to 1. Go to the last frame in your range, set another keyframe, and change the value to 0. Play the timeline and the bike should start at one end and drive straight through the crossroads.

8. The Auto-Bank factor will automatically make the bike the lean one way or another as it goes around a curve. In this take, the bike is just going forward so you don't need it. Either in the Parameter pane or in the Take List pane, RMB on it and choose Exclude from Take. The option is greyed out again and so is inheriting whatever is set in the parent take.

9. In the Take List, choose the hip take and then click Add Take and rename this one goLeft. If you had left the goForward take selected and then added a take, the new take would be a child of the goForward take, which is not what you want.

10. Include the Path Object, Position, and Auto-Bank factor parameters in the goLeft take.

11. In the Path Object parameter, navigate to and choose the turnLeftPath node.

12. Animate the Position parameter from a value of 1 at frame 1 to a value of 0 at the end frame. Scrub the timeline and you now have an animation variation in which the electron bike turns left at the crossroads.

13. Notice that as it turns, it leans way over. Set the Auto-Bank factor to 0 and now it stays upright in the turn.

14. Add another take as a child of the root take and name it goRight. Your take hierarchy should now look like Figure 7.17.

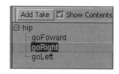

Figure 7.17
The take hierarchy.

15. Just as before, include the Path Object, Position, and Auto-Bank factor parameters in the goRight take. Set them to the appropriate settings, just as you did in the goLeft take.

16. Scrub through the timeline and you now have an animation variation in which the electron bike turns right at the crossroads.

17. Go back to the base take and, just for giggles, turn on the Display flag for the trail Object. Choose any of the child takes and play the timeline. Don't hit the wall, Ornt!

7. Animation

119

Flipbook to Preview Animation

On my machine, the complexity of creating the wall has made it play slower than real-time. If you force real-time, the wall won't be created as nicely as it should be. You can use the flipbook feature to do a quick OpenGL render of the viewport, which can then be played in real time. Dolly out enough so that you can see the whole path of the bike, then RMB on the render quick launch button and choose View: Flipbook. Toggle on Initialize Simulation Ops because you are using a particle system to create the wall and so always want to reset to frame 1. Change the Zoom if desired to a smaller percentage. This will save memory. Look at the bottom as you change the percentage and it will give you an approximation of the memory required for the current settings. When you are ready, press Accept. Sit back and relax for a few minutes.

Houdini will go through and cook each frame correctly and store the image building a sequence. Note that you cannot bring another window into focus during flipbook generation or it will mess up the flipbook render. It is a good time for a stroll anyway! Once it cooks all the specified frames, it will pop up a window and run through them once. After it is finished, you can play and scrub through the render with ease. Flipbooking is great way to quickly get a sense of the overall layout and timing of an animation.

Simple Rigging

The underlying structure for most characters is a hierarchy of bones called zee skeleton. It is the hard, unbending framework that all the muscles, tendons, and other tissues attach to and fondly call a friend. But you already knew that. You have one right inside of you. Or, if you are a powerful mutant from the galaxy Zebulon 6, you may also have an exoskeleton. If so, lucky you! The process of creating this skeletal structure with bones and then capturing geometry to it is called rigging.

Create Zee Skeleton

Look at your hand. Now, come on. I don't mean look at in the same way that you look at the mug before you pour grog in it. Really look at it—your hand, I mean. There will be enough time for staring at the bottom of an empty mug o' grog later. Marvel at the design and complexity of this wonderful machine. Move your fingers. Notice how you move the tip of your finger to where you want it to be. You do not have to think about how much to move each of the joints for the tip to arrive at the desired location. The study of this kind of motion is called Kinematics. Now, hold up two fingers displaying the number two. Now, move your hand up and down and start singing Little Bunny Foo Foo kept hoppin through the forest. Come on. You know the words. In Houdini, you have access to bones, though not bunnies, and you can move them in similar ways as you move your fingers.

1. Hop into a new session of Houdini. Over the viewport, choose the Bones state. Note that you are choosing the plural, Bones, state and not the singular, Bone, state.

2. Along the top of the viewport there are a few options to set before you get start creating bones. For this example, type `finger` in the Chain Name parameter and choose Inverse Kinematics in the Kinematics menu.

3. Go to quad view and, in the front view, click four times moving from left to right in a gentle arc. The first click will place the root of the bone chain. The next three clicks will draw the bones. After the fourth click (creating the third bone), RMB to complete the chain. You should have something like what is shown in Figure 7.18.

4. In the Tab menu over the viewport, choose the Pose state. Left click on the null (the cross) at the tip of the bone chain and RMB to accept the selection. This is called the *end affector*. Grab it and move the finger around. Isn't it glorious? It is almost as if you were moving your own finger around, without all the messy biology and having to grow old enough to understand that it really is amazing.

5. What happened here? As you were happily clicking away drawing the bones, Houdini was building the network you see in the Network Editor, which is also shown in Figure 7.18. The null Object called finger_root1 is the little ball at the base of the finger. All these nodes are named finger_* because you put finger in the Chain Name parameter. The three bone objects were added with their proper parenting and parameters set (orientation, length, and so on). At the end is another null Object named fin-

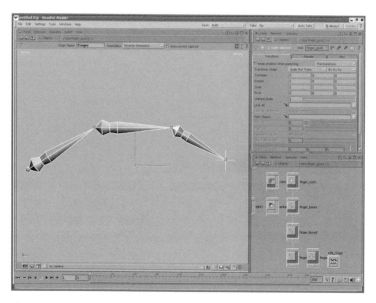

Figure 7.18
The bone chain as seen in the perspective viewport.

ger_goal1, which the kinematic solver uses to rotate the bones to the right angle to look like it's responding like a real finger. Next to the finger_goal1 node is a CHOP network called KIN_Chops. Inside it is a network of CHOPS that handle the hard math work for you. I recommend that you jump inside later to get a better feel for what is going on under the hood. For now, you can move on.

6. What if you don't want to move the tip around like you have done, but would rather pose the bones more explicitly? Then instead of Inverse Kinematics, you will want to use Forward Kinematics. But you already have the Inverse Kinematics on your finger. It is a simple matter to change the kinematics of a bone chain. First, save your work to a file called fingerIK.hip. You'll come back to it in a bit.

7. Enter the Bones state again. Ctrl+RMB anywhere in the viewport; a popup menu will appear, as shown in Figure 7.19. Because there are already kinematics on your chain, choose Remove Kinematics from this menu. Follow the prompts in the message bar. Select all the bones and RMB to complete. You have stripped the kinematics from the bone chain and are now ready to add the Forward Kinematics.

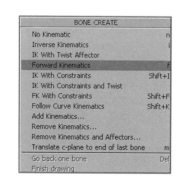

Figure 7.19
The bone create menu of the bones state.

7. Animation

8. At the top of the Viewer pane, change the Kinematics menu to Forward Kinematics. Then Ctrl+RMB again to get the menu again. This time choose Add Kinematics... and follow the prompts at the bottom of the screen. Click on the first bone (the one on the left) and RMB to complete. Then click on the last bone (the one on the right) and RMB to complete. Now you have a null handle for each bone.

9. Enter the Pose state and you can move the bones around however you like. Note that you are affecting the Translates of a particular null and the bone that is associated with it is aligned to the null's location. Be careful, because you can drag the null away from the bone tip, at which point you could get confused as to which null controls which bone.

10. The third most common style of kinematics is No Kinematics. This is a surprisingly easy way of moving your bones. Go back to the Bones state and Ctrl+RMB on a bone and choose Remove Kinematics and Affectors from the menu. Select all the bones and RMB to complete. If the nulls from the previous steps are still there in the network, select them and the CHOP network in the Network Editor and delete them. You will not be using them.

11. Now go back to the Pose state and select a bone. The handle should be fairly easy to figure out. You can grab the tip of any bone and move it. Notice here that you are affecting the Rotates of the bone itself even though the handle looks and acts like a Translate handle. If you move the handle away from where the bone can reach, the bone will still point to the handle and when you let go, the handle will snap back to the tip of the bone. Any bones further down the chain from there will follow along. If you press R (for Rotate) you can access the Rotates handle and even twist the bone around the axis of its length.

In other animation systems, they usually refer to what Houdini calls No Kinematics as Forward Kinematics. Houdini draws a distinction between them and actually has both. One of the main differences between No Kinematics and FK in Houdini is that although No Kinematics is simpler, it can lead to Gimbal lock, whereas FK is more like having IK between every bone and will therefore automatically avoid Gimbal lock. With No Kinematics, you are setting rotations about the root of the bone. With FK, you are setting the translates of goal positions (the nulls) for each bone. Which one you choose depends on which makes more sense to you and your situation.

Gimbal Lock

Gimbal lock is a situation that is brought about by using Euler angles to describe rotations. Sounds quite fancy, right? (Just so that you will sound overbearingly smart at parties, it is pronounced "Oiler angles.") If you think of each of the axes X, Y, and Z as actual gimbals, or separate pins to rotate about, this might make some sense. Each of the three rotations must be evaluated one at a time in a specified order. In the default setup, they are evaluated X first, and then Y, and then Z. Now, you'll run through a quick example to see what happens.

1. Create a new bone chain consisting of just two bones and using No Kinematics.

2. Go the Settings>Main Preferences>Handles menu and turn on the Color Transform Handles by Axis option. Over the viewport, choose a Transform state and select the parent bone. Press to make sure that the rotate handles are visible. RMB on the handle and toggle on Gimbal mode. Now you can clearly see the problem develop. Change the Rotate in X to 90 using the handle or the parameters. All is well thus far.

3. Change the Rotate Y value to 90. You can see the blue rz ring fold onto the red rx ring. Yes, it looks ominous and it means a bad situation has developed.

4. Try adjusting the Rotate Z value back and forth. You will notice that it is rotating along the same axis as the Rotate X value. The X axis is not recalculated and stays right where it was. But the Z axis turns about the Y axis when Y is rotated. This will cause the Z axis to align itself with the original X axis. So now when you rotate about the Z axis, you are really just rotating about the original X axis, and so you are only getting two degrees of freedom rather than the three you were expecting. The X rotation and the Z rotation are fighting against each other; this is the sad state of Gimbal lock..

5. There are a few ways to avoid this. The easiest way is to change your rotation priority so that the most important angles come first. Some trial and error will show you which is the most useful combination for your particular situation.

6. Another way is to use *quaternion angles*. This is another mathematical model for describing rotations that takes all the axes into account at once to calculate a master axis to use and a fourth value to determine how far to turn about that master axis. This method avoids Gimbal lock altogether, but is quite a bit harder to visualize in your head and so is not used as much. To use it in Houdini, it is straightforward though. Simply change the interpolation for all three rotations to `qlinear()` and set a couple of keyframes. Houdini will do the math for you. The main limitation with this is that there's no easing in or out.

7. Yet another way is to parent a null above the object and use it to only rotate in one or two axes by locking out `rz`. You ca then parent nulls in between the bones and the solvers would work just fine. Go ahead and turn off the Color Transform Handles by Axis option and continue.

Editing Bones

Go back to the hip file that you saved earlier, called `fingerIK.hip`. If you want to save the results of changing the IK style, go ahead and do that now. After saving that, open the `fingerIK.hip` file. It should still look like it did back in Figure 7.18. Once the bone chain is created, you still have freedom to adjust various characteristics about it such as the number of bones, the angles of the bones, and so on.

Changing a Bone's Position

Go into the Bones state and click on the purple boxes at the tip of each bone and you will get a translate handle. This handle is much different than what you get in the Pose state. If you watch the Translate channels as you move the end of a bone around, you will notice that they don't change in the Bones state, but they do in the Pose state. In the Bones state, you are actually adjusting the length of the bones and initial position. The kinematic solvers in the `Kin_CHOP` are updating their math to accommodate the changes. In the Pose state, the bones remain the same length and the CHOPs are solving for the static bone length.

Splitting Bones

You can split a bone into two by Ctrl+LMB on it. This seems simple, but you can lay out a rough bone structure quickly for a whole character, and then go back and add more detail later. Once you split a bone, you will probably want to move the new hinge point at least a little one way or another. This will give the solver a hint as to which way to bend the bone when the end affector is moved. It is like having one bone for your whole arm and then splitting it to create the elbow joint. You would want to move the hinge a little so the solver knew which way the arm was supposed to be able to bend.

Parenting Bones

You are probably reading this chapter because you want to create a character and make him, her, or it come alive. Unless your character is a finger (or a worm), you will need a more complex skeleton than a single chain can give you. The path to complexity is through parenting.

1. In the Bones State, change to the No Kinematics style. Then Shift+LMB on the first bone in the chain to draw from that bone. A new bone chain can be created that will begin from the tip of the bone selected. Any rotations made to the parent bone will be inherited by the new chain. Note that you can parent bone chains to anything, not just another bone. If you parent your new chain to a regular object (null or geometry), the parenting will be from the origin of the object as you would expect. But if you parent your new chain to another bone, the parenting will be from the tip of that bone. If you want your new chain origin to come from the base of a bone, choose the object that is the parent of that bone. This option is good for a situation like having a clavicle coming right out of the base of the neck.

2. Finish the bone chain and enter the Pose state. Move the parent bone of the new chain around; you will see the new chain follow with it.

3. Go back into the Bones state and this time Ctrl+MMB on a different bone to create a new chain. A blue dashed bounding box will be drawn around the parent bone to let you know which has been selected. Then as you move your mouse around, there will be a dashed red line connecting you back to your parent, kind of like an umbilical cord, as shown in Figure 7.20. Then just draw your new bone chain. You will notice that as you go to draw your new bone chain, it does not start at the parent—it starts from wherever you have made the first click. This option is good when you need an off-set joint like a hip.

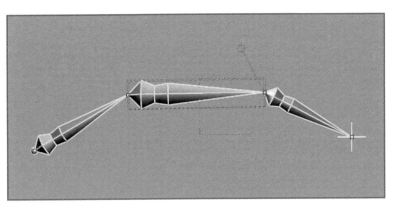

Figure 7.20
Using the Ctrl+MMB method to create a new bone chain.

Rigging the Hand

Now that you have got the hang of creating and moving bones around, you can work with some geometry. The bones themselves do not render. They are just a guide to use to move the real geometry around. You will take geometry of a hand, rig it with bones, and then capture the geometry to the bones.

Create Zee Skeleton

Your hand geometry needs the underlying structure of the bone chain. Let's create that now.

1. Load the `handStarter.hip` file. It contains a model of a skeleton's hand. Take a second to look around to see what is going on. The entire hand was built in the `fingersGeo` node and then just the palm was object merged into the `palmGeo` node. They are separated out because you will not be capturing them in the same way. You will get to that in a little bit.

2. In the Object viewport, press Tab and go into the bones state. Enter `index` in the Chain Name field at the top, as you will first build the bone chain for the index finger. Change the Kinematic type to Inverse Kinematics. Now you are ready to start rigging the hand. Normally, when you draw to create bones in the viewport, they will be built on the current construction plane. But because your fingers are not on a construction plane, you will use a different technique to line up the bones.

3. In the upper-right side of the Viewer pane, turn on snapping. Click on the point that is closest to the base of the index finger. As you move the mouse around, you will see the makings of a new bone following you around. Click again on or near the point at the back of the first knuckle of the index finger. Refer to Figure 7.21 for correct placement on each joint. Go ahead and create a bone for each geometry bone and RMB to complete the chain. The bones aren't exactly where you want them, but they are close. Turn off snapping. That way you can move the ends of the bones around in an unconstrained manner. Click on the root of the bone chain and a handle will appear. It is the small sphere at the beginning of the chain. Move the point until it is more in the middle of the mass of the ball of the first bone on the skeleton. Then click on the end of the first bone (which is also the beginning of the second bone) and another handle will appear. Move this handle down into the middle of the joint. Do the same for the next point on the chain. The tip of the bone chain should be aligned to the tip of the associated finger.

> If you make a mistake in drawing a bone, just press Delete to remove the bone you just drew while still staying in the Bones state. It effectively lets you undo the drawing of a particular bone.

4. Repeat this process for each of the other fingers and the thumb. Make sure to rename the Chain Name option to whatever the name of the digit is you are rigging. Most people think of their thumb as only having two bones, as opposed to their fingers that obviously have three bones. But the first bone of your thumb is actually down in your hand and it is a tri-boned digit just like your fingers. After you have drawn all the bones for the skeleton, your setup should look something like Figure 7.21. (You will add the null in the palm area in just a minute.)

5. In order to be able to move the whole hand around at once, you need to parent all the chains to a single Object. A Null will do nicely. In the Network Editor, create a Null Object and name it palm. In the viewport, move it to the center of the palm geometry.

6. Before you parent the bones' chains to the palm node, you want to first toggle on the Keep position when parenting option on the *_root node of each chain. This option can be found on the Transform tab. Houdini has a very handy and straightforward way of making adjustments to multiple nodes that share a particular parameter in a single stroke of mad genius. Select all of the root nodes, using Shift so that you can add to the selection or box select them all at once. In the parameters pane, you should see text in yellow that informs you that have five nodes selected, as shown in Figure 7.22. Once you see that, simply toggle on the parameter in the parameters of whichever node is currently being displayed and all five nodes will get the change. If you are using this feature later and you happen to select a node that doesn't share the parameter being changed, it will be ignored for that node and no harm will come of it.

7. Parent the root node of each bone chain to the palm node. If they are all still selected, just connect one of them to the palm node and the other four will do the same. You can't beat that with a stick, nor branch, nor bone.

8. Select all of the goal nodes, toggle on Keep position when parenting, and parent them to the palm node.

9. While all five goal nodes are still selected, click on the Pre-transform menu and select Clean Translates. This menu is to the right of the Keep Position When Parenting toggle. This basically "bakes" in each goal's offset to the palm node. Now, you can use the Pose state to move the goals around and play with the hand. When necessary, select all the goals, RMB on the Translate label, and choose Revert to Defaults to set all the Translate fields back to zero. But, this zero isn't truly zero. It is zero with a baked in pre-transform on it so all the goals jump back to their proper places. If you didn't bake in the pre-transform, whenever you did the Revert to Defaults, all of the goals would jump to 0, 0, 0 in the palm node's space and so the hand would get mangled.

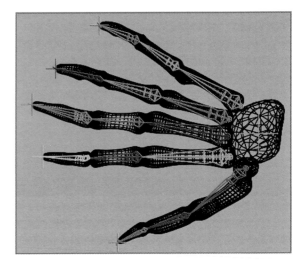

Figure 7.21
The completed bone chains.

Figure 7.22
Five nodes selected and ready to be modified at the same time.

You can change a particular parameter on multiple nodes by first selecting the nodes, and then making the change to any one of them.

10. Finally, toggle on Keep position when parenting on the `palmGeo` node and parent it to the palm node. As mentioned earlier, this geometry is "captured" differently than the bones and we will talk more about it in a few minutes.

11. Clean the Translates for the palm node also so that this position is considered its 0, 0, 0 default position.

12. At this point, you can go into the Pose state and test the motion of the bones to see if they do what you thought they would. You want to use the goal nodes and/or the palm null node to move the hand around. The bones and palm geometry move, but the finger geometries are not connected to the bones yet and so don't move around. Remember to use the Revert to Defaults on whatever nodes you moved before continuing so that the skeleton is in the right place for capturing.

Capture Geometry

You have some bone chains and you have some geometry, but will ever the two come together? Yes, they will, right now.

1. In the viewport, choose Capture Geometry from the Tab menu. Follow the prompts in the message bar. It tells you to select the geometry to capture, which is the fingersGeo node, and RMB to complete. You can select it in the viewport or in the Network Editor. It then says to select the root object, which is the palm node, and RMB to complete. The geometry is now colored according to which bone it is captured by. Now if you go into the Pose mode and move the bones around, the geometry moves with them. But you will see that there are some problems with the way the fingers were captured. Figure 7.23 shows what is happening in one problem area. Some of the bones in each chain are capturing an area that includes adjacent fingers. Sometimes this is fine and sometimes it is not. Revert to defaults if necessary and take a closer look.

2. In the viewport, choose Edit Capture Regions from the Tab menu. Click on the first bone in the pinky finger. The capture region is displayed by some guide geometry that looks like a pill or capsule that is enclosing the captured geometry. Any geometry inside the pill is captured by that bone. The capture pill is shown in Figure 7.24.

Figure 7.24
The capture pill of the selected bone.

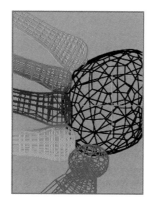
Figure 7.23
The capture of the digits needs a little tweaking.

3. Grab the little, solid arrows around the edges and move them in until the geometry is more accurately enclosed by the capture region. If you move it in too close, some of the points will turn white, which means that they are not captured any more.

Hold the Shift key while manipulating the capture region to mirror the change to the other end of the region. So, hold Shift and adjust the solid arrow at one tip in or out and it will also adjust the opposite tip in the same manner. You can use the technique with the other arrows and also the hoops that they lie on.

Sometimes it is hard to tell the difference between points that are white because they are not captured or because they have a specular highlight on them from the lighting. To fix this, temporarily turn off the OpenGL specular highlights with the Display Options window. Press d in the viewport and go to the Misc tab. At the far right, toggle off Specular Highlights. Don't forget to come back here and turn it back on when you are finished adjusting the captured geometry.

4. The circles at the top and bottom of the region can be slid up and down, and the end handles can be moved in to reduce the length of the region beyond the bone. It is fine that the top end extends into the next joint in the same bone chain, as shown in Figure 7.24. Overlap in that area will provide for some smooth blending at the joint. There is no difference between a point being just inside the pill region and it being in the core. If it is in, it is in and captured. If it is in more than one region, that can cause a problem and you will look at that next more closely next.

Over the viewport, type Shift+W to shade the pills. This can sometimes more clearly show what is captured and what is not.

5. Once you've adjusted all the Capture Regions that need it, there are probably still some points that aren't captured quite right. Now, you will do some fine-tuning.

A good method for capturing geometry is to first edit capture regions to get everything roughly in the right place and then edit capture weights for all the little areas of detail.

6. If you move the tip of the thumb back toward the palm a bit, you will likely see the side of the index finger getting pulled out in a very painful-looking way. Figure 7.25 shows the problem area. But you can't adjust the Capture Region any closer or you will start losing pieces of the thumb. This is where the Edit Capture Weights operation comes in handy.

7. In the viewport, press Tab and choose Edit Capture Weights. Select the points of the index finger that are sticking out. The first bone of both the thumb and index finger will be highlighted. On the center line of each bone will be a diamond-shaped handle that represents the relative weight each bone has on the selected points. Weight is another way to say influence.

Figure 7.25
A captured area that is yelping for some fine-tuning.

8. These points on the index finger should only have influence from the first bone of the index finger, so slide the handle in the center of the index finger's bone up towards the first knuckle. Because you have more than one point selected and the relative weight of the bones is somewhat different for each point, you may need to slide the handle up a few times until it stays at the top. Figure 7.26 shows the points with full weight to the index bone. The handle on the thumb also moves down toward the base of the thumb to indicate that it is losing influence over the points. The points should have moved back into place and not look quite so painful. Go ahead and go through and clean up any other problem spots you may find, particularly around the base and knuckles of the fingers.

Figure 7.26
The area is fixed by sliding the influence fully to the index bone.

7. Animation

9. When you have all the capture weights correct, all the points of the fingers should have color (not be white). In addition, you shouldn't be seeing any more of that painful pulling of points from undesired bones. Go to the Pose mode and select the tip of any of the fingers. Move it around and the geometry should move around following the motion of the bones. You no longer need to affect the bones directly, so you want to turn off their Display and Selectable flags. You could individually turn off each of the nodes or you could do the multiple selection trick. Or you could go one even better and use Hscript to do it.

10. Go to Windows>Textport to pop up a Textport. If necessary, cd into the /obj directory. Then type opset -d off -S off *bone* *root* and press Enter. Zoom! All of the bone and root nodes now have their Display and Selectable flags turned off. As you progress on your path with Houdini, you will most definitely learn to use Hscript more and more to make your life and living more pleasurable. Turn off the Selectable flag for the palmGeo and fingersGeo nodes, as you don't want to be able to select the geometry anymore either.

11. You do want to leave on the Display and Selectable flags for the goal nodes and the root node (the palm node) so you can still select them in the viewport. Now you can fly through in the Pose mode, clicking on the tips of the fingers or the palm and moving them around without fear of selecting the geometry or bones.

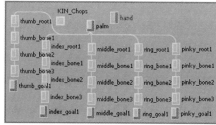

Figure 7.27
The organized network.

I cover one last organizational step before moving on to animate the hand. Look over in your Network Editor and it is likely that the node organization could be improved upon. It makes good sense to lay the bone chains out in a way that reflects their position in the scene. Figure 7.27 shows the result of organizing the nodes in this way.

Add a Little Automation

Next, take the fun a pinch further and add a little automation to the rig. You will create a single parameter that will clench and unclench the hand into a fist.

1. Select the palm node. Ctrl+RMB in the Network Editor and choose Add Spare Channel. In the dialog box, set the name of the object to palm if it isn't already, set the name of the spare channel to clench, and press Accept.

2. In the Parameters pane, click on the Spare tab so you can see the new clench parameter. RMB on the clench label and Delete Channels.

3. Move the fingers into a clenching position, something like Figure 7.28.

4. Now, edit each of the tx, ty, and tz channels of the five fingertip goals (the Null nodes) like this: if the value is −3.24597, add ch("/obj/palm/clench") * to the beginning so that it now reads ch("/obj/palm/clench") * -3.24597. Once you have edited all 15 of the Translate channels, the clench channel will now control the opening and closing of the fist. When clench is at 0, the hand is in its rest position. When it is at 1, the hand will be balled up in a fist.

5. To make this channel readily available, you'll turn it into a HUD slider. Click and drag on the clench parameter in the Parameters pane and drop it on the viewport. RMB on the HUD and choose Handle Parameters. Toggle on the Lock Low and Lock High options. Now, you can easily drag back and forth to get the clench action going. Figure 7.29 shows the final product with the color point attribute removed.

7. Animation

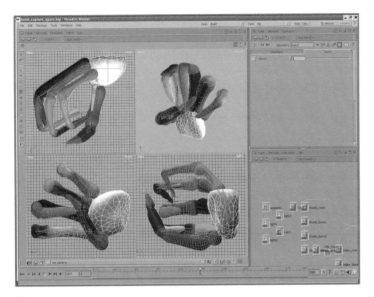

Figure 7.28
The clenched hand.

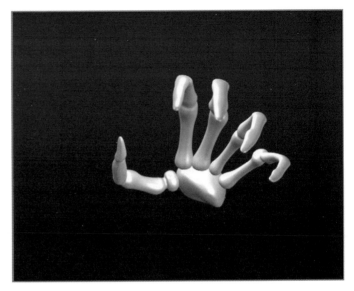

Figure 7.29
The hand will clencheth all.

Rigging the Dragonfly

This section goes through the rigging and capturing process again and covers some other possibilities of the process. You will then add a little automation to this exercise using channel operators. An interesting fact about your dragonfly is that it is symmetrical along the YZ plane. Because of this, you only need to rig one half and mirror the bones to the other half.

Create Zee Skeleton

First, you'll create the skeleton for the legs of the dragonfly.

1. Open dragonflyStarter.hip. Go into quad view to make bone placement easier.

2. You will start with the left side. Enter the Bones state. Again, that is the Bones, plural, state. Change the name of the chain to left_foreleg and change the kinematic style to IK With Twist Affector. Turn on snapping. You can adjust the exact placement later, but it is nice to be close even so. Draw a three-bone chain that ends up looking something like Figure 7.30. Turn off snapping after you RMB to complete the chain and do any fine-tuning that is necessary. Notice that because you chose With Twist Affector as the kinematic type, box geometry is snapped to the joint that it will govern. You will get back to that in a few minutes.

Figure 7.30
The left foreleg bone chain.

3. While all the nodes relating to this bone chain are still selected, it is probably a good idea to pull them over in the Network Editor and organize them in a way that make sense.

4. Change the Chain Name to `left_midleg` and repeat all the previous steps for the left `midleg`.

5. Change the Chain Name to `left_aftleg` and, masterfully this time as you have much practice, repeat all the previous steps for it.

6. The end affectors could probably be made more useful. Select all three twist nodes. On the Misc tab of one of them, change the Geometry Scale to 0.04 and turn Shaded Mode to off.

7. It would be nice to have the twist affector be the same color as the goal so you could easily see that they are related to the same bone chain. Select the foreleg's goal node and go to the Misc tab. RMB on the Color label and choose Copy Parameter. This copies all three channels. Go to the Misc tab of the foreleg's twist node, RMB on the Color label, and choose Paste Copied Relative Refs. Now each of these channels references back to the same channel on the goal node. And so, their colors in the viewport match.

8. Do the same thing for `midleg` and `aftleg`. Your setup should now look something like Figure 7.31.

9. And now for some wondrous and loving Houdini mojo. You have completed a good bit of work in rigging the three legs and yet, there are three more legs to go. Yarrrrrrr! But wait. Stay that Yarrrrrrr because it will be surprisingly painless.

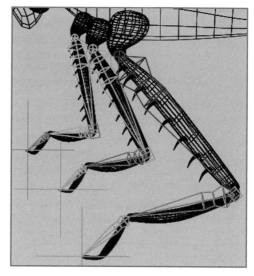

Figure 7.31
The completed rig for the left side.

In the top viewport, choose Mirror in the Tab menu. At the top, there is a field for renaming the mirrored objects. Change the word `mirror_` to `right_`. The next field says Remove old name up to and then there is a field with an underscore in it. Leave the underscore there. This will make it so that the `left_` is deleted and replaced with a `right_` in the naming of the mirrored objects. Much easier than renaming all the new nodes manually! The default mirror plane of YZ is fine also.

The message bar is asking you to select the objects you would like to mirror. First, turn off the Selectability flag for the `dragonflyGeo` node, as you don't want to accidentally select it and so mirror it. Back in the viewport, drag a selection box around all the bones, goals, and twist affectors to select them. Notice that as soon as you do that, Houdini is showing you what the mirrored objects will look like, as shown in Figure 7.32. It is a handy preview to verify you are mirroring across the correct plane. But, it is only a preview. You still need to RMB to complete the operation and actually create the mirrored magic. After you do, Houdini will build the right-side bones for you, renaming them and reworking all the connectivity. All the IK chains will work as they should. Notice too that the colors of the new goal and twist geometries are matching too. Even the layout of the nodes in the Network Editor has been duplicated! Tis a very robust operation indeed!

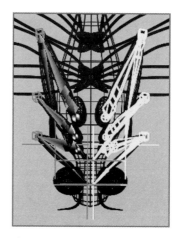

Figure 7.32
The mirrored preview.

7. Animation

131

10. While all of your new nodes are still selected, drag them over in the Network Editor to keep up a good visual layout.

11. Drop a Null Object and rename it body.

12. Make sure the Keep position when parenting option is toggled on for all of the root nodes. Then, parent all of them to the body node. Use the multiple selection trick so that you only have to make the connection once rather than once per each child node. Move the body node around and all of the bone chains follow, but the goals and twist nodes do not. You will address this later with a little CHOPs trickery.

13. They could use a little cleanup themselves though. Notice how the boxes that are the twist affectors are rotated off kilter a little. It would be better to have them also lined with up world space just as the goal handles are. Look in the Transform tab for the twist nodes and all the fields are set to 0. Hmmm, what is happening? Just as you manually did in the hand exercise, these twist nodes already have a pre-transform baked in. You need to extract it, revert the rotates to default so they are again aligned with world space, and then clean (or bake) the translates again.

Select all of the twist nodes. In the Parameters pane, choose Extract Pre-Transform. Then RMB on the Rotate label and choose Revert Selected to Defaults. Notice that all the boxes are now aligned correctly. In the Pre-transform menu, choose Clean Translates to bake back in the various off-sets. Take care on that last one. You want to choose Clean Translate and not Clean Transform.

Figure 7.33
The current state of the network.

My network layout looks like Figure 7.33.

"Capture" Geometry

There is usually more than one way to do rig a cat, especially in Houdini. You could rig the dragonfly the same way you did the fingers, but you'll look at another way. A dragonfly has an exoskeleton, which means that the outside of its body is not really flexible. It moves quite a bit like something mechanical, rather than like something fleshy. Because of this, you'll rig him like a machine.

It will require a bit of grunt work up front. The idea is that rather than using a Capture SOP and a Deform SOP inside the model, you will break the model apart into small sections that correspond to the bones. Then you will parent the pieces to the bones directly. If you recall, this is exactly what you did with the palm geometry in the hand exercise.

Isolate the Pieces

You first need to isolate the various geometry pieces before you can parent them to their respective bones.

1. Lay down a new geometry object. Rename it `left_fore_femur`. Jump inside and delete the default node. Drop Object Merge SOP and set the Object 1 field to the `displayRender` node inside the `dragonflyGeo` object. This will pull a copy of the geometry at that node into the current object. Because this is the entire geometry, append a Delete SOP and turn off the See One/See All button to clear up the visuals a little. Change the Operation to Delete Non-Selected and then choose the `GRLeftForeLeg` group. Because groups were made during the creation of the geometry, it makes it very easy to isolate out the various legs. Toggle the See One button on and off to verify that you do indeed have the left foreleg.

2. You just want the femur (the top leg segment) and not the whole leg though. Had I given the file a little more forethought, I would have also grouped out the various leg segments during creation. But, alas, I did not. So, use another Delete operation to only leave the femur and the spikes sticking out of the femur. You can also delete the round shoulder part at the top. Now is a great chance to play with the lasso selection tool and also change the selection to remove or add depending on what you need. Always remember to set this back to Replace after you are finished with all the legs because it can be very frustrating to forget that you left it on Remove and not be able to select anything.

3. Jump back up the Object context, copy and paste the `left_fore_femur` node, and name the copy `left_fore_tibia` (which is the middle leg segment). Jump inside this one and delete everything except the tibia. The easiest way is to press the backtick (`) key to reselect the geometry for the current operation, which should be the second delete. Then delete everything but the tibia segment.

4. Jump back up again, copy and paste the `left_fore_femur` node, and name the copy `left_fore_tarsus` (which is the bottom leg segment). Jump into it and delete everything but the tarsus segment.

5. That was a whole lot of manual labor for a computer nerd like myself and, I presume, you. Before you come to despair realizing that you have five more legs to go, take heart! All the legs were built the same way and all the poly counts will be topologically identical, which is a fancy way of saying that all you have to do is to copy all three of these new objects and edit one small thing in each to make them look at a different leg for their source. Yeehaa! Now you can consider forgiving me for not creating groups earlier for each segment.

6. Go ahead and copy the three `left_fore_*` objects and rename them `left_mid_*`. Then go into each one and change the Group parameter from using `GRLeftForeLeg` to using `GRLeftMidLeg`.

7. Repeat the process to create the three aft leg segments.

8. Next, copy all nine of these new nodes and change the `left_` in their names to `right_`.

9. Go into each of the new nodes and change the Group parameter to use the right versions of the group. You now have 18 new objects and they are all leg parts.

10. One more thing is needed and that is a body with no legs. Add a Geometry Object and rename it `body`. Jump inside and delete the default node. Drop an Object Merge SOP and set the Object 1 field to the `displayRender` node inside the `dragonflyGeo` object.

11. Append a Delete and choose all the leg groups so that you have just the body.

12. But, you still want the round shoulder geometries. MMB on the output of the object merge node and choose Delete to branch a delete operation off to the side. Choose the `GRnubbins` group and change the Operation to Delete Non-Selected.

7. Animation

133

13. Drop a Merge and wire in both of the delete nodes. You should now have all of the dragonfly geometry except for the legs. The Network Editor, with all of the newly created Geometry nodes, should look something like Figure 7.34.

Figure 7.34
The Network Editor showing the new Geometry objects.

Parent the Pieces

You aren't really going to "capture" the geometry in the sense of using the capture and deform operations. Instead, you are going to parent each isolated piece of geometry to its respective bone.

1. Before parenting any of the geometry pieces, you'll do a little viewport cleanup. You want to turn off the display and selectability of all the bone nodes, root nodes, and also the dragonflyGeo node. Pop up a Textport pane and cd into the /obj directory if needed. Type `opset -d off -S off *bone* *root* dragonflyGeo`. The task is performed for you with very little effort.

2. Next, you want to turn off the selectability of all the geometry pieces, being the legs segments and the bodyGeo node. Type `opset -S off *femur *tibia *tarsus bodyGeo`. The job is done.

3. Select all of the geometry pieces and then toggle on Keep position when parenting so that they all get the change.

4. Parent each leg geometry piece to its respective bone parent. For example, left_fore_femur is parented to left_foreleg_bone1, right_aft_tarsus is parented to right_aftleg_bone3, and so on. Parent the bodyGeo node to the body (a null) node. The network should now look like something like Figure 7.35.

5. Wipe the sweat from your brow, friend. You are in the promised land! Go into the Pose state and use the body null to move the whole dragonfly around; use the goals and twist affectors to move the legs around.

   As stated at the beginning of this exercise, rigging in this "mechanical" way can be a good bit of work. However, this kind of rig much more efficient to use because there isn't a Capture Geometry SOP or a Deform SOP in the geometry. It just has to follow the transforms of the bones. Of course, if you have something soft that needs to deform, this kind of rig will not work.

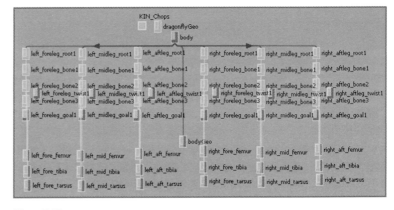

Figure 7.35
The final state of the Object network.

Chops-ify the Dragonfly

CHOPs (for channel operators) is one of the most interesting and least understood contexts in Houdini. Yet like any kind of magic, the determined mind will quickly find ease and even come to enjoy the arcane machinations. Channel operators are simply data processors. Data flows in, gets processed, changed, twisted, bent, smeared, mutilated, spindled, or reformatted, and then passed back out. You'll go through a simple example that demonstrates the good times that this context can afford.

1. If you are not continuing from the previous exercise, load `dragonflyCaptured.hip`.

2. Go to frame 1 and set a keyframe on the tx channel of the body node. Dolly out a bit so you have a good amount of work room to work in and move the dragonfly to the left side of the screen.

3. Go around one-fourth of the way through your frame range and set another keyframe on tx. Move the dragonfly over to the right side of the screen.

4. Go to around halfway through the range and set another keyframe on tx. Move the dragonfly back to the left side of the screen. Play back the animation and the dragonfly moves to the right and then back to the left. The goals and twist affectors are not following along and so are causing the legs to stretch out.

5. You could parent these nodes to the body node, but then they would just rigidly follow along. It would be more interesting to use CHOPs to inherit the motion of the body node and then add in a little extra crispy, non-chicken yumminess just because you can.

6. Here at the Object level, drop a CHOP Network and jump into it. Adding a CHOP operator is just like adding an operator in any other context. Over the Network Editor, press Tab to get the operator menu for this context. As in most cases, there are Generators and Filters. Look at the list of all the operators and try to guess what some of them do.

7. Choose a Fetch CHOP and rename it `fetchGoalsTwists`. This operator goes and gets channel data from elsewhere in your .hip file and pulls the data into CHOPs. Figure 7.36 shows a CHOP node. The node has an area for an input and an output. Notice that there is no arrow on the fetch node, which means it must be a generator type operator. There is a blue Display flag and an orange Export flag. Don't toggle on the Export flag for this node. The teal flag is the Audio flag. The node also has a bypass button and a lock button. As you can see, there are a number of similarities to the SOP node. One difference is the Export flag. As previously stated, this context is used to pull in data, manipulate it, and then push it back out. You don't want to export the data from this node and so you don't want to toggle on the Export flag. You will only turn this flag on at the last node in the chain. So be sure not to turn it on for any node previous to that.

Figure 7.36
The likeable CHOP node.

8. If you haven't already, turn on this node's Display flag. In this node, you will import the `tx` channels of all of the goal and twist nodes. Enter `/obj/*goal? *twist?` in the Node parameter. This means go to the Object level and look at every node that is named `*goal?` or `*twist?`. The * is a wildcard for anything and the ? is a wildcard for anything, but that occupies a single space. This will effectively go and look at every one of the goal and twist nodes. Enter `tx` in the Channels parameter. You should now see some colored, flat lines in the Viewer pane. MMB on the node icon and all the fetched channels are listed at the bottom. Because there is no animation on these channels, the lines appear flat in the CHOPs viewport.

9. Drop an unconnected Fetch and rename it `fetchBody`. Change the Node field to `/obj/body` and the Channels field to `tx`. You should see a curve in the viewport as shown in Figure 7.37. This is the animation that you previously created. The curve is labeled as `tx`, which is the channel it represents. Notice that the viewport shows values along the vertical axis and time along the horizontal axis. These give you a general idea of what is happening to the values in the channel.

10. To get a more exacting idea of what is happening, MMB on the node and you will get an info popup window, as shown in Figure 7.38. At the bottom, you can see the channel name, the min and max values of the entire channel, and the value at the current frame. There is, of course, other information, but this is not a chapter on CHOPs and so you must move one.

11. You have fetched the `tx` channels of the goal and twist nodes and also of the body node. Now, you need to get the goals and twists to inherit the body's animation. Drop an unconnected Math CHOP, and wire in the `fetchGoalsTwists` node and also the body node. In the viewport, you can see all the various channels together now. But, they are not combined in a useful way. On the OP tab, change the Combine CHOPs menu to Add. Do you see what happened? It was schweet! Every single goal and twist channel now has the body animation channel added to it. If you exported the data at this node, the goals and twists would rigidly follow the body node just as if you had parented them up at the Object level.

12. But this is CHOPs and you are looking for something more dazzling. Append a Lag CHOP to the network and, holding Shift, turn on its Display flag too. Yes, you can have multiple Display flags on. Leave everything at the defaults for now. You can come back later and play with the values to see what happens. Or, for more precise noodling, check out the help for the operator.

In the stowbar above the viewport, go to the Options menu and turn off Labels if the viewport is getting a little crowded. Figure 7.39 shows you the results. The purple curve is the channel before lag is applied and the pink curve is the channel after lag is applied. Isn't CHOPs pretty?

13. So, you have taken in the original goal and twist `tx` channels, added the body's `tx` channel, and then given them each a little lag. The only thing left is to export the channels back to their origins. Append an Export CHOP to the network and set its sets its Node field to `/obj/*goal? *twist?`. Now, finally, turn on the Export flag for the export node.

Jump back up to SOPs and look at the `tx` fields for the goal and twist nodes. They are all orange, indicating that they are being overwritten by CHOPs. If you toggle to expression view, it will tell you which CHOP node is exporting to that field.

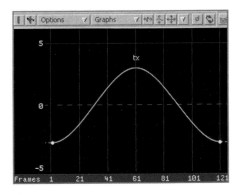

Figure 7.37
The CHOPs viewport.

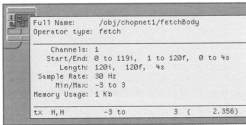

Figure 7.38
The info popup for the chosen CHOP node.

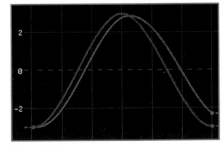

Figure 7.39
The channels before and after lag is applied.

14. If you haven't already, play the timeline and you should see something very simple, and yet very pleasing! As the dragonfly moves back and forth, the legs dangle and swing back and forth, giving a good feeling of momentum. Ahh, the sheer beauty of secondary animation is so rewarding. Just a little really starts to bring a character to life.

> If you save this file and later re-open it, the CHOPs will seem broken. This is because they need to initialize first. Simply jump into the chopnet to do this. You could also pop up a Textport and use the opcook command to force the initialization. For example, you can cd into the chopnet directory and then type **opcook -F export1** for that node to cook.

Summary

You are quickly becoming ready for a virtuoso virtual performance. Animation is what truly, and literally, brings to life the various elements of a CG scene. Although the process has evolved over time, the core principles are still the same as they were in the pioneering days of yore. From *Gertie the Dinosaur* to *Lord of the Rings,* it has always been up to the skill and artistry of the animator to make the work come alive. This chapter walked you through all of the basic concepts required to animate in Houdini and (hopefully) inspired a few ideas for adventures yet to come.

7. Animation

137

chapter 8
Particle Operators (POPs)

Hear Ye! Hear Ye! You have finally arrived at particles. When you first heard about Houdini, chances are it was in a context related to effects and particles. Houdini's particle operations are very robust tools for simulating natural phenomenon like water, smoke, fire, and pirouetting pyroclast. They are also very capable tools for mimicking the dynamics of group behavior as seen in hordes of locusts, squadrons of seagulls, and even schools of fish. Many of the high-end effects you see in movies every day were born in POPs and then marshaled back and forth through the various contexts of Houdini until the stunning final look was achieved.

Here, at the beginning of your adventure into POPs, I thought it would be most helpful to get a little perspective from one of the most experienced and talented Houdini users in the world, Caleb Howard. So, without further delay, here begins the magic of particles, in his words.

A WORD FROM CALEB HOWARD

"People are like Particles. We are each born in our own time. Our birth is predictable, based on a straightforward understanding of how such things come to pass. We live our lives with the semblance of self-control. We prefer to feel that we choose our goals and make the decisions for how to surmount the obstacles in our paths. Even so, it is impossible to say, on any given day, what unforeseen events we may face or how tomorrow will compare to today. The events of our lives are, to a large degree, unpredictable. Because of this, the course of our lives is also unpredictable. People and particles—to use a somewhat geeky term—are *nondeterministic* in their behavior.

As we grow and age, we gather spin and speed. We feel we are responsible for making the decisions which direct the course of our lives. In truth, we may wield a staggering degree of control over the universe around us. By applying our heads, hearts, and hands, in accordance with the greater forces which guide us, we may direct our lives to a great extent. We choose our schools. We choose our careers. We choose our mates... And yet, at times, we can clearly see the greater statistical guidelines of our society. There are systemic rules which govern and limit our behavior to a great extent. There are laws which regulate where and how we may choose to drive. There are fashions and social trends which indicate what we should wear and how we

---

should behave. We mate according to cultural dictates. We can feel free, and while paradoxically knowing that our context is governed by rules which constrain our decisions very narrowly. Like a sailor who knows the fixed currents and the fluctuating winds, and may work them both to move in any direction of his choosing, so too may we overcome the prevailing constraints of our lives to achieve the destinies of our own choosing. So may a particle manage to pull off unique and unexpected behavior despite its motion being defined by external rules and forces larger than itself.

The needs of life and society provide us with our goals from day to day, and even influence the greater arc of our lifetimes. In traffic and in careers, we seek similar objectives as do all people—food, fun, and a little sleep in between. The closer our current station is to that of our neighbor, the closer we will match their life's achievements, on the whole. We move in similar directions towards similar ends, and yet we never lose the overwhelming sense of unique purpose which defines each of us. We are so similar as to be indistinguishable, and yet so distinct that we often fail to recognize the kindred spirits with whom we share the world. All this, and then we die. Just like particles.

It seems like the great majority of applications that particle systems are used for in the film effects market miss the potential of philosophical introspection that particles truly provide. Born in the fire of a rocket's thrust, burning for an instant of pure acceleration, and then burnt out, gray, and drifting in a con-trail for 42 glorious frames of cinematic action. This isn't just the fate of a Hollywood Effects Artist, but is also often the microcosmic fate of the particles we create.

Birth rates and velocity curves, collision objects and wind vectors. These are the tools and jargon of we, the young gods of a particle's creation. Unthinking, we birth them by the millions, only to send them momentarily back to the oblivion from whence they came. This is fine. It pays the bills and, as mercenary work goes, it is no worse than much of what goes on. There is more available though. These crude forces are just the beginning—like training wheels. They barely hint at the graceful creations which an integrated environment like Houdini may help an aspiring creator bring to light. Like a simple chain of hydrocarbons gives rise to a complex planetary biosphere, a diverse set of interlocking control tools driving individuated agents in a particle system is sufficient to create life, in all of its diversity and detail. These needn't be daunting aspirations—even for someone new to Houdini, or to particles—for the secret to life's rich pageantry is the unstoppable emergence of complexity from simple rules which are iterated in a recursive environment.

On various occasions, Houdini particles have been given eyes, legs, gaits, brains, fingers, hungers, goals, and dreams. The true beauty of the tools in Houdini is that we, the creators for whom the tools are built, are in no way constrained by whatever preconceptions the tool builders may have held for how their tools should be used. Because of an excellent design philosophy, Houdini embodies tools of uniform, and unconstrained data flow amongst such diverse types of information as geometry, fields, images, files, and code. Amongst all of the different tools in Houdini, the seemingly humble particle has the greatest capacity to embody the complexity of life. This is because it is nondeterministic—just like people. So you want a stampede of ten thousand snakes? Well, particles are the solution. Do you need an army of thingies to fall into rank and then engage their common lifelong foe? Particles are the way. Do you need a monkey to climb a tree, and then hurl poo at the camera? Particles again are a good way to go.

I have a long history with particles. In the beginning, I simply wanted to try a few things out. The following was for a personal project, but it eventually made its way into a moderately public view. I built a valley by painting an elevation map and using a point SOP to lift the walls of a valley around a grassy plain. The valley walls rose to vertical cliffs. Nothing could enter nor leave an area of about 100 square miles. On this terrain, I painted a river, running from the mountain top to the marshy wetlands in the middle. With a smoothing algorithm, and a procedural shader (SHOPs), the terrain was textured according to region with grasslands, forests, marshes, ridges and more. Using this map as a guide, I wrote a script (Hscript) to distribute plants, rocks, trees, and initial populations of four species: Herbivores, Carnivores, Parasites, and Scavengers. Each population was a particle system (POPs) born according to the specie's breeding habits, and surviving according to fitness. They carried attributes of physical characteristics (height, sex, speed, color, and so on), and attributes of state (hunger, love, horniness, anger, and so on). For the sake of action, I created in them all a need for water, and in the valley only a single place to drink. I attached a camera object to each particle in turn, to let them see. In the compositing context (COPs), I attached a GL renderer (ROPs) and some image analysis networks (CHOPs) to make them understand what they saw. By these simple applications of different facets of Houdini's toolset, the creatures could see the water they craved. With some attribute communication trickery, they could tell their friends from their foes as well (Objects). Each particle was given a procedural body (SOPs), which worked to couple the particle's basic drives to the terrain.

Then I just turned it on. After just a week of the simulation, I had thirsty herbivores braving the predators to get to the water. The slower ones were eaten, the faster ones got away. The parasites evolved to avoid the heads of the creatures. The scavengers learned to wait until the predators were done before approaching the remains of a kill. All born from the simple particle, but empowered by advanced and diverse tools which could naturally and easily be associated with the simple, and yet complex, particle.

Do I feel anything when a particle I created is killed? I do. I identify greatly with particles, because particles are nondeterministic—like all life, like people. Because of resource issues, primarily a lack of near-infinite disk space, I haven't yet implemented the afterlife which I have designed for particles. It's in the works, though. It's the least I can do for them, as their loving creator.

God, I love Houdini. I really do. Magick, indeed."

Caleb Howard
C.T.O., Cognitive Imaging Corporation
C.G. Supervisor, Sony Imageworks

8. Particle Operators (POPs)

Salutations to the POP Node

As in every context, POPs also uses nodes. Figure 8.1 shows an example of a POP node; in this case, the Source POP. Based on what you have already learned about node functionality, you can probably guess what the features of a POP node do. The POP node has input and output connection points, a bypass arrow, a Display flag, a Cook flag (the purple flag), and a Template flag. The Cook flag is slightly new and it is used to tell the system to which node it needs to cook. Let's say you have three connected POPs and the Cook flag is on the second one. Even if the Display flag is on the third node, the simulation that you are viewing is only utilizing the input from the first two nodes. And finally, it has an icon displaying its type which can be MMB pressed to view a popup window containing all sorts of useful information about the state of the simulation at that node.

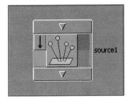

Figure 8.1
The POP node.

Particle Operations Are Cooked in a Simulation

Creating animation in POPs is somewhat different than creating animation in other parts of the package. In POPs, animation is achieved by creating a simulation based on a set of rules that you define. This means that the current state of a particular system is based on which conditions were present at the start and how those conditions interacted over time to get you where you are at the present. In other words, POPs are state dependent. This is different than your normal keyframed animation. Keyframed animation is created by setting keyframes at particular points in time and then having the software interpolate between those points based on some function.

For example, to animate a person doing a karate chop, you might set a keyframe with the hand above the head, and then set a keyframe of the hand at head level and out in front of the body, and finally set a keyframe with the hand below the head level and closer to the body. The software could take those three keyframes and create a smooth motion from start to finish. Although you can set keyframes on various parameters in POPs to gain finer control over the simulation, the particles are not simply interpolating from one keyframe to the next. The sum total of all the various forces at play are considered and the particles are affected by that calculation. Every discreet calculation of a simulation is called a *cook*.

So, the simulation cooks and then advances some defined period of time (which is often the next frame) and takes the state of the system at the previous cook and again calculates the sum total of all the rules and forces at play and applies the result to each particle, and so on, until your simulation is finished. Because of this, simulations cannot be cooked in reverse. If you scrub the playbar forward, Houdini will correctly update the state of the system at each frame based on the forces involved so long as it can cook the update faster than you are scrubbing through the timeline. However, drag backwards along the playbar and the system just stays at the latest frame to which it has progressed. This is because each cook is based on the one before it and it can't figure out how a particle should be affected going backwards in time.

Simulations Are the Result of Interconnected Forces

In a particle simulation, you are creating a system of interdependent forces. That is to say, choices you make are most often only meaningful when compared to how other forces and choices are being implemented. Compare this to animating at the SOP level for instance. You can animate a box going from 0 to 10 in the world Y axis and you can easily see the mechanics involved. It starts at a value of zero on some particular frame, and then moves to a value of 10 by some future frame based on an interpolation segment function. With particles, giving a system a positive world Y axis force of 10 will only give a tendency to the particles. Where they end up at any particular time is a combination of this force and also many other factors that could be at play like initial velocity, mass, charge, gravity, and more.

8. Particle Operators (POPs)

Particle Simulations Are Interactive

You can change POP parameters while the simulation is running and interactively view the changes. However, it is important to remember that you are viewing what the system looks like when a change is made at a particular time and not what the system would look like if that change had been present from the beginning. It is often efficient to interactively adjust parameters while the simulation is running to get your look in the right ballpark and then reset and play from the beginning to ensure the change still works as you expected. Remember that you can keyframe almost every parameter in POPs so that if the behavior you want only works when you animate a parameter midstream, you can easily do that too. I basically just said it, but I'll say it again more clearly because it is very important to remember. Any time you make a change in POPs, you want to reset the simulation by going back to the first frame and then playing it from there (unless, of course you are testing how an animated parameter would work.) Another way to update the system to reflect the change you made is to click the yellow flag in the upper-right corner of the viewport. Any time the simulation in the viewport is not accurate, the flag will turn yellow to indicate this. If you click on the yellow flag, the system will be reset and recooked up to the frame where you currently are. So, if you are frame 96, you won't see how the system is developing in the viewport from frames 1 to 95. The downside is that usually means you get to sit there for a while and wait for it to catch up. In addition, I usually prefer to reset to the first frame so that I can see the system developing from the beginning again.

> A quirk of cooking simulations is that sometimes when you drag the frame indicator back to the first frame, it doesn't actually reset the simulation. It is more reliable to press the Reset to First Frame button on the playbar anytime you want to reset the simulation. If you do run into this problem, you can fix it by scrubbing forward beyond the last frame cooked and then reset back to the beginning. If you cooked it to the final frame and then encounter the problem, temporarily move the Cook flag to another POP in the chain and then move it back to where it belongs. Then reset the simulation and it will work correctly.

The Real Time Toggle

Because POPs use a simulation approach to animation, it is often beneficial to turn off the Real Time Toggle button. This button is shown in Figure 8.2. Consider it a moment and you will understand why. A simulation is state dependent and so is based on the cook before it. If the simulation is complex enough that cooking it takes longer than the chosen frames per second, the simulation will be trying to update itself based on incomplete (and therefore incorrect) previous cooks.

Turn off the Real Time Toggle and run a simple simulation. The frame indicator will speed by, going faster than your FPS. However, crank up the complexity a bit and it may well take 30 or more seconds per cook (or greater than what your frames per second setting is). In this situation, if you were to turn back on the Real Time Toggle, Houdini would not play back the simulation in a way that was useful. You can turn off the Real Time Toggle in order to avoid this problem.

The Real Time Toggle button

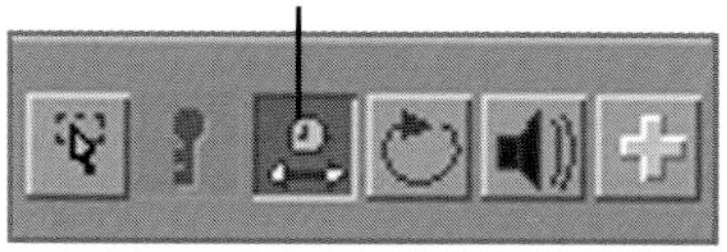

Figure 8.2
The Real Time Toggle button.

Perhaps the best setting when playing with POPs is to set the option called "Play every frame but never faster than FPS". Toggle on the Real Time Toggle and open the Global Animation Options window at the far right of the playbar and select that option under Realtime Behavior. When selected, the simulation will play as fast as possible but never faster than the designated frames per second, even if it could cook faster than that. As you can imagine, this is especially useful in the POPs context and it is often a good idea to have this option selected.

Particle SOP or Pop Merge SOP or Popnet SOP

When beginning the study of particle operations, there is sometimes some confusion about the various ways in which you can create a simulation. I'll first clarify the usage of the Particle SOP, and then the Pop Merge SOP, and finally the Popnet SOP. There are two main areas for creating particles: with a Particle SOP or inside a POP network. The POP network option can actually branch off and be in two places, as you can create a Popnet at the root /part level or inside SOPs using a Popnet SOP. Figure 8.3 shows these options. In this book, I most often use the latter method.

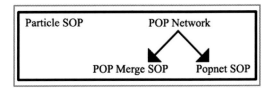

Figure 8.3
Particle creation possibilities.

If you were to create a Popnet at the root /part level, you would then use a Pop Merge SOP to bring the particle primitives into SOPs for further use. All of that may have sounded a bit like Hog Latin. So, let's walk through an example of each of these methods in order to translate Hog Latin into Pig Latin, which we can all readily understand.

> You can create a Popnet inside any of the other contexts following the networks within networks paradigm. However, you will most often be placing them inside the Geometry object with which they are associated.

Particle SOP

The Particle SOP is the simplest method of creating and manipulating particles. It is useful for simpler simulations involving only one source, collision object, and/or attractor input. Also, the Particle SOP is available in Houdini Select and Escape, meaning you do have some capable particle abilities available even in these less expensive packages. If your needs are relatively straightforward, this SOP can be faster to implement. In many cases that demand more complexity, you will want to go into POPs. POPs offer more control than the Particle SOP in that you have more exacting birthing options, have access to a wider variety of forces, have access to a large number of local variables that represent particle attributes, have control over how attributes are modified and inherited, have control over grouping of particles, and more. It is important to remember that even in cases where you expect the required behavior could easily be achieved with a Particle SOP, it may be wiser to create it in POPs so that any changes to design that might come later can be more readily accommodated. Before you make the assumption that the Particle SOP is ancient, useless technology and skip this section, let me assure you that this operator is strong in the ways of the force. It was the premiere particle generator for all visual effects work in Hollywood up until 1997, when POPs were introduced. It was the engine that drove all the smoke, water spray, and heat shimmer effects in *Titanic*, *True Lies*, and countless other films. So, let's check out a Particle SOP in action.

1. Open a spanky new session of Houdini if you don't have one open already. Dive into the default model object or create a geometry object and dive into it if the model object isn't present.

2. Lay down a Grid SOP and leave it at its defaults.

3. Append a Particle SOP. Press play and you will see that some particles are born, but they aren't doing anything to jump around about. If you don't see any particles, home your viewport to ensure the geometry is within your field of view. Also, to more clearly see the particles, you may want to toggle on the Display of Points button, which is located in the stowbar on the right side of the Viewer pane. To add a little interest, go to the Forces tab and add an External force of 1 in Y. Now you have some particles flying up. Notice how the particles are coming up kind of "in sheets" from the grid. That is

because you are birthing by point number and the grid's point numbers start at 0 in one corner and go back and forth all the way to the other end. The operation births points in cardinal order. So, it births the first particle at point 0, the second at point 1, and so on.

4. To see the point numbers, first put the Display flag back up on the grid and then turn on the display of point numbers and dolly in if necessary to get a better look. The point numbers toggle is also in the right stowbar. With point numbers turned on, you should be seeing something like what is shown in Figure 8.4.

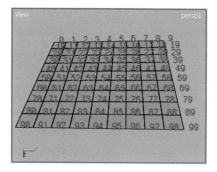

Figure 8.4
Point numbers displayed.

5. Because you can't make the operation birth from points randomly, instead you can randomize the position of the points on the grid before it feeds into the Particle SOP, which will effectively be doing the same thing. Insert a Sort SOP in between the grid and Particle SOPs. On the Point tab in the parameters for the Sort, change the Point Sort to Random. Make sure the Display flag is on the sort node and you should see that the numbers are now randomly arrayed across the grid. Go ahead and turn off the display of point numbers and continue.

6. Put the Display flag back on the particle node and view the simulation (remember to reset it first!). As a final touch to make it yet a wee bit more interesting, add 5 to Turbulence in X, Y, and Z in the Forces tab. Play the simulation again and you can see that it is starting to get exciting! Make sure to dolly out a bit to see all the interesting little twists and twirls the turbulence creates. Figure 8.5 shows you the results of this simulation after cranking up the Birth rate to 500 and running it to frame 300.

Figure 8.5
Result of some particle SOP play.

7. Using the Particle SOP, the particles are automatically brought into the SOP context. Why is this important? Most often, you will use POPs to create an interesting behavior and then export that behavior to other contexts for further manipulation. The most common context is SOPs, where you can attach geometry and shaders to each point in the particle system. Using the Particle SOP, the particles are automatically in SOPs and available for use.

Pop Merge SOP

If you create your POP network at the root /part level, you will need to use a Pop Merge SOP to bring the behaviors into SOPs. One reason you might want to use this method is if you want to reference the POP network several times from different areas of the package. Because a POP network is just a set of instructions with no specific geometry context, you can easily use that network in many different geometry contexts.

1. Using the context menu, jump over to the POPs context. In the path field for all of the panes, you should now see /part/popnet1/->. You are now inside a Popnet located at the root particle level (being /part).

2. Lay down a Location POP and press play. By default, you see an expanding cloud of particles. Go to the Attributes tab and set Velocity in Y to 1 and Variance in all axes to 0.3. Play the simulation and you now have a jet of particles shooting upwards. As you play the simulation, interactively adjust the variance in all axes (bring up the number ladder using the MMB on the Variance label and drag back and forth). You can see the width of the cone grow smaller or larger as you adjust the variance values.

3. Now, let's bring this simulation into SOPs so that you can later attach geometry to the particles. Jump over to the Objects context and create a Geometry object if one doesn't already exist.

4. Jump into it and lay down a POP Merge SOP. This SOP will allow you to import a simulation from the POPs context. Press the + button in the POP Path field and select the `location1` POP. You will need to expand the tree view to get down to it. Again, make sure that `location1` is selected and press Accept. Press play and you should now see the simulation playing here in SOPs. The POP Merge just goes to the specified POP and retrieves the state of the simulation at that node.

Popnet SOP (Called POP Network in the Tab Menu)

When a POP network is dropped inside an object at the SOPs level, it is called a Popnet SOP. For example, say you have an object called `lawnSprinkler` and inside it is all the geometry and animation necessary to make the spigot rotate back and forth. It would likely be a good idea to drop a Popnet SOP inside the object and access POPs from there (which might look like `/lawnSprinkler/popnet1`). That way, if you ever wanted to package it up and distribute it as a digital asset, the particle behavior would already be included. If you had created the water behavior in the root level particle context (`/part/popnet1`), you would have to first take the time to integrate it properly before packaging the asset. Besides that, when you have the popnet inside the object, it just seems easier to press Enter to dive in or the u key to go back up just as you jump into or out of SOPs. Having a popnet there at the SOP level also makes more visual sense if you are using geometry for birthing sources, collision, or attraction. Everything is in one place and easy to access. Let's jump through a quick example of this to see the glory.

1. Lay down a Geometry object and jump inside it. Press the Tab menu and drop a POP Network. Press Enter to jump inside it and you should now be in POPs.

2. Append a Location POP and press play. Turn on the display of points if necessary to better see the simulation. Currently, you have particles shooting off in all axes. Go to the Birth tab and change the Variance in Y to 0.1. Reset the simulation and press play. Tumble around in the viewport and you can see more of a pancake looking expansion.

3. Press u to jump back up to SOPs and you can see that you have the Popnet ready and willing to do your bidding. Most of the exercises in this chapter will use this method. Now that you understand where you can create particles, let's move on to exploring how to control their birthing.

Impulse or Constant Birthing

In the Location and Source POPs, you will find two types of birthing possibilities. *Impulse birthing* is based on a per time step increment while *constant birthing* is based on a per second time increment. Each of these birthing types is accompanied by an Activation field. These two birthing possibilities operate independently of each other. This means that that if you have both of their Activation fields set to 1 and some nonzero number in the Birth Rate fields, they will both be causing particles to be born simultaneously. The difference between impulse and constant birthing is a choice between pulse versus flow, respectively. If you want particles right now, use impulse birthing. If you want a nice flow of particles, use constant birthing.

The Impulse Birth Rate parameter births particles on a per time step increment, and this rate is affected by the oversampling set on the popnet node. By default, this oversampling is set to 1, which means one time step per frame. With this default oversampling, an impulse birth rate of 10 means that 10 particles are birthed per frame, because there are now 10 time steps per frame or 10 iterations through the entire POP network. What would happen if you set oversampling to some number other than 1? If you set it to 2, the popnet will cook twice per frame. Now, it will birth 20 particles per frame with 10 of those being birthed at frame 1 and 10 more being birthed at frame 1.5. If you set oversampling to 3 with the same impulse birth rate, 30 particles would be born per frame with 10 being born at frame 1, 10 being born at frame 1.33, and 10 being born at frame 1.66.

> One point to keep in mind when using impulse birthing and cooking between frames is that the geometry referenced by the POP network will be forced to cook as well if it too is deforming.

The Constant Birth Rate parameter births particles on a per second increment, and this rate is affected by what the global animation frames per second setting is. For example, if FPS is set to 24, and Constant Birth Rate is set to 10, 10 particles will be born by the time 24 frames have passed. If FPS were set to 30, 10 particles would be born by the time 30 frames had passed.

In case that discussion seemed a little too esoteric, let's put cement shoes on it and drop it into the lake of long-term memory.

1. Drop a Geometry object and jump into it. Next, drop a Popnet and dive into it as well.

2. Lay down a Location POP and go to the Birth tab. Change impulse activation to 1. This is saying that birthing particles based on a per time step increment is now activated. Because Oversampling for the Popnet is set to 1, the simulation will cook 1 time per frame. Next, set Impulse Birth Rate to 1. This says that you will now be birthing 1 particle per frame. Reset the simulation and advance to frame 2. MMB the location node and you can find out how many particles your system has birthed so far. The popup window shows that 9 particles have been born. Obviously, that seems a little high considering it should be birthing 1 per frame and you are on frame 2.

3. There is one more thing to tweak. There is another birthing option, Constant Birthing. As discussed earlier, because both Impulse and Constant Activation are set to 1, you are using both methods. This demonstrates why you will most often want to specifically use one method or the other. As you are currently looking at impulse birthing, set Constant Activation to 0. Now, no matter what number is in the Constant Birth Rate field, it is not activated and so won't be considered.

4. Reset the simulation and again advance to frame 2. MMB the popup window again and, yeehaa!, you have two particles, just as you would expect. Advance to frame 30 and what do you see but 30 particles birthed.

5. Lay down another Location POP, off to the side that is unconnected to the current one. Let's look at the constant birthing options now. Go to the Birthing tab and change Impulse Activation to 0 and Constant Birth Rate to 1. You are now looking at birthing on a per second basis. Reset the simulation and check the popup. You have birthed 1 particle as expected. Advance to frame 29 and check it again. You still have just 1 particle. As you have set the rate to 1, you are birthing 1 particle per second, which is every 24 frames because the frames per second is at the default of 24. (You might want to check what your FPS is set to in the Global Animation Options window.) Advance one more frame to 24 and check the popup window. You now have two particles.

So, when working with particles, remember that there are two rate options to choose from and, depending on the project at hand, it is likely that one or the other is more meaningful to use. Also remember to set the Activation field for the option not used to a value of 0 or you will be inadvertently using both methods.

8. Particle Operators (POPs)

Select a Source or Set a Context Source

Notice that there are four inputs on the Popnet node. These inputs can be used for referencing inside the network at the POPs level. For example, in the Source POP, the Geometry Source parameter says Use Parameter Values by default. With this selected, you use the SOP parameter field to navigate and choose the SOP you wish to use for the birthing source. As an alternative, you can change the Geometry Source parameter to First, Second, Third, or Fourth Context Geometry. These four choices correspond to the four inputs to the Popnet node. For example, you could connect a grid to the first input of the Popnet node and then use First Context Geometry in the Source POP to choose the grid for a birthing source. This is effectively no different than doing it the first way mentioned.

Select a Source

1. Lay down a Geometry object and jump into it. Drop a Grid SOP, which you will use for a birthing source. Lay down a Popnet and hop inside it.

2. Lay down a Source POP and click the + next to the SOP field to select a SOP node for a birthing source. Select the grid and press Accept. Go to the Attributes tab and change the Initial Velocity to Set Initial Velocity. Press play and you can see that particles are being birthed from the points that comprise the grid.

Set a Context Source

Delete the path reference in the SOP field so that it is blank again. Jump back up to the SOP level and now connect the grid node to the first input of the Popnet node. Jump back into the Popnet and change the Geometry Source to Use First Context Geometry. This tells the Source POP to go look for whatever is connected into the first input of the POP network of which it is a part and use the input as a birthing source. Press play and you see exactly the same thing as you did when selecting a source in the SOP field.

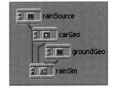

Figure 8.6
Example using context source inputs.

The latter method can sometimes be more visually informative. For example, let's say you have a particle system that is simulating rain falling from the sky and splashing off a car driving down the road. You lay down a Popnet, connect the birthing grid into the first input of the Popnet node, the car geometry into the second input, and the ground geometry into the third input. Now, it is easy to see that these three pieces of geometry are being used as part of the particle simulation. You can quickly visually identify that they are related. Figure 8.6 shows this network setup.

Each Particle Has Its Own Space

Just as every object has its own space and so has an origin where the X, Y, and Z axes meet, so too does each particle have its own unique space and associated axes as well. The axes are colored just as they are elsewhere in the package with x being red, y being green, and z being blue. Interesting things are possible because every particle has its own space, like the ability to apply unique transforms on a per particle basis. Figure 8.7 shows five particles with the display of particles origins turned on.

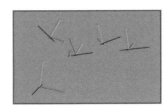

Figure 8.7
Several particles and their individual axes orientations.

A key concept to keep in mind when working with POPs or any other context in Houdini is to start simply when building a behavior and then build in the complexity. It often happens in production that you are working with complex files and run into an apparent dead-end. The first thing to always remember is to try to isolate what you are trying to do and determine whether it is achievable in a simple test-case scenario. This allows you, as much as possible, to remove all the other factors at play in the real file and just concentrate on the objective at hand. This also often has the benefit of making the test and tweak loop more responsive, as you don't have to wait for the complex calculations in the real file to run.

Z Axis Aligned to Velocity

A particle's Z axis is aligned to its velocity vector by default. In other words, a particle's Z axis is aligned to the direction in which it is traveling. In order to see a particle's axes indicator, you must turn on its display in the Pop viewport Display Options. On the Guides and Markers tab, toggle on the Particle Origin button. Before you close the Display Options window, check the size of the indicator display. If it is too small to see clearly, go to the Misc tab and increase the Scale Normal size until the axes are easily visible. Looking at Figure 8.7, you can easily determine which direction each of the particles is traveling by looking at the Z axis in blue.

At times, this auto-alignment can cause unwanted popping-like movement. For example, if you wanted to simulate a ball bouncing along the ground, this default behavior would cause problems. As the ball is falling down, the Z axis would point down, and when it started its bounce back up, the Z axis immediately flips to point in the upwards direction of travel. Let's create this example to see how this can be a problem and then look at one approach to solving it. Figure 8.8 shows you the result of this exercise.

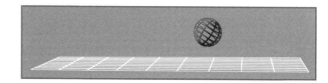

Figure 8.8
A colored ball bouncing on a grid.

1. Lay down a Geometry object and jump inside it.

2. Lay down a Grid SOP and change its Size in X to 20 and Size in Y to 5. This will be the ground geometry.

3. For the ball, drop an unconnected Sphere operation and change its Primitive Type to NURBs.

4. Give it some color so that you can easily see the rotation later. Append a Point operation to the sphere node and rename it ballColor. Change Keep Color to Add Color. Hold your pointer over the Color label and a little popup window tells you what the attribute name for each of the fields is. They are diffr, diffg, and diffb. This stands for diffuse red, diffuse green, and diffuse blue. Enter $TX < 0 in the diffr field and $TX > 0 in the diffb field. You can see that this has the effect of coloring red the half of the ball with TX values less than 0 and blue the half of the ball with TX values greater than 0.

5. Append a Popnet to the grid so that the grid node is piped into the first input of the popnet and then jump into the popnet.

6. Drop a Location POP and change its coordinates `locx` parameter to 10 and `locy` to –1. You'll birth a single particle at frame 1. Do you remember how? On the Birth tab, change the Constant Activation to 0, Impulse Birth Rate to 1, and Impulse Activation to `$FF == 1`. On the Attributes tab, change the Variance to 0, 0, 0, and then set Velocity in X to 2.

7. Append a Force POP and change its force in Y to –2.

8. Append a Collision POP and change the Geometry Source to Use First Context Geometry. This will use the first input of the Popnet node, which is the grid. On the Behavior tab, change its Behavior to Bounce on Collision. View the simulation and you can see you have a particle that looks like a ball bouncing along the ground. Figure 8.9 shows the state of the POP network.

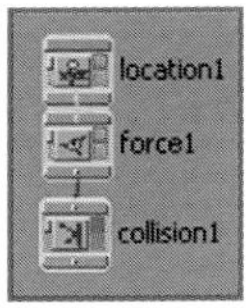

9. You can see the overall movement of the particle, but you can't yet see what is happening with its axes orientation. Turn on the display of the particle origins. Scale up their display if necessary. Close the Display Properties window and view the simulation.

Figure 8.9
The POP network thus far.

Remember that the blue axis is the Z axis. If you need a reminder as to which color corresponds to which axis, just look at the floating origin indicator in the lower-left corner of the viewport. Why is this default orientation a problem for the bouncing ball example? Move on to the next step to see.

10. Jump back up to SOPs and lay down a Copy operation. Connect the `ballColor` node to the left input and the pop-net node to the right input. Make sure the Display flag is on the copy node and reset and view the simulation. Notice how the ball seems to pop each time as it bounces up? This is because the ball is copied to the particle and is following its axes orientation. So, when the particle's Z axis snaps up as it travels upwards, so does the orientation of the ball. On the Copy tab of the copy node, toggle off the Rotate to Normal parameter. View the simulation and you can see that the ball's orientation is no longer popping; however, it would look better if it had some rotation as a real ball likely would. Your network should like Figure 8.10 at this point.

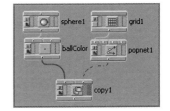

Figure 8.10
The SOP network thus far.

11. Append a Transform operation to the Copy operation and rename it to `rotateBall`. Set its Rotate Z field to `-$FF * 2`. View the simulation and you can see you are getting rotation; however, it is certainly not acting in the way that you desire. The problem is that the pivot point for the rotation is stationary at the origin of the object's space instead of at the center and following the ball geometry. Fix this by entering `$CEX`, `$CEY`, and `$CEZ` in the Pivot X, Y, and Z fields. These three local variables refer to the *centroid* of the input. So, by telling the pivot to go to the centroid of the input in X, Y, and Z, you are telling it to stay at the center of the ball geometry no matter where the ball geometry travels. View the simulation now and you have the beginnings of a ball bouncing with rotation.

12. Bring back in the ground geometry so you can see the whole simulation as it should be. Place a Merge SOP at the bottom of the network chain and pipe in the `rotateBall` and grid nodes. Play the simulation and you can see that the ball seems to be falling through the ground before bouncing back up. The reason this is happening is because the particle is what is actually colliding with the grid and it is much smaller and in the center of the ball geometry.

13. One way to fix this is to move the grid down to match the ball's radius. However, a more interesting method involves adjusting Collision Tolerance inside the Popnet. Jump back into it and look in the Collision tab of the collision node. Set this parameter to match the sphere's radius, which is 1. The reason this method is good deal crunchier in aggregate yumminess is because you can also use variables in the Collision Tolerance field. Say you made three particles and gave each of them a different $PSCALE attribute value. Copy a ball to each particle and each ball will bounce at the distance from the grid particular to its size. So, a small ball would go down farther than a larger ball. Now, that is nifty! Play the simulation and you have a ball bouncing along the ground (although it is going a little bit into the ground on each bounce). Jump back into SOPs and change Collision Tolerance to 1.3 and that should do it. Of course, you could further refine the animation by adding a little squash and stretch to the ball, diminishing the height of the bounce and the amount of rotation as it slows down, and more. At this point, your network should look like Figure 8.11.

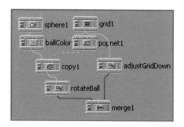

Figure 8.11
The completed SOP network.

$F and $FF

These are slightly different global variables that both relate to frame number. $F stands for integer frame number, whereas $FF stands for floating point frame number. An integer is a whole number like 1, 2, 3, and so on. A floating point number is a number than can contain a decimal like 1, 1.1, 1.2, and so on. As a particle simulation cooks forces between frames, it is more accurate to reference floating point frame numbers. So, it is recommended that you always use $FF inside the POP context. Remember that in order to see floating point frame numbers, you must bring up the Global Animation Options and toggle off the Integer Frame Values option.

POP Activation Field

Every POP node has an activation field that controls whether or not it affects the particles passing through it. It acts much like the node bypass toggle except that it is a string field and so you have the freedom to animate it and/or enter expressions. Whenever this field evaluates to greater than 0, it is considered true and is on. Whenever this field evaluates to 0 or less, it is considered false and is off. A common global variable often used in this field is $FF. For example, if you entered $FF<50 in the field, it would evaluate as true as long as the frame number was less than 50. So, whatever POP had this in its Activation field would be on for frames 1 through 49 and would be off at frame 50 and beyond. Another example that is often used is $FF==1, which means frame number equals 1. So this expression only evaluates as true at the first frame and so would be on only at that frame.

Popnet Oversampling

The Popnet node contains a parameter called Oversampling, which sets the number of time steps or times to cook per frame. By default, this is set to 1, which means that POPs will cook 1 time per frame. When at the default value of 1, the Impulse Birth Rate parameter, which is set in a number of generator type POPs, can be said to be birthing on a per frame basis. So, if you set Impulse Birth Rate to 50, 50 particles would be born per frame. It is important to remember that it technically refers to a per time step setting. For example, if you set Oversampling to 2 and left Impulse Birth Rate at 50, you would now be birthing 100 particles per frame because you have set the system to cook twice per frame. 50 particles would be born at frame 1, 50 particles would be born at frame 1.5, 50 frames particles would be born at frame 2 and then again at frame 2.5, and so on.

Initial Velocity, Force POP, Wind POP, and Fan POP

When a user is first learning about particles, there is often some confusion in choosing which force to use in which situation. Initial velocity, the Force POP, the Wind POP, and the Fan POP are similar in that they all affect the velocity of a particle; however, they each do so in a slightly different way and so are appropriate for different situations. Let's look at each now in order to minimize possible confusion.

Initial Velocity

Initial velocity is the velocity that particles are born with, basically a pre-existing velocity, like the velocity the ignited gunpowder imparts to a bullet. The bullet isn't being continuously pushed forward; it has been born with a certain velocity and will slow down over time if there is resistance, like the friction of air, to its motion. This velocity can either be set explicitly, inherited from a birthing source if one is being used, or a combination of the two. You can set these parameters on the Attributes tab of the relevant generator POPs.

Explicitly Set Initial Velocity

1. At the object level, ensure a geometry object exists and jump into it.

2. Drop a Popnet and dive into it.

3. Drop a Location POP. Reset the playbar and then play the simulation. You can see that a large number of points are flying off in all directions. If you can't see the simulation, you may need to home the viewport and/or turn on the display of points to more clearly see what is happening.

4. As always in Houdini, if you want to get to a clearer understanding of what is happening, simplify the conditions to zero in on what you are examining. In this case, go to the Birth tab and lower the Constant Birth Rate to 1. Now, one particle will be birthed per second. Press play and view the simulation.

5. You have fewer particles now but they are still flying off in various directions. Go to the Attributes tab and change Variance in X, Y, and Z to zero. View it again and now the particles don't move. In fact, it appears there is only one particle. In truth, you have the same number of particles as before. They just aren't going anywhere and so are overlapping each other. Turn on the display of point numbers and view the simulation from the beginning. Now you can see the point number zero by itself. Then, at frame 31, another particle is born and the number 1 is laid over the zero to accompany it.

6. Enter a value of -1 in the Velocity parameter's Y field and view the simulation. You may need to dolly out to see the system better. Each particle is now born with a velocity of negative one in the Y axis and so is instantly moving at that speed and in that direction when it is born. To verify this, RMB on the icon of the Location node and choose Spreadsheet.

7. You can see each of the particles has quite a few point attributes. MMB on the node's icon and you can see that each of the attributes listed in the popup window is available for viewing in the Geometry Spreadsheet pane. Narrow the range of display by LMB on the button that says Show/Hide Attributes and choose Hide All Attributes. Now, none of the attributes are shown. LMB again on the selector and choose v (for velocity) and then again on accel (for acceleration).

8. Reset the system and you can see that each particle is born moving at a velocity of −1 in the Y axis. You can also see that they are neither accelerating nor decelerating because all of the accel fields are zero. The reason they are staying at a constant velocity is because there are no additional forces speeding the particles nor slowing them down.

Inherit Initial Velocity

You have just seen how to explicitly set the initial velocity. If you are birthing from a source geometry, you can also set the particles to inherit their velocity from the source. If set to inherit velocity, POPs will look for the velocity and point normal attributes of the source geometry and use one of them to set the system's initial velocity. If the source doesn't have either attribute, no initial velocity will be set (or, a value of 0 will be set in all three axes). If the source contains only one of the attributes, that attribute will set the initial velocity. If the source contains both attributes, the velocity attribute will override the point normal attribute. Let's saunter through a little example to see these ideas in action.

1. Assuming you just finished the last example, delete the Location POP and lay down a Source POP. Before this POP will work, you need to create some geometry back up at the SOPs level and then come back to POPs and reference it.

2. Jump back up into SOPs and lay down a Grid SOP (unconnected to the Popnet). All of the defaults are fine. Jump back into the popnet.

3. On the Source tab of the Source POP, find the SOP parameter and select the grid you just created. Next, go to the Attributes tab and verify that Initial Velocity is set to the default Use Inherited Velocity. If necessary, reset and then view the simulation. Particles are being born; however, they aren't doing much of anything else. That is because they are inheriting velocity but there are no attributes to inherit.

4. Jump back up to the SOP level and MMB on the icon of the Grid node. You can see that there are no attributes listed. As stated earlier, the Source POP is looking for either a velocity or a point normal attribute. Give the grid a velocity attribute and see how it affects the simulation. Append a Point SOP to the grid node and rename it `addVelocity`. Go to the Particle tab and change Keep Velocity to Add Velocity. Next, RMB on the velocity label and choose Delete Channels. Now set the Y axis field to 1. You have just created a velocity point attribute for every point in the grid. If you scrub through the frame range, you can see the grid isn't actually moving anywhere. You didn't animate it up in Y with a value of 1. You just created a point attribute called v (or velocity) and gave it a value of 1. This is basically just a characteristic that each point now has that POPs can read and use for particle velocity.

5. Drop into the popnet and change the source SOP to the point operation you just created. View the simulation and you can see the particles are now flying up in the positive Y axis.

6. You can do the same thing with a point normal attribute. Go back up to SOPs and append another point operation and rename it `addPointNormal`. On the Standard tab, change Keep Normal to Add Normal. RMB on the Normals label and choose Delete Channels. Then enter a value of 0.1 in the Y field. MMB on the node's icon and you can see you now have two point attributes being v (for velocity) and N (for normal). Your network editor should now look like Figure 8.12.

   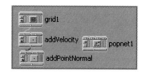

   Figure 8.12
   The SOP network thus far.

   RMB on the `addPointNormal` node and choose Spreadsheet. Hide all Attributes and then select the v and N attributes for viewing. You can now see that every point has these attributes and the values you set for them.

7. For now, toggle on the bypass flag of the `addVelocity` node so that the popnet won't see it. MMB on the `addPointNormal` node and you should no longer see the v attribute listed. That is because you bypassed and are no longer cooking the node that added the velocity attribute. Jump into the popnet and change the Source POP to birth from the `addPointNormal` node. Reset the simulation and view it. The particles are now going up in Y at a slower velocity. POPs is reading in the point normal attribute and using it to set the initial velocity.

8. Now jump back up to SOPs and toggle off the bypass flag of the `addVelocity` node. Go back into the popnet and view the system. The particles are now going up faster again at a velocity of positive 1 in Y. This illustrates the fact that if POPs finds both the v and N point attributes in the source geometry, the v attribute will override the N attribute.

Why are both attributes able to be inherited instead of just one? They seem to be functioning similarly in this example. Let's change the example a little and see how each attribute can be helpful in its own way.

9. Jump back up to the SOP level and delete the grid node. Lay down a Sphere SOP, change its Primitive Type to NURBs, and connect it in place of the grid. Make sure you connect it to the left input of the `addVelocity` node.

10. Ensure the Display and Render flags are on the `addPointNormal` node. Turn on the display of point normals in the viewport. You may have to zoom in on a particular point to see its normal. Alternatively, change the 0.1 to 1 and you will now visually see that all the point normals are straight up in the world Y axis. If you ran the particle simulation from this source, particles would be born from each point and travel upward as you just did previously with the grid. RMB on the Normals label of this node and choose Revert to Defaults. Notice the difference in the point normals. Each now juts out as if running from the sphere's origin through the point. Figure 8.13 shows the this.

Figure 8.13
The NURBs sphere with default point normals displayed.

11. Toggle on the bypass flag of the `addVelocity` node so it doesn't override the N attribute. Jump into the popnet and view the simulation. Particles are now shooting off in all directions instead of just going up in Y.

12. Next, let's change the example a bit and see how inheriting the velocity can be interesting. Jump back up to SOPs and insert a Transform operation after the sphere. Place the Display and Render flags on it. Change Pivot in X to 2 to offset the rotation a bit. Enter `sin($F*5)*50` in the Rotate Y field. Scrub through the animation and you can see the sphere is now swinging back and forth.

13. Go to the `addVelocity` node and toggle off the bypass flag. Then RMB on the Velocity label and choose Revert to Defaults. Each point is now set back to whatever its default is coming into that node. RMB on the node's icon and choose Spreadsheet. Scrub through some frames and you can see that velocity is zero across the board. So, even though the sphere is moving around, there is nothing yet that is measuring that movement.

14. Introducing the loveable and powerful Trail SOP! Insert one after the transform node. You will use this SOP to measure the movement of each point in the sphere and assign an appropriate velocity. Change the Result Type parameter to Compute Velocity. RMB on this node's icon and choose Spreadsheet. Scrub through some frames and you can see it has measured each point's individual movement and assigned the calculated velocity. Can you say, "Yum Yum?" Your network should now look like Figure 8.14.

Figure 8.14
The completed SOP network.

15. Jump into the popnet and run the simulation. Amazing sweetness cubed, Batman! The particles now inherit the velocity of the point at the time of their birth. The simulation mimics how sweat would fly off as you shake your head in mental exhaustion.

Ye Old Force POP

Oh, Force POP

Oh, light of the seven heavens

Do grace us with your celestial power

Do make our simulations flourish and flower

This operation applies a global directional force to the simulation and is often used to simulate gravity. In order to better understand how this POP works, let's go through a relatively painless refresher on basic physics.

```
Force = Mass x Acceleration
```

So, this is equivalent to saying

```
Acceleration = Force/Mass
```

Gravitational acceleration everywhere on the earth's surface is 9.8 meters per second squared (m/s^2). As Galileo proved long ago, one of the interesting things about terrestrial physics is that two free falling bodies of different masses will fall at the same rate (assuming no outside influences like air resistance).

Suppose you have two particles floating in the air next to each other and you want to add a force that simulates the behavior of gravity to them. As gravitational acceleration is basically constant anywhere a terrestrial being would simulate, it doesn't really matter if you use 9.8 or some other value, so long as it is constant in its effects to a mass's acceleration. With that in mind, you can just use a Y value of –1 to simulate the gravitational force. Let's set up this test case now.

1. Lay down a Popnet inside of a geometry object and jump inside it.

2. Drop a Location POP and rename it `lessMass`. Change its X Coordinate to –0.25 to scoot it over a bit. Go to the Attributes tab and change the Variance in all three axes to 0. Next go to the Birth tab and change Constant Activation to 0 because you won't be birthing particles based on a per second measure. Change Impulse Birth Rate to 1. To keep the test simple, you only want to birth one particle. Change Impulse Activation to `$FF= =1`. The = = signs is the correct syntax for saying equals. If you try using only one equals sign to signify equality, you will get an error. The Houdini expression language mimics the syntax of Boolean operations in the C programming language. So, whenever the floating point frame number equals one, this expression evaluates to true and returns a value of 1. Otherwise, it evaluates as false and returns a value of 0. Reset the simulation and play it through. The result of your efforts is that one particle is born on frame one only. To find out more about these operations, check out Chapter 6.

3. Append a Property POP and toggle on the Mass parameter. RMB on the Mass label and choose Delete Channels and enter a value of 2.

4. Now box select both of these POPs in the Network Editor and copy and paste them using the Ctrl+C and then Ctrl+V technique. Rename the newly created location POP to `moreMass`.

5. In the moreMass node, change its X Coordinate field from –0.25 to 0.25 to push it off to the other side. In the property POP below this node, change its Mass from 2 to 4.

6. Now you want to bring these two network branches together so that you can add a force that will apply to both. Lay down a Collect POP and wire in both of the property nodes. The Collect POP functions similarly in POPs as the Merge SOP does in SOPs. Your popnet should look like Figure 8.15.

7. Append a Force operation and set its Y field to –1. Home the viewport and zoom out enough to see both of them fall. Reset the simulation and view it. Reflecting the organization of the Network Editor, from the homed view, the viewport shows the particle with less mass on the left and the particle with more mass on the right. You will notice that the two particles are falling at different rates… and this, as discussed, does not reflect the reality of gravity.

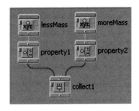

Figure 8.15
The POP network thus far.

However, this default scenario of the Force POP does reflect the idea of inertia and the fact that it is harder to change the state of motion of a larger mass than a smaller mass. Notice in your simulation that the particle with smaller mass gets moving much faster than the one with larger mass. This could be used, for example, to simulate the difference between a force trying to move a bike and a bus. View the Geometry Spreadsheet for this node and you can see that each particle has a constant, though different, acceleration.

Now, let's move on to set up a force that reflects gravity as discussed earlier. First, let's analyze the situation using the equations just discussed.

Acceleration= Force/Mass

The first particle's acceleration is –0.5 which is –1(Force)/2(Mass). The second particle's acceleration is –0.25 which is –1(Force)/4(Mass). You don't want to explicitly set acceleration, so you have to determine how to manipulate the other two variables to get a common constant acceleration. The force is the same for both particles, so that isn't the problem. The only variable left is Mass, which differs between the particles. Make Mass constant for both particles. On the force node, toggle on Override Mass and leave it at the default value of 1. This overrides the Mass attribute of all particles and sets it to 1 only for this node. Elsewhere in the network either before or after this node, Mass is equal to what was set in the property operations. Acceleration is now whatever force is set to because –1(Force)/1(Mass) equals –1. If force were changed to –10, you would have –10/1, which is –10.

Reset the simulation and view it. Notice that the two particles now fall at the same rate, which mimics gravitational acceleration on earth. Change the Force in Y from –1 to –7 and view the simulation. The particles now fall faster but still at the same rate. As you have demonstrated, overriding mass to a constant value across the board for any particles being affected has the result of creating a force that simulates gravity. Remember also that whether or not you are trying to imitate gravity or moving objects with different inertial properties, the acceleration of any particular particle is constant and will therefore continue to gain more velocity over time so long as no opposing forces are present to slow it down.

The Wind POP

The Wind operator functions similarly to the Force POP but does have an important distinction. The wind operation will only affect a particle up to the velocity of the wind itself. For example, if you have a stationary particle and then apply a wind strength of 5, the particle will never go faster than 5. In addition, its acceleration will slow as it approaches its maximum velocity. As you have seen, this is different than the Force POP because that operation will cause a particle to continuously accelerate based on the strength of the applied force. As a practical example, suppose a tangle of tumbleweed is blowing down a flat, empty highway just outside of Yuma, Arizona. The wind strength is at a constant 5 mph. The tumbleweed may be blown as fast as 5 mph but it won't ever be blown faster than that.

The Fan POP

The Fan POP acts similarly in that it does impart velocity to a particle. The distinction here is that this operation only functions within the area that the cone faces and within a certain distance. In addition, the cone has its strongest effect at the center and falls off towards the edges. This mimics the behavior of a real fan in that, if you stand right in front of it, you get a blast of air, and, if you stand off to the side a bit, you get more of a little breeze. As a simple exercise to verify this behavior, step through the following:

1. Lay down a Geometry Object and jump into it.

2. Now lay down a Grid SOP and change its Size in X and Y to 10. This will be your birthing source.

3. Next lay down a Popnet (unconnected to the grid) and jump inside it.

4. Drop a Source POP and choose the grid you just created for the birthing source. Go to the Birth tab and set Constant Activation to 0. Change Impulse Activation to $FF==1 and Impulse Birth Rate to 100. You have set it so that 100 particles will be born on frame 1 only. Next, go to the Attributes tab and change Initial Velocity to Set Initial Velocity and then change Variance in all axes to 0. Play through the simulation and you will see that you have 100 particles being born and not going anywhere.

5. Append a Fan POP. On the Location tab, enter -5 in the Y Origin field. Change the Direction to 0 1 0 in order to point the fan upwards in Y. Reset the simulation and play it through. You can see that the Fan POP is strongest in the center of the affected region, with the influence falling off as you move towards the edges of the fan's cone. Figure 8.16 shows this result.

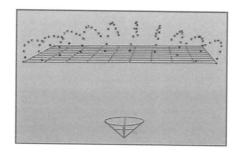

Figure 8.16
The fan pop has the strongest effect in the center of its cone.

Particle Charge

Charge is an important attribute that can be used in the context of certain POPs to determine the manner in which a force is applied. Basically, it controls whether a force is considered an attracting or repulsing one. It is important to remember that charge is only meaningful within the context of the POP that is using it. For example, using an Attractor POP will make positively charged particles move toward the attractor geometry (an attracting force); however, using an Interact POP will make positively charged particles move away from each other (a repulsive force). A Property POP can be used, among other things, to explicitly modify a particle's charge. Let's walk through a short example of using charge.

1. Lay down a Geometry Object and jump into it. Drop a Grid SOP, which will be the source geometry. Change its Size in X and Y to 2 and adjust it up in Y 1 unit. Turn on the footprint flag for this node.

2. Next, drop a Sphere SOP off to the side (not connected to the grid) and this will be the attractor geometry. Change the Primitive Type to Polygon. Set the Radius in all axes to 0.5. Type sin($F*1.5) * 0.5 in the Center X field. Change the frequency to 4. Hold the Shift key and then turn on this node's footprint flag (using Shift allows you to have the footprint flag on both nodes at once).

3. Drop a Popnet. This time use the context geometry approach to referencing. Connect the grid into the first input of the Popnet and the sphere into the second input. Then, jump into the Popnet.

4. Lay down a Source POP and change the Source Geometry to First Context Geometry. This will reference the first input of the Popnet node, which is the grid. Change Constant Activation to 0 to turn off birthing by seconds. Change Impulse Birth Rate to 10 so that it will birth 10 particles per frame.

5. Append an Attractor POP and change its Geometry Source to Second Context Geometry. The Scale parameter is at its default of 1, which means that it will create an attracting force. Always make certain that the Display and Render flags are where they should be when you run a simulation. Do so now and you can see that particles are being born; however, they aren't doing much of anything else. The reason is that the Attractor POP looks for geometry with forces attached to it and you don't yet have that.

6. Jump back up to SOPs and insert a Point SOP between the sphere and popnet nodes. Pop up a Parameters window so that you can have access to them even when inside the popnet by RMB on the point node and choosing Parameters. Go to the Force tab and change Keep Radius to Add Radius. This parameters allows you to set the radius of effect for each point. Next change Keep Radial F to Add Radial F. This allows you to set the amount of force directed toward each attractor point.

7. Jump back into the popnet and run the simulation. Aha! You still aren't seeing any movement of the particles. That is because you have a radial force of 0 set in the point operation parameters. Change the Add Radial F parameter from 0 to 1. Run the simulation; the particles are now birthed from the grid and then get powerfully sucked into the attractor sphere, shot out the other side, and then drawn back into and through the sphere again and on and on in that cycle.

8. In the attractor node on the Attractor tab, toggle on the Show attractor radius in guide. Reset the simulation and home the viewport. This shows a visual guide of the radius of effect around each point in the attractor geometry. In the point operation's Parameter window that you have up, drag the Add Radius slider from its default of 1 to 0 and you can see in the viewport its effect. Enter a value of 0.01. Run the simulation and the attractor points now have smaller areas of influence.

9. Just for fun, jump back up to SOPs and append an Add operation to the popnet. Go to the Polygon tab and change to By Group. Run the simulation and you get a pretty sweet-looking abstract design. The Add operation is creating geometry by adding edges between the points. Figure 8.17 shows the SOP network at this point.

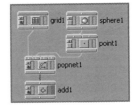

Figure 8.17
The SOP network thus far.

10. Right now, all of the particles are connected in kind of a jumble; however, you can set it up so that each point of origin on the birthing geometry has its own isolated set of points that are connected with edges. This can be easily understood visually. Change the Add parameter from All Points to Skip Every Nth Point. Next Change N (number) parameter from the default of 2 to 100. Now reset and run the simulation. Notice how all particles born from a specific point on the birthing grid are connected and not connected to particles born from other locations on the grid. How do you know what number to enter here? You simply had to look at the number of birthing points on the grid and place that number here. You could even use the npoints() expression so that N would automatically represent the number of points in the grid even if you went back later and changed its number of rows or columns.

11. You have seen how the Attractor pop can create an attracting force. It can also create a repulsing force and let's look at that now. Jump into the popnet and change the Attractor Scale from 1 to −1. Jump back up and play the simulation. Interesting things abound, eh? It starts to look like a crazy shock of hair or maybe seaweed under the ocean blue.

12. Let's make one final tweak to see another interesting look. In the sphere operation, cut and paste the expression from the Center X field to the Center Y field. You will likely need to delete the channel in the Center X field by RMB on the field and choose Delete Channels. Make sure that its value is also 0. Reset and run the simulation and now you get an interesting flower-looking creation. Figure 8.18 shows this geometry.

Collision Detection

It can sometimes be tricky to get particles to detect collisions as accurately as you might want. Getting the best possible accuracy in your collisions is usually a process of tweaking and often involves a tradeoff between speed and accuracy. Let's walk through an exercise to understand this process more clearly. In this example, you will create a drinking glass object and then bounce around particles inside with the goal of keeping them in and not letting them erroneously fall through the glass geometry. Figure 8.19 shows the glass with particles sloshing about inside.

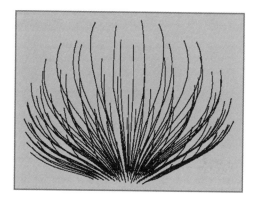

Figure 8.18
The result is some flower-like geometry.

1. Lay down a Geometry Object and jump into it.

2. First, let's create the glass geometry that will be used for collision. Drop a Tube operation and change its Primitive Type to Polygon and its Height to 2.

3. You want to cap one end of the tube so that you can trap particles inside the volume. With your pointer over the viewport, home the view and then select a Polycap operation. Press the w hotkey to go into wireframe shading mode. Press the 2 hotkey to choose the edge selection mask and choose one of the edges along the bottom rim of the tube as shown in Figure 8.20.

Figure 8.19
The glass with particles sloshing about.

Once you have the edge selected, RMB to complete the operation. Press w again to go back to your chosen shading mode and you can see that you have added a bottom to the tube.

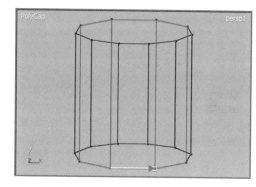

Figure 8.20
A bottom edge selected.

4. You now have a reasonable semblance of a drinking glass, which you will animate to rock back and forth. Append a Transform SOP and rename it rotateGlass. Go to frame 20 and set a keyframe on Rotate Z, leaving the value at 0. This will make it so there is a small delay before the glass starts to rock back and forth. Go to frame 100 and set another keyframe and change its value to −30. Next, go to frame 200 and set another keyframe with a value of 35. Finally, go to frame 300 and set another keyframe with a value of −40. Play the animation and you can see that you have a glass rocking back and forth.

5. Now let's create the birthing geometry. Drop an unconnected Circle SOP. Change its Primitive Type to Polygon, its Orientation to the ZX plane, its Radius in X and Y to 0.9, and its Divisions to 20.

6. Append a Convert operation and change the Convert Type to Mesh. As you can see, you added detail in the middle of the circle so that you can birth particles from those points.

7. Add a Duplicate operation and change its Number of Copies to 9. Set its Translate in Y to –0.1. You have created an area of points from which you can birth particles to smash around in the glass.

8. Append a Null node and rename it birthGeo. The null operation doesn't add anything to the network and is used here for organizational purposes only.

9. You can't readily play with POPs without adding a popnet. Do so now and connect the birthGeo node to its first input and the rotateGlass node to its second input. Your network should now look like Figure 8.21.

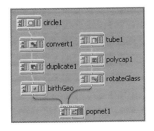

Figure 8.21
The SOP network thus far.

10. Jump into the popnet and add a Source POP. Change the Geometry Source to Use First Context Geometry. You want to birth one particle for every point in the birth geometry at frame 1 only. On the birth tab, change Constant Activation to 0. Change Impulse Birth Rate to $FF= =1. Enter npoints("../../birth_geo") in the Impulse Birth Rate field. This is an expression that returns the number of points existing at the SOP specified in the channel reference. The path you specified says to jump out of the POP in which the expression resides (../), then jump up one level to SOPs (../), and then find the SOP called birth_geo. On the Attributes tab, set the Variance to 0 in all axes.

11. Append a Force operation and set it to –0.5 in Y.

12. Append an Interact POP and change Particle Radius to Use Supplied Radius. Then specify a Radius of 0.05. This will get the particles to push away from each other as they bounce around the glass.

13. Append a Drag POP and change its Scale to 0.3. This will cause the particles to slow down over time as if being acted on by resistance.

14. Drop a Collision POP and change its Geometry Source to Use Second Geometry. On the Behavior tab, change the Behavior to Bounce on Collision and change Gain Normal to 0.5 so that the particles will lose energy each time they collide. Turn off the Template flag for the source node, as the display of the birth geometry is just obstructing your view of the particles. Make sure to leave the Template flag on for the collision node. You may also want to turn on the display of points in the viewport to more easily see the particles movement. Your POP network should look like Figure 8.22.

Figure 8.22
The POP network thus far.

View the simulation and you can see that you are losing all of your particles. Not exactly what you were hoping to see. One problem is that you are using geometry that is rotating, but you are using a detection algorithm meant for stationary objects (not translating, not rotating, and not scaling). On the Collision tab, change the Hint to Translating Geometry and view the simulation. That didn't seem to help much. Change Collision Tolerance to 0.1. This will cause the detection algorithm to look out for what is around each particle as it moves about. That seems to help a little bit, but you still have a long way to go. Set the Collision Tolerance to 1. This seems to help capture a few more but nothing startling. Go ahead and set it back to 0.1. On the Behavior tab, set the Oversampling to 20. This means that POPs will cook 20 times per frame to check for collisions, which should yield a more accurate result than just cooking once per frame. In this case, it didn't seem to make much of a difference. Go ahead and set it back to 1. On the Collisions tab, let's try the other Hint option, which is Deforming Geometry. Notice that as soon as you choose it, you get a red flag on your collision node. This is because, as the option says, you can only use triangular geometry for an input.

15. Jump back up to the SOP level and change the Connectivity of the tube node to Triangles. On the Polycap node, toggle on the Triangulate Caps option. If you put the Display flag on this node, you will see that your geometry is now composed entirely of triangles.

16. Jump down into pops again and view the simulation. Funky Fontaine, Danny! You are making progress! Crank Collision Tolerance back up to 1 and view the simulation. Yeehaa! You seem to only be losing a few particles now.

17. As there are only a few particles escaping the glass, let's use another method to rid ourselves of their errant behavior rather than fiddle endlessly with the collision geometry and parameters. Jump back up to SOPs and let's determine a clever way to do it.

    You could manually select them for deletion in the viewport, but that isn't very procedural, as any changes made later will likely result in different particles escaping the glass. A better way might be to first make the cup a closed volume, and then group the particles that are inside the cup, and finally delete any particles that aren't in the group. Using this method, no matter what changes you make to the POP network, you will always be deleting all particles that mange to escape. Let's do that now.

18. Put the Display flag back on the polycap1 node. Now, with your pointer over the viewport, bring up the Tab menu and type polyc to narrow down to your desired operation. Before you LMB select it, hold the Shift key down and then, while holding the Shift key down, LMB PolyCap. Make sure you are using the edge selection option and select an edge along the top rim of the glass so that you cap that end. Once you have made the correct selection, go ahead and RMB to finished the operation. You will notice in the Network Editor that you have laid down another Polycap operation and also that this one has branched off instead of being inserted into the network chain. Holding Shift while selecting it in the Tab menu enabled that functionality. One last thing, go ahead and toggle on Triangulate Caps, just as you did with the bottom earlier. Using the shading mode of your choice, tumble around in the viewport and you should see that the glass is now capped at both ends.

19. You have just created an enclosed volume that you can now use as criteria for grouping based on whether the particles are inside the glass or outside the glass. However, before you do that, you need to ensure that this bounding volume animates just like the glass does. RMB on the icon of the rotateGlass node and choose Reference Copy. This creates a node that has all of its parameters channel referenced back to the original. That way, anytime you make changes to the original, the copy automatically updates as well. Play through the frame range and you can see that you now have an enclosed volume that is animating just as the glass is.

20. In the Network Editor, lay down a Group SOP and connect the left input to the popnet1 node. MMB on the right input and a popup tells you it is expecting to wire in a bounding object. Connect the right input to the rotateGlass2 node. Let's create a group called inside by typing that in the Group Name field. Change the Entity to Points as that is what you will be grouping. Check Bounding and notice that all the options below are unavailable. You must first toggle on Enable to get access to the associated parameters. Change the Bounding Type to Bounding Object (points only). This is telling the Group SOP to go look at what is coming into its right input and see if it can determine an inside and an outside. If it can, it will then group all points found on the inside of the volume. Had you not capped the top of the glass before sending it into this operation, your grouping would have failed because you would not have been using an enclosed volume.

21. Next, append a delete operation in the Network Editor and (as always when adding a node in the Network Editor) ensure that the Display flag is on this node. To the far right of the Group field, LMB the triangle and select the inside group. Change the Operation to Delete Non-Selected and change Entity to Points. So, you have just set it so that any points coming into this node that are not a part of the inside group will get deleted, which is just spanktastically what you want to happen!

22. Let's add back the display of the glass so that you can see the particles bouncing around inside it. Append a Merge SOP and pipe in the delete node.

8. Particle Operators (POPs)

23. Go into wireframe shading and place the Display flag back up on the Polycap. This geometry wouldn't be that good to display because all the edges will get in the way of seeing the behavior of the particle system. RMB on the tube node and choose Reference Copy. Set the new reference copy's Primitive Type to Primitive. This will give you a much simpler geometry to view in the merge.

24. You need to add the rotation that your original glass has to this chain also. Select the `rotateGlass1` node and press Ctrl+C and Ctrl+V to copy and paste the node. You have now created a second reference copy which, just like the first, uses channel references to follow any changes made to the original node. Wire the new tube into the new `rotateGlass2` and then wire that into the merge at the bottom. Place the Display and Render flags on the merge node and view the simulation. You can now see the particle system clearly through a simplified version of the glass geometry.

25. You may see a yellow flag on the merge node indicating that inputs have mismatched attributes. It doesn't really matter in this case; however, to get rid of the warning, insert an Attribute SOP between the delete and the merge nodes. On the Point tab, enter an * (asterisk) in the Delete Attributes field and do the same on the Primitive tab. The final SOP network is shown in Figure 8.23.

26. Marvel at your skill and ingenuity!

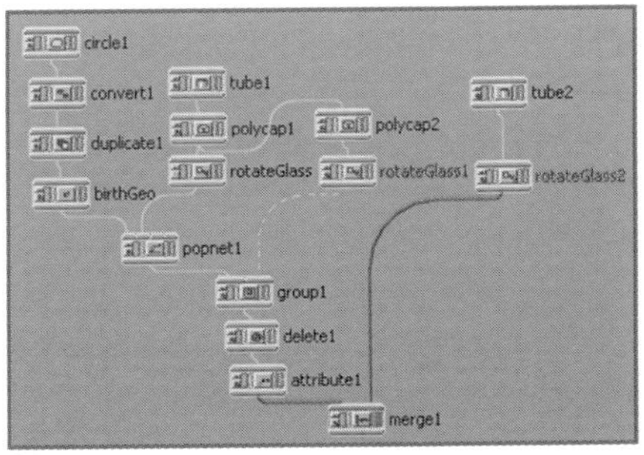

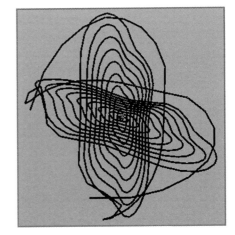

Figure 8.23
SOP network at the completion of the collision exercise.

The Particle Primitive

A particle primitive is just a collection of points with associated point attributes. These attributes are just characteristics that have been imported, created, and/or modified and then applied to each point as the simulation dictates. Some common attributes that particle systems use are velocity, life, and position. These attributes are initially classified as point attributes and work just like point attributes created in other areas of the package. See the Geometry Types section in the software help for more detail about the various types available in Houdini.

A particle primitive is defined as all particles birthed from a single source. Some examples of birthing sources are the Source, Location, and Split POPs. So, if your POP network is using three birthing sources, you are working with three particle primitives inside a single network. This is helpful to know because you can easily separate out the various primitives for individual modifications or rendering in layers, among other things. Let's walk through a simple example of separating out particle primitives for specific modification. Figure 8.24 shows the interesting result of this exercise.

Figure 8.24
Two particle primitives.

1. Throw down a new Geometry Object and jump into it. Drop a Circle SOP, which you will use as the birthing source. Change the Primitive Type to NURBs Curve so that you have more points to birth from and change Divisions to 30 to get even more points to comprise the circle. Also, change its Orientation to the ZX plane so that it lays flat relative to the default homed view.

2. RMB on the output of the circle node and append a Popnet SOP. You now have a Popnet that has geometry fed into its first input.

3. Jump into the Popnet and lay down a Source POP and change the Geometry Source to Use First Context Geometry. Next, go to the Birth tab and change Constant Birth Rate to 30. Play the simulation and you see particles being birthed along the circle but not doing much anything else.

4. Let's give it a little more interest by appending an Interact POP. Play the simulation again and you see a simulation that resembles a pinwheel with particles being born and then flying outward due to inter-repulsive force added by the Interact operation.

   MMB this node and you can see Primitive 0, which means that you have one particle primitive whose number is 0, which is comprised of a number of points (that number depending on where you are in the simulation and so the number of particles that have been birthed).

5. Copy and paste the source node so that you now have two birthing nodes. On the new node, go to the Source tab and change its Geometry Source to Use Second Context Geometry. Play the simulation and you will see a startling lack of particles. The problem right now is that you don't have anything running into the second input of the Popnet SOP.

6. Jump up to SOPs and MMB on the output of the circle node and choose a Transform operation. This will branch the operation rather than inserting it into the network chain. Change the Rotate Z value to 90 and wire this node into the second input of the Popnet SOP. Now, the second source node will be able to find a Second Context Geometry, which is the circle rotated on its side.

7. Jump back into POPs and let's see what you have. Currently, the second source node isn't being affected by the Interact operation because they aren't connected in any way. RMB on the output of the first source and insert a Collect POP. Then wire the second source node into it as well. Make sure the Cook flag is on the last node in the chain and let's view the simulation. You now have particles being born and flying out from each of the birth circles, one vertical and one horizontal. Figure 8.25 shows what your POP network should look like at this point.

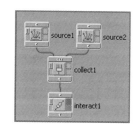

8. MMB on the Interact POP and you will see Primitive 0 and Primitive 1 listed. You are now working with 2 particle primitives that can very easily be split apart if desired. Oh, and you do desire it, my Primitivesssss!

Figure 8.25
The POP network thus far.

9. Jump up to SOPs and play the simulation. Turn on the display of points to better see them if needed. You are getting closer but it still doesn't look like the picture at the beginning of this exercise. In addition, you still haven't made use of the fact that you are working with two particle primitives.

   Append a Delete SOP to the Popnet node and ensure that the Display flag is on. In the Group field, enter 1 and play the simulation. You are only seeing the particles birthed from the horizontal circle, which is being used by the first source POP, which... drum roll please... is defined as particle primitive 0. So, putting the 1 in the group field told the delete operation to delete all particles that are a member of particle primitive 1.

10. Next, append an Add SOP and go to the Polygons tab. Toggle on By Groups and see what has automagically happened! The Add operation has created an edge between each point in the order that they are born. It is basically doing a grade school version of connect the dots just you like used to do. Can you say Supah Fly? I knew you could!

11. You are getting ever closer now. In the Network Editor, box-select both the delete and add nodes and then copy and paste them. In the new delete node, change the Group field to 0 so that you are now deleting the particle primitive 0.

12. Finally, lay down a Merge and pipe in both add nodes. Put your Display flag on the Merge and play the simulation for one last rousing performance. The interference between the two patterns creates an interesting moiré effect. Now, just hook up Houdini to a video projector and you have a good beginning to the trippy visuals needed at any banging soiree. Figure 8.26 shows the completed SOP network.

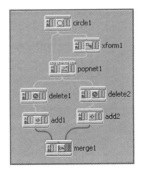

Figure 8.26
The completed SOP network.

POP Events and the `Popevent()` Expression

That trusty old codger Webster defines an event as "something that happens" and that works nicely for your purposes. A pop event is something that happens in POPs. Well, because a lot of things happen in POPs, you should be more specific. An event is an occurrence that can include a particle collision, change of state, or most anything else that can be detected about a particle. The reason an event is useful is because other POPs can be waiting for the event to occur before adding their input to the simulation. This is kind of like a stream of cars sitting idly at a red light waiting for the state of the light to turn green (the POP event). When the light turns green, the stream of cars surges forward, though in an orderly and lawful fashion. The cars (or, more precisely, the people driving the cars) were waiting on a particular event and then acted upon detecting that event.

In order to create an event, you must use either the Collision or Event POPs. Each of them has the ability to signal the rest of the particle system that an event has occurred. The Collision POP creates an event based solely on the occurrence of a collision. The Event POP creates an event whenever the defined rule (or expression) evaluates to greater than 0 for any of its input particles. You can check to see if an event has occurred by MMB on any of the node's in the network and look for a section called Events, which will contain the name of the event.

Now that your facile imaginations have created a POP event, how do you detect it? There is an expression called `popevent()` that is used to detect the named event. This expression is specific to POPs and so only works in this context. In the traffic example above, perhaps the `popevent()` expression would be `popevent(greenlight)` and so would be monitoring the simulation looking for an event called `greenlight`. The `popevent()` expression returns a 0 when it evaluates as false (whenever it isn't detecting the stated event) and returns a 1 when it evaluates as true (when it is detecting the stated event). It is important to understand that the `popevent()` expression is evaluated at every cook. So, in your traffic example again, just because the light turned green doesn't necessarily mean the cars can go forward indefinitely. At some point, the light will turn red again, the `popevent(greenlight)` will then again evaluate as false and the cars will stop.

Now that you know how to both create and detect a POP event, how do you put it to practical use? Basically, anyplace where a toggle of 0 to 1 would be useful, the `popevent()` expression can be useful. With that in mind, it is easy to see how it could be put to use in the Activation field for a particular POP. Using the traffic example, let's say that a Force operation is what will push the cars forward. If you entered `popevent(greenlight)` in the Force's Activation field, you would only see the force's input in the simulation when the `greenlight` POP event was being detected. Let's walk through a short exercise to see an interesting use for a POP event.

POP Event Generated with a Collision POP

One way to create a POP event is by using a Collision POP and setting it to generate an event upon collision. In this exercise, you will create a simulation that mimics how a meteor would impact the earth and kick up debris. You'll create a POP event every time the meteor collides with the ground and use that event to birth debris.

1. Lay down a Geometry Object and jump into it.

2. You will use a grid to simulate the ground as your collision geometry. Lay down a Grid operation and change its size in X to 16 and size in Y to 5 and its center in Y to −1.

3. Drop a Popnet and make sure that the grid is connected to the popnet's first input so that you can use the context method of referencing inside the popnet.

4. Jump inside the popnet and lay down a Location operation. On the Location tab, change its Coordinate in X to −8 and its Coordinate in Y to 0.5. On the Birth tab, change Constant Activation to 0, Impulse Birth Rate to 1, and Impulse Activation to $FF==1. On the Attributes tab, change the Velocity in X to 4 and Velocity in Y to −1. Change the Variance in all fields to 0. One particle will be born at frame 1 and will move down and to the right (when viewed from the default home axes orientation). This is your meteor of "Near Total Destruction"… It could not be considered total destruction because you know cockroaches will survive.

5. Append a Force POP and change its Force in Y to −1.

6. Append a Drag and leave it at the defaults. Later, you will come back and adjust this to give it a more realistic behavior.

7. Append a Collision and change Geometry Source to Use First Context Geometry. This will use the popnet's first input, which is the grid. Its pink template flag is on, which will enable you to see the collision grid in the viewport. If at some point you can no longer see the grid, remember that the template flag must be on in order to see it. Reset and run the simulation. The meteor flies down, strikes the earth, and dies. That isn't terribly interesting. Go to the Behavior tab and change the Behavior to Bounce on Collision. View the simulation again and you can see that the meteor seems to continue bouncing more like a rubber ball than a big solid piece of space junk. Let's turn down the amount of energy that it maintains from its collisions. Change Gain Normal from 1 to 0.5 and view the simulation. You don't want it to bounce forever. So, let's change Final Behavior to Stop on Collision and view the simulation. Notice that the Minimum Impulse value of 1 is reached too quickly because the particle seems to abruptly stop. Turn down Minimum Impulse to 0.01 and view the simulation. Now, the meteor seems to have a smoother deceleration; however, it slows very quickly. You will fix this by adjusting the drag in just a second. Finally, type `splitBirth` in the Collision Event field. Now, every time the particle collides with the grid geometry, an event will be generated called `splitBirth`. Remember that the event will only last for the duration of the cook in which the particle is in a state of collision. Basically, when the meteor bounces back up, it is no longer in a state of collision with the grid and so the event will cease to be generated. Your network should now look like the one in Figure 8.27.

8. Leaving the Display and Render flags on the collision node, let's go back and adjust the drag scale now. Change the Scale to 0.1 and view the simulation. The meteor is now traveling much further but it isn't slowing down fast enough at the end and so flies off the edge of the grid. You want it to come in fast and then slow down quickly as the friction of the collisions slow it down. So, what

Figure 8.27
The POP network thus far.

do you want in terms of drag? You want there to be low drag at first and then increasingly higher drag as the meteor bounces lower and lower and collides more and more. Just like channels up at the SOP level, channels here can be animated.

Make sure you are on frame 1 and set a keyframe on the Scale field. Change the frame number to 150 and set another keyframe. After setting the keyframe, change the Scale value to 1. View the simulation and you can see that it is looking better. Let's tweak the interpolation segment a little to make it look even more realistic. RMB on the Scale field and choose Scope Channels so that you can see the curve in the Channel Editor. Box-select the second keyframe at frame 150 and change its Slope to around 0.4. Now you have a scale that stays pretty small until around frame 90, where it starts to increase rapidly. Figure 8.28 shows what the adjusted interpolation segments looks like. Close the Channel Editor window and view the simulation.

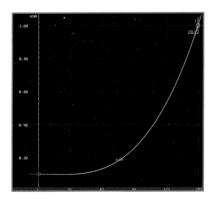

Figure 8.28
The modified drag scale animation curve.

9. You now have a decent-looking meteor flying out of the ether, striking the earth, and grinding to a halt. You could make the simulation look more compelling by adding debris that gets kicked up every time the meteor impacts the earth. (Remember that you are using your imagination and are seeing more than just a point and a grid!) The Split POP will work nicely for the task. Append a Split POP and view the simulation. There are a number of adjustments you need to make for this to look more realistic. First, you only want split particles to be born when the meteor impacts the earth and not constantly as it is doing by default. Ring in the POP event! In the Activation field for the Split, enter popevent("splitBirth") and view the simulation. You now see that every time the meteor strikes the earth, a POP event called splitBirth is generated, which the expression popevent("splitBirth") then detects. Upon detection, the expression evaluates as true (or 1) and so temporarily turns on the Split's Activation so that it can birth particles. On the Birth tab, change Birth Probability to 10 and 10. Now, 10 particles will be born every time the meteor collides. View the simulation and you can see that it still looks like just one particle is being born. You need to add variance to their birthing. Go to the Attributes tab and change Initial Velocity to Set Initial Velocity. Change Variance in X, Y, and Z to 0.5 and view the simulation. You can see debris being kicked out by the impacts, but some of the debris seems to be floating away.

10. One thing to remember is that you are now working with two particle primitives or systems. Forces acting on one system don't necessarily act upon the other. The result of this is that you need to append another Force POP below the split so that these new particles will also have a gravity like force pushing them down. Set its Force in Y to −1 and view the simulation. It seems the debris is now being pushed down to the exclusion of going up at all. More realistically, the meteor impact should send some debris showering up and out. On the Attributes tab of the Split operation, change Velocity in Y to 1 and view the simulation. As a last touch, change Variance in Y to 0.2, as some of the debris seems to be shooting up too much before it heads back down toward the ground.

11. What is left to tweak? The debris is falling through the ground and should be hitting the ground and stopping. Also, the meteor never comes to rest. Near the end of the simulation, it seems like the debris is shooting up like a water fountain. Let's address the first concern now. Append another Collision and change its Geometry Source to Use First Context Geometry, just like you did before. Go to the Behavior tab and change its Behavior to Bounce on Collision. Change Gain Normal to 0.2, as you want the debris to quickly lose energy and come to a stop. Change Final Behavior to Stop on Collision and view the simulation. It is starting to look pretty good; however, there is that problem of the water fountain look near the end.

12. Why is that happening? The problem is that the meteor is making such small bounces near the end that it is causing a large number of POP events and so loads of debris to be born. Let's take a look at how to verify this. Place the Display and Render flags back on the first collision node. Go to the Attribute tab and toggle on Add Num Hit Attribute. This adds an attribute that will keep track of how many times the meteor particle has collided. RMB the node and pop up the Spreadsheet so you can see its attribute values. Hide all attributes and then choose to show only the numhit attribute. Reset the simulation and scrub through the animation watching the numhit

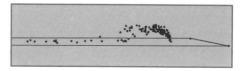

Figure 8.29
The meteor simulation.

attribute value. You can see it tracking the number of collisions and how that numbers shoots up near the end of the simulation. Remember that you have set it up so that the Split operation will birth particles every time one of those collisions occurs.

13. You need to manually stop the particle from colliding, sometime near the end of the simulation and before it starts looking like a water fountain. Insert a State POP between the first collision and the split node. Place the Display and Render flag back down at the bottom of the network chain on the last node. You want to set up the meteor so that after a certain number of collisions, it will change to a stopped state. You can use the if() expression to achieve this. On the Standard tab of the state operation, toggle on the Stopped parameter. Delete the default variable, type if($NUMHIT < 18, 0, 1), and view the simulation. Yeehaa and dosie-do with your partner to and fro! You've done it! Figure 8.29 shows the meteor simulation. But how? The if() expression takes an argument and then sets a value based on whether the argument is true or false.

```
if(argument, return when true, return when false)
```

So, you told it to look at the $NUMHIT attribute, which tracks how many times the meteor has collided and as long as it is less than 18 (the argument is true), returns a value of 0. As soon as $NUMHIT is 18 or greater (the argument is false), it returns a value of 1. The number 18 was arrived at by experimenting back and forth to see when it looked best for the debris to stop being generated. Change the 18 to some other number and you can see that it will either turn off the split births earlier or later in the simulation. You could have also thought up other ways to shut off the debris like using the meteor particle's velocity. Figure 8.30 shows the completed state of the POP network.

Figure 8.30
The completed POP network.

POP Event Generated with an Event POP

The second way to generate a POP event is with an Event POP. Let's use one now by creating a particle that flies up and then gets pushed back down by a downward force. You will then detect when it is moving down and birth particles from another generator only when the first particle is traveling down.

1. Lay down a Geometry Object and jump into it. Lay down a Popnet and jump into it. Ahhhh, the old familiar rhythm.

2. Drop a Location POP and set it so that you only birth one particle at the first frame. Do you recall how to do that? On the Birth tab, change Constant Activation to 0, change Impulse Birth Rate to 1, and change Impulse Activation to $FF= =1. On the Attributes tab, give it an initial velocity in Y of 2 and set variance to 0 in all three axes.

3. Append a force operation and set its Force in Y to −1. You now have a single particle that shoots upward and then gets overpowered by the downward force and falls back down.

4. Append an Event operation and enter ageBirth in the Event Name field. As you can see, there are a few predefined rules that can be used; however, none of them are going to be able to measure when the particle is traveling downward. There is an attribute which holds this information and that is the v (velocity) attribute. RMB on the event node and pop up the Spreadsheet. Hide all of the attributes and then show just the v attribute. View the simulation and you can see that v[y] shows a positive velocity when the particle is traveling up, and then a negative velocity when the particle is traveling down. Enter $VY < 0 in the Rule field of the event node. This is saying that whenever the velocity in Y is less than zero, this is true (and so return a value of 1) and whenever the velocity in Y is 0 or greater, this is false (and so return a value of 0). Stated another way, as soon as the particle stops going up and starts going down, this node will start generating an event called ageBirth. Run the simulation beyond where the particle turns down and then MMB the event node and you can see the event listed in the popup window.

5. Now, let's create the generator that will be controlled by the POP event. Drop another location POP off to the side somewhere (which is not connected to the current network). On the Location tab, change the X Coordinate to 2, which will push the birth location off to the side a little so that you can easily see everything together. On the Birth tab, change its Constant Activation to 0, change Impulse Birth Rate to 1, and change Impulse Activation to popevent("ageBirth"). This node will only birth particles when the POP event called agebirth is detected. On the Attributes tab, add a velocity in Y of 1.

6. Run the simulation and you will notice that you don't see anything happening. That is because the Display and Render flag is on the new location node and the node isn't connected in any way to the previous network. At this moment, the node has no way of knowing anything about the original particle because no information is being shared. Append a Collect POP and wire the event node and the new location node into it. Now information created on one side of the chain (specifically the POP event) is being passed back up the other side of the chain and you can see that particles start being born as soon as the original particle starts falling back down. Figure 8.31 shows the completed state of the POP network.

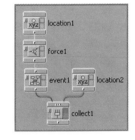

Figure 8.31
The completed POP network.

An initially perplexing observation about using the popevent() expression is that you never actually see it go from 0 to 1 and back to 0. For example, LMB on the Impulse Activation field of the location2 node so that you switch the field to numbers view. Play the simulation and you would expect to see the 0 go to 1 when the single particle starts moving downward. You can clearly see that it is working because you are birthing particles despite the confusion. The reason that the number doesn't appear to change is because the expression is not necessarily referring to just 1 particle. Just like local variables, because the value may not be the same for every particle in the network, it doesn't show anything.

The Dotted Line Connection

Just as at the SOP level, you will sometimes see POP nodes that are connected by a dotted line. Inside POPs, this type of connection means that one particle primitive is referencing another particle primitive in some way. You will see this situation whenever you use a Split POP that is using a previously created particle system as its birthing source. In this situation, it is important to remember that you are working with two distinct particle primitives (or systems) and that forces applied to one system won't necessarily affect the other. Let's look at an example to clarify the situation.

1. You know the routine... Drop a Geometry Object, go inside it, lay down a Popnet, and jump inside it.

2. Lay down a Location POP. On its Birth tab, set Constant Activation to 0 and Impulse Birth Rate to 0.1. This will birth one particle every 10 frames.

3. Append a Force operation and set its Force in Y to −1. View the animation and you can see that the particles spread out a little due to the Variance given in the location operation and then fall downward due to the force operation.

4. Next append a Split POP. Go to the Birth tab, and change Birth Probability Minimum (with is the left field) to 0. Leave the Birth Probability Maximum (the right field) at 1. This range means that each birth point, which are the particles coming from the location POP, will birth between 0 and 1 particles per cook. In the Network Editor, notice that the connection between the force and split POPs is a dotted line. As stated earlier, this is a visual indication that the split operation is only using its input as a reference and they are not a part of the same particle primitive or system. To prove this point, view the simulation and you can see that, although the original particles from the location POP are being affected by the downward force, the newly split particles are not.

5. Let's emphasize this separation by appending another Force to the chain and this time giving it a Force in X of 1. Always remember to ensure your Display and Render flags are correctly set and to reset the simulation. Then view the new state of affairs. Now, you can see that the downward force is only affecting the original particles and the horizontal force is only affecting the split particles. At this point, your network should like Figure 8.32.

6. What if you wanted a downward force to affect both particle primitives? You could, as just shown, add another force to the new particle primitive or you could use a Collect POP to merge the two systems and use a single force to affect both at once. Let's do that now. Go ahead and delete the force operation below the split POP. Remove the remaining force POP from the chain, making sure to leave the location POP as input for the split POP.

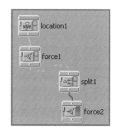

Figure 8.32
The POP network thus far.

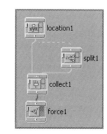

Figure 8.34
The completed POP network.

7. Lay down a Collect POP and wire both the location and split into it.

8. Append a new Force POP below the collect node and give it a value in Y of −1. Now view the simulation and you can see the a single force operation is affecting both particle systems. Figure 8.33 shows the resulting particle simulation and Figure 8.34 shows the completed POP network.

Figure 8.33
The result of the particle simulation.

Poppoint() Expression

The poppoint() expression has the same kind of utility as the point() expression, only it is limited for use inside of a POP network. This expression returns the value of an attribute of a specific POP and is most commonly used when inheriting custom attributes from SOPs. The syntax is defined as poppoint(point_number, attribute, index). For example, if you wanted to know the value of how much green was in particle number 17, you would type poppoint(17,"Cd",1) to find out. The specified attribute should always be placed within quotation marks. The index number refers to which component you wish to query. Cd (color) is a vector attribute and so has three components: Cdr (red), Cdg (green), and Cdb (blue). Index numbers always start at

0, which is the reason that you enter 1 if you want to find out about the second component, which is green in the example. If you wanted to find out how much red was in particle number 21, you would type poppoint(21, "Cd", 0) to find out. Figure 8.35 shows the result of the subsequent exercise.

Let's swagger through an example to see how this works.

1. Lay down a Geometry Object. Jump inside and lay down a Grid SOP and change its Orientation to XY so that it is facing you in the default homed view.

2. Append an AttribCreate SOP to create a custom attribute. Change its Name to bounds, its Size to 2, and enter $BBX and $BBY in the Value X and Y fields. As discussed previously in the book, these are two local variables that measure the bounds of the geometry in a particular axis and normalize that to a range of 0 to 1. With $BBX, the minimum position in X is assigned to 0 and the maximum position in X is assigned to 1, with values in between interpolated between the two. $BBY does the same thing using the Y axis. You have just created a custom point attribute named bounds that consists of two components. MMB on the node to see this in the popup window.

3. Append a Popnet SOP, making sure that the attribcreate node is wired in to its first input. Jump inside the popnet and lay down a Source operation. Set the Geometry Source to Use First Context Geometry. Set the Emission Type to Surfaces (random) and the Constant Birth Rate to 1000 so that you get a denser system.

   Note that in the Attribute tab, Inherit Attributes is set to *, which means that all attributes from the source geometry will be inherited. MMB on the node and you will see the bounds attribute here in POPs.

4. Append a Color POP and toggle on Param so that you can set a color. First, you must delete the existing channels by RMB over the blank space to the left of the color swatch and choosing Delete Channels. There are three fields, which are the red, green, and blue components of a color. In the red field, enter poppoint($PT, "bounds", 0) and in the green field, enter poppoint($PT, "bounds", 1).

   Play the simulation and you can see that you have colored the system, which is still in the shape of a grid, but what is the logic involved? Before I discuss that, let's make the display of the points larger so that you aren't straining to see them. You, the legion of computer geeks, have to take loving care of your peepers, you know.

Figure 8.35
Result of the poppoint exercise.

With your pointer over the viewport, press the d key to access the Display Options. On the Particles tab, change the Point Size to 5. Ahh, better! You can now easily see the grid's coloring. Later in the frame range, your viewport should now resemble Figure 8.36.

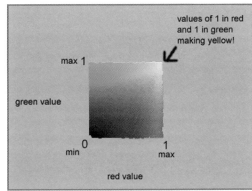

Figure 8.36
Particles colored with the poppoint() expression.

So, why is the system colored as it is? It looks like you have black in the lower-left corner, red in the lower-right corner, green in the upper-left corner, yellow in the upper-right corner, and interpolated values between them. In the red field of the Color POP, you are looking at the first component of the bounds attribute. As set up earlier in SOPs, the first component is using $BBX to evaluate the grid. So, here in POPs, particles born at the far left of the grid receive a 0 value of red, whereas particles born at the far right of the grid receive a value of 1 (a full value) of red. The same thing is happening in the green channel using $BBY with full values of green applied at the top of the grid. Notice again that the upper-right area is yellow, which is a combination of full values of red and green.

5. Let's try a better way. Insert an Attribute POP between the source and color nodes. Give it a name of origbounds with a Size of 2. RMB on the little blank area to the left of the color swatch in the Color POP and choose Copy Parameter. Back in the attribute node, RMB on the Value label and choose Paste Copied Expressions. This should paste in the poppoint expressions just as you used them in the Color POP.

6. In the Color POP, delete the poppoint expressions and instead enter $ORIGBOUNDS1 in the red field and $ORIGBOUNDS2 in the green field. The advantage of doing it this way is that these variables are now available to other POPs anywhere in the network. Using this method, you just have to type in the poppoint expression in one place and then use a variable referencing it everywhere else. In addition, this method is also much more efficient than using the poppoint() expression to do the same work.

7. Let's use these again to further solidify this heady experience. Append a Wind POP and use $ORIGBOUNDS1 in the Y Wind field. $ORIGBOUNDS1 is tied to the poppoint() expression referencing the first component of the bounds attribute which is, in turn, using $BBX to evaluate the grid. Coming all the way back then, the wind strength is lower on the left side of the grid and higher on the right side of the grid.

8. Let's try it one more way. MMB the color node and branch off a Fan POP and put the $ORIGBOUNDS1 variable in the Strength field. On the location tab, change its Origin to 0, −1, 0 and its Direction to 0,1,0. That should have faced the fan upwards and pushed it down a little. Press play and check out the new twist on the old color classic. There are now two balancing factors at play as the fan's strength is greater near the center of the cone, whereas the strength's value is controlled by the values represented in the variable. Your POP network should now look like Figure 8.37.

9. Jump back up to SOPs and drop a Copy operation. Wire the Popnet into its second input. Go to the Attribute tab and toggle on Copy Template Point Attributes. In the To Point Set field, enter Cd so that you are copying over the color attribute created inside the Popnet.

10. Throw down a Circle SOP and wire it into the first input of the Copy node. Reset the simulation and check it out. Magic mustered in a merry moment! Your SOP network should now look like the one shown in Figure 8.38.

Figure 8.37
The completed POP network.

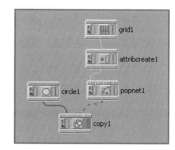

Figure 8.38
The completed SOP network.

Getting Colors and Alpha from POPs to Render

Once you have added color attributes inside of POPs, you will likely next want to render and see those colors. Confusion often arises because if you just render it out using a mantra output driver, the geometry will be its default grey. It seems so simple. You can see the colors in the viewport; why isn't the render showing those same colors? I recall pounding my forehead into the desk a number of times before learning what the problem was. It is simple once you understand what is happening. When you add color in POPs, you are adding a color attribute (Cd), which is composed of three components (Cdr, Cdg, Cdb), to the points and passing it up to SOPs. Before you can successfully see the color in a render, you have to first apply a shader that can understand the Cd attribute. It is as simple as that. Make sure the attribute is passed back to SOPs and that you apply a shader that looks for the attribute. Let's look at an example of how to do this by creating a simple network that will end up looking like Figures 7.39 and 7.40.

Figure 8.39
Render from the side.

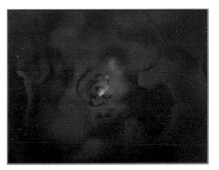

Figure 8.40
Render from the front.

1. Lay down a Geometry Object and dive in and drop a Popnet and jump inside it too.

2. Lay down a Location POP. On the Birth tab, set Constant Activation to 0 and Impulse Birth Rate to 10. Change Life Expectancy to 2 and Life Variance to 0.3. On the Attributes tab, set a Velocity in Y of 1 and a Variance in all three axes of 0.2.

3. Next append a Force operation and give it force in Y of –0.5.

4. To the meat of it, man! Append a Color operation next. Change from Pass to Param so that you can set a color. LMB on the black color swatch and select a bright yellow. Notice how it keeps snapping back to black? That is because you first must delete the three channels. Move your pointer just to the left of the three channels and the black color swatch. You will see an empty box highlighted. RMB on that "hidden" box and choose Delete Channels. You can now choose a bright yellow and it will accept the selection. This is the method you would use to assign a single color to the particles. However, you want to assign a color ramp based on the life of the particles. When the particles are born, you want them to be bright yellow, and then turn orange-red and finally black just before they die. Change Param to Ramp. Figure 8.41 shows the default ramp parameters with a few explanatory labels added.

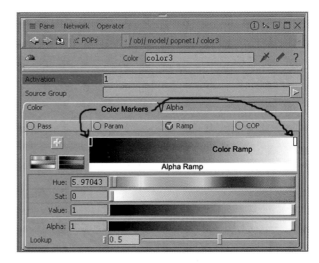

Figure 8.41
The color and alpha ramps.

The ramp has a 0 to 1 range, which is represented with the far left color marker being 0 and the far right color marker being 1. Each color marker holds a specific color and applies that color at the position in which it resides. To change the color for a particular marker, LMB on it and then adjust the hue, saturation, and value fields using the sliders or the fields themselves. To add another color marker in the range, just click on the color ramp where you want the new marker to be placed. To move the position of a marker, just LMB and drag it left or right. If you want to delete a color marker, LMB on it and hold while dragging it up off the ramp. LMB on the first marker and change it to a bright yellow color. LMB on the second marker and change it to black. Now add a marker about three-fourths of the way to the right and make it red. Your color ramp should now look like Figure 8.42.

Figure 8.42
Color markers on the color ramp.

5. Now you need to tell the popnet how to reference the ramp and you do that by using the Lookup Parameter at the bottom. Type $LIFE in the Lookup field and view the simulation. What did you just do? The $LIFE variable is the normalized value of the age of the particle. In this example, when the age of a particle is 0, $LIFE is 0. When the age of the particle reaches 2 and dies (not considering the variance you added), $LIFE is 1. No matter how long a particle lives, the $LIFE variable normalizes that time into a range of 0 to 1. As you can see in the simulation, this is very helpful. When the particle is born, $LIFE is 0 and so the lookup is at far left of the color ramp, which is bright yellow. When the particle is halfway through its lifespan at 1 second (again not considering any possible variance), its $LIFE is 0.5 and so the lookup is at the center of the color ramp, which is orange. Finally, when the particle dies, $LIFE is 1 and so the lookup is at the far right of the color ramp, which is black. Every single particle will individually have its own lifespan and hence $LIFE variable lookup.

As discussed in previous exercises, if you LMB the Lookup label to see a numbers view of the field, it always stays at a value of 0. This is because each particle has its own unique $LIFE value and so it doesn't know which one it should show in the field. As a result, it just leaves the value at 0.

6. Let's further refine the simulation by adding an alpha attribute. As shown in Figure 8.41 in the alpha ramp area, the alpha is at a full value of 1 (white) over the entirety of its life. Change from the Color to the Alpha tab. In the Lookup parameter, use the same variable of $LIFE. Ensure you have the far right marker selected and then change the Alpha parameter to 0. Next, click on the middle marker and change its Alpha parameter value to 1. You can now see that the alpha ramp shows that a particle's alpha will quickly drop to 0 near the end of its life (see Figure 8.43).

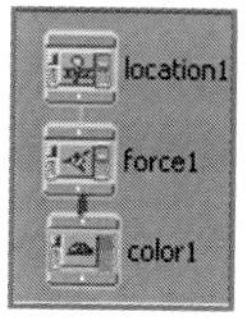

Figure 8.43
The POP network thus far.

7. Jump back up to SOPs and drop an unattached Copy SOP and a Metaball SOP. A metaball can be used to create geometry that behaves much like drops of mercury in that, if you get two of them too close together, their individual surfaces will suck together to form a single continuous surface. Change the metaball's Radius in X, Y, and Z to 0.1. Pipe the metaball into the left input of the copy operation and the popnet into its right input. Make sure the Display and Render flags are also on it and view the simulation. What happened to the colors?

MMB on the copy node's icon to bring up the info window and you can see that you don't have any point attributes. Specifically, you don't have the color and alpha attributes you added inside the popnet. On the Attributes tab of the copy node, toggle on the Copy Template Point Attributes parameter. This parameter tells the Copy SOP to pass along the chosen point attributes from the points in the popnet to the copied geometry that is attached to those points. Check the info popup again and you can see that you now have a number of attributes including the color (Cd[3]) and alpha (Alpha[1]) attributes.

When copying attributes from POPs back into SOPs, it is important to only bring in those attributes tbat you will be using. As seen in the example, by default, an asterisk is in the Set field and so all point attributes are taken along for the ride. In more complex simulations, this can eat up a lot of memory and also slow down operations downstream that only require particular attributes. Although this is a good habit to acquire, it means that you need to remember to specifically state whatever attributes you need for downstream work.

In the spirit of good habits and efficient workflow, on the Attribute tab of the Copy SOP, delete the asterisk in the To Point field and enter Cd and Alpha. MMB on the node's icon to view the popup information and you should now see these two Point Attributes listed. So, you have saved the memory and processing of all of those additional attributes, as you don't need them.

8. In the Viewport, RMB on the render selector and choose the fast mantra output. Mantra will popup an Mplay window and show you the render. Notice that the geometry in the render is still grey and also that the render took a while to complete.

9. The reason that the render took a while to complete is because mantra must convert the metaballs into polygons before rendering. You can do this process much faster in SOPs. Append a ConvertMeta operation to the end of the network and change the Step Size to 0.05 in all three axes. A smaller step size results in a more detailed conversion. Kick off another render and you will notice that this one is much faster.

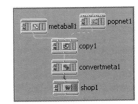

Figure 8.44
The SOP network thus far.

10. Now, let's get the colors that you see in the viewport to make it to the render as well. As mentioned in the beginning of this explanation, you need to apply a shader that looks for the color and alpha attributes that the points are carrying. Append a Shader SOP to the network and your chain should now look like Figure 8.44.

11. You will go into more depth about shaders and rendering in the SHOPs and VOPs chapters. For now, you will just dabble your toes in just enough to get the job done. You have a shader node that is ready and willing to apply a shader to your network; however, you still need to first create a shader for it to apply. Drop a SHOP Network SOP off to the side of your existing network. With it selected, press Enter to jump into it. This node operates in exactly the same way as the popnet SOP that you created earlier. With your pointer over the Network Editor pane, press Tab to bring up the menu and press the v key to bring up all options that start with that letter. Choose VEX Layered Surface. You can verify that this shader uses the color and alpha attributes that you set earlier by holding the pointer over the Diffuse and Alpha labels in order to see the field attribute names. Diffuse uses Cdr, Cdg, and Cdb and Alpha uses Alpha. Change the Lighting Model from Phong to Lambert. This turns off the bright highlights that you see in shiny objects.

12. Jump back up to the SOPs level. In the parameters for the shader node, click the plus button on the Surface field and choose the VEX layered shader you just created. You may need to expand the shopnet branch to find it. Make sure you have the geometry within view and kick off another render. By George, you dun done it!

13. Let's make one final cosmetic adjustment by pinching the scale of the metaballs when they are born and letting them grow over time. Jump into the popnet and append a Property POP to the existing network. On the Misc tab, toggle on Scale and enter $LIFE + 0.3 in its parameter field. What is this little expression doing?

Figure 8.45
The completed POP network.

You are using the $LIFE variable, so that means you are returning a value of 0 to 1 based on the birth and death of each particle. You then add the value of 0.3 to it. So, when a particle is born, this expression returns a value of 0 + 0.3= 0.3 and when it dies, it returns a value of 1 + 0.3 = 1.3. So, the particle's scale will smoothly interpolate between 0.3 and 1.3 over the span of its lifetime. Jump back up to SOPs and replay the simulation. You have achieved your heart's content, or at least achieved the goal of the exercise. Figure 8.45 shows the completed POP network.

Exercise: Flying Arrows

Hearken back to your favorite big-budget movie whose setting is in the idyllic medieval age. Well, at least many movies portray it rather idyllically. I'm not so certain it was common for everyone to be sporting glistening white teeth and abs of steels. Moving on, one of the shots you often see in this type of flick is a horde of arrows arcing across the sky speeding toward a soon-to-be crest-fallen enemy. Something about hundreds of deadly projectiles racing to their targets tends to elevate the tension of almost any scene. Besides being fun to watch, it's also fun to create. In this exercise, you'll make your own version of this Hollywood staple. Figure 8.46 shows the result of this exercise.

Overview

Because this exercise is a somewhat lengthy, I give you an idea of what you are going to cover here at the beginning:

1. Create the ground geometry.

2. Create the arrow geometry.

3. Create the birth geometry.

4. Create the particle simulation.

5. Attach the arrow geometry to the particles.

6. Add variation using the copy stamp technique.

7. Pop the top off a frosty beverage and enjoy your newly gained mastery!

The following sections discuss each of these steps in detail.

Figure 8.46
A bevy of arrows.

Create the Ground Geometry

First, you need some geometry to pound the arrows into:

1. Start a new session of Houdini and lay down two Geometry Objects. Label one `ground` and the other `arrows`. All SOPs related to the ground will be inside the former and all SOPs and POPs related to the arrows and how they fly will be inside the latter.

2. First create the collision surface, which is the ground. Jump into the ground Object and lay down a Grid SOP. Change its Primitive Type to NURBs so that when you deform it in the next step, those deformations will be smooth. Change its size to 50 by 50 to give you a larger area in which to launch and land your arrows.

3. Append a VEX Mountain SOP and change the height to 8.

4. Append a Convert SOP and leave it at the default settings. Converting the grid will give you a more detail for more accurate arrow collisions.

5. In the chapter mini-exercises, you often didn't label each node as thoughtfully as you could have. Because the size of the networks were relatively small, it wasn't absolutely necessary. However, when creating more complex networks, it is imperative to clearly label anything that might need it so that you and anyone else who may need to examine the file can quickly understand what is happening. So, append a Null SOP and name the node `collisionGeo` so that you can easily find it later.

6. Finally, append another Null SOP and name it `dispRender`. This is a quick and clear indication to any who view the file where the Display and Render flags should be. Although for this small five-node network, it is pretty obvious that it can get very confusing when working with 100's of nodes that are branching out in every direction. So, for now, it's just good practice. Figure 8.47 shows the SOP network that creates the ground geometry.

Figure 8.47
The ground SOP network.

Create the Arrow Geometry

Next, you need to create the geometry that you will fling through the air.

1. You'll first create the shaft, and then the fletching, and then the arrowhead. Jump over into the arrows Object and lay down a Tube SOP. Change its Radius in X and Y to 0.006 and its Height to 1.5. Rename the node to `arrowShaft` and toggle on the Template flag. You will use the shaft as a reference when creating the rest of the arrow.

2. First go to front view so that you make sure to create a flat curve. Then, with your pointer over the viewport, choose a Curve SOP. Create a closed, polygonal curve that resembles a bit of feather-like fletching near the top of the shaft. Check out Figure 8.48 for reference. Rename the node to `fletching`.

3. In the Network Editor, append a Transform operation to the fletching node and update the position of the Display flag. Notice where the pivot is (the little blue guide dot). It is below the geometry and not where you want. If you were to scale the fletching now, the scale would be incorrectly skewed. Go ahead and delete the node and let's do the same operation from the viewport. By doing it in the viewport, the pivot will automatically be correctly set to the centroid of the geometry. With your pointer over the viewport, choose

Figure 8.48
The arrow's fletching.

176

a Transform operation. Select the fletching geometry and RMB to complete and check your pivot values. They are no longer zeroed out. You can also see that the pivot guide is centered in the fletching geometry. Rename the node to `adjustFletching`. Leave it at its defaults for now. If you later want to come back and tweak the size of the fletching, this is where you would do it.

4. Lay down an unconnected Merge SOP and toggle on its Template flag. Then wire in the `arrowShaft` and `adjustFletching` nodes. At this point, your network should like Figure 8.49.

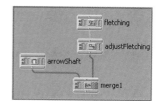

Figure 8.49
The SOP network thus far.

Figure 8.50
The curve that begins the arrowhead.

5. Also using the front view, throw down an unconnected Curve operation and create a closed, polygonal arrowhead shape something like Figure 8.50. You can create it down at the tip of the shaft or wherever, as you can position it correctly later.

6. Copy and paste this node and place it off to the side of the previous curve node. Append a Transform to the second curve node and uniformly scale it down to 0.8, 0.8, 0.8. Also, push it back just a little in Z. A value of −.013 should do nicely.

7. Now box-select the second curve node and the transform you just added and copy and paste them. Place them off to the side a bit and then connect each of the nodes into a Merge SOP as shown in Figure 8.51. On the `xform2` node, just remove the negative sign to push this curve in the positive Z direction.

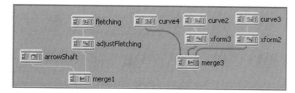

Figure 8.51
The SOP network thus far.

8. All you have done is gather the separate pieces of geometry together so that you can now perform a Skin operation on them. You have a diamond-shaped curve in the center with a smaller diamond-shaped curve on each side of it. Let's skin them all together now. Go back to the Perspective view if you are not already there. Be certain to select the pieces in the correct order, as the results will be different if the selection order is incorrect. So that you are clear on what that order is, turn on the display of Primitive Numbers in the viewport.

In the viewport, select a Skin operation and choose primitive 1, primitive 0, and then primitive 2. RMB to complete the selection and RMB again, as there is no need to select a V curves to skin. This will be the sharp edge of the arrowhead. Now you just need add back in the two sides to complete it. Your edge geometry should like Figure 8.52. If the geometry looks twisted and not clean as below, you have likely selected the curves in the wrong order. Just reselect the geometry for the current operation and correct the selection order.

Figure 8.52
The arrowhead edges.

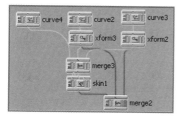

Figure 8.53
The arrowhead SOP network thus far.

9. You already have the sides, as they were used as profiles to create the edge geometry. Lay down an unconnected Merge and wire in the `skin1` node and the two `xform` nodes and you have the completed arrowhead. This part of your network should now look like Figure 8.53.

10. Box-select all of the nodes that make up the arrowhead geometry (all of the nodes shown in Figure 8.51). Hold Ctrl down and RMB on any one of the nodes and choose Collapse Selected Into Subnet. BAM! All of those nodes are now contained in this one node. Rename this node arrowHead. You can still modify its contents at any time by selecting the node and pressing Enter. Go ahead and jump inside it. Press u to jump back up. It's the same sort of navigation as jumping into or out of a Geometry Object.

> In order to better organize networks, it is sometimes helpful to collapse a group of related nodes into a subnet. This helps to keep things visually manageable and is very easy to do. The subnet node name will be colored blue to notify you that it is a subnet.

11. In the viewport, select a Transform operation, select the arrowHead geometry, and RMB to complete. Rename this node adjustArrowHead. Move the arrowhead down to the tip of the shaft if needed and let's mosey onward down the dusty trail of discovery.

12. Wire the adjustArrowHead node into merge1 to bring all of the arrow geometry together. Go ahead and rename this node arrowGeo. Your network should now look like Figure 8.54.

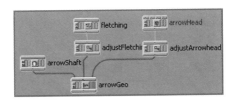

Figure 8.54
The SOP network thus far.

Create the Birth Geometry

Here, you create some geometry from which to birth the particles.

1. Create the geometry from which the particles will be born. Basically, you just want to shoot the arrows from one edge of the ground to the other. Drop an unconnected Grid SOP, leave it at the default settings, and rename it launchBirthGeo.

2. Append a Transform operation and rename it adjustBirthGeo. Now, lets place the birthing grid on one side of the Ground grid. Go to the Top View to more easily see where you are placing it and make sure you have the See One/See All toggle on so that you can see the Ground Object. Enter -23 in Translate Z and scale it up in X to 8. Go ahead and jump back into Perspective view. In Figure 8.55, the birth grid is in yellow.

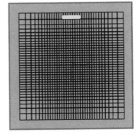

Figure 8.55
The birth grid's placement.

Create the Particle Simulation

You wouldn't have much of an arrow simulation without the simulation. It is time to create the flight behavior of the arrows using a particle simulation.

1. Now, let's get into the real guts and glory of this adventure. RMB append a Popnet SOP to the adjustBirthGeo node and dive into it. Would you have ever believed 3D work to be so physical? You are jumping, diving, moseying, throwing, and dropping things all over the virtual vista.

2. Lay down a Source POP and set Emission Type to Prim Center (ordered) and Geometry Source to Use First Context Geometry. You are going to set it up so that all of your arrows are born at once on frame 10. On the Birth tab, type $FF = = 10 in the Impulse Activation field. This says to only allow Impulse birthing on the instant you press frame 10 and at no other time. Set Constant Activation to 0.

Type $NPRIM in the Impulse Birth Rate field. This will go read the number of primitives of whatever source geometry is used and insert that number here. LMB on the label to go to numbers view and you can see that the birthing grid is comprised of 81 primitives. So, you will birth 81 particles at frame 10.

3. You now want to impart an "up and away" velocity to the arrows. Later, you will add a downward force that will overpower this upward velocity and so push the particles back down to the ground... much like gravity! On the Attributes tab, change Initial Velocity to Set Initial Velocity. Change Velocity in Y to 25 and Velocity in Z to 30. Play the simulation and you can see you now have the beginnings of arrow flight. Right now, they are packed a little too tightly together, so they would all land at once. Change Variance in Y to 5. This will make it so that some of the arrows land earlier than others.

> Signal the towers and sound the clarions! The Drag POP is sallying forth! Most simulations that you create will be in mediums that exert some kind of resistance or friction. Generally speaking, the denser the medium is, the greater the drag is. It is imperative for realistic simulations to account for this effect and the Drag POP is the answer.

Right now, the simulation is much like what might happen if you shot off a horde of arrows in space. They would just keep traveling forever at the velocity initially imparted upon them. Though that is fun to think about, you want to make the simulation a little more terrestrial.

4. Append a Drag POP and play the simulation. You can see that the particles now slow down very quickly. This looks like a medium much denser than air. Drop the Scale down to 0.2 and watch it again. You now have particles that speed out and gradually slow down. Now, you just need to push them back down.

As mentioned at the beginning of the chapter, it is important to remember that values in POPs are usually only meaningful relative to other values that they are interacting with. So, 0.2 for drag may not always be a good value for simulating the friction of air. If you changed the Initial Velocity or mass of the particles, you would find that a different drag value would be more appropriate.

5. Append a Force POP and rename it levelForce. Give it a value of −5 in Force Y and play the simulation to see what it adds to the simulation. This force is going to push down just a little bit on the particles so that they start to level off. As you can see though, they aren't yet actually making it back to the ground.

6. Append a Group POP and rename it GRpushDown. In the Group Name field, enter pushDown. Toggle on the Enable button below the Rule checkmark so that you can enter an expression to establishing grouping. Enter $AGE > 0.5 in the Rule field. So, now as soon as each individual particle is over half a second old, it will become a part of the pushDown group.

Reset the simulation and look at the MMB popup window every 10 frames or so, and you can watch the number of particles in the pushDown group grow from 0 to 81. Figure 8.56 shows the current state of the POP network.

7. Append another Force POP and rename it downForce. Choose pushDown for the Source Group and enter -25 in Force Y. View the simulation and you can see that the arrows are flying in a nice arc. If you don't see the pushDown group listed, make sure the Cook flag is on this node and reset the simulation.

Figure 8.56
The POP network thus far.

8. Append an Interact POP. You will use this POP to ensure that none of the arrows are able to run into each other while in the air. Change Particle Radius to Use Supplied Radius and enter a Radius of 0.5. In the Behavior tab, change the Force Multiplier to 0.1 so that you lessen the amount of repulsive force between them.

9. The last piece of this particle puzzle is to get the arrows to stop when they hit the ground, which is simple enough. Append another Group POP and rename it GRcanDie. With this POP, you will be limiting when the arrows can consider collisions. This will help you make certain that the particles don't try to collide with the Ground Object when they are born or try to collide with each other before the repulsive interact force has a chance to force some separation. Enter canDie in the Group Name field. Toggle on the Rule Enable and enter $AGE > 0.5 in the Rule field.

10. Append a Collision POP and rename it collideGround. Choose canDie for the Source Group. In the SOP field, choose the collisionGeo node inside the ground Object. On the Behavior tab, change Behavior to Stop On Collision because you want the particles to stop when they hit the ground. Play the simulation and shazaam! (that exclamation point is a make-shift lightning bolt), you have some particles flying like arrows would. Your POP network should now look like Figure 8.57.

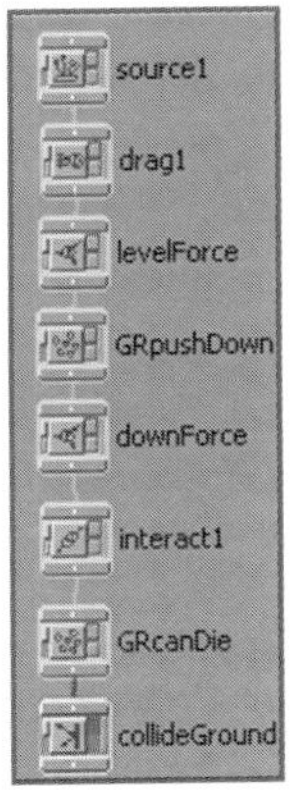

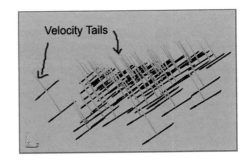

Figure 8.57
The completed POP network.

Attach the Arrow Geometry to the Particles

Now you need to get the arrow geometry attached to the particles so that you have something more interesting than a horde of points streaking across the sky.

1. So, you have particles that fly like arrows and you have arrow geometry. What is the missing link in the arrow flight evolution? Of course, you need to get the arrow geometry copied to each particle. Jump back up to SOPs and lay down an unconnected Copy SOP. Connect the arrowGeo node to its left input and the popnet node to its right input. As always, make sure the Display flag is on this node. Turn on viewing of the ground object and then play the simulation. You have one arrow attached per particle now, but the arrows aren't aligned correctly.

How do you go about aligning the arrows correctly? How can you know with precision what the angles are? Using velocity tails as a visual reference is one good way of doing it. As shown in Figure 8.58, notice in the viewport that there are blue lines coming off each particle that marks its path of travel. These are velocity tails and they can be seen in POPs as black tails and here in SOPs as blue tails. You can also see that they fade off in the direction from which they came. So, the tails in the Figure 8.58 indicate that the particles must be going down and to the right relative to the picture. Velocity tails offer an easy way of correctly aligning copied geometry.

Velocity Tails

Figure 8.58
Velocity tails.

2. RMB the output of the arrowGeo to append a Transform SOP and rename it `alignArrow`. Change the Rotate X value to −90 and you can see that now the arrow geometry is pointing along the direction of travel. Let's make one more small adjustment before moving on. Reset the simulation and play it through until all the arrows have collided with the ground. Notice how the arrows are stuck into the ground about halfway up the shaft. That would have to be a seriously heavy arrow. Set Translate in Z to −0.5 and you can see that the arrows have shifted up along their direction of travel so that now just the head is sticking in the ground.

Add Variation Using the Copy Stamp Technique

Although you now have a reasonably good arcing arrows effect, it can be better by adding some variation to make it look more natural.

1. Well, you have definitely achieved the basic goal of getting a horde of arrows to fly across the sky and punch into the ground. However, all the arrows are perfectly aligned to each other. That uniformity is just the sort of shortcoming that our brains can easily detect. Just as discussed in Chapter 5, "Surface Operators," let's use the copy stamp technique to add some variety so that you achieve a more organic feeling.

   RMB on the `alignArrow` node to insert a Transform SOP and then rename it `testParms`. You will use this node to first determine how much variation looks good. Then you can set up copy stamping to use the correct range of variation.

   Let's look at Rotation in X first. Change this value back and forth from positive to negative with the goal of determining a good range for variation. Play back the simulation using different values to see what the change looks like across the entire sim. To my eyes, it looks like −10 to 10 is about right. Much beyond either of those and it starts looking a little wonky. Archive that info on a piece of paper, in the deep cobwebbed recesses of your brain, or (in this case), let me remember it for you.

   Change Rotate in X back to 0 and do the same thing for Y. To me, it looks like a range of −10 to 10 looks good for Y as well. Set Rotate Y back to 0 and let's look at Z now. Change the value back and forth and notice that it is now rotating along its long axis. So, for this axis, any value between 0 and 360 should be fine.

   There is another logical possible variation that you can test in this node, which is how deeply the arrows penetrate into the ground. Experiment with the Translate Z value to determine a good range. It looks like 0 to 0.2 works pretty nicely. You have your ranges, so now you can determine how to use them. Make sure all values are back to their defaults on the `testParms` node and let's continue.

2. RMB append a Transform SOP to the `testParms` node and rename it `stampedParms`. Enter the following in the proper parameter fields:

```
in tz, stamp("../copy1", "penetratedepth", 0)
in rx, stamp("../copy1", "xrot", 0)
in ry, stamp("../copy1", "yrot", 0)
in rz, stamp("../copy1", "zrot", 0)
```

   The variables in the expressions are just made up and stand for:

```
xrot = x rotation
yrot = y rotation
zrot = z rotation
penetratedepth = z translation
```

3. Now, you need to go into the copy node and, on the Stamp tab, toggle on Stamp Inputs. Enter the variables created in the `stampedParms` node here, as shown in Figure 8.59.

4. Next, you need to build expressions that will give the arrows variation within the desired ranges. These expressions are entered into the associated fields to the right of each variable in the Stamp tab. Start with `xrot`, which you want to be randomized between −10 and 10. So, how do you go about building the correct expression? Step by step, of course! You know you want there to be randomized variation. So, let's use the `rand()` expression using `$ID` as its seed. The `rand` expression will return a random value from 0 to 1 based on a seed value. `$ID` is the unique ID of the particle to which the geometry is copied. So, you now have

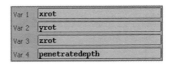

Figure 8.59
Stamp variables being used.

```
rand($ID)
```

which means that each copy has a value of somewhere between 0 and 1. What next? You need to fit that range to the desired range. −10 to 10 is an absolute range of 20 units. So, you want to fit 0–1 to 0–20. The fit expression is exactly what you want. Looking in the help, you see that the `fit` expression is:

```
fit(number, old minimum, old maximum, new minimum, new maximum)
After plugging in the components as appropriate, you now have
fit(rand($ID), 0, 1, 0, 20)
```

where the `rand` expression is the number you want to fit, 0 is the old minimum, 1 is the old maximum, 0 is the new minimum, and 20 is the new maximum. You aren't quite there yet though, as this now gives each copy a range of 0 to 20, which isn't −10 to 10 like you want. This is easily fixed by encompassing the entire expression in parentheses so that it is computed first, and then subtracting 10 from the result. You now have

```
(fit(rand($ID), 0, 1, 0, 20)) - 10
```

which works the magic! Play through the simulation and you will see that you now have variation in X rotation within the desired range. Yeehaa! Slap a saddle on cuz this thing'll ride! Remember that I am from Oklahoma, and so am allowed the occasional colloquial outburst.

5. As you want the same range for the rotation in Y, just copy and paste this expression into the field below, which should be listed as `Param 2`.

6. Next, you need to determine how to get a range of variation in Rotate Z of 0 to 360. That should be pretty easy for you to determine, having just used the expression for Rotate X, as you will use basically the same approach. The only difference is that you can simply create the new range without having to then offset it. So, the expressions associated with rotz will be

```
fit(rand($ID), 0, 1, 0, 360)
```

7. Finally, you need to create an expression that will set the range for `penetratedepth`. In the `Param` field associated with `penetratedepth`, enter

```
fit(rand($ID), 0, 1, 0, 0.2)
```

and there you have it! Refer to Figure 8.60 to see each of these expressions in their respective fields.

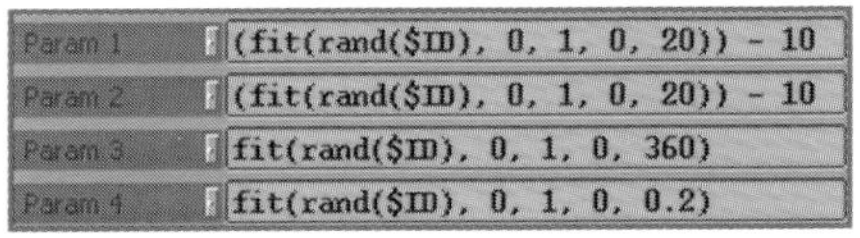

Figure 8.60
The final copy stamp expressions.

8. Replay the simulation and watch organic, loving kindness unfold. You now have a horde of arrows that scream across yon sky and pierce the earth with varying angles of entry and depth. Looks a good bit better, huh?

9. Finally, always keeping network organization in mind, append a Null SOP and rename it `dispRender`. That's it! Figure 8.61 shows the final state of the SOP network inside the `arrows` object. It is now high time you kick back, pop the top off a frosty beverage, and enjoy your newly gained mastery!

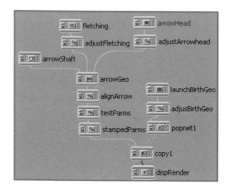

Figure 8.61
Final view of the SOP network of the arrows object.

Although you can't correctly cook or update a particle system by dragging backward in time, you can set up a Popnet SOP so that it can be viewed backwards after the simulation has been run. This is just like looking at a VCR tape in reverse. The content isn't changing. It's just being viewed going backwards in time. Append a Cache SOP to the Popnet SOP. Ensure the playbar is reset and then allow the particle system to play through one time as slow as it needs to in order to correctly cook. The information is now cached in memory and can be scrubbed back and forth for closer examination. Remember that it isn't actually recooking anything: it is just showing you the simulation played out in reverse. If you make further changes to your simulation, make sure to Clear Cache on the Cache SOP and play it through once again in order to place the new simulation in memory.

Summary

One of the most important things to remember is that POPs is an environment in which you define rules and create forces that interact in a simulation. This is opposed to the method of explicit animation found in SOPs and elsewhere. When you begin building a system, think about which factors are involved in the phenomenon you are trying to simulate and start by layering in forces that mimic them one on top of another. If you are in the thick of creation and running into problems, it is still helpful to use this approach in order to define the conditions that need to be present to get the simulation working properly. With the tools you now have at your disposal, you should be able to electrically slide into whatever simulation adventures await you.

chapter 9
Shader Operators (SHOPs)

E ven the most intricately delicate Lotus flower (see Figure 9.1) requires its accompanying hues to achieve the stunning beauty that is its birthright. If you were to take the same physical structure and apply a grey, shiny material to it, its beauty would be diminished. Thankfully, you visually experience the world in an almost overwhelming array of color and intensity. Up to this point in your adventure with Houdini, you have been limited to rendering with the default grey, shiny plastic material. For a final look, this is an imminently unsatisfying result.

How do you apply materials in Houdini, then? Well, you apply SHOPs. A SHOP is a *Shader Operator,* which is another way of saying a material. The difference between a material and a shader is subtle but important. In a lot of other packages, you are given a set of materials, and that's it. If you want to "roll your own," you're out of luck. In Houdini, shaders are little pieces of programming code that are compiled and then used by Mantra (Houdini's renderer) to define the look of the surface. This gives you great power and flexibility in defining the look of your surfaces.

An especially interesting aspect of SHOPs is that they are renderer agnostic. Does that mean that they believe that it is impossible to know for certain whether Buddha, God, Allah, or Saraswati exist? No. It does mean that you can use SHOPs with Mantra, Pixar's Photorealistic Renderman, or Mental Images' Mental Ray renderer. Other renderers may be added in the future if customers request them. The fact that SHOPs are a generic way of applying shaders means all shaders are used the same way, regardless of which renderer you're using. In the following exercises, you'll be using Mantra because it's included for free with the package. However, almost everything you learn here also applies to Photorealistic Renderman and Mental Ray.

Figure 9.1
A lotus flower found in Echo Park.
photo by Genevieve Bertone

What if you don't want to write any code? What if even the prospect of multiple lines of text with weird spacing and punctuation is enough to make you cross-eyed? Never fear, valiant seeker, for there is good news here! Houdini ships with a large number of pre-defined SHOPs that are quite capable for a lot of common shading tasks. Multi-layered texture mapping, glass, metal, stone, and so on, already exist as SHOPs in Houdini and so you can just dive in and put them to use. But, if you want to delve into the truly arcane, the powerful magic is to be found in VOPs. VOPs stands for VEX Operators and is the subject of the next chapter. In this chapter, you'll use the pre-defined SHOPs to explore the various ways SHOPs can be applied, where they can live in Houdini networks, and how you can animate and control them.

185

Shader Contexts

For the Mantra renderer, shaders are defined as being one of the following types: surface shader, displacement shader, light shader, shadow shader, fog shader, image3d shader, or photon shader. Other renderers such as Photorealistic Renderman have similar but not identical types. These types are known as "contexts" but most people just refer to them as "shader types."

♦ A surface shader is what you most commonly think of when talking about this topic, as it controls the surface appearance of the geometry. It controls the appearance of the color, opacity, and alpha.

♦ A displacement shader physically moves points of the geometry before rendering. This is often used to create small geometry details that would be too tedious or minute to physically model using surface operations. For example, a displacement map could be used to create the bumpy, complex skin of an orange or the ridged skin area on the knuckles of your hand.

♦ A light shader is used to control the illumination of a light source. For example, you might want to create a light shader that would set the behavior of the illumination to travel 10 units at full intensity and then fall off to 0 intensity over the next four units.

♦ A shadow shader is often used to determine where and how much a light source is occluded (blocked), thus creating a shadow. A special shadow shader might allow you to created colored shadows, or project texture maps into the shadowed region.

♦ A fog shader takes the result of the surface shader's computation and modifies it based upon an intervening medium like dust, smoke, fog, and so on.

♦ An image3d shader can create 3D texture files like clouds or smoke, which can then be read by a fog shader to create the rendered volumetric look.

♦ A photon shader is used to control the behavior of photons. These are typically used for things like global illumination and caustics.

Adding Instances of Default Surface and Displacement Shaders

Before you can apply a shader to geometry, you first need to create an instance of it. An important point to understand is that when you choose a shader inside a SHOP network, you aren't actually creating a new shader—in the sense that you started with nothing and defined a set of behaviors and so created a shader. You are really just making an instance of the particular shader available for use. The code and interface for the default shaders already exists. You are adding an instance and then are able to modify the available parameters. In order to make a new shader, you use either the VOPs graphical format or the VEX textual format. There you define the behavior of the shader and also the interface and parameters available. Once complete, you can then make it available for selection in a SHOP network.

1. Start a new session of Houdini and rename the default geometry object orange. Jump inside it and drop a SHOP network and jump inside it.

2. Over the Network Editor, bring up the tab menu. You will notice that the first level menu has both a RIB_Standard and VEX_Standard category. RIB shaders are renderman shaders and hence will function correctly only if you have a renderman-compliant renderer installed and are using it for output. Otherwise, you will be rendering using Mantra and so must use VEX shaders. Press the v key to bring up all shaders that begin with the letter v, which is all available VEX shaders. Choose a VEX Polka Dots shader and also a VEX Choppy Water Shader.

3. Notice that the layout in the Network Editor looks different than when in most of the other contexts. This is a list view of the nodes. They are still individual nodes just as in other contexts. You can see this by pressing the t hotkey to go into worksheet view. The nodes might initially be on top of one another and so you might have to drag one over a bit to see them both. The reason that SHOPs are displayed in list view by default is because you aren't normally connecting the nodes into a network as you are in some other contexts. Press t again to go back to list view.

The Shader Viewer

The shader viewer is the Viewer pane while you're in the SHOPs context and it is where you preview the shaders before you apply and render them. You can tumble and dolly just as you can in normal viewports. However, you can't track the object off the screen in the same way. Tracking will act just like tumbling in this viewer. The shader viewer is shown in Figure 9.2.

The Top Stowbar

Expand the stowbars on all three sides (top, left, and bottom) so that you can see all of the options. In the top stowbar, you have menus that you can use to select the desired shader. These allow you to see both a Surface and Displacement shader together on the same piece of preview geometry. In the Network Editor, select the polka dot shader. Now, in the viewer, select the `choppywater` displacement shader from the drop-down menu. You are now seeing both shaders simultaneously.

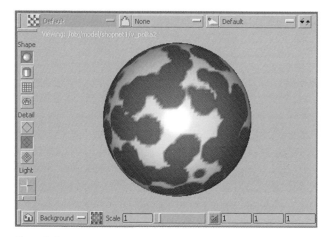

Figure 9.2
The shader viewer.

The Left Stowbar

The left stowbar contains a number of options to control how the shader viewer is displaying the selected shader.

1. On the left stowbar, the Shape options allow you to preview using a particular geometry type. For example, if you were going to put this polka dot shader on a banana-shaped piece of geometry, it would make the most sense to preview it using the tube geometry. Toggle between each of the Shape types and return to a sphere before continuing.

2. The Detail options offers three levels of details. These three options offer a trade off of speed versus display accuracy. When set on high detail, you may notice that the viewport is taking longer to redraw as you tumble the view around or change shader parameters. Toggle between these to see the different levels of detail and return to the medium level of detail.

3. The Light gizmo allows you to control how the preview light is hitting the geometry. LMB and drag in the upper part to position the light. Use the slider in the lower part to set how much the preview uses this light relative to a generic, frontal lighting position. Play around with the gizmo to get a feel for how it works. It is important to understand that this lighting is only applying to the preview you see here and won't have any effect on what is happening with the lights in the Object context (and hence, with how your renders will look).

The Bottom Stowbar

On the bottom stowbar, the Home button homes the viewport just like it does in other viewports.

The Background selector enables you to view the geometry in front of a particular background. When using transparency or raytraced reflection or refraction, it is very helpful to see the shader against something other than a gray background. The checkerboard pattern is a good one to use for most purposes and is especially helpful when previewing reflection and refraction. Cycle through the various preview backgrounds and return to No Walls.

9. Shader Operators (SHOPs)

187

The button with the checkerboard and red square is the Show Alpha button. If your shader uses transparency (often called Alpha or Opacity in the shader), toggle this button on in order to see through the those areas correctly.

The Scale parameter controls the scale of the preview geometry. This allows you to adjust the scale of the sphere to the size of the object that it is intended to receive this SHOP. It is difficult to see the change in size because the view is homed all the time and so the sphere looks the same size in the viewport. If the object that's receiving this shader is approximately 10 units in size, you need to set this scale value to 10 to see a reasonably accurate representation of the shader.

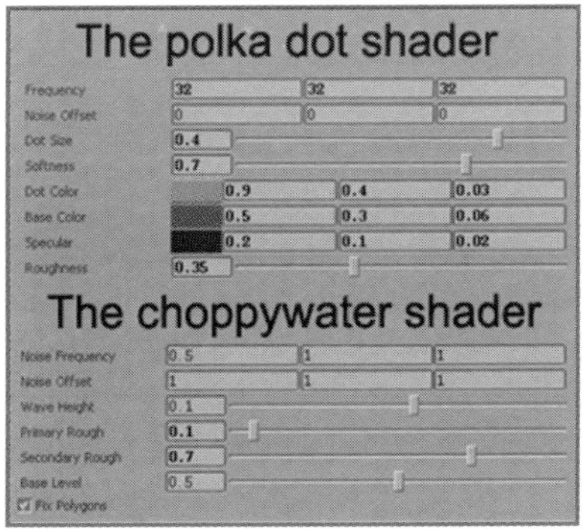

Figure 9.3
Values for the polka dot and choppywater shaders.

Play around the various parameters of the polka dot and choppywater shaders now. Adjustments made to their parameters will be reflected in the preview geometry in the shader viewer.

Notice that if you select the choppywater shader in the Network Editor, the polka dots disappear. That's no problem. Just go up to the top stowbar menu and select it from the drop-down menu. Now, both shaders will be previewed no matter which is selected in the Network Editor.

Adjust the parameters for the Polka Dot and Choppywater shaders so that they match those shown in Figure 9.3. You are going for a reasonable semblance of an orange.

Applying Shaders

There are basically two places to apply shaders in Houdini. The first, and simplest, is per object in the Object context. This has the advantage of simplicity because one shader will be applied to the entire object. The disadvantage is also the simplicity because it's rare that a single shader is appropriate for all parts of an object.

As with all networks in Houdini, shaders can be chosen in the root level SHOPs context or you can use the network within network approach and place a SHOP network inside of another type of network. You will most often use the second approach so that you can embed the shaders inside the object to which they apply.

Apply Shaders at the Object Level

If you have a simple object, like an orange, where a single surface shader and a single displacement shader will define the look for the whole object, you can apply the shaders at the Object level. This means that you are applying your shaders to the object no matter what groups are inside. Let's use the two shaders you have just created to turn a gray, shiny sphere into a decently delicious orange.

1. Reconfigure your panes so that you have Object viewer, Network Editor, and Parameters panes linked together and an unlinked SHOP Network Editor. Because you've already set the basic look of the orange, you don't need to keep the SHOP Viewer or Parameters panes around.

2. Inside the orange object, delete the file node if it exists. Drop a Sphere SOP and leave it at the defaults.

3. Move back up to the Object level. There are a few ways you can apply the shaders to the orange object. One way is to drag and drop each shader onto the object in the viewport. To do this, simply click and hold on the SHOP's icon and drag it into the viewport. When the mouse is over an area that can accept the shader, the mouse pointer will change to an arrow with a + below it. Release the mouse button and the shader will be applied to the object.

4. Alternatively, you can select the shader in the object's parameters. Go to the object's Shading tab and you'll see the SHOP Surface and SHOP Displacement parameters. If you already dropped both shaders, you'll see these filled in with the polka dot and choppywater shaders. If not, you can drag and drop the shaders into these fields as well. In addition, you can click the + button on the right side of the field and navigate through the tree view to the desired shader. Note that you cannot apply the polka dot shader to the displacement field, nor vice versa. The polka dot shader is of type Surface and the choppywater is of type Displacement. So they can only be applied to the correct field.

5. Use the Quick Render button to choose the fast_mantra output driver and render the sphere geometry with the shaders applied. You will need to reposition the light objects to get a better look. For more information about lights in Houdini, check out the software documentation.

Fly me to Florida on a freight rain! You have an orange nearly good enough to eat. I don't recommend trying it though. Go to your local market, buy an orange, study it, and play with these two shaders, or later roll your own, until you perfect the resemblance. Although this render is a rough approximation, it is a great starting point for further experimentation. When playing with the parameters, it is helpful to be looking at an orange and thinking, "What makes an orange look like an orange?" An orange isn't perfectly round. It has a dimpled kind of texture. It has small variations in color. There are some darker smudges here and there. Incorporate as many of the subtleties of the real object into its 3D equivalent as possible. The more you can do this, the more realistic and visually interesting your renders will be. With the parameters listed and minor changes to the position of the lights, your render should look something like Figure 9.4. Note that both of the shaders used in this exercise are completely procedural in that they don't depend on texture maps to generate the patterns. Houdini has a number of procedural shaders that are anti-aliased well and, like these two, can be used for a variety of purposes.

Figure 9.4
The rendered orange.

Apply Shaders Using the Shader SOP

It is also possible to apply shaders at the SOP level using the Shader SOP. This allows for more control than using the shading parameters at the Object level. At the Object level, the shader is applied to every piece of geometry contained within the object. Using a Shader SOP, you can have individual chains of SOPs using different shaders. Let's apply a couple of shaders to a very basic cloth simulation. This file is a simple example of one way to use a spring SOP and is not using DOPs, which is a context that is covered in Chapter 12, "Dynamic Operators."

1. Load clothStarter.hip from the Chapter 9>hips folder and jump into the swingingCloth object. Play the simulation through once or twice and you can see that cloth falls onto a bar and then swings around a bit.

9. Shader Operators (SHOPs)

189

2. Drop a SHOP network next to the `finalCloth` node and jump into it. Let's define for the appearance of the metal bar first. Choose a VEX Brushed Aluminum shader, rename it `barAluminium`, and enter the parameters shown in Figure 9.5.

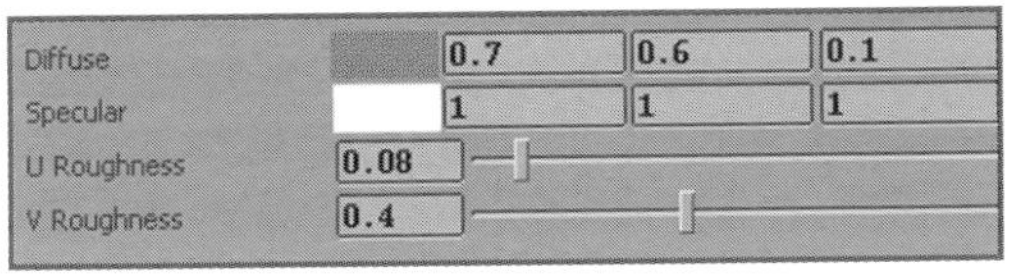

3. Jump back up to SOPs and insert a Shader SOP after the sweep node. Click the + button to the right of the Surface field at the top (not in the tabs), use tree view to find the `barAluminium` shader, and press Accept. You have just applied a shader to a portion of the geometry contained within the `swingingCloth` object, being the bar geometry.

Figure 9.5
Parameters for the `barAluminium` shader.

4. Jump back into the SHOP network and let's bring in a surface shader and a displacement shader for the cloth. Choose a VEX Gingham Checks shader and rename it `clothGingham` and leave it at the defaults. Next, choose a VEX Burlap shader and rename it `clothBurlap`.

5. Jump back up to SOPs and insert a Shader SOP after the `fixedGroup` node. In the Surface field at the top, choose the `clothGingham` shader. In the Displacement field at the top, choose the `clothBurlap` shader. That's all it takes. By placing a Shader SOP in a particular spot in a branch, you are applying a shader to everything feeding into that node. In order to see the shaders in the viewport, you will need to reset your playbar because the Spring SOP is a simulation. Figure 9.6 shows a render with these three shaders applied. Note how the `clothBurlap` displacement shader adds a nice bit of surface detail.

Figure 9.6
The rendered `swingingCloth` object.

Apply Shaders to Groups Using the Shader SOP

You have just looked at applying different shaders to different branches of a SOP network, but you can also apply different shaders to different parts of geometry in the same branch using a single Shader SOP that references groups. The concept is the same as before, with the addition of creating and using groups to gain more control. In this quick exercise, you'll apply three shaders to three groups at the SOP level using a single Shader SOP.

Create the Groups

Before you can apply shaders to groups, you first must define the groups. Makes good sense, don't you think?

1. Load up the file `treeTrophyStarter.hip`, which contains a simple model of a trophy anyone yearns most for... *Best Foliage in Show*.

2. Dive into the SOP network of the `treeTrophy` object. Notice that there is one SOP chain defining the tree and leaves, and another defining the base. These are merged, and then a Null SOP named `finalTrophy` has the Display and Render flags.

3. Your trophy will use one shader for the tree, a metal shader; one for the leaves, also a metal shader; and finally one for the base, a granite shader. First, you need to group the different pieces. Insert a Group SOP after the `lsystem` node. Rename this SOP to `treeGroup`. In the Group Name field, enter **treeGroup** and make sure the Number: Enable toggle is turned on. Ensure the Display and Render flags are on this node and you can see that both the leaves and the tree are included in the group, as they are both yellow. The Group SOP by default groups everything coming into it because the

Pattern field is empty, which is another way of saying everything is coming in. MMB on this node and notice the various geometry types that exist. The tree trunk parts are mesh, so choose Mesh in the Geometry Type menu. Because the tree trunk is the only mesh type of geometry feeding in, it is the only geometry included in the group.

4. Insert another Group SOP below the treeGroup node and rename it to leavesGroup. In the Group Name field, enter leavesGroup and make sure the Number:Enable toggle is turned on. Pull the Display and Render flags down on this node and you again see that, by default, everything is included in the newly created group. The leaves are primitive circles, so choose Circles in the Geometry Type menu and notice now only the leaves are members of this group. MMB on the leavesGroup node and you can see you have the two primitive groups you just created. (Actually, there is a third called lsysJ, which is automatically created in the lsystem node, but you won't be using it. So you can safely ignore it.)

5. Next, insert a Group SOP below the duplicate2 node and rename it baseGroup. Ensure that the Number: Enable parameter is turned on. In the Group Name field, enter baseGroup. MMB on the icon of the baseGroup node and you should see that there is 1 primitive group called baseGroup that is comprised of 3 primitives.

Create the Shaders

Now if you MMB on the merge node, you should see all the groups peacefully coexisting… or so you'd like to believe! These groups let you apply different shaders in one branch using a single Shader SOP.

1. RMB on the output of the merge node and insert a Shader SOP. It has a bunch of tabs with different shader types, each with a Group field and Shader field. However, you haven't yet created the shaders you want to use, so none of it is particularly useful just yet. Go ahead and set the Display flag back on the finalTrophy node.

2. Off to the side of the shader node, drop a SHOP Network. Your network should now look like Figure 9.7.

An important point to understand is that you can only apply shaders to primitive groups (except in special cases) because shaders must be the same across a single primitive. Let's say you have a single triangle with three points. On it, you applied a shader named zero to point number 0, a shader named one to point number 1, and a shader named two to point number 2. When this triangle is rendered, the renderer would have no way of interpolating those names to shade the middle of the triangle. Which one would it pick? How would it blend the names (shaders) to render the middle of the triangle? Basically, it can't. However, if you apply the shader to the whole triangle (the primitive), everything is happy and smiling. There are ways to get around this limitation. For example, you can use VOPs to create a shader that would blend across a primitive using an attribute.

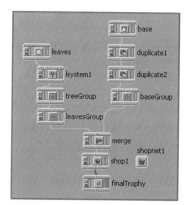

Figure 9.7
The current state of the SOP network.

Desktop layouts are very much a personal preference, but generally speaking when you are applying shaders to geometry, you'll want a pane configured to show you a SHOP list with parameters, while still being able to see and edit the SOP network. Figure 9.8 is one layout approach for customizing the interface to your advantage. Go ahead and save this as a customized desk. See Chapter 6 if you need a refresher as to how that is done.

3. Dive into the SHOP network and choose two VEX Metal shaders and a single VEX Gallery Granite shader. Rename one metal shader to treeMetal, the other metal shader to leafMetal, and the granite shader to baseGranite. The names don't matter except for organizational purposes so you can name them whatever makes the most sense to you.

4. For each of the shaders, enter the values shown in Figure 9.9. Only the areas that had non-default values are shown.

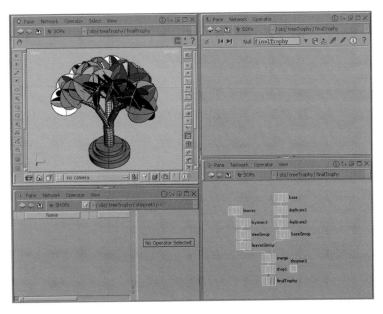

Figure 9.8
The desktop I am using for this exercise.

treeMetal shader

Ambient	1	1	1
Diffuse	1	0.8	0.2
Specular	1	1	1
Reflect	0.6	0.6	0.6

leafMetal shader

Ambient	1	1	1
Diffuse	0.6	0.9	0.5
Specular	1	1	1
Reflect	0.6	0.6	0.6

baseGranite shader

Base Light Model	VEX Specular		
Base Ambient	1	1	1
Base Diffuse	0.6	0.6	0.6
Splat Color 1	0.8	0.8	0.8
Splat Color 2	0.7	0.7	0.7
Base Specular	0.8	0.73	0.1
Base Roughness	0.2		
Base Reflect	0.8	0.8	0.8
Reflection Bias	0.01		
Disable Fog			

Figure 9.9
Parameter values for the three shaders.

Apply the Shaders

Now it's time to put those shaders to work to beautify the trophy.

1. In the shader node in the SOP network, make sure the Surface tab is visible, and click on the arrow to the right of the Group field. Select the treeGroup that you made earlier. You could also type this if you want, but the selector makes it easier and more importantly, prevents typing errors.

2. To assign a shader to this group, you can click the + button to the right of the Surface Shader field, and navigate the tree to find and apply the treeMetal shader. However, as you did in a previous example, you can also drag and drop the shader onto the field. LMB click and drag on the icon for the treeMetal shader and then drop it into the Surface Shader field.

3. You have one shader applied but where do you apply the other two? Simply click on the More button next to the Number Surfaces field and another empty pair of fields will appear. If you have a lot of shaders to apply, you can type the number of shaders you need in the Number Surfaces field. In this case create, you want a total of three.

4. In the next empty field down, select the leavesGroup and assign the leafMetal shader to it. On the last empty pair of fields, choose the baseGroup and assign its shader.

5. As you assign the shaders, you can see the color of the geometry change in the viewport (as long as you are using a shaded mode of viewing).

6. You'll notice that there are fields at the top of the SOP labeled Group, Surface, and Displacement that you have not used. These were used in the last exercise, as you only had one shader per field to apply.

7. Oh, I know you feel as though seven lifetimes have passed and you still have yet to bask in the glory of your hard-won *Best Foliage in Show* trophy. Wait not another minute longer! Render out a frame using the default View:Mantra output found in the quick launch button of the Viewer pane. Figure 9.10 has a render of your new most prized possession.

Figure 9.10
The trophy for *Best Foliage in Show*.

UV Coordinates

Application and use of UV Coordinates is essential to creating complex and realistic images. Houdini has a variety of powerful tools to apply and manipulate UV coordinates, as well as some useful utilities to help you use those UV coordinates to create texture maps. UV coordinates are simply numbers that usually range from zero to one in two directions. Then, the coordinates are tied to a texture map. The UV coordinates tell a shader where to find the parts of an image from a texture map.

The simplest case is a square grid (polygon or NURBs, it doesn't matter) geometry with orthographic UV coordinates applied. You will recall from Chapter 2 that orthographic simply means flat or without perspective. So, it's like projecting a grid of UV coordinates onto a grid of geometry.

A Simple UV Study

To get a sense of what is happening with the UV coordinates, let's saunter through a simple exercise that takes you through the application and analysis of the UV coordinates on a grid.

1. Load the file UVStarter.hip from the Chapter 9>hips directory. This files contains a grid and a planet already set up with shaders. The planet object should have its display toggled off. If you do see it, just turn off the display toggle on the node. Make sure you're looking through cam1 in the viewport and do a quick render with the mantra1 driver.

9. Shader Operators (SHOPs)

2. Notice that you see the mandrill four times. If you look at the wireframe, you'll see that there are four polygons. So, you're seeing the mandrill once on each polygon. If the shader doesn't find the uv attribute, it will use the parametric coordinates of the primitive, which is a fancy way of saying it applies its own UV coordinates to each primitive. This is what you are seeing right now. Each of the four polygons is a primitive and so each gets its own default parametric coordinates.

3. Jump into the grid object and change the grid Primitive Type to Mesh and render again. Now the mandrill is only seen once across the whole grid. A mesh type grid is a single primitive, so the default parametric coordinates are for the whole grid. Remember that you can always MMB on the icon of a SOP node to find out how many primitives are contained within it.

UV Texture SOP

The UV Texture SOP is a good choice for more straightforward texturing tasks.

1. Set the grid back to Polygon, and if you like, re-render to verify that you now have four mandrills again. Append a UV Texture SOP to the shader node and change the Projection Axis to Z. Make sure to set the Display and Render flags on the new texture node and render. Behold the result of this arcane lore! There is now a single mandrill even though the grid is polygonal and is comprised of four primitives. This is because you have applied a uv attribute and as soon as the shader sees it, the shader uses that attribute instead of the default parametric coordinates. MMB on the texture node to verify that have indeed added a uv point attribute.

> The order of the shader and UV Texture SOPs doesn't matter. You can place the texture before the shader and get the same result. It is common in complex networks to place the texture and shaders in arbitrary order near the top of the chain and have their effect reach through to the final node.

2. Go to smooth shading mode and you can see the mandrill in OpenGL. This is convenient, as it allows you to adjust the UV coordinates interactively without having to re-render the image constantly to see how it has changed.

3. Using the number ladder, interactively adjust the Offset U and note the mandrill sliding from side to side on the grid. To verify which field is the Offset U field, just hold your pointer over the Offset label and a tooltip will pop up, showing the names of each of the fields. Offset in U is the first one. Experiment with the other Offset fields and also the Scale and Angle fields as well to see their effects.

4. Note that when you MMB the texture icon, the uv attribute was listed as having three components. U and V are the first two; the third value is known as W and is only used in very special cases where you want to define the height of something off the surface. Most texture maps only use the U and V coordinates and ignore the W coordinate. You will also ignore this third coordinate when talking about texture maps.

5. Go to wireframe shading and turn on the display of Point Texture Coordinates from the viewport's right stowbar. Figure 9.11 shows the results captured from the side a bit so the numbers are more easily read.

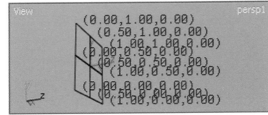

Figure 9.11
The grid with point texture coordinates displayed.

After the UV coordinates have been projected, there is a new attribute on each point of the grid called uv, which will be used by the shader. Showing Point Texture Coordinates allows you see in the viewport what those values actually are. Now, if you adjust the Offset or Scale, you will see the numbers adjusting. This is not something you use very often in production, but it's a great learning and debugging tool.

Now that you have a visual reference, it's easier to understand and see what the UV coordinates are doing. The UV coordinate (0,0) in the lower-left corner corresponds to the mandrill image's lower-left corner, and the UV coordinate (1,1) in the upper-right corner corresponds to the mandrill image's upper-right corner. The UV coordinate (0.5,0.5) corresponds to the middle of the mandrill, and so on.

6. If you increase the Rows of the Grid to 11, note that each V coordinate is now an increment of .1. But, go to a shading mode and the mandrill looks exactly the same. This is the power of UV coordinates. The resolution of the underlying geometry generally doesn't matter, as the UV coordinates will be interpolated across the points. Incidentally, this interpolation is exactly what Mantra is doing internally to get the UV coordinates from the areas inside each polygon where there are no points.

UV Project SOP

The UV Texture SOP is a fairly simple, automatic SOP that fits the UV coordinates to whatever geometry is fed in. This is great in simple cases but doesn't offer much control. The UV Project SOP is a more powerful and controllable SOP that also has some useful handles for viewport UV manipulation.

1. Jump over to SHOPs for a moment and find the v_layered1 SHOP. In the Texture Map parameter, navigate and find the planetMap.rat. Go to the second tab and select cloudsMap.rat for its Texture Map. Both maps have a file supplied on the accompanying Website in the Chapter 9>maps folder. Go back to Objects, turn off the display of the grid object, and turn on the display of the planet object. Then jump into the planet node.

2. Over the viewport, choose a UVProject operation and then select the primitive selection mask. Select the entire object and complete the operation. By default, you get an orthographic projection and the vertices are all highlighted, which prevents you from seeing the texture that has been applied in the shader node. The vertices may not be highlighted if you have previously toggled off that option in the preferences menu. RMB on one of the vertices in the viewport (or RMB on the uvproject node in the Network Editor) and select Highlight. This will remove the selected vertex highlighting and allow you to see the texture on the surface.

Applying UV coordinates requires you to select either points or vertices. You usually want vertices, as they help prevent edge wrapping problems. Houdini offers a handy shortcut to selecting vertices. If you use the primitive selection mask (as you just did in step 2), but the operation wants points or vertices, the primitive selection will automatically be converted into a vertex selection.

If you are doing a lot of UV texturing, you can turn off the auto-highlighting in Settings>Main Preferences->Objects and Geometry->Highlight Selected Geometry in Viewport.

3. You can now manipulate the handle directly in the viewport and see the UV coordinates move the texture around. Orthographic projection might be what you want in some cases on a sphere, but let's apply a spherical projection to the sphere. In the parameters for the uvproject node, change the Projection to Polar. You can still manipulate the handle if you want, but a better place to start from is the Initialize in the parameters. Click the Initialize button and the operation's guide geometry will snap to the sphere. It may not align exactly the way you want. You can change the Method parameter to specify a plane to snap to. Basically, the chosen plane specifies how the handle orients itself when you click Initialize. For example, set the Method to use the XY Plane and press Initialize again. The X and Y parts of the handle are now aligned to the XY plane in the viewport. There are several projection methods available, but generally orthographic, polar, and cylindrical are the ones most commonly used.

> The handles for UV manipulation work just like the handles in SOPs or Objects, or anywhere else in Houdini. If you RMB on the handle, you get a menu that allows you fine control of the handle and there are hotkeys associated with the various usages as well.

How to Layer Textures

Thus far you've only had a single layer of textures. However, most often you'll want to layer the textures for more complex and interesting effects. Also, you'll most likely want different UV coordinates for each layer for maximum control. Thank the gods of multiple planes of existence and the developers at Side Effects, for this task is quite easy in Houdini using either the supplied shaders or by making your own in VOPs. There are two parts to the puzzle when layering textures. The first is applying the UV coordinates so each layer has its own control. The second is knowing how to get the SHOP shader to actually use the different UV coordinates so as to apply the layers in a clever way.

The next chapter contains an exercise in which you texture a soccer ball and shows you how to access different UV coordinates in VOPs. Right now, you'll add the second set of UV coordinates in SOPs and then look at the supplied Layered Surface SHOP to see how to access them.

1. Continuing on from where you left off with the simple planet object from the previous exercise, rename the UV Project SOP in the network to applySphereUV so that looking at this network will be clearer later on.

2. In the viewport, choose a Layer operation and type the a hotkey to select all and RMB to complete. At the top of the viewport or in the parameters for the layer SOP, set the Current Layer to 2. Rename the layer node to setLayer2 for ease of identification. In the OpenGL viewport, it seems like your texture has disappeared! This is actually correct because you have moved to a new UV layer but have not yet applied the new UV coordinates. Soon the viewport will again be as right as rain (cue: foreshadowing literary device).

3. MMB on the setLayer2 node to access the info window and notice it tells you that you are "Working on layer 2 of 2". Now, that's handy.

4. In the viewport, select a UVProject operation, select all, and RMB to complete. Turn off the highlight if needed and shazaam! The OpenGL texturing came back! Just as you did before, set the projection type to Polar and in the Initialize tab, set the Method to XY Plane, and then click Initialize. If you adjust this handle, you can position your clouds over your planet's surface! Rename this new UV project node to applyUV2 and then MMB it to note that there are now two UV attributes, uv and uv2, which are the two being used by the planet's surface and clouds, respectively.

How It Works

It seems to work great, but why? If you have no Layer SOPs, you are always working on layer 1, which is the default layer. Once you add a new Layer SOP and set it to another layer, any SOP that you use after that creates attributes that will have the number of the layer appended to the attribute's name. SOPs like UV Project, UV Texture, the Point SOP, and many others are examples of ones that will use this feature. All your shader has to do is make sure it knows about these attributes and you're all set! If you want to explicitly set the first UV layer for file clarity or some other reason, you can place a Layer SOP before the first UV Project node, but it isn't necessary to do.

The Layered Surface SHOP

Let's take a quick look at the Layered Surface SHOP, which is what you are currently using. It is a default shader that comes with Houdini and is useful for many basic surfaces. Ultimately, you will probably find yourself heading in to VOPs to make your own custom shaders for specific effects or models. But, when starting out, the Layered Surface SHOP is great resource.

1. Select the shop1 node and look at its parameters. In the Surface tab, the Surface Shader is set to /shop/v_layered1, which is the name of the SHOP that is applying the planet's textures. If you click the Jump to Op button (the arrow to the left of the path), the parameters and all linked panes will jump to the SHOP specified. Use the back arrow on the pane navigation bar to jump back to where you came from. If you hold down Ctrl before you click on the Jump to Op button, instead of jumping you to the SHOP network, a new floating pane will appear that has the parameters for the SHOP being referenced.

   In fact, both methods are quite useful for particular situations. Jumping to the SHOP network quickly lets you see the shader ball and other shaders in the same network, but popping up the SHOP Parameters lets you make adjustments to the current object without leaving your network. If you're using IPR you can stay in the object, and make quick shader adjustments in the floating shader parameters window. For your look at the Layered Surface SHOP, you'll turn on IPR and use the floating popup parameters to make fast adjustments.

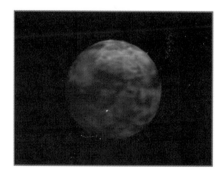

Figure 9.12
The happy mother.

2. Go back to the SOP network for the planet, if you aren't there already. Ctrl LMB on the Jump to Op button to pop up the floating parameters for the Layered Surface SHOP.

3. Change your viewport to IPR Viewer and toggle on Disable auto-update for a moment. Select the mantra1 output driver from the pull-down menu. Turn on the IPR flag and toggle off Disable auto-update. Figure 9.12 has a render of the wonder. And so appears Earth, in the year 2233. In that year, the gentle mother stood witness to the birth of the most swashbuckling, alien-loving, over-acting starship captain to ever cruise the space lanes! Yes, it was a good year.

4. The base tab is defining the texture that is on the bottom of the layers, which in this case is the land and ocean texture map. Switch to the 2 tab, which is defining the clouds. Play around with the various parameters. The help for the Layered Surface gives you some hints on what the parameters will do, but most are fairly straightforward. The ones I use the most are listed here.

◆ Compositing (on all tabs following the Base tab): Determines how the layer is overlaid on the layer before it. In this case, it determines how layer 2 is composited onto the base layer. Add gives you brighter clouds, whereas multiply gives you only clouds.

◆ Texture Map: The image file loaded from disk. When using Mantra, you should always use a RAT format image!

◆ Texture Tints: What will the map be applied to? Most common are Diffuse and Specular.

◆ S/T Map Filter: The type of filter applied to the texture map. Gaussian and Bartlett arguably look the best but are also somewhat slower to render. Point means no filtering will be used.

◆ S/T Map Blur: The amount of blur applied to the texture. You almost always want some blur applied. The default of a Box filter of size 1 really does little, but is often enough to make sure there are no aliasing problems.

◆ Ambient/Diffuse/Specular/Reflect: Depending on what your Texture Tints are set to, this allows you to modify the color of the texture map. In this example, adjusting the Diffuse will let you make differently colored clouds. Set this to orange to preview what your world might look like after another few centuries of emitting carbon dioxide at the current accelerating pace!

◆ Alpha: This lets you control the density of the Alpha channel of the texture map. If you set this above 1, you will get thicker clouds; below 1 gives you thinner clouds.

◆ Texture Source: Geometry Attribute: This just means that the UV coordinates are coming from the UV attributes you applied; in this case, from the UV Project SOP. I always apply my UV coordinates onto the geometry, so I've never changed this setting. However, you can use the Layered Surface SHOP to apply texture coordinates for you if you desire.

◆ UV Attribute: The name of the UV texture attribute to use. By default, this is uv2 for the second layer, but you could change this if you wanted.

The Base tab has some additional controls that affect the entire surface including Alpha Para and Alpha Perp (these allow you to fade off the edges or the center of your object), as well as the Lighting Model, which controls what type of specular highlight is applied.

The .rat image format is native to Houdini and is optimized to use minimal memory and various filtering options. That's great to know, but how do you turn an image of another format into a .rat file? If you have a .tga, a .tiff, or a .jpg, you should convert it to RAT using Mplay or the command-line tools icp or iconvert. If you do not use RAT, you will be using too much memory. Your renders will be slower and you will not be able to use the filtering options. One of the reasons the .rat format uses less memory is because it's a MIPMAP format, which contains four resolutions that Mantra can access in a tile by tile format. This allows Mantra to only load in a portion of the texture map, thereby saving memory.

Texturing the Dragonfly

Now that you have a good understanding of the UVs and texturing, let's now apply it to something more substantial than a sphere or grid. The dragonfly model used in various chapters seems an appropriate test subject. The dragonfly feels pretty good about itself, but I am sure it would much prefer more colorful plumage. It's not going to have much luck impressing the denizens of its world with only a shiny grey carapace. Let's bestow a blessing upon it and ourselves by putting your newly gained skills to work. Rather than spend time (and pages!) describing in detail applying textures to the whole dragonfly, you'll look at adding UV coordinates and textures to representative pieces of the dragonfly. Then, you can use that direction to finish the rest, or begin work on your own creation.

Apply UV Coordinates

In this case, you happen to have a live SOP network waiting to be modified, which is one aspect of the core power of Houdini. So long as you want it, you always have access to a history of construction. You'll jump and down the network adding operators where necessary to impart color to your little friend. In some instances, you might be required to use a model that was created in a less procedural software package with the result being that you don't have access to the SOP network to modify. Houdini has the tools for either job and only the approach differs. The following exercises demonstrate both approaches.

Apply UV Coordinates to the Legs

When doing UV texturing and applying shaders, it is helpful to have four panes on your desktop with three of them linked together. The way I work is to have a Viewer pane, a Parameters pane, and a Network Editor pane linked together, with a fourth pane unlinked and set to be a Network pane. You can start with the default Build desk and split the viewport top/bottom, for example.

1. Load the file `dragonflyTextureStarter.hip` from the `Chapter9>hips` folder. This file contains the complete SOPs network that was used to build the dragonfly. You want to apply textures to all six legs. Thankfully, due to the way the dragonfly was built, you only have to texture one leg and you get the rest for free! In the linked network pane, enter the dragonfly object. Spend a little time familiarizing yourself with the network. Don't forget you can put the Display flag at the top of a chain, then, in the viewport, use the Page Up and Page Down keys to move up and down the network to quickly view the changes interactively.

2. Note that there are two chains for the legs: one that ends in `SINGLE_LEG_SUBD` and another that ends in `LEG_STRAIGHT_SUBD`. The `LEG_STRAIGHT_SUBD` chain is not wired into anything right now. You added that to make this exercise a little faster. However, all you did was to copy all the SOPs after the Box SOP up to the `SINGLE_LEG_SUBD` SOP, then put the Display flag on the Transform SOP at the top, and work your way down using the Page Down hotkey in the viewport. On each SOP, you just rotated the handles in X so that they were straight. It took about two minutes to quickly zip down and straighten the leg. With a nice straight leg to work with, it will be very easy to apply UV coordinates. You could also do this trick with a model that did-n't have the SOP network, but having the SOP network makes future changes much more efficient. If you wanted to use a model imported from outside Houdini, you'd need to use the Edit operation to manually straighten the leg.

3. Using the RMB, append a UV Project SOP to the `LEG_STRAIGHT_SUBD` node and put the Display flag on it. Set the Projection parameter to Cylindrical and the Group Type to Vertices. Generally speaking, you will want to use Vertex UV attributes (as opposed to Point attributes) when doing texturing. Vertex texturing helps avoid texture seam problems.

   In the Initialize tab, click the Initialize button. The Method is set to To Best Plane, which works well in this case. The cylinder snaps to the leg nicely.

4. Append a UV Quickshade SOP to the uvproject node. In the Texture Map field, find and select the textureGrid.rat that is inn Chapter9>maps on the Website. Set the Display flag to this node and set your shading to smooth shaded in the viewport. You should see the textureGrid.rat texture applied to your leg. If you see a solid pink (some might even say salmon!) color, that means the texture was not found and you need to check the path.

5. You can see the texture on the straight leg, but you can also look at the UV coordinates unwrapped in the viewport to see their relationship with the texture map. In the viewport, press spacebar+5 to bring up the UV viewport. You now see a view of the geometry flattened out. Type **d** to pop up the Display Options interface. In the Background tab and Image Source subtab, set the Filename to the textureGrid.rat that you used previously. Turn off Apply Operation to All Split Views, then turn on Display Background Images. Your viewport should now look something Figure 9.13.

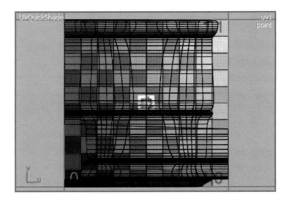

Figure 9.13
The UV viewport with the background map displayed.

Using the UV viewport with the background image displayed is a very powerful and intuitive way of visualizing your textures. By setting another pane to the normal perspective viewport, you are able to see the geometry in 3D and also flat in 2D "UV" space. You can translate vertices in this view and so intuitively push and pull the texture into place. Note that you aren't actually translating anything around in 3D space so you won't destroy your physical geometry. You are just adjusting how the geometry and texture relate to each other. For the purposes here, the textures coordinates are sufficient and so you can move on. Side Effects has some very good tutorials as part if you want learn more about this topic. Specifically, check out the UV Edit and UV Brush operations, which allow for finer control over the UV coordinates.

Transfer UV Coordinates

Regardless of whether you further modified the UV coordinates, you now need to transfer them back onto the original, bent leg. The Attribute Copy SOP is the tool for this job. You'll discover as you learn Houdini that the Attribute ops such as Attribute Copy, Attribute Transfer, Attribute Create, and others offer you direct access to the one of the core features of Houdini, which is the ease with which you can move attributes around.

1. Bring up the Display options again, turn off the display of the background image, and then go back to a perspective viewport.

2. RMB on the output of the SINGLE_LEG_SUBD node and insert an Attribute Copy SOP. Set the display dlag on it and you'll get a red flag indicating an error. MMB on the red flag to read a popup indicating the problem, which is that there are not enough sources specified. Wire the uvquickshade node into the second input of the attributecopy node and the red flag turns into a yellow warning flag.

A red flag means there is an error, whereas a yellow flag indicates a warning. A red flag breaks everything; no geometry is processed and you must fix the problem to make things work again. A yellow flag, however, will still allow the geometry to be processed. A yellow flag usually means something is not working as you might expect, but it's not fatal to the network.

3. MMB on the yellow flag to see what the warning is. It's a warning that the attribute Cd isn't used or is not recognized. That's because the default attribute that this operation looks for is Color, which is the standard Houdini attribute Cd. The problem is that the straight leg does not have the Cd attribute on it and so the Attribute Copy gives you a warning that it doesn't exist.

4. Change the Attribute menu from Color to Texture UV and the yellow flag goes away. MMB on the SINGLE_LEG_SUBD and then on the Attribute Copy. Notice that the SINGLE_LEG_SUBD node doesn't have UV coordinates, but the attribcopy node does. You have effectively copied over the UV coordinates from the straight leg to the bent leg. Thus far, only the UV coordinates were copied which is why you don't see the texture map on the bent leg. Change the Attribute menu from Texture UV to Other Attribute. Now, all the attributes are copied, over and so you can see the texture map on its new recipient. If you had many attributes and only wanted to pass along specific ones, you could enter those in the Attribute Name field. In this case, copying them all is fine.

   In fact, you don't need to keep any of the attributes except the UV coordinates. For now though, let's leave the texture on and later you can change the attribcopy back to UV Texture only.

5. Put the Display flag on the Leg_with_Hairs node and you get a yellow flag. If you MMB on the yellow flag, you'll get a really long, somewhat obscure warning about a mismatch of attributes. MMB on the copy node that is the second input to the Leg_with_Hairs Merge SOP. Notice that there are no attributes. This is the reason for the yellow flag. The leg has numerous attributes, but the hairs do not have any attributes and so the Merge SOP is bringing it to your attention.

The Merge SOP is used very often in Houdini, usually without problems. However, in the previous case, you see one of the issues that can arise. If you merge one piece of geometry that has attributes with another piece of geometry that does not have attributes, the geometry that did not have the attributes will be given the same attributes that the first piece had.

One of the most confusing cases of this arises when you have normals (attribute "N") on one piece of geometry and then merge it with some geometry with no normals. The geometry that did not have the normals turns black when you view it in smooth shaded mode and often when you render it too. This is because the "new" normals on the newly merged geometry are initialized to 0, which is an invalid normal.

You can easily see this by taking two polygonal spheres, applying normals to one (use the Facet SOP), and then merging them together. The sphere with no normals will be black. If you open the Geometry Spreadsheet on the merge node, you'll see that the second set of normals are 0,0,0.

---

6. The "new" attributes attached to the merged geometry will be initialized to a default value, which is usually 0. So, in this case, the leg hairs would now have UV attributes but they would be set to 0. Basically, they are useless and won't really hurt anything but your sense of flag-free network pride.

7. To appease the pangs of pride (but only a little!), let's apply some UV coordinates to the little leg hairs too. Simply insert a UV Project SOP after the tube1 node in the little network of SOPs that make the hairs. Set the Display flag to this node and press Enter over the viewport to see the blue guide geometry. Change the Projection to Cylindrical, the Group Type to Vertices, and then click the Initialize button.

8. Put the Display flag back on the `Leg_with_Hairs` SOP and, much to your consternation!, the yellow flag persists. If you MMB on the node, you'll notice that it has a number of Primitive attributes as well. These are from the UV Quickshade operation and contain the attributes needed to show the textures in the viewport. Go to the `attrib-copy1` node and change the Attribute to UV Texture. The yellow flag disappears because you're only copying the UV attribute now, but the texture disappears too. That's fine, as you'll see it again later.

9. Set the Display flag on the legs (Merge) node. This shows you all the legs merged together. Insert a UV Quickshade SOP after this node and turn on its Display flag. Select the `textureGrid.rat` in the Texture Map field. Figure 9.14 shows the test texture applied to the deformed legs.

10. Hmmm, you seem to be using this combination of UV Quickshade and the `TextureGrid.rat` image a lot. It sure would make life sparkly if that map was already chosen when you laid down new UV Quickshade SOPs. Say no more of how sparkly life could be when life is ready to sparkle for you right now! In the Parameters pane, LMB the Presets pull-down menu (the little down-arrow to the right of the name of the SOP) and choose Save As Permanent Defaults. From now on, the Texture Map will use the `TextureGrid.rat` by default. Now, that's sparkly.

Figure 9.14
The test texture applied to all of the legs.

Despite the number of steps you've taken, you've really only used only three operations to apply UV coordinates to all the legs and the hairs on the legs! The unadulterated joy of proceduralism. If you later edit the UV coordinates of the single original leg, all the legs are automatically updated as well.

Apply UV Coordinates to the Wings

When the wings were created, they were created as only tubes with no surface. Why? Because that's what looked sweeter for rendering with no textures, as was done when the exercise was originally created. That would be fine you wanted fully transparent wings. As you want to do a bit of learning here, you want a surface there for texturing. As you keep repeating, it's all pretty simple when you can go back up the network and make changes that cook down to the end. You might even say that is your "mantra." I promise to castigate myself later for that brutal laying down of a pun. You'll use one of the curves that created the veins in the wings to create the surface of the wing as well.

1. Find the SOP chain that ends with the `wingsFore` (Null) node.

To quickly find a particular node, go to the Operator->Find Operator menu or use the hotkey Alt+F and type the name of the node you seek. One limitation of this approach is that it will only search the current network level, meaning it wouldn't find a node named `wingsFore` in a different Object. If you didn't know in which network the particular node resided, you can use the `opfind` in the Textport to find out. Bring up a floating Textport with Windows>Textport (or Alt+T). No matter where you currently are in the path hierarchy, type **opfind -n wingsFore** and it will output the path to that node, which is `/obj/dragonfly/wingsFore` in this case. You can then jump into that network and use the Find Operator window to highlight the exact node.

2. Put the Display flag on the `curve1` node and notice that this curve is closed and, in a shaded mode, looks like a surface. Use the MMB to branch append a UV Quickshade SOP and move over the Display flag so you see this node's contribution. UV Quickshade will apply its own UV coordinates if it doesn't find any, as is the case here. In this case, they aren't what you want, but, by applying the UV Quickshade before you apply the UV Project, you can see the texture as you adjust the UV Project's handles.

3. Append a UV Project SOP to the `uvquickshade3` node and update the Display flag. Set the Group Type to Vertices and click the Initialize button. In the viewport, press Enter to enter the `UVProject` operational state. You should see the blue guide geometry around the wing shape. However, the grid is squished because UV Project tries to fit as much of the geometry into the UV square as possible, which results in squashing in this case.

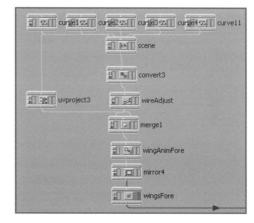

Figure 9.15
The current state of the `wingsFore` part of the network.

4. In the UV Project's Transformation tab, copy the X scale (using Ctrl+C) and paste it into the Scale Y field (using Ctrl+P). The projection is now square and so the texture is also square.

5. Insert a Merge SOP above the `wingAnimFore` node (after the `wireAdjust` node). Wire the `uvproject` node's output into this new merge node. Delete the UV Quickshade SOP, as you don't need that anymore. Put the Display flag on the `wingsFore` node and now the wings have a surface as well as veins. This part of your network should look like Figure 9.15. Repeat these procedures for the Hind wings. Some of the names are different but the concepts and procedures are the same.

Some people find it annoying to have "crossed wires" in SOP (or other) networks. Sometimes you can't avoid them and sometimes you can. In the parameters for each Merge SOP there is a section called Input Operators where you can drag and drop the inputs to re-order the operators, which will change the order of the wiring. This ordering then determines how the wires are shown to be feeding into the merge node. Operationally, the order of inputs doesn't usually matter and changing the order usually won't change the effective output of what the merge is passing along.

UV Coordinates for the Wing Hinges, Eyes, and Antennae

At this point, you have several methods you could use. The simplest is to just use a UV Project before the Mirror SOPs. If you wanted to be more sophisticated, you could model the hinges to make them more spherical or cylindrical, project the appropriate UV coordinates, and then use another Attribute Copy SOP to put the UV coordinates back on the deformed hinge. Texturing the eyes and the antennae covers the same ground, with the eyes being relatively spherical and the antennae being cylindrical. Choose whichever methods you wish to get more practice with to apply coordinates and let's move on to new material. Check out the `dragonflyWithShadersComplete.hip` on the Website to see how I went about it. If you do check it out, make sure to save your current hip file; you continue with it in the next section.

Apply UV Coordinates to the Body

Texturing the body requires a different approach. In this case, the more complex geometry of the body makes it hard to use a straight cylindrical projection. This is a perfect use of the UV Pelt operation. Side Effects provides an excellent tutorial on using the UV Pelt operation, so you won't cover it in all its gory detail here. (Yes, a second lashing is definitely in order as the wordplay is fast and fierce! If this doesn't seem particularly funny, it may be that you have yet to find out what a Pelt SOP does… or it could be that getting into Houdini beyond a certain level should not be recommended!)

1. Set the Display flag on the Body node and go to flat wire shading mode. This is a very useful view mode when selecting details like a polygon's edges in the viewport and also to easily examine the topology of a piece of geometry.

2. Go to a top view and, in the viewport, start a UV Pelt operation. Left click on an edge that is running from head to tail and is exactly in the middle of the geometry. The edge should have a red arrow on it, indicating you can select an edge loop. Ctrl+RMB to pop up the UV Pelt menu and choose Select Edge Loop (or use the hotkey Shift+L) to select a loop that goes completely around the body. If you made a mistake in the selection, just type ` (the backtick key) or click the Reselect Geometry for Current Operation button and try again. Figure 9.16 shows a close-up of the head and torso area so you can check that you are getting the right edgeloop. Once you have the loop all the way around the body, RMB to complete the operation.

Figure 9.16
A close-up of the correct edge loop around the dragonfly.

3. Change over to the UV viewport and note that UV coordinates are being applied but they are scrunched up in the middle. Crank up the Iterations and Boundary Springs really high until you get nice stretched out and relatively even UV coordinates. My settings were 1500 for Iterations and 20000 for Boundary Springs. Basically, you are using an edge loop to make a cut into the "pelt" of the dragonfly and then using the Iteration and Boundary Springs settings to stretch it out on a rack. Hence, the previous mention of gory detail!

4. Because you cut the geometry all the way around in the UV Pelt, it only applied UV coordinates to one half of the body. You need to determine which got them, cut off the other half, and then mirror back over so both sides have UV's and are ready to go. But, how do you know which one got the UVs? There are a number of ways to find out. You have used one possibility multiple times in this exercise. Do you know what it might be? <Insert a reasonable pause for pondering.> You'll the UV Quickshade operation.

5. Insert one under the pelt node and notice that now the `textureGrid.rat` is default and so saves you a little time going to find it. When viewed from above, the right side has UVs. Go ahead and delete the `quickshade` node; you no longer need it. Insert a Clip SOP after the `uvpelt` node. In the clip node, change the Direction to 1,0,0 to clip down the middle of the body.

6. Insert a Mirror SOP after the clip node. The default settings are fine. The body is whole again and now all of it has UV coordinates. If you want to, insert another UV Quickshade below the clip node to view the texture across the entire body. Eeet eez zat easy!

Apply Shaders and Textures

Not all models need UV coordinates because not all shaders will use texture maps. However, it's a pretty good bet that your models will need groups to assign shaders to unless the model is so simple that it needs only one shader. Just as you learned previously, there are basically two approaches when applying shaders in a SOP network like the dragonfly. The first is to put several Shader SOPs into the network, such that each Shader SOP applies a single shader to the geometry in its network branch. The second is to make one primitive group for each piece of geometry that will get a shader and then apply all the shaders in a single Shader SOP at the end of the network that references those groups.

There are advantages and disadvantages to each approach. Using multiple Shader SOPs allows you to quickly see in a network where each shader is being applied, and it means you can put the Render flag on that SOP and render only part of the model quickly and easily. However, using multiple Shader SOPs means that any time your geometry changes, you have to cook a lot of Shader SOPs, which on a complex model can be a bit slow. Also, if you haven't grouped your geometry, you lose the ability to split your model out into separate objects, which is a powerful way of setting unique render settings per group. The only real disadvantage to this method is that it's a little harder to see in the network where the shaders are being applied. Though, clever use of node coloring and naming can alleviate this. In most cases, the flexibility offered by using groups on your geometry more than outweighs the organizational issue and the small increase in memory usage. You will take the second approach and group out the parts of the dragonfly that require different shaders.

Create the Groups

Next, you'll create some useful groups that you can then individually apply shaders to.

1. You can either use the file you just finished applying the UV coordinates to or load the file dragonflyShadersStarter.hip that is provided. Enter into the dragonfly object and find the last SOP that defines the body of the dragonfly, which should be the mirror node and insert a Group SOP after it. As this network is already broken out into the various shading pieces, it will be quite easy to group. However, even if the entire model were just one chain, you can still select and apply groups in the viewport. Set the Group Name to be SHD_Body and also rename the node, to be the same.

It's generally a good idea to name the Group SOP node the same as the group that you're creating. This lets you see quickly in the network where the groups are being created. However, it's kind of a drag to have to type the name twice. So, rather than type things twice, you'll use a shortcut. In the Group Name field, enter $OS instead of the SHD_Body that you just typed in. $OS is a special local variable that gets replaced with the name of the current node. In the Presets menu, select Save As Permanent Defaults so that all future Group operations will already have $OS as the Group Name.

To remove the permanent defaults, use the Presets menu and select Delete Preset. This gives you a dialog box and lets you choose which default to remove.

2. Insert a Group SOP after the last node defining the Eyes, and rename the Group SOP to SHD_Eyes; doing this also make the Group Name SHD_Eyes because $OS is being used.

3. Repeat this and add groups for the antennae and legs. All the legs will get the same shaders. Put the Group SOP after the last Merge SOP that contains all the legs.

4. For the wings, it's a little more involved. Each wing has the surface that you projected the UV Coordinates onto and also the tubes. You want each wing surface to be a different shader, but the tubes from both wings get the same shader. In addition, the wing hinges will get their own shader. Insert a Group SOP after the UV Project for the forewing's surface. Name this group node to SHD_wingFore_Surface so it is clear what it is.

5. Insert a Group SOP after the polywire node that creates the fore wing's tubes and name this new node SHD_wingFore_Tubes.

6. Repeat the same steps for the hind wings, using appropriate names, of course.

7. The wing hinges will just get one group for them all, so insert a Group SOP after the Merge SOP that merges the hinges together. Name this node `SHD_wingHinges`.

   Why are all the groups prefixed with `SHD`? It's not essential, but it's a really good idea to name groups being used for specific things with a common prefix. In this case I chose `SHD` to indicate that these groups will be used to apply shaders. That doesn't mean these groups can't be used for other things.

8. MMB on the final Merge SOP that brings all the parts of the dragonfly together. Note that there are now primitive groups for all the various parts of the dragonfly. At last, at last! You are now ready to create and apply the shaders.

How to Save UV Images

Creating texture maps to apply to the materials is beyond the scope of this book, but there is a useful utility in Houdini to make creating those textures easier. Walk through using this utility on only the leg geometry. Feel free to get additional practice and repeat the technique for other parts of the model. When creating texture maps that are intended for specific parts of a model, it is very useful to have a representation of the UV coordinates as an image so that you can paint over it. Thankfully, this is easily accomplished.

1. Find the Attribute Copy node that is the single leg with UV coordinates applied. RMB on the icon of the Attribute Copy SOP and select Save Texture UV to Image. In the dialog box that appears, choose a filename and format. Choose a resolution for the image. 512X512 is generally considered the minimum useful resolution for a texture map, though you will often want a higher resolution if you are working in film or print. The UV Layer parameter allows you select the name of the UV coordinates to render. If you have layered textures, this allows you to specify which UV Layer to render out. In this case, you only have uv so there is no need to change this. Remove interior of connected regions should be off. This is a rarely used option that will give you just the outline of the UV region and not the detail within. You almost always want that detail for painting texture maps. Ignore visibility would be used if you have used any Visibility SOPs but want them to be ignored when you render the UV texture image.

Paint programs such as The Gimp, Adobe Photoshop, and Corel Painter can't read Houdini .pic or .rat images, so it's best to save the image to a standard format such as .tga.

If you want to preview the image before you save it, use the special filename md in the Output Picture field to render the image into Mplay. If you like it, you can use Mplay's Save Frame option to save the image to disk.

---

2. In `Chapter9>maps` on the Website, you will find a .tga of the saved UV image as well as a .rat image that has been painted. Mantra works best with .rat format images, and it is highly recommend you convert all your textures to .rat to save on memory and have access to filtering options.

3. Once you have painted the texture (or you can use the supplied one), you can use a UV Quickshade SOP to see it in OpenGL on the geometry. MMB to branch off and bring in a UV Quickshade SOP. Set the Texture Map to your .tga file or use the supplied `LegBentTextured.tga` image.

Quick Reloading of Textures

Hang on there! You just said .rat format is best for Mantra. Why then use the .tga in the UV Quickshade SOP? Good question. When you're painting your textures, you want to load them into Houdini as quick as you can to see them on your geometry. However, converting to .rat after every time you save from your paint package would make smiling faces go upside down. OpenGL doesn't care if it's a .rat image or not and doesn't achieve any efficiencies in displaying a .rat versus a .tga. A common workflow is to paint in your favorite paint package, save the image, and then refresh it in Houdini. Naturally, if you have a 3D Paint package such as Amazon Paint, Deep Paint 3D, or Body Paint, you don't need to worry about this as much. Refreshing the texture is accomplished with some simple Hscript commands. As you are constantly striving to avoid the tedium, you likely don't want to type an Hscript command to refresh every time. So, you will alias the commands to a function key. Then it's as simple as saving the texture from the paint package and pressing the function key in Houdini to see the texture on your geometry.

1. Open the Settings->Aliases and Variables floating window. In the Aliases tab, you may see a list of already defined function keys (F1-F8) that are usually defined to change desks. Function keys F9-F12 are generally not defined and are available for use. If you work in a non-standard Houdini environment, like at work, this may be different. Alternatively, you can redefine one of the other keys.

2. Assuming you are going to define F12 as the hotkey to reload the textures, click on any of the entries, then in the left field at the bottom, type in F12 to create a new alias definition. Type Tab to move to the right field, or just click in the right field. Click and hold on the UV Quickshade SOP that is showing your painted texture, and drag and drop it into the right side field. This should enter a path something like `/obj/dragonfly/uvquickshade2`, which is the path to the Quickshade SOP.

3. In the right field, insert `opupdate ; texcache -c ; opcook -F` before the path and follow it with a space. As syntax is a stickler for the rules, let's clarify what is happening, explicitly stating where the spaces should be. You can put a space after the semicolon if you want to improve readability, but it is not required. The field should now read something like:

   ```
   opupdate;texcache<space>-c;opcook<space>-F<space>/obj/dragonfly/uvquickshade2
   ```

Again, the path might be slightly different for you if the name of your UV Quickshade SOP is different. Now, when you type F12 on your keyboard, the texture on disk will be reloaded and the new one will be shown in OpenGL. The previous line basically executes three Hscript commands. The semicolons allow you to specify several Hscript commands on a single line. Each one will be executed in turn.

The `opupdate` command recooks operators if their referenced files have changed. However, it's not 100% reliable due to variations in the underlying operating system and sometimes doesn't recook the OpenGL viewport..

The `texcache -c` command clears the texture cache so that the old texture is flushed from memory.

And finally, `opcook -F /obj/dragonfly/uvquickshade2` forces a recook of the specified node, which in turn forces the .tga file to be reloaded and redisplayed. You could do the same thing by clicking the node's Bypass flag twice; however, it's a lot easier to have it on a hotkey.

9. Shader Operators (SHOPs)

Rest Position

So far you've been creating UV texture coordinates on the assumption that you will be applying 2D texture maps that map to the UV Coordinates. However, you also want to use 3D textures and they do not "attach" themselves to UV coordinates. If you don't attach them to something, however, the object will look strange when it deforms. The 3D texture will seem to swim through the deforming object. 3D textures are based on point positions in 3D space. When you don't attach them to the geometry in some manner, the texture stays fixed while the geometry moves through it.

> 2D textures are usually associated with UVs so that they can be mapped onto a 2D surface. 3D textures are usually associated with XYZ positions in space and so shade the surface depending on where it is in space. Basically, 2D generally means using texture maps and 3D generally means using procedural patterns.

So, to get them to "stick" to the object properly, you need to create what is called a rest position for them. All a rest position does is take a snapshot of the point positions and then makes sure those values don't change even if the geometry's actual point positions move around. You'll apply a rest position to the body, so if the tail is ever deformed, the 3D textures you apply won't incorrectly detach.

1. Locate the final SOP in the network that defines the body, which is likely the SHD_Body node, and insert a Rest Position SOP. Wire the second input of the Rest position SOP into the output of the same node as the left input. That's right, both inputs wire to the same place. That's it! You've applied a rest position attribute to the body.

2. Open the Geometry Spreadsheet on the rest node (RMB on the icon and choose Spreadsheet) and you'll see that the rest attribute is exactly the same as the point positions. However, if at some point in the future you bend the tail with bones, the point positions will move and change, but the rest attribute won't. Any 3D textures that are tied to the rest position attributes will therefore stick properly.

3. Also, don't forget that you only applied the rest attributes to the Body branch of the network. When this geometry is merged with the other geometry that does not have the rest attribute, the Merge SOP will give you a yellow flag warning. That's fine. It just means the rest attribute on the other parts of the dragonfly will be 0. If you do end up using 3D textures on other parts of the dragonfly, make sure you apply a rest attribute to those parts of the body just as you did here.

Assign the Shaders

Yeehaa! That was an action-packed lesson. What remains will be like sleeping in zero Gs... or so I imagine. You have UV coordinates. You have a texture map for the leg. You have rest attributes for the body. It seems there is nothing left but to assign the shaders and finally give the dragonfly the evolutionary edge! Where should you put the SHOPs? You could go to the default SHOP network in /shop but that will make it harder to turn your work into a digital asset later. For that reason, it would be best to create a SHOP network inside the dragonfly object.

1. You can use the .hip file you created in the previous exercise, or load the file dragonflyAssignShaders.hip from Chapter9>hips from the Website. Jump into the SOP network for the dragonfly object.

2. Drop a SHOP Network down by the last node in the network somewhere. Assuming you're using the four pane desktop with one pane unlinked and set to be a Network Editor, drag and drop the SHOPnet node onto the path of the unlinked network pane. The pane should change to point to the SHOPnet. Type Enter with your mouse over the unlinked network pane to jump inside the SHOPnet.

3. Change the Viewer pane to be an IPR Viewer. Make sure the Render flag is on the Dragonfly (Merge) node so that it renders what you want it to. In the IPR viewer, select the `mantra1` render output driver. This has been pre-configured to use IPR, so the IPR cache is created the first time it renders. (Hence, there is no need to Clear Cache to get what you expect.)

4. Append a Shader SOP to the Dragonfly node and update the Display and Render flags to it. This is the node where you will assign shaders to the groups you created earlier.

Shader for the Body

Next, you'll make a shader for the body so that the dragonfly doesn't feel naked.

1. The shader for the body geometry will be a 3D procedural shader. In the SHOP network, add a VEX Gallery Wood shader. Rename this SHOP to be `Dragonfly_Body`. It doesn't matter what you name it so long as you know what it is. You may end up with hundreds of shaders in a complex model and naming them logically will make your experience much the better!

2. In the Shader SOP, in the Surface tab, select the `SHD_Body` for the Group. For the Surface Shader field, find and select the `Dragonfly_Body` SHOP you just added. As mentioned earlier in the chapter, you can click the + button and find it, but it's a little faster to just drag and drop the SHOP into the Surface Shader field. Click and hold on the SHOP's icon and drag it up and release the mouse over the empty Surface Shader field.

> There are a lot of supplied shaders in Houdini! In fact, there are default shaders for three renderers: Mantra, PRman, and Mental Ray. Because you're only using Mantra for these exercises, turn off the other shaders. At the top of the SHOPs network, there is a little down-arrow for the pull-down menu that allows you to turn off the Renderman and Mental Ray shaders. Alternatively, bring up the Tab menu and Shift+V so only the VEX operators are shown.

Note that the IPR Viewer doesn't update. Even if you click the re-render button, you don't see the new shader. That's because changes to the SOP level require a re-creation of the IPR Cache. If this model was very slow to render, you would probably want to assign the groups and shaders all at once in the Shader SOP before generating the IPR cache.

3. Click the Clear IPR Cache button. Now, it re-renders with the body showing the new shader. At this point, you can start tuning the look of the shader. That's a very subjective thing, so we'll just give the values that look sufficient to us. This is your dragonfly friend though. Feel free to change it to whatever works for your vision. Only the values changed from their defaults are noted.

Base Light Model:	Blinn Specular	Noise Amplitude:	3.7
Base Diffuse:	.77 . 62 . 36	Noise Roughness:	.628
Ring Darkening:	.134	Bumping:	3D Fractal Dent
Base Specular:	.45 .45 .45	Base Amount:	.081
Base Roughness:	.15	Ring Amount:	.066
Ring Spacing:	.04	Groove Width:	.104
Noise Frequency:	5 5 5		

> Even with the IPR cache, re-rendering changes aren't instantaneous. You can speed up the re-rendering even more by setting an active region in the IPR viewer. Do this by holding down Shift and then drawing the region in the viewport. Use Shift+S to clear the active region or Shift and click outside the render view.

Shader for the Leg

The leg shader will use the texture map you created earlier or the supplied test map. Remember, and I can't stress this too often, make sure you use .rat format images when applying textures for Mantra!

1. Add a VEX Layered Surface SHOP, and rename it Dragonfly_Legs. In the Shader SOP, in the Surface tab, click the More button (or press 2+Enter in the Number Surfaces field) to add another slot for the additional shader. Select the SHD_Legs group for the Group field. Drag and drop the Dragonfly_Legs into the Surface Shader field.

   In the Texture Map field of the Dragonfly_Legs SHOP, select either your painted leg texture map or use the supplied LegBentTextured.rat image. Click the Clear IPR Cache button to make sure everything is up to date.

2. If you want to adjust the Diffuse color or any of the other parameters, feel liberty and inspiration in doing so. I adjusted the Diffuse to 1, 0.89, .7, which looks a little better.

Shader for the Wing Tubes

The tubes on the wings will use the VEX Hair shader even though they're not hair. You'll also apply a single shader to two different groups.

1. Add a VEX Hair SHOP and rename it to Dragonfly_WingTubes. In the Shader SOP, click the More button to create another slot. Select the SHD_wingHind_Tubes group. Also select the SHD_wingFore_Tubes group.

2. Drag and drop the Dragonfly_WingTubes shader into the Surface Shader field. Click the Clear IPR cache to regenerate the cache, and then tune the look as you like. I left it as the default values.

> By selecting two or more groups, you can apply a single shader to multiple groups. You can also use wildcards. So, you can also type *Tubes* instead in the Group field for the tubes, and any group containing Tubes would have the Hair shader applied to it! This is a great way to efficiently manage many groups.

Shader for the Wing Surface

The wing surface will use a supplied texture map, but in a somewhat different way. You'll use the texture map to define the transparency of the surface rather than the color.

1. Add a VEX Super Material SHOP and rename it to Dragonfly_WingSurface. In the Shader SOP, click the More button to create another slot. Select the SHD_wingFore_Surface group in the Group field. Replace the Fore in the group with an * (asterisk), which will match to both Fore and Hind. You could also select the SHD_wingHind_Surface group as well to get both groups in the Group field. Drag and drop the Dragonfly_WingSurface SHOP into the Surface Shader field. These are the non-default settings I used for the Dragonfly_WingSurface SHOP:

Diffuse:	1 .7 .37		Interpolate:	On
aparamap:	HexagonMonochrome.rat		Color Filter:	Scale to Min and Max
aparacoef:	.5		Min:	.5 .5 .5 .5
aperpmap:	HexagonMonochrome.rat		U scale:	5
aperpcoef:	.5		V scale:	5

The `HexagonMonochrome.rat` map is supplied on the Website in the `Chapter9>maps` folder. The `aparamap` and `aperpmap` parameters allow you to control the alpha (transparency) of the surface. *Apara* is the amount of transparency when the rays from the camera are parallel to the surface normals. *Aperp* is the amount of transparency when the rays from the camera are perpendicular to the surface normals. Basically, if you render a sphere with Apara set to 1 and Aperp set to 0, the edges of the sphere will fade out to nothing. If you set Apara to 0 and Aperp to 1, the edges will be solid and fade to nothing towards the center of the sphere. By making both of them the same, you have "regular" transparency, where the surface has the same transparency no matter what angle you look at it from.

The `aparacoef` and `aperpcoef` values are multipliers on the texture maps, so reducing them makes the surface even more transparent.

The Interpolate parameter increases the quality of the texture map when using the .rat format, but at the cost of slightly longer render times. Modern computers are fast enough that this can be on all the time with almost no noticeable change in performance.

Color Filter allows you to modify the texture map in conjunction with the Min and Max colors below. In this case, the texture map is purely black and white; however, you use the Scale to Min and Max to lift the minimum value from black to grey (.5) while not changing the Max (white) value. This effectively reduces the contrast on the image, making it more subtle.

U scale and V scale let you change how the UV Texture Coordinates are used. By increasing the U and V scale, you have increased the frequency of the textures. This is easier to do here than go back into the SOPs and modify the actual UV coordinates.

Shaders for the Eyes

For the eyes, you'll use a simple color shader and also apply a displacement map in order to add some surface detail and so make them more interesting. The IPR cache needs to be cleared whenever you make a displacement map change, so using the active region is very important here. The IPR cache will only be regenerated inside the active region, greatly speeding up iterations.

1. Add a VEX Gallery Spots SHOP and rename it `Dragonfly_Eyes`. In the Shader SOP click the More button to create another slot. Select the `SHD_Eyes` group in the Group field. Drag and drop the `Dragonfly_Eyes` SHOP into the Surface Shader field. Draw an active region in the IPR Viewer around the eyes area.

   The shader settings I used that are not at the default values are:

Base Diffuse:	.8 .75 .57	Use UV for dots:	On
Spot Light Model:	No Specular	Dot Frequency:	10 10 10
Spot Diffuse:	1 1 0	Dot Size:	.605
Dot Style:	Ringed Dots	Dot Jitter:	.5 .5 .5

   The only thing in the about this shader in particular is the Use UV for Dots parameter. This tells the shader to look for UV texture coordinates. Otherwise, it would be a 3D texture. For the displacement shader, the process is pretty much identical to the surface shader process, with a couple of extra considerations.

2. In the Shader SOP, change to the Displacement tab. There is already a slot available, so you don't need to create another one. In the SHOP network, add a VEX Displacement Layers SHOP. Rename it `Dragonfly_Eyes_D`.

3. Drag and drop the `Dragonfly_Eyes_D` SHOP into the Displace Shader field. In the Texture Map field, use the same `HexagonMonochrome.rat` texture map you used for the transparent wings. Turn off the IPR toggle above the IPR viewport. Displacement shaders will re-render if you have IPR turned on, but they are represented by bump maps, which is not an effective way of judging them. By using an active region and turning off IPR, you can get decent performance interactively adjusting displacement maps. Click the Force Re-render button above the IPR viewer. Adjust the Displacement Amount up very slightly. Even a value of 0.1 will give you crazy displacement. A value of .01 looks pretty good to me.

4. There are no apparent render artifacts. To be safe, go to the Object level of the dragonfly object and, in the Render tab, turn on Displace Bound and set it to .01 to make sure the displacement won't have any cracks. Go back into the SOP network and finish adjusting the displacement as you see fit. Then, turn back on IPR and click Clear IPR Cache to make sure it's fresh and wholesome.

> You can't have two SHOPs (or any other Houdini node) with the same name in the same network. You need to create or adopt a naming convention to differentiate between surface and displacement shaders, while making it clear that they are for the same surface. I use the suffix _D on my displacement shaders to indicate this, with no suffix on the surface shaders. This way, if you sort alphabetically, the surface and displacement shaders will appear together. It is also easy to tell which are the displacement shaders.

> You can quickly get to the parameters of a particular node by RMB on its name in the path window and choosing Parameters. For example, when you are inside the `dragonfly` object, you can just RMB on the word `dragonfly` in the path, as shown in Figure 9.17, and choose Parameters.

Figure 9.17
The dragonfly name in the path.

> When using displacement, you need to correctly set the Displace Bounds parameter to ensure you get a good render. Displace Bounds tells Mantra how far beyond the default geometry surface to look for the displaced surface at render time. If you don't set these bounds or don't set them large enough, some of the displaced geometry won't get rendered and you will end up with triangular-shaped holes that look like tears in the surface. Generally, a good rule to use is to set the bounds to the actual displacement amount. If the value is too high, too much of the geometry will be loaded in at render time and micropolygonized, which will unnecessarily eat up extra memory.

Shader for the Antennae

There is nothing much to mention here. You simply create a new Surface slot in the Shader SOP. I used a VEX Hair SHOP again with the following non-default values:

Specular Color: .6 .6 .6   Shinyness: 50

Shader for the Wing Hinges

Again, there is nothing extraordinary about this one. I used a VEX Gallery Spots shader with the following non-default values:

Base Diffuse:	.5 .3 .14	Dot Offset:	.4 .4 .4
Spot Diffuse:	.56 .4 0	Dot Size:	.4
Use UV for dots:	On	Number of Splats:	3
Dot Frequency:	20 20 20		

Can you believe you have finished? What a long, hard slog it has been. Fortunately, the slogging has put many new tools and techniques in your toolbox and so you can transition back to a comfortable saunter. You've applied several default shaders, texture maps, and a displacement shader and generally made the dragonfly look a good bit better. He/She/It thanks you for your kindness and promises to chow down on any mosquitoes you might have lurking around your yard. Figure 9.18 shows a render of the completed dragonfly.

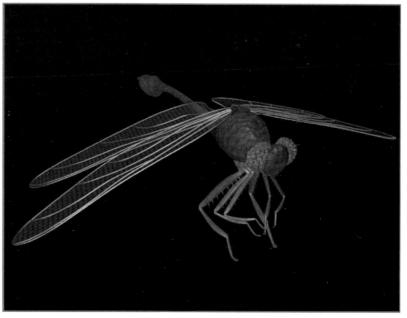

Figure 9.18
The completed dragonfly.

9. Shader Operators (SHOPs)

Summary

If you want, create your own shaders in VOPs, maybe with some procedural noises or mixing texture maps and procedural textures. Using the default shaders is great when they do what you want them to, but the whole point of creativity is to be able to make your own stuff. VOPs are great tools for this. There is nothing wrong with mixing default Houdini shaders with VOPs, too. The eyes particularly would benefit from some custom VOPs work.

chapter 10
VEX Operators (VOPs)

What Are VEX Operators?

VEX operators (or VOPs) are the graphical building interface to the VEX language. Each VOP node contains a snippet of VEX code. You can graphically wire together nodes, which essentially creates blocks of VEX code. If you already know VEX, you'll find VOPs a quicker way to create VEX code. However, if you don't know VEX, that's fine too! VOPs were designed to be useful to all levels of users.

You can use VOPs to create very simple, specific shaders or you can create very complex, general shaders, and anywhere in between. VOPs let you create new SOPs, so you can use them as a modeling tool. VOPs let you create new CHOPs, so you can use them as an animation tool. VOPs let you create new POPs, so you can use them to create effects. VOPs let you create new COPs, so you can use them to create cool compositing operations. For example, the Sprinkler POP was created using VEX, which means it can be created using VOPs. The VEX Mountain SOP was created using VEX, so you can create your own version in VOPs if you wanted to. VOPs can be used to make parts of a lighting system, designed so a new user just wires up the pieces and doesn't worry about the details. In a sea shell, VOPs is an extremely powerful context where your options and are both far and wide.

VEX, Expressions, and Hscript

There are at least three "scripting" languages in Houdini: Hscript, Expressions, and VEX. In fact, Hscript and Expressions are very closely related and can work together. Hscript gives you commands to directly control Houdini and its user interface. You can add new operators, wire them together, change their parameters, and do many other things with Hscript. Expressions are often used directly in an operator's parameters to create channel references, animate a channel like using a `sin()` expression, and more. You can also use expressions with Hscript, to create more complex scripts.

VEX is a whole different world. VEX is a very specialized programming language that does one thing, and does it extremely quickly: It modifies attributes. When you create a surface shader in VEX (or VOPs, because VOPs are really just a GUI for VEX), you are modifying attributes on the surface of the object being rendered. When you create a new SOP or POP with VEX, you are modifying attributes of the geometry's points, like color or position. When you create a new CHOP in VEX, you are modifying channel data. When you create a new COP in VEX, you are modifying pixels. As you continue through your journey in Houdini, you'll come to have more and more contact with each of these languages.

Salutations to the VOP Node

One example of a VOP, being a Stucco VOP, is shown in Figure 10.1. Most VOPs have inputs on the left and outputs on the right. So, the Stucco VOP has eight inputs and one output. There are some VOPs, like the Global Variables VOP, that only have inputs even though they are located on the right of the node. This is because you are bringing information from geometry into VOPs for use. The Output VOP only has inputs, because this node is the last node in a VOP network and all information computed in a VOPnet must pass its results out through the Output node. Just as in other contexts, you can LMB the icon in the upper-left to drag the node around the network editor pane or MMB to get an popup info window. You can collapse the display of the node to varying degrees by selecting the 1, 2, or 3 dots to the right of the icon. Connecting inputs and outputs works just like in other contexts.

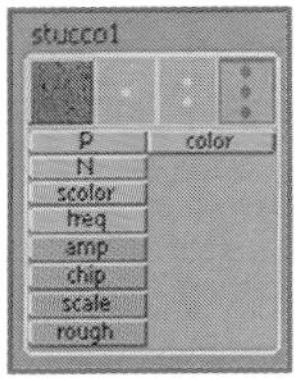

To wire the color output to some other input, LMB on color and then on the desired input. Say you had a P from the Global Variable VOP wired into P on the stucco node and you wanted to disconnect it. Just LMB on stucco's P input and then LMB again in a blank area anywhere in the network editor.

Some VOPs are actually a collapsed network of many VOPs, with particular parameters promoted to the top level. To see what is going on inside a VOP of this type (like the Stucco VOP shown in Figure 10.1), just select it and press Enter to jump inside. Jumping into existing VOPs to see how the logic works is a great way to learn about the VOP context.

Figure 10.1
The stucco VOP node.

Creating a Soccer Ball Surface Shader

The most common use of VOPs is to roll your own surface shaders. So, we'll walk through how to do this using the soccer ball you created in the Chapter 5. This is a great example of the power of VOPs as the default shaders aren't capable of some of the behavior that you can easily create in VOPs. The completed exercise is available for reference in the Chapter 10>hips directory in the soccerballCompleteVOPs.hip.

Analyze the Look

As discussed in the previous chapter, the first thing to do when shading an object is to think about what makes that object look like it does. You have to decide what you want the surface of the soccer ball to look like. At its simplest, a soccer ball is a collection of alternating black-and-white hexagons. However, most of us stopped playing with those balls back in the 1980s. Now, much more complex patterns exist. So, let's create an interesting pattern, with a few labels on the ball and some scuff marks to give it a bit of realism. For a more complex soccer ball, you'll use custom attributes based on groups for the black-and-white patches and build in some dents. Then you'll add another couple of layers to apply some labels.

Consider Approaches for Achieving the Look

In Houdini, there are usually multiple ways to accomplish the same task. Often, there is no single best way to achieve a goal...<ahem>. It is a matter of experience and creativity to conjure an elegant solution. To create the more complex surface for the soccer ball, you could use simple shaders to apply color to the black-and-white areas. But how would you then apply the label that will cover more than a single patch, and the scuff marks that will cover the entire ball?

One solution might be to have two pieces of geometry, two spheres, one inside the other. On the inner geometry, you could apply the black-and-white shaders to groups, which would be simple. Then, on the outer geometry, you could make it transparent except where the label and scuff marks are. This is perfectly valid, except it gets complicated when you start to do things like displacement, which actually pushes out the geometry. You could start to have problems with the inner sphere pushing out through the outer sphere.

Another solution is to use VOPs to create a single, more complex shader that is uniquely tied to the soccer ball and allows any level of complexity. As this is the better way and this chapter covers VOPs, you'll now pursue this method.

Visualize Groups on Existing Geometry

It is often useful to be able to visualize what geometry is a member of a particular group. The Visibility SOP allows you to easily do this.

1. Load the `soccerballComplete.hip` from the `chapter05` folder from the Website. You need to do a few things to it in preparation for using it in VOPs.

2. Jump into the `soccerBall` object. MMB on the `applyWhite` node and note that there are two groups, `coloredWhite` and `coloredBlack`. Quite often you will use a model or hip file from another artist and you will not have been involved in the creation of the model. Although for the soccer ball it's easy to tell which group is which, it is often not so easy.

3. To quickly visualize which group is which, branch append a Visibility SOP to the chain to the `applyWhite` node and rename it `visGroups`. In the Apply To menu, select Non-Selected Primitives and put the Display flag on the Visibility SOP. Nothing interesting has happened yet. If you set the Apply To menu to Selected Primitives, the whole soccer ball disappears. That's because the empty Group field actually means "everything."

4. Set the Apply To menu back to Non-Selected Primitives and use the arrow next to the Group Field to select the `coloredWhite` group. This now shows you only the white patches in the viewport. Use the arrow to select `coloredWhite` again and the selection will clear. Select `coloredBlack` group to see only the black patches.

5. MMB on the Visibility SOP and then the node above it. Notice that the point numbers and primitive numbers are the same. The Visibility operation is not deleting or modifying the geometry in any way. It is simply hiding part of it in the viewport.

Apply UV Coordinates

It is now the time in your life for applying some UV coordinates.

1. You're going to need UV coordinates on the soccer ball sooner or later, so you might as well apply them now. Drag the `dispRender` node down a ways and always keep it as the last node in the chain. Every time you need to insert or append the next operation, always ensure that the `dispRender` is still way down at yon bottom and is the last node in the chain.

2. Append a UV Project SOP to the chain (remember, above the `dispRender` node), and set the Display and Render flags to it. Move your mouse into the viewport and press Enter to go into the operational state. This should make the guide geometry visible, which by default is a blue grid indicating this is an orthographic (flat) projection. Set the Projection to Polar and the Group Type to Vertices. In the Initialize tab, click the Initialize button. You should

see the blue guide geometry of the texture projection snap to the size of the soccer ball, as shown in Figure 10.2. The UV Project SOP will apply various UV projections to geometry with interactive viewport handles so you can rotate, scale, and translate the UV projection if you want to. Because this is a simple sphere, you can leave it as it is. Setting the Group Type to Vertices will make sure that the seams of the texture (where it wraps around) match up nicely.

Figure 10.2
The initialized guide geometry using polar projection.

3. To see the UV coordinates in the viewport mapped into a 0-1 square, over the viewport, hold down the spacebar and Ctrl, then RMB and select UV viewport. Alternatively, use the hotkey spacebar+5 and the viewport will change to show you the UV coordinates you just applied in a flattened-out view. Use spacebar+1 to get back to the perspective view.

4. MMB on the uvproject node and notice that there is now a vertex attribute uv of size 3. These are your UV coordinates. Houdini applies them as three floats, because in fact they can be UVW, where W is the distance off the surface. This is normally not used; however, in rare situations where it is helpful, it is always available as the third number in the attribute.

Add a Custom Attribute

Speaking of attributes, you need to create a custom attribute as well. When you work in VOPs, you are creating a single shader that is applied to the entire soccer ball. This means that the two groups, coloredBlack and coloredWhite, can't be used directly to apply the black-and-white materials like you did with the Shader SOP in the Tree Trophy exercise. This is because a shader has no direct knowledge of the groups. However, shaders can look at an unlimited number of custom attributes and it is easy like pudding pie to embed the group information into a custom attribute.

1. Append an AttribCreate SOP to the uvproject node and rename makeBallColor so that the network is visually clear. This allows you create any attribute you want and apply it to the geometry. You are going to create a single attribute called ballcolor and set it to 1 where the ball is white and 0 where the ball is black. Your shader will then pick up and use this attribute to color the appropriate areas.

2. In the Name field, enter ballcolor for the attribute name. Note that capitalization matters, so I recommend that all attributes that you create always be lowercase to avoid confusion. In the end scenario, you can do what seems most logical, but you will need to match this attribute's name exactly later when you create the VOP surface shader. Change the Class to Primitive. You don't want the points to have different values. You want each polygon (primitive) to have a value of 0 or 1. Change the Type to Integer because you only want values of 0 or 1, with no decimals.

3. Before you apply the group, look at what values the geometry holds right now. RMB on the attribcreate node and select Spreadsheet. This table shows you the attribute values of every point, primitive, vertex, or detail on the geometry. It is extremely powerful and you will use it a lot when you get into more complex projects in Houdini. In the spreadsheet, change the type of information from Points to Primitives. In the Show|Hide menu, turn off everything else but ballcolor, which should give you a single column under the ballcolor heading. This is the value of the ballcolor attribute for every primitive in the soccer ball. Scroll down through the values and you can see they are all 0 because you haven't changed anything in the attribcreate SOP.

4. Change the first Value field in the parameters to 1. Notice in the spreadsheet that all the primitives now have a `ballcolor` attribute value of 1. In the Group field, select the `coloredWhite` group. Now, scroll through and notice what has happened in the spreadsheet. Some of the polygons have a `ballcolor` value of 1 and now some have a value of 0. When you use a group in an Attribute Create operation, you are actually setting two values. You are setting all primitives not in the group to the Default value and also setting all primitives that are in the group to the `Value` value.

5. To better understand this, change the first field of the Default parameter to 2. Notice in the spreadsheet that the primitives that previously were 0 have changed to 2. The primitives that previously were 1 have stayed at 1. Because you have used the `coloredWhite` group in the Group field, you know that the Default value (currently 2) is being applied to all primitives except those in the `coloredWhite` group, which get the Value (currently 1) applied to them. Set the Default value back to 0. You know that those are the black patches because you only have two groups. Close the spreadsheet and make sure the Display and Render flags are on the `dispRender` node.

Add the VOP Network

Now that you have the geometry set up with UV coordinates and custom attributes, it's time to jump into VOPs and stir up a heapin' helping of trouble. Actually, it's no trouble a'tall, as you'll soon see!

1. Change the desk type to `VEX_Builder`. This should show you a VOP network editor pane, a VOP shader ball, an empty VOP Parameters pane (all these three panes should be linked together), plus an Object viewport. If you don't see this, re-arrange your desktop so you see something similar. For more information on choosing desks and creating custom desks that can be saved, check out Chapter 6.

2. In the Network pane, add a VEX Surface Shader VOP network. At this level, you are actually adding a completely new network. The VEX Surface Shader VOP is ultimately used to build a new shader that's a new SHOP type. In previous exercises, the various SHOP types were pre-defined by Side Effects. Using VOPs, you can make your own SHOP types that do exactly what you want. Can you say, "Real ultimate power?"

3. Houdini only allows one uniquely named node type. The VEX Surface Shader field determines this name and also determines the name of the resultant SHOP. The SHOP Type Name field will become the name (or label) that you see when you type Tab or select Add Operator in SHOPs. How's that for a quick slip into confusing?

What you enter for the type of the VOPnet must be a legal Houdini name and also must be unique for all SHOPs. For example, you cannot use `v_metal` (an existing SHOP supplied by SESI) or you will get a yellow flag warning you that there was a conflict, and that your VOPnet has automatically been changed to `v_metal2`, or something like that. Ideally, you should avoid these types of conflicts; they cause confusion later on. Some studios use a standard prefix for the types of VOPnets. For example, artists at Rocking and Hocking might use `rh_` as the prefix for all their in-house SHOPs. That ensures that their new, custom, SHOP types won't clash with existing Side Effects SHOPs. Another option is to use your login name or initials as the prefix, so it's clear what you created. How you decide to work is up to you, but establishing some sort of system is a very good idea.

The SHOP Type Name does not have to be unique, but it's a really good idea to make sure that it is. This is what shows up in the Tab menu, and if there are two labels that read exactly the same, it would obviously be confusing to decide which one you wanted to use. Also, using the initials of your company or your login name as a prefix here means that all SHOPs you create are grouped together in the Tab menu and so are easy to find.

Finally, to add a little salt and pepper to the confusing soup you are concocting, the SHOP types you create in VOPs usually end up being written to disk, and then used from the disk file rather than directly from the VOPnet. You'll see why and how later on, but for now, just trust me that it is so. To save yourself some trouble later, append the suffix _VOPNET to the type, and VOPNET to the SHOP Type Name.

4. So, all that said, make the type of the VOPnet my_soccerball_VOPNET and the SHOP Type Name field VEX My Soccerball VOPNET, as shown in Figure 10.3. You have now created a new SHOP type, although right now it does nothing except make things turn white. Notice that the VOP Shaderball is a nice, constant white. You would be finished if you were doing self-illuminated snow, but you're not, so there is a bit more work to do.

Figure 10.3
The VOPnet type and SHOP Type Name fields, named correctly.

Add a New Material

It be time to plunge in and get to creating the materials necessary to make one good-looking soccer ball.

1. Enter into the VOP network just like you do any other Houdini network. RMB on the icon and select Edit Network, or select the network node and type **Enter**, or Alt-LMB on the node, or select the node and click the -> arrow next to its name in the path area just below the menus in any of the VOP context panes.

   Inside the VOP network is a single VOP node. All VOP networks always have one (and only one) Output node. These are often different for the different types of SHOPs you can create. For example, this VOP network creates a Surface SHOP, but a VOP network that creates a Displacement SHOP will have different output connectors. In VEX (which is the language the VOP network is actually writing for you), the different types of SHOPs are called *contexts;* you are in the Surface Context now.

   The Output node determines what this particular context delivers back by default. In this case, the Surface Shader, at a minimum, outputs color as Cf, opacity as Of, alpha as Af, and surface normals as N. For this reason, connectors on the Output node can be considered inputs (because they have other nodes connecting into them) and also outputs (because they output that information). You will only be using the Cf output connector. Cf is the output for color, which is all you need for this soccer ball. Of is opacity. If you were doing a shader for an object that had some transparency, you would need to use this output. Af is for the Alpha channel. This is not typically used, but allows you to do complex tricks with surfaces, like create special Matte objects. N is the Normal and is used to adjust the normals of the object. This allows for things like bump maps.

2. Woohoo! Here you are on the verge of making use of your first VOP operator. Breathe deeply and remember this moment, for there will come a day when you find it to difficult to imagine that you ever got along without using VOPs! Okay. Dally no longer; let's proceed. First, let's add an operator that at first doesn't seem like the right thing for the job: a concrete material. However, as you'll discover through experimentation, you can use seemingly unrelated materials to combine and fashion new materials.

   Bring up the Tab menu and notice there are many operator categories when working in VOPs. In fact, VOPs has the largest number of operators of any context in Houdini. Fortunately, the Tab menu organizes them for you into logical groups. Click on the Materials toolbar, and select Concrete.

Wire the color output of the concrete node into the Cf connector of the output node. Notice that the VOP shaderball now takes on the appearance of concrete! If you wanted a concrete-looking soccer ball, you would be done! But, as your feet would quickly be pulp after booting around a ball of that material, you have farther to travel yet. As you can see though, using VOPs can be as simple as picking an appropriate material and wiring it into the Cf on the output node.

3. Adjust the colors to be close to what would be good for the white base material of the soccer ball. The VOP shaderball works exactly the same as the SHOP shaderball, so you might need to increase the detail level to see the chips. The detail level can be accessed in the left stowbar or by using the hotkey d. The numbers I chose for this node are shown in Figure 10.4.

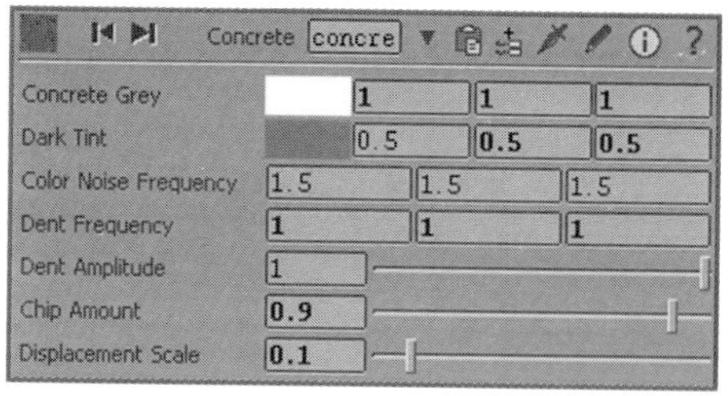

Figure 10.4
Parameters for the concrete node.

Apply the New Shader and Render

Now that you have something more interesting than a solid white shader, you can apply it to the soccer ball object and render it in Mantra.

1. Configure your desktop so that you have a SHOP network editor with a popup parameters pane within it, an Object viewer pane, an Object network editor, and an Object parameters pane. Make sure the three Object panes are linked.

2. In the SHOP network editor pane, choose the "VEX My Soccer Ball VOPNET" SHOP. Remember that you set the SHOP Type Name earlier and that this is what shows up in the Tab menu. Notice that there are no parameters for this SHOP! The VOP network that you were in was used to the build the new SHOP. In that network, you have to explicitly identify which parameters you want to promote up to the final shader interface. So, it's not a problem as you, because you just haven't added them yet. Fear not this apparent lack of control for two reasons. First is that you will be adding the controls soon and second is that it can be a very informative experience to relinquish your normally vise-like grip on what you believe you control.

3. In the SHOP Surface field of the Shading tab of the soccerBall object, find and choose the my_soccerball_VOPNET1 SHOP. Alternatively, because your panes are configured as they are, you can drag and drop the my_soccerball_VOPNET1 SHOP from the SHOP network editor directly into the SHOP Surface field. For yet another approach, you can drag and drop the SHOP directly into the viewport onto the soccerBall object; Houdini automatically places it into the correct field.

4. Ensure you are looking through cam1 from the camera menu at the bottom of the Viewer pane and render using the fast_mantra option in the Quick Render button, which is also at the bottom of the Viewer pane. You now see the somewhat poorly detailed soccer ball.

5. Set your desktop back to the way it was before so that you have a VOPs context viewer, parameters pane, and OBJ context viewer pane along the top, and a VOPs context network editor along the bottom. Again, remember to link all the VOPs context panes. You will be using what you see through cam1 to do subsequent test renders.

Use IPR to View Changes

Interactive Preview Rendering (IPR) rendering is a fast rendering system that allows you to make changes to SHOP parameters, and even VOP networks, and have the changes re-rendered in Mantra very quickly. In addition, you can even do some compositing of elements in the viewport without having to go into COPs. The reason IPR is a good deal faster than normal rendering for some tasks is that it takes a snapshot of the rendered geometry, so that things like motion blur, anti-aliasing, displacement, subdivision surfaces, and so on, do not have to be recalculated each time you re-render. Only things that have changed, like

10. VEX Operators (VOPs)

the color of the shader or the texture map, need to be recalculated, which makes the re-render very quick. It's important to note that raytraced reflections, refractions, and so on, are not cached and need to be recalculated each time you re-render. However, you still get a significant speed increase.

Change the Object Viewer pane to an IPR Viewer pane. In the Output Driver selector, choose the fast_mantra render driver and turn on (if it isn't already) the Enable IPR rendering toggle, which is just labeled as IPR. The soccer ball will be rendered into the viewport.

The render time will be "normal" speed the first time you render. However, subsequent renders will be much faster. If you need to force a re-render of the viewport for some reason, click the blue Force re-render button above the viewport. Remember to keep in mind that if your geometry changes (you add attributes, or change the model, and so on), you will need to click the Clear IPR Cache button to get the new geometry cached to disk. You will use IPR rendering for the rest of this exercise in order to quickly see your changes.

Access a Custom Attribute

Now that you have IPR ready, you can work on making this actually look like a soccer ball. First, you'll set up the black-and-white patches. Remember way back when you created a custom attribute on the soccer ball called ballcolor with the intention of using it later? Well, your planning is about to show the genius you always trusted it to be.

1. In the VOP network editor, drop a new Parameter operator. This is found in the Workflow category; however, as you already know, it is much faster to just type **par** to narrow down the options.

   A Parameter VOP does two useful things. Its most common utility is to create a parameter for the user to manipulate in the SHOPs context. You saw earlier how the my_soccerball_VOPNET SHOP didn't have any parameters that you could change. A Parameter VOP allows you to move controls from VOPs to the associated SHOP. You will do that later in the exercise. For now, you will first utilize its other major feature, which is to import attributes from geometry.

2. Set the Parameter Name field to ballcolor, which is the name of the custom geometry attribute you added earlier. It's also a good idea to set the name of the VOP to the same thing, so rename this VOP to ballcolor as well. Set the Parameter Type to Integer, which is the type you assigned to the custom geometry attribute earlier. Set the Parameter Label to also be ballcolor, just to be complete.

   If you don't remember these details, such as the name of the custom attribute or the type (as I often don't), use a handy popup floating pane (hotkey: Alt+Shift+W) to quickly check without changing the configuration of your desktop.

3. Notice that every time you change an attribute in the ballcolor node, IPR is re-rendering. It doesn't hurt anything really right now. But, if you wanted to have discrete control over when it re-rendered, you can turn on the Disable Auto-update button, and then just click Force Re-render anytime you wanted a render.

Use a Custom Attribute

The ballcolor attribute is available to your VOPnet, but how do you actually put it to use? Think about what you're trying to achieve. Wherever the ballcolor attribute is 1, you want to have white; wherever it is 0, you want to have black. Currently, you have just one concrete VOP that gives you the white color. So, you need to make another concrete material that will be black, and then mix the two concrete nodes based on the value of the ballcolor attribute.

1. Copy and paste the concrete node. Rename the first concrete VOP `white` and the new one `black`.

2. Drop a Null VOP and rename it `finalCf`. Enter `$OS` in the Output1 Name field. Then wire the output of the black node into the input on the `finalCf` node. Wire the output of `finalCf` into Cf on the output node. Now, you can have the black node wired into the `finalCf` node and the `finalCf` node wired into the Cf of the output node, but when you want to temporarily wire something directly into the output Cf, you can do so without forgetting what should usually be wired into it. Basically, the `finalCf` is just a placeholder node, so no matter what you might temporarily connect to the output node's Cf, you always know what needs to be wired in after the testing is over.

3. Change the Concrete Grey parameter of the black node to 0.13, 0.13, 0.13 to get a very dark grey. Because the black node is the only thing running into the `finalCf` node, you will see only its contribution to the shader. The IPR viewer should now have rendered a nearly black soccer ball. That should be fine for the black patches.

4. Drop in a Mix VOP. Wire the output of the black node into the first input of the mix node, and wire the output of the white VOP into the second input of the Mix VOP. Wire the output of the mix node into the input of the `finalCf` node. Your network should now look like Figure 10.5. Note that you just wired a green vector output into a seemingly dark green float input. The Mix VOP has some inputs that can change type based on their input. This is covered in more detail later in the chapter.

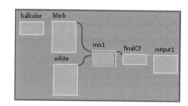

Figure 10.5
The current state of the VOP network.

   The IPR render should now be showing you a mix of 50% white and 50% black. Take a look at the mix node's parameters and notice the Bias parameter is set to 0.5, which is what gives you the 50/50 mix. Basically, the Mix VOP will show you 100% of `input1` when the Bias value is set to 0, and it will show you 100% of `input2` when the Bias value is set to 1. Anywhere in between will show you percentages of each input, depending on the value of the Bias parameter.

5. To verify this functionality, connect the output from the black node directly to the output node's Cf and IPR will render a very dark soccer ball. Now, connect the output of the white node directly to the output's Cf and IPR will render a very white soccer ball. Return the network to its normal state by connecting the `finalCf` node's output to the output Cf. IPR will again render the 50/50 mix.

6. Oh, but I have grander plans than that for the mix node. You happen to have an attribute that you can use to control the bias, which you have fetched in with the `ballcolor` Parameter VOP. Wire the `ballcolor` output of the `ballcolor` node into bias input of the mix node and see the magic! Well, the magic in this case is minimal because you now see red flags saying something is busted. MMB on the mix node's icon to see the error message. It says `"Input data type does not match output for…"` on all three inputs. Well, you know the first two had no problem before you wired in the `ballcolor` output. So, it's really just that one that needs a little spanking, errrm corrective therapy, I mean.

> As mentioned at the beginning of the chapter, VOP nodes are really just snippets of code that you can quickly wire together to create complex VEX code. To actually see the code being produced by the VOPnet, RMB on the icon of any one of the nodes in the network and choose View Code from VOP Network. A window pops up that shows the VEX code produced by the VOPnet.

Work with Different Data Types in VOPs

VOPs is capable of working with numerous data types, including float, integer, vector, and more. If you thrown down a Parameter VOP, you can see all these types in the Parameter Type selector. For easy visual identification, each type is represented with a different color. Generally speaking in VOPs, you cannot wire together parameters of different colors, which means they are of different types. So, in most cases, you can easily see that you can't wire a light blue (integer) into a dark green (float) without causing errors, as you just did by wiring the `ballcolor` output (an integer) into the bias input (a float). Has VOPs just abandoned you into the backwaters of electronic obsolescence? Happily, no. The issue is easily resolved using a conversion VOP.

1. RMB on the `ballcolor` output and go into the Convert category of operators. Here, you will find a wide variety of conversion VOPs. Can you guess which is the one you need based on this discussion? Of course, it is the Integer to Float operator. Behold the wonder! IPR is now showing a black-and-white soccer ball!

   The shaderball turns black because it does not have access to the geometry with the custom attribute, so it sets `ballcolor` to 0 for the whole sphere. Because a value of 0 results in black from the Mix VOP, the shaderball only shows black. This is why you almost always use Mantra IPR rendering. It gives very fast results, and the results are what your final render will look like! As you get more experienced, you might find yourself customizing your desktop such that you have no VOP shaderball, and only an Object viewport in which you use IPR rendering. Figure 10.6 shows the current state of the network. Now, on to the label!

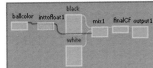

Figure 10.6
The state of the VOP network at this point.

Add a Texture Map

This next section illustrates an important point about VOPs: Although there are many useful VOPs supplied by Side Effects, they could not anticipate everyone's needs. So there will always be times where you have to roll (build) your own VOP systems. This is one of the most powerful aspects of VOPs—the capability to create your own unique VOP systems.

Let's think about what you want to do with the label. You have a nice black-and-white surface and you want to apply a label that will go across both the black-and-white patches. When you apply a label, you want to use the Alpha channel of the image to essentially composite it on, just as you might in COPs. You are going to create a simple "Over" Composite system, which will act just like an Over node in a compositing program. You will use this to composite the label over the black-and-white soccer ball surface.

1. Add a Texture VOP. This allows you to read in texture maps from disk for any of the formats that Houdini supports. However, you almost always want to use the RAT format, which is native to Houdini, as it provides the best memory savings and speed as well as quality options. Copy the `soccerballLabel01.rat` from the maps directory of Chapter 10 on the Website to a local location. Then, click the + button next to Texture Map to find the file and select it. Change the Signature to RGBA Values. A signature in VOPs-speak is simply the type of data you want. In this case, you want RGBA data, which includes the Alpha channel information.

2. Now you can try wiring this directly to the Cf output to see what the rendered texture looks like. Doh! The colors don't match! Recall though that you can easily remedy the problem. The generic data type of RGBA is known as a `vector4`, which just means it has four values—red, green, blue, and alpha. The Cf input is of type `vector`, meaning it has three values and does not have any other signatures. So, add `Vector4` to Vector conversion VOP between them.

If you forget what the colors mean, there is an easy way to find out. Hold your mouse over the input or output you are interested in and a tooltip will appear telling you what the data type is. In some cases, this might show you several data types, if an input allows several different types.

3. It's hard to tell what this image is doing, because it's mostly black with a little bit of red text on it. Harken to the image that has been used throughout the ages by computer people the world over. This near-mythical image is "the mandrill." Specifically, type `mandril.pic` in the Texture Map field and you'll see the mandrill in all his trippy rainbow glory all over your soccer ball. This is a default picture that is always available to Houdini. So you don't need to browse for it or specify a path. Just type it in and Houdini will find it. Yes, the mandrill is always lurking, waiting to be invited to the party.

Get and Use the UV Coordinates

"Why is the mandrill copied all over the place?", you ask. It isn't because he ate some rotten fruit or licked the backside of a toad and is happily split into numerous, distinct personalities. "I applied UV Coordinates, shouldn't those be used?" The answer, like so many things in Houdini, is "Yes, but only in a manner of speaking." UV Coordinates are not used by default in VOPs. You have to specifically fetch and then use them. Thus far, you have not done so. What you are seeing is the default s and t coordinates that all primitives have implicitly. The Texture VOP will use those defaults and t coordinates if there is nothing wired into the s and t inputs on the Texture VOP. Because each Polygon on the sphere is a primitive, you get one mandrill per polygon.

1. Bring in a Shader Layer Parameter VOP. The default action is to bring in UV Coordinates, which is exactly what you want. Notice, however, that the `shadinglayer` node's uv output is bright green, whereas the texture node's s and t inputs are dark green. You should know by now what to use here. Put your mouse over the uv output and you can see that its data type is a Vector. Put your mouse over the s or t input and you can see that their data type is Float.

2. Drop a Vector to Float VOP and wire the uv output from the Shading Layer Parameter VOP into the input of the Vector to Float. Wire the `fval1` output of the Vector to Float node into the s input on the texture node. Wire the `fval2` output to the t input. The `fval3` output is not used because normally UV coordinates have only two values. When your soccer ball renders, you should now see the mandrill wrapping over the entire ball, fitting to the UV coordinates nicely. You might need to clear the IPR cache for the vertex UVs to be picked up.

Apply Lighting to the Texture Map

There is still a bit of a problem. You can see in the IPR Viewer that there is no shading on the texture map. In VOPs, nothing is taken for granted. Unless you ask for it, your texture maps will be constant shaded, meaning they have no lights influencing them. This makes for a very flat-looking surface. The Concrete VOPs have operators in them that cause lighting to be calculated, which is why you were seeing the soccer ball as shaded by light when looking at it earlier. Select the black node and press Enter to jump into it. Check out the network and you can likely see which node is doing the lighting work—the Lighting Model VOP. Jump back up and let's add one to the texture map.

1. Drop a Lighting Model VOP and wire the vec output of the `hvectovec1` node into the diff input of the lighting node. Wire the output of the lighting node into output Cf. The render turns black, which isn't exactly right. You don't want the texture to have Specular or Ambient on it. So, we'll leave the **Lighting Model** parameter at VEX Specular because a brand new soccer ball has some shine to it, and we'll set the Ambient Color to 0,0,0 to remove any ambient contribution. You'll notice that IPR re-renders the image after every adjustment you make. Sometimes, like right now, that can get a little burdensome. Remember that you can temporarily toggle on the Disable auto-update button, make several changes, and then toggle it back off. It's

possible after doing that, your IPR may not update correctly. Just click Clear IPR Cache and all will be back to normal. Holy bananas, Mandrillman! The mandrill now looks like it's on the ball with proper shading.

2. Using the mandrill is a good way to quickly see where texture coordinates are. Now that they are sorted, replace the `mandril.pic` with the `soccerballLabel01.rat` image in the texture node's Texture Map field. The current state of the network is shown in Figure 10.7.

3. Go ahead and jump into the networks for the black-and-white nodes and change their lighting models to VEX Specular also, so that the materials are consistent across the ball.

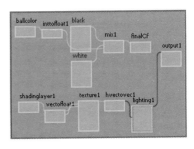

Figure 10.7
Your VOP should now look like this.

Composite the Label Over the Base Materials

You need to composite this image over top of the mix node that gives you the black-and-white patches of the soccer ball. You can do that inside VOPs with some simple compositing.

1. Wire the output of `finalCf` into the output's Cf so you can see the complete shader as you work.

2. Insert a Multiply VOP between the mix node and the `finalCf` node. Wire in the `hval4` output from the `hvectovec1` node into `input2` of the multiply node. This is taking the Alpha channel of the texture map and multiplying it against the base material. Because the Alpha channel is white where the text is (and so passes a value of 1), you only see the base material where the text is in the render. Coming at it another way, any value multiplied by 0 (where the alpha is black) is 0 and so renders as black. This is close to what you want, but not exactly. You need to invert the Alpha channel.

3. Drop a Complement VOP and wire the `hval4` output from the `hvectovec1` node into the second input of the multiply. Notice that this operator has a sweet yin-yang symbol... and continue. You have created an area on the background that is black where the foreground image's alpha is white. All that is left to do is add in the color from the foreground image.

4. Drop an Add VOP and wire the multiply node's output into it. Wire the lighting node's output into `input2` of the add node. Wire the add node's output into the `finalCf` node. Disconnect the first input, as there should always be just one connection going into this node. Then wire the `finalCf` output to the Cf on the output node and, can you believe it? You're done!

5. Okay, you must have realized by now that the learning process is never finished. Notice in the IPR render that the label is over on the side where you can barely see it. Now, let's say you wanted to leave the camera and the soccer ball in the same spot, but wanted the label to be centered in the render. Jump back over to your SOP network. In the `uvproject` node, change the Rotate in Y value to 0 and jump back to VOPs. This is one of those cases where you have to clear the IPR cache and start fresh to see an accurate update. So, press Clear IPR Cache and now the label is centered in the render.

All you did was rotate the UV coordinates 90 degrees and re-render. Now you can see the label in all its peaceful wordplay. You do realize, of course, that *ididthis* brand soccer balls are without equal. Change the output driver selector from `fast_mantra` to `mantra1` to get a better IPR rendering. Figure 10.8 shows the current state of the VOP network. Figure 10.9 is a rendered frame of your new creation.

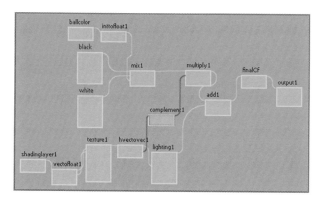

Figure 10.8
The VOP network that makes the soccer ball look good.

Figure 10.9
The rendered soccer ball.

Add User Parameters to the SHOP

So, what is there left to do? You have a working shader that gives you the look you want, but you have not yet made the controls available to the end user in the SHOP parameters. You will also want to save out this network as a SHOP on disk so that it can be more easily shared between users and maintained. First, let's add the parameters.

1. Pop up a floating pane (hotkey: Alt+Shift+W, or menu Windows->Floating Pane), make sure it isn't linked to any other panes, change the context to SHOPs, and press p to bring up a floating parameters pane inside the window. Select the my_soccerball_VOPNET1 shader and notice there are no useful user parameters. If someone came along and wanted to use this shader, all they could do is use whatever you have defined inside the VOPnet. That's not terribly versatile, because the user might want a different texture map, or different colors for the ball. Oh heavens above and hotter regions below, you must expose user parameters to the user and now!

2. You do see one parameter labeled ballcolor. However, it's not something the user will need or want to see because it is a parameter that is being used to grab and use a geometry attribute. Leave the floating pane up while you modify the VOPnet to affect the shader interface. Just push it over a little if needed. Select the ballcolor VOP and toggle on the Invisible parameter and it will disappear from the shader's interface. An Invisible parameter is most commonly used in exactly this situation, where you are importing attributes from geometry. Before you go on and makes lots of little additions to the shader interface, first disable IPR so it doesn't try to cook after every single change in the VOPnet.

3. MMB and hold on the map input of the texture node and select Create Parameter. A new Parameter VOP appears as if by magic, already wired in and already set to the correct data type. Look over in the shader interface and you can see that a new user parameter has appeared. A user can now select what texture map he or she wants to use as the label. It's so easy, it's like giving candy to a baby.

In the map node's parameters, change the Parameter Label to Label Map and notice that the SHOP user parameter's label has changed too. This is the beginning of how you customize the interface for your shaders. It's just a matter of repeating it for each parameter you want to expose.

4. In the Help Text field of the map node, type something like this:

```
This is the texture map for the label that\ngets composited over the patches base material.\nIt must have a valid Alpha channel
to work properly.
```

The Help Text field is a really great way of communicating with the end user who ultimately needs to understand how to use this SHOP. Hold your mouse over the Label Map label (whew, that's confusing) in SHOPs and the help text will appear in a tooltip. It's the little things that make life easy; you and others will appreciate your diligence in documentation when looking at this shader six months from now.

What's that strange \n for in the help text line? That's shorthand for "new line" and is often used in Houdini when you want to break a single typed line into several lines displayed lines. Each \n is just like typing Enter in a word processor; it adds a carriage return to the text. This technique is used here because the Help Text field is just a single line but you wanted a more compact, multi-line tooltip.

5. At this point you could go ahead and add the following parameters using the same method of creation:

On the black node: grey, tint, cfreq, dfreq, damp, chip, scale

On the white node: grey, tint, cfreq, dfreq, damp, chip, scale

However, that's a lot of senseless clicking and when your job is sitting in front of a computer for long hours each day clicking the mouse approximately 10 quadbazillion times, every single unnecessary click is a demon to be exorcised. It's much easier to add Parameter VOPs to all the inputs on the node and then delete the few you don't want.

RMB on the icon for the black node and select Create Input Parameters. This will add a Parameter VOP for every input and wire it in. The P and N inputs should not be wired in, as those are special global variables that the user should not alter directly. So, delete the P1 and N1 nodes. Do the same things for the white node.

6. Look over in the shader interface; you now have numerous parameters available for play. However, you can see that there are two copies of each parameter type, one for the black node and one for the white node. The problem is that they aren't currently labeled so that you can easily tell which is which. So, change the Parameter Label for each one to be prefixed with either Black or White, as appropriate. Also, although it's not strictly necessary, it's a good idea to change the Parameter Name for each to also include the new label, such as changing tint to black_tint in the Parameter Name for the black node. Now the shader interface has clear labels indicating which parameters control the black patches and which control the white patches. Figure 10.10 shows the finished state of the VOP network.

> When you want to create Parameter VOPs for numerous inputs on a particular node, creating each one individually can be a very tedious process. It can be much faster to RMB on the node's icon and choose Create Input Parameters. This will create and attach a Parameter VOP to every input in the original node. Each parameter node is named correctly and is set to the correct data type automatically.

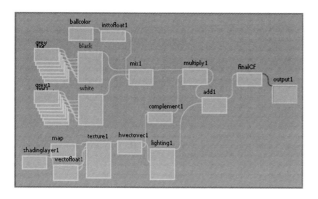

Figure 10.10
The finished VOP network.

Even though you can enter a name in the Parameter Name field using a space in the middle, you should always use an underscore to prevent parsing problems. For example, in the current exercise you could have name entered black tint. However, you want to be careful to actually enter black_tint. It's little things like that which can end up breaking something and be very, very difficult to track down. So, use a little due diligence up front to avoid throbbing temples down the road.

Organizing the User Interface

The interface is a little heavy right now and could be much better with a little slap and a shake. It would be clearer if the Black and White parameters had their own tabs. Each parameter gets its individual label, help text, and so on from a Parameter VOP, but the general organization of the SHOP interface is done from the top level of the VOP network.

1. Move to the root level of the VOP network by pressing the u key to jump up with the pointer over the network editor pane, or by clicking on the / at the end of the VOP network's path in the path area of the pane.

2. To create a tab (group) of parameters, you can select the parameters you want to group, and then click the arrow to the right of any of them. You can also drag and drop the parameters to re-order them or to drag them into a group. To rename the new tab, click on the New Group label and rename it Black Patches. Go ahead and finish grouping the parameters into Black Patches and White Patches tabs. Leave the Texture map field above the groups so it will not be in either tab. After you are finished, your shader interface should look like Figure 10.11.

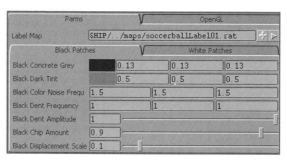

Figure 10.11
The finished shader interface.

Saving the VOPnet to Disk as a New SHOP Type

VOPnets are great for developing shaders, but you still need to save them to disk, which is known as "publishing" the shaders. Generally speaking, when you make a shader with a VOPnet, you are doing it for more than one shot, which means more than one person will use it and more than one .hip file needs to read it. By saving it to disk, you make all this possible and easy.

1. RMB on the VOPnet's icon and select Create Shop Type from Vop Network. The Create New Operator Type dialog box pops up, as shown in Figure 10.12. In it, you have the opportunity to specify the Operator Name, Operator Label, and where to save the new operator.

2. Leave this window alone for a second and RMB again on the VOPnet's icon and select Create New Shop from VOP Network. Notice in your floating pane that you now have two soccer ball shaders. So, this option just instantiates another shader into the SHOP context. You don't actually need the second one, so go ahead and delete it. Be careful to choose which you actually want—these two options sound very similar but do different things.

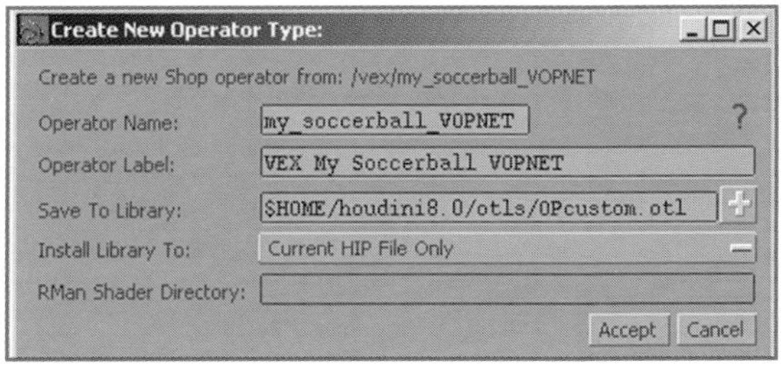

Figure 10.12
The Create New Operator Type dialog box.

3. Let's go back to the dialog box now. Remember when creating the VOPnet that it was suggested that you put _VOPNET on the end of the name and the label? Well, here's where you use it. Notice that the Operator Name is already filled in with the name of the VOPnet, and the Operator Label is filled in with the SHOP Type Name. That saves you some time. All you have to do now is remove the _VOPNET from the name and remove the VOPNET from the label. Make sure you delete the space before VOPNET in the label as well.

4. The Save To library is where the actual OTL file containing the shader will be stored. OTL files are a generic container format used by Houdini for holding various things, most often custom operators (also called digital assets). Because the SHOP you're creating from this VOPnet is a custom operator, this is most appropriate. You can also save digital assets, which are Objects or SOPs, to OTL files. When creating a new OTL file, like you're doing now, you need to specify where that OTL is saved and also where it is to be installed. Saving the OTL file simply creates the file with the asset inside. Installing it tells Houdini where to find it. If you don't install an OTL file, Houdini cannot use what's inside! It's really a two-step process, but it's important for flexibility that these two options be separated.

5. It is possible to save multiple assets into a single OTL file, but this is not recommended as it quickly makes things very confusing! There are some special occasions when you might want to do this, usually when you have very specialized operators that relate to each other, but generally, you want to keep one asset per OTL file. Unfortunately, the default in Houdini is to save all new assets into a generic OTL file called OPcustom.otl, as you can see in the Save To Library field.

   You are going to save the OTL file to your $HOME/houdini8.0/otls directory, but into an OTL file named appropriately for this new SHOP. You are going to install it to $HOME/houdini8.0 as well. In the Save To Library: field, leave the default path of $HOME/houdini8.0/otls, but change the OPcustom.otl file to SHOP_my_soccerball.otl. It's not strictly necessary but it's a really good idea to prepend the name of the OTL file with the type of operator it contains. In this case, you're creating a new SHOP, so use SHOP_ at the beginning. The rest of the OTL filename is the name of the new operator, with the .otl extension, of course. Now, if you ever want to find out what custom operators you have, you can look in the $HOME/houdini8.0/otls directory.

6. Another default is to install the library only to the current .hip file. This means that your new custom operator will only be found when using the current .hip file, and even then, only if you save the .hip file! This is almost never what you want. Change the Install Library To option to $HOME/houdini8.0 and click Accept. That's it. You've saved the VOP network to a new type of SHOP that many people can use and enjoy on that new summer blockbuster, *The Giant Soccer Ball That Attacked Milan*, you're working on. Of course it thought it was on a mission of peace, but the airhead didn't know the difference between a curtsey and an international incident.

On Unix-like systems, such as Linux, Irix, or OSX, you have a folder automatically defined for you as your "home" directory. This is where personal information like email or saved project files like .hip files are saved. This is typically in a directory like /home/pbowmar (or whatever your login name is) and is used by almost all programs.

On Windows systems, $HOME is also defined, but the default location is in a really long and somewhat arcane place. To see where your home is on Windows, in the Windows Explorer, type **%HOME%** in the navigation bar and it will take you there. You can change your HOME directory by RMB on My Computer and selecting Properties. Go to the Advanced tab, open the Environment Variables, and then create a new User Variable for yourself. For example, I use d:\user\willc, which is short and easy to find.

VOPnet Management

I recommend becoming familiar with the inner workings of Houdini. So for now, take a look in $HOME/houdini8.0 and check out the contents of the OPlibraries file in a text editor. It contains (at least) a single line that says ./otls/SHOP_my_soccerball.otl, which is simply a pointer telling Houdini where to find the OTL file. The ./otls is saying to Houdini that the OTL file lives in a directory called otls that is in the same directory as the OPlibraries file. This is known as a relative reference. If you wanted, you could also type the full path to the OTL file. However, this is really not recommended and is considered bad practice in production because it reduces flexibility considerably.

You've saved the VOPnet saved to disk as a new SHOP type. So what? Well, for one thing, if you installed it in an appropriate place on the network, all the users in the facility can access it. Also, because there are numerous problems with keeping your VOPnets "live," you can change the SHOPs you have applied to your objects over to use the ones from disk. "Live" means if you change the VOPnet and re-render, you'll immediately see the change on your object. After it has been saved to disk and you've used the on-disk version of the shader, if you change the VOPnet and re-render, it will use the disk version, and you won't see the change you made to the VOPnet until you re-save out the VOPnet to disk.

The main problem with using a "live" VOPnet is that you can't easily use it in different .hip files, unless you copy the VOPnet, which is very inefficient. If you save it to a SHOP on disk (in an OTL), many .hip files can use it, and if you make a change in the original VOPnet and save that again to an OTL on disk, all the .hip files that reference it immediately benefit from the changes you made.

1   In the floating SHOP pane, notice that the SHOP is still defined by the VOPnet in the file rather than the one on disk. You can tell this a couple of ways. The Label of the SHOP (next to the SHOP's name at the top) has the word VOPNET at the end. If you MMB on the icon, the Defined By line is also telling you that this SHOP is defined by a VOP network. Ah ha, so that's why you named them that way! You can now readily tell if your shader is defined by a VOPnet (when it has a VOPNET at the end of the reference) or by an asset on disk (when it doesn't have a VOPNET at the end of the reference).

2.   RMB on the SHOP's icon, and select Change Type. A little dialog box appears. Turn on Keep Name and Keep Parameters. Because this isn't a subnetwork, it doesn't matter if you turn on Keep Network Contents. The menu for the Operator: parameter currently says VEX My Soccerball, but it is actu-

ally set to VEX My Soccerball VOPNET; the menu is cutting off the rest. To be sure, you need to MMB the shader's icon and read the Defined By line. LMB the menu for VEX My Soccerball.

Eureka! You see another reason behind the madness of putting VOPNET on the end things when creating the VOPnets! There are two VEX My Soccerball entries in the list, but one has VOPNET at the end and one doesn't. It's pretty clear which is which, and this is one of the main reasons for making sure any operator defined by a VOPnet has VOPNET in the name and the label. Choose VEX My Soccerball and press Accept. The SHOP keeps its name and the values may have changed, but now the SHOP is defined from the disk file, not from the VOPnet in the current .hip file. MMB button on the icon to ensure that the shader is now defined by the file on disk.

3. If you wanted, you could remove the VOPnet. However, that is not recommended because you would no longer be able to make any changes to it. In production, what often happens is there is a library of .hip files that simply create VOP networks. That's all they do. If an artist needs to make a change to the shader that is shared across the network, he or she can load up the .hip file, make the changes to the VOPnet, and then re-save the operator to an OTL so the entire studio can access the new functionality. You can also institute simple versioning by renaming the .hip files appropriately. This seems a little clumsy when you first look at it, but in fact it's very powerful. You get the benefits of sharing operator assets with the ease of creation using VOPnets. But, you don't have to worry about each artist having his or her own, unique VOPnet in each individual .hip file. Down that path lies madness and the ruin of computerkind!

4. As mentioned at the beginning of the exercise, you can check out the `soccerballCompleteVOPs.hip` in the `Chapter 10>hips` folder on the Website. The only major difference between it and the exercise as written here is that the shader is defined by the VOPnet in the file so that you can open it and immediately see it working. If it were defined by a file on disk (as you do in the exercise), you wouldn't have access to my disk and so it wouldn't work correctly.

Summary

VOPs is just a graphical interface for accessing the VEX language. Because each operator contains a little snippet of code, you can quickly create complex operators by wiring nodes together. You explored building a VOPnet to create a new surface shader and had admirable success! VOPs are much more versatile than just for creating surface shaders, however. In the various VOP contexts, you can create new SOPs, POPs, CHOPs, COPs, and more with them too! The process is almost identical in terms of how you create the VOPnets and manage the OTL files. Only the objective and operators are different. As you progress in your adventure with Houdini, you will no doubt come to both depend and delight in the power of the VOP context.

chapter 11
Digital Assets

This chapter and the exercises in it are focused on the creation of Houdini Digital Assets, the cornerstone of high-end effects pipelines around the world. Houdini Digital Assets involve the creation of a new type of Houdini operator. Basically, you package some operators and then create an interface for the new operator type. When complete, the new operator appears to users just like any other Houdini operator, with a few minor caveats that you'll read about later in the chapter. Rather than rambling on about how powerful they are (because they are) or muttering about how much they will speed up your workflow (because they will), why not just jump in and actually make a Houdini Digital Asset? Oh yes, a Houdini Digital Asset is called an HDA or DA for short. You will likely also hear them called OTLs (operator type libraries) on the Houdini mailing list or in the various Houdini forums. That's a common way to refer to them, but it's not technically correct. You'll see why soon!

Kick the Tires!

As this chapter focuses on creating a Digital Asset, the objects, SOPs, and other operators that comprise the asset are already set up in the snowAssetStarter.hip, which is provided in the appropriate chapter directory. Go ahead and load it and take a look around. This file is commented internally with notes on each node to briefly explain what each node does. Any node whose name is in blue means that a comment has been added. As you recall, just MMB on the icon of the node to check it out. So, go ahead and take a few minutes to check out the various parts of the file.

Figure 11.1
Ol' man winter in a flurry.

Here are the highlights:

◆ The Collision_Geometry object contains the trees, ground, street, and sidewalk geometry. As far as this exercise goes, it's not specifically important because the DA will allow you to specify any object to collide with.

◆ The Alternate_Source object is used as an example to show how to change where the snow starts falling from. It's just a circle converted to a mesh.

◆ The Snow object is where everything is happening. Take a look at its Render tab. The Geometry is being rendered as a Procedural, specifically a sprite procedural. This is a special type of rendering that uses attributes on particles to replace each particle with a sprite image. You will also see that Motion Blur is set to none. This is because you will determine motion blur in the options of the sprite procedural.

Inside the Snow object, there are only a few SOPs, and most of those are just for flow control. The Source grid is a simple mesh grid that is used to determine the birthing origin of the particles.

◆ The get_external_source object Merge SOP will be used later in the exercise to change the source of the snow. It is not used right now.

◆ The get_external_collision object Merge SOP is used for merging in the street scene geometry. Later in this exercise you'll make it more generic, allowing the user to select what geometry the snow collides with.

◆ The choose_internal Switch SOP chooses which input to use as a birthing source, either the Source grid, or the get_external_source object Merge. An expression is used in the switch that detects if the get_external_source SOP contains any primitives. If it does, it uses that geometry. If it does not contain primitives, it uses the Source grid.

The Particles POP Network SOP contains the actual particles, which you'll dive into in a moment. Notice that the Render flag is on this node, but the Display flag is below on the show_source node. Note also that the choose_internal Switch SOP is wired into the first input, and the get_external_collision is wired into the second input. As mentioned in the POPs chapter, feeding connections into a POP Network SOP makes for clear visual relationships and allows you to easily refer to the context geometry inside the network.

◆ The show_source Switch node has the Display flag on it, and lets you switch between showing the particles (the default) or showing the source of the particles.

Inside the Particles POP Network, the source1 node uses the first input as its source. It is birthing randomly from Surfaces and gives the particles an initial velocity. Later, you're going to give the user direct control over this in the HDA interface.

◆ The wind1 Wind POP blows the snow down and also gives it the fluttery noisy motion.

◆ The collision1 Collision POP uses the second input to the POP Network to collide against, which right now is the street scene. It is set to Stick on Collision so if the trees were moving, the snow would stick to them as they moved. This POP also creates a group called *hit*. Particles that collide are placed in this group only for that instant. The Age POP works on these particles that have just collided.

◆ The age1 node resets the particle's age if it collides so that it won't die.

◆ Finally, the sprite1 Sprite POP applies the attributes needed to render the particles as sprites. Remember that the Snow object is set to render as a sprite procedural? Well, this is where the necessary attributes get created. A SHOP is applied, and the particles are given scale and rotation as well.

◆ The `sprite_shop` SHOP network contains a VEX Layered Surface SHOP that applies the sprite's texture map, sets the Diffuse brightness very high so that the snow actually is visible, and also sets the map to affect both the diffuse and alpha channels. You will make some of these controls available to the end user through the HDA interface.

When you're ready, let's proceed to encapsulate the various operators into a Houdini Digital Asset so that it can be quickly re-used, modified, and distributed to others.

Preparing for Assetization

Is assetization a word? My spell-checker doesn't think so, but I contend otherwise! But, what exactly does this newly formed word mean? If I'm going to make up a word, I should at least have the literary decency to define it. Basically, it just means to take a myriad of Houdini operators (or sometimes operator) and organize them and their parameters in such a way as to create a single asset that controls them all.

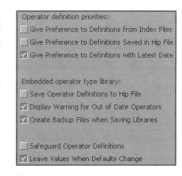

Figure 11.2
Make sure your Operator Type Manager>Configuration tab looks like this!

Important Note: Before you start creating Houdini Digital Assets, there are a few critical preferences that you need to check. If you don't, things may appear to work until you get to sharing your assets with other users. These preferences for creating HDAs will be explained later in the chapter. So for now, please just take it on faith that this is important! Open the main menu Tools->Operator Type Manager and switch to the Configuration tab. Ensure these preferences are set like the following. The most important ones are in **bold**. Figure 11.2 shows this settings you want for this tab. Click Close when done to exit the Operator Type Manager window.

◆ Give Preference to Definitions From Index Files: Off

◆ Give Preference to Definitions Saved in Hip File: **Off**

◆ Give Preference to Definitions with Latest Date: On

◆ Save Operator Definitions to Hip File: **Off**

◆ Display Warning for Out of Date Operator: On

◆ Create Backup Files when Saving Libraries: On

◆ Safeguard Operator Definitions: Off

◆ Leave Values When Defaults Change: On

11. Digital Assets

Collapsing Into a Subnet

The first step in making the asset is creating a subnet containing the operators that will comprise the asset. Generally, you take the operators you are making into the asset and collapse them into a subnet, which is exactly what you'll do here. In this case, you are taking a single object (which contains several networks and nodes) and collapsing it into a subnet.

1. Select only the Snow object. Then, select Operator->Collapse Selected into Subnet, or Ctrl+RMB and choose Collapse Selected into Subnet, or use the hotkey Shift+C to add a subnet and put the Snow object into it in one step.

2. Note that the new subnet has its own Transform and Subnet tabs. Later on, you'll actually hide these because you don't need them for this type of HDA. Different types of subnets (SOP, COP, and so on) will have different default tabs, but they can all be hidden if you don't want them.

3. Also note that all HDAs are created from subnets! That means all the components of your asset need to be inside that subnet! Houdini will warn you later in the process if you have components outside the subnet, but part of planning to create an asset is to make sure everything is inside. That's why it's generally a good idea to put the SHOPs for a model inside the model's geometry object, for example. Organizing your networks in this way from the outset helps to ensure a smooth assetization process.

> If you know you are making an HDA when you start, you can also simply add a subnet of the appropriate type, and then do your work inside it. However, because it's very easy to put your operators into a subnet at any time, *when* you do it really doesn't matter.

Creating the Asset

Once all the components are inside a subnet, you can transform the subnet into a living, breathing Houdini Digital Asset! Try it, it's fun!

1. RMB on the subnet you just created and select Create Digital Asset. Choose an Operator Name. I recommend using something like wmc_snow, which are my initials and then a name describing the asset. This step is critical because, once you name the operator, you generally try hard not to have change that name later. Everything else about the operator can be easily changed, including the contents of the subnet, the label, the number of inputs, and so forth. However, the name of the operator is what uniquely identifies the operator to Houdini. When you save a .hip file using your new operator, the name of the operator is how Houdini knows what operator was saved. If you later change the name (it is possible, just hard), those .hip files will break because when they load, they won't find the operator, due to the changed name. Much heartache and misery is in store for you down that road. So, simply avoid it by getting the name correct the first time.

It is a really good idea to name your own operators with a prefix that uniquely identifies the operator as one of your custom operators. Once you get into the groove of making your own assets, you'll find that the number of custom HDAs that you have grows very quickly. For your

> The Create New Digital Asset from Subnet window has a very useful Help page. Just click the ? in the upper-right corner to check it out.

personal HDAs, I recommend using your initials. If you are at a company, the initials of the company are a good idea. At Rhythm and Hues, for example, you use rh_ as the prefix for all the HDAs, and you have hundreds. For this exercise, I am going to use my initials and you will be using yours. So, anywhere you see mine, please do insert your own. My Operator Name will then be wmc_snow. Figure 11.3 shows this window after setting all of the necessary parameters.

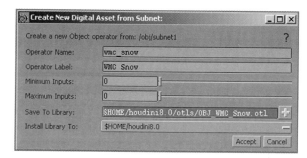

Figure 11.3
The window with all the parameters set and ready to go.

2. Give the operator a label; for example, WMC Snow. This part is not as critical as you can change it easily later. However, having a naming convention for this parameter is also a really good idea. The Operator Label is what you see in the Tab menu or when you use Operator->Add Operator. Using the same prefix on your labels lets you zero in on your HDAs very fast by typing the prefix, which narrows the Tab list down to just your own operators. For this exercise, I also use my initials, but using capital letters, so when I type Tab, I can then type Shift+W, Shift+M, and I instantly see only my own custom operators.

As a general rule, having the name of the operator and the label be similar is a good idea too. At the very least, having a common prefix will help make things clearer when you have a lot of HDAs.

3. For the Minimum Inputs, leave that at 0. For the Maximum Inputs, leave that at 0 also. The Minimum and Maximum Inputs are also easily changed later. So, if you change the design of your DA, you can readily change these to accommodate the change.

Minimum Inputs are the minimum number of inputs that are required to make the asset function. For this HDA, you don't require any inputs. But, there are times when an asset may not work unless it has at least one or maybe even two inputs. This is especially prevalent with SOP type assets that process and modify a geometry input. If you set the Minimum Inputs higher than 0, later when you use the HDA, you will get an error unless you have at least that number of inputs connected.

Maximum Inputs are the maximum number of inputs that are possible. Leaving this at 0 means there will be no input connector shown on the HDA node. However, you might want to allow people to connect one or more (up to four on object HDAs) inputs. In this case, you don't want to allow a parent for the Snow asset, so you'll leave this at 0 as well. You'll see in a moment that this causes no inputs connectors to appear on the HDA. The location of the Snow effect is determined by the source geometry, so having a parent for the asset doesn't make a lot of sense. This is something you can change later, however, if you find that having a parent would be useful for something.

4. For the Save To Library: location, use $HOME/houdini8.0/otls/OBJ_WMC_Snow.otl.

Whatever you do, don't use the default OPcustom.otl file! Well, okay, it's not the end of the world, but if you do keep saving HDAs to the same file, you'll end up with one huge file containing all your assets. That makes organization and control of particular HDAs really hard, and is a bit scary if something bad happens to that one file. Instead, I recommend installing each HDA to its own .otl file. Again, a naming convention is useful here so that you can look in the otls directory and quickly see what HDAs you have and also what type they are.

11. Digital Assets

I suggest using a convention that has the operator type as the first word, all capitalized, followed by the operator's label. So, as you can see from the name I suggested previously, the `otl` filename would be `OBJ_WMC_Snow.otl`, which should be pretty clear. The directory used, `$HOME/houdini8.0/otls`, is a good default location that should always be available. You are going to read about saving and installing .otl files later in this chapter in much more detail.

You can change where the HDA is saved and also where it is installed to after the fact, but it's good to get this right the first time, as changing the save to and install locations is a little tricky.

5. For the Install Library To: select `$HOME/houdini8.0`, which corresponds with the Save To location.

6. Once you have double-checked the Operator Name, Save To Library, and Install Library To fields (because they are the hardest to change), click Accept and you've created a Houdini Digital Asset! Well, nearly anyway.

7. Yaarrrggg! You got some sort of error message. Que pasa? Well, remember I said earlier that you had to have all the operators that make up an HDA inside the subnet? Houdini is being careful and warning you that it thinks you have broken this rule. It is telling you:

`/obj/subnet1/Snow/get_external_collision: references /obj/Collision_Geometry`

which is essentially saying you've got something inside your subnet that is referencing something outside your subnet. Aye yih yih! This is true, you do! However, it's fine in this case as that is part of the design of the HDA. Later in the exercise, you'll change the specific reference to be generic so that the user can specify what collision geometry will be used. For now, you will just respectfully ignore this error message. Click OK to skip the error and continue on. Now, you've really created a Houdini Digital Asset! Doesn't it just feel good?

Building the Asset's User Interface

As soon as you click OK, the Operator Type Properties window pops up. This is the main interface for creating HDAs, and you'll spend a goodly bit of time here every time you create a HDA. From this point on, creating your asset is a dynamic, non-linear process. I will offer suggestions on the order to proceed, but at this point, they are just suggestions and not hard and fast rules. Also, you can (and most likely will) re-open the Operator Type Properties many times as you discover additional features you want to add to your asset. There are also some options in the Operator Type Properties that are mostly personal preferences. Again, I will offer you my opinion. But in the end, you have to decide what you like and how you like to work. There is such freedom to be had!

Expose the Desired Parameters

You will spend a lot of time using drag and drop to configure the various parameters. This means that you need to arrange your Operator Type Properties window such that it won't disappear when you click on a Houdini node or parameter. On Linux, there are usually controls available in your Window Manager to prevent this, or simply RMB on the title bar and choose Always On Top. On Windows, this should automatically be the behavior of the window.

You will generally want to see the Parameters for your new asset while you build it, but building it means going inside the subnet. I use a 4 pane Desk with one of the panes not linked to the other three. Then set that one pane to be a Parameter pane looking at the asset's (top level) parameters. Go ahead and configure your desk like this now. Note that the Controls tab is currently empty, as you have not yet exposed any controls from inside the DA.

> As mentioned earlier, the order in which you do this is not critical; however, you'll discover as you make more and more HDAs that you have your own preferences with regards to the organization of the HDA. For example, the first parameters you will expose on the Snow object control various rendering parameters, and you will likely want to organize the various Rendering parameters into a single tab, which you'll do later. For now, you're just going to expose all of the desired parameters in a disorganized way and then clean up the UI afterwards.

1. In the Operator Type Properties dialog box, change over to the Parameters tab. This is where you create or expose the HDA's controls. In other words, this is where you promote parameters and controls from inside the asset to the top level of the asset. Usually, the end user will only have access to these top-level asset controls.

2. Enter into the HDA's subnet. Notice that the Snow object is inside, because you collapsed it into the subnet. You can now start exposing some of the parameters on the Snow object. In the Render tab of the Snow object, turn on the toggles for the Display, Matte, Phantom, and Shading Quality parameters. This activates (ungreys) the associated sliders.

3. Drag and drop the Display label into the blank Parameter area in the Operator Type Properties windows. Remember to drag and drop a parameter, you can LMB its label and hold. Then drag over to the desired area and release the LMB to drop it. The arrow will show a + sign next to it when it is over a valid drop location. Figure 11.4 shows where the Display label should be dropped. You'll drag over the other activated parameters later.

An entry appears named Snow_display and has a label Snow Display as well. For certain types of assets, for example, character assets where you want to promote 100s of bones parms that have nice names, this is a useful option. However, for the typical visual effects asset, it creates unnecessarily long channel names and so should be most often be turned off.

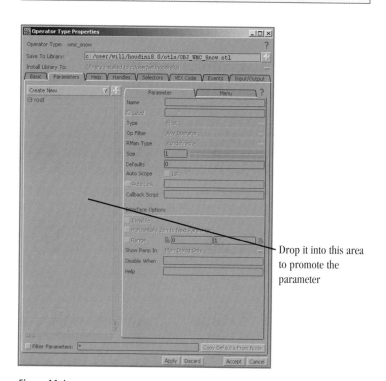

Drop it into this area to promote the parameter

Figure 11.4
Drop parameters from inside the asset to this area to expose them.

4. Delete this parameter by clicking on it in the Operator Type Properties' parameter list (it highlights in blue) and typing the Delete key. You can also RMB on it and select Delete Parameter. Change back to the Basic tab of the Type Properties window and turn off the two Prefix Linked Parameter options. Change back to the Parameters tab and drag over the Display parameter again. This time it is named `display2` and the Label is simply Display, which is better, in my opinion. Click Apply at the bottom of the Operator Type Properties, and you get the warning again about having external references. You'll turn this off in a bit; for now, just click OK. Make sure one of your panes is looking at the parameters for the new HDA subnet, and spanktastic! Your new control appears in the Controls tab!

You'll also notice that the Display parameter that you dragged in has turned green, indicating that a channel has been created. LMB on the Display label and you'll see that a channel reference `ch(display2)` has been inserted automatically. This is really at the heart of how HDAs work. Channel references are created automatically for you as you drag and drop (promote) parameters into the Operator Type Properties' parameter list. When you click Apply, the new channel reference is created and the change is committed to the asset.

> As in other parts of Houdini, if you click Accept, the Operator Type Properties will disappear. It's like clicking Apply and Close at once. Clicking Apply commits the changes without closing the window. If you inadvertently close the window, just RMB on the HDA's node icon and choose Type Properties. The Operator Type Properties window will open again. You can also RMB on the name of the asset in a path that is pointing at the asset or its contents and choose the same option.

5. The warning is coming from the Collision POP referencing the Collision Geometry object. This is expected and keeps popping up every time you applied the changes. For now, turn it off. The warning is very useful to prevent accidental inclusion of references that could break your HDA in various circumstances. Later, you'll turn it back on to double-check that the Asset is not accidentally referencing an external node. In the Basic tab, turn off Check for External Node References and click Apply. The warnings are gone.

6. Jump into the `Snow` object and select the `get_external_collision` node. Promote (drag and drop) the Object 1 label to the Operator Type Properties' Parameters area. Unlike the Display parameter you dragged in earlier, the name and label you get are not especially appropriate. Change the Name to collision and the Label to Collision object. Note that the Defaults field has been filled in with whatever was in the original parameter when you dragged it in. This is often useful, but in this case you do not want the default to be a specific object. So, clear out that field and apply the changes. Because you can't expect that `/obj/Collision_Geometry` will be present if this asset were to be used elsewhere, it is better to clear the field and so set the default state to avoid a potential error.

7. Use the + button for the HDA's Collision object and select the `Collision_Geometry` object. You could also drag and drop the `Collision_Geometry` object node's icon into the Collision object's parameter field.

Verify External References

Now is a good time to check the asset for external references.

1. You haven't finished yet, obviously, but now is a good time to see how using the Check for External Node References can be turned back on to check for external references. In the Basic tab, turn back on the Check for External Node References option and click Apply. The warning is there and tells you that the `get_external_collision` node has an external reference. This is correct even though it is the Collision object's parameter that seems to point to `/obj/Collision_Geometry`. In fact, the Collision object's parameter is simply passing down its reference to the `get_external_collision` node through the channel reference.

2. Use the Presets menu (accessed from little down-arrow next to the HDA's name) and select Revert to Default. This may switch the HDA's tab to Transform. Just click back on the Controls tab to see your controls again. Notice that the Collision Object field is empty, because you made the default empty. Now if you click Apply, you'll get a warning. Then click Apply again and the warning is gone. Turn off the Check for External Node References option and undo (Ctrl+Z) so that the Collision Object's field on the HDA's control tab again has the `/obj/Collision_Geometry/` reference.

   Although this might seem a little tedious, you don't have to do it very often. Basically, you can leave the Check for External Node References turned off until you have finished the asset or when you want to verify that all is going according to plan. The key idea here is to make sure your default values do not reference external nodes unintentionally. So, it's helpful when you revert to defaults to then turn on Check for External Node References and do a quick check.

Expose the Remaining Parameters

You now want to expose the rest of the desired controls. You are still not worried about the organization of the parameters just yet.

1. On the `Snow` object in the Render tab, promote the Matte, Phantom, Shading Quality, and Level Of Detail parameters. You know what this means by now, yes? It means to drag and drop them over into the Operator Type Properties' Parameter area. Let's leave the names and labels as they are. Click Apply to make sure these parameters show up in the Controls area and that the promoted fields turn green, indicating they have channel references.

2. In the SOP network for the `Snow` object, promote the Object 1 parameter on the `get_external_source` node. Rename this parameter `source` and relabel it Alt Source.

3. Expose the Select Input parameter of the `show_source` node. Rename this `showsource` and relabel it Show Snow Source.

4. Select the Particles SOP and expose the Preroll Time and Random Seed parameters. These names and labels are fine.

5. Go into the Particles network. On the `source1` node, expose the Const. Birth Rate and Life Expectancy parameters. Rename `constantrate` to `birthrate`. In the Attributes tab, expose the Velocity and Variance parameters. Rename the `vel` parameter to `initvel` and relabel it to Initial Velocity. Rename the `var` parameter to `initvar` and relabel it Initial Variance.

6. In the Noise tab, of the `wind1` node, expose the Turbulence, Roughness, Frequency, Amplitude, and Noise Type parameters.

11. Digital Assets

7. In the Behavior tab of the collision1 node, expose the Behavior parameter. Rename this hitbehavior and relabel it to Hit Behavior.

8. Enter into the sprite_shop SHOPnet. Expose the Diffuse and Texture Map parameters. Rename Cd to tint and relabel Diffuse to Tint. Rename map_base to map. Note that the Texture Map parameter has a default that is the SnowflakeSprite.rat texture. You can leave that as the default because it is useful. Go ahead and press Apply to see the asset's Control tab update with all of the new parameters.

> There are some parameters that you cannot drag and drop because they have no label. For example, the toggle next to the Display parameter on an object (the first parameter you dragged in earlier) has no label. So how can you promote it? If you RMB on it (or menus, or really any parameter), you can also select Export Parameter to Type Properties, which will export the parameter to the currently open Operator Type Properties. The hotkey for this is Alt+MMB. The only problem with using this method is that the parameters all end up at the bottom of the list. Dragging them in is a little simpler and you can organize your parameters as you expose them.

Organize the User Interface

Call the sheriff cuz I'm starting to feel a little too capable here! You have the controls exposed, but they're kind of a mess. So, let's slap a little spit shine on 'em! Looking through all of the parameters you have, it seems like you could logically break them into two categories: Behavior and Appearance.

1. In the Parameters tab of the Operator Type Properties, click the Create New button and select folder. Find it at the bottom and change the Label to Behavior. LMB on the Behavior folder in the Parameter list and drag it up to the top. The little line that appears will show you where it will be inserted. Drop it just below the root label at the top.

> Sometimes when you try to drag a Parameter like this, it doesn't drop where you want it to, or the little line doesn't appear, showing you where it is going to drop. You can fix this by clicking on a different parameter, and then clicking back on the parameter you want to drag, and finally dragging it into position.

2. Hold down Ctrl and then click on the following parameters to select them: Turbulence, Roughness, Frequency, Amplitude, Noise Type, Const.Birth Rate, Life Expectancy, Preroll Time, Random Seed, Hit Behavior, Velocity, and Variance. Once these parameters are selected, drag and drop them onto the Behavior folder. You can also do them one at a time if you have trouble selecting them or just prefer to do them individually. You can tell that the parameters are inside the Behavior folder because they are indented, just like what you see in Tree View. Figure 11.5 shows you the Behavior folder and its contents after they have been ordered in a sensible manner, which you'll do in a moment.

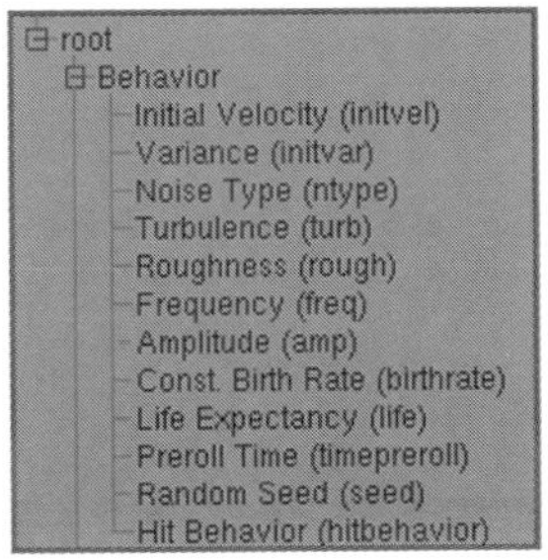

Figure 11.5
The Behavior folder and its parameters sensibly ordered.

3. Click the Create New button again and create another folder. Relabel this one to be Appearance. Drag the Appearance folder up and drop it just below the last parameter in the Behavior folder. To make dropping the Appearance folder easier, you can click the – (minus) button next to the Behavior folder to minimize its contents.

4. Drag the Alt. Source, Phantom, Display, Matte, Shading Quality, Level of Detail, Collision object, Show Snow Source, Tint, and Texture Map parameters into the Appearance folder. Click Apply whenever you want and you will see the Controls interface update.

5. Let's get rid of the Transform and Subnet tabs, as you are not going to use them. In the Basic tab of the Operator Type Properties, click the Hide Default Subnet Parameters toggle and click Apply again. Now, you have only the two folders: Behavior and Appearance. Back in the Parameters tab, you can now drag the parameters around to re-order the Snow Asset's interface more logically.

> You can select multiple parameters and move them around together, just as you did when dragging them into the folders.

6. In the Behavior folder, order the parameters in a way that makes sense. Figure 11.5 shows the order I thought most appropriate.

   There are actually three logical subgroups of parameters: noise-related parameters, basic particle parameters like Const. Birth Rate through Random Seed, and finally the Hit Behavior, which is kind of on its own. You don't want to make more folders that a user would have to dig through, but, you do want to visually separate these groups. Appropriately enough, you can use a few Separators to do this.

7. Click the Create New button and select Separator. You want to drag this Separator and drop it after the Amplitude parameter. However, for reasons I don't understand, you can't drag it there directly. You have to drag it (or any parameter) into the folder first and then drag it into the desired place.

   Drag the Separator and drop it onto the Behavior folder. Drag the Separator up and drop it after the Amplitude parameter. Click Apply and you'll see a line after the Amplitude parameter in the asset's parameters. Rather than create a new one, select the Separator you just dropped, RMB on it, and select Duplicate Parameter (hotkey d) to copy it. Drag this one down below the Random Seed parameter. Click Apply again and you now have a nicely organized interface without using too many folders. Figure 11.6 shows the Behavior folder in its final state.

8. Repeat the process for the Appearance folder. Figure 11.7 shows the organization I thought worked best.

Figure 11.6
The final configuration of the Behavior folder.

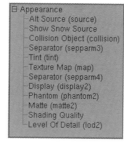

Figure 11.7
The organized parameters thus far in the Appearance folder.

Refine the User Interface

You have the basic parameters organized in a logical order, but there are still a number of things you can do to make the interface clearer and easier to use.

1. Notice the Show Snow Source is a numeric slider, but it would really be better if it were a toggle. Happily, any Integer parameter can be turned into a toggle (or a menu, but that's a topic I'll cover later) very easily. Click on the Show Snow Source parameter in the Operator Type Properties window to see its parameters. Hmmmm, click on a parameter to see its parameters; that is a wee bit confusing...

   Right under the Label field (where you typed in Show Snow Source, there is the Type menu. Currently it is Integer, which is what the default was when you dragged in the parameter from the Switch SOP. Click on this and change it to Toggle. Click Apply and it is now a toggle. Easy as pie, wouldn't you say? Or if not, insert a colloquialism of your choosing.

2. Take a look at the other parameters like Tint, Texture Map, or Collision object. They all have different Types. In fact, the base (or generic) type for Texture Map, Collision object, and Alt. Source are just strings, meaning just plain text. However, changing the Type to something more specific is known as hinting the parameter. Hinting adds useful interface widgets to the interface. For example, on Texture Map, setting it to Image File adds the + button and the -> (flyout) arrow to make it easier to select texture maps. Houdini was smart enough to recognize this when you exposed the Texture Map parameter and so automatically hinted the Type to the correct choice.

3. Another refinement can be made to the Hit Behavior parameter. Currently, it has a large number of options. Some of them aren't really appropriate for what snow would do, like Continue on Course, Stop, and Bounce. You can remove items from the menu that you exposed so that the user isn't confused by too many or erroneous options. Click on the Hit Behavior parameter in the Operator Type Properties window and switch to the Menu tab. Figure 11.8 shows the Menu tab.

   Note that there is a list of Menu Items for this menu. The Tokens, on the left side, are what are sent to the real menu on the node inside the HDA; in this case, to the Collision node inside the POP network. The Label column is what the users will see when they click the menu on the HDA's controls.

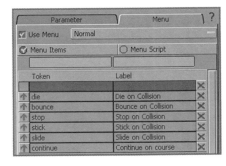

Figure 11.8
The Menu tab for the Hit Behavior parameter in the Operator Type Properties window.

4. Switch to the Parameter tab of the Hit Behavior parameter, and notice that the Type is integer. However, the Tokens are strings! This is very odd; why the mismatch? Well, it is due to the way that the Houdini menus are programmed internally. You don't need to worry about it; you just have to make a couple of small changes to get things to work. You can see that it isn't working by playing the simulation on watching what the particles do. They are bouncing even though the asset's Hit Behavior parameter says to Stick on Collision.

   Change the Type from Integer to String. In the Defaults field, replace the number with the word stick, which is one of the Tokens of the menu. Click Apply and nothing should change in the interface. However, internally, you are now passing the String Token to the Collision POP. Test the snow now and you should see that it is now sticking to the collision geometry as it should.

5. Switch back to the Menu tab, and click the red X next to the menu items you don't want. I kept die and stick and removed the others.

Create a Menu

Our HDA currently allows you to choose to see either the snow or the Snow Source. With two choices, a toggle works fine. However, what if you want a three (or more) choices? For example, what if you want to be able to show nothing from the snow? You could turn off the Display flag of course, but then it won't render. Instead, you might want to offer the user the option of displaying the snow, the source, or nothing.

1. Move to the SOP level of the HDA, where the `show_source` node is currently displayed. You'll recall that the `show_source` node's Select Input is controlled by the Show Snow Source parameter at the top level of the asset. Add a Null SOP and place it above and to the right of the `show_source` node. Rename this Null SOP `nothing` to indicate what it does. Wire the output of the nothing SOP into the `show_source` SOP's input. There should now be three wires going into the `show_source` node, from left to right: the Particles node, the `choose_internal` node, and finally the nothing node. This order is important, as the Choose Inputs Parameter on the Switch SOP uses this to determine which input is passed through to the output. Figure 11.9 shows the network correctly connected.

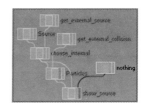

Figure 11.9
The Show Source node with its three inputs.

Now that you have three inputs to the `show_source` node, the toggle being used on the Show Snow Source parameter doesn't make sense. You'll replace it with a menu of choices.

2. In the Operator Type Properties, click on the Show Snow parameter to select it. Change the Type from Toggle to Integer, which doesn't actually change the underlying type of the parameter (a toggle is also an integer) but will change the user interface. Click on the Menu tab to show the Menu controls. Turn on Use Menu and leave the Menu Type to Normal.

> You might find that what you type in the first time disappears! This is a quirk of the menu entry fields. If this happens, just type the 0 and Snow Particles appear again.

3. Make sure Menu Items is selected. In the blank left field, type 0; in the right field, type Snow Particles; and then press Enter.

4. In the blank left field, type 1; in the right field, type Snow Source; and then press Enter.

5. Finally, in the blank left field, type 2; in the right field, type Nothing; and then press Enter. Click Apply in the Operator Type Properties and notice that you now have a nice menu with three options for the Show Snow Source parameter! Figure 11.10 shows the menu as it should appear after entering these choices.

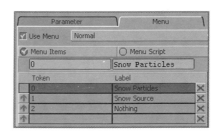

Figure 11.10
The correctly entered menu choices.

Understanding the Channel References

The HDA technology relies heavily on channel referencing, which basically means linking parameters (channels) inside an HDA with a control parameter at the top level of the HDA. It is important to understand how this channel referencing is done so you can troubleshoot your HDA when things seem to go wrong. Also, there is a lot of power derived from being able to intercept a channel reference and do clever things to it to make your HDA even more intuitive or flexible. Now, I'm not saying you could move into Castle GraySkull and proclaim your dominion over the universe. But, it is very helpful nonetheless!

There is a really handy tool called View Dependencies that will quickly find channel references and jump you to the correct location. You use this feature by simply RMB on a parameter's label, and selecting the View Dependencies. This pops up a small window that lets you see either channels that depend on this parameter (the default) or channels that refer to this parameter. You can then see the expression being used or even jump to the node with the dependency or reference. It is very useful when analyzing Digital Assets.

Dive down into the HDA's SOP network and then into the Particles POP network. Select the Wind POP and in its parameters, take a look at the Noise tab. Notice that the parameters you exposed earlier are all green, which is Houdini's way of indicating that they contain active channels. An active channel could be a channel reference, or it could be keyframed animation. The only way to tell is to click on the label and look at the expression. Click on the Frequency label to see the expressions. If you click inside the expression field, that field will expand to show you a wider view.

The channel reference for the Frequency X parameter is ch(../../../freqx), which simply says go up three levels and use the freqx parameter at that level. If you go up three levels, you will find yourself back at the HDA's main parameters. Notice the Noise Type parameter on the Wind POP. You promoted it earlier and the HDA does have a Noise Type parameter, but clicking on the label does not show you an expression. That is because the field is a menu. The only way to tell that there is a channel reference is the small (I would say tiny) green dot on the menu button. Figure 11.11 shows this miniscule green dot. Whatever you do, don't click the menu button! If you do, this will remove the channel reference, and then there will be much wailing and gnashing of teeth. The women will sing the lamentations and the men will join them for want of feeling included. Well, not really, but it's a bit of pain if you break the reference on a menu or toggle, which happens the moment you click on it.

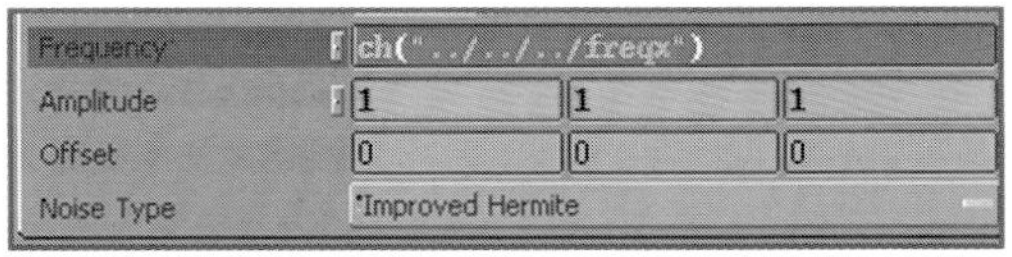

Figure 11.11
The green dot on the menu button signifies an active channel.

If you do accidentally click on a menu button or toggle that has a green dot (indicating there is a channel reference), you should immediately undo (Ctrl+Z) if you notice. However, if you don't notice and discover later that the link has been broken, the easiest way to fix it is to re-open the Operator Type Properties and first delete the old one, and then drag the parameter in again. Unfortunately, the linking of Menus and Toggles is the most fragile part of creating an HDA, so you need to keep an eye on it. It will also be the area that most often needs the most troubleshooting when you're building the interface.

Modify a Channel Reference

Let's say you want to offer your users the option of specifying the Life Expectancy in Frames rather than just in Seconds. The Source POP only offers the option of Seconds. Because you have direct access to the expression being used, it's pretty easy to make the change for your users using a simple expression. Better yet, you can make a new HDA control and offer users the choice of specifying the Life Expectancy in Frames or in Seconds.

1. Make sure the Operator Type Properties for your Snow asset is open. Dive down into the POP Network and select the Source POP where the snow is born. In the Birth tab, click on the Life Expectancy label to see the expression, which should be `ch(../../../life)`. This expression indicates that the HDA's top-level parameter controlling Life Expectancy is called life, as you would expect. Edit the expression to read `ch(../../../life)/$FPS`, which simply divides the channel referenced value by the current frames per second variable.

   Naturally, the value being used in the Life Expectancy at the top level of the HDA, which used to default to 20 Seconds, now defaults to 20 Frames, which is probably too short to be useful. For now, just leave it; you'll make the controls more intelligent a little later.

2. Now, let's make the new control that will let the user to specify Frames or Seconds. Open the Parameters tab on the Operator Type Properties, click the Create New button, and select Toggle. A new toggle appears at the bottom of the list. Rename your new toggle `useframes` and change the Label to be Use Frames for Life Expectancy. Set the Defaults to 0 so that this toggle is off by default. You want to drag this parameter up and place it above the Life Expectancy parameter. However, remember that you first have to drag it onto the folder containing Life Expectancy first. Then you can drag it where you want it above the Life Expectancy parameter. Click Apply to make the new toggle control appear.

   If you have a very long list of Parameters, drag the mouse above (outside) the Parameter area and the Parameter list will scroll. The farther you move it, the faster it will scroll. You can also use the − or + icons next to each folder to close folders you don't need, which will shrink the list and make it easier to drag things around.

   Remember also that sometimes when you click on a parameter to drag it, the line indicating where it will drop will not appear and you cannot drop the parameter. If this happens, click on a different parameter, and then click back on the parameter you want to drag and it should work.

Unfortunately, when you create a new widget, it always appears at the bottom of the list and you have to drag it back up into the folder where you want it. A trick to avoid this is to drag and drop a parameter you don't want to expose, which allows you to drop it wherever you want in the list. Then, if you turn off the Auto-link toggle, the parameter will appear but no link will be created inside the HDA. For this exercise, you'll continue using the newly created toggle.

---

3. Back in the Source POP, you are going to edit the expression used in Life Expectancy to utilize the new `useframes` control you just added. The expression is going to get too long for the relatively short space that the default entry field gives you, so you will open the Expression Editor. Click in the expression field for the Life Expectancy parameter, and press Alt+E, which will open the Expression Editor. You should see the same expression that you edited before, which is

   `ch(../../../life)/$FPS`.

> Any time you are editing an expression that is more complex than just a simple channel reference, you probably want to open and use the Expression Editor. Just click an expression field and press Alt+E to access it.

The Expression Editor gives you a lot of extra functionality, like an Apply button that will attempt to test your expression to make sure it is correct. Also, you can press Enter to create new lines, which lets you organize your expressions a lot easier. The formatting you give your expressions will be saved so if you re-open the Expression Editor, the formatting will still be there.

4. Modify the expression to read:

```
if( ch("../../../useframes") == 1,
    ch("../../../life")/$FPS,
    ch("../../../life")
)
```

This `if()` expression says if the `useframes` parameter (on the HDA's top level) equals 1, use the HDA's life parameter divided by the frames per second; otherwise, just use the life parameter without modification. You have just modified this parameter from a straight channel reference to a more complex one that does more interesting work. To explore Hscript expressions in more depth, the built-in Houdini documentation has several examples and a reference for all of the expressions available. Click Accept and test your newly created control.

5. Don't forget to click Apply or Accept on your HDA's Operator Type Properties to ensure your new channel modifications are saved! Then reset and play the frame range to ensure that all is working properly. When you have Use Frames for Life Expectancy toggled on, you should see the particles dying after only falling a short distance. You may have to dolly back a little in the viewport to see them. If you don't see any snow falling whatsoever, you may have inadvertently made an error whilst writing the expression.

Special Controls

So far you have been creating parameters mainly by dragging and dropping them. You did modify a channel reference and create a new toggle, but you were still essentially modifying a parameter that you had dragged in originally. Sometimes when creating an HDA, you want to create a completely new parameter that controls something that is normally not animated. For example, in the HDA, the `Snow` object is set to render as a Procedural, using the sprite procedural. There are two parameters to the sprite procedural that are especially important and you want to give the user control of them.

One is the `-v v` option, which indicates which attribute should be used to render motion blur. In this case, you are telling it to motion blur based on the velocity attribute. If the `-v v` option is not present, the snow will not motion blur.

The second is the -t option, which basically controls how big the motion blur is. It uses the expression SHUTTERSIZE/$FPS. So, if you want a shutter size of .5 (which is the normal default on film cameras), you would use -t .5/$FPS as the option. So, you want to create a Shutter Size parameter, and use it instead of the default of 1.0, and you want to create a Do Motion Blur parameter that will add the -v v option when it is turned on.

1. Move to the Object level of the Snow HDA, where the Snow object is. Select the Snow object to see the parameters. On the Render tab, note the sprite expression in the Mantra Procedure field.

2. In the Operator Type Properties for the Snow HDA, add a new Toggle. Rename the Toggle doblur, relabel it to be Do Motion Blur, and set the defaults to 0 so motion blur is off by default.

3. Add a new Float, rename it shuttersize, relabel it to be Shutter Size, and set the defaults to 0.5 so the default shutter size matches a real film camera.

4. Drag the two new parameters into the Appearance tab. You can leave them at the end of the list. If necessary, re-order the two new parameters so that Do Motion Blur comes first. Click Apply to ensure that the new parameters are saved.

5. You want to use the Shutter Size parameter in the Mantra Procedure field, but you can't drag and drop in this situation. You have to type in the channel reference… or do you? Here's a trick for situations like this. Temporarily use an unused parameter to get Houdini to type the correct expression for you.

   In the Snow object, below the Mantra Procedure field, the Ray Clip parameter is turned off and is not used for this asset. Turn on the Ray Clip parameter. RMB on the Shutter Size parameter in your HDA's controls and select Copy Parameter. RMB on the Ray Clip's label and select Paste Copied Relative Refs. There is the expression you want, which should read ch(../shuttersize).

6. Click in the Ray Clip's Expression field and press Ctrl+C to copy the expression. In the Mantra Procedure field, box-select the 1.0 and then press Ctrl+V to paste the expression you just copied. The 1.0 is replaced with the expression because you had it selected when you pasted. The entire expression should now read sprite -t 'ch("../shuttersize") / $FPS'. You don't want that expression in the Ray Clip field, so RMB on the Ray Clip label, select Delete Channels, and then again RMB to select Revert to Default if the value is not the default value of 1 to set it back to the default. Turn off the toggle too.

7. The Do Motion Blur is a little trickier to do. Basically, you want an expression that will return -v v when the toggle is on, but returns nothing when the toggle is off. That sounds like an if() statement! In fact, you'll use the ifs() expression, which is the same as the if() statement, except it returns strings instead of numbers.

   Click in the Mantra Procedure's text field, and press Alt+E to open the Expression Editor. Edit the expression to read:

```
sprite 'ifs( ch("../doblur"),
        "-v v",
        "" )' -t 'ch("../shuttersize") / $FPS'
```

   Click Accept on the Expression Editor and Apply in Op Type Properties to make sure your changes are saved into the HDA. Also, press Enter to exit editing the expression. If you accidentally press a key instead, the expression will get corrupted.

The `ifs()` statement is saying, if the `doblur` channel is 1, return `-v v`; otherwise, return nothing. The main difference between this and the `if()` expression you used earlier in the Life Expectancy parameter is that this one is a string field. That means any time you want to use an expression, you have to use backticks ` around the expression. This is because a string field does not know if you have entered an expression that should be evaluated unless you specifically tell Houdini, which is what the backticks are for. If you did not type the backticks, Houdini would think oh, OK, just use whatever you typed in, which would mean nothing to the sprite procedural.

> String parameters do not normally evaluate once the field has been edited. Only the final enter or when the node is first created or copy/pasted will cause the string field to re-evaluate. The backticks force the part of the string enclosed in them to evaluate as though it were a regular value parameter.

8. So, you've typed these expressions, but how do you tell if they are working? String fields in Houdini don't show you result of the expression the way a numeric field does. Basically, you need to use the Textport in this situation to see what the result of the string expressions are.

Open the Textport. You can either use main menu Windows->Textport... to get a floating Textport, or change one of your panes to be a Textport using the Pane->Textport menu of any pane. Type **opcf** in the Textport. Note that the `opcf` has a space at the end. Drag and drop the `Snow` object (the one inside the HDA) into the Textport. This will type the full path to the `Snow` object for you! You could also have typed it yourself, but really, that would just be brutally unnecessary, extra work. The line should now read `opcf /obj/subnet1/Snow`.

Type **Enter**. The `opcf` command is the same as the `cd` command in a DOS prompt or a Unix shell. It changes the current working directory to be the `Snow` object.

Type:

```
echo 'chs(detail_mantraproc)'
```

This should show you the sprite string the way Houdini sees it, with your expressions evaluated. It should read sprite –t 0.0208333. Now go to the assets parameters and change toggle on Do Motion Blur. Go back to the Textport and press the Up arrow key to access and enter the echo expression again. It should now read sprite -v v –t 0.0208333. Wahoo! It's working.

Remember from earlier that you need to use backticks to evaluate expressions in string fields? As it turns out, the whole Houdini Textport is a big string field! So, you use the `chs()` expression to look at the `detail_mantraproc` parameter on the `Snow` object and you enclose it in backticks to then evaluate it.

So, how did you find out that the parameter you wanted to look at was called `detail_mantraproc` anyway? If you hold your mouse pointer over the label for the Mantra Procedure parameter in the `Snow` object, a tooltip will pop up and tell you the parameter name! Almost all parameters in Houdini work this way.

> Using the `opcf` command to change the current directory to be the `Snow` object is a convenience, so in the `chs()` expression, you can refer directly to the parameter you are interested in. However, you could have also typed in the path to the operator in the `chs()` expression without first using the `opcf` command. Doing it this way, your `echo` expression is:
>
> ```
> echo 'chs(/obj/subnet1/Snow/"detail_mantraproc")'
> ```

Disabling Parameters

A very useful, standard user interface feature is greying out parameters that have no effect. On the Snow HDA, for example, if the Do Motion Blur toggle is off, the Shutter Size parameter has no effect. If you grey out the Shutter Size parameter when the Do Motion Blur toggle is off, the user knows immediately that the Shutter Size parameter is directly tied to the Do Motion Blur parameter and won't waste time adjusting that parameter. In the same manner, if the Collision Object field is empty, the Hit Behavior menu has no effect, and should be grayed out. Let's set this up now.

1. Go to the Operator Type Properties for the Snow HDA. In the Parameters tab, select the Shutter Size parameter. In the Disable When field, enter { doblur 0 } and click Apply. Turn on and off the Do Motion Blur parameter in the asset's parameters. When it's off, the Shutter Size should be greyed out.

2. In the Operator Type Properties window, select the Hit Behavior parameter. In the Disable When field, enter { collision "" } click Apply. When you clear the Collision Object field, the Hit Behavior menu should grey out.

   The Disable When field is quite simple. For single disable conditions like you just used, it's pretty clear what is going on. For the Shutter Size, the Disable When expression is saying, When doblur is 0, grey me out. Likewise for the Hit Behavior: It's saying, When collision is empty, grey me out.

These are simple cases; however, the Disable When fields can be more complex. Any Disable When expression contained in its own set of curly braces is like an OR statement. For example, { doblur 0 } { collision "" } is saying, If doblur is 0, OR collision is empty, so only one of those conditions has to be met for it to be disabled. If you put two or more expressions into a single set of curly braces, that becomes an AND statement. For example, { doblur 0 collision "" } is saying, If doblur is 0 AND collision is empty, both of these would have to be true before the parameter is greyed out.

One of the first things people want to do is create even more complex expressions, like grey out parameters if there is no geometry inside the HDA. Unfortunately, this is not currently possible. The functionality described here is basically all you get. However, for most HDA projects, it can see you through.

Expose Handles

Wouldn't it be nice to be able to drag the source of the snow around in the viewport? Well, that's where Handles come in. Generally speaking, you can attach handles to most parameters that can be animated on your HDA. There are two approaches to adding handles. If the parameters you want the handle on are linked to a node inside the HDA that already has handles, you can easily promote the handle to the asset level. Alternatively, if the parameter you want to control does not link internally to a node with handles, you can create your own handles, and attach whatever parameters you want to them. However, it's generally easier to just use a handle that already exists, which is what you will do in the following exercises.

For the Snow Source handle, the trick is to have the Operator Type Properties open, and then dive into the HDA and view the handle in the viewport. Once you have the handle you want, you can easily export it to the asset level.

1. Open the Operator Type Properties for the Snow HDA. Dive into the SOP Network and find the Source node. This is the Grid SOP, which is the default source for the snow. Make sure the viewport is linked to the same pane as the SOP network, so that you are viewing the SOP network you are working in. Click on the Display flag for the Source SOP. As you know, handles only show up in the viewport for operators that have their Display flags on. That is unless you make them persistent, as you've already learned.

   Move the mouse into the viewport and press Enter to access the handle. You may need to home the viewport to see it fully. RMB on the handle in the viewport and select Export Handle to Type Properties.

2. Notice at the bottom of the Parameters list in the Operator Type Properties there are three new parameters: Center, Size, and Orientation. When you export a handle like you just did, you are actually creating new parameters as well. This will happen unless the operator that has the handle already has links up to the HDA's top level. In that case, Houdini is smart enough to see the links, and only add the handle to the appropriate parameters. You don't need the Orientation parameter. Select just the new Orientation parameter and delete it. Rename the Center parameter name to be center instead of t2, and rename the Size parameter name to be sourcesize instead of just size to make it clearer.

3. Click on the Handles tab, and notice that there is a Grid_Transformer handle in the list. Change the Name to Snow Source, which can have spaces in it. This name is what will appear when the user uses the tooltips in the handle list in the left stowbar of the viewport. Don't forget in the SOP network to set the Display flag back on the show_source SOP or the snow won't be displayed correctly. Click Apply. The Source node should now have channel references up to the Center parameters in the assets controls.

4. Move up to the top level of the HDA, with the viewport showing you the whole scene. Make sure the Snow HDA is selected, and then move your mouse into the viewport and press Enter. The handle you just created should appear. If you change the Show Snow Source to Snow Source, you can now see the source and drag it around in the viewport as you like. Replay the simulation to ensure that the particles are now being born from the new location. The nice thing about creating handles for Digital Assets is that they automatically use all the great features of a Houdini handle. So, you can RMB on this handle and set keyframes, scope channels, and so on.

5. If you look at the controls for your HDA, the new parameters are sitting outside the tabs down at the bottom. Drag them up into the Appearance folder above the Alt. Source parameter. Your Appearance folder should now look like Figure 11.12.

6. Let's create a HUD (Heads-Up Display) slider for the Random Seed parameter. Drag and drop the Random Seed label from the asset's parameters into the viewport. Drag the slider to the lower-left corner of the viewport. RMB on the slider and select Locked, which will prevent it moving around. RMB on the slider again and select Name: Top to move the slider name to the top. The value on the left is fine. RMB on the slider and select Handle Parameters. Turn on the Lock Low toggle so that the slider will never go below 0 and close the Handle Parameters window.

Figure 11.12
The final ordering of the Appearance folder.

7. Make sure your Operator Type Properties for the Snow HDA is open. RMB on the slider and choose Export Handle to Type Properties. This time, it does not make a new Parameter in the HDA, because it's clever enough to see that the handle is already associated with the Random Seed parameter at the asset level. Click Apply to save the changes. The slider likely moved a little in the viewport! YARRRRRGGG!

8. When you drag and drop a HUD slider into the viewport, the slider becomes persistent, meaning even if you press Escape to go back into the View state, the slider remains visible. However, when you click Apply, the new slider that is actually part of the HDA is created, which confuses the HUD and makes it move. To fix this, simply RMB on the blue handle icon on the left side of the viewport and turn off Persistent. In the viewport, press Escape. Click Apply on the Type Properties to save the changes. Then in the viewport, press Enter again to refresh the handle.

9. Over on the Handles tab, rename the HUD slider to Random Seed and click apply again to finalize it. Note that when you change something about the HUD slider, like in this case its name, when you click Apply, it might get confused. If so, just press Escape in the viewport then Enter again to refresh it. This won't be a problem for your users, just a minor inconvenience for whoever is making the HDA.

Create Help

A new Digital Asset is never complete until you have some adequate Help for it. Even if you think you're the only one who will ever use it, spending the extra time documenting it will pay off in the long run. When you come back to the asset after not having looked at in ages and your brain is telling you that you likely didn't even create it, the Help will be there to hold your hand back into ownership. When you are creating the asset for others to use, Help is even more crucial. Just think of it this way... Every minute you put into clearly documenting the various features of the asset will likely save you five minutes of users asking you for assistance.

There are three areas where you want to create documentation for a Houdini Digital Asset. It's a good idea to put quick, simple comments on each node inside the HDA. For every parameter in the Op Type Properties Parameter's tab, there is a Help field. Whatever you type in here will appear as a tooltip when the user holds their mouse over the HDA parameter's label. These are really the quick reference tips that people use most often. Finally, the main operator help page is the one that pops up when you click the ? Help on your asset. This is where you describe what the operator is supposed to do and describe the parameters in detail. This is also where you would put any tutorials for using the HDA.

Operator Comments

This .hip file already has comments on the nodes. Just so you know, to add a note to a node, either RMB on the node and select Edit Comment, or click the Pen icon above the parameters for any node.

Tooltip Help

For the individual parameters, a quick summary is all that is needed. For example, in the Random Seed's Help field, you could type something like this:

```
This is the random seed for the whole particle system.\nChanging this will change where the particles start falling from.\nIf you
have several of these Snow effects, you might want to make each one have a different Random Seed so they don't all look the same.
```

As discussed earlier in the book, the /n is how you signify an Enter when typing in a single line field.

HTML Help

The main Help is actually using an embedded Web browser, a version of the open-source Mozilla browser. This means you can create quite sophisticated HTML pages for your help. The main limitation is that any images you want to use have to be on disk in a known location. This Help is added by typing in the Help tab of the Operator Type Properties window. It is possible to save images into the HDA, which the HDA can use, however, it is quite complicated and requires some complicated JavaScript and Hscript. If you really want to dive into that, there are some HDAs on the Houdini Exchange at the Side Effects Software Website that can show you how. This book can't go into the requisite depth with HTML and JavaScript; however, the Help doesn't have to be complicated to be useful. The main thing is to make sure the Help has a clear and complete description of how the HDA is supposed to be used. If you want to just type some simple help in, all you need to do is make sure you start and end the Help with correct HTML tags. For example:

```
<html>
<h1>Snow Effect</h1>
This Houdini Digital Asset will create a particle system, which when rendered will use Sprites to give the appearance of snow.
<br><br>
To have the snow collide with other geometry, simply select the object or SOP in the Collision Object parameter.
<br><br>
If you want a different source besides the default Grid, you can specify that in the Alt. Source parameter and it will automatically be used instead of the grid.
</html>
```

As long as you start your help with <html> and finish it with </html>, it will work. However, using other HTML tags like <h1> for the header, and <br> to create paragraph breaks, can significantly improve the readability.

If you are typing your HTML Help into the Help tab of the Operator Type Properties, you can quickly see what it will look like by clicking Apply on the Operator Type Properties, and then clicking the ? Help for the Snow HDA. After that first time, each time you want to see the Help properly formatted, just click Apply, and then click the Reload button at the top of the Help browser.

You can copy the Help from one operator and paste it to a file with an .html expression to edit in your favorite HTML editor. Save your changes and then copy and paste the actual text in to your HDA's help. You can also directly copy and paste the Help right into the Help. To do this, on a Houdini operator that has similar Help that you want to pattern yours after, RMB on that node to open its Operator Type Properties window, go to the Help folder, select all the text, and copy the Help using Ctrl+C. Now, RMB and open the Operator Type Properties on your HDA and paste using Ctrl+V in to the Help folder.

Conjure an Icon

Whew, you're almost done! There is one really important thing missing though: The icon! Right now the Snow HDA has the default Subnet icon, which makes me sleepy and want to think less of it. Fortunately, I quickly remember never to judge an asset by the appearance of its icon. Also, I know it can easily be changed to something more specialized.

You can use a Jpeg image, a Houdini .pic, or a Windows .bmp image file if you want. However, if you use an image file for the icon, it will cover the icon area completely. So, if you want to color the node, you won't see the color. Alternatively, you can select from a large selection of icons that ship with Houdini. The best choice, however, is to make native Houdini icons, ones that won't cover the whole icon area of the node.

Houdini includes a small standalone utility called gicon, which is used to make icons. Basically, you model your icon in SOPs, save out the geometry, and then use gicon to convert the geometry into a .icon file. If you apply a Primitive attribute Cd to the geometry, you can color the different parts of your icon as well.

1. Navigate to the top level Objects path and add a new Geometry object. Rename it makeSnowIcon. Enter the SOP network for the Jump inside it and make sure your viewport is linked and following along.

2. Delete the default File SOP. Add an Lsystem SOP. From the Presets pull-down menu, select the Koch Curve 3, which will configure the Lsystem to look a bit like a snowflake.

3. Append an Ends SOP to the Lsystem and in the Close U parameter, select Close Straight. This makes sure you have a closed polygon instead of wireframe. You can check this by turning on Smooth Shade in the viewport. Make sure your Display SOP is on the Ends SOP, of course.

4. Append a Primitive SOP. In the Attributes folder, change the Color parameter to Add Color, RMB on the label, and select Delete Channels. Select a color that would be appropriate for a snowflake. White seems to make good sense. This is the final icon, though you could create a more complex icon, using Merge SOPs, more Primitive SOPs for more color, and so on. Figure 11.13 shows the simple snowflake-like creation.

Figure 11.13
Ye simple snowflake geometry.

5. RMB on the Primitive SOP and select Save Geometry. Choose a directory to save to that will be easy for you to get to from a Unix shell or DOS prompt. I am going to use $TEMP, which is a variable that points to the temporary directory on both Unix-type and Windows systems. Give the geometry a name such as snowIcon.bgeo or something appropriate. This file is only a temporary file used to create the icon. So, the final name is $TEMP/snowIcon.bgeo and then click Accept to save it.

The following steps are slightly different depending on if you are on a Linux computer or a Windows computer. The steps labeled with "a" are for Linux, those labeled "b" are for Windows.

6a. In the Unix shell you launched Houdini from, type cd **$TEMP** and press Enter when you're done.

6b. In a Houdini Command Prompt (you can get one from the Start Menu in the Houdini menu folder and choosing Command Line Tools), type cd **%TEMP%** and press Enter when you're done.

Both of the steps will make your current working directory whatever the temporary directory is for your system.

Type gicon snowIcon.bgeo and if all goes well, you should see Converted snowIcon.bgeo to snowIcon.icon. That's it! Your icon is complete. Wasn't that easy?

7. In the Basics tab of the Operator Type Properties for the Snow asset, click the Icon button, browse to where you converted the icon, and select the snowIcon.icon file. Click Accept on the Operator Type Properties. The icon may not refresh properly on the Snow HDA, but if you dive inside it and then back out again, you should see your icon on the asset's node.

8. RMB on the Snow Asset and select Match Current Definition. This makes sure that the HDA is synchronized with the actual OTL file on disk. The finer points of this action will be discussed later in the chapter. Figure 11.14 shows the snow asset node with its spanking fresh new icon.

Figure 11.14
The Snow asset with its spanking fresh new icon.

Behold the wonder of creation! You now have a Houdini Digital Asset ready for all, or at least some!, of your snow production needs. That doesn't necessarily mean you are finished, though! As you work, you will most likely discover additional parameters that need to be exposed. That is one of the great features about the HDA concept. You can make upgrades and improvements while you work and immediately distribute those improvements to your colleagues.

For example, the Size parameters of the Sprite are currently hard-coded, but really should be exposed and so available for the user to modify. You don't want to expose the whole expression, because the $ID attribute is only available to you in POPs and not at the top level of the HDA. So, you might create two new parameters on your HDA's top level, and use those to control the min and max size in the expression. The expression in the Sprite POP might look something like this:

```
fit(rand($ID+6), 0, 1, ch("../../../minsize"), ch("../../../maxsize"))
```

Behind the Curtain

Creating the Houdini Digital Assets is only part of the picture. It is important to have a good understanding of what is happening behind the curtain, from a technical standpoint. Thankfully, this is all very logical and consistent with how Houdini works in other areas too.

New Operator Type

When you create a Houdini Digital Asset, you are really creating a completely new Operator Type. This is the core power of the Houdini Digital Assets! For the most part, these new Operators are equal citizens in the land of Houdini. You can animate their parameters, create channel groups for them, control them with Takes, use them in Bundles do and all the other things you might want to do with a regular Houdini operator.

You have always been able to create new Operators in Houdini, but only through the Houdini Developer's Kit (HDK), which requires knowledge of C++ programming. The HDK's strict programming requirements meant that only a small number of people were able to create their own Houdini Operators. Be gone, painful days of yesteryear! Now, any Houdini user can create his own Operators! These new Operators can range from a simple SOP tool to a more sophisticated effect like the one you just built and any number of things in between. Here are a few examples of real Houdini Digital Assets used by various companies. Note that these are examples of public HDAs. Every company will have special HDAs whose existence is not shared with the public.

◆ A special ROP that sends Houdini or Mantra tasks to the render queue.

◆ A SOP that deletes points based on their ID attribute, to allow quick culling of particles.

◆ A COP that does edge glows based on the Alpha channel or luminance of an incoming image.

◆ A customized Light object, with more controls and visualization tools than the standard Houdini Light.

◆ A custom, integrated interface to proprietary in-house software.

In fact, Houdini ships with several operators that are created as HDAs! The Platonic Solids SOP, the Fireworks POP, and many of the basic DOPs are actually Houdini Digital Assets. How do you tell, though? If the HDAs are represented as regular Houdini operators, they look just like any other operator. There are three ways to quickly tell, though. One is to MMB on the icon. If the info that pops up contains a Defined By line, you're looking at a Houdini Digital Asset. Another way is to select the Operator and press Enter. If you can jump into the operator, it's an HDA. Finally, type **d** in the Network Editor to pop up the display options for the pane, go to the Display tab and change the first entry under Name Highlights to Sub-Networks. Now, all subnets in the network will have a purple tinted node name.

The Houdini Exchange on the Side Effects Website has a large number of HDAs available that people from the community have shared. Many of these HDAs were created for productions and are shared through the generosity of the Houdini community. You can learn a lot from these HDAs just by looking through their networks and tinkering around.

A warning is in order here for users of the commercial version of Houdini. Be very careful when using HDAs from the exchange. If you install an asset that was made in the Apprentice version, your current session and any future sessions using that asset will become an Apprentice session with zero warning. This can result in much time lost if you don't notice it immediately.

As a commercial user, make sure you have first saved your .hip file. Then install the downloaded asset and immediately add it to the scene. If the Non-Commercial watermark appears, you should immediately un-install the asset (using the Operator Type Manager) and quit that session. Once a Houdini session has been "tainted" non-commercial, quitting and restarting the session is the only way to get back to a commercial version.

Design Philosophy

Once you get into the mindset of creating Houdini Digital Assets, you'll learn to create your networks with turning them into an HDA in mind. It's pretty simple, really. The key is using the Networks in Networks design philosophy. When building your networks, keep everything inside the top-level operator. In the case of the Snow asset, you put the POP Network and the SHOP network inside the original Snow object. When the Snow object was collapsed into the Subnet, everything just worked because all the required parts were already within the same network.

That is definitely not to say that you cannot make an HDA from networks that were not designed that way. It will just take more work to move the networks from outside the HDA into the HDA's subnet and ensure that everything is still being referenced correctly. Simply remembering and using the design philosophy of Networks in Networks essentially means you are always ready to create an HDA.

OTL Files

You will likely hear Houdini Digital Assets referred to as OTLs, which is not technically correct, but grew out of the file format that the HDAs are saved to. You'll recall back in the yonder blue at the beginning of the Snow exercise that you specified an .otl file to save the HDA to. You can save multiple HDAs to a single .otl file. Though, this is generally discouraged except in very special cases, like when one main HDA depends on another, smaller HDA. So, calling an HDA an OTL isn't really correct because the OTL is just the container file format. Incidentally, OTL stands for Operator Type Library, because creating an HDA is creating a new Operator Type.

Versioning Assets for Safety

When you create your HDA, each time you click the Apply or Accept button in the Operator Type Properties, or RMB on the HDA and select Save Operator Type, you are saving into the OTL file the custom interface and all the operators inside the HDA. That means other Houdini users can load this .otl file and get that custom interface and operator network. It also means if that .otl file is changed, all the other Houdini users getting their HDA definition from that OTL file can get the changes immediately, without exiting Houdini. This allows for a large, complex, multi-user environment (like a high-end film effects studio) to work together quickly and efficiently.

There are times when it's dangerous to make a change to an in-use HDA; for example, if you make a large change to an effect that causes the rendered appearance of the effect to change. In this case, a user who is already halfway finished with his shot probably does not want the changes and may even become a little unhappy if his work is changed just before crossing the finish line! To prevent unwanted changes, the easiest way is to use versions of your Digital Assets. There are several advantages to this. When a big change is made, you can make a new version of the HDA and the end user then explicitly chooses whether or not to use the new version. Also, the .hip files that use the various versions can always be loaded in and will work correctly, because instead of changing the HDA, you are essentially making a new one each time. This gives you the freedom to make changes to the HDA without fear that those changes will cause problems in the middle of a production.

The disadvantage of this is that it is extra work for the user to change versions, especially if you have a lot of HDAs of the same type in your .hip file. Also, you can't use the automatic updates features if you use versioning. However, the tradeoff for safety is usually considered to be well worth it.

To create a new version of an HDA, you simply copy the HDA, and give it a new Operator Name. To make a copy, you use the Operator Type Manager. There are two places you can access the Operator Type Manager. The first is from the Tools->Operator Type Manager... from the main menu. However, doing it this way means that you still have to go hunting for the operator you want to copy. The better way is to RMB on the HDA you want to copy and select Operator Type Manager. This will open the same Operator Type Manager window but will also open the OTL tree and select the current definition of the HDA you used the RMB on. Figure 11.15 shows the Operator Type Manager automagically opened to the desired asset.

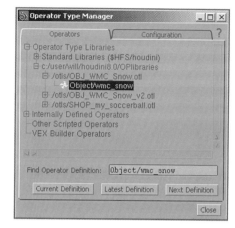

Figure 11.15
The Operator Type Manager opened to the desired asset.

1. For example, on the Snow HDA you created, let's create a new v2 version that you can safely modify without affecting whatever animation that may have already been created with the first version. RMB on the Snow HDA and select Operator Type Manager. You will see a list of Operator Type Libraries and another list of Internally Defined Operators, and your Snow HDA should be selected.

2. RMB on the selected HDA and select Copy. Hmmm, the dialog box that pops up looks familiar. In fact, it's identical to the first time you created a new HDA. For the Operator Name, add versioning to the name. For example, I would name it wmc_snow_v2. For the Operator Label, do the same thing without the underscore. Remember, this is what you see in the Tab menu. I used WMC Snow v2 for my Operator Label. For the Save To Library, I recommend using the same naming convention. $HOME/houdini8.0/otls/OBJ_PJB_Snow_v2.otl is what I used. For the Install Library To: use $HOME/houdini8.0, just as you did the first time around.

Click Accept and notice that the newly-created and installed .otl file appears immediately in the list. If you click the + button next to it to expand it, you will see the newly-created HDA.

3. Close the Operator Type Manager, and in the Object network, bring up the Tab menu. Notice that you now have two versions of your HDA: the original and the v2 version.

4. To version up, copy and paste your Snow HDA. Add a v1 to the name the copied version's node and turn off its Display flag. So you currently have two copies of the original version of the Snow asset. Now, let's change the displayed node to the second version of the Snow asset.

5. RMB on the original node (not the copy) and select Change Type. In the dialog box that pops up, make sure you turn on Keep Name and Keep Parameters. If you don't do this, you will still get the v2 version, but the name will be different and you will lose all the settings you had on your snow! From the Operator menu, select the Snow v2 item. When you're all ready, click Accept. Wow! Nothing of interest seemed to change. You have to look to the top of the Parameters to notice you're now using the v2 version.

By copying the original Snow operator, you always have it available should the v2 version turn out to have problems of any kind. The Change Type operation does its best to preserve parameter values. The only time it will have problems is if the Name (not the Label!) or Type of the parameter changes. If there are any new parameters in the v2 version, they will have their default values. If you deleted any parameters in the v2 version, they will disappear after you do the Change Type. You can now make changes to the v2 HDA secure in the knowledge that the original is sitting there waiting to be used should any problems arise.

11. Digital Assets

Another way to version Digital Assets is to version the library file. In this case, you simply copy the .otl containing the asset to another name. The asset inside is still the same name. You then use the Operator Type Manager to point at the new .otl file. This is a good way for substituting light assets with heavier ones at render time.

The Operator Type Manager

Every single operator available in any of the Network Editors is listed here! If you want to browse and see which operators are HDAs and which are C++ (those under the Internally Defined section), this is the place to look. At the top will be all the Operator Type Libraries (OTLs) and the operators they define. This includes your OTL files, plus all the Standard Libraries that ship with Houdini. As you can see, there are quite a lot of Houdini operators that are HDAs! The Internally Defined Operators are the operators written in C++ that are built in to Houdini. Other Scripted Operators is a list of old-style hand-crafted operators. These are still used mostly for writing shaders in VEX, as there are some advantages to having the shader exist on disk as a simple text file instead of as an OTL file. Finally, VEX Builder Operators will list any operators in your .hip file that are defined by a VOP network in this .hip file.

Generally, you'll use the Operator Type Manager to look at, copy, and manage your HDAs defined by OTL files. If you RMB on an .otl file entry, you can do some utility functions like Uninstall, Refresh, and Merge. Refresh is useful if you want to refresh a change in a single OTL file without reloading all of the OTL files, which is what File->Refresh Operator Type Libraries does in the main menu. Uninstall will remove the OTL file from the OPlibraries file, but it will not delete the OTL file. Merge allows you to move an Operator's definition into a different OTL file. This is a rarely-used command because you generally don't want multiple operators defined in a single OTL file. Expanding the .otl file entry will show you the operator (or asset) it contains. You can RMB on the operator and do various things here.

OTL Installation

When you install an OTL file, you are making Houdini aware that an OTL file exists and saying that Houdini should load the operator contained in the OTL file. Behind the scenes, Houdini is simply adding a reference to the OTL file in another file: the OPlibraries index file.

Using a filesystem browser, look in your $HOME/houdini8.0 directory. You will see (among other things) an OPlibraries file and an otls subdirectory. You saved your Snow OTL file to the otls subdirectory, and installed it to $HOME/houdini8.0, which means it was installed to the OPlibraries file in that directory. Using a simple text editor, open the OPlibraries file. You should see something like:

```
./otls/OBJ_WMC_Snow.otl
```

That's all that installing an OTL is doing. It adds a reference to the OTL file in a particular OPlibraries file. When Houdini starts up, or when you choose File->Refresh Operator Type Libraries, Houdini looks for OPlibraries files, looks inside each one it finds, and then loads whatever operators (or assets) are defined by the OTL files it finds. When you Uninstall an OTL file, it is simply removing the reference in the OPlibraries file. It does not delete the OTL file though!

Locked/Unlocked Status of an Asset

One of the many advantages that Houdini Digital Assets give you is that the network that makes up the HDA is saved into an OTL file. This means that the network is **not** saved into the .hip file, so long as the HDA is in a locked state. So, if you had a .hip file that only had locked HDAs in it, it would be a tiny .hip file, because all the networks would actually be in the OTL files on disk.

So, what does "locked" really mean? It simply determines if your HDA's network is being pulled from disk or from the .hip file. You can instantly tell if an HDA is locked or not by the color of the name of the node in the Network Editor. A locked HDA has a dark blue label, whereas an unlocked HDA has a red label.

If your Snow HDA's name is in red, it is still unlocked! That means that even though the custom user interface that you made is being loaded from the OTL file, the network is being saved in the .hip file. This is usually not desirable. RMB on the Snow HDA and select Match Current Definition. This is Houdini-speak for locking your HDA. All it is doing is making sure that the HDA is referencing the OTL file on disk, so that you are synchronized with the definition in the OTL file. However, you cannot edit a locked or synchronized definition. So, if you open the Operator Type Properties (by using RMB on the Snow HDA for example), make a change and then click Apply, you will get a warning that you can't do it. Also, if you go inside the subnet, you cannot change the wiring, alter parameters, add new nodes, or do anything else. You have to first RMB on the Snow HDA and select Allow Editing of Contents.

Selecting Allow Editing of Contents just means unlocking your HDA. Now, you can make changes to the parameters, click Apply or Accept, make changes to the contents, add new nodes, and so on.

The difference between a locked and an unlocked HDA is a very important concept. When you are creating an HDA, you of course have it unlocked as you work. It's important to realize that each time you click Apply or Accept, the work you have done on or in your HDA is saved to the OTL file! That means you really don't have to save the .hip file you work in, because all your work is saved to the OTL file.

When you save a .hip file that contains unlocked HDAs, you are also saving the HDA's network into the .hip file. This means that what is in the HDA in the .hip file might be different from what is on disk in the OTL file. This is generally undesirable. It means you can't automatically inherit changes from the OTL file, and really removes the advantages of having the network be in the HDA. There are rare times where you do want this ability, though. For example, you may need to do emergency fixes to an HDA to finish a shot. There is a better way, though, as you will see later.

It is also important to note that an unlocked asset still has its parameter interface being defined by the referenced HDA in the .otl file on disk. It can be quite alarming for the users if someone changes the interface in the referenced .otl while they are working with the unlocked asset, because the interface will change right before them as if by some fiendish witchcraft.

When you use an HDA, you generally want it to be locked so that it is always synchronized with the OTL file on disk. When an HDA is locked, it acts pretty much like any other Houdini operator. So, any changes you make to the HDA's parameters (or any other Houdini operator, HDA or not) are saved with the .hip file. Using the locked HDA approach allows you to save changes to the OTL on disk and have many users get those changes immediately, if you (and they) desire. Let's say you have 10 Houdini artists using the Snow HDA. The Technical Director that made the Snow HDA makes some changes, perhaps adding additional controls for the snow, or a more sophisticated shader. The TD simply saves those changes to the OTL file, and the 10 Houdini artists select File->Refresh Operator Type Libraries from the main menu and poof, all the changes the TD made are immediately available

11. Digital Assets

261

This can be taken to complex extremes. For example, a character rigger can create an HDA that will become a character. A crude model with basic rigging can be made into an HDA and then given to animators to start blocking or even doing final animation on. While the animators work, the character rigger, modeler, technical directors, and so on, can be working in parallel finishing the character. This means the animators don't have to wait until the character is fully rigged or the model finished before they start animating! This methodology is being used for complex commercial and feature film production and significantly reduces production time by allowing people to work in parallel. The Side Effects Website has some great articles discussing this type of pipeline in more detail. Although, with great power comes great re... re... repercussions, I think it was. This type of setup can allow the rigger or TD to defer important decisions to very late in the game, causing much consternation and fear amongst those using the asset.

Takes and HDAs

So, here you are in happy-happy land. You have locked HDAs that allow you to reference the effect or character from disk. What if you really want to change a parameter inside for some reason? You could unlock it, but that removes a lot of power from the HDA. The better solution is to use Takes. Takes allow you to modify the parameters inside an HDA without unlocking the HDA. If you are on any Take except the base Take, you can RMB on any parameter inside your HDA, and select Include in Take, which makes that parameter editable. This does not let you rewire things though, so it is not the solution for every situation. There will still be certain times where an artist will have to unlock the HDA to make emergency changes. Ideally though, the artist would be able to ask the Technical Director that made the HDA to make whatever changes are necessary and distribute those changes to everyone.

Multiple Definitions Using the Search Path

Another powerful feature of HDAs is having multiple installed copies of the same HDA operator. This allows you to have a base HDA, but be able to override it with shot-specific HDAs, or special-case HDAs, without affecting all your artists. This is controlled with the HOUDINI_PATH environment variable. By default, when looking for OPlibraries files, Houdini looks in the directory where your .hip file was loaded (known as $HIP). Then it looks in your $HOME/houdini8.0 directory. And finally, it looks in the $HFS/houdini directory, which is the base Houdini installation location. So, if you have an OPlibraries file in the directory where your .hip file is, any definitions in there will be used. However, if you have the same definition also in your $HOME/houdini8.0 directory, Houdini has to select which one to use. There is a preference in the Operator Type Manager that can be used to determine this: Give Preference to Definitions with Latest Date.

If this preference is On, the HDA with the latest date (most recently edited) will be used. However, if this is turned off, the order that Houdini finds the definition will be used. In the previous case, the $HIP definition will be used first, if found; the $HOME/houdini8.0 definition, if found. Just so you are clear, I'll see it again slightly differently. If Houdini finds a particular OTL definition in both the $HIP and $HOME/houdini8.0 directories, it will use the $HIP one.

You can customize this search process using the HOUDINI_PATH environment variable. This is a variable that contains the list of locations Houdini should search and in what order. For example, at Rhythm and Hues, you have a search path like this:

```
SHOT:SEQUENCE:JOB:STUDIO:$HOME:$HFS
```

Almost all production houses have very similar concepts for their search paths. This means an HDA can be installed only for a specific job (movie) or be distributed to the entire studio. If needed, you can copy the HDA to a specific shot, and make changes to the HDA only for that shot. This is getting into a pipeline discussion that's really outside the scope of this book. If you want to experiment, you can set the HOUDINI_PATH to search wherever you want. The most important thing is to make sure that $HFS/houdini is always the last thing listed. Otherwise, Houdini will not be able to find critical files and will fail to load whilst spewing an almost unending streams of warnings. To set the Environment variable in Windows, you would RMB on My Computer and select Properties. Then open the Environment Variables section and enter HOUDINI_PATH for the variable name and /somedir;/someotherdir;$HFS/houdini for the variable value. On Linux, assuming you use a Cshell, you can just type setenv HOUDINI_PATH /somedir;/someotherdir;$HFS/Houdini, where /somedir and /someotherdir are the locations on disk you want to search.

Embed an OTL

Remember at the beginning of this chapter when I suggested setting some preferences in the Operator Type Manager? Specifically, the following:

◆ Give Preference to Definitions Saved in Hip File: OFF
◆ Save Operator Definitions to Hip File: OFF

Well, now let's get to the understanding of why. If you have Save Operator Definitions to Hip File turned on, the OTL file is actually saved twice, once to disk in the .otl file you specified, and once in the .hip file! That means your .hip file gets bloated with extra, unneeded data. Even worse, it means things can quickly get very confusing determining which data should be used, modified, and saved. Saving to the .hip file is known as embedding the OTL file into the .hip file. It's great for putting all the HDAs you are using into the .hip file in case you want to email it to a friend or to Side Effects Support. However, embedding is very dangerous in production and should almost never be turned on. As you've read previously numerous times, if you use an HDA that is defined from the .hip file, you are missing out on any changes that might later be made to the disk file! Woe be unto you if you unknowingly put yourself in this situation.

Setting the Give Preference to Definitions Saved in Hip File: OFF preference helps to avoid this problem. So, if multiple definitions are found, it won't automatically use the one in the .hip file. However, if the Give Preference to Definitions with Latest Date is On (as it generally should be) and the definition in the .hip file is newest, it will still use the one in the .hip file. What a tangled web it can become if you don't strike out upon a sensible path from the beginning! The best way to avoid this problem is just to make sure the definitions are not saved into the hip file in the first place.

So, why do you have access to this somewhat bewildering array of options? Well, as usual with Houdini, power and flexibility are the number one considerations and there are times when you want to embed your OTL files into the .hip file. One example I already mentioned is sending things to Side Effects Support. Another example would be creating a custom, empty HDA that is just a custom interface with no network inside. This might be used to control various other Houdini operators. If it is specific to the .hip file, saving it into the .hip file makes sense too.

You can force an OTL file to be saved to the .hip file, no matter what the preference is set to, by using Embedded as the OTL file's location, as shown in Figure 11.16, instead of a file on disk. However, this should be used rarely and only in special cases, or chaos can result!

Figure 11.16
Where to specify the embedded option.

Summary

So, now that you've built a Houdini Digital Asset and have a better understanding of the details, what about an overview? Clearly, encapsulating an effect like you just did is one use for HDAs, but there are many more possibilities.

◆ Reuse: HDAs are ideal for reusing effects or techniques. Rather than having to copy a .hip file, or use tedious scripting methods, creating an HDA means you have the underlying networks always available, but you also have an interface and a clean, self-contained operator. This makes organization really easy, especially when you have hundreds of HDAs! It also means that when you have that next big snowstorm to make, you just drop down your Snow asset and away you go!

◆ Studio Deployment: If you have 50 Houdini artists, you want to maximize their efficiency. Using HDAs allows you to instantly share work by simply installing the HDA on the network. If changes have to be made, they can be distributed to the whole studio instantly. Each Houdini artist can create HDAs using his or her specialized skills or unique areas of knowledge, and everyone benefits.

◆ Encapsulation: On a TV show or large character-based feature film, you have characters, props, and sets that are used over and over in different shots. By encapsulating each item in a HDA, it makes managing all these individual items much easier, because textures, custom scripts, custom rigs, and so on can be packaged into a single file. If a set piece or character needs to change, you can make the change in a single location and every single shot in your production can receive the update instantly. Alternatively, you can create new versions of the character or prop, for shot-specific use, again without complicated management of the assets.

◆ New Tools: Another use for HDAs is creating new tools in Houdini. In the Snow exercise, you created a whole new effect. However, many HDAs are much simpler, basically they involve implementing a new tool in Houdini. For example, when modeling, you might find yourself having to cut slices into a model often. You can do this with the Clip SOP; however, making a HDA can speed things up significantly. This new HDA might contain the Clip SOP plus some other SOPs and expressions that automatically find the center of the model, and then apply the Clip with a random rotation.

◆ New Hires: You might find that hiring seasoned Houdini artists is tough, because there are almost never unemployed Houdini artists! HDAs allow you to take people new to Houdini and make them productive, fast. Rather than trying to teach someone everything about Houdini in a day (hah!), you can teach them the basics of the interface (perhaps, using this book) and then show them a few HDAs that were built to accomplish the effects that need to be done. As they work, they can dive into the HDA, and learn how the effects were actually done!

◆ Learning: The fact that HDAs are subnets containing Houdini operators means they are excellent learning tools as well. If you document the HDA well with comments on the nodes, people new to Houdini can use them as training tools!

Houdini Digital Assets have been part of Houdini since version 6, but even the most experienced users are still finding new and wonderful uses for them. Suggestions and tips can get you started, but ultimately, every shop both big and small will find their own needs and their own way of working. This is really what makes Houdini the premier 3D animation package: the capability to customize it almost endlessly to suit very specific needs and very different ways of working.

chapter 12
Dynamic Operators (DOPs)

The reality you experience is full of forces that interact in zanillions (that means a lot) of ways and are constantly changing and evolving according to the wondrous theories of physics. The universe abides by its own rules of behavior and, over time, we humans have come to understand some of them and even observed them consistently enough to feel reasonably confident in labeling some of them as laws. We particularly have a reasonably good grasp about how forces interact at the scale in which we exist. Although we have learned a great deal in such a speck of geologic time, we have much to learn yet about this thing we collectively refer to as reality. In particular, our knowledge is very limited when considering extremely minute or extremely large scales. Thankfully you don't have to be terribly concerned with those forces just now and because you have lived under the laws all of your life, you have gained an innate understanding of the motion and interactions described by physics.

Total Perspective Vortex

This innate understanding combined with a desire to dismantle and simulate the world around us brings us to believe that we can judge what motion looks real and what motion does not. And we can—for the most part. It turns out that we are pretty accurate at judging the gross movement of an object under physical simulation but we're not so great at judging the smaller and faster interactions. Think of a couple of dice bouncing across the table. You will never be able to predict what numbers they will land on, unless you are PrecipitationMan. But don't feel bad, as this is actually a very good thing! An effects artist must turn this fact to his advantage and use the simulation where necessary and also choose where to break it in order to get the most flamboyant and pleasing motion possible. That is why the craft is an artistic endeavor. You are not just trying to accurately simulate natural forces. You are trying to tell a story in a visual medium—employing artistically designed natural forces often furthers your goal.

The world of simulations is a chaotic one. There are thousands of forces that you will not be directly aware of even in the simplest scene. Often, it is useful to poke your head under the fabric of reality and tweak a variable here or there to see what happens. This is a great departure from the well-defined and purposeful approach to building illusions that you have encountered so far in the quest to grok Houdini. The effects of the laws of physics will not be fully understood by humanity in our current incarnation. Thankfully, you need only concern yourself with a simulacrum of reality, and even that is challenging. You will have tenuous control over this new world and you are going to need all the skills and tricks you can muster to keep the illusion convincing.

Ye Grand List

When you have a lot of things to remember to do, it's best to make a list. Perhaps even gods use lists because they obviously have a good deal to do. I suspect that the type of list such gods would use would be a little different than the "Walk the dog, take shower, figure out how to download directly to the brain" variety that is far more terrestrial in nature. Theirs may read something like "Create a universe of energy. Throw around some lightning bolts. Inspire the evolution of humankind." In this chapter, you get to draw up a list somewhat similar to that, more grandiose version!

The list you will create is actually pretty simple on the surface. The list contains a bunch of names of objects and some info about the objects. It also describes what to do with that information insofar as how objects may interact and influence each other. Throughout your experience with DOPs, you are going to be acutely aware of the list. You will keep an eye on it as each project evolves to gain an intimate understanding of what it is you are really requesting of the powers that be. To make this list easier to visualize and create, you don't even write it directly. You describe the complex interrelationships between the actors in the simulation using the DOP nodes available. Ye grand list is then populated by the nodes and the forces of nature take over. These forces never look at the nodes, only the list. They will even change some information in the list as they work too. In some ways, this should remind you of POPs, where all the POP nodes in a network really just build up a nice rule set for all the particles to follow but are not necessarily executed in a top-down way as are SOPs.

So where exactly is this most amazing and descriptive list? It is called the Details view pane. Launch Houdini. In the Objects context, drop a DOP network and dive into it. Split the Viewer pane Top/Bottom and change the lower pane to a Details view. Make sure that its path is looking at the newly created network, which is probably called `/obj/dopnet1`. The list looks a little empty at this stage of course, because you haven't added anything yet.

Divide and Conquer

Although it is true that all things in this fabricated universe are connected, the physics of it are broken up into a few well-understood categories. The categories, or disciplines, are broken apart in order to simplify and optimize the experience. In other words, it helps to keep things fast and fun. For objects that are not malleable or flexible in any way, certain mathematical assumptions can be made and this category is called Rigid Body Dynamics. For woven or flexible sheets, other assumptions can be made and this category is called a Cloth simulation. Another category uses a Wire Solver and capably defines the behavior for cords like rope, hair, wire, or cables. Houdini has operations that are aligned with each of these disciplines.

Salutations to the DOP Node

Just as in every other context, DOPs also uses nodes. Figure 12.1 shows a typical DOP node. There is an input and/or output connector. The blue flag is the Display flag and controls to what node the network is cooked. There is a Bypass flag for quickly removing the input of a particular node from the network. There is an icon that you can use for moving the node around. You can MMB on the icon to get a little information about that node, although not nearly so much as you find in other contexts. The Details view really takes over this role in DOPs. Some nodes in DOPs have unique capabilities and you will find out about those later in the chapter.

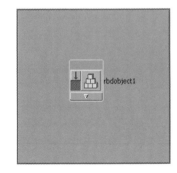

Figure 12.1
The DOP node.

Objects Level Objects and DOPs Objects

You are already familiar with objects in the Objects context and what they can do. The term *objects* is also used in the DOPs context to indicate DOP objects. Obviously, this can quickly get confusing when you are importing Objects level objects to be used as DOPs level objects. In an effort to clarify this muddled situation, I will call DOPs level objects *dobjects*, for DOP objects.

In the Beginning, There Was the Void (and RBDs)

Finalmente! It is time to do the deed. Rigid Body Dynamics will be covered first, as it is perhaps the simplest of the disciplines to understand. You will find that the defaults for the dynamics will attempt to simulate conditions on the planet Earth. This is fine for now, but don't forget that you can create simulations for many situations. From the bouncing ball to colliding starships, the forces of nature are now at your disposal... Though, they do demand the proper prayers.

1. The DOP network node is similar to the POP network node in that this is where simulations take place and, as with particle networks, they are completely separated from simulations inside other network nodes. This allows you to run as many independent simulations as you want, with each one playing at its own speed and time from the playbar frame. As with POP networks, these too can exist anywhere inside your scene, following the networks within networks paradigm. Make sure you are inside the DOP network and continue.

2. Drop an RBD Object DOP. You will see that a sphere appears in the viewport (just make sure your time slider is set to frame 1). This is the default geometry for this operation. You can see the path to it in the `Sop Path` parameter, which currently points to something called `./defaultgeo`. This is just the path to a default sphere and is sufficient for now. Press the plus button over in the Details view and then select the entry. Note the two sections, as shown in Figure 12.2. The left side contains the entries in the list and the right side contains the information for the selected entry.

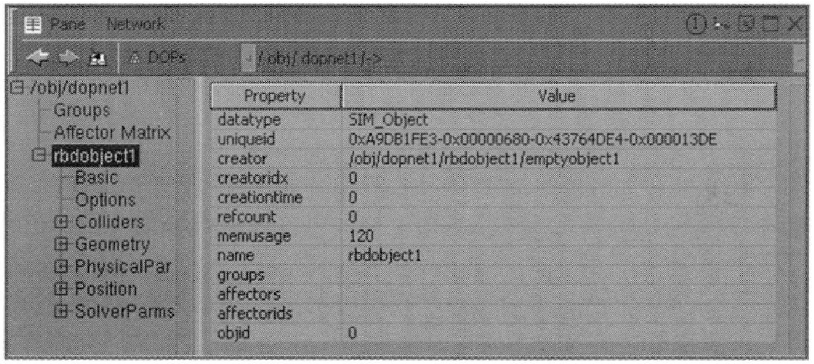

Figure 12.2
Ye grand list (the Details view pane).

3. Press Play—nothing happens. That wasn't very exciting. One problem is that you need to tell the dobject that it must be solved by a Rigid Body Dynamics simulation. Append an RBD Solver DOP. Set the Display flag on the RBD Solver node. Press Play and again nothing happens... and the reason this time is that there are no forces defined for this system. Currently your simulation is doing something but, it just isn't very interesting as there are no influences on the sphere.

4. Insert a Gravity Force DOP between those two operators and press Play. The sphere falls off the screen. Alas, you have movement! Note that although I have placed the solver at the end of the chain, it is actually completely unnecessary. As mentioned, DOPs don't act based on the top-down nature of SOPs but instead work off the compiled scene as shown in the Details view. The reason why I like to keep the solver as far down the chain as possible is purely to try and keep a "soft" order, which makes sense if you think about it in terms of a sentence. So the ball, which is affected by gravity, undergoes rigid body physics. Swap the gravity force node and RBD solver node, and there is no difference in the simulation. The reason is because there is no difference in the manner in which the objects and data in the Details view are built up when dealing with a simple simulation, whereby there is only one type of dobject (active RBD objects in this case) and one only type of solver. The order in which many of the operators are wired together in DOPs can become a personal preference, to a degree. Later in the chapter, you see two or more dobject types in one network where ordering becomes critical. For now, switch the two back and your network should like Figure 12.3.

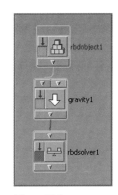

Figure 12.3
Your simple RBD network.

Let's examine this setup a little closer. You have performed the simplest possible simulation but you have still defined many things under the hood. Look over the in Details view and you will see an entry called rbdobject1. This is the internal name of the sphere and it happens to be named the same as the node that created it. In the parameters of the RBD object node, the Object Name field contains an opname() expression that just refers to the name of the operator. You can leave it as it is for now.

Back in the Details view pane, expanding the entry rbdobject1 will reveal all the data that was created for this dobject in the current DOP network. Each entry in this list is required data for the RBD solver to do its job. If you think about what an RBD solver would require, the data in the list bound to rbdobject1 starts to make sense. You see Colliders; yep, objects have to hit stuff. You see Forces and I bet the Gravity DOP builds this and, sure enough, bypassing the Gravity DOP in the network removes this entry from the list. You see an entry called PhysicalParms. Clicking on this item shows more, such as bounce, dynamic friction, friction, and more. There is also the Solver entry, which is defined by the RBD Solver DOP. Again, bypassing this node will remove this entry from the data associated with the dobject, called rbdobject1. The remaining data entries are defined by the internal guts of the RBD Object DOP. It is clear that DOPs creates data associated with dobjects. Make sure there are no unbypassed DOPs before you continue.

DOPs utilize Houdini Digital Assets to build many of the DOP operators that you will use extensively. These HDAs use many discrete DOPs, each one responsible for building a small piece of the data that represents a default generic dobject as an RBD, Wire, Cloth, or whatever type of dobject you want to create. Think of a dobject as a container that contains data that describes what it should do if it were to encounter a particular DOP solver.

The RBD object is one such asset. If you dive inside of a DOP object, you will see two more DOPs: an Empty Object DOP and yet another HDA called RBD Configure Object DOP. The Empty Object DOP is the start of every dobject. Without it, you might as well go home. Diving into the RBD Configure Object DOP, you see quite an impressive network. All these DOPs are used to build each bit of data in the Details view so the dobject will be properly interpreted and behave like an RBD object when it receives RBD Solver data. This is covered in more detail later on in the chapter.

5. Now you'll bring in some more spice. Remember, whoever controls the spice controls lots of sand. And sand, one day, may become a universally valued commodity. Drop a Ground Plane DOP off to the side in the Network Editor. In the Position parameter, move the plane down to 0, –5, 0.

6. Between the gravity node and the RBD solver node, insert a Merge DOP and wire then the ground plane node into it. Look at the network and you can logically see that gravity is only being applied to the sphere. The network should look like Figure 12.4. Reset the simulation (just as in POPs, always remember to do it here as well) and press Play. The ball drops to the ground and rolls around a bit. You can clearly visualize the data relationships in the Network Editor and you can also confirm that the ground plane (named GROUND in the Details view) does not have a Forces>Gravity data entry in it.

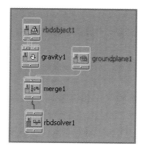

Figure 12.4
The DOP network causing the sphere to fall to the ground.

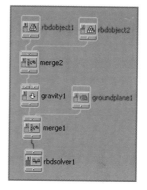

Figure 12.5
The final state of the DOP network.

7. Drop another RBD Object DOP off to the side somewhere. In the Position parameters, move it to over to 3,0,0.

8. Insert a Merge DOP between the original RBD object node and the gravity node, and wire the new RBD dobject into it. Your network should look like Figure 12.5. Press Play and both spheres do the stop, drop, and roll. While it's playing, go to either of the RBD object nodes and adjust the Velocity parameters to get the spheres to collide. Try putting 5 for the velocity in X on the rbdobject1 node and it will crash into the other sphere.

One thing that is to note at this stage is that a single wire connecting two nodes is carrying the data for more than one object. After the two spheres have been merged, that skinny, little wire is carrying both spheres down to the gravity node and beyond. Look in the Details view and you will also see that each one of the rbdobjects has its own information about the Forces>Gravity attached to them. The operations that a DOP performs will apply themselves to *all* the objects in the stream flowing down the wire.

> You can use the Display flag or, better yet, the Bypass flag, on the various DOP nodes to step down the chain to see how each DOP applies data to the simulation. This is an excellent way to see how Houdini builds up the final simulation from all the pieces. As Houdini cooks the DOP network, it is essentially moving the Display flag down one at a time and adding all the data and objects to the final simulation.

Objects versus Data versus Subdata

Thus far, there has been much casual reference to objects and data. Now, let's take a few minutes to more clearly define these concepts. You have gathered that in each simulation there are objects and they contain entries of data. Data belongs to each object in the scene and the various DOPs will read that data and modify it. This is a fundamental concept in DOPs as it provides a way that data can be attached and shared by any DOP operation or solver. For example, the exact same constraint data can be read by several solvers. There are many types of data that are globally recognized in this way. Gravity force and uniform force data are a couple of examples.

By now you may have noticed that many of the nodes have green or grey inputs and outputs. Grey stands for dobjects and green for data. The general rule is that you should be wiring grey to grey and green to green. However, Houdini attempts to make the task of attaching data to dobjects a little easier; most nodes that generate data can accept dobjects as inputs and will automatically attach the data to the input objects. As usual in Houdini, there are many ways to go about the task at hand. Look at Figure 12.6 and you will see two networks that have an identical effect. It is just that the one on the right happens to use more low-level, "atomic" operations. The setup on the left is just applying data internally in the Gravity DOP.

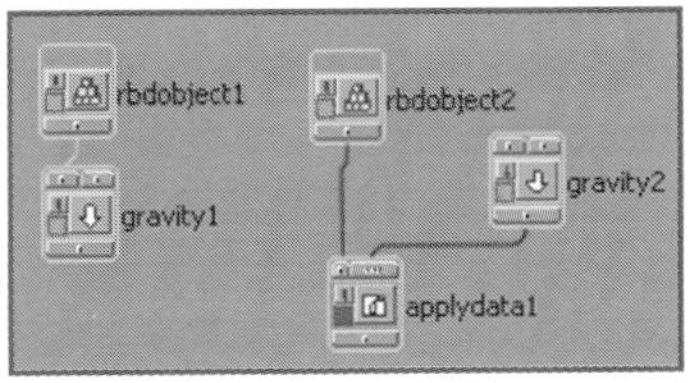

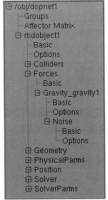

Figure 12.6
Two ways of doing the same thing.

Along these lines, it's actually possible to apply data to other data. This is called subdata in Houdini and it sounds a little esoteric, but it gets used all the time. Looking at the previous figure, you can see there is a green data input in the gravity force node. There is a Noise Field DOP, which is a general-purpose noise generator. Let's say you add one and wire it into the green input on the uniform force node. This would add a turbulent force to the scene. This is building a little subdata hierarchy. Noise subdata has been applied to uniform force subdata, which is attached to the Forces data, which is attached to the simulation object. Whew! That sounds complicated. Happily, it is made intuitively easy to grasp using the network of nodes in the Network Editor. It makes it very easy to visualize how the data is flowing through the network. Figure 12.7 shows the two networks again with the added noise (and also RBD solvers nodes as well). Notice that you can use the Apply Data DOP to apply data to data as well as data to dobjects. The left input on the apply data node will turn green when you use it in this way to indicate that it is reading in data and not dobjects. Remember that you would have to add an RBD solver node to add the correct RBD data to the dobjects for either of these networks to actually move as RBD objects in the simulation. It is the DOPs engine, not the RBD solver DOP, that moves the dobjects.

Take a quick gander at the Details view to get this more deeply embedded into the fibers of your wiggly worms. Look inside one of the objects, then inside the Forces data, and then inside the Gravity subdata, to finally find the Noise subdata. Figure 12.8 shows the expanded tree view of the rbdobject1 object. You won't have to delve this deeply into the oats and grits of Apply Data and such for a while yet. Later, you will do some pretty crazy stuff manipulating and copying data around.

The physics solvers in DOPs all look for common data names. Because of this, the same DOPs can often be used by various solvers. For example, all solvers will look for the Forces subdata and they all respect the Gravity Force subdata. The same goes for constraints and more. Naturally, the solvers will have certain unique demands because they are not doing the exact same thing. But, for the most part, they will attempt to read the same data.

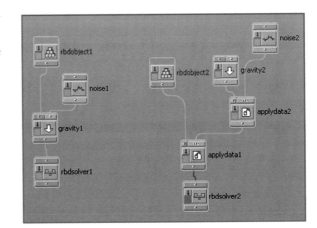

Figure 12.7
Example of applying data to data.

Figure 12.8
The expanded Details view of the rbdobject1 object.

Take a look at the Details view in Figure 12.8 again. Notice how there are several preset data names in there—Forces, Colliders, Solver, and so on. DOPs know a lot of what to do by looking into certain preset names. If you had renamed Solver to anything else, DOPs would not find the subdata inside the solver data name and so it wouldn't know how to solve the object. So in many ways, you will only ever deal with subdata, as the data are really a bunch of preset names that DOPs will search for and expect to find. You could turn this to your advantage later. For example, you could manipulate this data to stash Solver setups or Forces in custom data names and swap them around later. It will take a while for you to get fully comfortable with manipulating data and subdata. Once you get comfy with DOPs as a whole, don't be afraid to experiment! Remember, the mad scientists always have the suave stuff.

> The built-in Houdini Help files will often be specific about which data and subdata the particular solvers respect. Sneak a peak at the Cloth Solver DOP Help card and you'll see some good information regarding which subdata the solver is looking for. The generator DOPs, such as the RBD Object, Wire Object, and Cloth Object, go a long way toward ensuring that the correct subdata is created and named appropriately for the dobjects in the simulation.

Volume Representation

Several of the solvers in Houdini can take advantage of dobjects being represented as solid volumes instead of just being a large assembly of polygons. Technically, it's much faster to check to see if volumes are colliding as opposed to having to check potentially thousand of polygons for intersections. The RBD solver is especially optimized to check volumes but it can handle polygon-against-polygon intersection tests too. Unfortunately, it can sometimes be difficult to tell Houdini how to compute a valid volume for polygonal models that have modeling problems. If a polygonal model has problems such as holes, invalid surface normals, or simply be one-sided, it can prove a little tricky to get Houdini to generate a correct volume for it. Luckily, there are several options to coax Houdini into doing a better job of its approximation. This volume information is attached to the Geometry data and is called Volume subdata.

1. Start a new Houdini session and lay down a DOP network. Dive into it and drop an RBD Object. Jump into that and then into the `rbdconfigureobject` node. In this large network, you will find in the upper-right corner, a Volume DOP called `volume1` wired into a File DOP called `filedata1` and then into a SOP Geometry DOP called `sopgeo1`. These are the nodes being affected when you change parameters up at the top level `rbdobject` node. These DOPs add the correct data and subdata to the dobject. As you have just seen, it is just a more atomic view of the same capabilities.

2. Let's get some practice with generating good quality volumes. By good quality, I mean a representation that is as light as possible (for RAM and speed considerations) and that acceptably represents the nuances in the modeling of the outer hull of the object. Jump back up several levels to back to the Objects context. Delete the DOP network node you initially created and drop a Geometry object. Jump inside it, drop a Platonic Solids SOP, and set the solid type parameter to Utah Teapot.

3. While inside this object, create a DOP Network and then dive into that. Did you know working with Houdini would be so physical? You are practically jumping and diving to exhaustion! Following the networks in networks model, DOP networks too can be placed inside an object. This becomes useful if you want to build digital assets that can have the physics built into them.

12. Dynamic Operators (DOPs)

4. In the DOP network, drop an RBD Object DOP and enter ../.. in the SOP Path parameter. This is a relative path that points to whatever node holds the Display flag inside the Geometry object above it. The teapot should appear in the viewport. Wow! It looks like the teapot is imported in all its glory, but looks do not define the cook, and in this case, you need to get to the truth of this short-order sandwich. Switch to the Collisions tab and turn on the Show Collision Guide Geometry. Notice that there is a toggle above that called Use Volume Based Collision and that it is switched on. Go into wireframe viewing to more easily see the representation. The red wireframe is drawn badly and doesn't accurately represent the volume of the teapot, as shown in Figure 12.9. This is what Houdini is going use as the collision volume. Egad. That will never do!

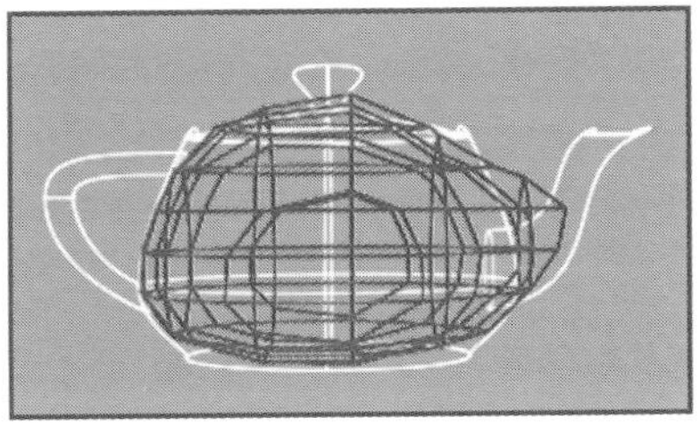

Figure 12.9
A badly represented teapot.

5. Change the Divisions to 20,20,20 to tell Houdini to divide up the bounding area of the input into this many cells to represent the volume. It looks better and worse. The handle is pretty badly defined, as it looks all solid. So change it to 40,40,40 and that looks better. There seem to be enough divisions that it should be able to capture how thin the handle is but it still has a bit of trouble.

6. Turn off Laser Scan. This casts rays at the object much like a 3D laser scanner does. Immediately it looks better and I would say acceptable. Figure 12.10 shows this more accurate representation. Turn off Show Collision Guide Geometry and your teapot is nicely and efficiently presented to the RBD Solver.

Figure 12.10
A more accurately represented teapot.

Taking Control

In the universe of DOPs, you have thus far created some forces and applied those forces to objects. But there is much room for better control of the simulation. It is time you reach and grasp the controls at your disposal! It is time for a revolution! This will be your own rose revolution!

Constraints

One effective tool in the DOPs arsenal is the power of constraints. You can constrain the position or orientation of simulation objects in any number of axes and with various forces. A hard constraint will fix the axes you want with unbreakable, divine measures. A spring constraint is a soft constraint with variable stiffness that you can use to softly influence a simulation. As usual, any constraints you set up will be attached to objects as subdata of the Constraints data. The RBD Constraint DOP and the RBD Rotational Constraint DOP will allow you to initialize constraints on the frame that you decide using the Activation field.

1. Using the teapot example you just finished, let's add some constraints to it. If you need the file, grab the volume.hip from the chapter12 directory.

2. Jump into the DOP network and append a Gravity Force DOP and then a RBD Solver DOP to the `rbdobject` node. Play the simulation and the teapot falls down out of view. Append an RBD Constraint DOP and a little ball appears near the middle of the teapot. The teapot will be pinned to this point and will only be allowed to rotate around this point and never move. Change the Object Location fields to 0.7, 0, 0, which places the pinned point closer to the spout of the teapot. Press Play now and watch the teapot dangle by the spout, as shown in Figure 12.11.

Houdini has initialized the goal position to be the same position as the point in the object's space. It did this the instant it was activated. Test this by entering `$SF > 15` in the Activation field. Press Play and the teapot is free to fall until frame 16. The teapot then jerks to a halt and swivels around with all previous rotational speed (angular velocity).

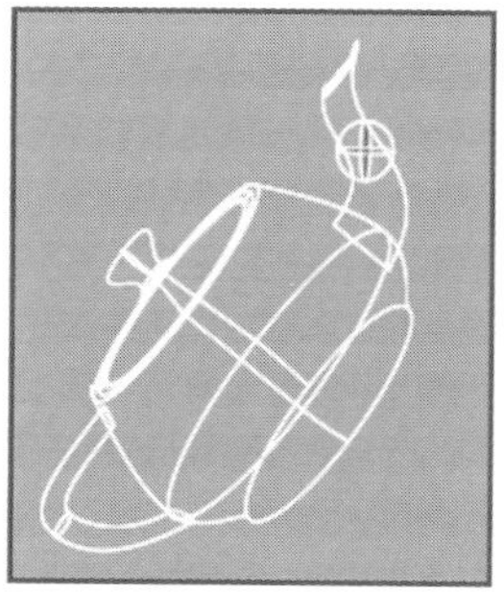

Figure 12.11
The teapot dangling by the spout.

The global variable $SF stands for the current Simulation Frame and is the replacement for $F or $FF, which you use in the rest of Houdini. There is the equivalent $ST for Simulation Time that replaces $T in DOP networks.

It is important to get into the habit of using $SF and $ST when using frames or time in your expressions. This allows you to use the powerful DOPs feature to freely scale time in the simulation. The Scale Time parameter is located in the Simulation folder of the DOP network node.

3. Next, let's look at rotational constraints. Branch off an RBD Rotational Constraint DOP from the `rbdsolver` node. Move the `rbdconstraint` node off to the side, as you don't need it any longer.

4. Drop an unconnected Ground Plane DOP and move its position down to 0, −4, 0.

5. Drop an unconnected Merge DOP, wire in the ground plane node, and then wire the `rbdrotconstraint` node into it. It is important that the ground plane gets wired in first and the reasons will be discussed shortly. Figure 12.12 shows the current state of the network. Press Play and the teapot drops to the floor but doesn't roll around when it bounces. The rotation of the teapot is totally fixed to 0,0,0, which doesn't look very believable. Breaking with realism is always a risk when directing physical simulations, but sometimes that is exactly what you want.

6. You want the teapot to have some rotational life to it. In the Relationship tab of the `rbdrotconstraint` node, switch to a Spring Constraint. Play it now and the teapot rolls about as if totally unconstrained. Temporarily bypass the rotation constraint and you will see the simulations look basically the same. Many values in the various force parameters in DOPs often take values much higher than you might expect. If you see no discernable effect, start increasing the values in greater and greater steps. For the scale of simulation, it looks like a Spring Strength value of around 1000 works. At this value, the spring constraint pulls the teapot upright, giving you lifelike physics while at the same time using a choreographed result.

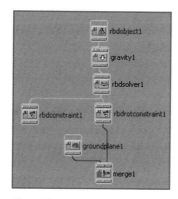

Figure 12.12
The network merging the ground plane and the teapot.

Multiple Constraints

It's possible for an object to adhere to more than one constraint, but you do need to be careful not to create conflicting constraints. For example, you can constrain an object to two separate destination (or goal) points as long as you make sure that the points on the object you want to pin down (so dubbed the anchor points) can both reach their destinations. If not, you'll get some horrible conflicts that will probably look like crazy jitter as the constraints vie for dominance. One great use for multiple constraints is to create hinge-like behavior.

1. Start a new session of Houdini and drop a Geometry object. Jump inside it, drop a Box operator, and change the dimensions to 1, 1, 0.1. This is going to serve as a door, so jump back up and rename the object `door`.

2. At the Objects level, drop a DOP Network and dive into it. Create an RBD Object DOP and point the SOP Path to your door object by entering `/obj/door`.

3. Append an RBD Constraint DOP and change the Object Location to –0.5, 0.5, 0 – (the top corner of the door). With the pointer over the viewport, press Enter to see the constraint's position relative to the door.

4. Append another RBD Constraint DOP and put it at –0.5, –0.5, 0, which is the bottom corner of the door.

5. Append a Gravity Force DOP and an RBD Solver DOP to the network chain. Press Play and the door doesn't fall nor swivel. The constraints are holding it in place at both points.

6. Go back up to Objects, create another Geometry object, and rename it `ball`. Put a Sphere SOP inside it with a radius of 0.3 in all axes.

7. Back in the DOP network, bring in this object using the RBD Object DOP with a SOP Path of `/obj/ball`, move the Position to 0.2, 0, 1, and set the Velocity to 0, 2, –5.

8. Append a Merge DOP to this new node and set the Affector Relationship menu to Mutual. This makes sure that all input objects will affect each other.

9. Wire the output of the second constraint (`rbdconstraint2`) into the merge and wire the merge node's output into the Gravity Force DOP, effectively inserting the merge before the gravity node. This ensures that all the input dobjects will have gravity and be solved. Figure 12.13 shows the network at this point. Press Play and the ball fires at the door, making the door swivel around the hinge you've defined as the axis between the two constraints. It is good, yes!?

10. It would be nice to make the hinge a little more realistic by adding a touch of friction to the system. You do this by adding some drag to the rotation of the door. In the door-only branch of the network—anywhere between the RBD Object for the door and the Merge DOP—insert a Drag Force DOP. You want to add drag to the rotation of the door, so you will use the Torque parameter. Set the Scale Torque to 50 and now the door swings and then comes to a gentle halt.

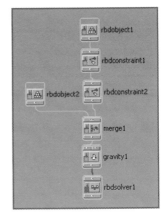

Figure 12.13
The DOP network used to smack the ball into the door.

Be aware that if you turn up the velocity of the `ball` dobject, you will find that it passes straight through the door and the door is none the wiser. If this happens, you need to inform the solver that it needs to be more careful and so take smaller time-steps when figuring out the high-velocity simulation. Do this by going to the solver node and setting the Maximum Substeps to 2, or more if you really start to push it.

Other useful types of joint configurations are things like piston and slider joints, which allow movement along an axis, and universal joints, which transmit rotational twist between two objects that are not in a straight line. Many joint types can set up with a small number of constraints. A piston joint can be set up with two positional constraints or one positional and one rotational constraint. The fundamental freedom of choice is yours.

Limiting Your Constraints

Often you may want to limit the range of your constraints. For example, with no drag, that door could easily just swing in circles forever. The simplest and most effective way of limiting the range of movement isn't the use of clever expressions or funny values in obscure parameters. The easiest and most intuitive way is to build physical collision objects, like a little doorstop for the door to collide with.

1. Building from the previous example (or load in the `multipleConstraints.hip`), reduce the torque scale of the drag from 50 to 20.

2. Go back up to Objects, create a new Geometry object, and then drop a Box SOP inside of it with dimensions of 0.1, 0.1, 0.1. Rename this object `doorstop`.

3. Back in the DOP network, import this box with an RBD Object DOP and move it to stand in the way of the door swinging. −1, −0.5, −0.5 worked for me. Wire this node into the Merge DOP.

4. Press Play and the doorstop falls away under the force of gravity and so doesn't prove to be very useful. Go back to its `rbdobject` node and toggle off Create Active Object. Press Play and now the cube stays put and doesn't even budge when the door swings open and collides with it. Figure 12.14 shows the final state of the network.

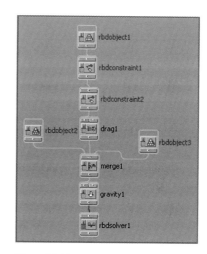

Figure 12.14
The final state of the DOP network.

Dobjects that you intend to be passive can also be placed after the RBD solvers without having to manipulate the Create Active Object toggle. In the previous example, you could have appended a Merge DOP to the RBD Solver DOP, thus changing it to a mutual relationship, and then wired in the RBD Object doorstop dobject into the Merge. Because the RBD object does not have Solver data attached to it, it will not be under that solver's influence. However, it still has all the properties or data to behave like an RBD passive object, and so it does.

Affectors and Active and Passive States

You can carefully control which dobjects are allowed to interact and, out of these, which affect each other mutually and which only affect others and so remain themselves impervious to the interaction. Dobjects that affect each other are called *mutual affectors*. You can also structure dobject interactions in a way called *ordered affectors*, where you specify that some dobjects will affect others but not be affected themselves. The concept of active and passive object states are closely related. It's possible to mark dobjects in a simulation as active or passive, as you have seen in the previous exercise. Active objects, the default for all dobjects, will affect other objects and also be affected by other dobjects. They are still governed by whether they are ordered or mutual affectors. Dobjects that are set to be passive objects will not be affected by any other dobjects or any forces, regardless of whether they were set up to be mutual or ordered. It's kind of a Get Out Of Jail Free card… from the prison of imperative forces! Viva la Revolucion Rosa!

It can be challenging to untangle these two concepts, so don't worry if you're a little confused. A simple approach (and definitely the easiest) is to consider making all dobjects mutual affectors and then just setting the dobjects you want to make invincible to be passive dobjects. When you get into some more intricate setups, you will likely find value in structuring your scenes with ordered affectors. There are a couple of ways to set up which objects are mutual and to adjust which are active or passive. Specifying which are mutual and ordered affectors happens in the Merge DOP. The Affector Relationship parameter allows you to set this to No Affector Relationship, Left Inputs Affect Right Inputs, or Mutual. The default for this operation is Left Affects Right, so why have you not been witnessing the effect of this in the previous examples? The reason is that the RBD solver has a toggle in it that says Make Objects Mutual Affectors and this has been overriding the settings in the Merge DOP. This option is on by default because DOPs is trying to go with the options that get things going quickly. You are left to turn this off yourself if you have designed your network to properly take ordered affectors into account. The active/passive setting of a dobject is set in the RBD Object DOP using the Create Active Object toggle. Simply switch this off for when you want to make an object impervious to impacts and forces and so be passive. If you want to animate whether an object is active or passive, you can use the Active Value DOP to do it.

Affector Matrix

In anticipation of getting utterly confused by intricate affector relationships across multiple dobjects, the Details view offers an affector matrix view. Look for the data called Affector Matrix and you'll be presented with a matrix of flags of every object versus every other object. The rectangle that cross-indexes two objects is colored based on whether there is a mutual relationship, a ordered relationship, or no relationship.

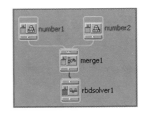

Figure 12.15
The simple DOP network.

1. Start a new session of Houdini. Drop a DOP network and dive into it.

2. Lay down an RBD Object DOP and rename it number1. Change its tx to –2.5.

3. Lay down another RBD Object DOP and rename it number2. Change its tx to 2.5

4. Append a Merge and wire them both in. Append an RBD Solver DOP. Your network should look like Figure 12.15.

5. Look in the Details view and find the Affector Matrix data to see the information. By default, the dobjects are mutual affectors because Make Objects Mutual Affectors is toggled on in the `rbdsolver` node and it overrides the Left Inputs Affect Right Inputs in the merge node. The cross-indexed rectangle for each shows green to indicate this mutual affectors relationship, as shown in Figure 12.16.

6. In the `rbdsolver` node, toggle off Make Objects Mutual Affectors; the affector matrix now looks like Figure 12.17. The Left Inputs Affect Right Inputs in the merge node is now determining the relationship and it is saying the dobject `number1` affects dobject `number2`. The blue flag at the cross index shown in the figure shows this. It seems a little backwards, but the list dobjects along the top are the affectors, whereas the dobjects along the side are the affected dobjects. So, it reads `number1` affects `number2`. You can verify this in the Network Editor.

7. In the merge node, click the up arrow for the `number2` input so that it becomes the first input and the wires are now crossed. The affector matrix changes to reflect this new relationship, as shown in Figure 12.18. Notice that the blue flag stayed in the same spot, but the column and row headings changed. Read it from column to row and you see that now, `number2` affects `number1`.

8. Switch the wires again so that `number1` is again the first input into the merge node. Now, toggle off Create Active Object in the `number2` node. This turns the `number2` dobject into a passive dobject, which means that it can affect other dobjects but can't be affected by them no matter what the relationship is set to in other nodes. The affector matrix, shown in Figure 12.19, reflects this because even though the merge node says that `number1` affects `number2`, it can't because `number2` is now a passive dobject.

9. In the `rbdsolver` node, toggle on Make Objects Mutual Affectors. Figure 12.20 shows the new affector relationship. Note that there is only a single blue flag and so there is not a mutual relationship. Again, that is because `number2` is set to be a passive dobject. But, `number2` can now affect `number1` and this is shown in the affector matrix. Remember to read from column to row. So `number2` affects `number1`.

Figure 12.16
Dobjects `number1` and `number2` are mutual affectors.

Figure 12.17
Dobject `number1` affects dobject `number2`.

Figure 12.18
Dobject `number2` affects dobject `number1`.

Figure 12.19
There is no affector relationship between dobject `number1` and dobject `number2`.

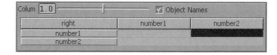

Figure 12.20
Dobject `number2` affects dobject `number1`.

12. Dynamic Operators (DOPs)

Crowd Psychology

If simulating one or two dobjects is fun, surely simulating many dobjects should be that much more fun. It would be a little tedious to have to create a new RBD Object DOP for every single dobject you wanted to throw into a system, especially if you wanted to simulate tens or hundreds or thousands of dobjects at the same time. This is one place where the DOPs context is very different from simulation contexts that exist in most other software packages. You have seen that dynamics in Houdini are built into a protected network (the DOP network) that makes no assumptions about where and how it gets it data. Each DOP network can even have its own offset in time, let alone completely independent sets of dobjects and physics. Like a particle system, DOPs can create thousands of dobjects to simulate that don't even exist anywhere in the normal object scene, and it can do this very efficiently. This makes it good fun and, above all, extraordinarily powerful. As previously discussed, each wire in a network can carry multiple dobjects, which I sometimes refer to as an object stream. All nodes in DOPs allow you to apply influence to individual dobjects in this stream by allowing local variable access to them. Just like POPs have access to $PT and $ID to identify particles, DOPs allows you to access the local variable $OBJID. The value in $OBJID is a unique number assigned to each object in a simulation.

All for One and One for All!

You are going to start by creating multiple dobjects in the RBD Object DOP. If you take another gander at the parameters in this DOP, you will see that there is a field called Number Of Objects. Increasing this number doesn't seem to do anything, but the reason is that all the objects you have created are lying exactly on top of each other. Check the Details view and you will see all the objects being defined. So you can be assured that it actually does work. As stated, the local variable $OBJID is available in all DOPs.

1. Open a new session of Houdini and drop a DOP network and dive into it.

2. Drop an RBD Object DOP and set the Number Of Objects to 5. Enter $OBJID * 2 in the X field of the Position parameter. In the Details view, open the /obj/dopnet1 field. You can see the five identical dobject entries called rbdobject1. To get unique names, edit the Object Name field to 'opname(" ")' $OBJID. Now you should see five dobject entries with unique names. In the viewport, you should see five spheres lying next to each other.. Again, it is good.

> With a little help from expressions and some simple math, you can create all kinds of interesting setups to watch. Experiment with the modulo function (%) and things like the rand() expression. Any parameter can be varied this way. Try varying the velocity parameter and the physical properties like Friction and Mass. With a bit of randomness, you can get some very realistic variation.

Another easy way to create a lot of dobjects is to use the Copy Objects DOP. This can make copies of any number of your input dobjects. By default, it's set up to copy a single dobject in the input stream a single time, but it can easily be set to copy the entire set of input dobjects once or many times.

1. Change the Number of Objects on the rbdobject node to 2. You now have two dobjects. Verify that by looking in the Details view.

2. Append a Copy Objects DOP. There is now only one dobject. Change the Number of Copies to 10 and there are now 10 dobjects.

3. Change the Object Index from 0 to 1. Now you are copying the second incoming dobject.

4. To get unique copy names, change the Object Name field to ${SRCNAME}_copy_$OBJID. Now see that there are unique names for the copies that inherit the base dobject name by using the local variable $SRCNAME. You need the curly braces around ${SRCNAME} to make the variable explicit to Houdini. Remember that you can see all the local variables for a particular operator by pressing the ? help icon in the parameters and going to the help for that parameter or in the Local variables tab.

Pulling in Point Instances

Outside of DOPs, you may have a situation where you have a few unique objects that you want to repeat hundreds or thousands of times, say, cars in a city or rocks in a landscape. One of the most common uses is in particle systems where you have, say, chunks of meteoritic rock falling from the sky in a very heavy shower. You might have to have individually modeled rock chunks named /obj/chunk1 to /obj/chunk10. Rather than copying these rocks onto particles, you can employ instancing, where you inform Houdini that at the time of rendering it should attach one of the rock chunks to a particle. You can do that with either an Instance POP inside the particle simulation or, after the particles have been output into SOPs, you can use a Point SOP to add an instance attribute and then define a path to these objects.

DOPs has a lovely operator called the RBD Point Object DOP that will pull in the positions of these points and yank in corresponding geometry that the instance attribute is pointing to in very much the same way as Houdini would instruct a renderer to do. This makes it extremely light because Houdini doesn't have to deal with a potentially huge amount of geometry. You can easily visualize the instances with the a Copy SOP or by rendering the instances directly with Mantra. It is usually a good idea to use low resolution stand-in geometry for the visualization. Lets try importing instances into DOPs with a simple example.

1. Open a new Houdini session and create five Geometry objects called geo1 to geo5 and in each, put one of the following: a Box SOP, a Sphere SOP, a Torus SOP, a Tube SOP, and a Platonic Solids SOP.

2. Create one more Geometry object and call it cloud. Dive into this object, create a Grid SOP, and change the Size dimensions to 25 x 25.

3. Append a Point SOP. Switch to the Particle tab and, at the bottom, select Add Instance and type in this expression /obj/geo'int(rand($PT)*5)+1' in the field. The expression takes a random value for each point returned from almost zero to almost one and multiplies by five to expand the range from almost zero to almost five. These are floating-point values, but the name requires an integer value (no decimal places). The int() function simply takes the floating point number and strips off the decimal place, leaving the integer number. Trivially, you then add 1 to shift the range from 1 to 5. You can verify that the instance attribute is working by looking the Details view for this node. You should see the correct path pointing to the geo1 through geo5 objects.

4. Jump back up to the Objects level, drop a DOP network, and jump into it.

5. Drop an RBD Point Object DOP. In the parameter called Point SOP Path, enter /obj/cloud/point1, which is the last node inside the cloud object. Immediately you'll see that all the objects have been brought into DOPs and they are ready to be abused at your leisure. Figure 12.21 shows the result. This approach is key to creating scenes populated with large numbers of objects ready to be simulated.

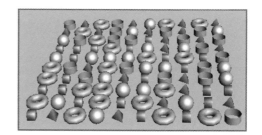

Figure 12.21
Importing point instances.

You might hear the dull clanging of warning bells ringing far off in the back of your mind as you realize that if you create many (in the hundreds or thousands) objects with this technique, that you might be asking Houdini to generate thousands of potentially heavy and slow-to-compute volume representations for all of the objects you want to play with. You would be correct in asking just how Houdini is ever going to deal with that amount of data. Happily, DOPs has been very carefully designed to share as much data between objects as is possible. The volume data that you would see attached to every object would be shared by as many objects as possible, hopefully resulting in the bare minimum of waste. You can actually prove this to yourself by going to the Details view, going down to the Geometry>Volume subdata, and examining the unique ID information. You will see a gigantic string value that doesn't look like anything very intelligible. If you're diligent and/or masochistic, you'll see that the same unique ID is used for all objects that are instancing the same object. And you can thank the heavens for this because it's what allows you to get away with simulating many thousands of objects with a minimal hit on memory consumption and avoid rigorous and redundant computation. It is pretty easy to set up a simulation of 30,000 instanced objects and not have any bad memory issues. Later in the chapter, you will learn how to combine particle systems from the POPs context with DOPs in order to leverage some of the existing functionality in POPs, such as the Instance POP and birthing new objects with the Source POP.

Fractured Objects

Now is an opportune moment to introduce a very cool feature in DOPs—the ability to import fractured objects. You have just learned how to import single objects, how to make many dobjects of a single object, and how to import many objects in the form of instances. How might you make many dobjects from the parts of a single object? The RBD Fractured Object DOP allows you to do this. In essence, you are asking that every primitive group in the source object be imported as a separate dobject. So if you have some geometry with 10 primitive groups defined, this operator will pull them in one-by-one and you will end up with 10 individual dobjects. Of course, you are given a lot of control over the process, but the real trick is to make sure that your groups are nicely defined in SOPs first.

1. In a new session of Houdini, create a Geometry object, jump inside it, and drop a Box SOP.

2. Append a Group SOP. MMB on the node to confirm that you have created a Primitive Group named group1.

3. Here in SOPs, drop a DOP Network and jump inside it.

4. Drop an RBD Fractured Object DOP and point the SOP Path to the group node you just created. Check the Details view and verify that a single dobject has been created. The RBD Fractured Object DOP has pulled in the geometry belonging to the group and defined a dobject for it.

5. Jump back up to SOPs and delete the group node. Append a Copy SOP and set the number of copies to 3 and the Translate in X to two. Toggle on Create Output Groups and you have created three groups of six primitives each.

6. Go back to the rbdfracturedobject node and set the SOP Path to point to the copy node. Look in the Details view and you will see that there are indeed three separate dobjects, as shown in Figure 12.22. If you had imported the Copy SOP node in with the vanilla flavor RBD Object DOP, only a single dobject would have been created.

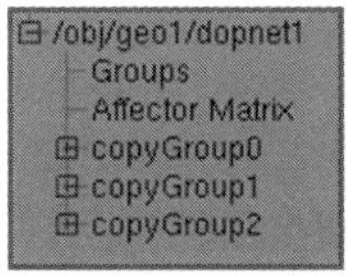

Figure 12.22
The Details view showing three dobjects.

12. Dynamic Operators (DOPs)

Create Primitive Groups Based on Connectivity

None of the DOP operators will attempt to recognize multiple connected meshes in the same object and import them separately. So if you have a model that you've shattered into several connected chunks or have imported from another software package and this geometry doesn't have all the geometry conveniently sorted into unique primitive groups, what do you do? The answer lies in SOPs, not DOPs. DOPs will just import primitive groups and you must ensure the geometry is lumped into the appropriate primitive groups.

1. Start up a spanking new session of Houdini and drop a Geometry object. Jump inside it and drop a Sphere SOP. Change its type to Polygon and its frequency to five.

2. Drop an unconnected Box SOP and set the size to 0.25, 2, 2.

3. Drop an unconnected Cookie SOP and wire the sphere into the left input and the box into the right input. Set the Operation to A minus B. You now have two pieces of the sphere but you don't have any groups set up for DOPs to import.

4. Append a Fuse SOP to make sure the dome sides and inner sides of the sphere are connected (sharing points).

5. Append a Connectivity SOP and set the Connectivity Type parameter to Primitive. This analyzes the geometry and sets a class primitive attribute.

6. Append a Partition SOP and enter chunk$CLASS in the Rule field. This sorts and names the geometry into two primitive groups. Check the info popup window to verify that you have chunk0 and chunk1 groups. The geometry is prepared for importing into DOPs with the RBD Fractured Object DOP.

7. Drop a DOP network and jump into it. Drop an RBD Fractured Object DOP and point it to the partition node. Build a little simulation where this hits on a ground plane. The two halves are treated as separate dobjects that can be confirmed in the Details view. Figure 12.23 shows the halves after their crash landing.

Figure 12.23
A sphere carved into two chunks for import as a fractured dobject.

Keep It Together! Use Some Sticky Stuff!

The RBD Glue Object is another really sweet operator available for play. RBD dobjects can be glued together until an impact makes them break apart. This can be treated fairly automatically with a minimal amount of setup. The only two things the user is required to do is to specify which dobjects are glued together (if not all) and to set a glue strength. The glue strength is a value which, if exceeded by the force generated by an impact, will break the bond. Glue doesn't only apply to the fractured dobjects but really applies to all RBD dobjects. It is just most commonly used to glue bonds between the pieces of a pre-shattered, single object.

1. Start a new Houdini session, drop a Geometry object, and jump inside it. Drop a Box SOP.

2. Append a Copy SOP and make eight copies. Enter a value of 1 in the Translate in X field and toggle on Create Output Groups.

3. Drop a DOP network and dive into it. Drop an RBD Glue Object DOP and point the SOP Path to the Copy SOP node. On the Internal Glue tab, set the Glue Strength to zero, effectively turning off the glue bonds. Go back to the Initial State tab and set the Rotation to 30 in Z.

4. Append a Gravity Force DOP.

5. Create a unconnected Ground Plane DOP and shift it down five units in Y.

6. Drop a Merge DOP and wire in both the ground plane and gravity force nodes.

7. Append an RBD Solver and press Play. The blocks fall about individually, exhibiting no evidence of glue at all, as shown in Figure 12.24.

8. On the `rbdglueobject` node, go to the Internal Glue tab and change Glue Strength to –1. –1 is a special number that causes the bonds to be infinitely strong. Press Play now and the blocks stay together and never break, as shown in Figure 12.25.

9. Finding out which value is reasonable for your scene is really just a matter of trial and error. As you have seen before, the values can be a lot larger than you might expect. In this case, a value of 20,000 results in only some of the blocks snapping off—the ones that take the initial impact and then the ones on the end that pendulum down, as shown in Figure 12.26. Experiment with increasing and decreasing the Glue Strength by increments of 5,000 to see the different results you can get.

> To see why you need 20,000, use the Details view to inspect the subdata type called Impacts. This is created only when one of the dobjects has collided with another dobject. When you scrub your simulation to a point where a collision has occurred, you should see the subdata Impacts created for those dobjects that have hit something. Dive in to this subdata and select the Impacts subdata field. You can see the energy absorbed by the dobject in the impulse column. Use these values as a guide in helping you determine ballpark values for the Glue Strength. The two values are of equal units of energy.

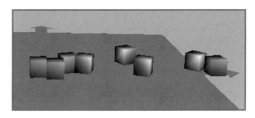

Figure 12.24
The falling blocks with a glue strength of zero.

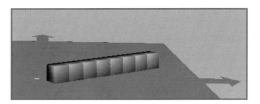

Figure 12.25
The falling blocks with a glue strength of negative one.

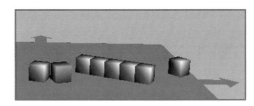

Figure 12.26
The falling blocks with a glue strength of 20,000.

10. What if you want to tell DOPs to hold the dobject together until you activate the glue. Well, this just boils down to animating the Glue Strength parameter. You'll find that the best way to do this is not to attempt to animate the Glue Strength in the RBD Glue Object DOP. In fact, you cannot do so, because all the atomic DOPs inside the RBD Glue Object are set to only initialize the dobject and then are never listened to again. This mode is called Set Initial and you'll learn about that in a moment. Insert a RBD State DOP between the `rbdglueobject` and the gravity node. On the Glue tab, change the Use Default to the left of Glue Strength to Set Always. Now the Glue Strength will be reset at every time-step allowing it to be animated

Enter `if($SF< 25, -1, 20000)` in the Glue Strength field. Press Play and the strength will be infinite before frame 25 and set to 20000 from then on. This is a simple way to animate the parameter.

DOPs will use a random seed when applying impact forces in order to fight any regular patterns in the solution. It picks this number based on the objects in your scene so you can expect similar and repeatable interactions while using the same objects. If you change the objects, it will select a new random seed. So, this is my excuse if you get solutions that look very different than the pictures.

Animating Values in DOPs

In this last exercise, you brushed up against an aspect of DOPs that is pervasive to the context. The Use Default/Set Initial/Set Always/Set Never toggles beside single every parameter. These are known as the parameter's operation. All the operations start off set to Use Default and this default is then set at the bottom of the parameters using the Default Operation parameter. By default, this parameter is Set Initial.

This information tells DOPs when to set these parameters. DOPs attempts to be as frugal as possible when setting data because some type of subdata (like the Volume subdata) can be very expensive computationally and so DOPs tries to set it only when absolutely necessary. By default, everything is configured as Set Initial and so DOPs will try to set the information the first time it's asked to and never again if at all possible. This is a bit of a diversion from the way in which POPs does things which, if you consider the Property POP for example, sets every attribute for every time-step.

The Set Always mode will set the parameters every time it is possible to do so. This is pretty safe for animating most parameters but you must be aware that you might be asking DOPs to do a lot of extra work if you inadvertently ask it to recompute heavy subdata. To prevent DOPs from worrying about parameters that are never going to change throughout a simulation, you should be as thrifty as possible when using this option. You might also be thinking that surely DOPs can be smart enough to automatically perform a Set Always operation for parameters that are animated. The reason that it is implemented in this way is to ensure that the choice is always a very conscious decision for the user. This allows you to be in full control over how and when DOPs sets data for those unexpected cases that always seem to come up.

This approach is really a philosophy in DOPs. Define your objects with the DOPs designed to create dobjects, import geometry, and set up all the useful attributes. After this, append the necessary DOPs that have the parameters that you want to animate and set only those fields' operations to Set Always. This will keep your networks as light as possible and not leave you wondering if you accidentally animated parameters in the general import DOPs or in other DOPs you subsequently added to the system. Basically, choosing Set Always needs to be a very conscious decision because it can be very expensive to implement.

Setting Never indicates to DOPs that no matter if this data has been set prior to this operator this parameter must not be set by this DOP.

With judicious use of Set Always and animating the Activation parameters, DOPs can keep the setting of data to a minimum and so make things faster and less complicated. For instance, you might have an RBD State DOP with an expression in one of the Position axes (with Set Always on) like sin($SF*5) *10. You then want to turn off this forced oscillation after two seconds. You don't have to build a large, complicated expression. You can just use the Activation parameter with the expression $ST<2. This deactivates everything about the DOP, including the Set Always nature of it.

Cloth

Now, its time to check out another discipline within DOPs and that is the area of cloth and the nodes that support this type of simulation behavior. So what defines cloth in Houdini? *Cloth* is a surface that tries to deform itself according to major cloth-like physical properties like friction, shear force, stretch force, and bend force. Cloth dobjects, like RBD dobjects, are added to the DOP object list in the same way. The second you create a cloth dobject, you will be struck with how similar everything looks. If you point at a Grid SOP, you'll notice that the grid will be imported and triangulated. This is because the cloth solver expects triangles and will divide the object into triangles in the import process. Dealing with cloth, as a whole, is much different than dealing with rigid bodies. Generally, you are dealing with far fewer cloth objects than in your typical RBD scene. Cloth is a far more intensive simulation process, as it requires loads of careful adjustments to keep the result both valid and believable.

Many of the techniques for dealing with cloth in Houdini are common techniques. You can stitch cloth panels together, pin certain areas of clothing to characters such as the wrists, waist and ankles, and more. In many cases, some of these techniques can be set up procedurally, which can be a great help in production, where the changing and evolving needs of a shot often require adjustments to the characters and elements involved.

Getting Started with Cloth

A free-falling grid of cloth in a perfect vacuum is remarkably boring. With this in mind, let's swaddle ourselves in more interesting material and cuddle up to some simple constraints. Constraints in cloth have a slightly different focus than those in RBD. Cloth constraints attempt to match up to actual geometry points on the cloth geometry and there are a couple of good reasons for this. First, cloth deforms and so you need to pin down one of these specific points and allow the other points to deform around it instead of trying to pin down many points near a specific anchor location. If this happened, too many questions would be have be answered as to which points around the anchor radius would be pinned down and which ones wouldn't, and the simulation would yak. Another reason is because a cloth simulation is a spring simulation and so it is sensitive to being suddenly yanked into a goal position. In this case, it could become severely unstable and require so much damping to fight the instability that it becomes unresponsive and unrealistic.

1. Start a new session of Houdini and drop a Geometry object and jump into it.
2. Drop a Grid SOP and switch the Connectivity from Quadrilaterals to Alternating Triangles. This just gets the geometry into the proper shape so DOPs doesn't have to do it.
3. Drop a DOP network and jump inside of it.
4. Drop a Cloth Object DOP and point the SOP Path to the grid node.
5. Append a Cloth Constraint DOP and pin down a corner by –0.5, 0, –0.5 in the Cloth Location.
6. Append another Cloth Constraint DOP and pin down another corner by putting 0.5, 0, –0.5.

7. Append a Gravity Force DOP and then a Cloth Solver DOP. Press Play; the cloth should droop and give you a decent-looking result as shown in Figure 12.27.

8. Insert another Cloth Constraint DOP after the second one and change the location to 0.5, 0, −0.5. Play the simulation; the cloth sags in the middle in a realistic way, as shown in Figure 12.28.

The Cloth Constraint DOP allows you to pin one point at a time to a specified position. If you pin enough points in a row, you're essentially pinning a seam. Instead of doing this one by one, the Cloth Stitch Constraint DOP allows you to define multiple points to constrain in one fell swoop. This allows you to constrain (or stitch) many

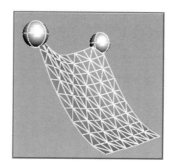

Figure 12.27
Cloth with two constraints.

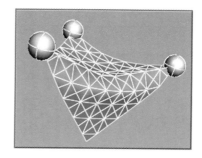

Figure 12.28
Cloth with three constraints.

points to many other points or to specified locations in space. These groups of points are most easily set up by the ClothCreateSeam SOP in that context. Seams have a number of great applications. They can define a row of constraints to static points in space to create, for example, banners or drapes. When simulating clothing, the seam around the waist of a shirt or pants can be constrained to the underlying deforming geometry. Often you may only need a couple of constraint points to do the job. So you may be able to get away with just a few soft damped spring constraints at the wrists to keep the sleeves form sliding up the arms. In other cases, you may need an entire row and so a seam to do the job. Another use for seams is for stitching cloth-to-cloth panels in the same way a tailor creates clothing from flat cloth panels. The concept here is to model geometry panels perfectly flat and facing each other, just as a tailor would in preparing to sew them together. You would then define the seams and tell DOPs to constrain them together with a Cloth Stitch Constraint DOP. The seams match up and your garment is ready. One big difference in the way in the electronic versus actual way is that you would put the character in between the cloth panels as you sew them together. Any tailor caught doing this might have an awful mess on his hands! Oh, the horror! The Cloth Constraint DOP will be used in a simple clothing exercise in just a moment.

Two-State Constraints

How would you go about sewing up two panels? The gritty details of the process are beyond the scope of this chapter, but let's discuss the method involved. As you have read, cloth is pretty sensitive to being yanked around at high speeds, which is why you must be as gentle as possible when constraining cloth points. This is why you usually have to make sure that the goal points are as close as possible to the anchor points. Otherwise, they can get yanked into position and destabilize the entire simulation. But, might there be a better way where you could have a spring constraint that gently pulls the cloth into position and then turns into a hard constraint to pin it there? Enter the magic of two-state constraints which, by the way, are available for RBD dobjects too. This type of constraint allows you to switch between spring and hard constraints depending on the strain placed upon that constraint. This allows the cloth to be pulled progressively together and then sewn up properly when the panels touch. They can also be used in the opposite manner where a constraint can start out being a hard constraint and, if it undergoes enough force, will then snap apart and become a spring constraint.

Cloth and Collisions

Causing collisions against other cloth and solid objects is done in exactly the same way as when using the RBD solver, by using the Merge DOP. There are three types of collisions that the cloth solver is capable of using: cloth against itself, cloth against other cloth, and cloth against solid objects. All of these have varying impacts on the speed of the solution. Cloth run with self-collisions will cause a big slowdown because it has to be aware of self-collisions continuously. Cloth against other cloth is much faster because it can pretty easily check to see if cloth dobjects are near enough to require testing for collisions. Solid dobjects are tested against pretty quickly using them in the form of their volume representations. Due to this, it is useful to use the RBD Object DOP (and other RBD import DOPs) to fine-tune the volume representation nice and easily.

In the Cloth Object DOP, you can choose between three models for cloth/volume (solid) collisions. They are foam, coarse, and fine. These collision models are listed here in order of ascending quality and computational expense. The foam model is like a soft collision where the intersecting cloth is slowly ejected from the solid object. The coarse model does rough collisions, which may be adequate for some situations. Generally, these two models are used during the setup phase to get faster results and fine is used when it is time to do more final, quality simulations. Let's sway through an example of cloth against solid collisions and also incorporate the use of the Cloth Stitch Constraint DOP by draping a skirt around some hips.

1. Start a new Houdini session, create a Geometry object, and dive into it. Create a Sphere SOP. This will serve as the hips that will give body to the skirt.

2. Drop an unconnected Tube SOP and change it to Polygons with Alternating Triangles connectivity. Change the Center to −0.6 in Y, the Radius to 0.8, 2, and the Height to 2.5. In the Detail tab, change Rows to 25 and Columns to 35.

3. Drop a DOP network and jump into it.

4. Bring in the tube in a Cloth Object DOP.

5. Append a Gravity Force and then a Cloth Solver DOP.

6. Create an RBD Object DOP and point it to the sphere.

7. Use a Merge DOP to merge both dobject streams together below the gravity node. The RBD Object must come first in the merge node, followed by the Cloth Solver DOP, because the merge node is set to have Left Inputs Affect Right Inputs. Press Play; the skirt just falls down and doesn't get a get enough grip to hang on to the hips.

8. The Cloth Stitch Constraint DOP can help out here. Jump back up to SOPs and append a Group SOP to the tube node. Set the Entity to Points and enter `0-'ch("../tube1/cols")-1'` in the Pattern field. This will add the first row of points to the group and will automatically adjust as you modify the resolution of the skirt geometry.

9. While here, let's make it a little more interesting by swirling the skirt a bit. Append a Transform SOP and enter `sin($T*200)*10` in the Rotation in Y field. Press Play and the rigid skirt geometry swings about a bit.

10. Jump back into the DOP network and point the clothobject node to the transform node. Toggle on the Use Animated Geometry option.

11. Insert a Cloth Stitch Constraint DOP after the clothobject node and set the Cloth Point Group to group1, which is the group of points that you want to pin down. The network should look like Figure 12.29. Press Play; the waistband stays put and the skirt swirls around realistically. This is a great time to investigate the differences between the Cloth/Solid collision models. Switch them out to get a feel for the different results and speeds. You might also want to turn on Cloth Self-Collisions too if you see a lot of interpenetration. You should end up with something like the skirt shown in Figure 12.30.

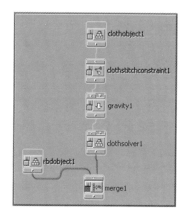

Figure 12.29
The final DOP network.

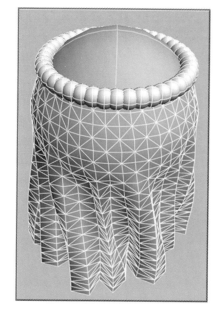

Figure 12.30
Cloth skirt with stitch constraints.

Cloth in a Vacuum = Yawn

The cloth simulator in Houdini simulates cloth as if it were in a vacuum. I'm not sure how often you've seen flowing robes in space, but I sure haven't. Some of the more interesting motion in real cloth movement is due to the resistance of the air against the cloth. Cloth displaces air and the air feeds back force against the cloth. A square of cloth in a vacuum and in Houdini will just drop perfectly flat to the floor and so you have to add in the effect of the air billowing up the material as it twists and drifts toward the ground. Houdini will not run the fluid dynamics required to do this in a way faithful to reality, which isn't an altogether bad thing because fluid simulations are not known be quick to compute nor easy to control. You are left to fakery and ingenuity.

1. Open a new session in Houdini and drop a Geometry object. Jump into it and drop a Grid SOP. Create a DOP network and jump into it.

2. Import the grid in a Cloth Object DOP. Append a Gravity Force DOP and then a Cloth Solver DOP. Press Play; the grid falls down in an immensely tame manner. So what do you need to bring this a little closer to reality? Cloth will be affected by the drag of the unmoving air.

3. Add a Drag Force DOP and play the simulation. It still looks verifiably boring, but you have guaranteed that the grid won't continue accelerating to infinity.

4. To simulate the turbulence, add a Uniform Force DOP. This operator will exert a totally uniform force throughout the entire scene on all dobjects in the current dobject stream. That doesn't sound like it's terribly interesting and it isn't yet.

5. Drop an unconnected Noise Field DOP and wire it into the green (the right) input of the uniform force node. This is wiring subdata to subdata and so the green connectors indicate this. Many DOPs will be able to use Noise Field subdata including the Uniform Force DOP. There are many familiar noise parameters including a Minimum Value and Maximum Value. Get the noise to blow in all directions by setting Minimum Value to –1. Go back to the Uniform Force DOP and enter **1,1,1** in the Force parameters. These values are used as overall scaling factors for the input noise for each axis. This is a common approach in DOPs. Press Play; the cloth bends and twists as it falls. Play with the different noise parameters to adjust the look of the turbulence imparted to the falling cloth.

> If you choose to animate any of these parameters, you must take care to set the parameter's operations to Set Always. It's fairly common to animate the Offset in noise fields to keep it evolving and interesting-looking, as well as the magnitude that appears in the Uniform Force DOP.

6. Another approach to creating some turbulence is to feed the Noise Field DOP into the second input of the Drag Force DOP. Drop another unconnected Noise Field DOP and wire it in as stated. If you consider that drag force is a force that operates against the velocity of each point, multiplying this direction vector by the turbulent vector generated by the Noise Field will cause the drag force to no longer act along the axis of the movement of each cloth point, effectively wrecking the concept of what drag actually is. So how do you go about fixing this problem? Notice that you force the Noise Field DOP to generate scalar values instead of vector values using the Generate Scalar Noise toggle. Now the noise is just a single scalar value and when you multiply a scalar by a vector, the resultant vector will remain along the same axis and just be of a different magnitude. Make sure the Minimum and Maximum Values for the noise are within the range of zero to one. If you have negative values in here, you will cause the drag force to be negative and so the drag direction is flipped over and will actually serve to increase the velocity of the associated cloth points. Figure 12.31 shows the far more interesting falling cloth result. Figure 12.32 shows the final network. Remember that your network for creating the Cloth dobject's data doesn't have to necessarily be in exactly the same order as the one shown. That is just what visually made the most sense to me.

Figure 12.31
The falling cloth with noise added.

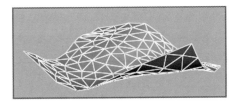

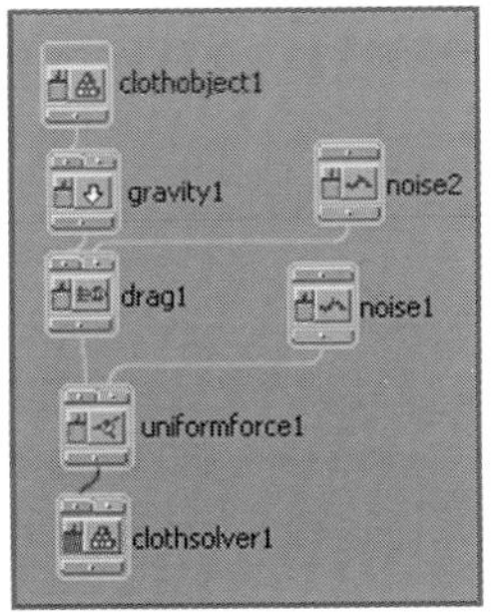

Figure 12.32
The final DOP network with noise added to falling cloth.

Per-Point Attributes and the Cloth Solver

One extremely powerful feature of the cloth solver is its ability to accept many of the physical parameters not only as a constant value for an entire piece of the cloth, but also as varying values across the surface of the cloth dobject. Having certain parts of the cloth be able to flex more, stretch more, or have more friction than other parts is both possible and easy to set up. All the different attributes that can be varied across the surface are documented in the Cloth Solver DOP's help card.

1. Start a new Houdini session and drop a Geometry object.

2. Jump into it and drop a Grid SOP. Make it a long strip of cloth by setting the size to 5, 1. Change connectivity to triangles. Change the Rows to 8 and the Columns to 20 so you get reasonably regularly-sized triangles. An even and nice topology is one where the triangles are close to equilateral and all have similar primitive areas. And when you are nice to the solver, it will be nice back to you. You have now entered the realm of interpreting solver vibrations. It is a tricky and arcane art.

3. Append an AttribCreate SOP. Enter friction in the Name field and enter $BBX * 0.8 in the value1 field. This creates a smooth ramp of friction values from zero to 0.8 across the X-axis of this long strip of cloth. The name friction is important because it is the same name that Houdini expects in the clothobject DOP.

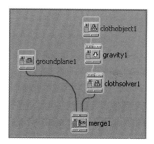

4. Drop a DOP network and jump into it. Create a Cloth Object DOP and pull in the result of the attribcreate node.

5. Append a Gravity Force and then a Cloth Solver DOP.

6. Drop an unconnected Ground Plane DOP and tilt it by entering 0, −2, 0 in the Position and 30, 0, 0 in the Rotation fields. This will be a nice sloping surface for the cloth dobject to fall upon.

7. Wire the groundobject node and then the clothsolver node into the merge node in the order stated. The network should now look like Figure 12.33. Press Play; the cloth drops onto the ground plane and then begins to slide down the sloping surface. You will notice that one side of the strip slides down the surface quite smoothly and the other side drags far more slowly. As a result, the cloth bends a bit in the middle to accommodate the differing frictions.

Figure 12.33
The DOP network importing the friction attribute.

You have to respect the Merge DOP. It does more than you might think. It knows how to create associations between different dobjects beyond the options of left affects right versus mutual relationships. Ah, so order *is* important! On top of that, the Cloth Solver DOP doesn't understand the ground plane for what it is! It thinks that it is a cloth object, but alas it does not have the requisite data to properly represent cloth, so it's rendered useless in the network. The ground plane wants to be a passive RBD object and has data associated with it that indicates to the Merge DOP that it is in fact a passive RBD object of infinite 2D dimensions. The Merge DOP builds the correct association between the Cloth Solver and the passive Rigid Body Object, or the infinite ground plane, or any other RBD object, for that matter.

The Merge DOP also likes its inputs to be in a specific order: first RBD dobjects with passive RBDs, then active RBDs, followed by wire dobjects, and finally, cloth dobjects. The wires and cloth can be interchanged.

Gleaning Some Meaning

The forces that occur in cloth simulations are numerous. Every point, edge, and primitive is constantly undergoing a slew of forces and it is often pretty hard to clearly tell them apart. To be able to examine the individual forces involved becomes very important when things are going to the dogs (or to put it more politely, unfolding in an unexpected way). At these times, you need to find the cause and root it out. Cloth dobjects have a useful Visualization mode that can help in the investigation. In the previous example, go to the Cloth Object DOP and switch to the Visualization tab. A large number of options are available and you should definitely experiment with them all, but wait! For now, toggle on Friction Force and play the simulation. You may not see too much because these forces are very sensitive to scene scale. At the top of the Visualization tab, there is a Force Scale parameter. Set this to 20 and you should see little vectors drawn from every cloth point. These vectors represent the direction and magnitude of the friction force vector (amplified by 20 right now). Notice that the vectors are longer on the right side where the friction is greater. You should see something similar to Figure 12.34.

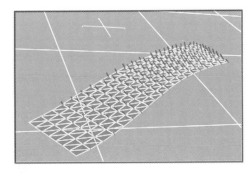

Figure 12.34
Cloth with varying friction across its surface.

> All of the visualizations possible in DOPs are there to keep you in the captain's seat. Always take care to check volume representations, constraint positions, cloth and wire visualizations and, above all, the Details view. You need to be aware of when she's giving you all she can, captain. And then you will know when you can ask for a bit more and take her to warp 3.

Getting Wired

Another major solver in DOPs is the wire solver. This solver's purpose is to simulate open curves that can be made of polygon edges or splines. The intention behind the solver is to simulate flexible threads, hair, or wires that can collide with themselves, other wires, or RBD objects in the scene. It is a lot more similar to the cloth solver than the RBD Solver for a few reasons. It is solving a deforming object and therefore must be careful to try to come up with a result that doesn't result in stretching or interpenetration. It is also designed to be able to set up a multitude of constraints at once. The sheer number of constraints involved in all those cloth seams requires methods to set up many constraints easily. Imagine setting up constraints for the root of every hair using the wire solver! One area in which the solver has an advantage over the cloth solver is because wires don't have a primitive area that it needs to try to preserve. It only has a segment length to preserve and so it can simulate many hundreds or thousands of wire dobjects pretty quickly.

1. Start a new Houdini session, drop a Geometry object, and jump into it.

2. Create a Grid SOP and sets its Position to 0, 2, 0. Set the Size to 3, 1. Set the Connectivity to Rows and it will generate 10 long lines of 10 points each.

3. Drop an unconnected Sphere SOP and leave it at default values.

4. Drop a DOP network and jump into it.

5. Drop a Wire Object DOP and point it to the grid node.

6. Append a Gravity DOP and then a Wire Solver DOP.

7. Import the sphere using an RBD Object DOP.

8. Append a Merge to the `rbdobject` node and then wire in the `wiresolver` node. Press Play; the wires fall down and bounce off the sphere. Hooray! It looks realistic for stiff wires, like long rods of steel.

9. Back up in the `wireobject` node, switch to the Force Model tab and you'll see four parameters related to Linear Spring and Angular Spring and their Damping constants. Turn down Angular Spring Constant to 0.1. Play the simulation and the wires have some sweet-looking flex happening.

10. Jump back up to SOPs and drop a Torus. Import that node using the `rbdobject` node and play the simulation. You should end up with something like Figure 12.35.

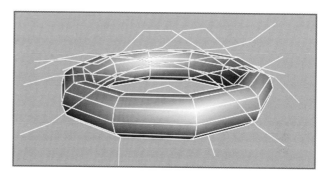

Figure 12.35
Wires falling onto a torus.

Springs and Damping

What are these and what do they do? Linear spring is the strength of the internal springs that act along each segment of the wire. A segment is between two points and this value is trying to ensure that the wires do not stretch or shrink. Angular spring is the amount of force that resists the change in the angle between each of the segments. That is, the bendy stiffness of the wires. I apologize for using such technical jargon, but it simply can't be avoided from time to time. Many simulated deforming surfaces are held together by a multitude of tiny internal springs. In wire dobjects being solved by a wire solver, the springs are laid out along each segment with the strength of each spring being influenced by the linear spring constant angular spring constant.

That makes a goodly amount of sense, but what is damping? The physical spring is a great analogy because it is easy to picture how a spring has a rest position. Picture a stiff spring that isn't 100 percent coiled up and so isn't as compressed as it could be, like one from an old car. When under no forces, it has a length (called the rest length). The spring will always endeavor to return to this length and the force it exerts to return to this length is what is called, quite naturally, the spring constant. In systems where you are stepping through time instead of being able to glide through it as you do in reality, you might find that the rate at which it snaps back into place is too fast or too slow. If there are many springs connected together, this erratic nature might cause some jitter that gets echoed through all the connected springs in the system. In bad cases, the reflected forces can cause some strong feedback resulting in uncontrolled amplification of the forces. This is a Bad Thing(tm) and you can sit back and watch your cloth or wire dobjects explode into "doblivion." The bad thing is that the system suddenly has to deal with large and escalating forces in what might have previously been a rather docile scene. These violent forces cause a lot of stress and unrest in solverland, and this manifests as exploding simulations and painful slowdowns.

12. Dynamic Operators (DOPs)

When stressed out, it is always a good idea to put a warm damp towel on your head until the pounding subsides. Likewise for springs; you can add a damping constant to take the edge off the amount of force that it needs to return to the rest length. There are dangers in soothing relaxation though. You (and springs) can become lazy and, frankly, boring. Remember that these values can be quite sensitive to the scale of the scene in the same way that all forces are in DOPs. So, what might make for an excitable spring in one scale will result in a lazy, dullard in another scale.

> The units in DOPs are called standard KMS units. All the equations in the solvers are geared to deal with forces, distances, and entities in kilograms, meters, and seconds. It is possible to force Houdini to perform a different conversion of units to these measurements in the Settings>Main Preferences>Hip File Options menu. Here, you can modify distance and mass mapping; there is no alternative time mapping.

Pin the Tail on the Ferengi: Wire Constraints

As mentioned before, constraints for wire dobjects are designed to be set en masse. So much so, in fact, that it seems there is no easy way to set up a single point constraint as you do for cloth. There is no Wire Constraint DOP. There is only a Wire Glue Constraint DOP, which is expressly designed to set many constraints in a way similar to the Cloth Stitch Constraint DOP. But wait, didn't you read earlier that constraints are just subdata? Well, I hope so. If you take a look at the subdata for RBD and cloth dobjects, you will see that they are made up of the very same components. The data type in the constraints subdata are both of SIM_Constraint and SIM_ConAnchorObjPointNumPos and such, with nothing in their names that seems to categorize them as being solely for the RBD or cloth solvers. How very interesting, yes? So perhaps you can just use the Cloth Constraint DOP to set up constraints for a wire dobject? And indeed you can! Continue in your quest, truth-seeker!

1. Continue from the previous example or load the getWired.hip.
2. Go back to the grid node and change number of Rows to one, which yields a single, long line.
3. Back in the DOP network, insert a Cloth Constraint DOP somewhere in the wire object stream. I chose above the wiresolver node. Set the Location to −1.5, 2, 0, which is the end point of the line. The little guide sphere will appear at the constraint point. This DOP is very useful because if you don't get the location exactly right, it will search around and give you the closest point to the location you specified. This is very useful when you are setting up constraints on a model using the viewport handles. Also, with many models (especially organic models), you won't know the exact coordinates of a point. You happen to know them here because you generated them in a very simple and controlled way with the Grid SOP. Press Play; the wire's end point remains constrained and swings down in a lovely way and collides with the torus, initially at least. Mine ended up exploding. One way to fix it is to throw a little damping on it. Change Angular Damping Constant to 0.1 and play the simulation. You should have something that looks like Figure 12.36.

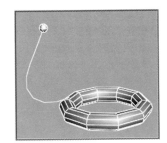

Figure 12.36
The constrained wire.

If you decide to increase the number of Rows in the Grid SOP, there will still only be a single constraint generated. This is because all of the wires from a single Wire Object DOP are still considered as a single dobject. Because it's a deforming dobject, it just looks like they are individual wires. Always look in the Details view to get the straight dope on the simulation situations.

12. Dynamic Operators (DOPs)

There is another way to determine which objects are individual objects and which are not. In the viewport, press d to bring up the Display Options. On the bottom-right side of the first tab, you will see two icons of boxes with red writing in them. Pressing the left one will show the names of the entities in the viewport. This is extremely useful because it shows constraint and force names as well. This display mode is shown in Figure 12.37.

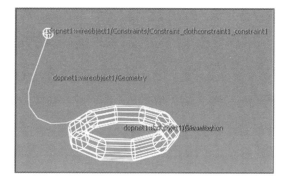

Figure 12.37
The viewport with object names turned on.

A Hairy Solution

Defining a single constraint point like you have just done is really most useful for when you are simulating a few hero wires, like a tail or a rope swaying beneath the hero. As soon as you start moving into setups where you want to procedurally set up a lot of constraints, you have two basic options. The first is to use the Cloth Stitch Constraint DOP. Oh, it is a trusty old friend by now. Let's use it to build a head with a shock full of hair.

1. Scare up a fresh batch of Houdini, drop a Geometry object, and jump into it.

2. Drop a Sphere SOP and switch the type to NURBs.

3. Append a Facet and turn on Pre-Compute Normals. This initializes point normals that point outward from the head.

4. Append a Scatter and set the Number of Points to 75. Notice that the geometry disappears. Turn on the display of points and point normals. These points will be the hair follicles.

5. Drop an unconnected Line SOP and change the direction to point down the Z axis by putting 0, 0, 1 in the Direction field. Allow the hair to bend a little by setting the points to 6.

6. Append a Group SOP and rename it `root`. Make sure the group name is also root. Set the Entity to Points and enter **0** in the Pattern field. Point 0 is now the root of the hair strand.

7. Drop a Copy SOP and wire the output of the scatter node into its right input and the root node into its left input, effectively copying a hair onto every point and aligning each hair to the associated point normal. If you check the geometry info, you will see that there are 75 points in the group called root. This is going swimmingly. Your SOP network should look like Figure 12.38.

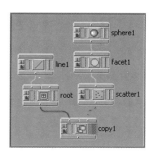

Figure 12.38
The SOP network building the hair geometry.

8. Drop a DOP network and jump into it.

9. Point a Wire Object DOP to the dangerously spiky hairdo by entering `../../copy1` in the SOP Path field. Switch to the Force Model tab and set the Angular Spring Constant to 0.1 to allow for more flexibility in the hair.

10. Append a Cloth Stitch Constraint DOP and enter `root` in the Cloth Point Group parameter.

11. Now the usual duo, a Gravity Force DOP and a Wire Solver DOP, to finish the dashing pair. You now see lots of balls indicating the various constraint points. Bring up the display options and turn off the display of guide geometry.

12. Point an RBD Object DOP to the head geometry, which is the NURBS sphere you previously created.

13. Use a Merge DOP to wire in the head and then the wire dobject streams. Play the simulation; it shows the hairs falling down and relaxing around the head, with all of their roots nicely fixed in place. You may get a yellow flag on the `wiresolver` node warning of unresolved collisions. The problem is that that the root points are colliding continuously with the head and much time and effort is being put into trying to solve for them. Go to the Collisions tab of the `wireobjects` node and change the Volume Offset to –0.1. Play the simulation now; it goes much faster and doesn't show the warning flag. The first few frames of the simulation provide a very mullet-like coif, as shown in Figure 12.39.

Figure 12.39
A mullet is worth a thousand wires.

> The volume offset feature will swell or shrink the volume for the sake of collision detection. You might find it necessary to swell it a bit for clothing-on-character collisions and you might shrink it a touch in cases like a hairy head where the roots are so close to the surface that Houdini might consider them colliding continuously and so spend too much time computing them. Either way, the volume offset feature is a very useful parameter and minimizes the amount of inflation, deflation, and offsetting you need to perform on the input models in SOPsland to achieve the same effect.

Feel the Power... Lines

Wire dobjects can also be constrained at multiple locations along the wire. This is most often used for constraining the tip and the root of the wire, but you can use it to constrain points along the length of the wire too.

1. Spark up a fresh Houdini session, drop a Geometry object, and jump into it. Do I ever tire of saying that? Do you ever tire of hearing it? Alas, we are mere mortals confined to the dictates of external communication… at least until our melons are so ungainly large that our puny bodies can no longer support their weight. And by that time it won't matter because we will have come to understand the power of thought itself. Thus will we locomote. Thus will we communicate.

2. Drop a Line SOP and orient it to the X axis by entering `1, 0, 0,` in the Direction field. Change its distance to 50 and its points to 10. These are going to be the constraint points. You might already be saying, "Hey! If those are the constraint points, where is the resolution in the line for the flexing?" Not to fret, as you will add that later.

3. Append an `AttribCreate` SOP and name it `goalpoint`. Enter `$PT` in the first Value field. This is saying that these points are going to be constrained to like point numbers. In fact, you are going to use this exact node as its own goal geometry. The attribute name `goalpoint` coincides with the data name in the DOP wire dobject and will be inherited automatically.

4. Append a Group SOP and change the Entity to Points to group the points.

5. Now, it is time to add in the detail needed for the wire to flex. Append a Refine SOP. Set the First U to 0, the Second U to 1, and the U Divisions to 50. This is going to insert 50 points along the length of the whole spline.

6. Next, you need to be able to easily determine which points are not supposed to be constrained. Append another Group SOP, change the Entity to Points, and switch to the Combine tab. Fill the fields out so that it reads as `group2 = ! group1`. This just creates a group out of the complement of `group1`. It is saying `group2` is not equal to `group1`.

Figure 12.40
The SOP network creating the powerlines geometry.

Figure 12.41
The final DOP network.

7. Check out the Details view to see what values the various points hold for the `goalpoint` attribute. Currently, due to interpolation, all the newly inserted points will have received some value in the `goalpoint` attribute and you don't want that. Append another `AttribCreate` SOP and set the Name to `goalpoint` and the Group field to `group2`. Enter -1 in the first Value field. The SOP network should look like Figure 12.40.

8. Drop a DOP network and jump inside. Drop a Wire Object DOP and point it at the `attribcreate2` node.

9. Give it some physics by appending a Gravity Force DOP and a Wire Solver DOP.

10. Drop an unconnected RBD Object DOP and point it to the `line1` node. Basically, you want to point it to any of the nodes before the refine node so that you retrieve the constraint points.

11. Drop a Merge and wire in the wire dobject stream and the `rbd` dobject stream.

12. Now that you have both objects, you need to constrain certain points on in the wire stream to the points in the RBD stream. Append a Wire Glue Constraint DOP. The network should now look like Figure 12.41. Set the Goal Object Name to `rbdobject1`. Press Play; the wires droop a little, but not much.

You might wonder why they hang at all because they were modeled tautly across the virtual posts. The reason is in the springs. You can adjust the Linear Spring Constant to get more or less droop. You may also notice that they don't pinch very much at the constraint points. They make a smoother kind of "S" shape. This is due to the Angular Spring Constant. Reduce that to zero (or near zero) and they should hang with pinching at each post (constraint point). Turn up the number of divisions in the Refine SOP and you should get a result resembling Figure 12.42. Now that is good droop!

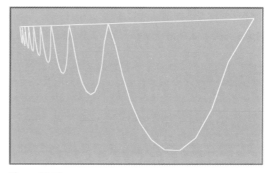

Figure 12.42
The powerlines with good droopiness.

All of the DOPs that define dobjects in DOPland can define the names of the dobjects that appear in the Details view. By default, there is an expression in the Object Name field of all of these DOPs and it is set to `'opname(" ")'`, which is the name of the node creating it. You can change this if you want. However, if the dobject name is the same as the name of the node that defined it, it's much easier to track. You can even search the network view for the DOPs using the / key when your mouse cursor is over a Network Editor. Try it and search for `rbdobject1`.

Reuse and Recycle—Use the POP Solver

Behold! You have just scratched the surface of the solver iceberg, for there are numerous other options available. Things can start to get a little abstract from this point forward, but you've made it this far so you should be fine. At this point, the concept of a solver gets broadened a bit. They no longer strictly refer to a completely contained system designed to emulate physics. A solver now becomes a tool to run against objects to which it is bound. Some of the following solvers are merely frameworks in which you can build your own simulations. Some of these solvers have very light demands upon the system and they don't require or care much about the subdata that gets acquired in a system.

You have invested a goodly bit of time in coming to grok the various tools available in POPs. If it ever seemed redundant to have two simulation contexts with similar, but different, ranges of operators, you will be happy to know that you can reuse and recycle all the utility of POPs inside of DOPs using the POP solver. The POP solver will execute a selected POP network for any dobject to which it is applied. This will let you generate particles during the DOPs simulation and use them for collisions against dobjects.

1. Start up a new session of Houdini and drop a Geometry object. Jump into it, drop a Grid, and change the Orientation to XY. At this level, drop a DOP network and jump into it.
2. Bring in the grid using a Cloth Object DOP.
3. Append the diligent duo of Gravity and then a Cloth Solver DOP.
4. Lets pin down the top two corners. Append a Cloth Constraint DOP and set the Object Location to 0.5, 0.5, 0. Append another to constraint and set it to –0.5, 0.5, 0.
5. Play the simulation and you have a hanging piece of cloth.
6. At this level, drop a POP network and jump into it. Create a Location POP and set the Coordinates to 0, 0, 2. Go to the Attribute tab and set Velocity to 0, 0, –2 and set Variance to 0.1, 0.1, 0.1. This creates a stream of spewing particles.

7. Jump back up to DOPs and create an unconnected POP Object DOP. This creates an empty dobject into which the POP solver can dump its particles. The reason for not just using a regular Empty Object DOP is the same reason why you use one for the RBD, cloth, or wire dobjects. The POP Object operator will initialize and add some very useful subdata. It can also help you set up some useful physical parameters for when the particles are causing collisions against other DOPs entities.

8. Append a POP Solver to the `popobject` node and point it to the popnet you just created.

9. Use a Merge to bring in the popsolver first, followed by the last `clothconstraint` node. The network should look like Figure 12.43. Play the simulation and the particles fly across and collide with the cloth dobject causing it to sway, as shown in Figure 12.44. It's the same kind of feel as using a water hose to spray the laundry on the line in the backyard.

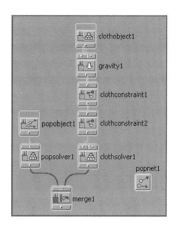

Figure 12.43
The DOP network using particles.

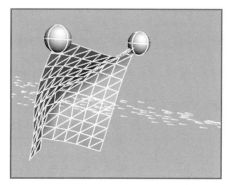

Figure 12.44
Spray that stinky shirt down.

The Power of Feedback—The SOP Solver

The SOP Solver is designed to let you run off to SOPs and modify each object to which this solver subdata is bound at every time-step of the simulation. What is so terribly special and exciting about that? The cloth and wire solvers push geometry around, but this one allows you to do whatever you like to the input geometry and feed it back into the simulation loop. For example, you could deform or decimate objects progressively through time. And that truly is, terribly cool.

1. Start up a new session of Houdini and drop a Geometry object. Drop a spanking new Grid. Drop a DOP network next to it and jump inside.

2. Import the grid with an RBD Object DOP.

3. Append a SOP Solver DOP. It wants a SOP Path so that it can execute whichever node it is pointed to and it does this for every object you've attached this Solver to. If it points to a SOP network, it will execute whichever node has the Display flag set, in the usual manner you have seen in other fields referencing SOPs.

4. Create a SOP network and drop it off to the side. In the `sopsolver` node, point the SOP Path to the new network.

5. Jump into sopnet1. This is where you are going to manipulate the geometry for each object in DOPs. Hmmm, now where do you get that geometry from? How do you usually fetch geometry from other networks? Yes, the Object Merge SOP is the answer. Create one of these and prepare for a little kung fu hustle, which will become clearer as you explore the freedom of data within DOPs. For now, close your eyes and enter '"../..:"+stamp("..", "OBJID", 0)+"/Geometry"' in the Object 1 field. The grid geometry should appear. What have you done? Basically, you have pointed the Object Merge to the Geometry subdata of a certain object in the parent DOP network, which you referred to by its ID instead of its name. Note that you can indeed refer to a name, but it's easier to extract the ID. Some information owned by the DOP network (referred to by the ../..) is able to be yanked out using the stamp() and stamps() expressions and so here you are just grabbing the OBJID from the dopnet. The plus operators merge the different string parts of the expression together. This *string concatenation,* common in many programming languages, is borrowed nicely in Houdini expressions.

6. Append a SoftPeak SOP; you are going to set it up so that one random point get pushed a little bit along the normal of the surface.. To grab a random point, enter 'int(rand($T)*npoints("../"+opinput(".",0)))" in the Group field of this node. This translates to "Generate an integer from a random number(based on time), which can be as high as the number of points that exist in the SOP that's wired into my (first) input." The backticks are needed to evaluate the expression inside a string field. Enter 0.1 in the Distance field and jump back up to the DOP network.

7. To be thorough, bypass and un-bypass the sopsolver node. This will force a re-cook because with some of the more delicate DOPs, you should be overly cautious in cooking in order to avoid errant feedback. Forcing a re-cook like this becomes a bit of a ritual but it is much better than feedback DOPs being over-cooked and causing Houdini to explode into a zajillion bytes. Press Play and yee haa! Look at that there grid get'n all banged up! The SOP network is being fed back into the simulation and is so getting dented over and over. See Figure 12.45.

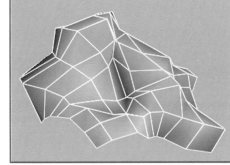

Notice how if you let it play for a while that the primitives get all horribly distended and it stops looking so interesting. Wouldn't it be a nice touch to further refine those areas that get too stretched? So how might you do this? You would want to find out the areas of the primitives and then subdivide those primitives that get larger than a certain size.

Figure 12.45
A grid getting progressively mangled by way of the SOP solver.

8. Jump back into the SOP network doing the damage, which is likely sopnet1.

9. Append a Measure SOP and set the Type to Area. This creates a primitive attribute that contains the value of a particular primitive's area.

10. Append a Group SOP and set the Group Name to be refineme. Enable the Number option and change the Operation to be Group By Expression. Enter $AREA > 0.015 in the Filter Expression field. This evaluates the expression for every primitive and asks whether each of their areas (as stored in the area primitive attribute) is greater than 0.015. If so, it evaluates to 1 and that primitive is part of the refineme group. If not, it evaluates to 0 and that primitive is not a part of the group.

11. Append a Subdivide SOP and set the Group field to refineme. This should refine all primitives whose area is greater than 0.015.

12. Append a Group SOP and, if necessary, switch off the Enable toggle under the Number radio button. Switch to the Edit tab. At the bottom, enter the refineme group in the Delete Group field. Why do this? You must clean up after yourself not only to be polite but also because, at the next time-step, the Group SOP above that creates the refineme group will error out because it will find that the refineme group already exists. This is a very important thing to realize when you are creating a recursive system. You have to be very careful and be as "respectful" as possible to the geometry that you are going to hand over for recursion. Also, keep in mind that it is possible that some other solver could get ahold of the geometry and do something with it you that you have no control over. The phrase is "program defensively" and the same thing applies to any closed system you build.

13. Jump back up to DOPs and do the force re-cook trick at frame 1 and then play the simulation. The grid gets more detail as it goes on its merry way. The value of this system is evident; as it could be used to modify geometry as RBD dobjects collide. Twist stuff, bend stuff, decimate stuff; your imagination is the limit.

14. There is one small improvement you could make before moving on. Jump back into the sopnet and move the softpeak node to the bottom of the chain. The reason is that you will get slightly softer and nicer bulges by pushing the point after the subdivision. Figure 12.46 shows the result of this smoother deformation. The SOP network should look like Figure 12.47.

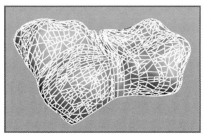

Figure 12.46
The grid getting mangled in more detail.

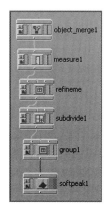

Figure 12.47
The SOP network—
the madness behind
the mangle.

The Script Solver

Along the same lines as the SOP Solver, the Script Solver is generally used for very customized solutions. The theory is simple but the application can be pretty advanced because it does nothing for you. It's like giving you a totally clean slate and saying "Do whatever you want, even if it's not drawing on the slate." The extremely abstract nature of this solver prevents the possibility of a suitably simple and yet interesting example. The basic duty of this solver is to execute Hscript .cmd files at every time-step. In each time-step, you are free to run any Hscript commands you want such as flipping switches and toggles, creating objects, manipulating the UI, running system commands, or even quitting the application. You are provided with a slew of Hscript commands to determine which objects are currently being executed against and you can, most commonly, change values in the object data and subdata. With these commands, you can actually create new custom subdata by any name you want and store information in it as the simulation runs. This can be extremely useful for keeping running totals and to refer to values you may have stashed away on previous frames.

Now that I've broached the topic of custom subdata, did you realize that you can do the same thing by using the Empty Data DOP? The Copy Data and Copy Data Solver DOPs can manipulate this information. This is an advanced topic, but please do look up the examples in the Help cards because there is some really yummy stuff in there.

Static Solver and the Copy Data Solver

These two solvers are rudimentary but totally necessary tools. The Static Solver will perform absolutely no actions on the dobjects. The Copy Data Solver will copy all the subdata from one subdata structure to another. This is often used to copy keyframed data into the Position subdata, for use with special solver types called multisolvers, which you'll learn about in the next section.

Only One Solver?

You may have heard from a little birdie somewhere that said you could make a system that would allow you to modify your objects when they impact something during an RBD simulation. That would suggest that your objects are going to be solved by two solvers, both an RBD Solver and a SOP Solver. What if I told you that you can only bind a single solver to an object and that if you attempt to bind more than one, that it would only execute one of them? Well, it is true. And the reason is because when you attach a solver to a dobject, it creates data called Solver and never Solver1, Solver2, and so on. It is a single unique name and two instances of it would cause a name clash. DOPs will look for and execute this name and only this name when it comes time to simulate stuff.

But, obviously, there is a way to get around it and that is by binding a single solver called the Multiple Solver to the dobject. This solver can take several solvers for input. Just be aware that when you use the Multiple Solver that you must ensure that the "Solver" data name that is generated is unique. Do this by toggling on Unique Data Name at the bottom of every solver that is being fed into the multisolver node. When the Multiple Solver gets executed by DOPs, it will execute all its input solvers sequentially.

This turns out to be a great strategy because it regulates how and when solvers get executed and brings about some excellent opportunities. There are currently several useful multisolvers—the Multiple Solver, the Switch Solver, and the Blend Solver. As mentioned, the Multiple Solver merely executes all of its input solvers one after the other. A common network setup for this is shown in Figure 12.48. Some of the more common uses are for denting and damaging objects due to impacts. It's conceptually plausible to make an object solved by both the RBD and the Cloth Solver, but there are some more involved technical considerations you'll need to work around first.

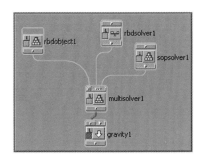

Figure 12.48
A common looking network using the Multiple Solver.

The Blend Solver will execute all the solvers that are input and blend the results. This solver can blend any data you want but is set to blend the Position subdata by default. The two (or more) input solvers may be any solvers you like but you'll discover that there are only a few combinations that make a lot of sense. One of the most direct and useful applications of this solver is to blend manually animated results with the results of a simulation.

The Switch Solver will switch between solvers either during the testing phase when you are jumping back and forth between possible solutions or even during the during the simulation by animating it. One use is that you can switch a dobject to be solved as cloth until a certain condition is met and then be solved as an RBD dobject. The condition could just be a certain frame number and often is. The switch also allows you to remove a solver by switching it out with a null solver, the Static Solver, which does nothing at all.

> The reason for the existence of the Static Solver is similar to other Null operators in Houdini. It is a placeholder that can be substituted into the multi-solvers to switch to or blend to. Those multisolvers won't allow you to blend to nothing. They want something to blend to, even if it is just a bunch of zeros.

Let's work through an example using the Multiple Solver to modify geometry during a cloth simulation.

1. Start a new Houdini session, drop a DOP network, and dive into it.

2. Lay down a Cloth Object DOP and leave it as the default cloth geometry.

3. Pin the corners down by appending two Cloth Constraints at −0.5, 0, −0.5, and −0.5, 0, 0.5, and set the constraint type on each to be a Spring Constraint with a Spring Strength of 50 and a Spring Damping of 20.

4. Append a Gravity Force DOP.

5. Append a Multiple Solver DOP. This DOP will run the other solvers sequentially from left to right with regard to their input order.

6. Drop an unconnected Cloth Solver and wire its output into the right input of the multisolver node. Remember that because you are setting this up to be used with a multisolver, you must toggle on Unique Data Name at the bottom.

7. Do the same with a SOP Solver DOP. Now you should have both solvers wired into the right input of the multisolver node. Toggle on Unique Data Name.

8. Create a SOP network node here. The network should now look like Figure 12.49.

9. In the sopsolver node, enter the ../sopnet1 in the SOP Path parameter. This is the network that will be called to modify the cloth geometry after the Cloth Solver has been called.

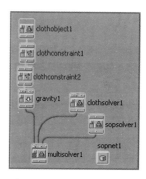

Figure 12.49
The DOP network using a multisolver.

10. Dive into the sopnet and create an Object Merge SOP. Enter `'stamps("../OUT", "DATAPATH", "../..:clothobject1/Geometry")'` in the Object 1 field. This will extract the geometry for the cloth object. Jump back up to the DOP Network and play the simulation. The cloth should fall and drape as expected. The SOP Solver will be doing exactly nothing because you have yet to actually modify the geometry. But, rest assured that it is indeed running through your SOP Solver network. This is just to confirm that everything is running as expected. If the cloth simulation explodes, you may need to raise its Minimum Substeps to 2 to get the desired result.

11. Jump back into the sopnet, append a Soft Transform SOP, and put 1 in the Group field and 0, 0.04, −0.02 in the Translate parameters. You should see one corner of the grid (along with surrounding points) get pushed up and out slightly. This next step is going to be quite delicate because it is very dangerous to make changes to the positions of points on cloth without considering the fact that every point on a piece of cloth has a unique velocity that has been carefully computed by the Cloth Solver to take into account the forces placed on it by the external forces and all the internal cloth forces as well.

If you are going to suddenly yank the cloth in some direction, you should take care to modify the point velocities to reflect the sudden manipulations. One thing to note about the v (velocity) attribute is that it is in units per second, not per frame. So, how do you calculate it? Basically, it is the change to the point positions you have just made multiplied by the number of frames per second, and you add the result to the original velocity. Append a Point SOP and wire the objectmerge node into its second input. This will inform it where the mesh was before the transforms were applied. Switch to the Particle tab and change Keep Velocity to Add Velocity. Enter `$VX + (($TX-$TX2)*$FPS)` in the Velocity in X field. That should make sense in light of the information just related. Now enter the Y and Z version swapping out the X so that it is comparing apples to apples and not X to Ys or Zs. Leave the Display flag on this SOP.

12. Jump back up to DOPs and play the simulation. Always remember with these touchier setups to reset to frame 1 and bypass and un-bypass the correct node, which is the multisolver node in this case. Play it now; the corner of the cloth tries to raise up, but gravity does overtake it eventually and it flops down. You have kind of modeled your own point forces! How exciting! During playback, you may notice that the simulation could become a little jittery and unstable. This is because the Cloth Solver has no real knowledge of what you have done in the SOP Solver and is left holding the bag and has to just make do with the result. To make sure you are getting a more stable cloth solution, switch to the clothsolver node and increase the Minimum Substeps to around 5, which instructs the solver to do a more thorough job of solving. You should end up with something like Figure 12.50.

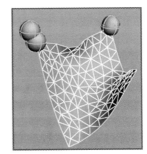

Figure 12.50
A cloth simulation being tweaked by SOPs.

The cloth example here might seem very simple, and it is. But armed with these techniques, you can really get in between the various solvers and do some things that would be impossible to achieve otherwise. For example, you could smooth wrinkles, color meshes based on strain or stretch, or even cause wrinkles. Anyhow, whatever you end up playing with, remember that its takes a fairly gentle hand with finely balanced solvers like the Cloth Solver. They can be quite skittish and it is common to have to increase the minimum substeps in order to battle the instabilities you introduce into the system.

Now What?

You have long slaved away in the mines of the DOPmasters, but what can you do with the results of your long toils? Are the simulations stuck there smoldering in the underbelly of the beast? Are you forced to render them straight out of the DOP network?

The Three Rs: Readin', Ritin', and Renderin'

It is guaranteed that some of the simulations you run, especially if you are running them in a production context, will take quite a long time to complete. And when I say "some" simulations, I mean "all." All cases except the simpler RBD cases require some lengthy computation and so it is likely that you will want to spend as little time as possible in unnecessary re-computation. There are a few avenues to help avoid this.

There is an operator called the File DOP. This node will read in and then write the input dobject stream. This is conceptually similar to the other file operations in Houdini where it will store everything in the input object stream to disk. This is an extremely useful tool to check-point certain non-simulation steps to. If, for example, you have a complex model that is being used for collisions by some solver and that solver would like to collide against it in the form of a volume, you may want to generate a hi-fidelity volume representation for it. Calculating accurate, high resolution volumes can take a while and it is a tricky task. But once you have managed to get a volume result you are happy with, there might be little reason to compute it again. At this stage, you might want to "check-point" this with an intermediate cache-to-disk type operation. Enter the File DOP. Simply append this to your RBD Object DOP and you take full control over how and when it writes the dobject stream to disk. The File DOP is set up to be able to write entire animated simulations to disk by default as it references the simulation frame number ($SF). To bake out single initial states of a dobject stream, use two File DOPs. Set one to write a file and set the other to read it back in. In this way, you can keep explicit control over how often these DOPs might be executed. These files have a .sim extension and contain everything in the current dobject stream and nothing about the current state of the DOP network.

> The .sim files can get rather large if you have thousands of objects being cached out to disk. At this stage, I would recommend using a .sim.gz extension, which writes compressed files to disk instead. The performance hit in computing the decompression often is on a level with the long file reads and disk-space issues when using uncompressed files.

Another way to write out the .sim files is to use the render driver called the Dynamics ROP. This driver is exactly like a File DOP. Because it is a ROP, it can be executed in the same way as any other ROP. This is mostly useful in the context of production when you want to use the command-line hrender or rscript applications to invoke computations of offline simulations. This is really handy when you want to run several lengthy simulations with various parameter settings. Writing and reading .sim format files with the File DOP and Dynamics ROP are extremely useful ways of getting simulation data in and out of Houdini. However, that is only half the battle and although knowing is half the battle, there is still the other half to consider. That other half is how to move the simulation data around inside Houdini.

The Freedom of Data Act

You may have noticed that DOP networks will try to emulate a full scene with multiple objects and their rendering characteristics, however, in many cases, it is not meant to replace the general scene. Sure, they will attempt to preserve all of the geometry information applied to them (all SOP level attributes, shader assignments, and such), but DOPs makes no effort to try to pull any of the source's Objects level parameters into the mix. You may be thinking that if you import single objects into DOPs, you can often just turn off the display of those objects and just keep the Display flag on the DOP network. This is where the power of DOPs to create multiple objects that are not represented in the regular scene in the Objects network can come back to bite you... and not in a good way.

If you have had any experience with dynamics in other software packages, you will expect that dynamics can only occur between objects that explicitly exist in the scene. As you have learned, this is not the case in Houdini. There can be multiple objects nested at various levels and in various DOP Networks within Houdini and, at first, this can seem like a lot of work to overcome, both mentally and physically. After a short while, you come to understand the abstracted nature of multiple DOP networks and grow to appreciate it, and so you will happily deal with the necessary discomfort in manipulating the results.

You are asking for trouble if you are looking to just select a few objects at the Objects level and then simulate them as RBD dobjects or Cloth dobjects by just pressing Play. Houdini requires a step of separation for these types of things. Houdini allows you to extract geometry, manipulate it and access simulation information from all contexts in a way that is very consistent across contexts. But, there are a few things in DOPs that you haven't had to deal with before you first stepped foot in this land.

As mentioned, a DOP network is not meant to be a replacement for the regular scene in the base Objects network (/obj). However, it is possible to render the DOP network directly as if it were the entire definition of the scene. This often happens because it is fully supported and easy to do. All you need to do is make sure that your shader assignments are all assigned at the SOP level by Shader SOPs (and so become geometry attributes) and you should be good to go. The reason for this is that DOPs does not attempt to copy any parameters like shader assignments and such because it is very possible that the geometry being sourced by a RBD Object DOP does not even exist inside of a Geometry object. It could just as easily be sourced from a SOP network that resides inside the DOP network itself.

Controlling Visibility with the Rendering Parameters DOP

You have probably noticed the conspicuous lack of Display and Render flags on the DOP nodes like you see on SOP nodes. Take a moment to consider the difference between DOPs and SOPs and it should be become clear that having these flags on DOP nodes wouldn't allow you to set display and render characteristics on a per-dobject basis if there were multiple dobjects in the stream. This is solved by having each dobject carry Display and Render flags in subdata called RenderParms. You can create and switch this information easily using the Rendering Parameters DOP. There is one odd thing to note about this DOP. Its intention is to be applied as subdata to the Geometry data. It will not work if it appears under any other Data or directly under the dobject itself. So, it is important to realize that the default Data Name must be changed to Geometry/RenderParms. By default, it is designed to be plugged into the SOP Geometry DOP, but these are generally hidden inside of read-only custom objects like the RBD Object DOP, Cloth Object DOPs, and others. So, remember to change the Data Name to Geometry/RenderParms if you want to manipulate the display and render characteristics downstream.

Object Merge SOP Skullduggery

DOP networks come in two basic flavors. One flavor exists in the Objects network and is the DOP Network object. The other flavor is all the DOP networks that exist under other network types (SOPs, CHOPs, ROPs, and so on). Although everything about the nature of the DOP network parameters and the DOPs themselves is identical between these flavors, there is one major difference. The Objects level DOP network has a Display flag. This means that the result of its simulation is automatically output to the viewport and fed to renderers. It is treated as an ordinary object. With the DOP networks that exist under the other networks, it is left up to the user to extract the simulated geometry and you do so with the Object Merge SOP. The Object Merge can fetch the result-ant geometry from a simulation dopnet. It can either extract some or all of the dobjects from the simulation. Now, you'll sprint through a simple example to see this.

1. Spark up a new Houdini session, drop a Geometry Object, and jump into it.

2. Create a DOP network and pop inside for a short visit.

3. Create two RBD Object DOPs and move the second over two units in X using the Position parameter.

4. Merge them and make sure the flag is on this node. You should see both objects in the viewport.

5. Jump back up to the SOP level and they are no longer visible. It is your task to extract the dobjects from the DOP network. Drop an Object Merge SOP and point it to the DOP network in the Object 1 field. The spheres happily appear and are ready for further SOP modifications. At one time or another, you will find yourself performing all kinds of modifications to geometry extracted in this way. Cloth interpenetration issues are commonly in need of repair or simply post-processed and remodeled for artistic purposes.

   This shows that the DOP network will cough up the resultant simulated geometry and nothing else. That is, there is a lot of information in DOP net-works. Out of all those pages of lovely information in the data and subdata of a dobject, the only thing that gets output is the Geometry subdata.

6. You will experience one implication of this right now by attempting to extract just one of the `rbd` dobjects. Change the Object Merge now to yank out `rbdobject1` by entering **../dopnet1:rbdobject1/Geometry** in the Object 1 field. Here you see that as soon as you start accessing the contents directly, you must explicitly specify that you are interested in the Geometry subdata.

> You can specify wildcards in the Object Merge SOP. Setting the Object 1 field to /obj/dopnet1 is the equivalent to setting it to /obj/dopnet1:*/Geometry.

Now that you have full access to the resultant geometry, you can choose to use the File SOP or Geometry ROP to store the simulation as baked-out geometry as opposed to using the .sim format. Both methods have their advantages and the decision is really up to you in deciding how much of the simulation data you want to store.

Extracting and Processing Simulation Information

There are many reasons why you might want to extract simulation information to post-process in CHOPs. One primary use is that you can easily set it up so that RBD simulation positions will directly affect objects in your scene, as I mentioned is more the norm in other software packages.

1. Start a new session of Houdini, drop a Geometry object, and jump into it. Create a Torus. Back up at Objects, create another Geometry object, jump inside, and create a Sphere.

2. Jump back up to Objects, drop a DOP network, and jump into it.

3. Create an RBD Object DOP, change the SOP Path to be `/obj/geo1`, and also change the node name to `geo1`. The Object Name will automatically be called this as well because of the `opname()` expression that it uses. By doing this, you are easily identifying from where you fetched the dobject. Lift the object into the air by putting 0,2,0 into the Position and tilt it over a little by putting 40,0,0 in the Rotation parameters.

> Another way to name your dobjects is to enter `'opname(chsop("soppath"))'` in the Object Name field. The Object Name is extracted from the operator name that the SOP Path field is pointed at. If you think you might be doing this type of thing in the future, save a Preset for it.

4. Duplicate the RBD Object DOP and change the SOP Path to `/obj/geo2`. It should automatically pick up the new node name and so be called `geo2`. Set the Position to 0.2, 4, 0, and zero out the Rotations.

5. Merge these two nodes and set the Affector Relationship to Mutual.

6. Follow with a Gravity Force DOP.

7. Create an unconnected Ground Plane DOP.

8. Drop a Merge and wire in the `groundplane` node and then the gravity node.

9. Append an RBD Solver and toggle off Make Objects Mutual Affectors. This will speed up the simulation because the ground plane shouldn't be affected by the sphere and torus. In the merge that brings them all together, note that the Affector Relationship is set to Left Inputs Affect Right Inputs and so the ground plane will affect the torus and sphere. Press Play; the two shapes should fall and collide with each other. Now, you are going to export this animation back out to the objects from which they originated.

10. Jump back up to the Objects level and turn off the Display flag on the dopnet.

11. Drop a CHOP Network node and dive into it.

12. Put down a Dynamics CHOP. Point the DOP Path parameter to the DOP network (`/obj/dopnet1`) and turn on its Display flag. The Dynamics CHOP fetches the current state of the simulation. Click the middle mouse button on the node icon to see the multitude of channels that have been pulled into this operator. Now notice that the name of the dobject has been prepended to the CHOP channel names. You have already taken some care in properly naming things, so go ahead and turn on the Export flag (the orange one) for this node.

13. Jump back up to Objects and the numerous channels for each object have been overridden by the Dynamics CHOP. You now have the freedom to perform all the usual things in this scene and treat it all as normal.

14. You may remember that in the CHOPs channel info, there were references to the ground plane dobject, called GROUND. You don't actually need this information. Jump back into the chopnet. Narrow the scope of the fetched data by entering /obj/dopnet1:geo*/Position in the DOP Path field.

    You have seen that the Object Merge SOP is only interested in the Geometry subdata. The Dynamics CHOP finds the Position subdata most useful. You could actually ask for any subdata that interests you; the Impacts subdata is another common request. Checking the channel information now reveals that only the geo1 and geo2 dobjects are being read in. You can confirm the whole thing is still working back in the Objects network. Currently, you

```
Full Name:      /obj/chopnet1/dynamics1
Operator type: dynamics                                          dynamics1

     Channels: 12
   Start/End: 5.67 to 5.67i,   137 to 137f,   5.67 to 6.67s
      Length: 1i,    24f,   1s
 Sample Rate: 1 Hz
    Min/Max: -58.82 to 10.64
Memory Usage: 1 Kb

geo1:tx  H,H    -0.0105 to     -0.0105 (    -0.0105) /obj/geo1/tx
geo1:ty  H,H     0.476 to       0.476 (     0.476) /obj/geo1/ty
geo1:tz  H,H    -0.568 to      -0.568 (    -0.568) /obj/geo1/tz
geo1:rx  H,H -1.09e-005 to  -1.09e-005 (-1.09e-005) /obj/geo1/rx
geo1:ry  H,H     9.838 to       9.838 (     9.838) /obj/geo1/ry
geo1:rz  H,H  5.61e-006 to   5.61e-006 ( 5.61e-006) /obj/geo1/rz
geo2:tx  H,H   0.00676 to     0.00676 (   0.00676) /obj/geo2/tx
geo2:ty  H,H     1.578 to       1.578 (     1.578) /obj/geo2/ty
geo2:tz  H,H    -0.556 to      -0.556 (    -0.556) /obj/geo2/tz
geo2:rx  H,H -58.82329 to   -58.82329 ( -58.82329) /obj/geo2/rx
geo2:ry  H,H  -28.8533 to    -28.8533 (  -28.8533) /obj/geo2/ry
geo2:rz  H,H  10.63833 to    10.63833 (  10.63833) /obj/geo2/rz
                                                              192
```

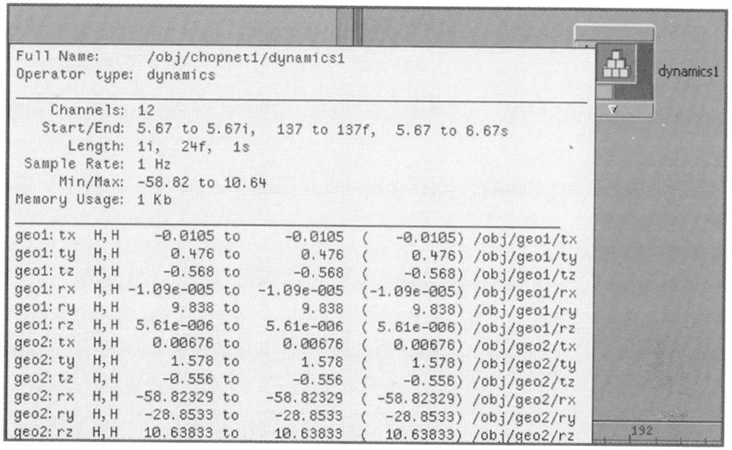

Figure 12.51
The final subdata being fetched.

are really only interested in the transformation values, so narrow it down by putting t? and r? into the Field Names field. This will match tx, ty, tz and rx, ry, rz from the subdata. The information popup should now look like Figure 12.51.

15. Let's do one more thing to demonstrate how much fun it is to post process dynamics in CHOPs. Make sure you are in the chopnet and append a Stretch CHOP. Turn on its Export flag. Enter **10** in the End parameter field and play the simulation. Notice that there is no difference in the animation. The reason is that the Stretch CHOP relies on there being access to past and future values and because you don't see this CHOP actually making a difference, it must not have the access it needs. The reason is that the Dynamics CHOP is not caching/recording anything by default. It is merely serving as a lightweight conduit for the current state of the DOPs simulation. In the Dynamics CHOP, set the Method to Cached and press Update. This will zip through the simulation and record everything.

Play the simulation and now you will see that the animation is being stretched out over a longer period of time. Hold down Shift and turn on the Display flag for the dynamics node too so that you can see the data from both nodes in the CHOPS viewport. Play with the End parameter and you will that you are stretching out the animation data so that it occurs over a longer period of time. Play with adding other CHOPs to see their effects. One thing to keep in mind is that you must manually press the Update button on the Dynamics CHOP if you change the DOP network simulation parameters at all. You have learned how to pull a ton of information out of a DOP network in a single little Dynamics CHOP and then cause post-processed output to be sent to multiple objects with minimal setup. Yes, it is good.

12. Dynamic Operators (DOPs)

Enough Impact?

In the previous example, I alluded to something called the Impacts subdata. The Impacts subdata is a flighty piece of information that gets added by the various solvers to record the collision points and the impulse forces required to keep the dobjects apart. This information is recorded per dobject. That is, the impacts that occur to a dobject. There can be scores of impacts per frame, especially if the dobjects are resting on each other.

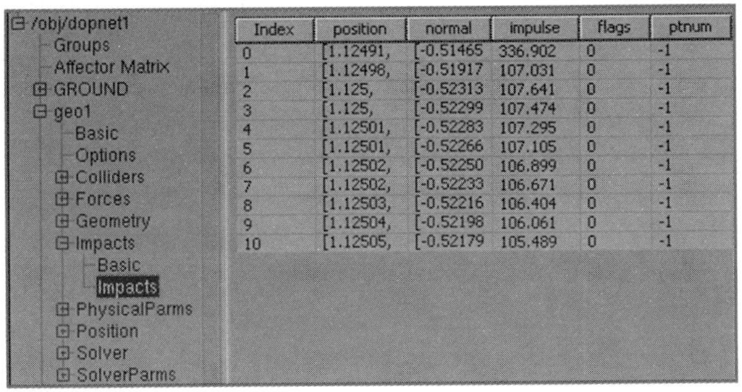

Look in the Details view inside the DOP network to step through the simulation. When collisions are occurring, Impacts subdata will be listed. Open up the Impacts subdata and notice another Impacts section. In here you will see ranks of numbers, as shown in Figure 12.52. These are all the impacts that occurred to poor geo1 in the last time-step. Note there is a large amount of information returned. Generally, the most useful of it is the positions of the impacts, the normal (the angle) and the impulse (the magnitude). There is also some other information that might be populated by other solvers like the Cloth Solver.

Figure 12.52
A peek at some of the Impacts subdata.

There are a goodly number of commands and expressions to access these impact records. You are not limited to extracting this information purely with the Dynamics CHOP. One excellent use of this information is to create birth points for particles to create easy secondary effects for collisions. Dust and sparks can be generated from these points, adding to the illusion of a powerful impact. Let's create a simple scenario that does just that. You will use the Impacts subdata to create secondary particles, perhaps sparks, at the points of impact.

1. Fire up a new session of Houdini and drop a Geometry object. Jump inside it and drop a Torus. You can set it to NURBs to make it look a little prettier. One thing to be aware of is that many of these tools rely on polygons and so will convert the input geometry to polygons internally.

2. Back in Objects, drop a DOP network and jump into it.

3. Import the torus using an RBD Object DOP and push it by setting 0, 5, 0 in Position. Rotate it over using 20, 0, 0.

4. Append a Gravity Force and then an RBD Solver DOP.

5. Create an unconnected Ground Plane DOP.

6. Drop a Merge and wire in the groundplane node and then the rbdsolver node.

7. Ahh, this simple RBD setup just never gets old, does it?

8. Jump back up to Objects and create a new Geometry object. Rename it sparks and jump into it. At this point, make sure that you have a Details view open on the DOP network somewhere and step through the simulation until some Impacts subdata appears. Expand it and see how many impacts it created. There could be anything from 1 to, say, 20 impacts for the current frame.

9. In a seashell, you want to create geometry (a single point) for every impact in the Impacts subdata. So, drop an Add SOP and toggle on Point 0. This creates a single point at 0, 0, 0. Make sure that you are displaying points so that you see it.

10. Append a Copy SOP and enter `dopnumrecords("/obj/dopnet1", "rbdobject1", "Impacts", "Impacts")` in the Number Of Copies field. This expression is fairly easy to read. Give me the number of entries in the Impacts subdata for the simulation object known as `rbdobject1` in the `dopnet1` network.

11. You have numerous points now, but they are all on top of each other. Append a Point SOP. Replace the Position in X field with `dopfield("/obj/dopnet1", "rbdobject1", "Impacts", "Impacts", $PT, "positionx")`. Place the same expression in the Y and Z fields and substitute in `positiony` and `positionz`, respectively. The points should hop to the collision positions. Press Play; the points hop around. Notice how many impacts are generated for those frames where the torus comes to rest. You don't need to generate dust impacts when the torus is still.

12. Append an `AttribCreate` SOP and enter `impulse` in the Name field. In the first Value field, enter `dopfield("/obj/dopnet1", "rbdobject1", "Impacts", "Impacts", $PT, "impulse")/5000` to extract the impulse subdata. Notice the division by 5000? This is just trying to scale the values down to a more intuitive range. Feel free to examine the impulse attribute now in a Geometry Spreadsheet if you want to check the values.

13. Append a Delete SOP and set the Entity to Points. Enable the Number option if necessary and choose Delete by Expression. Enter `$IMPULSE < 0.2` in the field. This culls out the low magnitude collisions.

14. Play the simulation; only the major collisions are generating impact points. Great stuff! Just so you know, the numbers used to divide by and as a threshold are discovered purely through the experimentation. You can make educated guesses about these values by looking at the spreadsheet and Details view. Note that they are very scene dependent and could be much higher or much lower depending on the particular scene.

15. Append a POP Network SOP and dive inside it. Create a Source POP and set the Geometry Source to Use First Context Geometry. On the Attributes tab, set the Initial Velocity parameter to Add to Inherited velocity, the Variance to 2, 1, 2, and the Velocity to 0, 2, 0.

16. Append a Drag POP and set the Scale to 3.

17. Append a Force POP, set the force to −9.81, and click on Ignore Mass to simulate the effect of gravity. Play the simulation; you have the simplest puffs of particles occurring at the high impact points. Of course it doesn't look so realistic right now, but you should be able to tweak the simulation to look more realistic using what you learned in the POPs chapter (Chapter 8). One suggestion is to make the velocity of the particles' burst scale with the impulse as well as the number of particles being emitted. Another is to remember that you have access to the impact normal too and by pulling that direction into the Normal attribute in the Point SOP, you could drive some other aspect of the effect. In any case, you should end up with something similar to Figure 12.53. This section on impacts is really just to demonstrate that there is a lot of data in simulations that you can ferret out with the proper expressions.

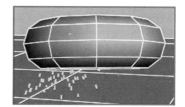

Figure 12.53
Sparks generated using Impacts subdata.

Summary

DOPs in Houdini are not just an afterthought that has been wedged into the package to give it the feeling of completion. There is a multiverse of options available, and with that power comes complexity. Great effort has been made trying to keep much of the complexity under control with DOP subnets that wrap up the seemingly complex configurations into much simpler interfaces. Keeping a steady eye on the Details view, coupled with inquisitive investigation into DOP, will take you ever farther down the path of discovery. Sooner or later, you are going to experiment with mangling the subdata. Although the system imparts an initial impression that DOPs are compartmentalized into an area that's separate from the rest of Houdini, it is good to remember that there are a multitude of tools that facilitate the import and export of information through this context. It behooves you to interpret the protection of the DOP networks as a boon and to try to take full advantage of it. The key to DOPs, and indeed any dynamics context, is experimentation. The results are often unexpected. You need to gain enough familiarity to have fun tweaking and changing the scene until you get the results that you seek.

chapter 13
Render Outputs (ROPs)

So much work. So much toil. And where is the reward? The reward is in the render. The time has come to render your work! This can often be the most fun part of working in CG because once you click the Render button, you're free to go out to a movie, spend time with the family, or go to sleep. Just watch where your head falls because you don't want to interrupt any work in progress. If things are set up properly, the computer might chug along for hours or even days without needing your intervention. It is making sure things are set up properly that is the trick!

When people first start working in Houdini, or in any 3D package, their renders are typically output to a specific location on disk and not much more thought is put into it. However, this quickly becomes a problem if you want to send your scene to someone else, or render multiple elements in one render session. Also, initial renders are rarely as fast or at the highest quality they could be. This chapter will cover various and sundry rendering topics, starting with having an organized file structure and using variables to make sure the scene is always portable.

File Structure

In a professional studio, the organization of data can get quite complex. One common system is to have a set of disks that contains critical data that is backed up regularly, and another set that contains reproducible data that does not need to be backed up. You don't need to go to that extent; however, you do want to make sure that the scene files are easily portable and logically organized.

At the core of all organization is well considered thought and creating a useful file structure is no different. There is nothing worse than having all sorts of directories scattered about your hard disk or, even worse, just dumping everything into a single directory. At the minimum, you want to have your texture maps, your geometry files, and your rendered files in different directories.

> On some systems, *directories* are called *folders*, but they mean exactly the same thing. For the purposes of this book, they are interchangeable.

The Hip-Centric Approach

The most basic approach, known as a hip-centric system, makes everything relative to the .hip file that requires the data. There is a special variable in Houdini called $HIP that gets replaced with the directory path to the .hip file that was loaded. The nice thing about using $HIP is that you can rely on it for all your .hip files, and if properly used, means that your .hip files are completely portable without any extra work for you or anyone who may be receiving the .hip file.

Let's assume you're starting with a new project, although this can be easily adapted to existing projects too. If you always start new projects the same way, using this hip-centric system will just become the natural way that you work. First, create a directory with the project name that will contain all files related to the project. For this test project, I'm going to create a fictitious project called "Hammurabi Goes to Hollywood" and use the project's initials for the directory name. So, you start with a new directory called hgh, which will contain the .hip files and all subdirectories pertaining to that project. You want to create directories called map, geo, and render inside the main hgh directory. That's really all you have to do to get started. There is one important point to understand if you are starting a new project. Before you can use the $HIP variable inside the file, you must first save the .hip file to its proper location inside the hgh folder. Saving (or loading) the file sets the $HIP variable and thus makes it a meaningful variable. As an example, if your project is called Hammurabi Goes to Hollywood, here is what you do to get set up.

1. Create a new directory called hgh.
2. Create new subdirectories inside hgh called map, geo, and render.
3. Start a new Houdini session and immediately save the .hip file to the hgh folder.

Now you can use the variable $HIP anywhere you would load or save a file, geometry, texture map, and so on. In the desired field, just type $HIP and it will always point to the hgh directory. If you copy or move the hgh directory somewhere else, everything will still work! For rendering, this means that in the Mantra (or any other) ROP, in the Picture field, you could use $HIP/render/TestRender.$F4.pic. Of course, it would probably be better to create subdirectories inside the render directory to better organize things. For example, it might behoove you to create shot1, shot2, and so on. Likewise, loading a texture map in SHOPs would look something like $HIP/map/MyTexture.rat.

One disadvantage of using $HIP is that it is integrally tied to a single .hip file. By that, I mean all the textures and .bgeo files need to live in the directories underneath the main $HIP directory. If you are using a lot of textures or geometry that are shared between different projects, that means a lot of duplicated files. Also, because the render directory is part of the $HIP file structure, it makes it hard to back up the $HIP directories but exclude the render directory. Because renders are relatively easy to reproduce when you have all the source files, it is usually best to save disk space and not back them up.

The Job-Centric Approach

The job-centric system requires a little more manual setup but is the way that most production systems work. It allows you to have a common location for referenced files (like texture maps) no matter how many different .hip files you're working on. It also affords the advantage of having a separate area for renders that is easy to skip when making backups of the job.

The key to the job-centric system is creating and using your own variables. In the hip-centric system, the $HIP variable is created and defined automatically for you by Houdini as soon as you save the file. In the job-centric system, you create your own variable(s) to use throughout your projects. If you want to send the job to someone else, you have to tell that person what your special variables are called and where they should point to.

First, identify a directory that you want to contain all of your jobs. Optionally, if you want your rendered data to be in a different hierarchy, identify a different directory for your rendered data. For this example, on Linux I have a directory called /myuserdata and on Windows I have a directory called e:\myuserdata; both are empty. (If you only have a c: drive partition, substitute e: for c: in the subsequent example.) From here on, I will just use /myuserdata. Replace this with whatever is appropriate for your system. Inside /myuserdata, create two directories, one called job_root and the other called data_root. These folders will be the top level of the job-centric system.

Inside the job_root directory, create the actual job directory. In this example, you would create the hgh folder inside the job_root folder. Inside the hgh folder, create the geo and map subdirectories. In this case, do not create the render directory here. Inside the data_root directory, also create a hgh directory and inside that, create the render directory. If you want, create subdirectories inside the render directory to hold different shots.

Now, you need to create two environment variables that point to these two directories. Doing this is quite different on Linux and Windows, but not especially hard on either platform. On Linux (or any supported Unix-based system), simply edit your .cshrc or .bashrc file, depending on which shell you use. The default Linux shell is Bash, which will use the .bashrc file, but many people prefer Tcsh (an extension of Csh), which will use the .cshrc file.

For .cshrc, add these two lines:

```
setenv JOB_ROOT /myuserdata/job_root
setenv DATA_ROOT /myuserdata/data_root
```

For .bashrc, add these lines (no spaces around the equals signs):

```
export JOB_ROOT=/myuserdata/job_root
export DATA_ROOT=/myuserdata/data_root
```

On Windows, you need to:

1. RMB on My Computer and choose Properties. If you don't have that icon, go to the Start Menu>Settings>Control Panel>Settings or, yet another possibility depending on the OS version, go to the Start Menu>My Computer and click View system information.
2. Go to the Advanced tab.
3. Go to Environment Variables.
4. In the User variables section, click New.
5. Set the Variable name to JOB_ROOT.
6. Set the Variable value to e:\myuserdata\job_root.
7. Click OK.
8. Click New again.
9. Set the Variable name to DATA_ROOT.
10. Set the Variable value to e:\myuserdata\data_root.

13. Render Outputs (ROPs)

313

11. Click OK.

12. Click OK to close the Environment Variables tab.

13. Click OK to close the window.

Now, you're ready to use these variables. When Houdini starts, any environment variables that it finds are automatically available to be used within Houdini! So, you can now use the $JOB_ROOT variable in your SHOPs to load in textures. For example, the path might be $JOB_ROOT/hgh/map/SomeTexture.rat. For rendering, you can use the $DATA_ROOT variable. In the Mantra ROP's Picture field, you might enter $DATA_ROOT/hgh/renders/shot001/Shot001.$F4.pic as the sequence to render out.

The advantage of this system is that it doesn't matter where you save your .hip files and you can set up a "permanent" directory structure that can easily absorb new jobs. Also, if you want to share data (texture maps, geometry, and so on) between jobs, it is very easy to reference that data. Also, by splitting out the JOB_ROOT and DATA_ROOT directories, you can easily make backups of your job data without backing up the render data. Backing up data requires time and space, both of which are commodities in high demand in a production environment. Save on both whenever you can!

The only real downside to this system is that when you transfer the data to someone else, the recipient has to create JOB_ROOT and DATA_ROOT variables that point to the correct location. However, this is not that harsh of a scenario. In fact, these variables can easily be created inside the .hip file! If you want to override an Environment variable, you can create your own in the Settings -> Aliases and Variables window. If you type JOB_ROOT here and set it to a path, Houdini will use that path wherever you have typed $JOB_ROOT. This is an easy way for the recipient to get around having to create system operating system variables. Note that you don't want to do this as a general rule, as you'd end up with .hip files with "hard coded" locations. If you have 200 .hip files and you want to change the location of $JOB_ROOT, that would be a painful amount of work.

Render Dependencies

Render dependencies are a way to ensure that all the elements in a shot are rendered, in the correct order. Basically, you wire together ROP nodes to create the dependencies. Then, you click Render on the last node in the chain, and the ROPs "upstream" will get rendered too, before the one you clicked Render on. This is often used in a situation where you want to dump out geometry with a Geometry ROP (discussed later in this chapter) to be loaded directly into Mantra (also discussed later in this chapter) for efficiency. Then, you render several Mantra renders for different elements, such as background, static props, and animated geometry. Finally, you have a COP network that composites these elements together, which has its own Composite ROP (discussed later in this chapter) to render out the final images.

In this scenario, you would have the Geometry ROP wired into several parallel Mantra ROPs, all of which wire into the Composite ROP. When you click Render on the Composite ROP, the Geometry ROP would actually render first, and then the Mantra ROPs, and finally the Composite ROP. This process ensures that all the elements are indeed rendered before the Composite ROP finally tries to put it all together. This is discussed in the Houdini documentation in some detail. See Shading and rendering -> Rendering -> Control dependencies between renders for more information.

Common ROP Options

Almost all ROPs have a number of very similar basic controls. I'll go over these first. Then, I'll cover the differences in the commonly used ROPs.

Valid Frame Range

The two most common options are Render Any Frame and Render Frame Range. The Render Frame Range Only (strict) is a less used option, and specifically when using the Render Dependency features.

Render Any Frame, at its simplest (when there is nothing wired into the ROP), just renders the current frame when you click Render. If you have the ROP wired into another ROP, when you render the child ROP, Render Any Frame will let the child ROP control the frame range.

Render Frame Range, when not using Frame Dependencies, renders the frames specified in the Start/End/Inc fields. When using Frame Dependencies, any inputs to the ROP will also have their frames set by this ROP. The exception is if they use the strict option, as discussed next. Any child ROPs can request frames outside the Start/End range.

Render Frame Range Only (strict) is used when you do not want a child ROP to request frames outside the parent ROP's Start/End/Inc range. For detailed information on using the Render Dependency features, please see the Houdini documentation in Shading and Rendering -> Rendering -> Control dependencies between renders. This is a very useful and powerful way of ensuring your renders are highly automated.

Render Control

Please see the Houdini documentation in Shading and Rendering -> Rendering -> Render control window for detailed information.

Start/End/Inc

Sets the start frame to render, the end frame to render, and the increment. For example, setting 1, 100, and 2 would render frames 1, 3, 5, 7, and so on, up to 100. These fields are editable when you have specified rendering to a frame range.

Render with Take

This controls what the Take menu will be set to before the render of this ROP starts. It is highly recommended that you change this to be explicitly set to the Take you want. The default, unfortunately, is (Current), which means that you might accidentally click Render while on a different Take than what you had intended, thereby rendering the wrong thing. It is much better to explicitly choose the Take that you want, even if it is just the base take, which is usually called hip.

Initialize Simulation OPs

Having this turned on will force any simulation operators (POPs, DOPs, and so on) to recook from their first frame. There are numerous strategies for rendering, so having this on or off depends on how you like to work. In most production studios, simulations are never rendered directly. They are first dumped out to sequences of geometry (.bgeo files) by the Geometry ROP as a separate render. That way, if something is wrong with the render (lighting is wrong, shaders are wrong, and so on), the simulation does not have to be recooked, which can waste additional hours or even days. In this situation, only the Geometry ROP that actually dumps out the simulation would have the Initialize Simulation Ops toggle turned on. All the Mantra ROPs would have it turned off.

13. Render Outputs (ROPs)

Alternatively, for the user working at home who might be more concerned with convenience rather than efficiency, it might be easier to have it turned on in the Mantra ROP. Be warned though that it has to cook from the beginning (usually frame 1) up to the frame you actually want to render! That means if it takes 10 minutes to cook your POPs to frame 250, rendering frame 250 will require a 10 minute wait before Mantra even starts rendering.

Pre-Render, Pre-Frame, Post-Frame, Post-Render Scripts

These fields allow you to specify scripts to be run at specific times during the rendering of the ROP. Pre-render is run once right after you click Render and before any rendering is done. Pre-frame is run once per frame before rendering that frame. Post-frame is run once per frame after the rendering of that frame. Post-Render is run once after everything has finished rendering.

The scripts are written in Houdini's Hscript language. You can type simple scripts directly into the fields provided or have the fields reference more complex scripts from files on disk. These scripts give you a lot of power for automating routines in overnight renders. There are numerous things you might want to do. A few suggestions are listed here:

- Have a Post-frame script that checks the frame just rendered to see if it's roughly the size expected. This allows you to run a "sanity check" to see if the rendered image actually contains useful information. If it doesn't, your script could raise an error message and halt rendering.
- Have a Post-frame script that scans the verbose output of the frame just rendered for error messages.
- Have a Pre-render script that checks to make sure the destination for the frames actually exists. If it doesn't, either raise a warning, or automatically create the directories.
- Have a Post-render script that takes the rendered sequence of images and creates a QuickTime or AVI movie from it, using mcp on Windows or Mencoder on Linux. Part of this script could then move the AVI or QuickTime to some common location on your network. Now, you could arrive bleary-eyed and befuddled in the morning and click a single a button to view all of your renders.
- Have a Pre-frame script that checks the amount of free disk space of the destination. It could then pop up a warning, or better yet, it could change the destination of the image to a disk with more free disk space.
- Have a Post-frame script that submits an .ifd file from the ROP to a render queue, such as Sun's GridEngine or Rush. GridEngine from Sun Microsystems is an open-source distributed process manager that distributes batch jobs consisting of script wrappers. When used with Houdini, it can script most any task involving the creation of any data files, such as rendered images and geometry sequences. See http://gridengine.sunsource.net/ for more information. Currently, GridEngine is only supported on Sun, SGI, and Linux operating systems. Rush is a very powerful network render queue solution that manages the generation of image files across a network of computers. It works with script wrappers to execute jobs. See http://seriss.com/rush/ for more information.
- Have a Post-render script that emails you or sends you a page or text message when it is done! Naturally, other software outside of Houdini that does this sort of thing via the command-line would be required.

Using Local and Global Variables

Using variables in ROPs is essential due to the way frame numbers are specified. When writing out a sequence of images or .ifd files, you must use a variable to indicate how the frame will be numbered on disk. The most commonly used variable is $F, which is the current frame number. So, in the Output Picture field of most ROPs, you would use something like $DATA_ROOT/shot0001/shotA.$F4.pic, where $DATA_ROOT is a directory on disk, shot0001 is a subdirectory, and shotA.$F4.pic is the actual image file. $F4 will be replaced by the current frame number padded with zeroes so that the total number will always be four digits. Frame one will become shotA.0001.pic, frame 543 will be shotA.0543.pic, and so on. You don't need to use padded frame numbers; however, most industry types use them so that the frames are listed in order in a Linux shell or Windows Explorer. The exception is when using floating point frame numbers, which are discussed next.

There are some other variables that are important to know about. $FF is the floating point frame number. This means that you are rendering on subframes and will output files that are named like shotA.1.5.pic. In addition to using the $FF global variable, you must also make sure to set the Inc field to a value that will be useful, like 0.5. This would render frame 1, 1.5, 2, 2.5, and so on. This is not commonly used but is helpful if you want to do special motion blur tricks or over-render your animation for various special effects.

> Note that you cannot use $FF4 for padded frame numbers if you are using floating point frames.

Finally, $N gives you the current frame from the sequence being rendered. This always starts at 1 regardless of what your Start/End/Inc settings are. So, if you had a Start frame of 55 and an end frame of 100, $N would evaluate to 1 on frame 55 and 46 on frame 100. Likewise, if you are using subframe rendering, you might find it more useful to use $N instead of $FF. In a case where you have Start of 1, End of 10 but an Inc of .5, $N will evaluate to 1 on frame 1, 2 on frame 1.5, 3 on frame 2, 4 on frame 2.5, and so on. Unfortunately, $N4 does not work to do padded numbering either. Though, you can use a simple expression instead. If you want to use $N with padding, use an expression like shotA.'padzero(4, $N)'.pic. The padzero() expression will take the second number and pad it out to however many digits you specify. You have to use the backticks to make sure the expression evaluates in the string field.

Common ROPs

There are quite a number of ways to get data out of Houdini. Almost always, using ROPs (Render Operators) will be the method for the madness. Fear not intrepid, and by now experienced, explorers. As you have already learned from previous experience in this book, madness can sometimes be refreshing and innovative.

But, never let it be said the madness be embarked upon unnecessarily. The Networks in Networks flexibility is not usually a feature that you will want to use with ROPs. It can be quite confusing tracking down where things are being written from if the ROPs are scattered throughout a Houdini session. I generally recommend that all ROPs be located in the /out directory so that anyone looking at the scene will know quickly where all the "deliverables" are located. That is not to say you should never, upon your life and luck, do it that way; however, in production, having all ROPs located in /out greatly simplifies the management of outputs. There are quite a few output operators available. I will discuss the most commons options forthrightly.

Mantra ROP

The Mantra ROP is likely the most commonly chosen option, unless you happen to be using a different renderer like Photorealistic RenderMan or Mental Ray. Typically, you will create several of these ROPs, each configured for different quality and speed settings, and named appropriately for its settings. Let's set up some typical ROP variations and look at some quality versus speed settings while you are it.

1. In a new session of Houdini, load the ROPStarter.hip file.

2. In the Build desk, split the Network Editor pane. Unlink the new pane and change it to the Outputs (ROPs) context and notice that there is a ROP already there called mantra_sel. You will examine it a little bit later.

3. Add a new Mantra ROP using the usual Tab key or Operator->Add Operator menu. Rename this operator mantra_default.

4. Click the + button next to the Render Command field and in the Output tab, turn on Verbose, and choose Render Time and Memory from the menu. Click Accept when done. When you render, this will output the render time and the amount of memory used. On Linux or other Unix-based systems, this information is output to the shell where you launched Houdini. On Windows, this information is output into a pop-up Houdini Console window.

5. Click the Render button and note how long the render took. On my machine (a Pentium 4 running at 3.2Ghz), it takes about 50 seconds. Leave the Mplay window open, so that subsequent renders will be output to the same Mplay window for comparison.

6. Add another Mantra ROP. Rename this one mantra_VeryFast. Check that the Camera field is pointing to the correct camera. In this case, the default /obj/cam1 camera is being used.

7. In the Render Command field, click the + button to the right to call up options for the Render command. In the Standard folder, turn on Ray Tracing Level of Detail and set it to 0.01, which will speed up raytracing renders at the expense of raytracing quality.

8. In the Micro Polygon folder, turn on Shading Quality and set it to 0.4, which will significantly speed up rendering at the expense of quality.

9. Turn on Micro Polygon Cache Size and set it to 65536, which will use more memory to retain a larger cache of micro-polygons. In some cases, it can help to speed up rendering.

10. Turn on Render Quality (fine control) and set it to No ray-traced motion blur. This will make sure that any raytraced shadows won't use motion blur. Motion blurred raytraced shadows are excruciatingly slow! In this test scene, there is no motion blur, so it won't make any difference. Stow that knowledge somewhere in the sock drawer of your mind because for motion blurred scenes, it will make a huge difference.

11. In the Output folder, turn on Verbose and set it to Render Time and Memory as you did before.

12. When you're done in the Render Command dialog box, click Accept. The Render Command dialog box is *modal* (or *exclusive*), meaning you can't do anything else in Houdini until you click Accept (or Cancel if you want to forget the changes you just made).

13. Set the Super Sampling to 1 and 1, which effectively turns off Anti-Aliasing. This parameter has a huge impact on speed if you are doing raytracing or motion blur. Super-sampling for raytracing is very expensive, so keeping this as low as possible for raytracing is desirable. However, you don't want it too low or quality will suffer. 3×3 is the default and is generally fine for most work. To speed things up with raytracing, you can turn on Decouple ray sampling (right below the Super Sample field) and this will allow you to set different values for micro-polygon super-sampling and raytrace super-sampling. When you have Decouple turned on, Super Sample will only control the super-sampling for the micro-polygon, non-raytraced render, and Ray

Samples will control super-sampling for any raytraced parts of the scene. For example, you might have Super Sample set to 4×4 but have Ray Samples set to 2×2 and in scenes with a lot of raytracing, render times will be much better. You just have to keep an eye on the quality of the raytraced anti-aliasing to make sure it is acceptable.

14. Set the Jitter to 0. Jitter is used to reduce aliasing artifacts in raytraced rendering. Basically, instead of sending out rays in regular intervals, jitter causes the rays to be sent out somewhat randomly within a certain area. However, when you set super-sampling to 1×1 (turn it off), the jitter will make the edges look like, well, dung. It doesn't have much impact on speed and should generally be turned off when rendering still images with no super-sampling.

15. Click the Render button and note how long the render took. On my machine, it now takes about 10 seconds! That's quite a speed improvement. Looking at the images though, you can see they won't win any beauty contests and are clearly unsuitable for final output. For rough tests, this tradeoff may be exactly what you want. Go ahead and experiment with different combinations of settings, rendering each one in turn so that you get a sense of the speed versus quality options that are available.

16. Although this seems obvious, it's important to state: The resolution of the image affects speed! When doing tests, try to render at the lowest possible resolution that still gives you the information you need. Many people erroneously render at a high resolution when doing lighting tests, for example, but this is often not needed and slows down the render. Use the Override Default Res option and use a lower resolution for your VeryFast Mantra ROPs.

17. Another use for the Mantra ROP is to create the .ifd file instead of actually rendering. This allows you to dump out all the information needed to render and then have a render farm or even just a second CPU on your computer render the .ifd files. To learn more about .ifd files, check out the Houdini-Mantra Connection section later in this chapter.

> For any object using raytracing, on the Object's Render tab, set the Reflect and (if appropriate) Refract Bounce parameters as low as possible. This controls how many times rays are bounced around. The lower the number of bounces, the faster the render will be. This will, of course, affect the look of your render. A single mirror needs a single bounce, but a hall of mirrors needs a number of bounces to look right. Our brains have a great deal of difficulty accurately resolving reflections, so high values are usually not needed. A default of three to five is generally enough to capture the required detail.

Render Command Options

The following list shows the Render Command options that can affect speed. Each option has a brief description of how it can affect the balance of speed versus quality.

◆ Remote Hosts: This allows you to use multiple CPUs across multiple machines (or just one machine) to speed up rendering. Unfortunately, this is not available to Apprentice users due to licensing restrictions. Assuming you have Houdini installed on all the machines you want to render on and enough Mantra licenses (you need one Mantra license per CPU), you enter the list of machines names you want to render on separated by commas (no spaces!). Make sure you have hserver run-

> Once you are familiar with the options, you can type the flags directly into the Render Command field. In fact, when you click the + button to get the dialog box for the Render Command field, it is offering an interface for creating, choosing, and inserting those same flags.

ning on all the machines you want to render on as well. This can be a very tricky option to set up and get working correctly! You also need to make sure that any texture maps are on a network server and available to all the machines you are rendering on. You can also set this to render on the local machine if its name is entered here. You enter the machine name once for each processor you want to use on a particular machine. So, for a dual processor system, you might want to enter the machine name twice.

◆ Number of processors: Set the number of processors to be used on the local machine only.

◆ Turn off micro-polygon rendering: This one little toggle can radically change how Mantra renders! When this is turned on, Mantra becomes a pure raytracer, not a micro-polygon, renderer. If you are doing very heavy raytracing, turning this on may speed things up. Unfortunately, anti-aliasing and motion blur can suffer or become even slower! This is something to experiment with and results will change on a per-scene basis. Generally, you do not want to use this option unless you are getting really slow renders when using a lot of raytracing.

◆ Bucket Size: This is how big each rectangle of the render is. If you are doing a lot of displacement, making this bigger might speed things up at the expense of using more memory. Brush Size principally determines how many micropolygons are held in memory and the portion of the .rat texture maps referenced in. This is one of the more "tunable" features for affecting the speed and memory usage of a render.

> Rules of the raytracing road: Any render that has Fast or Filter shadows, reflections, or refractions is doing raytracing. However, unless you turn off micro-polygon rendering, only the areas of the scene that need raytracing will have raytracing applied to them. So, for a regular (micro-polygon) render, the ray tracing level of detail only affects areas that are raytraced. If you turn off micro-polygon rendering, the entire scene is raytraced even if it has no reflections/refractions/raytraced shadows. In that case, the Ray Tracing Level of Detail affects the entire scene.

◆ Ray Tracing Level of Detail: For any geometry rendered using raytracing, this is how detailed that geometry will look. Lowering this to 0.5 often speeds things up without a visible reduction in quality. You can adjust this on a per-object basis as well. It is important to note that if you do adjust the level of detail in the Object's parameters as well as in the ROP, the two values will multiply together! So, if you set a level of detail of 0.5 on an object, and set a level of detail of 0.5 in the ROP, you will get a combined level of detail of .25 when the object renders.

◆ Variance: For any geometry rendered using raytracing, this is the threshold at which anti-aliasing (super-sampling) is performed. Super-sampling in raytracing is quite slow, so increasing this value can speed things up for renders with raytracing. If you turn it up too high, you can get aliasing artifacts that are unacceptable for a final render. Generally, values below 0.1 are useful. The threshold is basically the amount of difference between two pixels. If that difference is bigger than the threshold, the pixel is anti-aliased (super-sampled) to reduce jaggies.

◆ Quantization: This is simply the amount of data that is stored in the image file. The default of 8-bit data means there are only values between 0–255 for each pixel being stored. This is fine for previews but is not considered production quality, especially for film work. 32 bit float is the highest quality and can hold numbers above 1 and below 0 so the image is never clipped at white or black. This means you can use the Houdini compositor and have a lot of latitude in adjusting the brightness levels. This has almost no impact on the speed of the render, but it does result in larger file sizes.

◆ Render Quality and Render Quality (fine control): These can be used to turn off various features of the render, which obviously can speed things up a good deal. Remember that you will almost always face a tradeoff of speed and image quality.

◆ Shading Quality: When this is set to 1, there is roughly one micro-polygon for each pixel in the final render. Reducing this to 0.5 means there is roughly one micro-polygon for four pixels, which means it will render a lot faster and look a lot worse. If you turn it up to two, you get four micro-polygons for each pixel, resulting in a much better-looking image at the expense of speed and memory. See "How Rendering in Mantra Worketh" later in the chapter for more insight into this powerful option.

◆ Micro Polygon Cache Size: This is how much memory is used to cache micro-polygons. In more complex renders, raising this can speed up rendering at the expense of using more memory. In simpler scenes, it often will have no noticeable effect.

◆ Micro Polygon Splits: This is used in special cases where a primitive (polygon or NURBs) intersects the camera plane. In this case, the renderer has to keep subdividing the primitive until it is in small enough pieces that none of the pieces intersect the camera plane. In this case, lowering this number can speed up renders and use less memory, though render errors (disappearing geometry) can occur. Raising this number above 10 will usually allow intersecting geometry to render correctly at the expense of memory and time. This is not a commonly used option. It is important to remember that shader displacements count in pushing the geometry through the camera plane. They are the most common reason you might run into the eyesplits problem.

Geometry ROP

The Geometry ROP is another commonly used option. It references to a SOP node and dumps out the state of the network at that node to disk. In a complex .hip file, you will likely have quite a few of these. They are useful because you can dump out slow cooking SOP networks to disk and then read them back in with File SOPs. This optimizes the network and helps to keep networks more responsive.

Channel ROP

Although it's not used as often, the Channel ROP is very similar in concept to the Geometry ROP except it dumps out data from CHOPs. For example, if you are doing motion-capture editing or other complex processing of CHOP data, you will probably want to dump out the data via the Channel ROP and then read it back in with a File CHOP to keep your networks more responsive.

> The Channel ROP is unusual in that you generally do not want to specify a frame range. This is because CHOPs usually has already processed the whole frame range that you are dumping out. As a result, if you do specify a frame range, you will end up dumping out the same file many times over, wasting time and disk space. The exception to this is if you have used Time Slicing in CHOPs, in which case dumping one .bclip per frame is appropriate.

Object Scene and OpenGL ROPs

These two ROPs are almost identical, except that the OpenGL renderer offers some control over the line appearance when using Wireframe or Hidden Line modes. Generally, opt to use the OpenGL ROP. The Object Scene ROP is designed to be extended through the HDK (Houdini Developer's Kit) and really offers nothing beyond what the OpenGL ROP offers in its current state. The OpenGL output allows you to output Wireframe, Hidden Line, Shaded, or VEX Shaded renders without tying up your viewport like the Flipbook renders do. It is important to note that the OpenGL ROP does not use hardware for its rendering, so you can use it on the render queue with Houdini-NG (Non Graphical), and so on. This does mean that Flipbook renders will generally be faster, but often less convenient than OpenGL ROP renders. Unfortunately, the OpenGL output renders cannot render things like handles, viewport labels, and so on the way Flipbook renders can.

Wren ROP

Wren is Houdini's line renderer. Like Mantra, Wren is a standalone renderer that reads a script file and can be run on its own in the command line. Houdini does not have a "cartoon" renderer built-in like some other packages, but in true Houdini fashion, you can pretty easily make your own! There are a few important things to know about Wren. The first is that lines show up where there are unshared edges. That means, by default, you will not get lines on the interiors of geometry. If you want lines on the interior of geometry, use a Facet SOP set to Unique Points. Naturally, this will only work on Polygonal geometry, so convert NURBs to Polygons if you want to see their interior edges. In certain modes, you need to apply a Primitive color to color the filled geometry. This is done with the Primitive SOP set to Add Color. A lot of the time you will just want the wires with an Alpha channel so you can composite the wires over the geometry rendered with custom "toon" shaders. Wren is also used when you want to save out "flattened" UV coordinates to disk. This means you can make your own custom systems to dump out UV images of your geometry. This almost definitely requires unique points so that you see the interior wires of the geometry. Another really cool use for Wren is outputting PostScript files! Yes, Wren can output a Postscript file or even output polygons into a Postscript file.

All of these options are found in the + button for the Render Command. Basically, the Shade Mode option is most important. The White Wire/Black or PrimColor fill option, which is the default, will give you white wireframe rendering over the top of either black or whatever the primitive color is of the geometry. Black Wire/White or PrimColor fill is similar except with black wireframe over white, or whatever the primitive color is. White (or Black) Wire/Ghost or PrimColor fill will do almost the same as the previous options, except if there are no primitive colors, a ghost color will be used. Probably the most useful options are the last two, White (or Black) Wire/Matte fill. This will draw only the wires with the Alpha channel holding the matte for the wires, which means they are ready to composite over other images, like toon shaded geometry. If you turn on UV Style Render, the uv attribute specified will be rendered "flat" such that 0–1 in U will be left to right in the output image, and 0–1 in V will be from bottom to top. This is exactly what happens when you RMB on a SOP and select the Save Texture UV to Image option.

Motion Blur

Motion blur is an integral part of almost any rendering that attempts to be photo realistic. Even non-photorealistic rendering will usually use motion blur to avoid a choppy look. Mantra supports several types of motion blur and generally has good overall motion blur support. The following exercises take you through the different types of motion blur and review some controls regarding the ever-present quality versus speed choice.

Motion blur can be controlled in two places and, by default, uses a system of inheritance for ease of setting motion blur on all your objects. Geometry objects have their Motion Blur set to Inherit Behavior by default and this has two meanings. The first is that it will inherit the motion blur used by its parent, if it has one. The second is that it will inherit what the "global" Motion Blur type as specified in the ROP. Because the default is Inherit Behavior, you can actually set the type of motion blur for all your objects just by setting it in the ROP's Motion Blur parameter. The ROP can also be used to globally turn on and off the motion blur. As it turns out though, it is very rare that you want to turn on motion blur for everything in the scene. You will most generally be controlling the blur on a per-object basis, which is what the remainder of this topic covers.

Transformation Blur

First, you learn how to get transformation type motion blur working.

1. Load the file MotionBlurStarter.hip and go to frame 5. You will bear witness to a fascinating, flying cube moving through the view.

2. Go to a frame where the cube is in view. In the Object viewport, render using the fast_mantra ROP. You can use the quick launch under the viewport or the Render button on the ROP itself if you prefer. Figure 13.1 shows you the result.

3. Ooooo, you may think. A shiny cube with a shadow is not all that impressive. In the Render tab of the Flying_Cube object, set the Motion Blur parameter to Transformation Blur Only and render it again. The Ooooo turns to Woooo as you can now see some pretty good blur. But, it is a little too noisy as shown in Figure 13.2.

4. Render using the good_mantra ROP, and the blur looks satisfyingly suave as shown in Figure 13.3.

   This exercise illustrates the simplest use of motion blur in Mantra. Transformation blur simply means any transforms on the Object will be blurred. In this case, there is only a simple move in the X direction. If you want, add to the translate animation and keyframe rotations or scaling on the cube. These will also motion blur correctly when using Transformation motion blur.

   Transformation blur is the fastest type of motion blur, as Mantra has to do the least amount of work to get the blur working. The primary influence on speed when rendering Transformation motion blur is the Super Sample setting in the ROP. The fast_mantra ROP has a Super Sample setting of 2×2 whereas the good_mantra ROP has a Super Sample setting of 5×5. The Super Sample setting will directly impact both the speed of the render and the quality of the motion blur. However, remember that there is another factor at play here that is important to be aware of. By default, Mantra renders all raytracing with motion blur! This significantly slows down rendering and is often not needed.

Figure 13.1
The zooming cube with no motion blur.

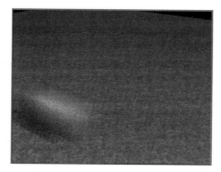

Figure 13.2
The zooming cube with lower quality
transformation blur.

Figure 13.3
The zooming cube with higher quality
transformation blur.

13. Render Outputs (ROPs)

5. In the `fast_mantra` ROP, click the + button next to Render Command. On the standard tab, turn on Render Quality (fine control) and set it to No ray-traced motion blur, which turns off raytraced motion blur. Click Accept to close the dialog box. Render the cube again with `fast_mantra` and notice the render is even faster. However, the shadow is not motion blurred, as shown in Figure 13.4. If you do need motion-blurred shadows, reflections, or refractions, you probably only want to render them when doing final renders to save time. Generally, a test ROP will have the No ray-traced motion blur option on, while a final render ROP will not have this turned on. Even when rendering with ray-traced motion blur turned on, use the Decouple Ray Sampling to lower the sampling on the ray tracing, which will speed up the render and usually does not make a huge impact on the quality of the blurred shadows.

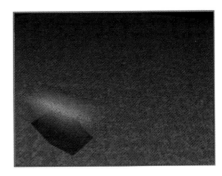

Figure 13.4
The zooming cube with no raytraced motion blurred shadows.

Another point to keep in mind is to view this stuff in motion! A still frame highlights problems with blur, such as a noisy appearance when sampling is too low. In motion, your eye will often not see these problems, which means you can actually render with lower super-sampling than you would expect from viewing the still images.

Deformation Blur

You have motion blur on objects that are moving around and that is simply super. What about if the object is changing shape? Well, that is where Deformation Blur flies in and says simply super is not enough, man. Remember this general rule of thumb. If the only animation on an object is in the Object's Transform tab, you can just use Transformation Blur and be done with it. However, if anything is animated inside the object at the SOP level, Deformation motion blur will be required. It is important to note that Deformation motion blur also includes Transformation blur, so if you have animation inside the object and animation of the object itself, use Deformation blur and you will get the correct results.

It is even more important to remember the following fact. If your geometry changes point numbers from frame to frame, deformation blur will not work! Deformation blur works by comparing the point positions at the current frame to the point positions at the next frame. If the point numbers or point count change from frame to frame, your motion blur will freak out! Thankfully, Velocity Blur can save you and you will look at it in just a moment.

1. Load the `MotionBlurStarter.hip` file, if you don't already have it open.
2. Turn on the Display flag of the `Tree` object. Turn off the Display flag of the `Flying_Cube` and `Debris`, if they are not already off.
3. Play the animation back and you will that the tree is deforming. If you want, check out the SOP network for the tree; it's just a Twist SOP with a simple expression moving the tree back and forth.
4. Move to a frame where the tree is moving quickly. Frame 59 seems like a good choice.
5. Render with the `fast_mantra` ROP. OooOoo and there is no blur.

> When testing motion blur, it is usually a good idea to render a frame without motion blur, and then another with motion blur to the same Mplay window. That way, you can quickly compare the two renders. Very often, a render with motion blur will be very subtle, making it hard to tell if there is any blur at all!

6. On the `Tree` object, set the Motion Blur parameter to Deformation Blur. On the `fast_mantra` ROP in the render commands dialog box, toggle off Render Quality (fine control) so you are again motion blurring raytraced shadows. Render the frame. Woowoo; there is now blur. Figure 13.5 shows this using the `good_mantra` output.

7. If you want, toggle back on the Render Quality (fine control) option so that the raytraced shadow is not motion blurred and generate an image sequence to see the blur across numerous frames. All the tips from the Transformation blur section apply here too.

Velocity Blur

Ahhhhh, wonderful, fanciful, imaginative, save you in the end, Velocity Blur. How many times has this saved a project? By my count, countless times! And I hope that you understand that I can count to at least 89. Velocity Blur is the true unsung hero of Mantra. Well, you can start the singing and tell the tale! I think you may know what comes next. Yes, a bit of poetic prose.

> Oh Velocity Blur,
>
> Oh Velocity Blur,
>
> What is it in your essence
>
> That so readily makes my renders purr?
>
> If at times I overlook your contribution,
>
> Please take this, a poem, a song, as my ablution.

Velocity Blur works by taking a vector attribute on the points of the object being rendered and using that to blur the geometry at render time. A vector is simply a direction relative to the point. So, Mantra has all the information it needs to blur the geometry within a single frame! The really cool thing about Velocity Blur is that changing point counts do not matter, so you do not have to worry about your geometry's point counts changing frame to frame. Also, you can create your own attribute and actually "motion blur" static geometry for very interesting effects. Before you can fly like a flamingo, you must slither like a snake.

1. Load the `MotionBlurStarter.hip` file. Make sure the `Tree` and `Flying_Cube` objects are not displayed.

2. Make sure you reset to frame one, as this next part uses particles.

3. Turn on the Debris object's Display flag and move to a frame where you can see the rocks. Frame 67 looks fine.

4. Render with `fast_mantra`, which will render the "rocks" with no motion blur, as shown in Figure 13.6.

Figure 13.5
The swinging tree with deformation blur.

Figure 13.6
The flying debris with no motion blur.

5. In the Render tab of the Debris object, set the Motion Blur parameter to Velocity Attribute Blur. Render again and you now see motion blur as shown in Figure 13.7. So far, nothing too exciting, as you have seen motion blur numerous times already. However, go into the SOP network for the Debris object and there are a couple of interesting things to note.

The first is that you are rendering particles and the number of particles changes per frame. All particle systems have the v (velocity) attribute on them by default. So as long as particles are rendered with Velocity Attribute Motion Blur, it is all well and good.

The second is that there is a Copy SOP copying a polygonal sphere onto the particles. This is a pretty common thing to do (copy geometry onto particles), so it is important to highlight an extra step here. Look at the Copy SOP's parameters in the Attribute page. Use Template Point Attributes is turned on and the To Point is using v in the Set column. This is copying the v attribute from the particle to the sphere that is being copied. This lets the spheres render using velocity motion blur.

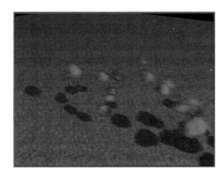

Figure 13.7
The flying debris with velocity motion blur.

Velocity Motion Blur—The Remix

Now that the basics are out of the way, you can proceed into the realm of sweet delights.

1. Still inside the Debris object, append a Point SOP to the end and turn on its Display and Render flags.

2. In the Particle tab, change Keep Velocity to Add Velocity. Multiple each of the variables by five to get $VX*5, $VY*5, $VZ*5.

3. Render with fast_mantra and whoa! Those particles sho 'nuff do have long motion blur! Figure 13.8 shows this. In fact, it is as simple as just multiplying the v attribute to control the length of the blur when using Velocity Attribute Motion Blur. When using Deformation or Transformation blur, the only way to control the length of the blur is using the Camera's shutter parameter. In this .hip file, the Camera's shutter is set to 2, which is very unrealistic. A "real" film camera has a shutter that is open for only half a frame, so a realistic setting is 0.5. You had it set to 2 so that it was easier to see the blur for the exercises.

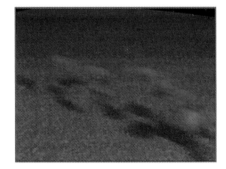

Figure 13.8
The flying debris with a multiplied velocity motion blur.

4. You can now conjure another trick of the craft using velocity motion blur. You can create your own velocity attribute and have non-moving objects "blur" for cool effects. Go up to the Object level and turn off the display of all the objects except Ground.

5. Enter the Ground Object's SOP network and append a Point SOP at the bottom and don't (never!) forget to turn on its Display and Render flags.

6. Change Keep Velocity to Add Velocity. Delete the channels and set the parameters to 0,1,0, which will define a velocity pointing straight up in the Y axis.

7. Render with the `fast_mantra` renderer. The ground looks as you would expect, as shown in Figure 13.9.

8. On the `ground` object's Render tab, set the Motion Blur to Velocity Attribute Blur and render again. Hmm, more interesting! Figure 13.10 shows the result.

9. In the `ground` object's SOP network, turn up the value of the Velocity attribute to 0,10,0 and render it again. Hearken me to the days of hallucinatory ruminations already! Ponder it, ye scalawags. The ground itself be smearing, as shown in Figure 13.11.

10. Wave the wand one last time and pull a blurred bunny out of the stove top ether. In the Y field, enter `fit(rand($PT*5),0,1,-10,10)` and render again. Sakes alive! Now there is random motion blur going up and down, between −10 and 10. Try turning up the number of divisions in the Grid SOP for a more patchy-looking rendered grid.

Figure 13.9
The `ground` object with no motion blur.

Figure 13.10
The `ground` object with "artificial" velocity motion blur.

Figure 13.11
The `ground` object with a greater "artificial" velocity motion blur.

How Rendering in Mantra Worketh

There is a lot going on when you click the Render button. Although it's not essential to understand all the details, having some idea of what is happening on the anvil in the forge will help with diagnosing problems. This knowledge will also give you more power in coming up with your own special effects. Can one say special effects in special effects? Well, you get the idea.

One of the most important concepts is that Mantra (or any renderer that Houdini can use, such as Pixar's Photorealistic RenderMan, or Mental Images' Mental Ray) is a separate program. In other words, Mantra can render just fine without Houdini. In fact, Mantra has no interface other than the command line! Normally, however, you use Houdini as the interface to Mantra so you do not have to go typing commands to get the Mantra train rolling. You get a lot of power and flexibility by having Mantra as a separate program.

So, if Mantra is a separate program, how are your objects, lights, cameras, shaders, and textures given to Mantra to render? Well, Houdini uses the ROP to output a file format called *IFD*, which stands for Instantaneous Frame Description. This is basically a snapshot of a frame from Houdini and it contains all the information Mantra needs to render a frame. If you are familiar with PRman or Mental Ray, the .ifd file is equivalent to a RIB or MI file from those two renderers. The .ifd file normally contains:

◆ The geometry (the polygons, or NURBs or whatever)

◆ Each object's position, rotation, scale, and so on

◆ What shaders to attach to each bit of geometry

◆ Each light's location, brightness, color, and so on

◆ Render quality settings (super-sampling, raytracing settings, and so on)

◆ Where to write the file to and what file format to write

Note that the list is a general overview and that the actual contents of each .ifd file vary from render to render.

Once the data has been dumped from Houdini into the .ifd file, Houdini is no longer needed. The file contains all the information needed to render. There is the caveat that sometimes things like texture maps, shaders, or even geometry live on disk outside the .ifd file. Regardless, once the file has been dumped from Houdini, it is a standalone description of what Mantra should render. This means that you can render on computers that have no graphics cards or have less memory than a normal workstation. Most professional render farms are simply stripped-down CPUs, with RAM and a hard disk, but no graphics or other fancy peripherals. This allows them to render with maximum efficiency because graphics (like the Linux KDE or Gnome, or the entire Windows interface) take up memory and CPU resources that could be devoted to rendering.

Having said all that, most of the time the creation of the .ifd and Mantra being a separate program are hidden from you. When you click Render in Houdini, the .ifd is automatically sent to Mantra (in technical terms, through a "pipe"), which then renders the information and returns the rendered image (again, automatically) to Mplay, Houdini's image viewer. It is beyond the scope of this book, but if you are interested in exploring the .ifd files, all you have to do to is go into a ROP and turn on Generate Script File. Also, you will want to turn off Binary Script so that you can check it out in a text editor. Included is a simple .hip file that renders a displaced Sphere and a reflective Tube. There is a single ROP that is configured to dump the script file to $TEMP/TestIFD.ifd for you to look at.

> Note that $TEMP will be in a different location depending on which platform you're working. To see where $TEMP is on your system, open a Houdini Textport from the Windows->Textport main menu and type echo $TEMP to see what the variable is set to.

Once you have the .ifd file on disk, you can render it directly in Mantra from a Unix shell or from a DOS prompt. As stated earlier, you could shut down Houdini, as it is no longer needed. Simply change directory into the $TEMP directory, and type mantra < TestIFD.ifd (or whatever you called the file) to see the render.

On Linux or any other Unix-based operating system, you can simply go into the shell you started Houdini from to render the .ifd file. On Windows, you need to use the command prompt that is in the Start Menu subfolder where you launched Houdini. This ensures that the environment is configured correctly for Houdini. Windows users very often install Cygwin (www.cygwin.com) so they can use a Unix-like system on Windows, because it is generally much more powerful and flexible than the DOS prompt.

Once you have the .ifd file rendering, you can start to experiment with the Mantra command-line options. Some of these options were discussed earlier in the Render Command Options sections. As stated in that section, this is a case where you would enter the flags directly rather than setting them through a dialog box. Type `mantra -h` to get a list of the options. For example, type `mantra -V 4 < TestIFD.ifd` to get a verbose output of what is happening in the render. Most professional effects shops use this as the default, as it makes it easier to quickly spot and diagnose render problems. Using the < is called the "redirection" prompt and basically is telling Mantra to use the contents of the .ifd file to render with.

You can also edit the .ifd file with a text editor such as Kate, vim, or wordpad to make changes. For example, you can edit the .ifd file and change the `ray_sample` line to `ray_sample 8 8`. Doing so will increase the anti-aliasing quality to maximum. This is exactly the same as setting the Super Sample line to 8 8 in the ROP. Really, all Houdini and the ROP do is organize and output these various commands to the .ifd file, which Mantra then interprets at render time.

Mantra Rendering Is All About the Micro-Polygons

The actual rendering in Mantra, after it has loaded the .ifd file, is fairly complex and is especially so when raytracing is involved. Again, you do not need to know this in detail, but the more you know, the faster you will be able to diagnose problems and come up with special ermmm… things. Rather than go into painful detail on what Mantra is doing when it renders, let's look at a gross over-simplification at a micro-polygon render.

Mantra picks a bucket to work on. A bucket is simply a rectangle part of what the camera sees. By rendering in buckets, Mantra is able to efficiently use memory and throw away stuff it doesn't need in order to preserve memory. Any geometry not "seen" in the bucket is ignored. The geometry that is seen in the bucket is "diced" into micro-polygons. A micro-polygon is a tiny polygon that is approximately the size of a pixel. If you turn up the Shading Quality on an object, this makes even smaller micro-polygons for that object, which can add detail in some cases. As part of the "dicing" process, any attributes on points or vertices are interpolated across the micro-polygons.

The micro-polygons are then "shaded," meaning that any shaders attached to them are executed. The shaders are executed in this order:

1. Displacement—Move the micro-polygon.
2. Surface, Light and Shadow—Color the micro-polygon.
3. Fog—Color the micro-polygon, again.
4. If a Surface shader (or Shadow shader) requires raytracing, call the raytrace engine to color those micro-polygons.

5. Filter (anti-alias) the resulting pixels.

6. Output the bucket's image.

7. Start over with a new bucket until the image is finished.

The main difference when doing "raytrace only" mode (using the -r flag to Mantra) is that inside of dicing the scene into micro-polygons, rays are fired from each pixel into the scene, and wherever the ray hits, that point is then colored using the shaders. To get anti-aliasing to work properly, many rays per pixel are usually needed, which can significantly slow down rendering.

> Any book that covers writing shaders in the RenderMan Shading Language is very useful to people writing shaders in VEX because the two languages are quite similar in concept and syntax. However, it is important to note that the .ifd scene descriptions used in Mantra are very different from the RIB scene descriptions used in RenderMan. Shader writing and scene descriptions in Mental Ray are quite different from Mantra (and RenderMan) so the Mental Ray book(s) listed below are mostly for overall concepts and not so much for specific implementation.

For a detailed look at rendering, I recommend the following books.

◆ *The RenderMan Companion: A Programmer's Guide to Realistic Computer Graphics* by Steve Upstill—The original! Despite its age, it contains much useful information about shader writing and rendering generally in RenderMan.

◆ *Advanced RenderMan: Creating CGI for Motion Pictures* by Anthony A. Apodaca and Larry Gritz—This, along with *The RenderMan Companion,* are the definitive books on RIB and RenderMan shader writing. They are highly recommended for anyone writing shaders in either Mantra or RenderMan.

◆ *Rendering for Beginners: Image Synthesis using RenderMan* by Saty Raghavachary—This is a good place to start if you are working with RenderMan or Mantra.

◆ *Essential RenderMan Fast* by Ian Stephenson—Another good starter for those diving into RenderMan or Mantra shader writing.

◆ *Texturing and Modeling: A Procedural Approach, Third Edition* by David S. Ebert, et. al—This is a somewhat more technical look at how various aspects of rendering work, and how to use various algorithms to create cool images. It includes some shader writing applicable to RenderMan and Mantra, and quite a lot of theory. Suitable for somewhat more advanced shader-writers or programmers.

◆ *Rendering with Mental Ray* (Mental Ray Handbooks) by Thomas Driemeyer—Although this deals with the Mental Ray renderer (which is not a micro-polygon renderer), it has valuable information about rendering that is generally applicable to most production renderers.

◆ *Production Rendering,* Ian Stephenson (editor)—This is the definitive book on the guts of a production quality micro-polygon renderer. Mark Elendt, Senior Mathematician at Side Effects and creator of Mantra, contributed to this book along with several other luminaries in the field of rendering. If you are interested in writing your own renderer or just delight in the most intimate details of production rendering, this is the book for you!

Rendering from a File

Now that you have seen how the .ifd file works, you can do some things to optimize the renders even more. One of the most important and widely used methods in production is to render from a file. Basically, instead of having the geometry for each object be saved to the .ifd file, you run a pre-process that sends the geometry to disk for each object. Then, you tell the .ifd file to read the geometry from disk when it actually needs to render it. This will mean that the .ifd files are significantly smaller (because the geometry is almost always the biggest part of the file) and a lot less disk space is wasted. It can also help reduce memory usage and speed up the rendering. There are two parts to setting up a Render from File render scheme. First, you need to save out the geometry to disk. Second, you need to specify how it is read back in to the .ifd file.

1. Load the `ROP_Starter.hip` file and select the `Ring` object. It will be highlighted in yellow when the node is selected.

2. In the `mantra_sel` ROP, turn on Generate Script File and turn off Binary Script.

3. In the Script File field, type **$TEMP/test.ifd** and click Render.

4. Edit the `$TEMP/test.ifd` file you just wrote to disk. Generally, any text editor other than Notepad will work fine as it, in particular, will format things poorly and so make the file more difficult to read. You only are rendering one object so there should only be one Geometry definition. This definition is the line that reads `ray_detail -s /obj/Ring stdin`. The word `stdin` means Standard In, which in the .ifd file means read the geometry from the following line. The next line is `PGEOMETRY V5`, which indicates the start of some Houdini geometry. If you scroll down, the line `endExtra` indicates the end of the geometry definition.

   As you can see, the geometry definition for just one simple object is already more than half the size of the file. If you were doing an animation using this geometry, every single .ifd file will have a copy of the `Ring` object embedded in it, even though the `Ring` object does not change over the animation. What a waste of time and disk space!

5. In the `Ring` object, go to the Render tab and turn on Render from File.

6. In the Geometry File field, enter **$TEMP/${OS}_archive.bgeo** (the curly braces around OS are important!). Curly braces are needed when the actual name of the variable is ambiguous. The curly braces clearly define the variable as `${OS}` to Houdini and Mantra.

7. Set Auto Archive to Auto-archive (no overwrite).

8. Click Render in the `mantra_sel` ROP and edit the `$TEMP/test.ifd` file again. Woowoo! The Geometry Definitions section is now a single line that reads something like `ray_detail -s /obj/Ring d:/temp/Ring_archive.bgeo`. The actual path to `$TEMP` (`d:/temp` in the previous example) will be different on Windows and Linux. Also, you normally would not use `$TEMP`. Rather, you would use a network-mounted directory accessible by all your render machines. Now, when you render, the .ifd file will load the .bgeo file from disk. This means that if you dump out a series of .ifd files, there is only one copy of the geometry in `Ring_archive.bgeo`. Now, each .ifd file is much more efficient.

A bit of explanation for some of the steps:

◆ Render from File requires that you enter a path to a file (usually Bgeo) on disk. Whatever is typed here is used on the `ray_detail` line in the .ifd file for that object.

◆ `$TEMP` is replaced with whatever the TEMP variable is on your system. `${OS}` is replaced with the name of the current object, which is `Ring` in this case.

13. Render Outputs (ROPs)

◆ You need to use curly braces around OS. Otherwise, $OS_archive would be interpreted as the name of the variable and you would get nothing.

◆ The Auto Archive (no overwrite) option will save out the geometry from this object, but only if the file on disk does not already exist. Once the file exists, you can turn Auto Archive off entirely if you want. The Auto Archive option will always dump out a new .bgeo even if it already exists on disk. This is not so useful. You do not have to use the Auto Archive option at all. There is an Archive ROP that you can use, or even just the Geometry ROP will do the job. These have the advantage that you can control them in ROPs via the Render Dependencies and are easier to script. However, they have the disadvantage that they will not (natively) detect if the file exists on disk like the Auto Archive (no overwrite) option you just used.

9. All is swell. You have your geometry (for the Ring object) loading from disk. But what if the Ring object is out of the camera's view and is not reflected in any other object? In this case, loading the Ring object wastes time and memory too. You really should be able to specify that you do not want to load the object at all if it is not seen in the render. Thankfully, you can do this too. This is known as Bounded File (explicit bounds). It requires an extra step that is not automatic (unless you write a script), but is easy to do. Also, it only has to be done once unless the geometry is deforming. That step is specifying the Bounding Box of the object. When Mantra renders, it will first check to see if the bounding box of the object will be seen in the render. If yes, it will load the geometry when mantra sees any part of the bounding box inside the current render bucket during the render. If the bounding box is never detected in any of the buckets, the geometry is never loaded, thereby saving time and memory! In renderman speak, this is called *delayed read-archive* in that the archived file is read in only if the bounding box is contained inside the currently rendered bucket. Larger buckets can cause more objects to have their bounding boxes detected and therefore cause more memory to be consumed. In the Ring object, change the Geometry option to Bounded file (explicit bounds).

> If you build monolithic objects that have bounding boxes that occupy the entire rendered image, the bounded file feature is completely negated. If you are building large sets, it is best to build them in small object components so their bounding boxes are small, thus taking full effect of the bounded file feature. Planning for this in the early stages can allow you to render insanely large scenes effectively.

10. Leave the Geometry File and Auto Archive options the same as before.

11. Go into the Ring object's SOP network, and MMB on the SOP with the Render flag. Write down the Bounds numbers. The top line is the Max bounds, the bottom line is the Min bounds. I got these numbers:

```
Max:  0.759, -0.477,  1.879
Min: -2.874, -1.190, -1.576
```

12. In the File Min Bounds fields (in the Ring object's Render tab), enter the minimum values that you recorded. Do the same for the File Max Bounds fields.

> A lot of people find it confusing that when you MMB on a SOP, the Max bounds is listed above the Min bounds, but when you type the values in the File Min/Max Bounds fields, you enter Min first. Double-check that you have entered the values correctly; it's a common mistake to enter the Max values into the Min fields.

You can use the Textport to output the operator info to aid in copying and pasting the values. Just cd to the node in question and type **opinfo** to return the information of that node to the Textport. Now, select the particular values and cut and paste them into the appropriate areas.

13. Click Render on the `mantra_sel` **ROP** and edit the `test.ifd` file again. Now, the `ray_detail` line includes the bounding numbers that were entered.

14. There is an option called Bounded File (render SOP defines bounds), which will automatically detect the bounds from the Render SOP. It might be useful in some unusual situations, but, it requires that the SOP network be cooked, which defeats the purpose of Render from File! As a result, this option is generally not used.

15. There are "File" versions of the three main render types. You've looked at regular geometry, but there is also a Subdivision from file (explicit bounds) option that you would use with the `TreeTrophy` object that is rendering as Subdivision Surfaces. It works exactly the same as what you have just discussed. Likewise, there is a Points from file (explicit bounds) option that would be used if you are rendering as points.

You want to make the bounding box a little bigger than the strict bounding box numbers you get from the MMB information. It's a good idea to add five percent of the total size to each of the Max numbers, and subtract five percent of the total size from each of the Min numbers. Hmm, that really screams out for the automation that a script provides, does it not? Well, ask and ye shall receive! Included in this chapter's downloads are a couple of scripts that will add this functionality. Put the OPmenu file in your $HOME/houdini8.0 directory (if one already exists, add the lines in the file provided to what is in your file). Put the `minmaxbounds.cmd` file in your $HOME/houdini8.0/scripts directory. The next time you start Houdini, all your Geometry objects will have a RMB menu that will automatically fill in the File Min/Max Bounds fields with an extra five percent added to the bounding box size.

When calculating the size of the bounding box for the object in question, you have to allow for any displacements on the geometry. If there are large displacements occurring, you need to add that to the initial bounding box calculations and then apply the five percent padding factor.

13. Render Outputs (ROPs)

Summary

This chapter dealt with how to get all the wondrous work from the various contexts in Houdini out for the world to see. There are numerous kinds of render outputs and each has a specific utility. By far, the most common ROP is the Mantra ROP because it allows you to render your scene to an image file. As you learned, the process of rendering almost always involves a tradeoff between speed and quality. Exploring what each of the render options controls is a requisite task in learning how to output both efficient and attractive images.

13. Render Outputs (ROPs)

chapter 14
And So It Ends?

Alas, you are coming to the final pages of this book, but your adventure with Houdini is just beginning! Where might you want to go and what might you want to do with your newly gained skills? You could make animations to entertain your friends at parties. You could make visualizations to help forward the sciences and to better mankind. You could create a custom Valentine for the one you love. You could even decide to take the plunge and do this kind of work for employment.

Occupations in the Computer Graphics Industry

So you have decided that you are enthused and stalwart enough to want to create this kind of content for a living. What is the first step? One of the initial decisions that affects your continued learning path is deciding on a vague area of occupational interest. The choices are expansive and although they are related, each has its own set of responsibilities and often a particular stratum of software package associated with it. The various roles can be explained in terms of the chronology in which they fit into the post-production process. The positions described are generalized in nature and sometimes occur at the same time or in sequences other than that listed, depending on the needs of the project. Many of the positions list useful areas of knowledge for a person working in that capacity. Understand that these are only suggestions, because many people in this industry come from wildly varying backgrounds and succeed at what they do through determination and skill. Also, this is only a sampling of the available positions in the industry.

◆ **The Designer**—The designer develops the look of a project and creates drawings, sculptures, and schematics that are passed on to the next role in the process. Obviously, the designer must have extensive training or ability in traditional art-related subjects such as drawing, perspective, color theory, design, and so on.

◆ **The Software Engineer**—The software engineer most often develops in-house tools that might be completely proprietary or add-ons to commercial software. When particular needs arise during a production, a software engineer can often save the day by coding custom solutions for a particular issue. Solid programming skills are required and high-level math skills are usually also a necessary part of the package.

◆ **The Motion Capture Technician**—The motion capture technician is responsible for capturing computer animation data based on the movement of actors who are specially rigged with sensors that record positional and rotational data. A good knowledge of still cameras, video cameras, perspective, and character rigging are important.

- **The Tracker**—The tracker takes information gathered on the set or created virtually and ensures that the computer animation elements are synched with the live-action elements. It is often necessary to have the computer camera and models match their live counterparts in order to believably combine them. A solid knowledge of still cameras, video cameras, perspective, storytelling, and other topics assist the tracker in his job.

- **The Modeler**—The modeler receives the design materials and uses them as reference to create 3D models. Often, the modeler benefits greatly from these same traditional subjects that serve to assist in visualizing how volumes are established and how lines create form.

- **The Texture Artist**—The texture artist receives the models, props, or characters, and creates and applies appropriate maps to help meet the design and technical objectives. Likewise, many traditional art topics come in handy when painting maps and backgrounds.

- **The Character Animator**—The animator is engaged to impart the desired motion and emotion to the model. To animate, or give life, is one of the most difficult areas of computer animation and studios often look to employ artists trained in traditional 2D animation because they already have experience with this creative and difficult process. Convincingly imparting emotion, motive, or thoughts to a 3D model will likely be the enduring challenge facing our medium.

- **The Effects Animator**—The effects animator handles animating almost everything that isn't considered character animation. Digital effects include everything from fanciful pixie dust and visual psychedelia to simulating natural phenomenon like waterfalls, explosions, tornados, shock waves, and much more. This effects animator benefits from an artistic background in drawing, lighting, color theory, and so on, and also a science background where physics and the like help to form an understanding of the motion of nature. In addition, strong programming skills are very useful for scripting and creating or modifying shaders. This position truly benefits from a wide variety of disciplines.

- **The Lighter**—The lighter takes the textured and animated models and creates the lighting and camera elements that capture and render the scene. It is her job to take all the work done before and output the look desired. The lighter often renders out many layers so the next step in the pipeline, the compositor, has a fine degree of control in creating the final look. For example, the lighter might render a diffuse (color), specular, reflection, shadow, or "problem-fixing" layer to give the compositor what she needs. Knowledge of traditional lighting schemes, cinematography, design, perspective, and more are helpful in this position.

- **The Compositor**—The compositor uses the multiple layers and combines them with each other and the live action or CG plates to create the end result. By operating on various layers individually, the compositor has great control over the amount to which each layer contributes to the final look. In addition, 2D effects are generally must faster than their 3D counterparts and so things like distortions, noise, and so on, are often incorporated at this stage. Many traditional art topics like design, color theory, and drawing are helpful in this role.

The following positions don't neatly fit into a phase of the process and so are listed outside of the chronology of the pipeline.

- **The Pipeline Technician**—The pipeline technician keeps a diligent eye on the pipeline to ensure that the flow of data through the studio is both useful and efficient. Strong programming skills are helpful, due to the large number of tasks that require scripting.

- **The "Area" Lead**—This job is labeled slightly differently at various studios and positions in the hierarchy of positions. But basically, she is a user that has several years of production experience under her belt and so has taken on the role of guiding a team of folks working at a particular task, usually in the areas of tracking, modeling, animating, or lighting. The required skills include whatever area that person is managing in addition to communication skills, project management skills, and more.

◆ **The Visual Effects Supervisor**—The visual effects supervisor is basically like the top of the pyramid sequence supervisor. His job is to ensure the quality and look of all the sequences that the studio is responsible for. Usually, this person interacts personally with the director in trying to come to understand the director's vision for the film and, in particular, the vision for the sequences being worked on. The visual effects supervisor is usually the last stop in the chain before the work is sent over for review by the director. This is another one of those positions where the helpful background of skills is so varied, it is easier just to say that you should learn as much as you can at every opportunity.

◆ **The Educator or Trainer**—The trainer usually helps new employees acclimate to the particular processes of the studio, focusing on the pipeline and any non-standard conventions that might give rise to confusion for employees. Often in studios, classes are offered from time to time to help workers broaden their knowledge of the various packages used in the studio. An educator must be skilled in the areas being taught in addition to having good communication skills.

◆ **The Intern**—Last, but not least, is the venerable intern. He most often does a combination of administrative tasks and project work. This is a well-trod path that many an expert Houdnik has traveled on the way to greatness. The energetic and attentive intern can almost always find ways to expand his opportunities and is in the perfect position to meet future peers.

> *Houdnik*—a Houdini beatnik; that is, a Houdini user who lovingly embraces the unconventional and creative methodologies employed by the software and enjoys waxing poetically on those same attributes. Thanks to one Valerie Berney for that moniker.

Houdini in Production

Now that you have a general notion as to some of the available roles, you might be wondering which of these roles most often involve the use of Houdini. It is a complete solution and as such includes tools to model, animate, create special effects, light, render, and composite any scale of animation project. The open nature of the architecture and the straightforward approach of the procedural node-based system also means that Houdini is often used as the pipeline backbone that can ably import, process, and export data from and to various other packages. So, the short answer is that it is possible to encounter Houdini at numerous stages (and therefore positions) of the production process and pipeline. If you have researched the industry, you will know that Houdini usage is well established for modeling, effects, pipeline glue, and rendering. With the production of *The Wild* by Core Feature Animation in Toronto and *The Ant Bully* by DNA Productions in Dallas, Houdini is also making significant inroads in the areas of character animation and compositing.

One aspect of a career using Houdini that is not often discussed relates to good old Adam Smith and his theory on the law of supply and demand. Digging way back into the vault of a bachelor's degree gone awry, I recall that, generally speaking, as supply of a good or service is increased, the price for it will decrease. For various reasons, there has historically been a relatively constant over-demand (or under-supply) for Houdini talent. Generally speaking, this translates to less competition for jobs and higher pay for those same jobs. With many other packages, there is an abundant supply of labor, which has the effect of keeping compensation lower on average. That is not to say that you can't make a good living working with any particular package. A skilled artist in any medium will always be in demand. In addition, as a Houdini artist, you are more likely to be given more responsibility earlier simply because there are fewer folks to choose from who understand the software. The most important thing you need to do is be prepared and knowledgeable so that when the opportunity presents itself, you are equal to the task.

A Parting Word

Wow! You made it! I made it! We are all in it together! I hope you have learned as much in reading this book as I have in writing it. The challenges you face in your future dealings with Houdini will no doubt test the limits of your intuition and skill. But, I can assure you that having a solid foundation in the basics will help carry you as far as you are willing and wanting to go with the adventure. It has been a number of years now since I first started learning Houdini and I still feel a sense of excitement whenever beginning a new shot or lesson. It is my earnest wish that you too will find that same sense of wonder and intrigue in exploring the magic of Houdini.

Index

Index

Numerics

2D, UV Coordinates, 208
3dbuzz forum, 17
3D
  building blocks, 8–10
  overview of, 7–8
  viewing, 11

A

Academy of Motion Pictures, Arts, and Sciences, 4
accessing attributes, 222
activation fields, POPs, 151
Activation parameters, 283
active channels, keyframes, 109
active states, DOPs, 276–277
adding
  CHOP operators, 135
  instances (SHOPs), 186
  materials (VOPs), 220–221
  movement, 93–94

  operations, 63
  parameters (SHOPs), 227
  spare parameters, 66
  subnets, 236
  texture maps, 224–225
  variation, 181–183
  VOP networks, 219–220
Add Spare Parameter button, 65
affectors, DOPs, 276–277
age1 node, 234
alignment
  arrows, 180
  axis, 149–151
All Channel Groups, 116
Alternate_Source object, 234
angles, Euler, 122
animation, 109
  autokeys, 111–112
  Channel Editor, 112
  dragonflies, 130–132
  expressions, 64
  gimbal locks, 122–123

  history of, 2
  manually set keyframes, 109–111
  previewing, 120
  rigging, 120
    automating, 129–130
    hands, 125–130
  skeletons, 120–124
  takes, 117–119
  values (DOPs), 283
  zones of utility, 113–116
antennae (dragonflies)
  shaders, 213
  UV Coordinates, 203–204
apertures, creating, 91–93
appending Visibility SOPs, 100
apples, 81–87
applying
  attributes, 222–223
  data to data, 270
  labels, 224
  lag, 136
  lighting (to texture maps), 225–226

live VOPnets, 231
shaders
    dragonflies, 204–213
    VOPs, 221
SHOPs, 188–193
textures (to dragonflies), 204–213
UV Coordinates, 199–204
Apprentice (Houdini), 5
arches, creating, 95–97
archSize node, 95
area lead, 336
arrows
    aligning, 180
    creating, 176–178
    ordering inputs, 101
assetization, preparing for, 235
assets. *See* **Digital Assets**
assignment of shaders, 193, 208–213
attaching geometry, 180–181
attack of the be-tentacled sphere, 89–94
AttribCreate SOP, 79
attributes
    accessing, 222
    applying, 222–223
    ballcolor, 222
    Details View pane, 70
    friction, 289
    per-point, 288–289
    position, 71
    VOP customization, 218–219
autokeys, animation, 111–112
Automatically Adjust toggle, 53

automating rigging, 129–130
auto-numbering nodes, 45
axes, 7
    orientation, 148
axis
    alignment, 149–151
    movement along, 275

B

backticks, 71
ballcolor attribute, 222
balldobject, velocity, 275
bareAluminium shader, parameters, 190
base materials, compositing labels, 226
behavior
    folder organization, 242
    Hit Behavior parameters, 244
birds (totem poles), 52–54
birthing POPs, 146–150
black boxes, 4
blank spaces, filenames, 62
Blast SOP, 103–104
Blend Solver, 300
Blend state, Objects context, 37
bodies (dragonflies)
    shaders, 209
    UV Coordinates, 204
bones
    creating, 121
    deleting, 125
    editing, 123
    indexing, 128

moving, 123
parenting, 124
splitting, 123
bottom stowbars, SHOPs, 187
Bounded File, 332
bounding boxes, sizing, 333
boxes, 9
Box SOP, 281
boys (totem poles), 54–57
brush operations, SOPs, 74–79
building
    blocks (3D), 8–10
    monolithic objects, 332
    user interfaces (Digital Assets), 238–256
bulls (totem poles), 58
buttons
    Add Spare Parameter, 65
    mouse, 16
    Pane Linking, 69
    presets menu, 73
    Quick Render, 78
    Real Time Toggle, 143
    See One/See All, 101
    Shading Selector, 38
    Update, 46

C

cables, 266
calculating size of bounding boxes, 333
Camera object, 33
Capture Geometry, 127–129, 132–134
centroids, 150

Channel Editor
animation, 112
channel groups, 116
channel lists, 115–116
zones of utility, 113–116
Channel Operators (CHOPs)
dragonflies, 135–136
overview of, 31
Channel ROP, 321
channels
groups, 116
keyframes, 109
lists, 115–116
references, 86, 65–68, 246–248
Tooltip window, 67
ty, 116
character animators, 336
charge POPs, 157–159
choose_internal object, 234
CHOPs (Channel Operators)
dragonflies, 135–136
overview of, 31
circles, 10
of arches, 96–97
clipping
distances, 53
pane, 11
Cloth Constraint DOP, 285, 292
cloth DOPs, 284–290
Cloth Object DOP, 286
Cloth Solver DOP, 288–289
collapsing
nodes, 52
subnets, 236

Collision_Geometry object, 234
Collision POP, 165, 240
collisions
cloth, 286–287
detection, 159–162, 294
colors
particles, 170
rendering, 172
combine tab, 73
Comb SOP, 75
commands
opcf, 250
opcook -f, 207
opparm, 79
opupdate, 207
Render (options), 319–321
texcache -c, 207
communities (Houdini), 17
compositing labels, 226
Compositing Operators (COPs), 31,
97–98
compositors, 336
concave polygons, 10
Concrete VOPs, 225
configuration
behavior folders, 243
context sources (POPs), 148
conjuring icons, 255–256
connections, dotted line, 168–169
connectivity, creating primitive groups,
281
constant birthing, 146–150
constant( ) function, 114

constraints, 275–276
multiple, 274–275
two-state, 285
wire, 292–293
construction plane grid, 42
containers, objects as, 33
contexts
interfaces, 28–31
POP sources, 148
SHOPs, 186
controlling visibility, 304
controls
DOPs, 272–275
special, 248–250
convex polygons, 10
cooking
POPs, 142
simulations, 143
coordinate spaces, 12
coordinate systems, 7
COPs (Compositing Operators), 31,
97–98
Copy date Solver, 300
Copy operator, 90
Copy/Paste SOP, 104–105
Copy SOP, 76–79, 104–105
Copy Stamp technique, 181–183
Copy state, Objects context, 36–37
cords, 266
Create New Digital Asset, 236
Create New Operator Type dialog box,
230
crossed wires (in SOP), 203
cubes, 9

cubic( ) function, 114
curves
  NURBS, 81
  transforming, 83
customization
  attributes
    accessing, 222
    VOPs, 218–219
  subdata, 300
cylinders, 9

D

damping springs, 291–292
data, DOPs, 269–271
data types, VOPs, 224
Davidson, Kim, 31
defaults, deleting, 205
defining groups, 190
deformation
  blur (ROPs), 324–327
  transformations, 13
Delete operation, 53
Delete SOP, 85, 99, 103–104
deleting
  bones, 125
  defaults, 205
dependencies, rendering, 314
Descartes, Rene, 7
designers, 335
desks, creating, 118–119
Detail View pane, 69
  attributes, 70
  DOPs, 267
detection, collisions, 294

dialog boxes
  Create New Operator Type, 230
  Operator Type Properties, 239
Digital Assets, 233
  assetization, 235
  creating, 233–235, 236–238
  design overview, 256–263
  DOPs, 268
  Help, 253
  interfaces, 238–256
  locked/unlocked status, 261–262
  subnets, 236
  versioning, 258–260
directories, home, 231
disabling parameters, 251
Display flag, 49
display options (Viewer pane), 20
Dissolve SOP, 103–104
DNA, duplicating, 61–65
dobjects, 275
  DOPs, 278–280
  streams, 303
  viewing, 280
documentation, 16
dollying, 20
Do Motion Blur, 249
DOPs (Dynamic Operators), 30, 265
  active/passive states, 276–277
  affectors, 276–277
  animation values, 283
  cloth, 284–290
  controls, 272–275
  data, 269–271
  dobjects, 278–280

fractured objects, 280–281
glue, 281–283
POP solver, 296–297
RBDs, 267–269
rendering, 303–309
Script Solver, 299–300
single solvers, 300–302
SOP solver, 297–299
total perspective vortex, 265–267
volume representation, 271–272
wire, 290–296
dotted line connections, 168–169
dragging, 22. See also moving;
  navigating
  parameters, 242
dragonflies
  antennae
    shaders, 213
    UV Coordinates, 203–204
  bodies
    shaders, 209
    UV Coordinates, 204
  CHOPs, 135–136
  creating, 130–132
  eyes
    shaders, 211
    UV Coordinates, 203–204
  legs
    applying UV Coordinates, 199–200
    shaders, 210
  shaders, 204–213
  textures
    applying, 204–213
    SHOPs, 199–213

wings
    hinge shaders, 213
    surface shaders, 210
    tube shaders, 210
    UV Coordinates, 202–203
dropping parameters, 239, 242
Duplicate SOP, 83, 104–105
duplicating DNA, 61–65
Dynamic Operators (DOPs), 30, 265
    active/passive states, 276–277
    affectors, 276–277
    animation values, 283
    cloth, 284–290
    controls, 272–275
    data, 269–271
    dobjects, 278–280
    fractured objects, 280–281
    glue, 281–283
    POP solver, 296–297
    RBDs, 267–269
    rendering, 303–309
    Script Solver, 299–300
    single solvers, 300–302
    SOP solver, 297–299
    total perspective vortex, 265–267
    volume representation, 271–272
    wire, 290–296
Dynamics CHOP, 308
Dynamics ROP, 303

E

easeout( ) function, 114
echo $TEMP, 328
Edit Capture regions, 127
Edit Capture Weights, 128
editing
    bones, 123
    expressions, 248
editors
    Channel Editor
        animation, 112
        channel groups, 116
        channel lists, 115–116
        zones of utility, 113–116
    Expression Editor, 249
    expressions, 67
Edit SOP, 81, 106–107
educators, 337
effects animators, 336
embedding OTL, 263
entering subnets, 239
equations, primitives, 9
Escape (Houdini), 5
Euler angles, 122
Event POP, 167–168
events, POPs, 164–168
explicitly set initial velocity, 152
Export CHOP, 136
exposing
    handles, 251–253
    parameters, 238–242
Expression Editor, 249

expressions
    animation, 64
    editing, 248
    editors, 67
    filter, 72
    point( ), 101
    popevent( ), 164–168
    poppoint( ), 169–171
    rand( ), 94, 278
    sin, 64
external references, verifying, 241
extracting simulation information,
    306–307
eyes (dragonflies)
    shaders, 211
    UV Coordinates, 203–204

F

$F, 151
falling blocks, 282
Fan POP, 157
Fetch CHOP, 135
fetching subdata, 307
$FF, 151
fields
    activation (POPs), 151
    Help Text, 228
    Mantra Procedure, 249
    Sin Expression, 65
    Transform Object, 103
File DOP, 303
filenames, blank spaces, 62

files
Bounded File, 332
.ifd (rendering), 329
OTL, 258
rendering, 331–333
.sim, 303
structure (ROPs), 311–314
File SOP, 305
filter expressions, 72
Find feature, 18
flags
Display, 49
footprint, 50
lock, 50
red, 200
Render, 49
Template, 83
flipbooks, previewing animation, 120
flying arrows, POPs, 175–183
folders
behavior organization, 242
home directories, 231
Follow Path state, Objects context, 35
footprint flag, 50
formatting
profiles, 81
.rat image format, 198
forms
non-planar geometric, 10
planar geometric, 10
forums, 17
fractured objects, DOPs, 280–281
frames, start, 315
framing viewpoints, 23

Frequency X parameter, 246
friction attributes, importing, 289
functionality of object nodes, 25
functions
constant( ), 114
cubic( ), 114
easeout( ), 114
linear( ), 114
modolo (%), 278
Fuse SOP, 101

G

Generate Scalar Noise toggle, 288
geometry
attaching, 180–181
Capture Geometry, 127–134
ground, 176
hair, 293
isolating, 133–134
navigating, 21–23
non-planar geometric forms, 10
planar geometric forms, 10
powerlines, 295
shaders, 186
transformations, 13
types of, 9
VOPs, 217
Geometry Object, 25, 134
Geometry ROP, 305, 321
get_external_collsion object, 234
get_external_source object, 234
gimbals, locks, 122–123
Global Animation Options window, 143

global space, 12
global variables
ROPs, 317–322
$SF, 273
glue, DOPs, 281–283
goForward take, 119
Go menu, 17
Gravity Force DOP, 268, 282
GRcolorBlack node, 72
green dots, 246
grids
node values, 62
SOP solvers, 298
UV Coordinates, 194
Grid SOP, 284
ground geometry, creating, 176
Ground Plane DOP, 273
Group operator, 73
groups, 71
channels, 116
creating, 205–206
defining, 190
primitive, 281
shaders, 190–193
tacked, 116
VOPs, 217
Group SOP, 99, 191, 298
naming, 205

H

hair, 266
geometry, 293
Halo (Houdini), 5

handles
exposing, 251–253
persistent (Objects context), 36
Snow Source, 252
UV manipulation, 196
hands, rigging, 125–130
HDAs (Houdini Digital Assets), 257. *See*
also **Digital Assets**
takes, 252
HDK (Houdini Developer's Kit), 257
heads (totem poles), 50–52
Heads Up Display (HUD), 252
Help
Digital Assets, 253
pane, 16–18
Text field, 228
Hermanovic, Greg, 3
h hotkey, 23
hierarchies, takes, 119
highlighting, 128
hip-centric approach, 311–312
Hit Behavior parameter, 244
Hole Faces parameter, 86
home directories, 231
home pages, Settings tab, 18
homing
viewpoints, 23
viewports, 45
hotkeys, 20
h, 23
keyframing, 110
q, 51
viewing, 60

Houdini
family of products, 5
history of, 2
Houdini Developer's Kit (HDK), 257
Houdini Digital Assets. *See* **Digital**
Assets; HDAs
Houdnik, 17
Howard, Caleb, 139–141
Hscript, 215
HTML (Hypertext Markup Language)
Help, 254
HUD (Heads Up Display), 252
sliders, 35
Hypertext Markup Language. *See* **HTML**

I

icons, conjuring, 255–256
.ifd files, rendering, 329
ifs( ) statement, 250
images
previewing, 206
.rat image format, 198
UV Coordinates, 206
Impacts subdata, 282, 308–309
importing friction attributes, 289
impulse birthing, 146–150
indexing bones, 128
info popups, CHOPs, 136
initializing simulation, 315–316
initial velocity, POPs, 152–157
inputs
nodes, 5
ordering, 101

installing OTL, 260
instances
points, 279–280
SHOPs, 186
Interactive Preview Rendering (IPR),
221
Interact POP, 157
interfaces
contexts, 28–31
Digital Assets, 238–256
Help pane, 16–18
optimizing, 229, 244–245
organizing, 242–243
panes, 18–27
Parameters pane, 27–28
zones, 15–16
internal springs, 291
interns, 337
intersections, 7
Invert COP, 98
IPR (Interactive Preview Rendering),
221, 226
isolation, pieces, 133–134

J

job-centric approach, 312–314
joints, sliders, 275

K

keyframes
  manually set animation, 109–111
  moving, 113
  navigation, 111
keys, autokeys, 111–112
KMS units, standard, 292

L

labels
  applying, 224
  compositing, 226
lag, applying, 136
lassos, 82
Layered Surface SHOP, 196, 197–198
layers
  textures, 196
  VOPs, 216
layouts, viewports, 42
Left mouse button (LMB), 17
left stowbars, SHOPs, 187
legs (dragonflies)
  applying UV Coordinates, 199–200
  shaders, 210
lighters, 336
**lighting, applying to texture maps,
  225–226**
Lighting Model VOP, 225
Light object, 33
linear( ) function, 114
Linear Spring Constraint, 295
linear springs, 291

lines, 294–296
Line SOP, 294
lists
  channels, 115–116
  DOPs, 266
live VOPnets, applying, 231
LMB (Left mouse button), 17
Localization POP, 147
local space, 12
local variables, ROPs, 317–322
locked status, Digital Assets, 261–262
locks
  flags, 50
  gimbals, 122–123
Look At state, Objects context, 40

M

main menu bar, 15
**Make Object Mutual Affectors toggle,
  306**
management
  Operator Type Manager, 259
  VOPnet, 231–232
Mantra
  Procedure field, 249
  ROPs, 318–321, 327–333
**manually set keyframe animation,
  109–111**
maps (textures)
  adding, 224–225
  applying lighting, 225–226
Master (Houdini), 5

materials
  compositing labels, 226
  VOPs, 220–221
matrices, affector views, 276–277
Maximum Inputs, 237
Measure SOP, 298
menus
  creating, 245
  Go, 17
  mouse (keyframing), 110
  Operators, 25
  Take (rendering), 315
Merge DOP, 273, 289
merge node, rewiring, 93
Merge operation, 102
Merge SOP, 201
message bar, 15
middle mouse button (MMB), 17
Minimum Inputs, 237
MMB (middle mouse button), 17
modelers, 336
modes, Visualization, 290
modifying
  channel references, 247
  clipping distances, 53
  multiple nodes, 126
modolo function (%), 278
monolithic objects, building, 332
moons, creating, 97–98
Morph state, Objects context, 41
motherspheres, creating, 89–90
**Motion and Audio Channel Operators
  (CHOPs), 31**

motion blur
    ROPs, 322–324
    testing, 324
    velocity, 326–327
motion capture technicians, 335
mouse
    buttons, 17
    menus (keyframing), 110
movement, adding, 93–94
moving. *See also* **navigating**
    bones, 123
    geometry, 21–23
    keyframes, 113
multiple constraints, 274–275
multiple definitions, 262
multiple nodes, 126
multiple parameters, 243
Multiple Solver, 300
Multiply COP, 98

N

naming
    Group SOP, 205
    objects, 306
    viewing object names, 293
navigating
    keyframes, 111
    Viewer pane, 20
    viewpoints, 24
Near Clipping Plane, 53
Network Editor
    nodes, 59–62
    operations, 26, 63
    panes, 16, 24, 69

networks, 26–27
    COPs, 97–98
    nodes, 4
    objects as containers, 33
    SHOP, 190
    VOPs, 219–220
new Operator Types, 256–257
night, creating, 100–102
nodes, 4
    archSize, 95
    auto-numbering, 45
    collapsing, 52
    Digital Assets, 233–235
    DOPs, 266
    GRcolorBlack, 72
    grid values, 62
    input, 5
    merge, 93
    multiple, 126
    object functionality, 25
    output, 5
    POPs, 142
    rbdfracturedobject, 280
    rbdrotconstraint, 273
    rbdsolver, 277
    reference copies, 86
    SOPs, 49–50
    unwiring, 93
    viewing, 59–62
    VOPs, 216
Noise Field DOP, 288
non-planar geometric forms, 10
Null COP, 98
Null operations, 64

Null operators, 301
Null SOP, 87
numbers
    auto-numbering nodes, 45
    ladders, 28
    pseudo-random, 94
NURBS modeling
    curves, 81
    SOPs, 80–87

O

Object Merge SOP, 102–103, 305
objects
    Camera, 33
    as containers, 33
    Digital Assets, 233–235
    DOPs, 267, 269–271
    fractured, 280–281
    Geometry, 134
    Light, 33
    monolithic, 332
    naming, 293, 306
    node functionality, 25
    rbdobject1, 270
    RBD Object DOP, 267–269
    searching, 45
    shaders, 188–189
    snapping, 42–43
    space, 12
    states, 33
    swingCloth, 190
    viewport layouts, 42
Object Scene ROP, 321

Objects context
auto-numbering nodes, 45
Blend state, 37
Copy state, 36–37
Follow Path state, 35
HUD slider, 35
Look At state, 40
Morph state, 41
Parent state, 37
Path state, 34
persistent handles, 36
Pose state, 44
Shading Selector button, 38
Sticky state, 39
OBJs (Objects Operators), 29
occupations in the computer graphics industry, 335–337
onherit initial velocity, 153
opcf command, 250
opcook -f command, 207
OpenGL ROP, 321
operations
adding, 63
Network Editor pane, 26
networks, 26–27
Operations view pane, 25
operators
CHOPs, 31, 135–136
COPs, 31
Copy, 90
DOPs, 30, 265
active/passive states, 276–277
affectors, 276–277
animation values, 283

cloth, 284–290
controls, 272–275
data, 269–271
dobjects, 278–280
fractured objects, 280–281
glue, 281–283
POP solver, 296–297
RBDs, 267–269
rendering, 303–309
Script Solver, 299–300
single solvers, 300–302
SOP solver, 297–299
total perspective vortex, 265–267
volume representation, 271–272
wire, 290–296
Group, 73
new Operator Types, 256–257
Null, 301
OBJs, 29
outputting info, 333
PolyExtrude, 57
PolyKnit, 56
POPs, 30, 139–141
activation fields, 151
axis alignment, 149–151
birthing, 146–150
charge, 157–159
collision detection, 159–162
cooking, 142
dotted line connections, 168–169
events, 164–168
$F/$FF, 151
flying arrows, 175–183
initial velocity, 152–157

nodes, 142
Particle SOPs, 144–145
POP Merge SOP, 145–146
Popnet oversampling, 151
Popnet SOPs, 145–146
poppoint( ) expression, 169–171
primitives, 162–164
Real Time Toggle button, 143
rendering colors, 172
simulations, 142–143
space, 148–149
ROPs, 31
SHOPs, 30, 185
adding instances, 186
applying, 188–193
contexts, 186
texturing dragonflies, 199–213
UV Coordinates, 193–198
viewers, 187–188
SOPs, 29, 49
attack of the be-tentacled sphere, 89–94
Blast, 103–104
brush operations, 74–79
Copy, 103–104
Copy/Paste, 104–105
Delete, 103–104
Dissolve, 103–104
Duplicate, 104–105
Edit, 106–107
nodes, 49–50
NURBS modeling, 80–87
Object Merge, 102–103
Point, 105–106

polygonal modeling, 50–61
Primitive, 104–105, 105–106
procedural modeling, 61–74
Stonehenge, 95–102
Transform, 106–107
VOPs, 30, 215
    expressions, 215
    nodes, 216
    saving VOPnet, 229–231
    surface shaders, 216–229
    VOPnet management, 231–232
Operators menu, 25
Operator Type Library. *See* **OTL**
Operator Type Manager, 259
**Operator Type Properties dialog box,
    239**
opparm command, 79
optimizing
    interfaces, 229
    user interfaces, 244–245
options
    Render command, 319–321
    ROPs, 314–316
opupdate command, 207
ordering
    inputs, 101
    shaders, 194
    transformations, 13
organizing
    behavior folders, 242
    user interfaces, 242–243
orientation, axes, 148
orthographic projection, 11

OTL (Operator Type Library), 258
    embedding, 263
    installation, 260
output
    nodes, 5
    operator info, 333
oversampling, Popnet, 151

P

PageDown key, 54
PageUp key, 54
Paint SOP, 75
Pane Linking button, 69
panes, 15, 69
    Detail View, 69
        attributes, 70
        DOPs, 267
    Help pane, 16–18
    interfaces, 18–27
    Network Editor, 16
        operations, 26
        panes, 24
    Parameters pane, 16, 27–28
    Take List, 117
    Tear pane, 16
    Viewer pane, 19–24, 69
    View pane, 25
parameters
    Activation, 283
    bareAluminium shader, 190
    disabling, 251
    dragging, 242

dropping, 239, 242
exposing, 238–240, 241–242
Frequency X, 246
Hit Behavior, 244
Hole Faces, 86
Random Seed, 252
selecting, 243
SHOPs, 227
string, 250
Parameters DOP, rendering, 304
Parameters pane, 16, 27–28
Parameter VOPs, 228
parenting
    bones, 124
    pieces, 134
Parent state, Objects context, 37
Particle Operators (POPs), 30, 139–141
    activation fields, 151
    axis alignment, 149–151
    birthing, 146–150
    charge, 157–159
    collision detection, 159–162
    cooking, 142
    dotted line connections, 168–169
    events, 164–168
    $F/$FF, 151
    flying arrows, 175–183
    initial velocity, 152–157
    nodes, 142
    POP Merge SOP, 145–146
    Popnet oversampling, 151
    poppoint( ) expression, 169–171
    primitives, 162–164

Real Time Toggle button, 143
rendering colors, 172
simulations, 142–143
sources, 148
space, 148–149
particles
DOP network using, 297
simulation, 178–180
Particles Operators (POPs)
Particle SOPs, 144–145
Popnet SOPs, 145–146
passive states, DOPs, 276–277
Paste SOP, 84
paths, 62, 66
Path state, Objects context, 34
Pennie, John, 3
per-point attributes, 288–289
persistent handles, Objects context, 36
perspective projection, 11
pieces
isolating, 133–134
parenting, 134
pipeline technicians, 336
piston joints, 275
planar geometric forms, 10
playbar, 15
playing simulations, 307
point( ) expression, 101
Point Normal, 74
points, 9
instances, 279–280
per-point attributes, 288–289
selecting, 56
UV Coordinates, 195

Point SOP, 74, 105
PolyExtrude operator, 57
polygonal modeling, SOPs, 50–61
polygons, 10
PolyKnit operator, 56
PolySplit operation, 50, 55
Polywire SOPs, 62
popevent( ) expression, 164–168
poppoint( ) expression, 169–171
POP solvers, DOPs, 296–297
POPs (Particle Operators), 30, 139–141
activation fields, 151
axis alignment, 149–151
birthing, 146–150
charge, 157–159
collision detection, 159–162
cooking, 142
dotted line connections, 168–169
events, 164–168
$F/$FF, 151
flying arrows, 175–183
initial velocity, 152–157
nodes, 142
Particle SOPs, 144–145
POP Merge SOP, 145–146
Popnet
oversampling, 151
SOPs, 145–146
poppoint( ) expression, 169–171
primitives, 162–164
Real Time Toggle button, 143
rendering colors, 172
simulations, 142–143
sources, 148
space, 148–149

popup windows, 72
Pose state, Objects context, 44
position attribute, 71
positive Z axis, 90
post-frame scripts, 316
post-render scripts, 316
powerlines geometry, 295
preferences, Digital Assets, 235
pre-frame scripts, 316
preparing for assetization, 235
pre-render scripts, 316
presets, 11, 73
previewing
animation, 120
images, 206
IPR, 221
primitives, 9
groups
applying shaders, 191
creating, 281
POPs, 162–164
viewing, 70
Primitive SOP, 100, 104–105
PRISMS, 3
procedural modeling, SOPs, 61–74
procedural paradigm, 4–5
processing simulation information,
306–307
production, 337
profiles, creating, 81
Profile SOP, 86
projection, 11
Project SOP, 85

Property POP, 157
pseudo-random numbers, 94
pulling in point instances, 279–280

Q

q hotkey, 51
quads, 10
quick reloading, textures, 207
Quick Render button, 78

R

rand( ) expression, 94, 278
Random Seed parameter, 252
random seeds, 283
.rat image format, 198
Ray SOP, 99
RBD Constraint DOP, 274
rbdfracturedobject node, 280
RBD Glue Object DOP, 281
RBD Object DOP, 303
rbdobject1 object, 270
RBD Point Object DOP, 279
RBD (Rigid Body Dynamic), 267–269
rbdrotconstraint node, 273
RBD Solver, 290
rbdsolver node, 277
RBD State DOP, 283
Real Time Toggle button, 143
red flags, 200

references
    channels, 65–68, 246–248
    copies, 86
    external, 241
    points, 9
Refine SOP, 295
regions, capture, 127
Relationship tab, 273
reloading textures, 207
Render command options, 319–321
Render control window, 315
Render flag, 49
rendering
    dependencies (ROPs), 314
    DOPs, 303–309
    file, 331–333
    .ifd files, 329
    IPR, 221
    Parameters DOP, 304
    Quick Render button, 78
    ROPs, 327–333
    Take menu, 315
    VOPs, 221
Renderman Shading Language, 330
Render Outputs (ROPs), 311
    deformation blur, 324–327
    file structure, 311–314
    global variables, 317–322
    local variables, 317–322
    Mantra, 327–333
    motion blur, 322–324

options, 314–316
render dependencies, 314
rendering, 327–333
Rest position, 208
Revolve operation, 81
rewiring, merge node, 93
rigging, 120
    automating, 129–130
    dragonflies, 130–132
    hands, 125–130
right-hand coordinate systems, 7
right mouse button (RMB), 17
Rigid Body Dynamic (RBD), 267–269
RMB (right mouse button), 17
rope, 266
ROPs (Render Outputs), 31, 311
    deformation blur, 324–327
    file structure, 311–314
    global variables, 317–322
    local variables, 317–322
    Mantra, 327–333
    motion blur, 322–324
    options, 314–316
    render dependencies, 314
    rendering, 327–333
rotations
    constraints, 273
    gimbal locks, 122

S

Save To Library, 237
saving
    images (UV Coordinates), 206
    VOPnet, 229–231
Scatter SOP, 76
scripts
    post-frame, 316
    post-render, 316
    pre-frame, 316
    pre-render, 316
Script Solver, DOPs, 299–300
scrubbing timelines, 98
Sculpt operation, 74
searching objects, 45
Secure Selection, turning off, 82
See One/See All button, 101
Selectable Links toggle, 93
Select (Houdini), 5
selecting
    multiple parameters, 243
    operations, 25
    points, 56
    POP sources, 148
selection options (Viewer pane), 19
Separator, 243
Set Always, 283, 288
Settings tab, 18
$SF global variable, 273
Shader Operators (SHOPs), 30, 185
    adding instances, 186
    applying, 188–193
    contexts, 186

texturing dragonflies, 199–213
UV Coordinates, 193–198
viewers, 187–188
shaders, applying, 221
Shading Selector button, Objects
    context, 38
shading wireframes, 82
Shape COP, 98
SHOPs (Shader Operators), 30, 185
    adding instances, 186
    applying, 188–193
    contexts, 186
    texturing dragonflies, 199–213
    UV Coordinates, 193–198
    viewers, 187–188
show _source node, 234
Side Effects Software, 3
.sim files, 303
simulation
    extracting information, 306–307
    initializing, 315–316
    particles, 178–180
    playing, 307
    POPs, 142–143
sin expression, 64
Sin Expression field, 65
single solvers, DOPs, 300–302
sizing bounding boxes, 333
skeletons, creating, 120–124
sliders
    HUD (Object context), 35
    joints, 275
smoothing wireframes, 54
Smooth operation, 85

snapping objects, 42–43
Snow object, 234
Snow Source handle, 252
software engineers, 335
SOP solver, DOPs, 297–299
SOPs (Surface Operators), 29, 49
    attack of the be-tentacled sphere, 89–94
    Blast, 103–104
    brush operations, 74–79
    Copy, 104
    Copy/Paste, 104
    Delete, 103–104
    Dissolve, 103–104
    Duplicate, 104
    Edit, 106–107
    nodes, 49–50
    NURBS modeling, 80–87
    Object Merge, 102–103
    Point, 105
    polygonal modeling, 50–61
    Primitive, 104, 105
    procedural modeling, 61–74
    Stonehenge, 95–102
    Transform, 106–107
sources, POPs, 148
space, POPs, 148–149
spare parameters, adding, 66
sparks, 309
special controls, 248–250
spheres, 9
    attack of the be-tentacled, 89–94
splitting bones, 123
Spring Constraint, 273
springs, damping, 291–292

Sprite POP, 234
Stamp tab (copy node), 78
standard KMS units, 292
start frames, 315
state indicators (Viewer pane), 19
statements, ifs( ), 250
states
    Blend, 37
    Copy, 36–37
    Follow Path, 35
    Look At, 40
    Morph, 41
    Object, 33
    Parent, 37
    Path, 34
    Pose, 44
    Sticky, 39
Static Solver, 300
Sticky state, 39
Stonehenge, creating, 95–102
stowbars
    SHOPs, 187
    Viewer pane, 19
streams, dobject, 303
string parameters, 250
structure, files (ROPs), 311–314
subdata
    customizing, 300
    DOPs, 269–271
    fetching, 307
    Impacts, 282, 308–309
    Volume, 271
Subdivide SOP, 298

subnets
    adding, 236
    collapsing, 236
    entering, 239
Surface Operators (SOPs), 29, 49
    attack of the be-tentacled sphere, 89–94
    Blast, 103–104
    brush operations, 74–79
    Copy, 104
    Copy/Paste, 104
    Delete, 103–104
    Dissolve, 103–104
    Duplicate, 104
    Edit, 106–107
    nodes, 49–50
    NURBS modeling, 80–87
    Object Merge, 102–103
    Point, 105
    polygonal modeling, 50–61
    Primitive, 104, 105
    procedural modeling, 61–74
    Stonehenge, 95–102
    Transform, 106–107
surface shaders, VOPs, 216–229
Surfsect operation, 83
Sweep operation, 86
swingCloth object, 190
Switch Solver, 300

T

tabs
    Relationship, 273
    Visualization, 290

tacked groups, 116
tails, velocity, 180
Take List pane, 117
Take menu, rendering, 315
takes
    animation, 117–119
    goForward, 119
    HDAs, 252
Tear pane, 16
$TEMP, 328
Template flag, 83
tentacles, creating, 90–91
testing motion blur, 324
texcache -c command, 207
Textport, 78
textures
    artists, 336
    dragonflies
        applying, 204–213
        SHOPs, 199–213
    layers, 196
    maps
        adding, 224–225
        applying lighting, 225–226
    reloading, 207
    UV Texture SOP, 194
time, moving keyframes, 113
timelines, scrubbing, 98
Tooltip
    Help, 253
    window, 67
top stowbars, SHOPs, 187
torii, 1
torus wires, 291

total perspective vortex, DOPs, 265–267
totem poles, 50–61
Trace COP, 98
Trace SOP, 97
trackers, 336
tracking, 20
trainers, 337
transferring UV Coordinates, 200–202
transformations
    blur, 323–324
    curves, 83
    deformation, 13
    order, 13
Transform COP, 98
transform handles (Viewer pane),
    21–23
Transform Object field, 103
Transform SOP, 106–107
triangles, 10
troubleshooting Digital Assets, 253
tubes, 9
tumbling, 20
Twist operation, 62
two-state constraints, 285
ty channel, 116

U

Unique Data Name toggle, 300
unlocked status, Digital Assets, 261–262
unwiring nodes, 93
Update button, 46

user interfaces
    Digital Assets, 238–256
    optimizing, 229, 244–245
    organizing, 242–243
user parameters, adding to SHOPs, 227
UV Coordinates
    applying, 199–204
    2D, 208
    images, 206
    SHOPs, 193–198
    transferring, 200–202
    VOPs, 217–218, 225
UV Project SOP, 195
UV Quickshade SOP, 207
UV Texture SOP, 194

V

vacuums, cloth in, 287–288
valid frame ranges (ROPs), 315
values
    animation, 283
    grid node, 62
    keyframes, 113
    pseudo-random numbers, 94
variables
    global
        ROPs, 317–322
        $SF, 273
    local (ROPs), 317–322
variation, adding, 181–183
velocity
    axis alignment to, 149–151
    balldobject, 275

blur, 325–326
initial (POPs), 152–157
motion blur, 326–327
tails, 180
verifying external references, 241
versioning Digital Assets, 258–260
vertices, 9
    UV Coordinates, 195
VEX Operators (VOPs), 30, 215
    expressions, 215
    nodes, 216
    surface shaders, 216–229
    VOPnet
        management, 231–232
        saving, 229–231
Viewer pane, 19–24, 69
viewers, SHOPs, 187–188
view indicators (Viewer pane), 19
viewing
    dobjects, 280
    Geometry objects, 134
    hotkeys, 60
    nodes, 59–62
    object names, 293
    options (Viewer pane), 20
    primitives, 70
    subdata, 308
View pane operations, 25
viewpoints
    3D, 11
    framing, 23
    homing, 23
    navigating, 24

Index